ALGEBRA 1
for Christian Schools®

ALGEBRA 1

for Christian Schools®

Second Edition

Kathy D. Pilger, Ed.D.
Ron Tagliapietra, Ed.D.

 Bob Jones University Press
Greenville, South Carolina 29614

ALGEBRA 1 for Christian Schools®
Second Edition

Kathy D. Pilger, Ed.D
Ron Tagliapietra, Ed.D.

Contributing Authors	**Consultants**
Larry L. Hall, M.S	Wendy H. Alsup
Larry D. Lemons, M.S.	Kathy Kohler
	Anita R. Sedivy

Produced in cooperation with the Bob Jones University Department of Mathematics of the College of Arts and Science, the School of Education, and Bob Jones Academy.

for Christian Schools is a registered trademark of Bob Jones University Press.

ISBN 1-57924-325-8

15 14 13 12 11 10 9 8 7 6 5 4 3 2

Contents

Chapter 1: Integers x

1.1 Locating Integers on a Number Line 2
1.2 Opposites and Absolute Value 6
1.3 Adding Integers 9
1.4 Subtracting Integers 14
Algebra Through History: Isaac Newton 18
1.5 Multiplying Integers 20
1.6 Dividing Integers 23
Probability and Statistics 1: Terms 26
1.7 Exponents 27
1.8 Factoring and Prime Numbers 31
1.9 Greatest Common Factor and Least Common Multiple 35
Algebra and Scripture 40
Chapter 1 Review 42

Chapter 2: Real Numbers 44

2.1 Kinds of Numbers 46
2.2 Adding and Subtracting Rationals 51
2.3 Multiplying and Dividing Rationals 56
Probability and Statistics 2: Averages 61
2.4 Order of Operations 63
2.5 Symbols for Grouping 66
2.6 Square Roots and Radicals 69
Algebra Around Us: Science 74
2.7 Sets and Operations 76
Algebra and Scripture 80
Chapter 2 Review 82

Chapter 3: The Language of Algebra 84

3.1 Variables 86
3.2 Word Phrases and Algebraic Expressions 90
3.3 Negative Exponents 93
3.4 Evaluating Algebraic Expressions 96
3.5 Combining Like Terms 99

3.6 Removing Parentheses 103
3.7 Using Formulas 107
Probability and Statistics 3: Probability 113
3.8 Properties of Equality 115
Algebra Through History: The Bernoullis 118
3.9 Word Sentences and Equations 120
Algebra and Scripture 124
Chapter 3 Review 126

Chapter 4: Solving Equations 128

4.1 Using Properties of Equality 130
Probability and Statistics 4: Multiplication Principle of Counting 134
4.2 How to Attack Word Problems 136
4.3 Equations of the Form $ax + b = c$ 140
4.4 More Work with Equations 143
4.5 Equations of the Form $ax + b = cx + d$ 147
4.6 Absolute Value Equations 150
4.7 Clearing Equations of Fractions 154
4.8 Coin and Interest Problems 157
4.9 Motion Problems 163
4.10 Mixture Problems 169
Algebra Around Us: Medicine 174
Algebra and Scripture 176
Chapter 4 Review 178

Chapter 5: Solving Inequalities 180

5.1 Inequalities 182
5.2 Properties of Inequality: Addition and Subtraction 186
5.3 Properties of Inequality: Multiplication and Division 188
5.4 Solving Inequalities 192
5.5 Conjunctions 194
5.6 Disjunctions 197

Probability and Statistics 5:
    Addition Principle of Counting 200
Algebra Through History: René Descartes 202
5.7 Absolute Value Inequalities 204
5.8 Word Problems Using Inequalities 208
Algebra and Scripture...212
Chapter 5 Review...214

Chapter 6: Relations, Functions, and Graphs 216

6.1 Coordinates in a Plane 218
6.2 Relations and Functions...............................223
6.3 Graphs of Relations and Functions...............228
6.4 Graphs and Intercepts of Linear Equations ...234
6.5 Slopes of Lines 238
Algebra Around Us: Business..............................244
6.6 Slope-Intercept Form
    of a Linear Equation 246
Probability and Statistics 6:
    Rules of Probability 250
6.7 Point-Slope Form of Linear Equations..........252
6.8 Finding the Equation of a Line
    Given Two Points...255
6.9 Direct Variation...258
6.10 Graphing Linear Inequalities 262
Algebra and Scripture...266
Chapter 6 Review...268

Chapter 7: Systems of Equations and Inequalities 270

7.1 Solving Systems of Equations
    by Graphing 272
7.2 Using the Graphing Method 276
7.3 Solving Simple Systems of Equations
    by Substitution 280
7.4 Solving Systems by the Substitution
    Method 284
Probability and Statistics 7: Permutations...........288
7.5 Solving Simple Systems of Equations
    by the Addition Method..................................290
Algebra Through History: Carl Gauss.................294
7.6 Solving Systems of Equations
    by the Addition Method..................................296

7.7 Motion Problems...300
7.8 Interest Problems 304
7.9 Mixture Problems 309
7.10 Systems of Inequalities 314
Algebra and Scripture..318
Chapter 7 Review...320

Chapter 8: Polynomials.........................322

8.1 Classifying and Evaluating Polynomials.......324
8.2 Adding Polynomials 327
8.3 Subtracting Polynomials 330
8.4 Multiplying by a Monomial...........................332
Algebra Around Us: Skilled Trades 336
8.5 Multiplying Binomials...................................338
8.6 Multiplying Polynomials 342
Probability and Statistics 8: Combinations 345
8.7 Special Products..347
8.8 Dividing by a Monomial................................350
8.9 Dividing Polynomials 354
Algebra and Scripture..358
Chapter 8 Review...360

Chapter 9: Factoring Polynomials....362

9.1 Factoring Common Monomials.....................364
9.2 Factoring the Differences of Two Squares 366
Probability and Statistics 9: Variability 369
9.3 Factoring Perfect Square Trinomials 371
9.4 Factoring Trinomials
    of the Form $x^2 + bx + c$.................................374
Algebra Through History: Albert Einstein 378
9.5 Factoring Trinomials
    of the Form $ax^2 + bx + c$...............................380
9.6 Factoring Trinomials
    of the Form $ax^2 + bxy + cy^2$.........................384
9.7 Factoring Completely 386
Algebra and Scripture..390
Chapter 9 Review...392

Chapter 10: Radicals.........................394

10.1 Expressing Square Roots 396
10.2 Simplifying Radicals...................................400
10.3 Multiplying Radicals...................................403

10.4 Dividing Radicals and
Rationalizing Denominators.......................406

Probability and Statistics 10:
Standard Deviations.......................................412

Algebra Around Us: Quality Control.................414

10.5 Adding and Subtracting Radicals...............416

10.6 The Pythagorean Theorem 418

10.7 The Distance Formula...............................423

10.8 Multiplying Radical Expressions...............428

10.9 Dividing Radical Expressions....................431

10.10 Radical Equations.....................................435

Algebra and Scripture 438

Chapter 10 Review..440

Chapter 11: Quadratic Equations.....442

11.1 Zero Product Property...............................444

11.2 Solving Quadratic Equations
by Factoring 446

11.3 Solving Equations by Taking Roots...........450

Algebra Through History:
John Von Neumann 454

11.4 Completing the Square...............................456

11.5 Completing the Square
with Leading Coefficients 459

11.6 The Quadratic Formula 463

Probability and Statistics 11:
Empirical Rule 468

11.7 Solving Quadratic Equations 470

11.8 Word Problems Using
Quadratic Equations 471

Algebra and Scripture 476

Chapter 11 Review..478

Chapter 12: Rational Expressions 480

12.1 Simplifying Rational Expressions..............482

12.2 Multiplying Rational Expressions..............485

12.3 Dividing Rational Expressions...................489

12.4 Adding and Subtracting Rational
Expressions..491

12.5 Adding Rational Expressions
with Different Denominators 495

Algebra Around Us: Engineering.......................498

12.6 Subtracting Rational Expressions
with Different Denominators 500

Probability and Statistics 12:
Intersecting Sets and Probability 504

12.7 Complex Rational Expressions 506

Algebra and Scripture 510

Chapter 12 Review..512

Chapter 13: Rational Equations........514

13.1 Numerical Denominators 516

Probability and Statistics 13:
Independent and Dependent Probabilities 518

13.2 Polynomial Denominators...........................519

13.3 Work Problems...522

13.4 Investment Problems...................................527

13.5 Motion Problems...531

13.6 Literal Equations...535

Algebra and Scripture 538

Chapter 13 Review..540

Chapter 14: Quadratic Functions 542

14.1 Quadratic Functions of
the Form $f(x) = ax^2$.......................................544

14.2 Quadratic Functions of
the Form $f(x) = ax^2 + k$ 548

14.3 Quadratic Functions of
the Form $f(x) = a(x - h)^2 + k$...................551

14.4 Zeros of a Function 555

Probability and Statistics 14:
Standard Normal Distribution.......................558

14.5 Applications of Quadratic Functions 560

Algebra and Scripture 564

Chapter 14 Review..566

Glossary 568

Selected Answers 572

Table of Normal Curve Areas....................593

Symbols...594

Index 594

Introduction

What Is Algebra?

The Arabic word *al-jabr* from which we get our word *algebra* carries the idea of the reunion of broken parts, such as the reduction of fractions to whole numbers. Algebra takes the fragmentary information of a word problem, symbolizes it in abstract form, and derives the answer. Algebra is a structured system for expressing and analyzing the relationships between quantities that may themselves be unknown. The resulting formulas, equations, and expressions are built from symbols, numbers, and operations. The power of algebra is seen when we determine an unknown quantity simply by manipulating the symbols.

Khorasan Gate in Baghdad, Iraq

Historically, algebra grew out of more elementary topics such as arithmetic and algorithms. Some would even call it sophisticated arithmetic. The best known of the ancient Arabic mathematicians, Al-Khwarizmi, wrote a very important book called *Kitab al-jabr wa'l muqabalah*, roughly meaning "the book of integration and equation." From this lucid ninth century book algebra took shape as a separate mathematical discipline. His work made algebra general enough to solve problems of great variety. The book eventually found its way to Europe, where algebra developed further.

Algebra, like geometry, models the relationships of nature and science. The complex dynamics of our physical world defy understanding unless we can approximate them with mathematical models. All scientific inquiry from physics to business depends on the power and abstraction of algebra to find values for unknown quantities.

Why Is Algebra Important?

Language is important because it is our means of communication. Algebra is also a language in which a single symbol may express complex relationships.

Technology in everyday life

Since the language of algebra encapsulates the concepts and principles for studying related quantities, our entire technological culture depends on algebra. From medicine to psychology, and from engineering to auto repair, many professions depend on precisely related quantities.

Algebra has become imbedded in the fabric of our culture. Someone has said "life is one big problem," and certainly, problem solving is critical to daily life. Such problem solving requires proper tools for organized thinking and the formulation of equations from relationships. Writing equations that describe the characteristics of unknown quantities demands a thorough knowledge of algebra. Unless one knows enough algebra to do this, he will never become adept at problem solving.

Algebra, as a tool of analysis, comprehension, and deduction, helps people solve problems in business, science, engineering, building, medicine, technology, and manufacturing. For some, algebra hides inside the instruments of their trade as an unseen partner, but for others it is never any farther away than the end of their pencil or the display of their calculator.

But Is It Worth the Effort?

Algebra is a worthwhile study for all students. Even trades use computers or other tools that depend on algebra, and the most effective use of such tools requires an understanding of what it does. The study of a subject such as algebra requires diligent effort, but it provides either specific skills or practical background knowledge for every type of work. Furthermore, the diligent development of mental discipline has its own rewards.

The hand of the diligent shall bear rule: but the slothful shall be under tribute (Prov. 12:24).

Skyline of Cleveland, Ohio

1 Integers

$$y = mx + b$$

Why do we study numbers and their operations? Numbers are essential in science, business, and even history. The sixteenth king of the Maya, Yax Pac, depicted his accession to the throne on this altar at Copan, Honduras. He used numbers to record the date, which appears left of his head.

A number is an idea, an abstraction that represents that which is concrete. Numerals are symbols or letters used to denote numbers. We can refer to the number of wheels on a car by the word *four* or the Arabic numeral 4. Civilizations have developed various systems of enumeration. For example, one hundred may be represented in Arabic numerals as 100, in Roman numerals as C, in ancient Egyptian numerals as ⁹, and in Greek numerals as ρ.

Look at the following mathematical representations.

- 5382
- 5.382×10^3
- $\overline{\text{V}}$CCCLXXXII
- ⚙⚙⚙⚙⚙⁹⁹⁹⁹∩∩∩∩∩∩∩‖
- 1010100000110_2

All of them mean 5382, but you need to be familiar with each system to determine the number represented. Although the symbolic representations of the number differ, the number itself is a specific, absolute number that remains fixed as God established it. God also made an orderly numerical system. In this chapter you will review the orderly laws that govern God's number system.

After this chapter you should be able to

1. locate numbers on a number line.

2. give the opposite of any number.

3. give the absolute value of any number.

4. add, subtract, multiply, and divide any integers.

5. use the laws of exponents.

6. identify properties of numbers

7. use prime factorization to find LCMs and GCFs.

8. translate word phrases into math symbols.

1.1 Locating Integers on a Number Line

Many times in mathematics, particularly algebra, graphs and number lines will aid your understanding of algebraic ideas. Later in this chapter you will review how to use number lines to perform basic operations on integers. In other chapters you will learn about graphs and how to use them.

Numbers can be represented in picture or symbolic form. The picture form of a number is shown on a number line.

You can construct a number line by following these four steps.
1. Draw a line.
2. Mark an arbitrary point and label it 0.
3. Mark a point to the right of 0 and label it 1. (The distance from 0 to 1 determines a unit on the number line.)
4. Mark off equal units (as determined in step 3) on both sides of 0.

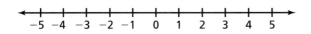

Measuring temperatures requires both positive and negative integers.

The arrows at the ends of the number line indicate that the number line extends without limit in both directions. Can you think of anything else that has no end? Does eternity end? Will everyone live forever? Yes, even you will live forever somewhere. Will it be in heaven or in hell?

INTEGERS

29 30 31 32 33 34 35 36 37 38

Continue without limit in both directions

Now THIS job has a future!!!

Since the line continues, what would the mark after 5 represent? The arrow indicates 6, 7, 8, and so on. What system of numbers is pictured on the number line above? Note that the numbers increase in value as they go from left to right. All numbers to the right of 0 are called *positive numbers*.

What number would be on the left of 0? On this graph, the numbers to the left of 0 are called *negative numbers*. The arrow on the left end of the number line, indicating the continuation of the number line in that direction, includes numbers less than the last number on your line. Is −6 less than −5? Is 6° below 0 colder than 5° below 0? On the number line, any number to the left of a given number is less than the given number.

Graphing a Number on a Number Line

1. Draw a line.
2. Mark the line with segments of equal length.
3. Number the marks consistent with the numbers to be graphed.
4. Place a dot at the indicated number on the number line.

The dot on the number line is called the *graph* of the number, and the number is called the *coordinate* of the graph.

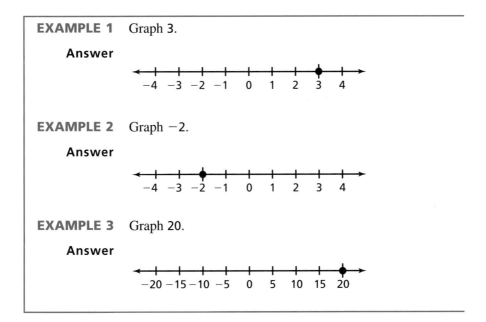

EXAMPLE 1 Graph 3.

Answer

EXAMPLE 2 Graph −2.

Answer

EXAMPLE 3 Graph 20.

Answer

The number line does not always have to be partitioned into units of one. It can be partitioned into units greater than one or into units smaller than one, which will be fractions. You will usually graph on a horizontal number line, but you can also graph on a vertical number line.

On a horizontal number line, positive is always to the right, negative to the left. On a vertical number line, positive is always up, negative down.

Two numbers when plotted on the same number line define a segment. The coordinate of the midpoint of this segment can be found by averaging the coordinates of the endpoints. For example, the midpoint between 4 and 10 is found by averaging 4 and 10.

EXAMPLE 4   Graph -22.

Answer

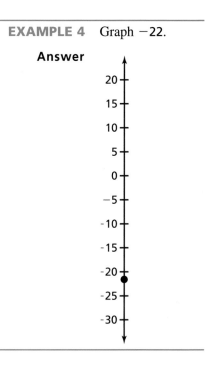

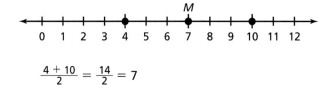

$$\frac{4 + 10}{2} = \frac{14}{2} = 7$$

Therefore, the coordinate of the midpoint, *M*, of the segment joining 4 and 10 on the number line is 7.

▶ A. Exercises

Locate each integer on a horizontal number line.

1. 4
2. -3
3. -24
4. 80
5. -1

Locate each integer on a vertical number line.

6. -4
7. 9
8. -25
9. 100
10. -144

What integer is indicated by the dot on each number line?

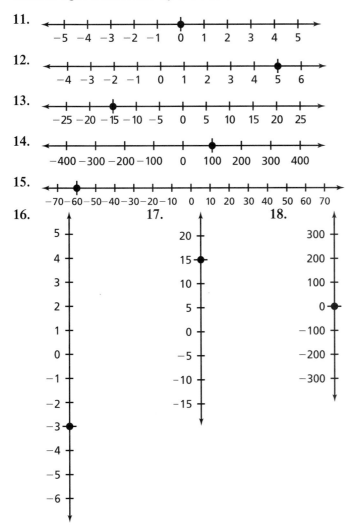

11.

12.

13.

14.

15.

16.   **17.**   **18.**

▶ B. Exercises

Find the midpoint, *M*, of the segment defined by each pair of numbers.

19. 0 and 4   **21.** 137 and 259   **23.** 102 and 16

20. 12 and 22   **22.** 25 and 13

▶ C. Exercises

24. Nineteen is the midpoint of a segment determined by two numbers, one of which is 7. Find the other number.

25. If −1 is the midpoint of a segment 4 units long, what numbers determine the endpoints of the segment?

1.2 Opposites and Absolute Value

You can locate any integer on a number line. When you graph the integer 5, notice that the dot is five units to the right of 0.

What number is five units to the left of 0?

Opposite numbers (or additive inverses) are numbers that when located on a number line are the same distance from 0 but on opposite sides of 0.

Opposites are easy to find. The opposite of 3 is −3.

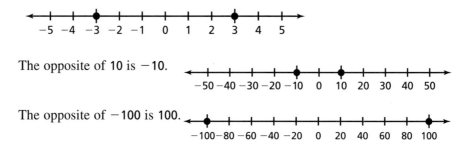

The opposite of 10 is −10.

The opposite of −100 is 100.

For an example of opposites, read Romans 5:19. Heaven and hell, also opposites, are found in II Corinthians 5:1 and Matthew 5:22 respectively.

Before you can become proficient in algebra, you must become very skilled in performing the basic operations of addition, subtraction, multiplication, and division with negative integers as well as positive ones. If you can perform these calculations quickly and accurately, you will have an advantage later in the course. A thorough knowledge of number lines and absolute value will aid you in your operations with numbers.

At this point the definition of absolute value is not a formal one but an adequate and understandable one. In Chapter 4 you will see a more formal definition.

Opposite times of day at the Arc de Triomphe in Paris

Definition

Absolute value is the number of units (distance) between an integer and **0** on a number line.

The absolute value of an integer *a* is denoted by vertical parallel bars, $|a|$. This symbol is read "the absolute value of *a*."

EXAMPLE 1 Find $|4|$. How far is **4** from **0** on the number line? By counting the units, you find that 4 is four units from 0.

$$\overset{\overbrace{1\quad 1\quad 1\quad 1}}{\underset{-7\,-6\,-5\,-4\,-3\,-2\,-1\ \ 0\ \ 1\ \ 2\ \ 3\ \ 4\ \ 5\ \ 6\ \ 7}{\longleftrightarrow}}$$

Answer $|4| = 4$

EXAMPLE 2 What is the absolute value of −7?

Answer Find $|-7|$. How far is **−7** from **0** on the number line? To find out, count the units from −7 to 0.

$$\overset{\overbrace{1\quad 1\quad 1\quad 1\quad 1\quad 1\quad 1}}{\underset{-7\,-6\,-5\,-4\,-3\,-2\,-1\ \ 0\ \ 1\ \ 2\ \ 3\ \ 4\ \ 5\ \ 6\ \ 7}{\longleftrightarrow}}$$

$|-7| = 7$

Notice that the negative sign does not influence the absolute value of 7 or -7 because both numbers are seven units from 0. Remember that absolute value represents distance, so the answer is always positive.

Care must be taken when applying operations to absolute values of numbers. Example 3 indicates the absolute value of a difference while example 4 takes the difference of two absolute values.

EXAMPLE 3 Find the $|\ 82 - 31\ |$.

    Answer $|\ 82 - 31\ | = |\ 51\ | = 51$

EXAMPLE 4 Find $|\ 74\ | - |\ -24\ |$.

    Answer $|\ 74\ | - |\ -24\ | = 74 - 24 = 50$

▶ A. Exercises

Find the opposite of each integer.

1. 38
2. -14
3. 42
4. -56

5. 134
6. -368
7. -412

8. -3247
9. -5
10. 34,892

Find the absolute value of each integer.

11. $|\ 8\ |$
12. $|\ -17\ |$
13. $|\ -382\ |$
14. $|\ -147\ |$
15. $|\ 0\ |$

16. $|\ 123\ |$
17. $|\ 84\ |$
18. $|\ -234\ |$
19. $|\ 4\ |$
20. $|\ -4\ |$

▶ B. Exercises

Perform the indicated operation.

21. $|\ 341 - 26\ |$
22. $|\ 18 + 27\ |$
23. $|\ 1246 - 389\ |$
24. $|\ 64 - 32\ |$
25. $|\ -12\ | + |\ 3\ |$

26. $|\ -9\ | + |\ -4\ |$
27. $|\ 18\ | - |\ -6\ |$
28. $|\ -25\ | + |\ 30\ |$
29. $|\ 86\ | - |\ -10\ |$
30. $|\ -5\ | - |\ 5\ |$

31. What is true about the absolute value of a number and the absolute value of its opposite?
32. Find the difference between the absolute value of a number and the absolute value of its opposite?

► **C. Exercises**

Perform the indicated operations.

33. $\mid 18 - 7 \mid - \mid -4 \mid + \mid 2 - 5 \mid$
34. $\mid -12 - 5 \mid - \mid -12 \mid - \mid 5 \mid$

■ Cumulative Review

Give the integer represented by each point.

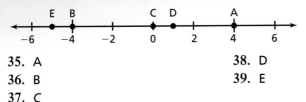

35. A
36. B
37. C

38. D
39. E

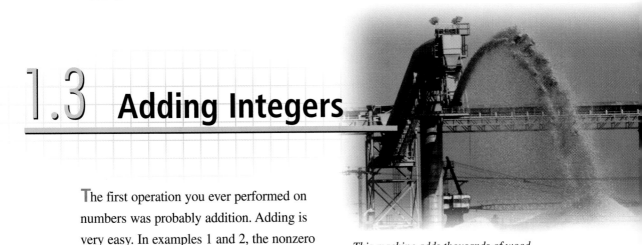

1.3 Adding Integers

The first operation you ever performed on numbers was probably addition. Adding is very easy. In examples 1 and 2, the nonzero numbers (addends) have the same sign.

This machine adds thousands of wood chips to a pile.

Condition 1 Both numbers (addends) have the same sign.

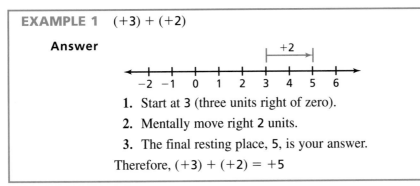

EXAMPLE 1 $(+3) + (+2)$

Answer

1. Start at 3 (three units right of zero).
2. Mentally move right 2 units.
3. The final resting place, **5**, is your answer.

Therefore, $(+3) + (+2) = +5$

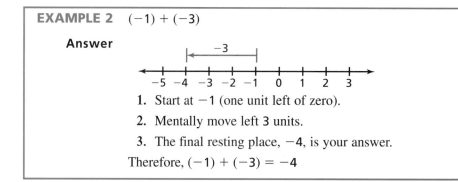

EXAMPLE 2 $(-1) + (-3)$

Answer

1. Start at -1 (one unit left of zero).
2. Mentally move left 3 units.
3. The final resting place, -4, is your answer.

Therefore, $(-1) + (-3) = -4$

When the numbers have the same sign, find the sum of the absolute values and use the sign of the original numbers. Now consider two examples of addends with opposite signs.

Condition 2 One addend is positive and the other is negative.

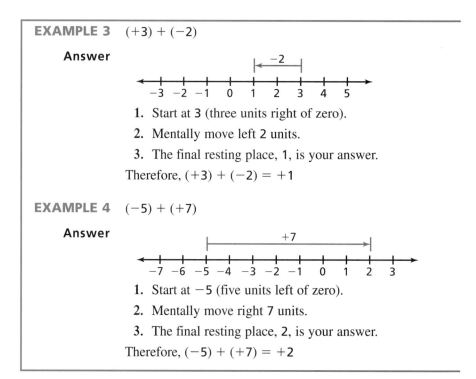

EXAMPLE 3 $(+3) + (-2)$

Answer

1. Start at **3** (three units right of zero).
2. Mentally move left 2 units.
3. The final resting place, **1**, is your answer.

Therefore, $(+3) + (-2) = +1$

EXAMPLE 4 $(-5) + (+7)$

Answer

1. Start at -5 (five units left of zero).
2. Mentally move right 7 units.
3. The final resting place, 2, is your answer.

Therefore, $(-5) + (+7) = +2$

Adding integers on number lines is time consuming, especially if you are working with very large or very small numbers. Instead of always adding on the number line, you can add by using the following procedures.

Adding Integers

Condition 1
Like-sign addends

1. Add the absolute value of the addends.

2. Give the sum the sign of the two addends.

Condition 2
Unlike-sign addends

1. Subtract the smaller absolute value from the larger.

2. Give the difference the sign of the addend with the greater absolute value.

EXAMPLE 5 $(-1) + (-3)$

Answer

$\mid -1 \mid + \mid -3 \mid = 1 + 3 = 4$	1. Add absolute values (condition 1).
$(-1) + (-3) = -4$	2. The sign of the sum must be negative.

If there is no sign in front of a number, assume that the number is positive

This number has a sign in front of it; it must be a negative number!

EXAMPLE 6 $(8) + (-3)$

Answer

$\mid 8 \mid - \mid -3 \mid = 8 - 3 = 5$	1. Subtract absolute values (condition 2).
$8 + (-3) = 5$	2. The sum is positive because $+8$ has a larger absolute value than -3.

EXAMPLE 7 $(4) + (-10)$

Answer

$\mid -10 \mid - \mid 4 \mid = 10 - 4 = 6$	1. Subtract the smaller absolute value from the larger.
$(4) + (-10) = -6$	2. The sum is negative because -10 has a larger absolute value than $+4$.

You have learned in previous math classes that numbers have special properties. These properties have been named so that mathematicians can talk about them. Several properties related to addition follow the next definition.

Definition

A **mathematical property** is an equation or statement that is true for any value of the variable. Properties are sometimes called identities.

Properties of Numbers

1. The *commutative property of addition* shows that if you add two numbers together in different orders, the sum is the same. $3 + 5 = 5 + 3$. In symbols: $a + b = b + a$

2. The *associative property of addition* shows that if you group numbers together differently when adding, the sum is the same. $2 + (9 + 4) = (2 + 9) + 4$. In symbols: $a + (b + c) = (a + b) + c$

3. The *additive identity property* shows that if you add zero to any number, or add the number to zero, you get the original number. $3 + 0 = 3$ and $0 + 3 = 3$. In symbols: $a + 0 = a$ and $0 + a = a$

4. The *additive inverse property* shows that the sum of a number and its opposite is always zero (the additive identity number). $3 + (-3) = 0$. In symbols: $a + (-a) = 0$

▶ A. Exercises

Find each sum.

1. $(+3) + (+21)$
2. $(-13) + (+32)$
3. $(+26) + (-28)$
4. $(-7) + (-8)$
5. $(-126) + (+35)$
6. $(+781) + (+243)$
7. $(+7) + (-3)$
8. $(-14) + (-7)$
9. $(+36) + (+19)$
10. $(-7) + (+37)$
11. $(+384) + (-24)$
12. $(+6) + (-6)$
13. $(-10) + (+10)$
14. $(+4) + (0)$
15. $(-14) + (0)$

▶ B. Exercises

Find each sum.

16. $342 + (-463)$
17. $141 + 891$
18. $(-147) + (-684)$
19. $(-4897) + 387$
20. $(-426) + (-741)$

Find the midpoint, *M*, of the segment defined by each pair of numbers.

21. 23 and 17
22. −8 and −16
23. −15 and 3
24. 0 and −8
25. −5 and 5

Translate into symbols. Do not calculate.

26. Five plus two
27. Nine added to four
28. The sum of two and seven
29. Eight increased by three
30. Five more than six
31. What property does $(-3) + 0 = -3$ describe?
32. What property does $(27) + (-27) = 0$ describe?
33. If the temperature on a January day is 0°F at 7:00 A.M., increases 14° by noon, and then decreases 20° from noon to 10 P.M., what is the temperature at 10 P.M.?
34. A motorboat travels an average speed of 17 knots in still water. Set up an integer equation and solve to find the actual speed the boat is traveling if it is traveling against a current of 5 knots.

▶ C. Exercises

Perform the following operations.

35. $-7 + (-8) + 18 + (-5)$
36. $14 + (-9) + 6 + (-28)$
37. $-8 + |-10| + (-9) + |17|$
38. Give the steps in thinking when solving $(-349) + (+684)$.

■ Cumulative Review

Compute the following.

39. $|(26) + (-30)|$
40. $|26| + |-30|$
41. $|(-8) + (-2)|$
42. $|-8| + |-2|$

43. Is the absolute value of a sum always equal to the sum of the absolute values?

1.4 Subtracting Integers

Subtraction is simply addition of the opposite.

Definition

$a - b = a + (-b)$ for any integers a and b.

A farmer subtracts eggs from the henhouse.

Read the definition as "*a* minus *b* equals *a* plus the opposite of *b*." Since you already know how to subtract numbers such as $8 - 3$ where a smaller number is being subtracted from a larger, continue to do them as before.

Subtractions such as $4 - (-2)$ or $-3 - 2$ often cause confusion and can best be understood as addition.

---

1 Subtract as indicated: $(+4) - (-2)$.

Answer $(+4) - (-2) = 4 + (+2) = 4 + 2 = 6$

Since **2** is being added, mentally move **2** units to the right of four.

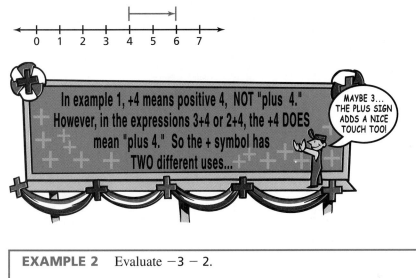

In example 1, +4 means positive 4, NOT "plus 4."
However, in the expressions 3+4 or 2+4, the +4 DOES
mean "plus 4." So the + symbol has
TWO different uses...

MAYBE 3...
THE PLUS SIGN
ADDS A NICE
TOUCH TOO!

EXAMPLE 2 Evaluate $-3 - 2$.

Answer $-3 - 2 = -3 + (-2) = -5$

Since a negative is being added, mentally move **2** units to the left of negative three.

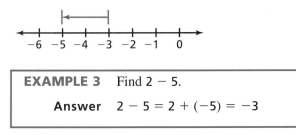

EXAMPLE 3 Find $2 - 5$.

Answer $2 - 5 = 2 + (-5) = -3$

Since a negative is being added, mentally move **5** units to the left of two.

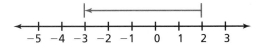

Subtracting Integers

Change to the addition of the opposite.

EXAMPLE 4   Evaluate $-15 - 7$.

Answer $-15 - 7 = -15 + (-7) = -22$

EXAMPLE 5   Find $3 - (-8)$.

Answer $3 - (-8) = 3 + 8 = 11$

▶ A. Exercises

Find the difference.

1. $+3 - (-2)$
2. $+4 - (+5)$
3. $-12 - (+5)$
4. $-8 - (-2)$
5. $-29 - (-5)$
6. $+7 - (-3)$

7. $+6 - (+8)$
8. $-16 - (-31)$
9. $-83 - (+47)$
10. $+4 - (-9)$
11. $-27 - (-41)$
12. $-12 - (-3)$

▶ B. Exercises

Find the difference.

13. $-247 - 82$
14. $-313 - (-629)$
15. $34 - (-241)$

16. $392 - (-78)$
17. $571 - 1324$
18. $387 - (-27)$

19. If the temperature on January 5 increased from $-3°$ to $14°$, how much did it increase?

Translate from words to symbols. Do not compute.

20. The difference of 6 and 2
21. Seven minus four
22. Three subtracted from eight
23. Sixteen less than five
24. Sixteen less five

Compute the following.

25. $-4 - 7 + (-2) - 6$
26. $-3 + (-6) - 8 - (-7)$
27. $-5 + (-5) - 10 - (-6)$
28. $4 + (-9) - (-8) + (-6)$

► C. Exercises

Compute the following.

29. $7 - \left| -6 + 18 \right| - (-9)$
30. $\left| -8 \right| - \left| 7 \right| - \left| -8 - 7 \right|$
31. $4 - (-5) + \left| 2 - 19 \right| - (-6) - 4$

■ Cumulative Review

Compute the following.

32. $\left| (-12) - (+7) \right|$
33. $\left| -12 \right| - \left| +7 \right|$

34. Is the absolute value of a difference always equal to the difference of absolute value?
35. Is subtraction commutative? Explain by giving an example.
36. Graph 5 and its opposite.

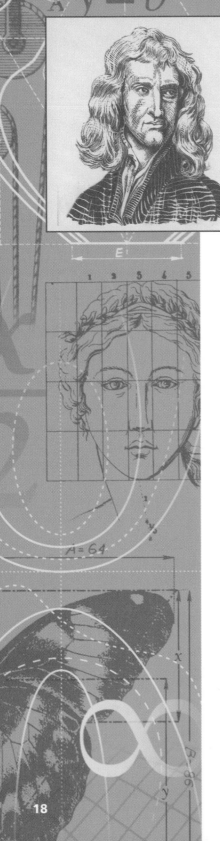

Isaac Newton

Like many children of modern times, Isaac Newton cared little for school studies. Isaac entertained numerous ideas of "modern inventions" in his active child's mind. He found more enjoyment in inventing things, such as a water clock, a windmill, a sundial, and even a self-propelled carriage, than he did in studying. He neglected his studies so much so that others considered him a poor student.

Isaac was born on Christmas, 1642 (the year Galileo died). Isaac's father died several months before Isaac was born, and Isaac's mother, Hannah, had to care both for the family farm and for her sickly child, Isaac. When Isaac was only three, his mother remarried, leaving him in the care of his grandmother. At twelve, he entered grammar school at Grantham but left two years later and began working on his mother's farm. Because he spent more time reading books than working, he was sent back to school. In spite of such an unpromising childhood, he soon became one of the greatest men in the history of mathematics.

In 1661 Newton entered Trinity College at Cambridge University. He soon mastered Descartes's work on analytic geometry. Under the tutelage of Dr. Isaac Barrow, Newton then made several mathematical discoveries, including the binomial theorem, or the expansion of $(x + y)^n$, where n is a natural number. In these ways Newton developed mathematical skills but did not show any exceptional aptitude. His teachers would not have guessed that even his binomial theorem would aid the development of higher math or that Newton himself would later become one of the founders of a branch of mathematics called calculus, which would one day become one of the four main branches of math.

$$ax^2 + bx + c = 0$$

Newton continued to enjoy science. He studied how prisms bend light rays to form rainbows and developed a 6" reflecting telescope, with which he viewed Jupiter's moons. He also studied the effects of gravity upon objects as diverse as an apple and the moon. His study of gravity led him to the development of his three laws of motion.

By the time he was thirty, Newton had been elected to the famed Royal Society, the oldest scientific society in England.

Newton had become a professor of mathematics at Cambridge University in 1669. During his twenty years there, he made most of his contributions to mathematics. Because Newton was sensitive to criticism and sought to avoid controversy, he had published few of his findings. However, his contemporaries soon discovered that Newton had proved their own conjectures and persuaded him to publish his works for the benefit of all mankind.

Through Edmund Halley's financial assistance, Newton's *Mathematical Principles of Natural Philosophy* (or *Principia*) appeared in three volumes in 1687. This work was the first to discuss relationships between celestial bodies and earthly objects; consequently, it greatly changed man's view of himself and his world.

His years of research eventually brought due recognition. In 1701 Newton was elected to Parliament. Two years later he became president of the Royal Society and was reelected each year until his death. In 1705 Queen Anne knighted him and gave him the title Sir Isaac Newton. He died on March 20, 1727, and was buried in Westminster Abbey, a burial place for many famous Englishmen.

Newton may have been a Christian and had written discussions of the books of Daniel and Revelation, which were published after his death. Certainly, he acknowledged God as the Creator of the universe and recognized that the order he found in math and science came from God.

His study of gravity led him to the development of his three laws of motion.

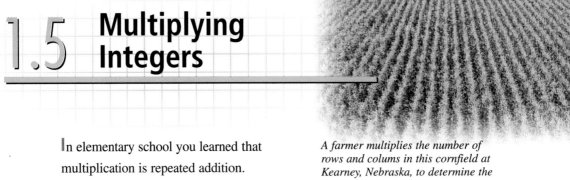

1.5 Multiplying Integers

In elementary school you learned that multiplication is repeated addition.

A farmer multiplies the number of rows and colums in this cornfield at Kearney, Nebraska, to determine the number of plants and then mutiplies by the average number of ears per plant to estimate his harvest

$$3 \cdot 5 = 5 + 5 + 5 = 15$$

Since algebra uses letters extensively, especially *x* for any unknown quantity, you may have difficulty distinguishing when *x* means "multiply" and when it is an unknown. From now on you will use a small dot in the middle of the line to indicate multiplication. Also, when no sign is shown, as in **3x** or **3(2 + 5)**, multiplication is intended. So **3x** means **3 · x** and **3(2 + 5)** means **3 · (2 + 5)**.

Properties of Numbers

1. The *commutative property of multiplication* shows that if you multiply two numbers together in different orders, the product is the same. **3 · 5 = 5 · 3**. In symbols: *ab = ba*

2. The *associative property of multiplication* shows that if you group numbers together differently when multiplying, the product is the same. **2(5 · 3) = (2 · 5)3**. In symbols: *a(bc) = (ab)c*

3. The *multiplicative identity property* shows that if you multiply any number by one (or one by any number), you get the original number. **1 · 5 = 5 · 1 = 5**. In symbols: **1 · a = a** and **a · 1 = a**

4. The *distributive property* of multiplication over addition shows that the product of a number with a sum gives the same result as multiplying each addend by the number and then adding. In symbols: *a(b + c) = ab + ac*
   $$3(6 + 7) = (3 \cdot 6) + (3 \cdot 7)$$
   $$3(13) = 18 + 21$$
   $$39 = 39$$

5. The *zero property of multiplication* shows that the product of a number and zero is zero. **4 · 0 = 0**. In symbols: *a · 0 = 0*

Factors, like addends, can be positive or negative. Look at the following illustrations of multiplication as repeated addition. Watch carefully the signs of the factors and the resulting products.

$3 \cdot 5$	$3(-5)$
$5 + 5 + 5 = 15$	$(-5) + (-5) + (-5) = -15$

Notice that in the first example both factors are positive and the product is also positive. In the second, one factor is positive and the other negative. The product is negative.

If we apply the commutative property of multiplication to the second example, we see that it does not matter which term carries the negative sign. $3 \cdot -5 = -5 \cdot 3$. If exactly one factor of a multiplication problem is negative, the resulting product is also negative.

Do you know what will happen if both factors are negative? Observe the pattern in these products.

$(3)(-5) = -15$
$(2)(-5) = -10$ found by using the illustration above
$(1)(-5) = -5$

$0(-5) = 0$ found by the zero property of multiplication

$(-1)(-5) = 5$
$(-2)(-5) = 10$ found by continuing the pattern
$(-3)(-5) = 15$

As the first factor decreases by one, the product increases by five. Notice that the product of a negative factor and a positive factor is negative but that the product of two negatives is positive.

Multiplying Integers

1. If the factors are both positive ($a > 0$, $b > 0$) or both negative ($a < 0$, $b < 0$), the product is positive.
   In symbols: $ab = |a| \cdot |b|$

2. If one factor is positive ($a > 0$) and the other is negative ($b < 0$), the product is negative.
   In symbols: $ab = -|a| \cdot |b|$

EXAMPLE 1 $(-2)(+9)$

Answer   Since $-2 < 0$ (negative) and $+9 > 0$ (positive), condition 2 applies.

$-|-2| \cdot |9| = -18.$

EXAMPLE 2 $(-4)(-6)$

Answer   Since $-4 < 0$ (negative) and $-6 < 0$ (negative), condition 1 applies.

$|-4| \cdot |-6| = (4 \cdot 6) = 24$

► A. Exercises

Multiply.

1. $(+3)(-2)$
2. $(+7)(+8)$
3. $(-4)(-6)$
4. $(-8)(+6)$
5. $(-3)(-1)$

6. $(+3)(-7)$
7. $(+4)(+9)$
8. $(-32)(+3)$
9. $(-41)(-7)$
10. $(+79)(-8)$

11. $(-25)(-5)$
12. $(-182)(+3)$
13. $(-10)(+3892)$
14. $(-964)(-81)$
15. $(+372)(-46)$

► B. Exercises

Multiply.

16. $1234 \cdot 369$
17. $-374(-941)$
18. $-76(-423)$

19. $-471 \cdot 34$
20. $462(-491)$

Translate each phrase into symbols. Do not compute.

21. Five times four
22. Seven multiplied by three
23. The product of two and nine
24. Twice eleven
25. Six sets of eight objects each

Apply your knowledge of integers to solve these word problems.

26. On successive days, Jim's newspaper sales profit (or loss) is represented by signed numbers as $7.50, -$1.95, $3.75, -$0.70. Find his profit for the four-day period.

27. Mr. Hendricks represented his bank deposits as positive numbers and checks as negative numbers. If his transactions in dollars were represented as $-37, -9, 157, -6, -140,$ and $118,$ by how much did his account balance change during this period?

28. A northern city had the following temperatures one winter week. Find the average temperature for the week: $-7, -15, 2, 9, -1, 17, 23.$

► C. Exercises

Look at each pattern and express it as a property by using a variable.

29. $-3 = -1 \cdot 3$
    $-4 = -1 \cdot 4$
    $-7 = -1 \cdot 7$

30. $-(-1) = 1$
    $-(-3) = 3$
    $-(-6) = 6$

31. Write $8(-3)$ using the definition of multiplication as repeated addition.

Simplify.

32. $-(-2)$

33. $|-4|$

34. $(-5) + (-3)$

35. $(-5)(-3)$

36. $(-5) - (-3)$

1.6 Dividing Integers

Just as subtraction is the inverse operation of addition, division is the inverse operation of multiplication. Every multiplication problem has two corresponding division problems, and every division problem has a corresponding multiplication problem.

A section of this stadium has 16 rows and seats 480. If you distribute fliers, how many should you pass down each row?

$9 \cdot 2 = 18$	so	$18 \div 2 = 9$	and	$18 \div 9 = 2$
$6 \cdot 4 = 24$	so	$24 \div 6 = 4$	and	$24 \div 4 = 6$
$-5 \cdot 3 = -15$	so	$-15 \div -5 = 3$	and	$-15 \div 3 = -5$

Because division and multiplication are inverse operations, the sign rules for division correspond to the sign rules for multiplication.

Dividing Integers

1. If the divisor and the dividend have like signs, the quotient will be positive.

2. If the divisor and the dividend have unlike signs, the quotient will be negative.

EXAMPLE 1 $+14 \div +2 = +7$	**EXAMPLE 3** $+105 \div -21 = -5$
EXAMPLE 2 $-72 \div +9 = -8$	**EXAMPLE 4** $-864 \div -36 = +24$

A good way to check your division is to multiply the quotient by the divisor. The answer should be the same as your dividend.

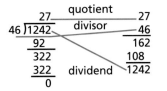

Remember that division is also indicated by a fraction bar.

Now here's a division problem for you.

$$\frac{18}{0} = 18 \div 0$$

Change it to a multiplication problem.

$$0 \cdot ? = 18$$

What number can you multiply by 0 to get 18? According to the zero property of multiplication, the product of any number and 0 is always 0. Therefore, there is no number that when multiplied by 0 gives a product of 18. Consequently, division by 0 is not possible and is, therefore, undefined.

$18 \div 0$ is undefined, but what about $0 \div 18$? There is a definite answer to this problem. $18 \cdot ? = 0$? The answer is 0.

In conclusion, $\frac{0}{18} = 0$, but $\frac{18}{0}$ is undefined.

Now that you have reviewed all four operations on integers you should be able to identify and use all of these properties.

Property	of Addition	of Multiplication
commutative	$a + b = b + a$ $3 + 4 = 4 + 3$	$a \cdot b = b \cdot a$ $4 \cdot 2 = 2 \cdot 4$
associative	$a + (b + c) = (a + b) + c$ $2 + (3 + 4) = (2 + 3) + 4$	$a(b \cdot c) = (a \cdot b)c$ $5(3 \cdot 2) = (5 \cdot 3)2$
identity	$a + 0 = a$ and $0 + a = a$ $3 + 0 = 3$ and $0 + 3 = 3$	$a \cdot 1 = a$ and $1 \cdot a = a$ $5 \cdot 1 = 5$ and $1 \cdot 5 = 5$
inverse	$a + (-a) = 0$ $3 + (-3) = 0$	
zero		$a \cdot 0 = 0$ $6 \cdot 0 = 0$
distributive		over addition and subtraction $a(b + c) = (a \cdot b) + (a \cdot c)$ $4(3 + 2) = (4 \cdot 3) + (4 \cdot 2)$

▶ A. Exercises

Divide.

1. $(+27) \div (+3)$
2. $(-56) \div (+8)$
3. $(+36) \div 0$
4. $(-20) \div (-4)$
5. $(+54) \div (-6)$

6. $(-48) \div (+6)$
7. $\frac{+198}{-22}$
8. $\frac{0}{-37}$
9. $\frac{-516}{+86}$
10. $\frac{-6584}{-823}$

Translate each phrase into symbols, using the fraction bar to denote division.

11. Eight divided by three
12. Divide four into twelve
13. The quotient of nine and two
14. Divide fifty by six
15. The ratio of eleven to four

▶ B. Exercises

Divide.

16. $588 \div (-84)$
17. $\frac{-124}{0}$
18. $\frac{-732}{-61}$
19. $3403 \div 41$
20. $-1768 \div -52$

21. $\frac{1075}{-25}$
22. $-1953 \div 31$
23. $-2352 \div (-56)$
24. $\frac{-3136}{56}$

▶ C. Exercises

25. $(14{,}175 \div -5) \div (-2916 \div -36)$
26. The product of two numbers is **7904** and the absolute value of one of the numbers is **247**. Find two possible solutions for the other number.

■ Cumulative Review

Simplify.

27. $34 + 25 - 84$
28. $(3)(5)(-18)$

Give the property that justifies each step.

29. $(56 + 0) + (79 + 44) \quad = \quad 56 + (79 + 44)$
30. $\qquad\qquad\qquad\qquad = \quad 56 + (44 + 79)$
31. $\qquad\qquad\qquad\qquad = \quad (56 + 44) + 79$
$\qquad\qquad\qquad\qquad = \quad 100 + 79$
$\qquad\qquad\qquad\qquad = \quad 179$

32. Is division commutative? Explain and give an example.

Probability and statistics are topics that affect your life daily. In this study, you will learn the difference between these topics. In future studies in this series, you will study these topics in greater depth to help you evaluate the vast amount of information that you receive in the form of probability and statistics.

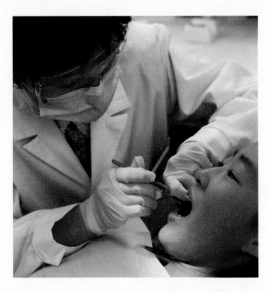

The integers that you studied in this chapter are the basis for probability. A **probability** is a ratio of two integers used to express a likelihood. For instance, an advertiser may tell you that **3** out of **4** dentists recommend a certain brand of toothpaste. The phrase "**3** out of **4**" describes the ratio $\frac{3}{4}$. By division, it could also be expressed as a percentage. The same advertiser could have said that **75** percent of all dentists recommend that toothpaste.

Probabilities reported as percentages are all around us. A weather reporter may say that there is a **60** percent chance of rain, or a newscaster may report that **34** percent of the people favor a political candidate. Studying probability will help you understand and evaluate these integer ratios and percents.

In contrast, **statistics** are real numbers that describe or characterize a set of data. For instance, when you took standardized tests in eighth grade, your teachers and parents looked at your scores in relation to the scores of all the eighth graders in the nation. They compared your score with the average score. Perhaps the average was the real number **78.4**. Averages are one of the important statistical measurements for comparisons.

Classify each of the following as a probability or a statistic.
1. Twenty percent of all fatal traffic accidents involve a speeding motorist.
2. The average age at which children learn to walk is **11** months.
3. The highest score on today's quiz was **97** and the lowest was **44**.
4. The ratio of teachers to students at this school is one to ten.
5. Stan has made five out of every six free throws this season.

1.7 Exponents

Do you know a short way to write $6 \cdot 6 \cdot 6$ or $5 \cdot 5$? To save time and space, you can use the exponential form. *Exponential form* is a shorter way to write repeated multiplication just as multiplication is a shorter way to write repeated addition. In exponential form, $6 \cdot 6 \cdot 6 = 6^3$ and $5 \cdot 5 = 5^2$. In 6^3 the 3 is the *exponent,* and the 6 is the *base.* The expression 5^2 is read "5 to the second power," or "5 squared," and 6^3 is read "six to the third power," or "six cubed."

The reasons for this terminology are illustrated by the area of a square and the volume of a cube.

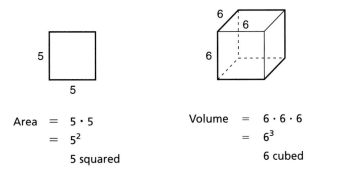

Area $= 5 \cdot 5$
$\quad\ = 5^2$
5 squared

Volume $= 6 \cdot 6 \cdot 6$
$\qquad\ = 6^3$
6 cubed

Definition

Exponential form is a simplified form of writing repeated multiplication.

Can you use exponents to simplify problems? Here are a few examples.

EXAMPLE 1 Write $2 \cdot 2 \cdot 2 \cdot 2$ in exponential form.

Answer The base is 2, which is used as a factor four times.

$$2 \cdot 2 \cdot 2 \cdot 2 = 2^4$$

EXAMPLE 2 Write $4 \cdot 4 \cdot 4 \cdot 4 \cdot 4$ in exponential form.

Answer $4 \cdot 4 \cdot 4 \cdot 4 \cdot 4 = 4^5$

Now we can expand and evaluate exponential forms. To "evaluate" means to change from exponential form to a number. For example, the evaluation of 2^2 is 4.

EXAMPLE 3 Evaluate 5^3.

 Answer $5 \cdot 5 \cdot 5 = 125$

EXAMPLE 4 Evaluate 8^4.

 Answer $8 \cdot 8 \cdot 8 \cdot 8 = 4096$

EXAMPLE 5 Evaluate $(-3)^2$.

 Answer $-3 \cdot -3 = 9$

EXAMPLE 6 Evaluate $(-7)^3$.

 Answer $(-7)(-7)(-7) = -343$

What happens when you multiply like bases?

$$5^2 \cdot 5^3 = (5 \cdot 5)(5 \cdot 5 \cdot 5) = 5^{2+3} = 5^5$$

When the bases are the same and the operation is multiplication, add the exponents.

What happens when you divide like bases?

$$8^5 \div 8^2 = \frac{8^5}{8^2} = \frac{8 \cdot 8 \cdot \overset{1}{\cancel{8}} \cdot \overset{1}{\cancel{8}} \cdot 8}{\underset{1}{\cancel{8}} \cdot \underset{1}{\cancel{8}}} = 8^{5-2} = 8^3$$

When the bases are the same and the operation is division, subtract the exponents.

What happens when you raise an exponential expression to a power?

$$(3^2)^4 = 3^2 \cdot 3^2 \cdot 3^2 \cdot 3^2 = (3 \cdot 3)(3 \cdot 3)(3 \cdot 3)(3 \cdot 3) = 3^8$$

When the bases are the same and the operation is raising an exponential expression to a power, multiply exponents.

Properties of Exponents

1. The *multiplication property* shows that if you multiply like bases, the exponents must be added.

   For integers x, a, and b, $x^a \cdot x^b = x^{a + b}$.

2. The *division property* shows that if you divide like bases, the exponents must be subtracted.

   For integers, x, a, and b, with $x \neq 0$, $\frac{x^a}{x^b} = x^{a - b}$.

3. The *power property* shows that if you raise a power to a power, the exponents must be multiplied.

   For integers x, a, and b, $(x^a)^b = x^{ab}$.

4. The *zero property* shows that for any base $x \neq 0$, $x^0 = 1$.

$$5^0 = 1 \qquad (-5)^0 = 1$$
$$10^0 = 1 \qquad 14^0 = 1$$

Since $\dfrac{3^4}{3^4} = 3^{4-4} = 3^0$

and $\dfrac{3^4}{3^4} = \dfrac{\overset{1}{\cancel{3}} \cdot \overset{1}{\cancel{3}} \cdot \overset{1}{\cancel{3}} \cdot \overset{1}{\cancel{3}}}{\underset{1}{\cancel{3}} \cdot \underset{1}{\cancel{3}} \cdot \underset{1}{\cancel{3}} \cdot \underset{1}{\cancel{3}}} = 1$

$3^0 = 1$

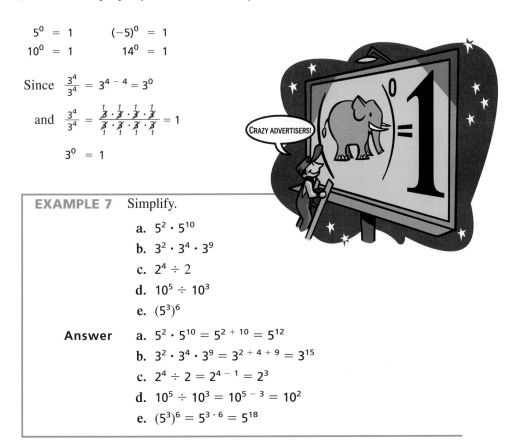

CRAZY ADVERTISERS!

EXAMPLE 7 Simplify.

    a. $5^2 \cdot 5^{10}$

    b. $3^2 \cdot 3^4 \cdot 3^9$

    c. $2^4 \div 2$

    d. $10^5 \div 10^3$

    e. $(5^3)^6$

Answer   **a.** $5^2 \cdot 5^{10} = 5^{2 + 10} = 5^{12}$

    b. $3^2 \cdot 3^4 \cdot 3^9 = 3^{2 + 4 + 9} = 3^{15}$

    c. $2^4 \div 2 = 2^{4 - 1} = 2^3$

    d. $10^5 \div 10^3 = 10^{5 - 3} = 10^2$

    e. $(5^3)^6 = 5^{3 \cdot 6} = 5^{18}$

EXAMPLE 8   Simplify.

  a. $3^2 \cdot 3^5 \cdot 2^4 \cdot 2^6$

  b. $4^3 \cdot 4^5 \cdot 4 \cdot 5^3$

Answer   **a.** $3^2 \cdot 3^5 \cdot 2^4 \cdot 2^6 = 3^7 \cdot 2^{10}$

  b. $4^3 \cdot 4^5 \cdot 4 \cdot 5^3 = 4^9 \cdot 5^3$

▶ A. Exercises

Write as repeated factors; then evaluate.

1. 4^3
2. $(-2)^4$
3. $(-3)^5$
4. 1^4
5. 2314^0
6. 6^4

Write in exponential form. Do not evaluate.

7. $7 \cdot 7 \cdot 7 \cdot 7$
8. $5 \cdot 5 \cdot 5 \cdot 5 \cdot 5 \cdot 5$
9. $(-4)(-4)$
10. $127 \cdot 127 \cdot 127$

Simplify, leaving the answer in exponential notation.

11. $3^2 \cdot 3^3$
12. $4^{16} \div 4^{-2}$
13. $(8^3)^5$
14. $(3^{11})^0$
15. $12^2 \cdot 12^7$
16. $(10^{10})^5$
17. $7^2 \cdot 7^9$
18. $10^{12} \cdot 10^3$
19. $8^7 \div 8^3$
20. $17^{81} \div 17^{12}$
21. $3^{148} \div 3^{140}$
22. $(7^2)^3$
23. $(28^4)^2$
24. $5^3 \cdot 5^2 \cdot 5^{10}$
25. $2^3 \div 2$

▶ B. Exercises

Simplify, leaving the answer in exponential form.

26. $2^2 \cdot 2^3 \cdot 3^4 \cdot 5^2 \cdot 5$
27. $10^2 \cdot 10^4 (-2)^3 (-2)^6$
28. Identify any of the following that are positive.
   $(-2)^3, (-2)^4, (-3)^2, (-3)^5$
29. If you raise a negative number to an odd power, is the answer positive or negative?
30. If you raise a negative number to an even power, is the answer positive or negative?

Translate each phrase into symbols. Do not evaluate.

31. Two to the seventh power
32. Nine to the fifth power
33. The tenth power of six
34. The square of eight
35. Four cubed

Simplify, leaving answers in exponential notation.

36. $\dfrac{2^3 \cdot 3^{10} \cdot 2^7 \cdot 5^3}{2^4 \cdot 5^4 \, (3^5)^2}$ **37.** $\dfrac{2^4 \cdot 7^8 (11^9)^2}{2^3 (3^2)^3 \cdot 3^5}$

■ Cumulative Review

Simplify (do all indicated operations).

38. $37 - 85$ **42.** $-389 + (-27)$

39. $126 + 395$ **43.** $23 + (-82)$

40. $27(-82)$ **44.** $(-83)(-24)$

41. $-135 \div 5$ **45.** $-146 + (-29) + 35$

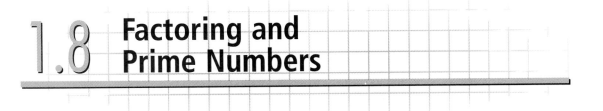

1.8 Factoring and Prime Numbers

Two integers multiplied together are called *factors* of the product. For example, to factor **12**, you must think what numbers multiplied together equal **12**. There are several: -4 and -3 are factors of **12** because $-4(-3)= 12$; 6 and 2 are factors of **12**; 1 and 12 are factors of **12**. In fact, ± 1, ± 2, ± 3, ± 4, ± 6, and ± 12, are all factors of **12**. (The symbol $\pm$ means "positive or negative.") What are the factors of **8**? The factors of **8** are ± 1, ± 2, ± 4, and ± 8.

Definition

A **prime number** is an integer greater than 1 whose only positive factors are 1 and itself.

What is the smallest prime number? The first prime number is 2, because the only positive factors of **2** are 1 and **2**.

Definition

A **composite number** is a nonprime positive integer greater than 1.

By definition 0 and 1 are neither prime nor composite.

Every natural number greater than 1 is a prime or can be factored uniquely into a product of primes. The product of the factors will give the original number. When all the factors of a given number are prime, we say that the number has been factored into the product of its prime factors. Factor trees can help you organize your work.

EXAMPLE 1 Find the prime factors of 12.

Answer

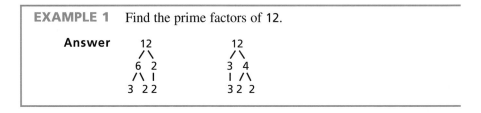

First, divide 12 by 2. Notice that 2 is prime but 6 is not. Continue factoring until all factors are prime. Factors of 6 are 3 and 2. Since 3 and 2 are primes, the prime factorization of 12 is $2 \cdot 2 \cdot 3$ or $2^2 \cdot 3$.

If you start the factorization with 3 and 4, are the results the same?

EXAMPLE 2 Find the prime factors of 36 three ways.

Answer

```
    36              36              36
   / \             / \             / \
  6   6   or      4   9   or      12   3
 /\  /\          /\  /\          /\   |
3 2 3 2         2 2 3 3         4 3   3
                              /\ | |
So 36 = 3² · 2²              2 2 3   3
```

EXAMPLE 3 Find the prime factors of 86.

Answer The prime factors of 86 are 2 and 43.

```
    86
   / \
 43   2
```

You should be able to find the prime factors of any composite number. Here is a large number to factor into primes.

EXAMPLE 4 Factor 14,175 into primes.

Answer

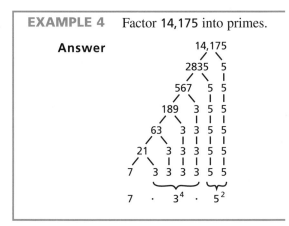

The prime factorization of 14,175 is $3^4 \cdot 5^2 \cdot 7$ in simplified exponential form. Another method for factoring a number into its prime factors is called the ladder method, or successive division.

EXAMPLE 5   Factor **18** into primes.

Answer

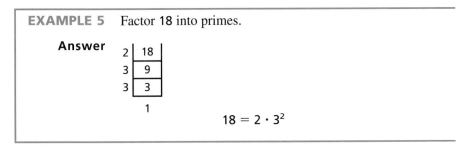

$$18 = 2 \cdot 3^2$$

In this method, divide by prime numbers until the quotient is one, writing the prime numbers on the left of the ladder. These are the prime factors. Always begin with the smallest prime number that divides into the number you are factoring and use it until it no longer divides into the previous quotient.

EXAMPLE 6   Give the prime factorization of **3780**.

Answer

$$
\begin{array}{r|r}
2 & 3780 \\ \hline
2 & 1890 \\ \hline
3 & 945 \\ \hline
3 & 315 \\ \hline
3 & 105 \\ \hline
5 & 35 \\ \hline
7 & 7 \\ \hline
& 1
\end{array}
$$

The prime factorization is $3780 = 2^2 \cdot 3^3 \cdot 5 \cdot 7$ in exponential form.

▶ A. Exercises

Use either method to factor each number into its prime factors. Give answers in exponential form. List bases in ascending order. Show factoring.

1. 48
2. 158
3. 873
4. 840
5. 820
6. 14,553
7. 1384
8. 978
9. 94
10. 89

▶ B. Exercises

Factor each number into its prime factors, listing bases in ascending order. Give answers in exponential form.

11. 27,783
12. 6048
13. 20,160
14. 11,664
15. 2688
16. 104
17. 1081
18. 531
19. 28,561
20. 2023

▶ C. Exercises

Translate each phrase into symbols. Do not simplify.

21. The sum of the squares of five and six
22. The difference between the cube and the square of seven
23. The cube of negative seven
24. The opposite of the cube of seven
25. Three less than the square of five
26. Three more than the square of five

▪ Cumulative Review

Perform the indicated operations.

27. $87 + 98 - 378$
28. $48(-5)(7)$
29. $387 - 873 - 278$
30. $-75 + 78 + 98$
31. $(-8)(-4)(-27)$
32. $3 + 4 - 9 + 6 - 28$
33. $4500 \div -36$
34. $-8978 \div -67$
35. $-129 - 35 - 69 - 72$

1.9 Greatest Common Factor and Least Common Multiple

Once you have factored numbers into primes, you can easily find the greatest common factor (GCF) and the least common multiple (LCM) of the two numbers. The GCF is used to simplify fractions. To rename a fraction in lowest terms, divide the numerator and the denominator by the GCF of the two numbers.

Definition

The **greatest common factor** (GCF) is the largest positive integer that divides evenly into two numbers.

The greatest common factor of two numbers is the product of the prime factors that the numbers have in common.

EXAMPLE 1 Find the GCF of 18 and 56.

Answer 1. Find the prime factors of 18 and 56.

```
      18              56
     / \             / \
    9   2          28    2
   / \  |         / \    |
  3  3  ②       14  2    2
                / \ |    |
               7  ②2     2
```

2. Circle the prime factors common to both numbers. Here 2 is the common factor.

3. The GCF of 18 and 56 is the highest power of 2 common to both numbers. Although 3 factors of 2 are contained in 56, it is a factor of 18 only once. Therefore, the GCF of these numbers is 2.

Finding the Greatest Common Factor

1. Factor both numbers into primes and write in exponential form.

2. Circle each factor common to both numbers and determine the highest common power of each factor.

3. Find the product of the common factors found in step 2.

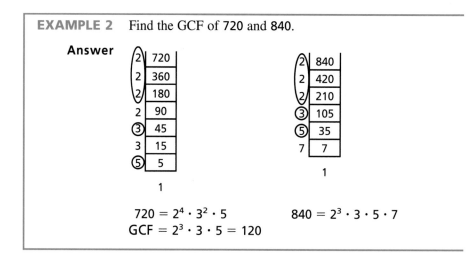

EXAMPLE 2   Find the GCF of 720 and 840.

Answer

$$720 = 2^4 \cdot 3^2 \cdot 5 \qquad 840 = 2^3 \cdot 3 \cdot 5 \cdot 7$$
$$\text{GCF} = 2^3 \cdot 3 \cdot 5 = 120$$

These two numbers have several common factors: **5**, **3**, and **2**. Since the factors **2** and **3** have different exponents, we choose the smaller exponent for each factor. The GCF is the product of these common primes. The largest integer that will divide evenly into both **720** and **840** is **120**.

The least common multiple of denominators is frequently used in arithmetic and in algebra when adding or subtracting fractions or irrational expressions because it is the lowest common denominator.

The **least common multiple** (LCM) is the smallest positive integer that is a multiple of two numbers.

EXAMPLE 3   Find the LCM of 12 and 42.

Answer

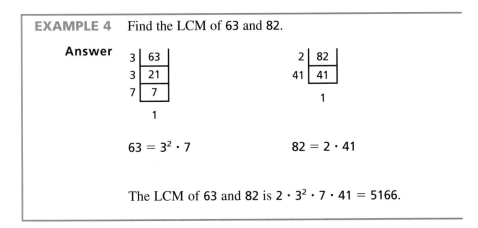

$3 \cdot 2^2 = 12$ $3 \cdot 2 \cdot 7 = 42$

$LCM = 2^2 \cdot 3 \cdot 7 = 84$

1. Factor each number and write the prime factorizations in exponential form.

2. Multiply the largest exponential form of each factor.

The product of these factors is 84, the smallest number that both 12 and 42 will divide into evenly.

EXAMPLE 4   Find the LCM of 63 and 82.

Answer

```
3 | 63          2 | 82
3 | 21         41 | 41
7 |  7              1
     1
```

$63 = 3^2 \cdot 7$ $82 = 2 \cdot 41$

The LCM of 63 and 82 is $2 \cdot 3^2 \cdot 7 \cdot 41 = 5166$.

Finding the Least Common Multiple
1. Factor both numbers into primes written in exponential form.
2. Circle the highest power of each prime factor.
3. Find the product of all circled factors.

▶ A. Exercises

Find the GCF of the integers given.
1. 34 and 784
2. 358 and 934
3. 792 and 392
4. 5760 and 34,560
5. 3780 and 420
6. 4725 and 378

Find the LCM of the integers given.
7. 140 and 34
8. 82 and 54
9. 38 and 95
10. 924 and 36
11. 504 and 352
12. 92 and 38

▶ B. Exercises

Find the factored form of the LCM and GCF.
13. $2^5 \cdot 3^4 \cdot 7$ and $2^3 \cdot 3^4 \cdot 5^2$
14. $2 \cdot 3^7 \cdot 5^2$ and $3 \cdot 5^3$

Translate each phrase into symbols. Do not simplify.
15. Five more than eight
16. Five less than eight
17. Five multiplied by eight
18. Five divided by eight
19. Five less eight

▶ C. Exercises

If a is a factor of b, find the following.
20. The GCF of a and b
21. The LCM of a and b

If a and b are relatively prime, find the following.
22. The GCF of a and b
23. The LCM of a and b

Use a, b, the GCF of a and b, and the LCM of a and b. Assume $a \neq b$, a and b are not relatively prime, and neither divides into the other.
24. Which is always the largest?
25. Which is always the smallest?

Cumulative Review

Complete the following computations.

26. 689(−4)
27. −27 ÷ 3
28. 142 + 386 − 1024
29. 82 − 79 − 38 + 124
30. 6(−3)(−18)4

31. 42 + 38 − 147 + 25
32. 12(−15)(3)(10)
33. −176,295 ÷ 69
34. −56 + 29 + 186
35. 192 − 35 − 81

Algebra *and* Scripture

In this chapter you studied numbers and their properties, which are basic to the study of algebra.

The Bible provides a basis for the study of numbers. God used numbers during Creation week to describe the orderliness and exactness of His creation. A biblical study of the numbers in the Creation account follows.

1. List the numbers in Genesis 1 that signal the end of a paragraph.
2. What do these numbers count?
3. Since God cannot do evil, what can you conclude about counting?
4. What does the number in Genesis 1:16 describe?

Genesis 2 through 8 illustrate seven purposes for numbers.

5. Order. The counting in Genesis 1 shows the order in which God created living things. What number draws the order to conclusion in Genesis 2:1-3?
6. Counting. What does God count in Genesis 2:10-14? How many are there?
7. Time spans. All 28 numbers in Chapter 5 are time spans. What is being measured by them?
8. Measurement. Give the dimensions of the ark (Gen. 6).
9. Totals. How many of each creature did Noah count (Gen. 7)?
10. Dates. Supply the first dates from Genesis 7:11 and 8:13.
11. Depth. Give the first depth (Gen. 7:20).

There are other purposes for numbers, but these are enough to show that numbers can be used to describe a variety of things. What could you call this property of numbers?

ℕumbers glorify God in describing the order of creation, in counting created objects, measuring distances and sizes, registering dates and counting spans of time. What is the word used to describe such concepts that cannot be touched and handled?

12. What does Isaiah 55:9 imply about God's knowledge?

Scriptural Roots

𝔉OR AS THE HEAVENS ARE higher than the earth, so are my ways higher than your ways, and my thoughts than your thoughts. ଈ

ISAIAH 55:9

Chapter 1 Review

Graph these integers on separate horizontal number lines.

1. 1
2. 24
3. Graph the integer -2 on a vertical number line.
4. Find the coordinate of the midpoint, *M*, of the segment joining -3 and 7 on a number line, and graph all three points as a check.

Identify the opposite of each number.

5. 29
6. -10

Identify the absolute value of each number.

7. $|-13|$
8. $|6|$

Simplify.

9. $14 + (-18)$
10. $(-14)(2)$
11. $12 - 32$
12. $(-2)^3$
13. $-32 \div -8$
14. $-5 + 3$
15. 15^0
16. $7 - 18$
17. $(-37)(-12)$

Perform the indicated operation and leave in exponential form.

18. $8^9 \cdot 8^6$
19. $4^5 \cdot 4^8 \div 4^2$
20. $(3^4)^3$

Give the prime factorization of these numbers. Show factoring.

21. 75
22. 210

Find the LCM of the numbers given.

23. 9 and 24
24. 18 and 27

Find the GCF of the numbers given.

25. 216 and 308
26. 270 and 330

Match the properties to the correct symbolic statement.

    A. associative property of addition
    B. associative property of multiplication
    C. commutative property of addition
    D. commutative property of multiplication
    E. distributive property
    F. identity property of addition
    G. identity property of multiplication
    H. zero property of multiplication
    I. additive inverse property

27. $a \cdot 0 = 0$
28. $a + 0 = a$
29. $(a + b) + c = a + (b + c)$
30. $a + (-a) = 0$
31. $ab = ba$
32. $a \cdot 1 = a$
33. $a(b + c) = ab + ac$
34. $a + b = b + a$
35. $a(bc) = (ab)c$

Translate each phrase into symbols. Do not simplify.
36. The opposite of negative six
37. Eight less than five
38. The product of fifteen and three
39. The sum of four and the square of nine
40. Explain the mathematical significance of Isaiah 55:9.

2 Real Numbers

$y = mx + b$

Numbers are found in every field of study, so it is important to learn what these numbers mean and how to use them. This chapter will review the different types of numbers and four basic operations governing them.

Many forms of numbers are used in our society. You will soon be able to classify them into sets of numbers.

Cost of a shirt	$15.95	**decimal**
Recipe amount	$\frac{1}{3}$ cup sugar	**fraction**
Traffic statistic	5.7 accidents daily	**decimal**
Scientific distance	4.39×10^{13} mi.	**decimal, exponent**
Peanut butter survey	5 out of 7 prefer creamy	**ratio**
Temperature	$-14°$	**negative integer**
Package weight	3.2 lbs.	**decimal**
Area of a circular table	4π sq. ft.	**irrational numbers**
Population— bacteria culture	$5 \cdot 2^{15}$	**exponent**
Size of bacterium	1.3×10^{-4} mm	**decimal, exponent, negative integer**

After this chapter you should be able to

1. identify types of numbers and locate them on a number line.

2. add, subtract, multiply, and divide rational numbers.

3. find the specified root of certain numbers.

4. find the intersection and union of sets.

5. identify and use properties of real numbers.

6. use grouping symbols and the order of operations to simplify expressions.

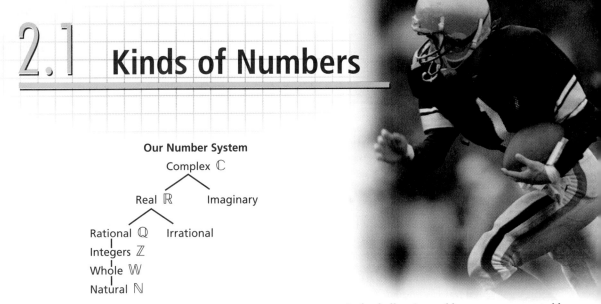

2.1 Kinds of Numbers

Our Number System

Complex $\mathbb{C}$

Real $\mathbb{R}$ Imaginary

Rational $\mathbb{Q}$ Irrational
Integers $\mathbb{Z}$
Whole $\mathbb{W}$
Natural $\mathbb{N}$

In football, gains and losses are represented by positive and negative real numbers respectively.

Can you remember when you learned to count? Slowly and deliberately you probably learned to count to ten; 1, 2, 3, 4, 5, 6, 7, 8, 9, 10. But you soon learned to count beyond ten. The numbers you used are called the *natural numbers,* or *counting numbers,* because they are numbers that describe what people see in nature. The natural numbers begin with 1 and continue infinitely.

Another set of numbers is the *whole numbers,* which have only one more number than the natural numbers. What one number is a whole number but not a natural number?

The numbers 0, 1, 2, 3, and so forth, are whole numbers. Sometimes the symbol . . . is used for "and so forth." Thus, you can write, "The whole numbers are 0, 1, 2, 3, . . ." Whole numbers are the steppingstones for our entire number system.

The next set in the number system is the integers. The word *integer* comes from a Latin word that means "entire." *Integers* are whole numbers and their opposites.

    . . . , −4, −3, −2, −1, 0, 1, 2, 3, 4, . . .

Notice that the integers have no smallest number and no largest number. Integers smaller than 0 are preceded by a negative sign. You learned to work with integers (including natural and whole numbers) in Chapter 1.

Mr. Weber, the football coach at East Park High School, wants his players to perform to the best of their ability in the weekly scrimmage. Each time a play is run the coach records a positive integer if the offense gains yards and a negative integer if they lose yardage. For example, if the offense gains **5** yards the coach records **+5** and if they lose a yard he records **−1**. At the end of the scrimmage, he totals the results. If the sum is positive **100** yards or more, the defense runs laps after practice. If the total is less than **100** yards, the offense runs laps instead. Do you think these boys will understand integers?

Notice that fractions have not yet appeared in our number system, but they are in constant use in our society.

In drama class, girls must sew costumes using a pattern. For her costume, each girl must purchase $\frac{3}{4}$ of a yard of $\frac{5}{8}$-inch-wide elastic. Do you think it is important to know the difference between $\frac{3}{4}$ of a yard and $\frac{1}{4}$ of a yard? Could the girls finish their costumes if they got $\frac{1}{4}$ of a yard of elastic?

How about decimal fractions? Just changing a spark plug in a car requires gapping spark plugs to the correct setting of thousandths of an inch. A setting of **.030** of an inch might be typical. Set it wrong and the car runs poorly or not at all.

All numbers presented so far are rational numbers. The word *rational* comes from the word meaning "ratio." *Rational numbers* are numbers that can be written as a ratio. All fractions produced by placing one integer over a nonzero integer are rational numbers. Because any integer can be written over **1**, integers are rational numbers.

In sewing, real numbers describe portions of yards of cloth.

A **rational number** is a number that can be expressed as a ratio of two integers when the denominator is not equal to **0**.

EXAMPLE 1   Which is not a rational number?
$\frac{5}{8}$, $-\frac{17}{12}$, 0, $4\frac{2}{3}$, -9, $\frac{3}{0}$, $\frac{341}{3}$

Answer   Only $4\frac{2}{3}$ is not a ratio of the integers. But it can be written as the improper fraction $\frac{14}{3}$. However, $\frac{3}{0}$ is undefined. Thus, $\frac{3}{0}$ is not a rational number.

Decimals that can be written as a ratio are also rational numbers. To understand which decimals represent rational numbers, you must be able to convert between fractional form and decimal form.

Such decimals either terminate or repeat. The repeating portion is signified by a line across the repeating sequence of digits.

EXAMPLE 2   Convert $\frac{12}{5}$ and $\frac{4}{11}$ to decimals.

Answer   1. Divide to convert
2. If the decimal repeats, write the sequence only once and place a bar over it.

$$
\begin{array}{r}
2.4 \\
5\overline{)12.0} \\
\underline{10} \\
20 \\
\underline{20}
\end{array}
\qquad
\begin{array}{r}
.3636 \\
11\overline{)4.0000} \\
\underline{3\,3} \\
70 \\
\underline{66} \\
40 \\
\underline{33} \\
70 \\
\underline{66} \\
4
\end{array}
$$

$$\frac{12}{5} = 2.4 \qquad \frac{4}{11} = 0.\overline{36}$$

EXAMPLE 3   Which rational numbers terminate? Which are repeating?
$\frac{5}{8}, \frac{1}{3}, -\frac{3}{4}, -\frac{1}{7}, \frac{5}{12}, \frac{22}{5}, 3\frac{1}{9}$

Answer   Terminating Decimals
$\frac{5}{8} = 0.625, -\frac{3}{4} = -0.75, \frac{22}{5} = 4.4$

Repeating Decimals
$\frac{1}{3} = 0.333\ldots = 0.\overline{3}$

$-\frac{1}{7} = -0.142857142857\ldots = -0.\overline{142857}$

$\frac{5}{12} = 0.41666\ldots = 0.41\overline{6}, 3\frac{1}{9} = 3.111\ldots = 3.\overline{1}$

Notice that the repeating decimal $0.\overline{3}$ can be represented as $\frac{1}{3}$, a ratio of integers. All repeating decimals can be so represented.

Numbers that cannot be expressed in fractional form are called irrational numbers. God's creation displays irrational numbers such as π, $\sqrt{2}$, and $\sqrt{6}$. The decimal form of these numbers does not terminate and never repeats. Therefore, to compute with them, we use a rational approximation of their value.

EXAMPLE 4   Give rational numbers approximately equal to π and $\sqrt{2}$.

Answer $\pi = 3.14159\ldots$ $\qquad\qquad$ $\sqrt{2} = 1.414213562\ldots$

Rational approximations $\qquad$ Rational approximation

$3.14 = 3\frac{14}{100} = \frac{314}{100}$ $\qquad\qquad$ $1.414 = 1\frac{414}{1000} = \frac{1414}{1000}$

$3\frac{1}{7} = \frac{22}{7}$

EXAMPLE 5   Which numbers are rational?

$\qquad$ 5 $\quad$ $\sqrt{3}$ $\quad$ 4.53 $\quad$ π $\quad$ $\frac{\pi}{8}$ $\quad$ $0.1\overline{6}$ $\quad$ $0.\overline{34}$ $\quad$ $0.121122111222\ldots$

Answer   These four are rational because they can be converted to a fraction (ratio of integers).

$5 = \frac{5}{1}$ $\qquad\qquad\qquad$ $0.\overline{34} = \frac{34}{99}$

$4.53 = 4\frac{53}{100} = \frac{453}{100}$ $\qquad\quad$ $0.1\overline{6} = \frac{1}{6}$

$0.121122111222\ldots$ is neither a repeating decimal nor a terminating decimal since you cannot put a bar over any combination of digits to represent a repeating pattern. It is therefore not rational.

Natural numbers, whole numbers, integers, rational numbers, and irrational numbers are all included in a larger set of numbers called real numbers. Algebra 1 will deal primarily with numbers in the real number system. From the diagram at the beginning of the lesson, you can see that there exist numbers that are not part of the set of real numbers. The complex number system including imaginary numbers will be explained in Algebra 2.

The Venn diagram shows the relationship of the different sets of numbers discussed.

Notice that irrational numbers are outside the circle representing rationals, indicating that they are not rational. Every number inside the rectangle however is a real number.

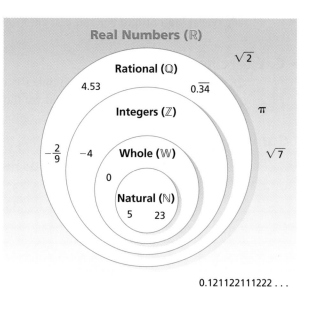

▶ A. Exercises

Convert each ratio to a decimal.

1. $\frac{11}{2}$
3. 23%
5. $\frac{5}{7}$

2. $\frac{4}{3}$
4. $\frac{18}{9}$
6. 3 out of 6

Convert each number to a fraction in lowest terms.

7. 4.3
9. $\sqrt{9}$
8. 82%
10. 0.57624

▶ B. Exercises

Draw a Venn diagram like the one above. Label the number systems. Then place each real number below in the innermost position possible. You need to simplify first.

11. −6
16. −0.721721172111 . . .

12. 4.868668666 . . .
17. 0

13. 0.5
18. $\sqrt{5}$

14. 0.313131 . . .
19. $\frac{3}{1}$

15. $-\frac{4}{11}$
20. $\sqrt{4}$

Graph on a number line.

21. π
22. $-\frac{11}{5}$

23. Does the real number system have a smallest number? a largest number?
24. Does the whole number system have a smallest number? a largest number?
25. Does the natural number system have a smallest number? a largest number?
26. What kind of number represents the population of a town?
27. What kind of number can you enter into your calculator?

▶ C. Exercises

28. Why is it that an irrational number is never given for a person's weight? If we chose larger units, would we then get such numbers?

■ Cumulative Review

Translate each phrase into symbols. Do not evaluate.

29. Half of twelve
32. Ninety percent of six

30. Seventeen thirds
33. Eight more than seven

31. Twenty-six out of thirty

2.2 Adding and Subtracting Rationals

If Bill needs $\frac{1}{2}$ gallon of paint for the bathroom and $\frac{3}{4}$ gallon for the bedroom, how much paint should he buy?

To solve his problem, Bill will have to know how to work with rational numbers. What are rational numbers? Rational numbers are often thought of as fractions, but remember integers are rational also.

Sometimes a rational number may not look like the usual ratio. The decimal **1.3** equals $\frac{13}{10}$, so **1.3** is a rational number. The whole number **8** equals $\frac{8}{1}$, so **8** is a rational number too. What does a rational expression such as $\frac{6}{7}$ actually mean? It means that something is divided into seven parts and six parts are represented, or that six items must be divided into seven equal portions.

Therefore, $\frac{6}{7}$ is **6** times $\frac{1}{7}$ of the objects, or $6 \cdot \frac{1}{7}$. In general, a rational number can be expressed as $\frac{a}{b}$ where *a* and *b* are integers and *b* ≠ **0**. Therefore, for any rational number, $\frac{a}{b} = a \cdot \frac{1}{b}$ where $\frac{1}{b}$ is the *multiplicative inverse* of *b*.

When working with rational numbers, always state the number in its lowest form. For example, if you have $\frac{6}{21}$ as a solution to a computation, you would simplify, or reduce, the fraction to $\frac{2}{7}$. To simplify a fraction, cancel the greatest common factor (in this case GCF = 3) from both numerator and denominator.

$$\frac{6}{21} = \frac{2 \cdot \overset{1}{\cancel{3}}}{7 \cdot \underset{1}{\cancel{3}}} = \frac{2}{7}$$

The GCF of **12** and **32** is **4** and the simplified form of $\frac{12}{32}$ is $\frac{3}{8}$.

Before you can add or subtract rational numbers, you must express them using equivalent fractions with the same denominator. To rename $\frac{2}{3}$ as an equivalent fraction with a larger denominator, multiply the fraction by **1**, the identity element for multiplication, in the form of any natural number over itself.

$$\frac{2}{3} \cdot \frac{2}{2} = \frac{2 \cdot 2}{3 \cdot 2} = \frac{4}{6}$$

$$\frac{2}{3} \cdot \frac{3}{3} = \frac{2 \cdot 3}{3 \cdot 3} = \frac{6}{9}$$

$$\frac{2}{3} \cdot \frac{4}{4} = \frac{2 \cdot 4}{3 \cdot 4} = \frac{8}{12}$$

As you can see, $\frac{4}{6}$, $\frac{6}{9}$, and $\frac{8}{12}$ are all equivalent to $\frac{2}{3}$.

Suppose the denominator of the equivalent fraction is given. To rename the fraction, first find the factor used to determine the given denominator. Then to find the numerator of the equivalent fraction, multiply the numerator of the original fraction by the same factor.

The simplifying and renaming procedures use the following principle.

> **Fundamental Principle of Fractions**
>
> If a is an integer and b and c are nonzero integers, $\frac{ac}{bc} = \frac{a}{b}$

Here is the principle applied to simplifying. $\frac{25}{45} = \frac{5 \cdot \cancel{5}}{9 \cdot \cancel{5}} = \frac{5}{9}$

Here is the principle applied to renaming. $\frac{2}{3} = \frac{2 \cdot 6}{3 \cdot 6} = \frac{12}{18}$

To add or subtract rationals with different denominators, you must first rename the fractions to equivalent fractions that have the same denominator.

EXAMPLE 1   Add $\frac{3}{7} + \frac{2}{7}$.

Answer   Since the denominator of both rationals is the same, add the numerators. The resulting rational number cannot be reduced.

$$\frac{3}{7} + \frac{2}{7} = \frac{5}{7}$$

Why does $\frac{3}{7} + \frac{2}{7} = \frac{5}{7}$? All computations follow basic principles set down in mathematics. Each step of a mathematical computation works for a reason. Here is the reasoning behind this computation.

$\frac{3}{7} + \frac{2}{7}$	
$3\left(\frac{1}{7}\right) + 2\left(\frac{1}{7}\right)$	1. $\frac{a}{b} = a \cdot \frac{1}{b}$
$(3 + 2)\left(\frac{1}{7}\right)$	2. distributive property
$5\left(\frac{1}{7}\right)$	
$\frac{5}{7}$	3. $a \cdot \frac{1}{b} = \frac{a}{b}$

EXAMPLE 2   Simplify $\frac{3}{4} + \frac{2}{3}$.

Answer

$4 = 2^2;\ 3$	1. Factor the denominators completely.
$LCM = 2^2 \cdot 3 = 12$	2. Find the LCM.
$\frac{3}{4} + \frac{2}{3}$ $\frac{3 \cdot 3}{4 \cdot 3} + \frac{2 \cdot 2^2}{3 \cdot 2^2}$ $\frac{9}{12} + \frac{8}{12}$	3. Rename the fractions as equivalent fractions with the same denominators, using the fundamental principle of fractions.
$\frac{17}{12}$	4. Add the numerators.

Although $\frac{17}{12}$ can be changed to $1\frac{5}{12}$, mixed fractions are not normally used in algebra because $\frac{17}{12}$ is more convenient for computation and fits the rational form $\frac{a}{b}$.

EXAMPLE 3   Subtract $\frac{3}{7} - \frac{5}{28}$.

Answer

$7 = 7 \quad 28 = 2^2 \cdot 7$	1. Factor the denominators completely.
$LCM = 2^2 \cdot 7 = 28$	2. Find the LCM.
$\frac{3}{7} - \frac{5}{28}$ $\frac{3 \cdot 4}{7 \cdot 4} - \frac{5}{28}$ $\frac{12}{28} - \frac{5}{28}$	3. Rename the fractions as equivalent fractions with the same denominators, using the fundamental principle of fractions.
$\frac{7}{28}$	4. Subtract the numerators.
$\frac{1}{4}$	5. Reduce the fraction.

EXAMPLE 4   Subtract $\frac{3}{32} - \frac{5}{8}$.

Answer $32 = 2^5 \quad 8 = 2^3$

$LCM = 2^5 = 32$

$\frac{3}{32} - \frac{5}{8}$

$\frac{3}{32} - \frac{5 \cdot 2^2}{8 \cdot 2^2}$

$\frac{3}{32} - \frac{20}{32}$

$-\frac{17}{32}$

Adding and Subtracting Rationals

1. Factor each denominator into primes.
2. Find the LCM of the two denominators and use it for the common denominator.
3. Change each rational number to an equivalent fraction having the LCM as the denominator. Do this by multiplying both the numerator and the denominator of the rational number by the factor that will make the denominator equal to the common denominator.
4. Add (or subtract) the renamed numerators. Place the sum (or difference) over the LCM.
5. If possible, reduce the rational expression.

Do you remember how to add and subtract rationals in decimal form? Look at these examples.

EXAMPLE 5	Add 2.39 + 14.682.	
Answer	2.39 14.682 17.072	Write the addends in vertical form, lining up decimal points. Add.
	2.39 + 14.682 = 17.072	
EXAMPLE 6	Subtract 39.27 − 112.6.	
Answer	39.27 − 112.6	When subtracting, add the opposite.
	39.27 + (−112.6)	
	−73.33	

Remember, when adding a positive and a negative, take the difference of the absolute values and choose the sign of the one with the larger absolute value.

If **no** denominator is written... the denominator is... 1

▶ A. Exercises

Simplify.

1. $\frac{10}{14}$ 2. $\frac{3}{6}$ 3. $\frac{12}{36}$ 4. $\frac{8}{32}$

Rename each rational number as an equivalent fraction having the given number as the denominator.

5. $\frac{4}{9}$; 81   7. $\frac{5}{7}$; 56   9. $\frac{2}{5}$; 105

6. $\frac{2}{3}$; 9   8. $\frac{1}{6}$; 30   10. $\frac{8}{3}$; 24

Rename the following fractions so that the denominator equals 48.

11. $\frac{1}{2}$ 12. $\frac{5}{12}$ 13. $\frac{3}{8}$ 14. $\frac{11}{16}$

▶ B. Exercises

Perform the indicated operations.

15. $\frac{2}{9} + \frac{5}{9}$ 22. $\frac{3}{4} - \frac{8}{9}$

16. $\frac{4}{7} - \frac{11}{7}$ 23. $\frac{1}{7} + \frac{14}{5}$

17. $\frac{14}{9} + 4$ 24. $\frac{4}{27} - \frac{8}{21}$

18. $\frac{3}{5} - \frac{2}{15}$ 25. $3.896 + 11.42$

19. $\frac{2}{11} - \frac{3}{8}$ 26. $527.69 + 89.41$

20. $\frac{3}{5} - \frac{7}{2}$ 27. $1876.31 - 1026.48$

21. $\frac{12}{21} + \frac{10}{3}$ 28. $621.4 - 0.23$

29. Sue is making a dress for school chorus. She needs $\frac{3}{8}$ yard of lace for the cuffs and $\frac{1}{4}$ yard of the same lace for the decoration on the front of her dress. How much lace should she buy?

▶ C. Exercises

30. $\frac{3}{7} + \frac{5}{14} - \frac{7}{21} + \frac{9}{28}$ 31. $2.9 + 13.05 - 26.472$

■ Cumulative Review

Name each property.

32. $15 \cdot 0 = 0$
33. $(2 + 8) + 5 = 2 + (8 + 5)$
34. Give the GCF of 99 and 363.
35. What kind of number is 12.36333?
36. Find the sum of 11.25 and $0.\overline{3}$.

2.3 Multiplying and Dividing Rationals

After rounding up horses all day, Chip filled his $2\frac{1}{2}$ gallon bucket with water and he gave $\frac{2}{3}$ of it to his horse. How many gallons of water did the horse get?

To solve this type of problem, you must be able to multiply rationals. Do you need a common denominator for multiplying or dividing rationals? No, you can simply multiply the numerators and then the denominators. Consider this example.

EXAMPLE 1 $\frac{3}{4} \cdot \frac{7}{8}$

Answer $\frac{3}{4} \cdot \frac{7}{8} = \frac{3 \cdot 7}{4 \cdot 8} = \frac{21}{32}$

Why does the product equal $\frac{21}{32}$?

$\frac{3}{4} \cdot \frac{7}{8}$	
$3\left(\frac{1}{4}\right) \cdot 7\left(\frac{1}{8}\right)$	$\frac{a}{b} = a \cdot \frac{1}{b}$
$\left(3 \cdot 7\right)\left(\frac{1}{4} \cdot \frac{1}{8}\right)$	commutative and associative properties of multiplication
$21\left(\frac{1}{32}\right)$	
$\frac{21}{32}$	$a \cdot \frac{1}{b} = \frac{a}{b}$

When you multiply rational numbers in fractional form, you can reduce the terms before or after you multiply.

Cancel first

$\frac{12}{7} \cdot \frac{14}{3}$

$\frac{2^2 \cdot \overset{1}{\cancel{3}}}{\underset{1}{\cancel{7}}} \cdot \frac{2 \cdot \overset{1}{\cancel{7}}}{\underset{1}{\cancel{3}}}$

$\frac{2^3}{1}$

8

Multiply first

$\frac{12}{7} \cdot \frac{14}{3}$

$\frac{168}{21}$

$\frac{2^3 \cdot \overset{1}{\cancel{3}} \cdot \overset{1}{\cancel{7}}}{\underset{1}{\cancel{3}} \cdot \underset{1}{\cancel{7}}}$

$\frac{2^3}{1}$

8

Now consider this problem: $\frac{43}{31} \cdot \frac{31}{74}$.

Cancel first

$\frac{43}{31} \cdot \frac{31}{74}$

$\frac{43}{\cancel{31}_{1}} \cdot \frac{\cancel{31}^{1}}{74}$

$\frac{43}{74}$

Multiply first

$\frac{43}{31} \cdot \frac{31}{74}$

$\frac{1333}{2294}$

$\frac{\cancel{31}^{1} \cdot 43}{2 \cdot \cancel{31}_{1} \cdot 37}$

$\frac{43}{74}$

This time, the first method is so easy that you can do it in your head. However, the second method is hard. You not only have to multiply and then factor large numbers but you also waste time doing it since you already know the factors! Furthermore, if you leave $\frac{1333}{2294}$ as your answer, it will be wrong since it is not reduced.

You should always reduce first to save time and avoid possible errors. Reducing first will also prepare you for reducing fractions with variables later.

Multiplying Rationals

1. Factor numerators and denominators into prime factors.
2. Cancel when possible.
3. Place the product of the reduced numerators over the product of the reduced denominators.

EXAMPLE 2 Multiply $\frac{3}{4} \cdot \frac{18}{7}$.

Answer $\frac{3}{4} \cdot \frac{18}{7}$

$\frac{3}{\cancel{2^2}_{2^1}} \cdot \frac{3^2 \cdot \cancel{2}^{1}}{7}$

$\frac{3^3}{2 \cdot 7}$

$\frac{27}{14}$

EXAMPLE 3 Multiply $\frac{12}{35} \cdot \frac{42}{27}$.

Answer $\frac{2^2 \cdot \cancel{3}^{1}}{5 \cdot \cancel{7}_{1}} \cdot \frac{2 \cdot \cancel{3}^{1} \cdot \cancel{7}^{1}}{\cancel{3^3}_{3^1}}$

$\frac{2^3}{15}$

$\frac{8}{15}$

Since division is the inverse operation of multiplication, each division problem can be restated as multiplication by the reciprocal of the divisor.

Definition

Reciprocals (multiplicative inverses) are two numbers whose product is 1.

The reciprocal of $\frac{2}{3}$ is $\frac{3}{2}$ because $\frac{2}{3} \cdot \frac{3}{2} = 1$, and **5** and $\frac{1}{5}$ are reciprocals because $5 \cdot \frac{1}{5} = 1$.

The *multiplicative inverse property* states that the product of a number and its reciprocal is always **1** (the multiplicative identity number).

In symbols, $a \cdot \frac{1}{a} = 1$ and $\frac{1}{a} \cdot a = 1$.

Dividing Rationals

To divide rational numbers, multiply by the reciprocal (multiplicative inverse) of the divisor.

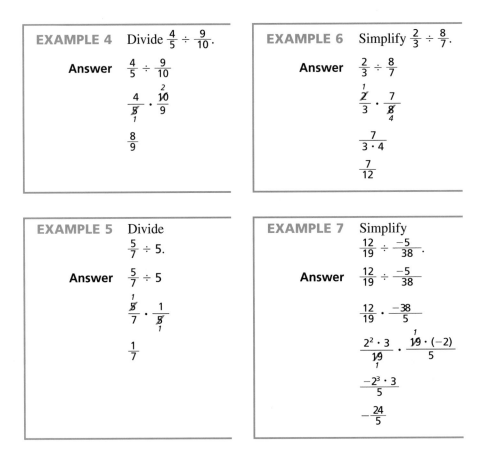

EXAMPLE 4   Divide $\frac{4}{5} \div \frac{9}{10}$.

Answer $\frac{4}{5} \div \frac{9}{10}$

$\frac{4}{\cancel{5}} \cdot \frac{\cancel{10}^{2}}{9}$

$\frac{8}{9}$

EXAMPLE 6   Simplify $\frac{2}{3} \div \frac{8}{7}$.

Answer $\frac{2}{3} \div \frac{8}{7}$

$\frac{\cancel{2}^{1}}{3} \cdot \frac{7}{\cancel{8}_{4}}$

$\frac{7}{3 \cdot 4}$

$\frac{7}{12}$

EXAMPLE 5   Divide
$\frac{5}{7} \div 5$.

Answer $\frac{5}{7} \div 5$

$\frac{\cancel{5}^{1}}{7} \cdot \frac{1}{\cancel{5}_{1}}$

$\frac{1}{7}$

EXAMPLE 7   Simplify
$\frac{12}{19} \div \frac{-5}{38}$.

Answer $\frac{12}{19} \div \frac{-5}{38}$

$\frac{12}{19} \cdot \frac{-38}{5}$

$\frac{2^2 \cdot 3}{\cancel{19}_{1}} \cdot \frac{\cancel{19}^{1} \cdot (-2)}{5}$

$\frac{-2^3 \cdot 3}{5}$

$-\frac{24}{5}$

Do you remember how to multiply and divide decimals? These examples may remind you. Be sure you know how to perform these operations.

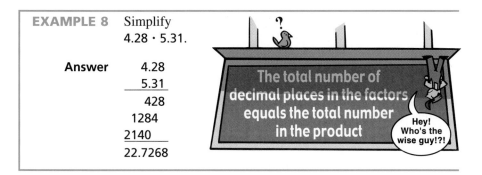

EXAMPLE 8   Simplify
4.28 · 5.31.

Answer

```
     4.28
     5.31
      428
     1284
    2140
   22.7268
```

The total number of decimal places in the factors equals the total number in the product

Hey! Who's the wise guy!?!

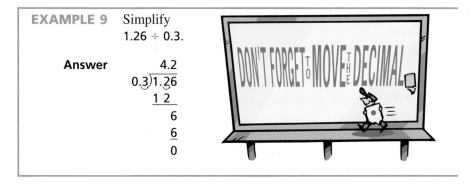

EXAMPLE 9   Simplify
1.26 ÷ 0.3.

Answer

```
        4.2
  0.3)1.26
      1 2
        6
        6
        0
```

DON'T FORGET TO MOVE THE DECIMAL

▶ A. Exercises

Perform the indicated operations.

1. $\frac{4}{7} \cdot \frac{5}{12}$

2. $\frac{34}{9} \cdot \frac{3}{17}$

3. $\frac{21}{8} \cdot \frac{7}{3}$

4. $\frac{1}{6} \cdot \frac{18}{19}$

5. $\frac{3}{7} \cdot \frac{84}{15}$

6. $\frac{4}{9} \div \frac{8}{11}$

7. $\frac{1}{4} \div \frac{9}{16}$

8. $\frac{5}{11} \div \frac{3}{22}$

9. $\frac{2}{17} \div 8$

10. $\frac{54}{19} \div \frac{18}{7}$

11. 14.1 · 5.6

12. 3.9 · 8.42

13. 56.4 ÷ 0.2

14. 61 ÷ 12.2

15. 6.09 ÷ 7

16. Give the reciprocals of $\frac{5}{6}$, $-\frac{7}{3}$, and 4.

▶ B. Exercises

Perform the indicated operations.

17. $-\frac{4}{11} \cdot \frac{7}{12}$

18. $\frac{18}{6} \cdot \frac{10}{-9}$

19. $-\frac{1}{10} \cdot -\frac{15}{4}$

20. $\frac{18}{-35} \cdot \frac{-7}{-16}$

21. Chip's bucket contains $2\frac{1}{2}$ gallons of water. If he gives his horse $\frac{2}{3}$ of the water, how much water does the horse get?

22. Beth, Brad, and Ben picked $1\frac{1}{2}$ gallons of blackberries and divided them evenly among themselves. How many gallons of blackberries did each get?

23. If one side of a square is $\frac{3}{8}$ inches, what is the perimeter of the square?

24. What is the product of a number and its reciprocal? What property does this problem illustrate?

25. Use $\frac{a}{b} = a \cdot \frac{1}{b}$ to rewrite $\frac{5}{2}$

26. Does the zero property of multiplication hold true for all rational numbers?

▶ C. Exercises

27. Use $\frac{a}{b} = a \div b$ to rewrite and calculate $\dfrac{\frac{2}{3}}{\frac{5}{4}}$

28. Rename $\dfrac{\frac{3}{7}}{\frac{2}{5}}$ by changing it to an equivalent fraction with a denominator of 1.

29. Distinguish $\dfrac{4}{\frac{3}{5}}$ from $\dfrac{\frac{4}{3}}{5}$

30. Evaluate $-\frac{13}{42} \div -\frac{5}{7} + \frac{1}{15} - 0.427$

■ Cumulative Review

31. Graph $\frac{8}{3}$.

32. Write $10 \div 5 = 2$ as a multiplication.

33. Simplify $|-4.3|$.

34. Explain why division by zero is undefined.

35. Write the zero property of multiplication as a division principle.

Find the digit that will properly fill in each space in these multiplication problems.

```
1.    ___          2.   7___           3.      _2_         4.      5_4_
       39                  _8                   _81                   _3
     47_3                _81_2                 __6                17__8
     1__1                14__8                 _4_8               ____2
    2__53               _03_92                _278              43_0_8
                                            1_2_06
```

Averages

Suppose that a group of ten students took a math test and that their scores were as follows.

83	97	77	62	89
92	83	75	94	86

There are three main methods of averaging. The *mean* is the most familiar. The symbol for the mean is $\bar{x}$ (read *x* bar). Each score is an *x* value, *n* represents the number of scores (**10**), and Σ is the symbol for adding up a total.

$$\bar{x} = \frac{\Sigma x}{n} = \text{sum of scores over number of scores}$$

For the math test above,

$$\bar{x} = \frac{83 + 97 + 77 + 62 + 89 + 92 + 83 + 75 + 94 + 86}{10}$$

$$= \frac{838}{10}$$

$$= 83.8$$

The other methods of averaging are easier to determine if you list the scores in order:

97	94	92	89	86	83	83	77	75	62

The *mode* is the score that occurs most frequently. Since **83** is the only score that occurs twice, it is the mode. Some sets of data have more than one mode and some have no mode at all.

$$\text{Mode} = \text{most frequent} = 83$$

The *median* is the middle score. Half of the scores always exceed the median, and half of the scores are always lower. Since there are an even number of scores (**10**), calculate the midpoint between the two middle scores.

Median = middle score (of an odd number of scores)

Median = midway between the two middle scores (for an even number of scores)

For the scores shown, the median $= \frac{86 + 83}{2} = \frac{169}{2} = 84.5$

Because we usually use the term average to refer to the mean, mathematicians often avoid the word average when referring to other measurements. Instead, the more technical phrase "measures of central tendency" is used since all the measures describe an aspect of the center of the set of data. You should also recall that these measures are statistics because they are real numbers that describe the central tendency in a set of scores.

▶ Exercises

Jay delivers 24 pizzas on Monday, 30 on Tuesday, 27 on Wednesday, 29 on Thursday, and 37 on Friday.

1. Find the mean number of pizza deliveries per day.
2. Find the median number of deliveries.

The temperature on January 5 was $-16°$ in 1994, 12° in 1995, 23° in 1996, $-6°$ in 1997, 30° in 1998, and 23° in 1999. For the period from 1994 to 1999, find the average temperature on January 5 as directed.

3. mean temperature
4. median temperature
5. modal temperature

2.4 Order of Operations

Solve this problem. $3 + 2 \cdot 4 - 6 \div 3$

What is your answer? Did you get $\frac{14}{3}$? $\frac{5}{3}$? $-\frac{10}{3}$? 9? 18? confused? If you are confused, you have good reason because all of those numbers are possible answers; but only one of them is correct.

If you think a math problem with more than one solution is confusing, what do you suppose a life without purpose or direction is like? Perhaps you wonder, "How do I know what is right and what is wrong? How do I determine which answer is right?" God did not put man on earth and leave him without directions. He gave man a rule book, the Bible, in which He tells sinful man that he needs a Savior. Then He tells the saved man how to live like Christ. God established absolute truths that never change. His Word is truth (cf. John 17:17) and will never pass away (cf. Matt. 24:35). You do not have to wonder what the purpose of life is, for you can turn to God's Book and find the answers. You must follow God's rules.

This Renaissance painting by Tintoretto reminds us that salvation is through the blood of Christ, shed on the cross in our behalf.

In mathematics we are not left to wonder which answer is correct. Certain guidelines have been established so that you can correctly solve a problem such as the one above. You need only learn the order of operations.

Order of Operations

Numerical expressions without grouping symbols are evaluated as follows.
1. Evaluate all exponential expressions.
2. Perform all multiplication and division from left to right.
3. Perform all addition and subtraction from left to right.

Once you have the rules, you can easily solve the introductory problem correctly. Try it again. Since this problem has no grouping symbols and no exponential expressions, you perform the multiplication and division first.

$$3 + 2 \cdot 4 - 6 \div 3$$

Multiply **2** and **4**. Then divide **6** by **3**. Now the problem looks like this.

$$3 + 8 - 2$$

Perform the addition and subtraction from left to right; you now know the correct answer is **9**.

EXAMPLE 1   Evaluate $2 + 3^2 - 4 \div 2 \cdot 3$.

Answer   Since there are no grouping symbols, look for exponential expressions.

$2 + 3^2 - 4 \div 2 \cdot 3$

$2 + 9 \ - 4 \div 2 \cdot 3$ 1. The exponential expression 3^2 equals 9.

$2 + 9 \ - \quad 2 \quad \cdot 3$ 2. Find the first multiplication or division
$2 + 9 \ - \quad\quad 6$ left to right and follow with any other
                            multiplication or division.

$\quad 11 \quad - \quad\quad 6$ 3. Add 2 and 9. Then subtract 6 from the
$\quad\quad\quad 5$ sum. The answer is 5.

EXAMPLE 2   Evaluate $2 \cdot 5 - 3 \cdot 5 + 8 \div 4$.

Answer $2 \cdot 5 - 3 \cdot 5 + 8 \div 4$
$\quad 10 \ - \ 15 \ + \ 2$ 1. Multiply and divide left to right.

$\quad\quad -5 \quad + \quad 2$ 2. Add and subtract left to right.
$\quad\quad\quad -3$

EXAMPLE 3   Evaluate $2^3 - 1^2 + 5 \cdot 4 - 3^2 + 9 \div 3$.

Answer $2^3 - 1^2 + 5 \cdot 4 - 3^2 + 9 \div 3$ 1. Evaluate exponential
$8 \ - 1 \ + 5 \cdot 4 - 9 \ + 9 \div 3$ expressions.

$8 \ - 1 \ + \ 20 \ - 9 \ + \ 3$ 2. Multiply and divide left to right.

$\quad\quad\quad 21$ 3. Add and subtract left to right.

▶ A. Exercises

Evaluate.

1. $3 \cdot 4 + 5$
2. $8 - 3 \cdot 2 + 10 \div 2$
3. $10 + 7 - 3 \cdot 2$
4. $8 + 10 \div 5$
5. $1 + 9 \div 3 \cdot 2$

6. $-10 - 2 \cdot 4 \div 4 + 3$
7. $4 + 6 \cdot 2 \cdot 3 \div 9$
8. $3 \div 1 \cdot 3 + 7$
9. $2 + 1 - 4 \cdot 1$
10. $8 + 2 \div 2 + 6$

▶ B. Exercises

Evaluate.

11. $2^3 \div 4 + 7$
12. $1 + 7^2 \cdot 2 - 50$
13. $27 - 3^2 + 8 \div 2$
14. $17 + 4 \cdot 8 \div 2$
15. $22 - 11 \cdot 2$

16. $-81 - 14 \cdot 3 \div 1 \cdot 2$
17. $3 + 4 - 2 - 6 \cdot 3$
18. $2 \div 2 + 4 - 2 + 7$
19. $6 \cdot 2 + 10 \div 5$
20. $7 - 3^2 - 1 + 4^3 \div 2$

Translate into symbols. Do not calculate.

21. Five more than twice the square of four
22. The product of five and six increased by the quotient of twenty and five
23. The sum of nine and the next consecutive odd number
24. Seven less than the product of eleven and the reciprocal of 9
25. Reduce 9 by the absolute value of the sum of two and negative fifteen.

▶ C. Exercises

26. Evaluate $\frac{5}{6} \div \frac{4}{3} + \frac{1}{3} \cdot \frac{2}{5}$.
27. Decrease one-half the square of the absolute value of negative one-third by twice the product of the reciprocals of negative four-thirds and seven.

■ Cumulative Review

28. Which number is not an integer? $\frac{4}{2}$, $\sqrt{9}$, $\frac{\pi}{9}$, 2^6
29. Give the reciprocal of -2.
30. What number does not have a reciprocal?

Simplify.

31. $(-30) - (-6)$
32. $(-30) \div (-6)$

2.5 Symbols for Grouping

Sometimes you may want to perform a sequence of operations in an order different from the one prescribed by the order of operations. For instance, you may want to add two numbers before you divide. If so, you must have some way to indicate the revised order. *Grouping symbols* let you indicate which operation to perform first.

Consider $3 + 2 \cdot 4 - 6 \div 3$. If we wanted to add 3 and 2 and subtract 6 from 4 first, we would have to write the problem like this.

$$(3 + 2)(4 - 6) \div 3$$

$$(3 + 2)(4 - 6) \div 3$$
$$5 \quad (-2) \div 3$$
$$-10 \quad \div 3$$
$$-\frac{10}{3}$$

Is the answer still 9? No, it is $-\frac{10}{3}$. Why? The parentheses are grouping symbols. They tell you to do any operations inside them first. Then you can follow the usual order of operations.

Now let's group the numbers another way.

$$[(3 + 2)4] - 6 \div 3$$
$$[(5) \quad (4)] - 6 \div 3$$
$$20 \quad - \quad 6 \div 3$$
$$20 \quad - \quad 2$$
$$18$$

Notice the two sets of grouping symbols. Do the innermost grouping first, indicated by parentheses. Then finish the operations in the brackets. After performing these operations, follow the usual order of operations.

There are three grouping symbols that you will see in mathematical expressions. They are *parentheses* ( ), *brackets* [ ], and *braces* { }. These grouping symbols indicate that the operations enclosed by them are to be performed prior to any other operations.

Using Grouping Symbols

1. Find the innermost set of grouping symbols.
2. Perform operations inside these grouping symbols according to the order of operations.
3. If there are any more grouping symbols in the expression, go back to step 1.
4. When all grouping symbols are removed, evaluate the expression by following the order of operations.

EXAMPLE 1   Evaluate $2 + 3(5 + 7) \div 2$.

Answer

$2 + 3(5 + 7) \div 2$

$2 + 3 \cdot 12 \div 2$

$2 + 36 \div 2$

$2 + 18$

20

First remove the parentheses by performing the operation within them.

Then evaluate by following the order of operations.

EXAMPLE 2   Evaluate $9 - 3[2 + 7 \cdot 8(3 + 5)] - 4$.

Answer

$9 - 3[2 + 7 \cdot 8(3 + 5)] - 4$

$9 - 3[2 + 7 \cdot 8 \cdot 8] - 4$

$9 - 3[2 + 56 \cdot 8] - 4$

$9 - 3[2 + 448] - 4$

$9 - 3 \cdot 450 - 4$

$9 - 1350 - 4$

$-1341 - 4$

-1345

Compute inside parentheses first and remove them.

Compute inside brackets and remove them.

Evaluate by order of operations.

Now that you know how to solve problems containing grouping symbols, you can also insert grouping symbols to produce a specific value.

EXAMPLE 3   Insert grouping symbols so that the expression represents -50.

$24 \div 4 + 8 \cdot 3 - 10$

Answer   Without grouping symbols, the solution is 20, but the desired value is -50. How can the terms be grouped to equal -50? Since the order of operations says that multiplication and division should be performed first, insert grouping symbols so that addition or subtraction can be performed first. You will need to try several ways to find the correct one.

$24 \div (4 + 8) \cdot 3 - 10$
$24 \div 12 \cdot 3 - 10$
$2 \cdot 3 - 10$
$6 - 10$
-4 (not -50)

$24 \div (4 + 8)(3 - 10)$
$24 \div 12(-7)$
$2(-7)$
-14 (not -50)

$(24 \div 4 + 8) \cdot 3 - 10$
$(6 + 8) \cdot 3 - 10$
$14 \cdot 3 - 10$
$42 - 10$
32 (not -50)

$24 \div 4 + 8(3 - 10)$
$6 + 8(-7)$
$6 - 56$
-50

▶ A. Exercises

Evaluate step by step. Show all your work.

1. $5 + 4(3 + 7)$
2. $3 \cdot 2 + 4(5 + 8)2$
3. $4 + 5 + [(8 + 2 \cdot 4) - 5]6$
4. $6 \cdot 3 \div (5 + 4) + 1 - 6$
5. $8 \cdot 4 + 3(1 + 6) \div 2 \cdot 9$
6. $3 + \{[(4 \cdot 8 - 2) + 2 + 7 \cdot 4] - 7 \cdot 2\} - 8$
7. $9 - [(4 \cdot 2 + 6) - 9] + (4 + 2 \cdot 6)$
8. $4 - \{3 + [2(8 + 9) \div 4] + 9\}2$
9. $\{1 \cdot 3 + 2[5 + 7 \cdot 2(3 + 9)]4\} + 2$
10. $10 + 3 - [4 \cdot 8 - (7 - 8)6]9$
11. $7 - 5 + \{[6 + 2 - (3 - 4)6] + 5\} + 9$
12. $8 \div 2 + (3 - 6)(8 + 2) - (3 + 1)4$
13. $6 + (2 - 5)8 - [3 + (4 - 7)3] + 6$
14. $4 + (2 - 3)6 + 8 - 9(3 + 2)$

▶ B. Exercises

Evaluate step by step. Show all work.

15. $1 + [3(4 + 2) - 6] + (3 - 5) - 8 + 6$
16. $2\{[4 - (5 + 2)](-3 - 6) \div 9 - 3\}$
17. $3 - [2(6 - 2) \div 4 + (7 - 9) \div 2]$
18. $5\{3 + 5 \div 4 - (4 - 7)(-3 + 6) - 2\}$

Insert grouping symbols so that each expression will have the given value.

19. $2 + 4 \cdot 7 \div 2 = 21$
20. $3 + 9 \cdot 2 - 6 = -33$

Translate into symbols. Do not calculate.

21. The product of five and the sum of six and seven
22. The square of the difference of twenty and thirteen
23. The difference of the squares of twenty and thirteen
24. The sum of two and five, times six
25. The sum of two, and five times six

▶ C. Exercises

Insert grouping symbols so that the expression will have the given value.

26. $14 + 5 - 10 \div 2 \cdot 7 - 2 - 3 = 15$
27. Find all possible values of the following by using any combination of parentheses, brackets, and braces. $3 + 4 \cdot 5 \div 2 - 7$

Simplify, leaving the answers for exercises 30-32 in exponential form.

28. $6^0 - 6^2$
29. $(3 + 1)^4 \div (5 - 7)^3$
30. $5^{43} \div 5^{17}$
31. $2^8 \cdot 3^7 \cdot 2^5 \cdot 3^4$
32. $(4^3)^9$

2.6 Square Roots and Radicals

If Nancy has a square garden encompassing an area of **16** square feet, what are its dimensions?

To find the dimensions of the garden, you must find the equal factors whose product is **16**. The factors have to be equal because the garden is a square. The process needed to answer this problem is called finding the square root.

Definition

A **square root** is one of a number's two equal factors. The symbol for square root is $\sqrt{}$.

The number whose square root you are trying to find is called the *radicand*. For example, in $\sqrt{16}$, 16 is the radicand.

EXAMPLE 1   Take the square root $\sqrt{25}$.

   Answer $\sqrt{25} = \sqrt{5^2} = 5$ since $5 \cdot 5 = 5^2 = 25$

EXAMPLE 2   Evaluate $\sqrt{36}$.

   Answer $\sqrt{36} = \sqrt{6^2} = 6$ since $6 \cdot 6 = 6^2 = 36$

Since $3 \cdot 3 = 3^2 = 9$, a square root of 9 is 3. Since $-3(-3) = (-3)^2 = 9$, -3 is a square root of 9 too. A positive number always has two square roots: one positive and one negative. You should use the positive square root (*principal square root*) unless you are instructed to use the negative root.

Some radicals, such as $\sqrt{5}$, do not have rational numbers as square roots. These numbers are called irrational numbers.

The concept that $\sqrt{x^2} = |x|$ will be used in many of these problems.
—*The Management*

EXAMPLE 3   Find $\sqrt{4}$.

   Answer $\sqrt{4} = \sqrt{2^2} = 2$

Notice that the negative sign is outside the square root in example 4. Therefore the opposite of the principal square root is taken.

EXAMPLE 4   Find $-\sqrt{16}$.

   Answer $-\sqrt{16} = -\sqrt{4^2} = -4$

Don't confuse taking the square root of a number with squaring a number. Finding the square root is the inverse of squaring.

The radical sign is used to indicate other roots as well as the square root. All such roots of numbers are therefore called *radicals*.

$\sqrt{}$ denotes square root

$\sqrt[3]{}$ denotes cube root

$\sqrt[4]{}$ denotes fourth root

$\sqrt[5]{}$ denotes fifth root

The small number above the radical sign is called the *index*. It indicates the type of root to be taken. Since square root is the most common root taken, no index is shown. If it were, it would be two.

Definition

A **cube root** is one of a number's three equal factors.

You can extend this definition for all indices. Notice that roots undo powers if the index matches the exponent. As in square roots, they are inverse operations.

Definition

An ***nth*** root is one of a number's *n* equal factors.

EXAMPLE 5   Find $\sqrt[3]{27}$.

Answer $\sqrt[3]{27} = \sqrt[3]{3^3} = 3$

EXAMPLE 6   Simplify $\sqrt[3]{-8}$.

Answer $\sqrt[3]{-8} = \sqrt[3]{(-2)^3} = -2$ since $(-2)(-2)(-2) = (-2)^3 = -8$

EXAMPLE 7   Evaluate $\sqrt[4]{625}$.

Answer $\sqrt[4]{625} = \sqrt[4]{5^4} = 5$

EXAMPLE 8   Find $\sqrt[5]{1024}$.

Answer $\sqrt[5]{1024} = \sqrt[5]{4^5} = 4$

EXAMPLE 9   Find $-\sqrt{\dfrac{4}{9}}$.

Answer $-\sqrt{\dfrac{4}{9}} = -\sqrt{\left(\dfrac{2}{3}\right)^2} = -\dfrac{2}{3}$

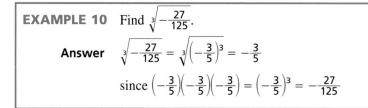

EXAMPLE 10 Find $\sqrt[3]{-\frac{27}{125}}$.

Answer $\sqrt[3]{-\frac{27}{125}} = \sqrt[3]{\left(-\frac{3}{5}\right)^3} = -\frac{3}{5}$

since $\left(-\frac{3}{5}\right)\left(-\frac{3}{5}\right)\left(-\frac{3}{5}\right) = \left(-\frac{3}{5}\right)^3 = -\frac{27}{125}$

The following examples involve applying the definition of roots.

EXAMPLE 11 Write $\sqrt{25} = 5$ using exponents.

Answer $5^2 = 25$

EXAMPLE 12 Write $4^3 = 64$ using radicals.

Answer $\sqrt[3]{64} = 4$

You should recognize that radical signs as well as fraction bars and absolute value symbols can serve as grouping symbols. In each example below you must add or subtract first because of the grouping symbols.

EXAMPLE 13 Simplify $8\sqrt{5 + 4}$.

Answer $8\sqrt{5 + 4} = 8\sqrt{9} = 8 \cdot 3 = 24$

EXAMPLE 14 $\frac{7 + 11}{3}$

Answer $\frac{7 + 11}{3} = \frac{18}{3} = 6$

EXAMPLE 15 $2\left|\, 5 - 14 \,\right|$

Answer $2\left|\, 5 - 14 \,\right| = 2\left|\, -9 \,\right| = 2 \cdot 9 = 18$

There is great benefit to your study of mathematics in memorizing the squares of the numbers from 1-20. For instance, if you know that $17^2 = 289$ and $18^2 = 324$, then when faced with finding $\sqrt{305}$, you immediately know the answer is between 17 and 18.

▶ A. Exercises

Find the indicated roots.

1. $\sqrt{49}$

2. $-\sqrt{36}$

3. $\sqrt{81}$

4. $-\sqrt{121}$

5. $\sqrt{1}$

6. $\sqrt{\dfrac{49}{16}}$

7. $\sqrt{\dfrac{81}{25}}$

8. $\sqrt{100}$

9. $\sqrt{\dfrac{9}{16}}$

10. $\sqrt{\dfrac{144}{9}}$

11. $-\sqrt{225}$

12. $-\sqrt{196}$

13. $\sqrt{361}$

14. $\sqrt{\dfrac{400}{100}}$

15. $\sqrt[3]{216}$

16. $\sqrt[4]{1}$

17. $\sqrt[3]{-27}$

18. $-4\sqrt[4]{256}$

19. $-\sqrt[3]{-343}$

20. $\sqrt[3]{\dfrac{27}{125}}$

▶ B. Exercises

Write without radicals (use exponents).

21. $\sqrt{16} = 4$

22. $\sqrt[3]{13.824} = 2.4$

Write using radicals.

23. $11^2 = 121$

24. $\left(\dfrac{1}{2}\right)^7 = \dfrac{1}{128}$

Simplify.

25. $3 - \sqrt{17 + 19}$

26. $\dfrac{8 - 11 \cdot 4}{7 \cdot 2 + 4 \cdot 3^0} + 2$

27. $-5(6 - 11) + |\, 2 - 7 \,|$

28. $\sqrt[5]{8(129 - 2^0)}$

29. $\dfrac{2^2 - 4^3}{\sqrt[3]{-125}} - |\, 9^2 - 1 \,|$

30. $-\sqrt{6(70 \cdot 20 - 50)}$

▶ C. Exercises

31. Explain when the root of a negative number is real.
32. Insert symbols so that $3 - 5 \cdot 36 = 12$.

■ Cumulative Review

Identify the kind of number. Give the most specific set. Remember, the appearance of a radical does not necessarily mean a number is irrational.

33. $\sqrt{5 \cdot 2 + 39}$

34. $7 \cdot 9 \div 14$

35. $6(-3) - 5(-2)$

36. $|\, 5 - 9 \,| - \sqrt{16}$

37. $\sqrt{8 - 3 \cdot 2}$

ALGEBRA AND SCIENCE

Is God calling you to be a scientist? The broader and more intense your education, the greater will be the number of professional options available. Mathematics is essential for advanced work in the sciences. Most fields of study require at least six years of mathematics beyond Algebra 1.

Scientists use many real numbers in their research. The speed of light is one example of a real constant used in astronomy. Planets and satellites shine by reflecting sunlight, but they also emit infrared and radio waves because their surface temperatures are above absolute zero (0° K; −273° C; −460° F). The mass of the moon is $\frac{1}{81}$ times the earth's mass, making it much larger than most satellites in comparison to their central planet (usually less than .001 times). Supernovas are rare and violent, being as bright at maximum as a whole galaxy (10,000,000,000 times the sun's luminosity).

A physicist also uses real numbers. Models of atoms were proposed in the beginning of the twentieth century. Ernest Rutherford in 1911 showed that the scattering should be proportional to $\sqrt{t}$, t = foil thickness, for the Thomson atom.

Niels Bohr in 1913 used the real number π in his study of atoms. He stated that for a singular electron moving in an orbit around the nucleus, the angular momentum is an integral multiple of $\frac{h}{2\pi}$, h standing for a constant 6.63×10^{-34}. Remember that π is a real number

Astronomers in southern California took this photograph of the Andromeda galaxy about two million light years away. What real number describes its size? the number of stars in it?

Nuclear physicists at the LEP Accelerator split atoms and describe the sizes and speeds of the resulting particles with real numbers.

that equals 3.1415926 . . . What kind of real number is π? A nuclear physicist also uses the irrational number denoted by e, which equals 2.71828 . . . , when doing radioactive dating. He can calculate how much time has passed since the "beginning" (t) using this equation.

$$N = N_0\, e^{-\left(\frac{0.693}{t_{\frac{1}{2}}}\right)t}$$

In the physical world, real numbers measure continuously varying quantities such as sizes and times. A scientist cannot accomplish his work without the use of real numbers, both rational and irrational.

This research chemist uses real numbers that represent atomic weights of chemical elements.

2.7 Sets and Operations

CALVARY CHRISTIAN ACADEMY CLASS SCHEDULE

	English 1	Basic Science	Bible	Algebra 1
Beth	X		X	X
Julie	X	X	X	
Kevin	X		X	
Martin	X	X	X	X
Michael		X	X	X
Sara	X	X	X	

The principal wants to know how many students are taking both basic science and Algebra 1. The group of students taking science are Julie, Martin, Michael, and Sara. Those taking Algebra 1 are Beth, Martin, and Michael. Martin and Michael are the only ones taking both.

Definition

A **set** is a collection of objects.

In algebra you will usually deal with sets of numbers. For example, the number system discussed at the beginning of the chapter is made up of sets of numbers. Sets are denoted by capital letters, and $\mathbb{N}$ represents the natural numbers. Using set notation, you can describe the natural numbers as follows.

$$\mathbb{N} = \{1, 2, 3, 4, \ldots\}$$

The { } are called *set braces* and are read "the set of." The *ellipsis* (. . .) means that the numbers continue in the same pattern. The numbers 1, 2, 3, 4, and so forth, in the set above are called *elements,* or *members,* of the set. The symbol $\in$ means "is an element of" and $\notin$ means "is not an element of." Therefore, these are true statements: $4 \in \mathbb{N}$ and $-2 \notin \mathbb{N}$.

If the number of elements in a set is a whole number, then the set is called a *finite set.* An *infinite set* is a set that is not finite. The set of natural numbers is an example of an infinite set since there is no largest number. A set that has no elements is called the *null set,* or *empty set,* denoted by { } or $\varnothing$. The empty set is considered a finite set.

$$A = \{1, 3, 7, 9, 10\} \quad B = \{1, 4, 6, 10\}$$

Are A and B finite or infinite sets? If you put the elements from A and B together into one set, you would get the set $\{1, 3, 4, 6, 7, 9, 10\}$. This set is called the union of A and B and is denoted $A \cup B$.

$$A \cup B = \{1, 3, 4, 6, 7, 9, 10\}$$

If you identify the elements that A and B have in common (1 and 10), you recognize the intersection of A and B, denoted $A \cap B$.

$$A \cap B = \{1, 10\}$$

A **union of sets** is the set of elements that appear in any of the sets.

An **intersection of sets** is the set of elements common to all of the sets.

Each skewer of shish kabob represents a set of food items.

Sets are often represented in picture form in a Venn diagram. From it you can easily determine the elements in the union and in the intersection of the sets.

$$C = \{1, 2, 3, 4, 5, 6\} \quad D = \{2, 4, 6, 8, 10\}$$

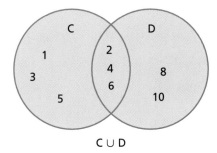

$C \cup D$

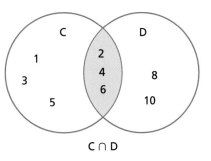

$C \cap D$

$C \cup D = \{1, 2, 3, 4, 5, 6, 8, 10\}$ Numbers in circle C or D are in the union of the sets.

$C \cap D = \{2, 4, 6\}$ Numbers in the overlapping area of the circles C and D are in the intersection of the sets.

One set is a **subset** of another set if every element of the first is contained in the second. $A \subseteq B$ means set A is a subset of set B.

EXAMPLE	Which are not subsets of set C above? Why? Write any sub-sets using symbols.
	$C \cup D$ $\{5\}$ $\varnothing$ 6 C $C \cap D$

Answer	$C \cup D$ is not a subset of C	$10 \in C \cup D$ but $10 \notin C$
	6 is not a subset of C	6 is not a set
	$\{5\} \subseteq C$ $\varnothing \subseteq C$ $C \subseteq C$ $C \cap D \subseteq C$	You can't find an element in any of the other sets that is not in C, so all the others are subsets of C.

▶ A. Exercises

$\mathbb{Z} = \{\ldots -2, -1, 0, 1, 2, \ldots\}$
$A = \{1, 3, 5, \ldots\}$
$B = \{-2, -1, 1, 3\}$
$C = \{-1, 2, 5, 6\}$

Identify these sets using set notation.

1. $A \cap B$
2. $C \cup \mathbb{N}$
3. $B \cap C$

4. $(A \cup B) \cap C$
5. $(A \cap B) \cup (A \cap C)$

True or False. Use sets A, B, and C above.

6. $3 \in B$
7. $\varnothing \in B$
8. $\{3, 5, 7\} \subseteq A$

9. $\{2, 3\} \subseteq C$
10. $5 \notin C$

▶ B. Exercises

$D = \{$all U.S. states that border the Mississippi River$\}$
$E = \{$all U.S. states that begin with the letter $M\}$
$F = \{$all U.S. states that border the Gulf of Mexico$\}$
$G = \{$all U.S. states with 2 words in name$\}$
$H = \{$all states that have a land border with Canada$\}$

Find the following sets.

11. $D \cup E$ **15.** $D \cap E$ **18.** $E \cap H$

12. $D \cup F$ **16.** $E \cap F$ **19.** $F \cup H$

13. $E \cup F$ **17.** $D \cap G$ **20.** $(D \cap E) \cap F$

14. $F \cup G$

21. Write in set notation the set of whole numbers.

22. Write in set notation the set of integers.

23. Draw a Venn diagram to represent the following sets.

$A = \{-5, -3, -1, 0, 1, 2, 3\}$ $B = \{0, 2, 4, 6, 8, 10\}$

► C. Exercises

24. Name the identity element for union.

Translate into symbols.

25. Nine is not an element of the union of sets A and B.

26. The set containing 5 and 7 as elements is a subset of the set containing the odd positive integers.

27. The intersection of sets A and B is commutative.

28. Identify the finite and infinite sets in exercise 26.

■ Cumulative Review

Factor into primes.

29. 558   **31.** Find the LCM of 558 and 264.

30. 264

Simplify.

32. $7 - \dfrac{15 + 13}{2} + \left| \sqrt[3]{8} - 5 \right|$

33. $9^0 + 3 \cdot 5 - 6 \cdot 4 + 12 \div (-\sqrt{10 + 6})$

Algebra *and* Scripture

Number systems provide an important tool for classifying numbers. Another method is to use their relation to sets.

Cardinal numbers describe sizes of sets. A cardinal number gives the total number of elements: one, two, three, . . .

Ordinal numbers describe the order of elements. An ordinal number identifies the position of an element in a list: first, second, third, . . .

Give the number in each verse below and classify it as cardinal or ordinal.

1. II Kings 15:13
2. Ezra 2:10
3. Nehemiah 2:1

4. Esther 5:1
5. Jeremiah 32:9

THE NTH DEGREE
Find verses to illustrate 100 in both cardinal and ordinal form.

Ordinal numbers stress order and sequence, as you noticed in Chapter 1. Order is an important attribute of God. The Bible tells us that God is a God of order. The number systems reflect God's character.

6. How does I Corinthians 14:33 describe this attribute?

The number zero is a whole number. Although the word *zero* does not occur in Scripture, the concept is the numerical representation of the words *none* and *nothing*, which occur often in Scripture. Because it describes the size of the empty set, it can be considered a cardinal number.

7. How does Romans 3:10 define *none* (zero)?

Every book of the Bible except Lamentations and III John includes a natural number. However, even these books contain the concept of the whole number zero.

8. Give a verse from Lamentations 1 and III John containing the concept zero.

The whole numbers and real numbers share the element zero and reflect the orderliness of the Creator. They also reflect another characteristic of God.

9. What does Psalm 147:5 say about God?

Infinite means **not finite**. A piece of paper is finite because its size can be specified by real numbers ($8\frac{1}{2}$ by 11 in.). Your hometown has a finite population. How many pets do you have? Even if you don't have any (zero), it is a finite set (zero is a specific real number). Since no specific number can describe the size of our number systems, they are infinite. Since no physical being or object is infinite, number systems help us understand this important characteristic of God.

> ### Scriptural Roots
>
> **A**S IT IS WRITTEN,
> There is none righteous,
> no, not one.
>
> ROMANS 3:10

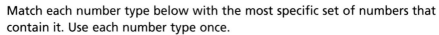
Match each number type below with the most specific set of numbers that contain it. Use each number type once.

1. 7.2727727772 . . .
2. 7.27272727 . . .
3. −7
4. 0
5. 2

A. Integer
B. Natural
C. Rational
D. Real
E. Whole

Give the symbolic form of each property listed below.

6. Commutative property of addition
7. Associative property of multiplication
8. Distributive property
9. Identity property of multiplication
10. Additive inverse property
11. Multiplicative inverse property
12. Fundamental principle of fractions

Simplify.

13. $4 + 6 \cdot 8 \div 2 - 14$
14. $\frac{1}{8} + \frac{3}{8}$
15. $\sqrt{36}$
16. $3 + 8 - 5 \cdot 4 + 6$
17. $\frac{4}{7} \div \frac{3}{8}$
18. $5 + 3(2 - 6 \cdot 2) - 4 + 6$
19. $3 + 6^2 - 7 - 2 \cdot 4 - 9$
20. $\frac{1}{9} \cdot \frac{4}{5}$
21. $\frac{5}{8} - \frac{7}{9}$
22. $6 - 2(9 \div 3 + 8) - 6 \cdot 4$
23. $\sqrt[3]{-8}$
24. $2^3 + 2[4(3 + 9) - 7] - 15 + 3 \cdot 6$
25. $\frac{2}{3} \div \frac{1}{3}$
26. $4^2 - 1 \cdot 8 + 3 - 7 + 10 \div 2$
27. $\sqrt{9} + \mid -9 \mid (2 - 6) + 4 \cdot 5^0$

27. $\sqrt{9} + |-9|(2 - 6) + 4 \cdot 5^0$

28. $\frac{2}{9} + \frac{3}{21}$

29. $\sqrt{\frac{4}{16}}$

30. $2 + \{[3 - 6(2 - 9) + 4(6 + 3)] - 8\} \cdot 4$

$A = \{2, 4, 6, 8, 10\}$
$B = \{0, 1, 2, 3, 4, 5\}$
$C = \{2, 8, 14, 20, \ldots\}$

Find.

31. $A \cup C$

32. $B \cap C$

33. $A \cap B$

34. $A \cap \varnothing$

35. $A \cup B$

36. $B \cup \mathbb{N}$

37. Which sets in exercises 31-36 are infinite? Which ones are finite?

Complete each statement using sets A, B, and C above.

38. $32 \in$

39. $\{2, 10\} \subseteq$

40. What is the mathematical significance of Romans 3:10?

3 The Language of Algebra

Cheryl works for the Quality Quilts Company, making patterns from which the company manufactures quilts. Her designs combine pieces of material cut into geometric shapes. Many designs utilize triangular or square pieces; others incorporate pentagons or hexagons.

Cheryl is designing a quilt that will be made from hexagonal pieces of material. The quilt for a twin bed must be 72 inches wide and 108 inches long. The formula for the area of a regular hexagon is $A = \frac{1}{2}ap$, where A represents the area of the hexagon, a the length of the apothem (the shortest distance from the center to a side), and p the perimeter.

Cheryl must determine how many hexagonal pieces to cut for her pattern. How many square inches must the quilt cover for a twin bed? If her hexagons have a perimeter of 12 inches and an apothem of 1.73 inches, how many square inches does each hexagonal piece cover? How many pieces should she cut?

Cheryl needs to decide which formulas to use, how to apply the formulas to the problem, and how to answer these questions. She needs to be familiar with equations and formulas in which variables are represented as letters. You will begin to use letters as variables, and write equations using them in this chapter.

After this chapter you should be able to

1. evaluate expressions containing variables.
2. simplify exponential expressions and use negative exponents.
3. use formulas.
4. combine like terms.
5. give examples of the properties of equality.
6. change word problems to algebraic expressions and equations.

3.1 Variables

A church is planning a fall cookout. The food committee decided to shop for the best buy in canned soft drinks. Here is what they found.

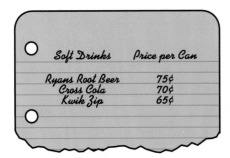

Soft Drinks	Price per Can
Ryans Root Beer	75¢
Cross Cola	70¢
Kwik Zip	65¢

Brand	Price per Can p	Total Price $62p$
Ryans	0.75	$46.50
Cross	0.70	$43.40
Kwik	0.65	$40.30

The committee chairman asked for the total cost of each brand based on one can for each of the 62 members. So the committee multiplied each p value by 62.

If symbols are written next to each other with no operational sign between them, multiply them.

On the sheets above, p represents three different values: {$0.75, $0.70, $0.65}. We say p is a variable because its value varies. A variable is denoted by a letter that stands for any member of a set. This set of possible replacement values is called the *domain* of the variable. Variables are used extensively in algebra to indicate an unknown quantity. Frequently a mathematical expression will contain a constant, a number or letter whose value does not change. The Greek letter pi (π) represents a constant approximately equal to 3.14. The constant in the table above is 62.

A **variable** is a symbol used to represent any element of a given set of numbers. The set of numbers is the domain of the variable.

A **constant** is a fixed number.

Is God variable or constant? Does He do what He says He will do? Read James 1:17, Hebrews 13:8, and Malachi 3:6. Can God make the answer plainer? When you get discouraged, you can rest in God, knowing that He is always the same. Man is changeable and doesn't always keep his promises, but God is always the same. What other verses tell of God's steadfastness?

You already know how valuable variables are for summarizing properties. It is much easier to write $a + b = b + a$ than to try to list all number statements separately ($2 + 3 = 3 + 2, 2 + 4 = 4 + 2$, etc.). Variables are also valuable for problem solving.

To be able to solve problems, you must learn how to read a word phrase and convert it into an algebraic expression containing variables.

An **algebraic expression** is the result of performing mathematical operations on any collection of variables and constants.

EXAMPLE 1   If c represents the cost of one pencil, what is the cost of ten pencils?

Answer   Let c = the cost (in cents) of one pencil. Then $10c$ is the cost of ten pencils.

EXAMPLE 2   If the domain for c is {5, 10, 17}, what is the cost of the pencils?

Answer   If $c = 5$, then $10c = 10 \cdot 5 = 50$.
If $c = 10$, then $10c = 10 \cdot 10 = 100$.
If $c = 17$, then $10c = 10 \cdot 17 = 170$.

Thus, the cost of the pencils in each case is 50 cents; 100 cents, or $1.00; and 170 cents, or $1.70.

EXAMPLE 3	Write an algebraic expression to represent the sum of 5 and any real number n
Answer	Let n = any real number Then $n + 5$ represents the algebraic expression.
EXAMPLE 4	If the domain of x is $\{-5, \frac{1}{2}, 2, 3\}$, find the corresponding values of $x + 9$.
Answer	If $x = -5$, then $x + 9 = -5 + 9 = 4$. If $x = \frac{1}{2}$, then $x + 9 = \frac{1}{2} + 9 = 9\frac{1}{2}$. If $x = 2$, then $x + 9 = 2 + 9 = 11$. If $x = 3$, then $x + 9 = 3 + 9 = 12$. The corresponding set of values is $\{4, 9\frac{1}{2}, 11, 12\}$.

▶ A. Exercises

Write an algebraic expression for each word phrase.

1. The product of 8 and any number x
2. The number of spider legs in a box containing s spiders
3. The calories Joe consumes eating n sweet rolls when one sweet roll has 325 calories
4. A number that is four more than five times another number
5. Joy's keyboarding speed if Joy types twice as fast as Lynn
6. The number of history books a bookstore has if it has four more than three times the number of math books
7. The perimeter of a rectangle 24 units long and w units wide
8. The amount Evelyn makes the week she gives x haircuts at $15 each and y permanents at $45 each

Assume the domain of the variable is $\{-4, 1, 3, 8\}$ in exercises 9-14. Evaluate each expression and give all possible solutions.

9. $x - 4$
10. $y + 6$
11. $3z$
12. $a + 4$
13. $\frac{1}{2}n$
14. $|b^2 - 10|$

Name the variables and constants in each expression.

15. $3x + 6$
16. $\frac{ab}{3}$
17. $c + d - 5$
18. $\frac{t}{4} + 6$

▶ B. Exercises

State the properties described.

19. $x + y = y + x$

20. $a(b + c) = ab + ac$

21. $t(sq) = (ts)q$

22. $n \cdot \frac{1}{n} = 1$

23. $(ab)c = (ba)c$

▶ C. Exercises

Write an algebraic expression to represent the following.

24. The amount of water in a pool if three pipes deliver water at the rates x, y, and z gallons per hour respectively. The first and third are used to fill the pool while the second is a drain pipe. The fill pipes are opened and run for 4 hours, and the drain pipe is inadvertently left open for 2 hours and then shut off.

25. The amount of sales tax paid at 6% for x shirts at $24 each and y pairs of socks at $4 each.

▮ Cumulative Review

Perform the operations.

26. $-18 + (-6)$

27. $-18 - (-6)$

28. $-18(-6)$

29. $\frac{-18}{-6}$

30. List the order of operations.

3.2 Word Phrases and Algebraic Expressions

As a student of algebra, you must be able to take information from our God-created universe and translate it into algebraic language. After you have symbolized the problem, you can solve it and relate it back to the physical world. In this section you will change verbal problems into algebraic symbols. Look for words that indicate certain operations. Of what operations do the following words make you think?

times	divided by	add
less	more	subtract
quotient	diminished	decreased
sum	half	increased
twice	difference	product

Symbolize the following.

EXAMPLE 1   The sum of *n* and 4

Answer $n + 4$

EXAMPLE 2   The difference between a number and 5

Answer $n - 5$

EXAMPLE 3   One-third of a number

Answer $\frac{1}{3}n$

EXAMPLE 4   A number divided by 6

Answer $\frac{n}{6}$

EXAMPLE 5   The sum of 3 and 8 times a number

Answer   Let *x* stand for the number. Since "8 times a number" means 8*x*, the desired sum is $3 + 8x$.

EXAMPLE 6 8 more than 3 times a number

Answer $3n + 8$

EXAMPLE 7 The quotient of the difference of a number and 8, and twice the number. Let *n* represent the number.

Answer The difference: $n - 8$
Twice the number: $2n$
The quotient of them: $\dfrac{n - 8}{2n}$

EXAMPLE 8 The opposite of the reciprocal of the square of a number. Let *s* be the number.

Answer $-\dfrac{1}{s^2}$

▶ A. Exercises

Express in algebraic form.

1. A number decreased by 17
2. The product of a number and 4
3. *x* increased by *y*
4. *n* less 10
5. The sum of twice a number and 6
6. The difference between a number and twice the number
7. 24 greater than a number
8. The sum of a number and 82 times the number
9. The square root of a number
10. The average of three numbers *p*, *q*, *r*
11. The midpoint between *m* and *n*
12. A number *q* to the fifth power
13. The cube of the length *s* of one edge of a cube
14. Five degrees less than the outside temperature *t*

▶ B. Exercises

Express in algebraic form.

15. A number cubed plus the number squared
16. The quotient of twice a number, and the sum of the number and 7
17. 126 diminished by the product of a number and 1 less than the number
18. Three less than the product of a number and 2 more than the number
19. The sum of the squares of *a* and *b*

20. The reciprocal of the absolute value of a number

21. The amount spent if a customer buys 6 large sodas at *d* dollars each and 12 hot dogs at *h* dollars each at a baseball game

22. The number of animal legs on a farm containing *x* horses, *y* cows, and *z* chickens

23. The number of points a basketball player gets in one game when he makes *x* three-point baskets, *y* shorter field goals, and *z* free throws

24. Sue's score and Jim's score if Sue got six more points on the test than Mark and Jim got ten fewer than Mark. Mark's score was *m*.

▶ C. Exercises

Write two word phrases to describe each algebraic expression.

25. $2a + 5$

26. $a - 9$

27. $3(x + 2)$

28. $\frac{4}{x}$

■ Cumulative Review

$A = \{\text{prime numbers}\}$ $B = \{\text{odd integers}\}$ $C = \{1, 4, 9, 16, 25\}$

29. Write in symbols any set that is a subset of $\mathbb{N}$.

30. Write in symbols that the number 9 is or is not an element of each set above.

31. $A \cap B$

32. $A \cap C$

33. $A \cup C$

3.3 Negative Exponents

In Chapter 1 you learned that instead of writing $4 \cdot 4 \cdot 4$, you can write 4^3. The same shortcut applies to variables. If you wish to represent three factors of some number, n, you can write n^3. This shorter form is the exponential form. In the expanded form, n^3 would be nnn. Since the base is now a variable, the exact value of the expression is unknown until the value of n is established.

EXAMPLE 1	Write *aaabb* in exponential form.
Answer	a^3b^2

EXAMPLE 2	Write x^4yz^5 in expanded form.
Answer	*xxxxyzzzzz*

The properties of exponents that you learned in Chapter 1 apply to variables as well as to known values. Here are those properties again with variables and numbers.

$$x^a \cdot x^b = x^{a+b} \qquad 2^4 \cdot 2^2 = 2^{4+2} = 2^6$$

$$x^a \div x^b = x^{a-b} \qquad \frac{2^5}{2^3} = 2^{5-3} = 2^2$$

$$(x^a)^b = x^{ab} \qquad (2^2)^3 = 2^{2 \cdot 3} = 2^6$$

$$x^0 = 1, \text{ if } x \neq 0 \qquad 321^0 = 1$$

Following the above laws, simplify the next division problem by subtracting exponents.

$$5^2 \div 5^3 = 5^{2-3} = 5^{-1}$$

As you know, a division problem can be written as a fraction, which can then be expanded and simplified.

$$5^2 \div 5^3$$

$$\frac{5^2}{5^3}$$

$$\frac{\overset{1}{\cancel{5}} \cdot \overset{1}{\cancel{5}}}{\underset{1}{\cancel{5}} \cdot \underset{1}{\cancel{5}} \cdot 5}$$

$$\frac{1}{5}$$

Based on these computations, we represent $\frac{1}{5}$ as 5^{-1}.

A fractional expression such as $\frac{1}{8}$ can be expressed in exponential form as $\frac{1}{2^3}$. You can also express this fraction in exponential form as a whole number with a negative exponent.

$$\frac{1}{8} = \frac{1}{2^3} = 2^{-3}$$

By following the properties of exponents, you can understand this general reasoning.

$$\frac{1}{x^a} = \frac{x^0}{x^a} = x^{0-a} = x^{-a}$$

Negative Exponent Property

$x^{-a} = \frac{1}{x^a}$, if a is any real number and $x \neq 0$.

When you multiply, divide, or raise the power of exponential expressions with negative exponents, use the same rules that you used when working with positive exponents.

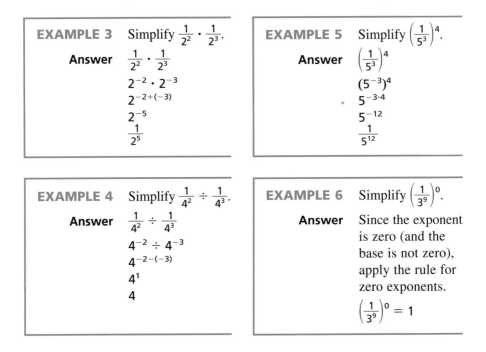

EXAMPLE 3 Simplify $\frac{1}{2^2} \cdot \frac{1}{2^3}$.

Answer
$\frac{1}{2^2} \cdot \frac{1}{2^3}$
$2^{-2} \cdot 2^{-3}$
$2^{-2+(-3)}$
2^{-5}
$\frac{1}{2^5}$

EXAMPLE 5 Simplify $\left(\frac{1}{5^3}\right)^4$.

Answer
$\left(\frac{1}{5^3}\right)^4$
$(5^{-3})^4$
$5^{-3 \cdot 4}$
5^{-12}
$\frac{1}{5^{12}}$

EXAMPLE 4 Simplify $\frac{1}{4^2} \div \frac{1}{4^3}$.

Answer
$\frac{1}{4^2} \div \frac{1}{4^3}$
$4^{-2} \div 4^{-3}$
$4^{-2-(-3)}$
4^1
4

EXAMPLE 6 Simplify $\left(\frac{1}{3^9}\right)^0$.

Answer Since the exponent is zero (and the base is not zero), apply the rule for zero exponents.

$\left(\frac{1}{3^9}\right)^0 = 1$

► A. Exercises

Write in exponential form.

1. aaa
2. xx
3. kk
4. $qqqqq$
5. $ddpppp$
6. $uuvw$
7. $vvvvvvv$
8. $mnoo$
9. $ruaa$
10. $zzzzzzzzzz$

Write in expanded form.

11. x^5
12. n^2b^7
13. c^3
14. jo^4
15. t^6

Write each expression with positive exponents.

16. 3^{-2}
17. x^{-5}
18. 4^{-8}
19. y^{-2}
20. $x^{-3}y^{-4}$
21. 4^{-3}

Write each expression with negative exponents.

22. $\dfrac{1}{4^3}$
23. $\dfrac{1}{8^2}$
24. $\dfrac{1}{x^4}$
25. $\dfrac{1}{x^2y^9}$
26. $\dfrac{1}{3^2x^3}$
27. $\dfrac{1}{x^2yz^3}$

► B. Exercises

Compute, leaving the answers in positive exponential form.

28. $\dfrac{1}{3^2} \cdot \dfrac{1}{3^3}$
29. $4^{-2} \div 4^{-9}$
30. $\left(\dfrac{1}{7^3}\right)^4$
31. $\dfrac{1}{9^2} \div \dfrac{1}{9^4}$
32. $(3^{-6})^0$
33. $4^{-5} \div \dfrac{1}{4^2}$
34. $8^{-3} \cdot \dfrac{1}{8^5}$
35. $\dfrac{1}{3^{-2}} \cdot \dfrac{1}{3^2}$
36. $x^{-5} \cdot x^3$
37. $y^{-4} \div y^{-2}$
38. $z^4 \cdot z^6$
39. $x^2 \cdot x^5 \cdot x^3$
40. $(x^4)^{-3}$

► C. Exercises

Compute, leaving the answers in positive exponential form.

41. $(3x^{-2} \cdot x^5)^{-4}$
42. $(-2x^{-3}y^4)^{-2}$

■ Cumulative Review

43. Give the GCF of 1200 and 792.

Find the following.

44. π^0
45. 0^5
46. $\dfrac{0}{10}$
47. $\dfrac{-3}{0}$

3.4 Evaluating Algebraic Expressions

What does the noun *value* mean? The mathematical definition is "an assigned or calculated numerical quantity." To evaluate means to find that quantity.

Does your life have any value? Can you calculate its worth? Many people evaluate their lives as without value because they have not accepted Jesus Christ as their Savior. The Christian, however, recognizes that his life has value in God's sight. He also evaluates his life every day to see whether he is living up to God's standard. He should compare himself not with those around him (II Cor. 10:12) but with Christ. The Christian must daily read and study God's Word (James 1:23-25) so that he can become more like Christ, the only standard by which he should evaluate his life.

This pond reflects the white tail deer. Does your life mirror biblical principles or peer opinions?

To find the value of $x + 10$ when $x = 5$, replace x with its value of 5, and the expression becomes $5 + 10$, which equals 15.

Definition

To **evaluate** is to calculate the numerical value of an expression.

EXAMPLE 1   Evaluate x^2 when $x = 3$.

Answer $x^2 = 3^2 = 3 \cdot 3 = 9$

EXAMPLE 2   Evaluate $x + y + z^2$ when $x = 4$, $y = 9$, and $z = 2$.

Answer $x + y + z^2$
$4 + 9 + 2^2$
$4 + 9 + 4$
17

EXAMPLE 3   Evaluate $3a^2 - b + c^3$ when $a = 1$, $b = 4$, and $c = 3$.

Answer $3a^2 - b + c^3$

$3 \cdot 1^2 - 4 + 3^3$

$3 - 4 + 27$

26

EXAMPLE 4   Evaluate x^2yz^2 when $x = -\frac{1}{2}$, $y = -2$, and $z = \frac{1}{4}$.

Answer x^2yz^2

$\left(-\frac{1}{2}\right)^2(-2)\left(\frac{1}{4}\right)^2$

$\frac{1}{4}(-2)\left(\frac{1}{16}\right)$

$-\frac{2}{64}$

$-\frac{1}{32}$

Definition

Substitution is the process of replacing a variable with a value or an algebraic expression.

Evaluating Expressions

1. Substitute the given values for the variables.
2. Evaluate by following the order of operations.

▶ A. Exercises

Evaluate with $x = 4$, $y = -2$, $z = 3$, and $h = -1$.

1. $x^2 y$
2. $x + yz$
3. $\frac{x + y}{h}$
4. $x^2 + h - 3$
5. $\frac{x}{y} + \frac{z}{h}$

6. $(x + y)(x - y)$
7. $x^3 - z^3$
8. $h(x + z)$
9. $h^2 + y^2 - x^3$
10. $\frac{3x^2 y - z}{5}$

▶ B. Exercises

Evaluate $xy^2 z$ when

11. $x = 2$, $y = 3$, $z = -2$.
12. $x = 5$, $y = n$, $z = 3$.
13. $x = a$, $y = a$, $z = a$.

If $p = 12$, $q = 196$, and $r = -13$, evaluate.

14. $r^2 + \sqrt{q}$
15. $\frac{|p + r|}{p + r}$

Evaluate with $x = \frac{1}{2}$, $y = -\frac{1}{4}$, $z = 1$, and $h = \frac{1}{3}$.

16. $x^2 + h - 3$
17. $(x + y)(x - y)$
18. $h^2 + y^2 - x^3$

19. $3x^2 y - \frac{z}{5}$
20. $\frac{z - h^2}{2y}$
21. $\frac{xy - zh^2}{2yh}$

▶ C. Exercises

Evaluate when $a = -\frac{2}{3}$, $b = \frac{4}{7}$, and $c = -3$.

22. $|a - b| - \frac{c^2}{b}$
23. $\sqrt{|14abc|} + \left(\frac{1}{a}\right)^2$

■ Cumulative Review

Match each phrase to its most literal translation.

A. $4 - 9$ C. $4 + 9$ E. $4 \cdot \frac{1}{9}$ G. $\sqrt{4} \cdot 9$ I. $9 - 4$
B. $\sqrt{4 \cdot 9}$ D. $\frac{4}{9}$ F. $\frac{9}{4}$ H. $\sqrt{4} \cdot \sqrt{9}$ J. $9 + 4$

24. The sum of four and nine
25. Four more than nine
26. Four less nine
27. Four less than nine

28. The quotient of four and nine
29. The square root of the product of four and nine
30. The product of the square roots of four and nine
31. The product of the square root of four and nine
32. The product of four and the reciprocal of nine

3.5 Combining Like Terms

The statement "Simplicity is truth's most becoming garb" means that God's truth is never complicated. In II Corinthians 11:3, Paul warns the Corinthian Christians not to believe anyone or anything who would turn their minds "from the simplicity that is in Christ." God's plan of salvation is that one simply believe the gospel. The gospel—that Christ died, was buried, and rose again—can be no simpler. But Satan corrupts that simplicity and says there are other things to do besides believe. Christians need to guard themselves against Satan's complications by trusting fully in the simplicity of Jesus Christ.

Mathematical expressions are written as simply as possible. When you speak of a group of apples and bananas, how would you most simply express 11 apples, 8 bananas, and 6 more apples? You would say 17 apples and 11 bananas. In other words, you would combine the two sets of apples into one set.

Likewise, to simplify an algebraic expression, you need to combine *like terms* by performing the indicated operations. In algebra, as in all math work, always express your final answer in simplest form.

A display at Tonala in the state of Jalisco, Mexico

Definitions

A **term** is a constant, a variable raised to a power, or the product of a constant and one or more such variables.

Like terms are terms that have the same variable (or variables) with the same exponents.

The expression $3x - 4y + 5x$ has three terms: $3x$, $-4y$, and $5x$. There are only two variables: x and y. The terms $3x$ and $5x$ are like terms because both have the same variable, x, and the same exponent, 1. Like terms can be combined into a simpler form, but unlike terms cannot. The expression in its simplest form is $8x - 4y$.

The **numerical coefficient** is the numerical factor (constant) accompanying the variables in a term.

The numerical coefficient of $3x$ is 3 and of $-4y$ is -4. If there is no expressed numerical coefficient of a variable, the coefficient is 1.

When you combine like terms, you are actually applying the distributive property $a(b + c) = ab + ac$.

EXAMPLE 1   Combine $3x + 5x$.

Answer $3x + 5x = (3 + 5)x = 8x$

Use the distributive property in reverse.

EXAMPLE 2   Simplify $3x + 4y - 5x$.

Answer

$3x + 4y - 5x$ $3x - 5x + 4y$	1. Rearrange the terms (commutative property of addition).
$(3 - 5)x + 4y$	2. Apply the distributive property.
$-2x + 4y$	3. Perform the operations.

Since $-2x$ and $4y$ are unlike terms, they cannot be combined. Now the expression is in simplest form.

EXAMPLE 3   Simplify $7x^2 + 8x - 4x^2 + 10x$.

Answer $7x^2 + 8x - 4x^2 + 10x$
$7x^2 - 4x^2 + 8x + 10x$
$3x^2 + 18x$

The terms containing x^2 and those containing x are unlike terms because the exponents of x are different.

WRITE ANSWERS IN DESCENDING POWERS OF THE VARIABLE
NOT $18X + 3X^2$, BUT $3X^2 + 18X$!

Combining Like Terms

1. Find all like terms.
2. Combine like terms by adding coefficients.

Remember your rules for adding and subtracting positive and negative numbers.

EXAMPLE 4	Simplify $2x + 4y - 8x + 3z - 5y$.
Answer	$2x + 4y - 8x + 3z - 5y$ 1. Find all like terms. (Mark them if necessary.)
	$-6x - y + 3z$ 2. Add the numerical coefficients.
EXAMPLE 5	Simplify $4x^2y + 5xy - 10x^2y + 22xy - 8x + y$.
Answer	$4x^2y + 5xy - 10x^2y + 22xy - 8x + y$ $-6x^2y + 27xy - 8x + y$

REMEMBER THAT ANY VARIABLE WITH NO WRITTEN COEFFICIENT HAS A COEFFICIENT OF ONE.
$X^2 = 1X^2$

EXAMPLE 6	Simplify $8x^3 - x^2 + x^3 + 4x^3 - x^2 + 6x^3$.
Answer	$8x^3 - x^2 + x^3 + 4x^3 - x^2 + 6x^3$ $19x^3 - 2x^2$
EXAMPLE 7	Simplify $2x^2y + xy^2 + 4x^2yz - 3xyz$.
Answer	This cannot be simplified because there are no like terms.

▶ A. Exercises

For each algebraic expression, list all numerical coefficients. Then tell which terms are like terms.

1. $3x + 4x - 5y$
2. $8x^2 + 3x + 6x^2$
3. $xy - 2xy - 9xy$
4. $x^2yz - xy^2z + 3x^2yz$
5. $2x^3 - 17x + 5x^3$

Simplify by combining like terms.

6. $3a + 7a$
7. $19k - 13k$
8. $12xy + 4xy$
9. $21b - 2b$

▶ B. Exercises

Simplify by combining like terms.

10. $2x^2 + 3x + 5x$
11. $d - 4d + 3f + 7f$
12. $\frac{1}{2}x + \frac{3}{2}x$
13. $12ab + 9ab - 7ab$
14. $2.46m + 1.6n - 8.4m$
15. $6x^2 + 3x^2y - 4x + 8x^2$
16. $21c^2 + 3d - 5cd + 6c^2 + 8cd$
17. $y - 9y + 3y^2$
18. $8x^2 - 6x^2y + 2xy + 7x^2y + xy$

Simplify first and then evaluate the result with $x = 2$ and $y = -3$.

19. $4x + 3y - x + 6y - 8y$
20. $x^2 + 2x - 7x + 4$
21. $xy - 3x + y^2$
22. $3y - x^3 + 1 - y$
23. $(4x)^0 + xy^2 + x$

▶ C. Exercises

Find the terms that should be added to obtain the indicated expression.

24. $3a^2 + ? = 2a^2 + 3a + 4$
25. $x^2 + x + 7 + ? = 5x^2 + 3x - 8$

■ Cumulative Review

Provide the correct reason (property) for each step.

Simplify $3x^2 + x + 2x^2 - 3x$.

26. $3x^2 + 2x^2 + x - 3x$
27. $3x^2 + 2x^2 + 1x - 3x$
28. $(3x^2 + 2x^2) + (1x - 3x)$
29. $(3 + 2)x^2 + (1 - 3)x$
30. $5x^2 - 2x$

3.6 Removing Parentheses

An algebraic expression enclosed in parentheses, braces, or brackets is treated as one term. For example, $(2x + 5)$ is considered one term. It $(2x + 5)$ should be read "the quantity $2x$ plus 5." If a number precedes the parentheses indicating multiplication, you can remove the parentheses by applying the distributive property. Remember that the sign preceding a number can be considered part of the number. Observe how parentheses are removed from each expression.

EXAMPLE 1	$4(a + 3b)$	
Answer	$4(a + 3b)$	
	$4a + 4 \cdot 3b$	1. Apply the distributive property.
	$4a + 12b$	2. There are no like terms.
EXAMPLE 2	$-2(3x^2 - 4x + 5)$	
Answer	$-2(3x^2 - 4x + 5)$	
	$-2(3x^2) + (-2)(-4x) + (-2)(5)$	1. Apply the distributive property.
	$-6x^2 + 8x - 10$	2. There are no like terms.

Notice that the signs inside the parentheses changed when the parentheses are removed because each term is being multiplied by a negative.

THE + IN FRONT OF THE PARENTHESES REPRESENTS +1. DISTRIBUTE THE +1 TO ALL TERMS INSIDE PARENTHESES WHEN REMOVING PARENTHESES.

EXAMPLE 3 $(2x + 5) + (3x - 9)$

Answer

$(2x + 5) + (3x - 9)$

$2x + 5 + 3x - 9$	1. Remove parentheses by distributing the coefficient of 1.
$5x - 4$	2. Combine like terms.

EXAMPLE 4 $(5x - 7) - (x - 6)$

Answer

$(5x - 7) - (x - 6)$

$5x - 7 - x - (-6)$	1. Distribute the -1.
$5x - 7 - x + 6$	2. Since subtracting a negative is the same as adding a positive, $-(-6)$ becomes $+6$.
$4x - 1$	3. Combine like terms.

EXAMPLE 5 $4a(a + b) + 3(a^2 + 2)$

Answer

$4a(a + b) + 3(a^2 + 2)$

$4a^2 + 4ab + 3a^2 + 6$	1. Apply the distributive property.
$7a^2 + 4ab + 6$	2. Combine like terms.

EXAMPLE 6 $2(3x^2 + 4x) - 8(x^2 + 2x)$

Answer

$2(3x^2 + 4x) - 8(x^2 + 2x)$

$6x^2 + 8x - 8x^2 - 16x$	1. Apply the distributive property.
$-2x^2 - 8x$	2. Combine like terms.

Removing Parentheses

1. Apply the distributive property.
2. Combine like terms.

When an expression contains more than one set of GROUPING SYMBOLS, START with the INNERMOST SET and follow the ORDER OF OPERATIONS.

EXAMPLE 7	Remove grouping symbols and simplify the expression. $7x^2 - [3x + 4y(2x - 8y) - 4x] + 5xy$

Answer	$7x^2 - [3x + 4y(2x - 8y) - 4x] + 5xy$	
	$7x^2 - [3x + 8xy - 32y^2 - 4x] + 5xy$	1. Apply the distributive property to remove parentheses.
	$7x^2 - \left[-x + 8xy - 32y^2\right] + 5xy$	2. Combine like terms.
	$7x^2 + x - 8xy + 32y^2 + 5xy$	3. Remove brackets, changing signs.
	$7x^2 + x - 3xy + 32y^2$	4. Combine like terms.

EXAMPLE 8	Remove parentheses and simplify the expression. $3k(k + 2) - k(k - 1)$

Answer	$3k(k + 2) - k(k - 1)$	
	$3k^2 + 6k - k^2 + k$	1. Apply the distributive property to remove parentheses.
	$2k^2 + 7k$	2. Combine like terms.

Simplify and show all work.

1. $4a + (2a + 9)$
2. $(7b - 8c) - (3b + 2c)$
3. $4(x + 2y)$
4. $-2(3z + 7)$
5. $5 - (2x - 18)$
6. $2x - (8y + x)$

7. $-5a - (3a + b) + (2a - 7b)$
8. $3x + 2y + (5x - 7y)$
9. $(2a - b) - (3a + 4b) + (6a + b)$
10. $9m + 11n + (3n - m)$
11. $7b - 3(2b + 6)$
12. $-4(x + 3) + 5(x - 7)$

► B. Exercises

Simplify.

13. $5x(x + y)$
14. $(x + y) - (x - y)$
15. $(x + y) + (x - y)$
16. $10(2x^2 - 3x + 4) - 5(x^2 + 2x - 9)$
17. $4a - (2a^2 + 3z) + 7(a^2 - 2a + 8)$
18. $2x(x - 4) + 3x(x + 2)$
19. $6(m^2 - 2m + 4) - m(m + 3)$
20. $4 - 3p - 6(p + 5) + 9$
21. $2r^2 + 5r + 3r - r(6r + 2)$
22. $a + 6a + 2 - a(a + 4) + 5 - 2$
23. $u^2 + 3(u^2 + 4) - 5(u^2 + 4u + 6)$
24. $x(x + y) - y(x + y)$
25. $x(x + y) + y(x + y)$

► C. Exercises

Simplify.

26. $2x^2 - 5x(4x - 3) - x(x^2 - 5x + 3)$
27. $4x^2(x - 9) - 3(x - 9) - 2x(5x^2 - 3x + 4)$

■ Cumulative Review

Simplify.

28. $x + x + x + x + x$
29. $x \cdot x \cdot x \cdot x \cdot x$
30. $x - x - x - x - x$

31. $x \div x \div x \div x \div x$
32. $(5x)^0 + 5x^0 + 5^0x$

3.7 Using Formulas

When Ahmed dives, he feels additional pressure on his ears above normal atmospheric air pressure. Near the surface he feels less pressure than when he dives for pearls. Underwater the amount of additional pressure (p) in pounds per square inch (psi) depends upon the height (h), or depth, of the water. The relationship is shown in the formula $p = 0.433h$. Diving to a depth of 20 feet, he feels $0.433(20) = 8.66$ psi of additional pressure. At a depth of 3 feet he feels only $0.433(3) = 1.299$ psi of additional pressure.

A **formula** is an equation that expresses the relationship between related quantities.

The metric system is used more frequently in today's scientific world than the English measurements used here. Instead of measuring in pounds per square inch, a scientist measures in newtons per square meter, which is called a pascal (Pa). The formula for converting pounds per square inch (psi) to pascals (Pa) is $Pa = 6894 \times$ pressure in psi.

In chemistry class Sara found that the temperature of the chemicals in her experiment registered 35°C. She was to make sure the chemicals reached at least 100°F. She had to use the formula $F = \frac{9}{5}C + 32°$ to convert Celsius readings to Fahrenheit equivalents. Had the chemicals reached the desired temperature yet? Should she continue to heat the chemicals?

$$F = \frac{9}{5}C + 32$$

$$F = \frac{9}{5}(35) + 32$$

$$F = 63 + 32$$

$$F = 95°$$

The Fahrenheit temperature is 95°, so the chemicals have not reached the desired temperature. Sara must continue to heat them.

Formulas are used extensively in science, business, engineering, carpentry, and many other professions. You use formulas every day.

Using Formulas

1. Write the correct formula.
2. Substitute given values for the variables in the formula.
3. Evaluate the expression.

Formulas are mathematical sentences. You can distinguish mathematical phrases and sentences by identifying a verb—just as you distinguish phrases and sentences in English grammar. Can you find the verb in the sentence $P = 2l + 2w$? In words, the sentence reads, "Perimeter is twice the length plus twice the width." The verb "is," or "equals," is symbolized by "=." Here are other mathematical verbs you should know.

Math verb	Meaning	Math verb	Meaning
$=$	is, equals	$\notin$	is not an element of
$\neq$	is not equal to	$>$	is greater than
$\approx$	is approximately equal to	$<$	is less than
$\subseteq$	is a subset of	$\geq$	is at least, is greater than or equal to
$\in$	is an element of	$\leq$	is at most, is less than or equal to

You should know these formulas.

Perimeter (distance around) formulas		
Rectangle	$P = 2l + 2w$	perimeter equals 2 lengths plus 2 widths
Square	$P = 4s$	perimeter equals 4 times the length of a side
Circle	$C = 2\pi r$	circumference equals 2π times the radius

▶ A. Exercises

Write the appropriate formula, substitute the given values into it, and then do the indicated calculations.

1. How much additional pressure would you feel from the water if you dove to a depth of **32** feet?
2. Convert **8°C** to Fahrenheit.

3. Mr. Denton wants to put a fence around his rectangular garden, but first he needs to know the perimeter. If his garden is **60** feet long and **20** feet wide, how many feet of fencing does he need?

4. A picture that is **11** in. by **14** in. is to be framed using wood one inch wide. Find the perimeter of the picture and then explain why this length would not be enough to frame the picture.

5. A carpenter plans to cut Formica to go around the outer edge of a circular table. To find out how long he needs to cut it, he must find the circumference of a circle. If the radius of the table is **2** feet and the constant π is approximately **3.14**, how long should he cut the Formica?

The volume of a rectangular box can be found with the formula $V = lwh$. Find the volume of boxes having the following dimensions.

6. $l = 4"$	7. $l = 10"$	8. $l = 8"$
$w = 2"$	$w = 3"$	$w = 7"$
$h = 5"$	$h = 2"$	$h = 6"$

Use the given formula to answer each question.

9. The formula $d = rt$ gives distance as the rate multiplied by the time. If a bus carrying spectators to a soccer game travels **47** mph for **2** hours, how far does the bus travel?

10. The formula for normal weight is $w = \frac{11(h - 40)}{2}$. The variable h represents height in inches. If Ben is 5'2" tall and weighs **154** pounds, what is his normal weight? Should he lose or gain weight to be at his normal weight? How much?

$R = xp$ means revenue (business income) equals number of items sold (x) times price per item (p).

11. If **48** cans of Ryan's soda are sold at **79¢** per can, how much revenue is collected?

12. The senior class washed **110** cars and charged **$3.50** per car. How much money did they raise?

13. A company sold **33** bicycles for **$129** each. How much revenue did they receive?

$t = pC$ means sales tax (t) = tax rate percentage (p) times the cost (C).

14. Find the tax on a **$23.95** shirt with a **5%** tax rate.

15. How much tax is on a **$2300** computer in a state with a **7%** tax rate?

16. In a state with a $5\frac{1}{2}$% tax rate, how much tax would there be on the **$2300** computer?

When using percent, change the percent to a decimal

For example, 4% means...

A. 4 per hundred

B. $\frac{4}{100}$

C. 0.04

I'd say... all of the above.

▶ B. Exercises

$G = wh + \frac{1}{2}wE$: gross pay (G) is computed by multiplying the hourly wages (w) by the number of hours worked (h). If you work overtime (more than 40 hours), multiply the number of extra hours (E) by half the hourly wage ($\frac{1}{2}w$) and add it to the previous product.

Find your gross pay if you work

17. 20 hours at $6.75 per hour.
18. 40 hours at $8.12 per hour.
19. 45 hours at $8.50 per hour.
20. 47 hours at $10.92 per hour.
21. The amount of simple interest that Shanda receives on the money she saves from baby-sitting is expressed by $I = Prt$. In this formula, I is simple interest, P is the principal (or amount invested), r is the percentage rate of the investment per year, and t is the time or length of the investment in years. If Shanda invests $150 at 5% interest, how much interest will she gain in one year?

Write the following mathematical formulas in symbols.

22. Distance (d) divided by rate (r) equals time (t).
23. The perimeter (P) of a triangle is the sum of the lengths of the three sides (a, b, c).
24. The diameter (d) of a circle is twice the radius (r).

Translate these mathematical sentences into words.

25. $5 < 7$
26. $\sqrt{5} \approx 2.24$
27. $\emptyset \subseteq \mathbb{N}$
28. $-1 \notin \mathbb{N}$
29. $\pi \neq 3.14$

▶ C. Exercises

30. Chris plans to paint a cylindrical gasoline tank. After he finds the number of square feet of surface area on the cylinder using the formula $A = 2\pi rh + 2\pi r^2$, he can compute the amount of paint needed. If the height of the cylinder is 5 feet and the radius is 2 feet, what is the total surface area of the cylinder?

31. If a circle has radius *r*, find

  a. The effect on the circumference when the radius is increased by 50%. ($C = 2\pi r$)

  b. The effect on the area if *r* is increased by 50% ($A = \pi r^2$).

Displacement for an engine is given by $D = \frac{\pi}{4} nsb^2$, *where* n *is the number of cylinders,* b *is the bore (diameter of cylinder), and* s *is the stroke (distance piston moves).*

■ Cumulative Review

Simplify.

32. 7^{-2}

33. $3(6 - 2) - (9 + 7)$

Evaluate if $x = -2$ and $y = 3$.

34. y^{-2}

36. $(x^{-1} + y^{-1})^2$

35. $3x + 4y$

Here is a 3 x 3 magic square. Use the numbers 1 through 9 to fill in the square so that the sum of each row, column, and diagonal is equal to $\frac{n^3 + n}{2}$.

n = the length of one side of the square

You can make a magic square for any odd number by following the instructions given here. Try a 5 x 5 square.

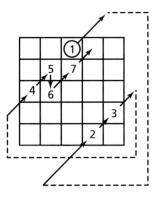

1. Place 1 in the top row center square.
2. Move up diagonally to the right. Since you have moved out of the top of the square, put 2 in the square at the bottom of that column.
3. Move up diagonally to the right from 2 and put 3 in the square.
4. Move up diagonally to the right again. Since you have moved out of the right side of the square, put 4 in the square at the left end of that row.
5. Move up diagonally to the right and put 5 in the square.
6. Since you cannot move up diagonally to the right from 5, put 6 in the square below 5. Then proceed with the steps as given above.

Can you finish this magic square? Can you make a 7 x 7 magic square? What is the sum of each row? column? diagonal? What is the sum of the four corners and the center square?

If you move out of the top of the square, put the next number in the empty square closest to the bottom of the column. If you move out of the right side of the square, put the next number in the empty square closest to the left end of that row. If you cannot move up diagonally to the right within the square, put the next number below the previous number.

If you always begin your magic square with 1, you can use the formula $\frac{n^3 + n}{2}$ to find the sum of the rows, columns, and diagonals.

Probability

Probability measures how likely something is to happen. If you flip a coin, what is the probability that it will land head-side up? There are two possible results or outcomes—"heads" and "tails." Since we are interested in the coin landing with the head-side up, only one of these two results constitutes a successful outcome, namely "heads." **Probability** is the ratio of the number of successful outcomes to the number of *possible outcomes.*

$$P = \frac{\text{number of successful outcomes}}{\text{number of possible outcomes}}$$

You can summarize this formula as $P = \frac{s}{t}$ ($\frac{\text{successes}}{\text{total}}$). You should learn this formula as the definition of probability. For the coin flip, the probability is $P = \frac{1}{2}$, which can also be written in decimal form (**0.5**) or percent form (**50%**). From our limited human perspective, this tells us that on the average a balanced coin will land heads up **50%** of the time.

When finding probabilities, be sure to reduce your fractions. Suppose there are **20** marbles in a box. If eight marbles are yellow, five are red, four are green, two are blue, and one is black, find the probability of drawing a yellow marble. $P = \frac{8}{20} = \frac{2}{5}$

You should also remember that from God's perspective there is no probability. He knows which marble will be drawn. The probability is 1 ($\frac{1 \text{ success}}{1 \text{ possibility}}$) or **100%** that the marble of God's choosing will be drawn. The study of probability considers possibilities from a human perspective to help us make informed decisions as God's stewards.

Notice that probabilities range from **0** to **1** or from **0%** to **100%**.

EXAMPLE 1	What is the probability that a random point chosen on the earth will be on land if water covers **71%** of the earth's surface?
Answer	If **71%** is water, then **100** $-$ **71** $=$ **29%** is land. The probability of randomly selecting a land location from all the locations on the earth is **0.29** (or $\frac{29}{100}$ or **29%**).

▶ Exercises

Suppose that you are one of 15 men and 20 women at a banquet and the host selects one of the names out of a hat to receive a door prize.

1. What is the probability that you will win the prize?

2. What is the probability that a woman will win?

Suppose you have a 12-sided paperweight showing a calendar month on each face. If you roll the paperweight along the floor, what is the probability that it will land with the top face showing

3. the current month?

4. a month beginning with *J*?

5. a month with exactly 30 days?

6. Is it more probable that it will land on a month beginning with *J* or on a month that has thirty days?

The maitre d' welcomes guests to the banquet.

3.8 Properties of Equality

Equality means the condition of being equal. Are all men equal in man's eyes? Read James 2:1-10. Do you show such favoritism? Are all men equal in God's eyes? Yes, all men are sinners, for "there is none righteous, no, not one" (Rom. 3:10). "Whosoever" in Romans 10:13 means anyone. Any person can have heaven for his home if he will accept Jesus Christ as his personal Savior.

In algebra you will use mathematical equalities often. An equality contains an equal sign and two expressions, one on each side of the equal sign. When two expressions represent the same number, the expressions are equal. For example, 2^4 and $22 - 6$ have the same numerical value, 16. Therefore, $2^4 = 22 - 6$. Read the equal sign ($=$) "is," "equals," or "is equal to."

Definition

An **equation** is a mathematical sentence stating that two expressions are equal.

Equations are either true or false. You can tell whether a numerical equation is true or false by simplifying both sides to see if they are equal.

$$3^2 - 5(7) = -2(13) \qquad 4(5) = 3 + 2(4)$$
$$9 - 35 = -26 \qquad\qquad 20 = 3 + 8$$
$$-26 = -26 \qquad\qquad 20 = 11$$

Therefore, the first equation is true and the second is false.

An *algebraic equation* is an equation with a variable such as $x + 4 = 7$.

$$\text{If } x = 3 \qquad\qquad \text{If } x = 2$$
$$x + 4 = 7 \qquad\qquad x + 4 = 7$$
$$3 + 4 = 7 \qquad\qquad 2 + 4 = 7$$
$$7 = 7 \text{ is true} \qquad 6 = 7 \text{ is false}$$

You can see that $x + 4 = 7$ is true when x is 3 and false when x is 2. Finding values that make algebraic equations true is called *solving* the equation. It is important to identify the truth, and solving algebraic equations is one of your main objectives in algebra. To do this effectively, you must understand the four properties of equality below.

PROPERTIES OF EQUALITY

Operation	Used to Solve	Example	Symbolization
Addition	$x - 29 = -58$	$5 = 3 + 2$ $5 + 4 = 3 + 2 + 4$ $9 = 9$	If $a = b$, and c is a real number, then $a + c = b + c$.
Subtraction	$x + 18 = 122$	$7 = 4 + 3$ $7 - 3 = 4 + 3 - 3$ $4 = 4$	If $a = b$, and c is a real number, then $a - c = b - c$.
Multiplication	$\frac{x}{8} = -34$	$4 = 1 + 3$ $2(4) = 2(1 + 3)$ $8 = 2 + 6$ $8 = 8$	If $a = b$, and c is a real number, then $ac = bc$.
Division	$4x = 62$	$8 = 2 + 6$ $\frac{8}{2} = \frac{(2 + 6)}{2}$ $\frac{8}{2} = \frac{2}{2} + \frac{6}{2}$ $4 = 1 + 3$ $4 = 4$	If $a = b$, and c is a real number not equal to zero, then $\frac{a}{c} = \frac{b}{c}$.

▶ A. Exercises

In each problem below, the left side of the equation has been changed. What must you do to the right side of the equation to maintain balance?

1. $3 = 1 + 2$
   $3 + 5 =$

2. $x + 7 = 15$
   $x + 7 - 7 =$

3. $8 - 2 = 6$
   $8 - 2 + 2 =$

4. $x - 3 = 24$
   $x - 3 + 3 =$

5. $5 = 2 + 3$
   $2 \cdot 5 =$

6. $8 + 4 = 12$
   $3(8 + 4) =$

7. $24 = 12 \cdot 2$
   $\frac{24}{2} =$

8. $20 = 4x$
   $\frac{20}{4} =$

9. $5x = 75$
   $\frac{5x}{5} =$

10. $\frac{x}{2} = 8$
    $2\left(\frac{x}{2}\right) =$

Label each equation true or false.

11. $5 \cdot 6 = 2 + 3 \cdot 6$

12. $8 + 6 = 2 \cdot 7$

13. $3(5 + 2) = 11 + 5 \cdot 2$

14. $2 + 3(1 + 5) = 2^2 - 3(-8 + 5) - 7$

Is the given number the solution to the equation?

15. $5x + 1 = 2$ if $x = 5$ **17.** $6x + 5 = x$ if $x = -1$

16. $x - 7 = 9$ if $x = -2$ **18.** $10 = 12 - x$ if $x = 2$

▶ B. Exercises

Which property would be used to solve each equation?

19. $5x = 20$ **21.** $\frac{x}{18} = 3$

20. $x - 5 = 20$ **22.** $8 + x = 15$

Use the properties of equality to transform the equation $x = a + 4$ in each of the following problems.

23. Subtract 10 from both sides.   **24.** Multiply both sides by five.

Translate each sentence into symbols.

25. Twice the sum of nineteen and twenty is seventy-eight.

26. Three less the quotient of twenty and four is negative two.

27. Five more than the square root of four hundred is the square of five.

28. The reciprocals of three and five add up to eight-fifteenths.

▶ C. Exercises

Translate each sentence into symbols.

29. One more than one-half the reciprocal of a number is 9 less than the square root of 3 times the reciprocal.

30. Twice the square of a number increased by five times the product of the number and three more than the number is the opposite of the quotient of six and the number.

▪ Cumulative Review

If $x = 3$ and $y = 6$, evaluate each formula.

31. $D = \sqrt{(x + 1)^2 + (y - 3)^2}$ **34.** $D = |x - y|$

32. $L = \sqrt{x + y}$ **35.** $M = \frac{x + y}{2}$

33. $R = 130x$

THE BERNOULLI FAMILY

The Bernoulli family of Switzerland (who escaped from Belgium under religious persecution from Catholics) contributed greatly to the field of mathematics. In three generations the family produced eight mathematicians. Two of these mathematicians, Jakob and Johann Bernoulli, made calculus practical for the common man.

Although his father intended for him to study theology, Jakob Bernoulli (1654-1705) favored mathematics and astronomy. At age twenty, he took the chair of mathematics at the University of Basel, which he held until his death in 1705. His accomplishments included the development of differential and integral calculus, discovery of the isochrone, implementation of polar coordinates, the Bernoulli distribution, and the Bernoulli theorem. Jakob's work in differential and integral calculus is applied today in electrical engineering, and the Bernoulli theorem is widely used in statistics and insurance studies. In fact, Jakob's book *The Art of Conjecturing*, published in 1713 after his death, was the first thorough treatment of probability.

Johann Bernoulli (1667-1748), like his brother, did not follow his father's plan for him to run the family business but sought instead a degree in medicine. After obtaining his M.A. degree, he left medicine to study mathematics. At age thirty, Johann took his first post as professor at Groningen University, leaving eight years later to succeed his brother at Basel. Johann wrote on various mathematical topics, including optical phenomena, analytical trigonometry, and exponential calculus. In 1696 he compiled the first calculus textbook.

$$ax^2 + bx + c = 0$$

Nikolaus Bernoulli (1687-1759), a nephew of Jakob and Johann, worked mainly in the fields of probability theory and infinite series. Encouraging Nikolaus to study mathematics were his friends Isaac Newton, Edmund Halley, and Gottfried Leibniz. Besides being an expert in mathematics, Nikolaus was also a lawyer. From 1722 to 1731 he was a professor of logic, and in 1731 he changed to a professorship in law.

Like their father, the sons of Johann all became famous mathematicians and scientists. Nikolaus (II) (1695-1726) wrote about curves, differential equations, and probability. Daniel Bernoulli (1700-82), the most famous son, is well known for his work in probability, astronomy, physics, hydrodynamics, and calculus. Johann (II) (1710-90), who originally studied law, spent his later years as a professor of mathematics at the University of Basel. He received the distinguished Paris Prize three times for his outstanding work in physics. His sons, Johann (III) (1744-1807) and Jakob (II) (1759-89), also were great mathematicians.

The Bernoullis contributed greatly to the field of mathematics. In three generations the family produced eight mathematicians.

3.9 Word Sentences and Equations

The sum of a number and 5 is 23. Find the number.

Can you translate this word problem into a numerical equation? First, analyze it very carefully. The statement *find the number* tells you that the variable will stand for the number. Choose a letter as a variable to represent *the number*. Next, translate the phrase *the sum of a number and 5* as $x + 5$. Since the word *is* means *equals*, put $=$ in your algebraic sentence. The final number, 23, is the sum. $x + 5 = 23$

After you have read and analyzed a word problem systematically and methodically, you should be able to write an equation that symbolizes it. Consider some further examples.

EXAMPLE 1 The difference of a number and 10 is 37.

Answer Analyze: Let the number be x

difference means $-$

is means $=$

Equation: $x - 10 = 37$

You have had a lot of practice translating expressions. To translate an equation, translate both expressions and connect them with the verb *is* ($=$).

EXAMPLE 2 If 23 is added to 4 times a number, the results is 143. What is the number?

Answer Analyze: Let the number be n

23 added to four times a number $4n + 23$

is $=$

Equation: $4n + 23 = 143$

EXAMPLE 3   Six subtracted from three times a number equals thirty-six decreased by four times the number. Find the number.

Answer   Analyze: Let the number be x

                         6 subtracted from 3 times a number $3x - 6$

                         equals $=$

                         36 decreased by 4 times the number $36 - 4x$

             Equation: $3x - 6 = 36 - 4x$

If you learn to analyze problems carefully, you will have no difficulty setting up algebraic equations.

Translating Words into Equations

1. Read the problem carefully.
2. Analyze the problem.
3. Substitute algebraic symbols for words.
4. Write the equation.

EXAMPLE 4   The sum of two consecutive integers is 49. Find the two integers.

Answer   Analyze: Let the first integer be x

                         the second integer $x + 1$

                         sum $+$

                         is $=$

             Equation: $x + (x + 1) = 49$

                        $2x + 1 = 49$ Combine like terms.

EXAMPLE 5   One number is 6 more than 3 times another number. The difference of the numbers is 34. What are the two numbers?

Answer   Analyze: Let the number be x

                         the second number $3x + 6$

                         difference $-$

                         is $=$

             Equation: $(3x + 6) - x = 34$

                        $2x + 6 = 34$ Simplify.

Now that you can translate words into equations, you need to learn how to solve these equations. This is the topic of the next chapter. For now, concentrate on getting the equation from the words.

▶ A. Exercises

Analyze each word problem. Write the equation you would use to solve the problem, but do not solve it.

1. The product of a number and 12 is 780. Find the number.
2. Four times a number plus 8 is 28. What is the number?
3. The quotient of 3 times a number and 16 is 12. Find the number.
4. The absolute value of a number is five. Find the number.
5. Fifteen percent of what number is 41?
6. If a five percent sales tax comes to $3.32, what is the price of the item?
7. Sue bought two new dresses, paying $100 for the pair. One of the dresses cost $12 more than the other. How much did each dress cost?
8. The total attendance for Sunday's services was 266. If there were 18 more people at the morning service than at the evening service, how many attended the evening service?
9. In a basketball game, the teams combined to score 96 points. The winners scored twice as much as the losers. What was the final score?
10. Find two consecutive integers whose sum is 175.
11. Find two consecutive odd integers whose sum is 178. (If x is the first odd integer, how do you represent the next odd integer?)
12. Find two consecutive even integers whose sum is 90.

▶ B. Exercises

Analyze each word problem. Write the equation you would use to solve the problem, but do not solve it.

13. The sum of the angles of a triangle is 180°. Angle A is 3 times as large as angle B, and angle C is 120° more than angle B. What is the measure of each angle?
14. The sum of three numbers is 40. The first number is 4 more than the product of 6 and the second number. The third number is 9 less than twice the second number. Find the three numbers.
15. Jim and Bill share a bookshelf in their room. Jim has 4 more than twice as many books as Bill. There are 22 books on the shelf. How many of the books belong to Jim and how many belong to Bill?
16. The number of girls in Mrs. Conn's math class is 2 less than 3 times the number of boys. She has 26 students in her class. How many boys are in the class?

17. Kenny is 7 years older than his sister. The sum of the ages is 31. Find the age of each child.
18. The sum of three consecutive integers is 84. Find the numbers.
19. Find three consecutive odd integers whose sum is 57.

▶ C. Exercises

Analyze each word problem. Write the equation you would use to solve the problem, but do not solve it.

20. The sum of two numbers is 85, and their difference is 29. Find the two numbers. Write two separate equations, either of which can be used to find the numbers.
21. The sum of the first and twice the third of three consecutive integers is equal to four times the second decreased by 5.

■ Cumulative Review

Each word problem requires a perimeter formula. Write the equation needed to solve the problem, but do not solve it.

22. How long is a rectangular park that is 80 yards wide if it takes 600 yards of fence to enclose it?
23. Joe used 108 inches of weather stripping around a square window. How wide is the window?
24. The General Sherman Tree has a trunk that is 103 feet around. What is its radius?
25. Mr. Collins is going to enclose his rectangular garden with 74 feet of fencing. The length is 7 feet longer than the width. What are the dimensions of his garden?
26. The long side of a rectangular pasture is along a river and does not require a fence. The long side is $\frac{1}{4}$ mile longer than the width. Find the dimensions of the pasture if one mile of fence is required.

The General Sherman Tree at Sequoia National Park in California contains more wood than any other tree in the world.

Algebra *and* Scripture

This chapter introduces variables and their uses.

1. In John 3:16 which word is a variable?
2. Write John 3:16 with your own name substituted for the variable.
3. Which of the groups below are part of the domain for the variable in John 3:16?

angels	God
men	demons
animals	women
plants	Jesus

The variable in John 3:16 enables us to write a general statement without having to list everyone separately. Likewise, mathematical variables enable us to write formulas without having to list all the values separately. For example, the area of a rectangle is $A = bh$.

4. Give another example of a formula.

Just as John 3:16 summarizes many statements about different people all at once, so the formula for the area of a rectangle summarizes many relationships. If the base and height are 6 and 8 inches respectively, then the area is 48 square inches. If the base and height are 2 and 10 inches respectively, then the area is 20 square inches. The list of such true statements summarized by the formula is endless.

5. According to Colossians 2:1-3, from what source do these truths come?

6. What does Philippians 4:8 say about things that are true?

7. Who is truth according to John 14:6?

Some truths apply to all numbers. Such truths are called properties. The commutative property is true for all real numbers and can be expressed with variables: $a + b = b + a$. Since this is true for an infinite number of values, it reflects in a small way that God is infinite. Since it is true in all times and all places, it also reflects two other attributes of God. He is both omnipresent and eternal. Omnipresent means that God is present everywhere at once.

Some people confuse infinite and eternal. Each describes something as limitless and without measure, but one refers to time and the other to space.

8. Which term refers to limitless time? which to limitless space?

9. Psalm 90:2 shows that God has one of these two qualities. Which one?

THE Nth DEGREE

Find a verse to show that God also has the other characteristic.

10. What else is eternal according to Psalm 119:89 and Psalm 117:2?

Scriptural Roots

FOR GOD SO LOVED THE WORLD, that he gave his only begotten Son, that whosoever believeth in him should not perish, but have everlasting life.

JOHN 3:16

Using the domain $\{-4, 2, 3, 8,\}$, evaluate each expression, giving all possible solutions.

   1. $x - 8$

   2. $y^2 + 4$

   3. $z + 4z - 2$

   4. $w^2 + w - 3$

What are the variables and the constants in the following expressions?

   5. $3x - 4$

   6. $\dfrac{5ab}{c}$

   7. $4a^2 + 3a - 7$

Write with positive exponents.

   8. 5^{-3}

   9. x^{-8}

  10. 1^{-4}

Write with negative exponents.

  11. $\dfrac{1}{3^2}$

  12. $\dfrac{1}{8^3}$

  13. $\dfrac{1}{x^4}$

Compute, leaving answers in positive exponential form.

  14. $3^{-2} \cdot 3^{-8}$

  15. $7^2 \div 7^8$

  16. $4^2 \div 4^{-3}$

Evaluate, if $x = 3$, $y = -4$, and $z = 2$.

  17. $4x^3 y$

  18. $2x + 3y - 6z$

  19. $x^2 + yz$

  20. $2x - 3y + z^3$

  21. $5x^2 + 2x + 7$

Combine like terms.

  22. $4x^2 + 3x - 8x^2$

  23. $2a - 4a + 3b$

  24. $x + 2y - 4x - 6x + y$

  25. $2a - 3b + 4a - 6b$

  26. $2x^2 + 3x - 8 + 4x^2 - 5x + 2$

Simplify.

27. $2a - (4a + 3b) - 6a$
28. $8 - [3x + (2y - 4) - (8y + 3)]$
29. $3x^2 + (2x + 7) - (5x + 6)$
30. $(a^2 + 2a + 5) + (3a^2 + 4a - 9)$
31. $x + 3y - [(4x + 2y) - (8x - 9y)]$

Express in algebraic form.

32. A number increased by 8
33. The total number of legs in a barnyard containing m cows, p pigs, and n chickens
34. The product of any number y and the sum of the number and 5
35. The sum of three times a number and the number squared
36. Five less than the quotient of a number and 27
37. The formula for finding the volume of a cube is $V = e^3$, where e is the length of one edge. If the edge of the cube is 4 inches, what is the volume of the cube?

Place in equation form. Do not solve the equations.

38. The sum of twice a number and 8 is 24.
39. In a football game the total score for one team was 20 points, which included 2 extra points after touchdowns. How many touchdowns did the team score if it made no field goals or safeties?
40. Brent is 3 years older than Jan. The sum of their ages is 59. Find each of their ages.
41. Explain the mathematical significance of John 3:16.

4 Solving Equations

$$y = mx + b$$

Three rocket engines provide the power to lift the space shuttle into orbit. During every minute of flight, each engine uses 64,000 gallons of liquid fuel that is 86% oxygen and 14% hydrogen. Together the three engines use 192,000 gallons of fuel each minute to create 1,410,000 pounds of thrust. Even so, two additional booster rockets are needed in the first few minutes to generate enough thrust to put the space shuttle into orbit.

A mixture of liquid oxygen and liquid hydrogen powers the three main engines used at blastoff. An external tank 154 feet long and 27 feet in diameter holds 520,000 gallons of these fuels with the oxygen in the upper third. When the mixed fuels are ignited, they combust to produce energy that makes the shuttle rise into orbit. After combustion the hydrogen and oxygen form water, creating the white billows of steam seen at liftoff. NASA engineers must mix the liquid fuels precisely using correct percentages so that the shuttle will blast off with the proper power. In this chapter you will learn methods for solving mixture problems. Would the shuttle get into orbit if you were responsible for the amounts of oxygen and hydrogen to mix? Word problems provide the basis for the problem-solving skills you will use throughout life.

After this chapter you should be able to

1. solve equations of the form $ax + b = c$.
2. solve equations of the form $ax + b = cx + d$.
3. solve absolute value equations.
4. solve equations containing fractions.
5. set up and solve coin and interest problems.
6. set up and solve mixture problems.
7. set up and solve motion problems.

4.1 Using Properties of Equality

$x + 10 = 142$ $x - 17 = -35$ $3x = 9$ $\frac{x}{5} = 21$

Can you find the number that should replace x to make each of the above examples true? Each number is called the solution of the equation. To *solve* these equations you have to undo an operation.

Cheetahs can cross 100 yards in 3 seconds flat. Solve $D = rt$ for r to determine the cheetah's speed.

Definition

An **inverse operation** is the operation that will reverse (undo) a given operation.

$$7 + 8 - 8 = 7 \quad 10 - 1 + 1 = 10 \quad 7 \cdot 5 \div 5 = 7 \quad 21 \div 3 \cdot 3 = 21$$
$$x + 4 - 4 = x \quad x - 4 + 4 = x \quad x \cdot 4 \div 4 = x \quad x \div 4 \cdot 4 = x$$

In the first column above, subtraction is used to reverse the process of addition. Subtraction is the inverse operation for addition. What inverse operations do you see in the other columns?

Review the properties of equality on page 116, which show that if you perform an operation on one side of an equation you *must perform that same operation on the other side of the equation* to keep the equation true. You know that $4 + 2 = 6$. If you subtract 2 from the left side only, then $4 + 2 - 2 = 6$, or $4 = 6$. Since $4 \neq 6$, the statement is now false; thus, it is not a balanced equation. To keep the equation balanced, you must subtract 2 from both sides.

$$4 + 2 - 2 = 6 - 2$$
$$4 = 4$$

To solve an equation like $x + 10 = 142$, first notice the variable x. What is being done to x? Ten is being added to it. The inverse of adding 10 is subtracting 10.

OH!

To solve an equation, find what is happening to the variable. Do the inverse operation on both sides.

EXAMPLE 1   Solve $x + 10 = 142$.

Answer

$x + 10 = 142$	1. Observe that 10 is added to x.
$x + 10 - 10 = 142 - 10$	2. Subtract 10 from both sides.
$x + 0 = 132$ $x = 132$	3. Simplify both sides.
Check. Does $132 + 10 = 142$?	4. Check your solution by substituting it for the variable. If the resulting equation is true, the solution is correct.

EXAMPLE 2   Solve $x - 17 = -35$.

Answer

$x - 17 = -35$	1. What is happening to the variable? Seventeen is being subtracted from it.
$x - 17 + 17 = -35 + 17$	2. What is the inverse of subtracting 17? Add 17 to both sides of the equation.
$x = -18$	3. Simplify.
Check. $-18 - 17 = -35$ $-35 = -35$	4. Check.

Since you can check mentally, show the check only when directed.

EXAMPLE 3   Solve $3x = 9$.

Answer

$3x = 9$	1. What is happening to the variable?
$\frac{3x}{3} = \frac{9}{3}$	2. Since the inverse of multiplication by 3 is division by 3, divide both sides by 3.
$x = 3$	3. Simplify. (What is $\frac{3}{3}$?)

EXAMPLE 4   Solve $\frac{x}{5} = 21$.

Answer

$\frac{x}{5} = 21$	1. What is happening to the variable?
$\frac{x}{5}(5) = 21(5)$	2. Multiply both sides of the equation by 5.
$x = 105$	3. Simplify.

Solving Equations

1. Determine the operation performed on the variable in the equation.
2. Perform the inverse operation on both sides of the equation.
3. Simplify both sides of the equation.
4. Check your answer.

Sometimes an equation will have other letters in it besides the variable. This type of equation is called a *literal equation.* You solve a literal equation exactly as you solve a numerical equation.

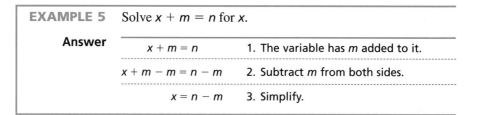

EXAMPLE 5 Solve $x + m = n$ for *x.*

Answer

$x + m = n$	1. The variable has m added to it.
$x + m - m = n - m$	2. Subtract m from both sides.
$x = n - m$	3. Simplify.

▶ A. Exercises

Solve each equation. Show all steps on your paper. Check your answers.

1. $x + 3 = 12$
2. $x - 4 = -23$
3. $a + 7 = -3$
4. $\frac{y}{5} = 24$
5. $2x = 16$
6. $b - 14 = 62$
7. $\frac{y}{2} = -28$
8. $\frac{c}{-9} = -8$
9. $4x = 164$
10. $x + \frac{1}{2} = \frac{3}{4}$
11. $m - 20 = 14$
12. $3z = 12$
13. $\frac{z}{4} = -7$
14. $8x = -56$

15. $y + 12 = 2$
16. $\frac{n}{-21} = -46$
17. $18 = y + 27$
18. $b + 14 = 36$
19. $\frac{m}{2} = -146$
20. $15n = 1020$
21. $3 + x = 9$
22. $32x = 160$
23. $\frac{b}{2} = 14$
24. $9n = 9$
25. $\frac{x}{4} = 1$
26. $\frac{y}{10} = 20$
27. $a - 127 = -2$
28. $y + 17 = -24$

▶ B. Exercises

Solve each equation for x.

29. $rx = d$

30. $x + a = c$

31. $x + 0.93 = 1.42$

32. $x - 3.89 = 0.49$

33. $2x = \frac{1}{2}$

34. $82 = x - 24$

35. $40 = 5x$

36. $\frac{x}{13} = 1.24$

37. $102 = 3x$

38. $x + 0.7 = 21.2$

39. $0.8x = 0.24$

40. $\frac{1}{2} + x = 2\frac{1}{4}$

41. $0.3x = 0.96$

42. $\frac{x}{12} = 4.69$

▶ C. Exercises

Solve each literal equation for x.

43. $b - x = d$

44. $a = bx$

45. $\frac{x}{n} = q$

■ Cumulative Review

Give a property to justify each step in solving this equation.

$(7 + x) + 9 = 53$

46. $(x + 7) + 9 = 53$

47. $x + (7 + 9) = 53$

48. $x + 16 - 16 = 53 - 16$

49. $x + 0 = 37$

50. $x = 37$

Use clues to find the digits to solve each addition problem. No two letters represent the same number

1.	Four + One Five	2.	Soft + Ball Game	3.	Four − Two Ten
Clues		**Clues**		**Clues**	
$V = 2E$	$R =$	$B = 2T$	$O =$	$W = 3$	$F =$
$E = F - U$	$N =$	$F = A^2$	$S =$	$N = R + E$	$E =$
$U = 5$	$O =$	$E = 8$	$A =$	$O = 8$	$W =$
$F = 2^3$	$E =$	$L = 5$	$T =$		$R =$
	$I =$		$F =$		$U =$
	$U =$		$L =$		$N =$
	$V =$		$B =$		$O =$
	$F =$		$G =$		$T =$
			$E =$		
			$M =$		

4 Probability and Statistics

Multiplication Principle of Counting

In Chapter 3, you learned that to find the probability of an occurrence you must count the number of outcomes. This means that shortcuts in counting are important for finding probabilities. The most important tool is the multiplication principle of counting, or the Fundamental Principle of Counting.

> ### Multiplication Principle of Counting
>
> If A can occur a ways and B can occur b ways, then A and B can occur in $a \cdot b$ ways.

EXAMPLE 1   A group will select a chaplain and a secretary. The nominations include **4** boys for chaplain and **7** girls for secretary. How many possible ways are there to fill out a ballot?

Answer   Since they must select one of **4** possible chaplains and one of **7** secretaries, there are **4** · **7** = **28** possible ballots.

EXAMPLE 2   How many two-letter abbreviations are possible?

Answer   Choose one of **26** letters for the first position *and then* (multiplication) one of **26** letters for the second position.

26 · **26** = **676** abbreviations

How many lists of four different states could begin with Texas?

EXAMPLE 3   A teacher wants to assign reports on different states. She has students write down their top **4** choices in order and hopes to assign each student one of his choices. How many possible lists are there?

Answer   Choose one of **50** possible first choices and one of **49** remaining second choices and one of **48** remaining third choices and one of **47** remaining fourth choices.

50 · **49** · **48** · **47** = **5,527,200** possible lists

Examples 2 and 3 should convince you that using the multiplication principle of counting is much faster than listing all the possibilities and counting them one by one. In example 2, letters can be repeated or used more than once, so the choices for consecutive letters are the same (26 · 26). However, in example 3, no state can be listed twice; thus the number of choices for consecutive states is lowered by 1 each time (50 · 49 · 48 · 47). Always consider whether repeats are allowed and calculate accordingly.

Finally, read the question carefully to see whether the answer should be the total number of occurrences or the probability that something will occur.

EXAMPLE 4   Suppose each letter of the alphabet is written on a slip of paper and placed in a container. One is drawn out and read. This is an example of a process called random selection. The slip is then replaced and a second drawing made. What is the probability of randomly selecting a two-letter abbreviation in which both letters are vowels out of all possible two-letter abbreviations?

Answer   In example 2 you found that the number of possible outcomes is 676. Since there are five vowels, there are 5 · 5 = 25 abbreviations formed from two vowels. Thus, the probability is

$$P = \frac{\text{successful outcomes}}{\text{possible outcomes}} = \frac{25}{676} \approx 0.04$$

▶ Exercises

1. How many ways can a travel writer select a U.S. state and a continent for feature stories?
2. How many possible 5-digit zip codes are there?
3. What is the probability of randomly selecting a zip code for which all five digits are positive even numbers?
4. How many ways can a basketball coach fill 5 positions from his 12-member team?
5. How many three-digit area codes are possible if the middle digit must be 0 or 1 and the first digit cannot be 0 or 1?

4.2 How to Attack Word Problems

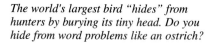

When a problem arises in your life, how do you solve it? Do you hide your head in the sand and hope the problem will go away? Do you consider it unimportant? Do you worry and fret? Or do you plan a solution to the problem and attempt to put it into action?

The world's largest bird "hides" from hunters by burying its tiny head. Do you hide from word problems like an ostrich?

A Christian must always be prepared, especially against the craftiness of the Devil. Ephesians 6:10-18 tells the Christian how to prepare himself to overcome the problems he will encounter. He must put on armor before he goes into battle. He cannot defeat the enemy unless he is prepared.

In mathematics you must also be prepared and have a plan of attack. Follow the procedures below, practice on many different problems, and finish the job. If you quit partway through, you will never get the answer. The key to success is hard work and perseverance.

Solving Word Problems

1. **Read** the problem several times, looking for operational words.
   a. *Draw a picture* (if possible) to be sure you understand the problem.
   b. Assign a variable to the main unknown and express any others in terms of it.
2. **Plan** a method of attack.
   a. *Make a table* (if possible) to organize relevant information.
   b. Translate word phrases into expressions using the variable. Express each unknown and any other key quantities in terms of the variable.
3. **Solve** an equation.
   a. *Write an equation.* Find the mathematical verb to translate the sentence into an equation. Use any pictures or tables to help you identify two quantities that are equal.
   b. *Solve your equation* using the methods and properties that you have learned.

Continued ▶

4. **Check** your solution. Ask yourself these three questions.

   a. *What do the numbers represent?* Interpret your answers in the context of the problem. Include units.

   b. *Have I answered all of the questions in the problem?*

   c. *Are the answers reasonable?* A negative distance is impossible and a car speed of 100 mph is unlikely (and illegal). Impossible and improbable answers are clues that you made a mistake. Check your work.

EXAMPLE 1   The sum of five times a number and two times the number is 161. Find the number.

Answer
1. **Read** the problem carefully, noting the operational words *sum, times,* and *is.* You cannot draw a picture for this problem. The unknown quantity is a number, so let the variable *x* represent the number.

2. **Plan** a strategy. You cannot make a table, but you can translate each phrase.
   $5x$ = five times a number $2x$ = two times the number

3. **Solve.** The verb *is* identifies the equal expressions. Since the sum $5x + 2x$ is 161, write the equation.

$5x + 2x = 161$	
$7x = 161$	Combine like terms.
$\frac{7x}{7} = \frac{161}{7}$	Divide both sides by 7.
$x = 23$	

4. **Check.** Interpret the solution: The number is 23. Have you answered all the questions? Yes, there is only one question. Is it reasonable? Yes, and it checks.
   $$5 \cdot 23 + 2 \cdot 23 = 161$$
   $$115 + 46 = 161$$
   $$161 = 161$$

ALWAYS
Check your answer in the original equation!!!

And they said this wasn't a good idea!

EXAMPLE 2 In 14 years Joe will be 42. How old is Joe now?

Answer

1. **Read** carefully. What operation does "in 14 years" indicate? No picture is needed. What is the unknown quantity? Let n = Joe's age now.

2. **Plan.** No table is needed. How do you express "in 14 years"? Since Joe will be 14 years older, his age in 14 years is $n + 14$.

3. **Solve.** Identify the verb *will be* and translate it as (*will*) *equal* (=). Subtract 14 from both sides to solve.
$$n + 14 = 42$$
$$n + 14 - 14 = 42 - 14$$
$$n = 28$$

4. **Check.** Interpret: Joe's age is 28. There is only one question and the answer is reasonable since $28 + 14 = 42$.

▶ A. Exercises

Solve, using the procedures for solving word problems. Show all your work.

1. A number added to 27 gives -14. Find the number.
2. On vacation the Hill family traveled an average of 300 miles each day. How many days did they travel if they went a total of 1800 miles?
3. The difference of a number and 72 is 12. Find the number.
4. A number multiplied by 12 is 60. Find the number.
5. When Laura is six times as old as she is now, she will be 84. How old is she now?
6. In triangle *ABC*, side *AB* is 9" and side *BC* is 5". How large is *AC* if the perimeter is 21"?
7. Donna canned 24 quarts of beans, which was four times as many as Ann canned. How many quarts did Ann can?
8. Kent has three times as many stamps in his collection as Joan has in hers. If Kent has 243 stamps, how many stamps does Joan have?
9. A train going 80 miles per hour moves ten times as fast as I move on my bicycle. How fast can I ride my bicycle?
10. The elephant at the circus weighs 5075 pounds, which is twenty-five times Mr. Lee's weight. How much does Mr. Lee weigh?

11. I can buy a candy bar for **65¢**, which is **13** times the amount I pay for a piece of hard candy. What is the price of a piece of hard candy?

12. A paper boy delivers thirteen papers to an apartment complex. If these deliveries compose one seventh of his route, how many papers does he deliver?

▶ B. Exercises

13. One number is four times another, and the sum of the two numbers is **155**. What are the two numbers?

14. If you subtract eight times a number from four times a number, you get -52. What is the number?

15. The difference of a number and -9 is -74. Find the number.

16. How many feet of fencing should be added to the **24** yards that the school owns to enclose a field that has a perimeter of **89** feet?

17. Jeanie paid **$0.48** in sales tax for a doll for her sister. If the tax rate is six percent, what was the price of the doll?

18. Write a word problem for the equation $\frac{x}{2} = 87$.

▶ C. Exercises

19. Write a word problem for the equation $0.05x = \$2.30$ and then solve it.

20. Miss Miller teaches three times as many students first hour as she does third hour. Her second-hour class has twice as many as her third-hour class. If she has a total of **72** people in her three morning classes, how many does she have in each class?

21. A triangular lot has a perimeter of **590** feet. The road frontage is twice as long as one side, and **50** feet shorter than the third side. Find the dimensions.

▪ Cumulative Review

22. What kind of number is $2.\overline{3}$?

23. Graph -3.

24. Simplify $2x - 3(5x + 4) + 8$.

25. Evaluate $2x + yz + 1$ if $x = -3$, $y = \frac{7}{2}$, and $z = 4$.

26. Translate: Four more than a number is ten less than three times the number. Do not solve.

4.3 Equations of the Form $ax + b = c$

$$2x + 6 = 21 \qquad 4y - 36 = 16$$

These two examples are in the form $ax + b = c$, in which the letters a, b, and c represent real numbers and x is an unknown variable. There is nothing new about this type of equation; it is just a combination of two operations on a variable instead of one.

Solving Equations of the Form $ax + b = c$

1. Combine any like terms on each side of the equation separately.
2. Determine the operation or operations performed on the variable in the equation.
3. Perform the inverse operations in reverse order on both sides of the equation.
4. Simplify both sides after each operation is performed.
5. Continue until the variable is alone on one side and its numerical coefficient is 1.
6. Check your answer.

EXAMPLE 1 Solve $2x + 6 = 21$.

Answer

$2x + 6 = 21$	1. There are no like terms to combine.
	2. The variable is multiplied by 2 and then 6 is added to the product.
$2x + 6 - 6 = 21 - 6$	3. Since x is multiplied by 2 and then 6 is added to the product, division and subtraction are the inverse operations. Using reverse order, subtract 6 from both sides first.
$2x = 15$	4. Simplify.
$x = \frac{15}{2}$	5. Continue by dividing both sides by 2.

Check.
$$2 \cdot \frac{15}{2} + 6 = 21$$
$$15 + 6 = 21$$
$$21 = 21$$

6. Check.

EXAMPLE 2 Solve $4y - 36 = 16$.

Answer

$4y - 36 = 16$	1. There are no like terms to combine.
	2. y is multiplied by 4 and 36 is subtracted from the product.
$4y - 36 + 36 = 16 + 36$	3. Perform the inverse operations (division and addition) in reverse order.
$4y = 52$	4. Simplify.
$\frac{4y}{4} = \frac{52}{4}$ $y = 13$	5. Continue with the second inverse operation.
Check. $4 \cdot 13 - 36 = 16$	6. Check mentally.

EXAMPLE 3 Solve $-2x + 5x + 9 = 87$.

Answer

$-2x + 5x + 9 = 87$	
$3x + 9 = 87$	1. Combine like terms.
	2. x is multiplied by 3 and 9 is added to the product.
$3x + 9 - 9 = 87 - 9$	3. Perform the inverse operations in reverse order.
$3x = 78$	4. Simplify.
$\frac{3x}{3} = \frac{78}{3}$	5. Continue with the other inverse operation.
$x = 26$	6. Check (not shown).

▶ A. Exercises

Solve for the variable.

1. $3x - 10 = 14$

2. $5x + 24 = -36$

3. $17 = 3x + 2$

4. $12 = 2x - 28$

5. $4x - 8x + 9 = 41$

6. $9x + 17 = 71$

7. $\frac{x}{5} - 13 = -84$

8. $4 + \frac{x}{6} = 9$

9. $12b - 18 = 474$

10. $3x + 4 - 5x + 9 = 15$

11. $2x + 24 = 52$

12. $\frac{n}{7} + 12 = -27$

13. $162 = 24m - 86$

14. $\frac{p}{4} - 7 = 10$

15. $\frac{2n}{5} = 14$

▶ B. Exercises

Solve each word problem. Show all work.

16. If **47** is added to three times a certain number, the result is **68**. What is the number?

17. Sue's salary is **$240** a week plus a commission of **$13** for every piece of furniture she sells. How many pieces must she sell to make **$500** per week?

18. One number is **4** more than another, and their sum is **120**. Find the two numbers.

19. If Bill's salary is **$25** and he gets a **20¢** commission on every newspaper he sells, how many must he sell to make **$47**?

20. How many quarters must be added to **$1.89** to make a total of **$2.64**?

21. What number increased by $1\frac{1}{2}$ is $5\frac{1}{4}$?

▶ C. Exercises

22. Five reduced by twice a certain number is two. Find the number.

23. The sum of twice a number and seven less than four times the number is fifteen. Find the number.

24. Eight more than five times a number is twenty thirds. Find the number.

■ Cumulative Review

Simplify.

25. $51 - 0$

26. $0 - 51$

27. $\frac{0}{51}$

28. $\frac{51}{0}$

29. $\frac{51}{51}$

30. $\frac{0}{0}$

4.4 More Work with Equations

The foundation on which a structure is built is the most important part of the construction. If the foundation is weak, the house will be weak. Read Matthew 7:24-27. Who is the Rock that must be the Christian's foundation?

*The largest monolith in the world, Ayers Rock in Australia, is **4** miles long by **1.5** miles wide.*

Equations are the foundation upon which algebra is built. To be successful in algebra and higher math, you need a good foundation in solving equations.

HEY BUDDY! DOESN'T THE EXPRESSION, $d = \frac{1}{2}(9.8m/sec^2)(t)^2$ MEAN ANYTHING TO YOU?!?

YOU MEAN THE LAW OF FALLING BODIES? SO WHAT?!?

ALGEBRA

WRONG WAY!!

EXAMPLE 1 Solve $3x + 2 + 5x - 7 = 28$.

Answer

$$3x + 2 + 5x - 7 = 28$$

$$8x - 5 = 28 \qquad \text{1. Combine like terms.}$$

2. Solve.

$$8x - 5 + 5 = 28 + 5 \qquad \leftarrow$$

$$8x = 33$$

$$\frac{8x}{8} = \frac{33}{8} \qquad \leftarrow$$

$$x = \frac{33}{8}$$

Check. $\quad 3 \cdot \frac{33}{8} + 2 + 5 \cdot \frac{33}{8} - 7 = 28 \qquad$ 3. Check.

$$\frac{99}{8} + \frac{16}{8} + \frac{165}{8} - \frac{56}{8} = 28$$

$$\frac{224}{8} = 28$$

$$28 = 28$$

The steps designated by an arrow in example 1 may be done mentally from now on as shown in example 2. Remember that you can check mentally also. If parentheses appear in the equation, remove them by applying the distributive property before solving the equation.

EXAMPLE 2 Solve $4(x + 5) - 3x = 24$.

Answer

$4(x + 5) - 3x = 24$	
$4x + 20 - 3x = 24$	1. Remove parentheses by applying the distributive property.
$x + 20 = 24$	2. Combine like terms.
$x = 4$	3. Solve.
	4. Check mentally.

EXAMPLE 3 John's mother is four times as old as John, and John's brother is twice as old as John. If you find the sum of their ages and add 3, you get 80. What is the age of all three people?

Answer

Let x = John's age	1. **Read** the problem carefully to find the main unknown. All ages are described based on John's age.
$4x$ = John's mother's age $2x$ = John's brother's age	2. **Plan.** Define the other ages using x.
$4x + 2x + x + 3 = 80$ $7x + 3 = 80$ $7x = 77$ $x = 11$	3. **Solve.** Write an equation and find its solution.
$4x = 44$ $2x = 22$	4. **Check.** Find the other ages, interpret them, and notice that they are reasonable since $11 + 44 + 22 + 3 = 80$

John is 11 years old, his mother is 44 years old, and his brother is 22 years old.

You may be surprised that it is necessary to solve equations to convert repeating decimals to fractions.

EXAMPLE 4   Convert $2.\overline{3}$ to fraction form.

Answer

Let $x = 2.\overline{3}$

$10x = 23.\overline{3}$ 1. Multiply both sides of the equation by 10 to move one repeated pattern to the left of the decimal.

$\begin{array}{r} 10x = 23.\overline{3} \\ x = 2.\overline{3} \\ \hline 9x = 21 \end{array}$ 2. Subtract equal amounts from each side of the second equation (x from the left and $2.\overline{3}$ from the right) to eliminate the repeating decimal.

$x = \frac{21}{9} = \frac{7}{3}$ 3. Solve for x.

On your calculator find the value of $\frac{7}{3}$ by dividing 7 by 3. The result **2.33333** verifies the result that $2.\overline{3} = \frac{7}{3}$. Therefore, $2.\overline{3}$ is a rational number because it can be written as a fraction.

EXAMPLE 5   Convert **7.292929 . . .** to fraction form.

Answer

Let $x = 7.\overline{29}$

$100x = 729.\overline{29}$ 1. Multiply both sides of the equation by 100 to move one repeated pattern to the left of the decimal.

$\begin{array}{r} 100x = 729.\overline{29} \\ x = 7.\overline{29} \\ \hline 99x = 722 \end{array}$ 2. Subtract to eliminate the repeating decimal.

$x = \frac{722}{99}$ 3. Solve for x.

Therefore, $7.\overline{29} = \frac{722}{99}$ 4. 722 over 99 cannot be reduced.

▶ A. Exercises

Solve for x.

1. $4x + 8x = 12$
2. $3x + (2 + 4x) = 23$
3. $2(9x + 3) - 4x = 34$
4. $5x - (3 + 2x) = 9$
5. $(x + 3) + 2(x + 5) = 34$
6. $5x + 9x - 4 - 6x = 12$
7. $3x - 4(x + 5) = -17$
8. $4(x - 7) = 8$
9. $-8x - 4x = 24$

10. $3(x + 2) = 66$
11. $2x - 4(x - 3) = 26$
12. $6 - 2(x + 4) = 108$
13. $-7(x + 3) = 77$
14. $3x + 9x + (12 - 2x) = 2$
15. $-2(x - 1) + 3(x + 4) = 8$
16. $3.2x + 4(x + 0.7) = 38.8$
17. $4x + 9x = 26$

▶ B. Exercises

Solve each literal equation for *x*.

18. $3x - (x + n) = m$
19. $ax + b + a(x + b) = b$
20. $a(x + c) + b(x + d) - ax = e$

Set up an equation and solve.

21. The freshman class has **11** more girls than boys. There are **63** students in the freshman class. How many of each are in the class?
22. One number is **23** more than another number. The sum of the two numbers is **83**. Find the two numbers.
23. A calculator costs **$12** less than a camera. Both together cost **$87**. What is the cost of each?
24. The difference of two numbers is **12**, and the sum of the two numbers is **40**. What are the two numbers?
25. Stan wants to make a rectangular garden. He has **34** feet of fencing to put around the perimeter. He wants the length to be **5** feet more than the width. How wide and how long should he make the garden?

Convert to decimal form.

26. $\frac{2531}{1000}$

27. $\frac{371}{99}$

Show that each decimal below represents a rational number by finding its reduced fraction form.

28. 0.0704

29. 90.7

▶ C. Exercises

Find the reduced fraction form.

30. $0.151515\ldots$

31. $2.4\overline{395}$

32. $0.6\overline{381}$

$A = \{-13, -5, 1, 9, 17\}$ $B = \{10, 20, 30, \ldots\}$ $C = \{20, 15, 10, 5, 0, -5 \ldots\}$

33. $A \cap B$
34. $B \cap C$
35. $A \cup \{1, 4, 9\}$
36. $B \cup C$
37. $C \cap \mathbb{N}$

4.5 Equations of the Form $ax + b = cx + d$

$$2x + 5 = x - 2 \qquad 3(x - 4) = 4(x - 6) \qquad 5x + 3x - 4 = x - 2$$

Why are these equations different from the ones in the last two sections?
The only difference is that these equations have variables on both sides of the
equal sign.

Move all the variables to one side of the equation and all other terms to the
other side.

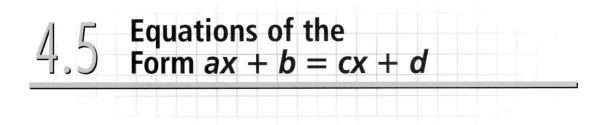

| EXAMPLE 1 | Solve $2x + 5 = x - 2$. |

Answer   To place all the variables on the left, you must eliminate
the x on the right. Remember the coefficient of the x term
is $+1$. To eliminate x from the right side, subtract x from
both sides of the equation.

$2x + 5 = x - 2$	
$2x + 5 - x = x - 2 - x$ $x + 5 = -2$	1. Subtract x from both sides. Notice that all the variables are now on the left.
$x = -7$	2. Subtract 5 from both sides.
Check. $2(-7) + 5 = -7 - 2$	3. Check mentally.

If there are any parentheses in the equation, remove them first.

EXAMPLE 2 Solve $3(x - 4) = 4(x - 6)$.

Answer

$3(x - 4) = 4(x - 6)$

$3x - 12 = 4x - 24$	1. Remove parentheses by applying the distributive property.
$3x - 12 - 3x = 4x - 24 - 3x$	2. To move the variables to the right, subtract $3x$ from both sides.
$-12 = x - 24$	3. Solve.
$12 = x$	

Will you get the same answer by moving the variables to the left?

$3(x - 4) = 4(x - 6)$

$3x - 12 = 4x - 24$	1. Remove parentheses.
$3x - 12 - 4x = 4x - 24 - 4x$	2. Subtract $4x$ from both sides.
$-x - 12 = -24$	3. Solve.
$-x = -12$	
$\dfrac{-x}{-1} = \dfrac{-12}{-1}$	
$x = 12$	

Yes, you will get the same answer regardless of the side you put the variable on.

Solving Equations of the Form $ax + b = cx + d$

1. Remove any parentheses in the equation and combine like terms.
2. Use inverse operations to move the variables to the desired side of the equation.
3. Solve the equation according to procedures on page 140.

EXAMPLE 3   Solve $5x + 3x - 4 = x + 2$.

Answer

$5x + 3x - 4 = x + 2$	
$8x - 4 = x + 2$	1. Combine like terms.
$8x - 4 - x = x + 2 - x$	2. Move variables to the left.
$7x - 4 = 2$	3. Solve.
$7x = 6$	
$x = \frac{6}{7}$	

Getting the correct answer should give you a sense of satisfaction. However, complete satisfaction comes only through Jesus Christ. He supplies your needs, hears your prayers, and even helps you with your math. You should do your math unto the Lord (Col. 3:17; I Cor. 10:31).

▶ A. Exercises

Solve. Show all work.

1. $3x + 5 = 8x - 5$
2. $7x - 20 = 2x + 25$
3. $3(x + 1) = 8x - 12$
4. $7(x - 9) = 3(x - 2) - 1$
5. $3x = 5x - 2$
6. $11x - 8 = 12x + 9$
7. $4(x - 9) = 3x - 8x$
8. $6x - 1 = x + 4$

9. $82b - 3b + 7 = 71b + 19$
10. $5(x - 4) + 4x = 3x - 14$
11. $7n - 13 = 4n - 9$
12. $y + 9 = 2y - 4$
13. $3x - 7 = 2x$
14. $8a = 4(a - 9)$
15. $4 - 9a + 10 = 3a - 10$

▶ B. Exercises

Solve each equation.

16. $4(m - 6) - m(3 + 4) = 8m - 2$
17. $8(2t + 1) - (t - 9) = -52 - 8t$
18. $3x = 9x$
19. $0.25z - 3.09 = 0.75z + 8$
20. $5(y + 2) - 4y = 8y - (2 + y)$

Solve each literal equation for x.

21. $mx + n = 2mx - n$
22. $a(x + c) = 2ax + d$
23. $Pn = qx - r$

24. $amx = 3a$

25. $\frac{x}{r} = r$

26. Eight times a number equals the number increased by **504**. Find the number.

27. Find two consecutive integers such that twice the smaller is **10** more than eight times the larger.

28. If **3** subtracted from twice a number is equal to **31** more than three times the number, what is the number?

▶ C. Exercises

29. The length of a rectangle is three times the width. The perimeter of the rectangle is equal to the perimeter of a triangle that has one side equal to the length of the rectangle. The sum of the other two sides of the triangle equals **85**. What is the length and width of the rectangle?

30. Find two consecutive even integers such that four times the smaller is equal to four more than three times the larger.

Cumulative Review

31. Factor **4096** into a product of primes.

32. Simplify $\sqrt[12]{4096}$.

33. What is the GCF of **4096** and **64,512**?

34. Reduce $\frac{4096}{64,512}$.

35. Add $\frac{1}{4096} + \frac{1}{64,512}$.

4.6 **Absolute Value Equations**

Do you remember the definition of *absolute value*? Look back to page 7 if you need to refresh your memory.

$$| \, 6 \, | = 6 \qquad | \, {-6} \, | = 6$$

If x is a positive number, such as **6**, then $|x| = x$.

If x is a negative number, such as -6, then $|x| = -x$
(opposite of x) $= -(-6) = 6$.

$$|x| = \begin{cases} -x \text{ if } x < 0 \\ x \text{ if } x \geq 0 \end{cases}$$

Let's look at the equation $|x| = 4$. Consider the possible cases involving x to apply the definition of absolute value.

If $x \geq 0$, then $|x| = x = 4$ If $x < 0$, then $|x| = -x = -(-4) = 4$

We see that the two solutions to the equation are $x = \pm 4$. The symbol $\pm$ indicates two solutions, in this case $+4$ and -4.

What are the two solutions to $|x| = 3$? Notice that the solution is always both the positive and the negative values of the number that the absolute value equals.

$$|x| = 3$$
So $x = 3$ or $x = -3$

To graph these solutions on a number line, place a dot on both answers. Notice that **3** and -3 are both **3** units from the origin (zero).

EXAMPLE 1   Solve $|2x + 5| = 11$.

Answer   Remember that absolute value measures the distance from zero on a number line. Since $2x + 5$ is eleven units from zero, $2x + 5$ must be 11 or -11. Solve for x in both equations.

$2x + 5 = 11$	or	$2x + 5 = -11$
$2x = 6$		$2x = -16$
$x = 3$		$x = -8$

Check. $|2 \cdot 3 + 5| = 11$ $|2(-8) + 5| = 11$

            $|6 + 5| = 11$ $|-16 + 5| = 11$

                 $11 = 11$ $11 = 11$

The two solutions are $x = 3$ and $x = -8$.

Solving Absolute Value Equations

1. Simplify as much as possible within the absolute value signs.
2. Isolate the absolute value on one side of the equation and all other quantities on the other side of the equation.
3. Write two equations by applying the definition of absolute value.
4. Solve each equation separately.
5. Check your solutions.

EXAMPLE 2   Solve $5 + |\, 2y + 4 - 5y \,| = 21$.

Answer

$5 + |\, 2y + 4 - 5y \,| = 21$	
$5 + |\, -3y + 4 \,| = 21$	1. Simplify inside the absolute value.
$|\, -3y + 4 \,| = 16$	2. Subtract 5 to isolate the absolute value.
$-3y + 4 = 16$ or $-3y + 4 = -16$	3. Use the definition of absolute value to write two equations.
$-3y = 12$ $-3y = -20$ $y = -4$ $y = \frac{20}{3}$	4. Solve both equations.

Check.   5. Check both answers mentally (or in writing if necessary).

$5 + |\, 2(-4) + 4 - 5(-4) \,| = 21$ $5 + \left|\, 2\left(\frac{20}{3}\right) + 4 - 5\left(\frac{20}{3}\right) \,\right| = 21$

$5 + |\, -8 + 4 + 20 \,| = 21$ $5 + \left|\, \frac{40}{3} + 4 - \frac{100}{3} \,\right| = 21$

$5 + |\, 16 \,| = 21$ $5 + |\, -16 \,| = 21$

$21 = 21$ $21 = 21$

▶ A. Exercises

Graph.

1. ± 5 2. $x = 3$ or $x = 12$

Solve and graph.

3. $|\, x + 5 \,| = 7$
4. $|\, 7x \,| = 4$
5. $|\, x + 1 \,| + 2 = 8$

Give the solutions to each equation.

6. $|x| = 16$
7. $|y| = 129$
8. $|x + 2| = 37$
9. $|x - 8| = 14$
10. $|3z + 4 - z| = 16$
11. $|2y - 5| - 9 = 24$

▶ B. Exercises

Solve the following equations.

12. $|2x - 3| = 2$

13. $|5y + 12| = 24$

14. $|7x + 9| = 51$

15. $19 = |12x - 5|$

16. $|7x - 4| = 9$

17. $|3z - 10 + 4z| = 18$

▶ C. Exercises

Solve the following equations.

18. $26 = |3y + 4 - 6y|$

19. $|2x + 4 - 5x| + 3 = 17$

20. $172 = |12x - 5| + 82$

■ Cumulative Review

Calculate.

21. $|-3 \cdot 4|$
22. $|-3||4|$
23. $|-5(-6)|$
24. $|-5||-6|$
25. Can you state a principle of absolute values based on exercises 21-24? Use variables to express the multiplication property of absolute values.

4.7 Clearing Equations of Fractions

The coach has developed a drill that requires a rectangular field with the width being $\frac{1}{3}$ of the length. The perimeter of the field is **280** feet. What length and width should the field liner mark off?

To solve this problem and others like it, you must be able to work with equations containing fractions.

Tom paints a foul line on a baseball field with an athletic field maintenance machine.

$$\text{Let } x = \text{ the length of the field}$$
$$\tfrac{1}{3}x = \text{ the width of the field}$$
$$x + x + \tfrac{1}{3}x + \tfrac{1}{3}x = 280$$

First you need to clear the equation of fractions by multiplying both sides of the equation by the LCM of the denominators of the fractions, which in this equation is **3**.

$$3\left(x + x + \tfrac{1}{3}x + \tfrac{1}{3}x\right) = 280 \cdot 3$$
$$3x + 3x + x + x = 840$$
$$8x = 840$$
$$x = 105$$
$$\tfrac{1}{3}x = 35$$

The length of the field is **105** feet, and the width is **35** feet.

EXAMPLE 1 Solve $\frac{2x + 5}{3} = 7$.

Answer

$$\frac{2x + 5}{3} = 7$$

$$3\left(\frac{2x + 5}{3}\right) = 3(7) \qquad \text{1. Multiply both sides of the equation by the denominator 3.}$$

$$2x + 5 = 21 \qquad \text{2. Solve.}$$
$$2x = 16$$

$$x = 8 \qquad \text{3. Check mentally.}$$

EXAMPLE 2   Solve $\frac{x}{4} + x - \frac{1}{3} = 3$.

Answer   To solve for x in this equation, first find the common denominator (LCM), which for 4 and 3 is 12. Multiply both sides of the equation by 12, using the distributive property to remove parentheses.

$$\frac{x}{4} + x - \frac{1}{3} = 3$$
$$12\left(\frac{x}{4} + x - \frac{1}{3}\right) = 12(3)$$
$$3x + 12x - 4 = 36$$
$$15x - 4 = 36$$
$$15x = 40$$
$$x = \frac{40}{15}$$
$$x = \frac{8}{3}$$

EXAMPLE 3   Solve $\frac{x + 2}{6} - \frac{x - 1}{3} = \frac{1}{9}$.

Answer   The LCM of 6, 3, and 9 is 18.

$$\frac{x + 2}{6} - \frac{x - 1}{3} = \frac{1}{9}$$
$$18\left(\frac{x + 2}{6} - \frac{x - 1}{3}\right) = 18\left(\frac{1}{9}\right)$$
$$18\left(\frac{x + 2}{6}\right) - 18\left(\frac{x - 1}{3}\right) = 18\left(\frac{1}{9}\right)$$
$$3(x + 2) - 6(x - 1) = 2$$
$$3x + 6 - 6x + 6 = 2$$
$$-3x + 12 = 2$$
$$-3x = -10$$
$$x = \frac{10}{3}$$

REMEMBER THAT THE COMMON DENOMINATOR **IS THE LEAST COMMON MULTIPLE OF THE** DENOMINATORS

MORE $$$$

Now THAT'S a sign!

Solving Equations Containing Fractions

1. Find the LCM of the denominators.
2. Eliminate fractions by multiplying both sides by the LCM.
3. Solve the resulting equation.
4. Check the solution in the original equation.

▶ A. Exercises

Solve.

1. $\frac{x}{4} = \frac{1}{2}$

2. $\frac{x}{3} + \frac{x}{8} = \frac{11}{24}$

3. $\frac{2x}{9} + \frac{1}{3} = 5$

4. $\frac{x}{6} - \frac{3x}{2} = \frac{16}{3}$

5. $\frac{y}{2} - \frac{2y}{7} = \frac{25}{7}$

6. $a + \frac{3a}{2} = \frac{15}{2}$

7. $\frac{b}{3} - \frac{8b}{7} = \frac{68}{21}$

8. $9m - \frac{3m}{8} = \frac{345}{8}$

9. $\frac{x}{3} - \frac{x}{4} = 1$

10. $y = \frac{3y}{5} + 12$

11. $\frac{x + 2}{9} - \frac{x}{3} = 10$

12. $0.5x = 0.3x + 9$

13. $1.4y + 0.09y = 1.49$

14. $0.67a + 3.06 = 0.84a$

15. $2b - 8 = 0.4b$

▶ B. Exercises

Solve each equation.

16. $\frac{4y - 4}{8} + \frac{26}{2} = \frac{1}{4}$

17. $\frac{a - 3}{2} - \frac{a + 3}{4} + \frac{a}{8} = 6$

18. $3k + \frac{k - 4}{9} = \frac{1}{3}$

19. $\frac{107}{6} = \frac{7m}{2} - \frac{3m - 1}{3}$

20. $0.8(x + 4) - 0.3x = 1.7$

Solve each literal equation for P.

21. $\frac{P}{6rn} = \frac{7}{9nx}$

22. $f + \frac{P}{3} = \frac{P}{8}$

23. $\frac{2P}{m} - \frac{r}{s} = \frac{Ps + q}{ms}$

24. What properties do you use to clear fractions?

25. What is the difference between an equation and an expression?

▶ C. Exercises

26. Solve for x. $ax - \frac{2b}{c} = 3$

27. Solve for x. $pq + \frac{2x}{d} = 4b$

■ Cumulative Review

28. Simplify $3(x + 5) + 2(3x - 1)$.

29. Solve $3(x + 5) + 2(3x - 1) = 4$.

30. Evaluate $3(x + 5) + 2(3x - 1)$ if $x = 7$.

31. Simplify $3(x + 8) + (5 + 4x - 9)$.

32. Solve $3(x + 8) = 5 + 4x - 9$.

4.8 Coin and Interest Problems

What happens when you offer a small child a choice between one quarter and five pennies? Frequently, children prefer the five pennies because they do not yet understand the value of the coins.

How many coins do you have in your pocket or purse? Find the total value. If you have five dimes, you must multiply the number of dimes (5) by the value of a dime (10 cents). Your five dimes have a total value of 50 cents. How many cents do you have if you have 3 nickels, 4 quarters, and 6 pennies? To find the worth of all the coins, you must multiply the value of each by the number of coins of that type and then find the sum of these products.

	Number of coins	Value of coin	Total value
Nickels	3	0.05	0.15
Quarters	4	0.25	1.00
Pennies	6	0.01	0.06

The total value of all the coins is $0.15 + 1.00 + 0.06 = \$1.21$.

In elementary school you learned to count coins and figure up their value. The coin problems that follow are somewhat more difficult in that they state a total value and the type of coins but ask you to compute the number of each type of coin. Tables like the one above will help you organize information and solve the problems.

Suppose you have 20 coins in dimes and nickels. If eleven are dimes, how many are nickels? Yes, there are nine, but do you see that you subtracted the part (11) from the total (20) to obtain the second part? This principle is used with variables in problems in which a total amount is given.

EXAMPLE 1 Chris has 17 coins, and they are all dimes and quarters. If he has a total of $2.45, how many of each coin does he have?

Answer

Let x = number of quarters

$17 - x$ = number of dimes   1. Name one part x; subtract the part from the total to name the other part.

Continued ▶

2. Make a table. Multiply across to complete the last column.

	Number of coins	Value of coin	Total value
Quarters	x	0.25	$0.25x$
Dimes	$17 - x$	0.10	$0.10(17 - x)$

3. Solve an equation.

$0.25x + 0.10(17 - x) = 2.45$

a. Write an equation using the last column of the table and solve it.

Clear decimals by multiplying both sides of the equation by 100.

$25x + 10(17 - x) = 245$

b. Solve the equation.

$25x + 170 - 10x = 245$

$15x = 75$

$x = 5$

$17 - x = 12$

Chris has five quarters and twelve dimes.

4. Answer the rest of the question, and interpret the answer. Are the answers reasonable?

Solving Coin Problems

1. **Read** the problem, carefully looking for the main unknown value. Assign a variable to it; then express any other unknowns in terms of it.
2. **Plan** and organize by making a table indicating the number of each kind of coin, the value of each type of coin, and the total value of each type.
3. **Solve** an equation obtained by using the information in the total value column and any other information from the problem.
4. **Check** that your answers relate to the numbers in the problem, answer all questions, and are reasonable.

EXAMPLE 2   A coin bank contains four more quarters than nickels, twice as many dimes as nickels, and five more than three times as many pennies as nickels. If the bank contains $22.25, how many of each coin are in it?

Continued ▶

Answer

Let x = the number of nickels

Read

$x + 4$ = the number of quarters
$2x$ = the number of dimes
$3x + 5$ = the number of pennies

Plan

	Number of coins	Value of coin	Total value
Quarters	$x + 4$	0.25	$0.25(x + 4)$
Dimes	$2x$	0.10	$0.10(2x)$
Nickels	x	0.05	$0.05x$
Pennies	$3x + 5$	0.01	$0.01(3x + 5)$

Solve

$0.25(x + 4) + 0.10(2x) + 0.05x + 0.01(3x + 5) = 22.25$

Multiply both sides of the equation by 100.

$25(x + 4) + 10(2x) + 5x + 3x + 5 = 2225$
$25x + 100 + 20x + 5x + 3x + 5 = 2225$
$53x + 105 = 2225$
$53x = 2120$
$x = 40$

Check

Since $x + 4 = 44$, $2x = 80$, and $3x + 5 = 125$, there are 44 quarters, 80 dimes, 40 nickels, and 125 pennies.

The formula for simple interest on a bank account or for a loan is $Prt = I$, where P = principal (amount invested), r = rate, and t = time. Rate and time are usually given in years.

The first bank built in America still stands in Philadelphia.

This formula helps you organize a table for investment problems. These problems are similar to coin problems and the same procedure can be used.

EXAMPLE 3

Chris invests the same amount of money in each of two accounts and gets $36 interest at the end of one year. If the accounts earn 5% and 7% interest respectively, how much was the total amount invested?

Answer

1. **Read.** Let x = the amount in each account.

2. **Plan.** Make a table using $Prt = I$. Fill in the first three columns, and then multiply across to fill the last column.

Continued ▶

P	r	t	=	I
x	0.05	1		0.05x
x	0.07	1		0.07x

3. **Solve.** The total interest is $36.

$$0.05x + 0.07x = 36 \qquad \text{Multiply by 100 to clear}$$
$$5x + 7x = 3600 \qquad \text{decimals.}$$
$$12x = 3600$$
$$x = 300$$

4. **Check.** Chris invested $300 in each account.

EXAMPLE 4 Robert borrowed $500 at a simple rate of 6%. Two months later he borrowed an additional $900 at 8%. If he paid off both loans at the same time and paid $47.50 in interest charges, for how many months did he borrow each amount of money?

Answer 1. Let x = the time of the longer loan.
2. Make a table and remember to express the time in years. This means 2 months must be written $\frac{2}{12} = \frac{1}{6}$.

P	r	t	=	I
500	0.06	x		$0.06(500)x$
900	0.08	$x - \frac{1}{6}$		$0.08(900)\left(x - \frac{1}{6}\right)$

3. The sum of the interest amounts is $47.50.

$$0.06(500)x + 0.08(900)\left(x - \frac{1}{6}\right) = 47.50$$

Multiply both sides of the equation by 100.

$$6(500)x + 8(900)\left(x - \frac{1}{6}\right) = 4750$$
$$3000x + 7200\left(x - \frac{1}{6}\right) = 4750$$
$$3000x + 7200x - 1200 = 4750$$
$$10{,}200x = 5950$$
$$x = \frac{5950}{10{,}200} \approx 0.58\overline{3} \text{ years}$$

In months this would be

$$12(0.58\overline{3}) = 7 \text{ months for the } \$500$$
$$x - 2 = 5 \text{ months for the } \$900$$

▶ A. Exercises

Solve.

1. Jill has $9.96 in nickels, pennies, and dollar bills in her bank. If she has 12 more pennies than nickels and 5 less dollar bills than nickels, how many of each does she have?

2. One Saturday Bill collected from his newspaper customers twice as many one dollar bills as fives and one less ten than fives. If Bill collected $58, how many tens, fives, and one dollar bills did he get?

3. Lynn has $8.58 in quarters and pennies. If she has eight times as many pennies as quarters, how many of each does she have?

4. Jim has a jar of dimes, nickels, and pennies. He has one dime more than five times the number of nickels and four times as many pennies as nickels. How many of each coin are in the jar if the total value is $7.77?

5. A bank teller knows that she received 34 dimes and nickels from a customer. If the change totaled $2.05, how many dimes and nickels did she receive?

6. In his pocket Chip has 4 more dimes than quarters. If the quarters and dimes total $2.85, how many quarters and dimes does he have?

7. Sam has five more dimes than quarters and four less nickels than quarters. If he has 34 coins, how many of each does he have?

8. A teller has 36 rolls of coins in his drawer, consisting of quarters ($10 per roll), dimes ($5 per roll) and nickels ($2 per roll). He has three times as many rolls of quarters as nickels and twice as many rolls of dimes as nickels. The total is $252. How many rolls of each does he have?

9. Mike said, "Guess how many coins and dollar bills I have in my pocket. Their value is $13.40, and I have three times as many dimes as dollar bills and half as many quarters as dimes. How many of each coin do I have?"

10. Josh has seven times as many nickels as quarters. If the coins total $2.40, how many of each does he have?

11. Mr. Mooney has invested money in three separate accounts. The amounts invested in the second and third accounts are respectively twice and three times the amount invested in the first account. If the total invested is $22,500, how much does he have in each account?

12. Mrs. Jones invested $10,000, some in each of two separate accounts. One pays 5% interest and the other 6%. If her combined annual interest is $575, how much does she have invested in each account?

13. An investor has $500 more invested at 7% than he does at 5%. If his annual interest is $515, how much does he have invested at each rate?

14. Ruth borrowed $2000, part from each of two different sources, for a 6-month period. One charged 6% interest and the other 8%. When she paid them off, she paid a combined total of $68 interest. How much did she borrow at each rate?

15. An investor has $7500 invested at one rate and $6200 invested at a different rate. If the second investment is at a rate 2% lower than the first, find the rate for each investment if his annual interest is $698.

16. The Grand Bank loaned one borrower $25,000 and another borrower $50,000 at an interest rate that was twice that of the first. If the combined annual interest received by the bank was $7500, what was the interest rate for each loan?

17. The Halls borrowed $1800 at 12% and took out a second loan for $2500 at 9%. If the time period for the second loan was twice as long as that for the first, and the total interest paid for both combined was $499.50, find the time of each loan.

18. An investor placed her money in a venture paying 7% interest. If she had another $1500, she would have been able to invest her money at 10% and gain an additional $255 in annual interest. How much did she invest?

▶ **C. Exercises**

19. A finance company offers cheaper interest rates if you borrow a larger sum of money for a shorter time period. A borrower is offered $7000 at 12% or $10,080 at 10%. If the time for the larger loan is 6 months less but the total interest is the same, find the time to repay for each loan.

20. An automobile buyer is trying to decide whether to buy a new car and finance it for 5 years at 7% interest or a used car costing $11,500 less at 11% for 2 years. The new car loan will cost $5130 more in interest than the used car loan. Find the cost of each car.

■ **Cumulative Review**

Simplify.

21. $\sqrt{361}$

22. $-\sqrt{784}$

23. $\pm\sqrt{16}$

24. $\sqrt{-25}$

25. $\sqrt{\frac{49}{64}}$

26. $\sqrt{(-2)^2}$

27. $\sqrt[3]{216}$

4.9 Motion Problems

Air traffic controllers direct planes from the tower.

A jet leaves O'Hare Airport in Chicago at 7:00 A.M. and flies south toward Atlanta, 606 air miles away, at an average rate of 420 mph. An hour later a jet leaves Atlanta and flies toward Chicago at an average rate of 500 mph. Because of an error in calculations, the jets are flying at the same altitude and on the same route toward each other. How much time do the air traffic controllers have to change the direction or altitude of the jets before they collide?

This is a motion problem. To solve it, you need to use the formula $d = rt$, in which d stands for distance, r for rate, and t for time.

How far will a car travel if it goes 50 mph for 3 hours?

$d = rt$
$d = 50 \cdot 3$
$d = 150$ miles

How far will a car travel if it goes 50 mph for x hours?

$d = 50x$ miles

At what rate is a car traveling if it goes 225 miles in 5 hours?

$225 = r \cdot 5$
$\frac{225}{5} = r$
$r = 45$ mph

Often you can simplify motion problems if you make a diagram and a table and fill in the known quantities.

When you have two quantities in any horizontal row, find the third quantity by using the formula $rt = d$ as written in the top row of the table.

rate ·	time	= distance
50	3	150
50	x	$50x$
r	5	$5r$

EXAMPLE 1   Jim rides his bicycle at a rate of **8 mph** for *t* hours. How far does he ride?

Answer   **1.** Let *d* = the distance he rides

He rides **8t** miles.

r ·	*t*	= *d*
8	*t*	8t

EXAMPLE 2   The junior and senior high Sunday school classes are going on a hike. The junior high class leaves the church and travels east at **3** miles per hour. The high school class leaves an hour later traveling at **5** miles per hour on the same route. How much time will pass before the senior high class catches up with the junior high class?

Answer   **1. Read** the problem carefully. Identify the main unknown in the problem (the time that passes before the senior high class catches up).
   Let *x* = the amount of time the senior high class hikes
   Also draw a picture to represent the problem.

2. Plan your strategy.
   a. A table will help you organize the information. Since the junior high class traveled one hour longer, they traveled *x* + 1 hours.
   b. Fill in both times using your variable expressions. Fill in the rate column using the specific numbers in the problem.

	r ·	*t*	= *d*
junior high	3	*x* + 1	
senior high	5	*x*	

   c. Since two columns of the table are complete, fill in the third column using *rt* = *d* without looking at the problem.

	r ·	*t*	= *d*
junior high	3	*x* + 1	3(*x* + 1)
senior high	5	*x*	5x

3. **Solve.** Now locate information about the column filled in last, which was the distance column. The problem states that the high school class will catch up with the junior high class. This statement or your picture will remind you that both groups walk the same distance. Since the distances are equal, equate the distance expressions from your table.

Now solve your equation.

$$3(x + 1) = 5x$$
$$3x + 3 = 5x$$
$$3 = 2x$$
$$\frac{3}{2} = x$$

4. **Check.** Look back at the table and see what x represents. In this problem x represents the amount of time the high school class hikes. Does this answer the question in the problem? Interpret the answer (as a mixed number) in hours. In $1\frac{1}{2}$ hours the high school class will catch up with the junior high class. Observe that this is reasonable.

Solving Motion Problems

1. **Read** the problem carefully.
   a. Find the unknown in the problem and let the variable stand for this unknown.
   b. Draw a picture to represent the problem.
2. **Plan** a strategy.
   a. Make a table and fill in two columns. One column will be specific numbers from the problem and the other column involves expressions using the variable.
   b. Using $rt = d$, fill in the third column.
3. **Solve** an equation.
   a. Use the problem or your picture to identify the relationship between the expressions in the last column that you filled in. Write an equation using this relationship.
   b. Solve your equation.
4. **Check** that you answered the question, that you interpreted the answers with proper units, and that the answers are reasonable.

EXAMPLE 3 Two trains leave Mattoon at the same time. The northbound train travels **5** mph faster than the southbound train. What is the rate of each train if after **3** hours they are **333** miles apart?

Answer **1. Read.**

a. Let x = the rate of the southbound train
   $x + 5$ = the rate of the northbound train

b. Make a sketch.

Mattoon

southbound   northbound

──────── 333 mi. ────────

2. Plan. Make a table.

a. Fill in two columns.

b. Fill in the third column: use $rt = d$.

	r $\cdot$	t =	d
northbound	$x + 5$	3	$3(x + 5)$
southbound	x	3	$3x$

3. Solve.

a. Since d was the last column completed, determine what the problem says about the distances. After three hours the trains are **333** miles apart, which is the total distance the two trains have traveled (as in the sketch). $3(x + 5) + 3x = 333$

b. Solve the equation.

$$3(x + 5) + 3x = 333$$
$$3x + 15 + 3x = 333$$
$$6x + 15 = 333$$
$$6x = 318$$
$$x = 53$$

4. Check.

Look back at the table to see what x represents. In this problem x = the rate of the southbound train. So the southbound train travels **53** mph, and the northbound train travels $x + 5 = $ **58** mph. Check this solution.
$$53(3) + 58(3) = 333$$

▶ A. Exercises

Fill in the following tables.

	r	$\cdot$	t	$=$	d
1.	3		18		
2.			2		132
3.	19				x
4.	52		x		
5.			$\frac{3}{16}$		$\frac{15}{4}$

	r	$\cdot$	t	$=$	d
6.	35		$x + 2$		
7.			16		$16x$
8.	$x + 12$				$4(x + 12)$
9.	a		$7b$		
10.	16				x

11. Andy won a race by sailing **20** mph for $6\frac{1}{4}$ hours. How far did he sail?
12. A train is traveling **62** mph and has to go **372** miles. How long will it take the train to make the trip?
13. A jet travels the **2800** miles from New York to Los Angeles in **7** hours. What is the average speed of the jet?
14. Sue leaves Lewiston for Clarksville **388** miles away and drives **52** miles per hour. Monica leaves Clarksville for Lewiston at the same time and travels **45** miles per hour. How soon will the two meet?
15. Brent rides a moped down the country road in front of his house. Brent's wife, Jan, and her two sons ride bicycles in the opposite direction on the same road. If they leave at the same time and Brent travels **24** mph and Jan and the boys travel **8** mph, how much time will pass before they are **24** miles apart?

▶ B. Exercises

16. Brandon and Shanda walk to Grandma's house at a rate of **4** mph. They ride their bicycles back home at a rate of **8** mph over the same route that they walked. It takes one hour longer to walk than ride. How long did it take them to walk to Grandma's?
17. Steve, a cyclist, leaves the corner of First and Maple on his bicycle and travels **9** mph. Two hours later his brother leaves from First and Maple and comes after him on a moped traveling **27** mph. How long will it take him to catch up with Steve?
18. Ted runs two thirds as fast as Frank. In two hours Frank runs eight miles farther than Ted. How fast does each run?
19. A fishing boat leaves Tampa Bay at 4:00 A.M. and travels at **12** knots. At 5:00 A.M. a second boat leaves the same dock for the same destination and travels at **14** knots. How long will it take the second boat to catch the first?

20. A passenger train leaves Charleston, W.Va., heading east at the same time a loaded coal train leaves Charleston heading west. The passenger train travels 23 mph faster than the coal train, and in 4 hours the two trains are 412 miles apart. What is the speed of each train?

21. A roller coaster goes down the first grade eight times faster than it goes up the other side. If the distance down the hill is 100 feet more than the distance up the hill and if it takes 70 seconds to go up and 10 seconds to go down, what is the speed in feet per second of the roller coaster when it goes up the hill and when it comes down the hill?

22. In 5 hours, how far can a car go and return if the average speed going is 48 mph and the average speed returning is 52 mph?

23. A freight train leaves Centralia for Chicago at the same time a passenger train leaves Chicago for Centralia. The freight train moves at a speed of 45 mph, and the passenger train travels at a speed of 64 mph. If Chicago and Centralia are 218 miles apart, how long will it take for the two trains to meet?

24. At the auto race one car travels 190 mph while another travels 195 mph. How long will it take the faster car to gain two laps on the slower car if the speedway track is $2\frac{1}{2}$ miles long?

25. John and Jay run the 220-yard dash, and Jay wins the race by 10 yards. If Jay runs the race in 30 seconds, what is the rate of each boy in yards per second? How long would it take John to run the 220-yard dash?

▶ C. Exercises

26. Mr. Thomas drove his old truck to the city at a speed of 40 mph and drove back home on the interstate at a rate of 60 mph. The total trip took 6 hours. How far is Mr. Thomas's house from the city?

27. Joe and Peter bicycled at 12 mph to a lake and then canoed at 4 mph across it. The entire trip took $4\frac{1}{2}$ hours. If they bicycled 6 miles more than 3 times the distance they canoed, how far did they travel by each method?

■ Cumulative Review

28. Simplify $\frac{1}{14}x + \frac{1}{8}x$.

29. Solve $\frac{1}{14}x + \frac{1}{8}x = 22$.

30. Simplify $\frac{2}{3} + 5x + \frac{1}{9} + 2x$.

31. Solve $\frac{2}{3} + 5x + \frac{1}{9} + 2x = 0$.

32. Simplify $5x - 3(2x - 7) + 4$.

33. Solve $5x - 3(2x - 7) = 4$.

34. Simplify $3x + 17 - 12x + 5$.

35. Solve $3x + 17 = 12x + 5$.

4.10 Mixture Problems

Mixture problems involve the combination of different substances. To solve such problems, make a table similar to those for coin and interest problems. Read the following problem and collect all the necessary facts.

EXAMPLE 1   A feed store owner wants to mix corn and barley to make 150 bushels of silage additive for cattle feed. If corn costs $2.40 a bushel and barley costs $2.20 a bushel, how many bushels of each grain should he mix to yield an additive worth $2.34 a bushel?

Answer   1. **Read** carefully to find the unknown quantity.
We want to know how many bushels of corn and of barley should be combined to yield 150 bushels. Name one part x and subtract from 150 to get the other part just as you did with coins.
$$x = \text{number of bushels of corn}$$
$$150 - x = \text{number of bushels of barley}$$

2. **Plan.**
a. Make a table and fill in two columns.
b. Fill in the third column by multiplying the number of bushels by the price per bushel to get the total price.

	Number of bushels	Price per bushel	Total price
corn	x	2.40	$2.40x$
barley	$150 - x$	2.20	$2.20(150 - x)$
mix	150	2.34	351

3. **Solve.**
a. The total price of the corn plus the total price of the barley equals the total price of the mixture.
$$2.4x + 2.2(150 - x) = 351$$
b. $24x + 22(150 - x) = 3510$
$$24x + 3300 - 22x = 3510$$
$$2x = 210$$
$$x = 105$$
$$150 - x = 45$$

Continued ▶

4. **Check.**
   The additive should contain 105 bushels of corn and 45 bushels of barley.

EXAMPLE 2   Nickel silver, often used for coating tableware, is an alloy containing 15% nickel along with copper and zinc. How much pure nickel must be melted with 70 pounds of nickel silver to make an alloy that is 20% nickel?

Answer   Let x = pounds of pure nickel
1. **Read.**
2. **Plan.**

	Pounds of alloy	% of nickel	Pounds of nickel
nickel silver	70	0.15	
pure nickel	x	1.0	
mix	$70 + x$	0.20	

Percents are changed to decimal form. Note that pure nickel is 100% nickel and that 100% = 1.00 in decimal form.

Using the fact that the pounds of metal multiplied by the percent of nickel produces the pounds of nickel, fill in the third column.

	Pounds of alloy	% of nickel	Pounds of nickel
nickel silver	70	0.15	(0.15)70
pure nickel	x	1.0	x
mix	$70 + x$	0.20	$0.20(70 + x)$

3. **Solve.** Now form an equation from the column you just completed. The pounds of nickel in nickel silver plus the pounds of nickel in pure nickel will equal the pounds of nickel in the mix.

Continued ▶

$$(0.15)70 + x = 0.20(70 + x)$$
$$(15)70 + 100x = 20(70 + x)$$
$$1050 + 100x = 1400 + 20x$$
$$80x = 350$$
$$x = 4.375$$

To eliminate decimals, multiply both sides by 100.

4. **Check.** The amount of pure nickel that must be melted with the nickel silver is **4.375** pounds.

Solving Mixture Problems

1. **Read** the problem carefully to find the unknown quantities. Translate each into an algebraic expression.
2. **Plan.**
   a. Make a table to organize the information in the problem. Fill in all columns except the last one.
   b. Complete the last column without looking back at the problem.
3. **Solve.**
   a. Write an equation using the information in the last column.
   b. Solve the equation.
4. **Check.**
   a. Did you answer all the questions?
   b. Did you interpret the answer using proper units?
   c. Are your answers reasonable?

▶ A. Exercises

Find the missing value in each row of the table.

	Amount of mixture	Percent of salt	Amount of salt
1.	20 gal.	0.70	
2.	x pounds	0.65	
3.	90 oz.	0.08	
4.	15 grams		4.95 grams
5.		0.18	14.4 liters

	Number of items	Value per item	Total value
6.	20	$1.26	
7.	x	$5.21	

	Amount of mixture	Percent of ingredient	Amount of ingredient
8.	80 liters	0.20	
9.	x liters	0.50	
10.		0.25	

In the next four exercises, you will not need variables. Make a table to help you answer each question.

11. Ten gallons of a **12%** salt solution are mixed with eight gallons of an **80%** salt solution. What is the total amount of solution? How much salt is in the mixture? What is the percentage of salt in the mixture?

12. Four gallons of pure iodine are added to **46** gallons of **2%** iodine. How much of the final solution do you have? How much iodine is contained in the mixture? What is the strength (percentage) of iodine in the mixture?

13. Dilute **35** gallons of **40%** acid with **7** gallons of water. What is the amount and strength of the mixture?

14. If you boil **3** gallons of **10%** salt water until there are only **2** gallons left, what is the percent of salt when you finish?

15. Mr. Harper, the candy store manager, wants to mix butterscotch candies and cinnamon balls to make a deluxe mix to sell for **$3.00** a pound. Butterscotch sells for **$3.40** a pound, while cinnamon balls sell for **$2.90** a pound. How many pounds of each should he use to make **20** pounds of the mix?

16. How many gallons of cream that is **30%** butterfat must be mixed with milk that is **3%** butterfat to make **45** gallons that are **12%** butterfat?

17. Mr. Lee owns a tea company and wants to make an exotic blend of tea. He has two brands to mix. One brand is an Indian tea that sells for **$3.25** per pound. The other is a Chinese tea that sells for **$4.00** per pound. If he wants a mix of **35** pounds that will sell for **$3.70** a pound, how many pounds of each should he mix?

18. Chris has **3** gallons of a solution that is **30%** antifreeze that he wants to use to winterize his car. How much pure antifreeze should he add to this solution so that the new solution will be **65%** antifreeze?

19. How many gallons of pure water must be added to **10** gallons of **30%** salt water to make a solution that is **25%** salt water?

Solve.

20. Kim sells Pistachio Pleasure containing **80%** pistachios and Pistachio Surprise containing **30%** pistachios. How much of each should she mix to make twelve pounds of a new mix that is **40%** pistachios?

21. A chemist has **2** liters of a solution that is **20%** hydrochloric acid, and she wants a solution that is **25%** hydrochloric acid. How much pure hydrochloric acid must be added to the solution?

22. How many gallons of pure alcohol must you add to **25** gallons of **28%** alcohol solution to obtain a solution that is **40%** alcohol?

23. A nurse wants **4** liters of **5%** iodine solution. She already has **3** liters of **3%** iodine solution. What percentage of iodine should the additional liter contain?

24. A butcher makes meat loaf by mixing hamburger, which sells for **$1.89** per pound, and sausage, which sells for **$2.99** per pound. How many pounds of each should he mix if he is to make **30** pounds of mix and sell it for **$2.33** per pound?

25. Jo makes fruit salad with grapefruit and pineapple. Grapefruit costs **$1.25** per 12-ounce can, and pineapple costs **$0.83** per 12-ounce can. How many cans of each should she mix to obtain **84** ounces of a mixture that will cost **$1.01** for every **12** ounces?

26. How much water should you boil off a 30-gallon solution of **10%** salt to increase it to **15%** salt?

► C. Exercises

27. Babbitt metal, named for its developer, Isaac Babbitt, who first made the metal in 1839, is used primarily for machine gearings. This metal alloy is composed of **90%** tin, **7%** antimony, and **3%** copper. How many ounces of pure tin must be added to the alloy to make **6** ounces of a metal that is **94%** tin?

28. One 1700-pound load of feed mixture contains **25%** corn, **40%** bran, and the rest roughage. How many pounds of corn should be added to a load of feed mixture to make the feed **40%** corn?

Cumulative Review

Solve.

29. $7x - 15 = -99$

30. $3(x - 2) + 2 = 23$

31. $12x - 6 = 5x + 8$

32. $|x - 2| = 5$

33. $\frac{x}{4} + 3 = 7$

34. $\frac{x + 2}{3} + \frac{x}{6} = 4$

ALGEBRA AND MEDICINE

S uppose you want to be a nurse, so you inquire about prerequisites to enter that area of study in college. You will find that mathematics and science are the most important subjects and you need as many classes as you can fit into your schedule. One 20-year veteran nurse claimed that not a day went by that she did not use math in some way. She often set up ratios and proportions and also frequently used algebra.

Anesthesiologists prepare and monitor patients for surgery by using dosage formulas for anesthetics.

EXAMPLE 1 A nurse is preparing a dose of amoxicillin for a boy weighing **18** kg. She knows the correct dosage requires no more than **20** mg per kg of body weight. If the product comes as a liquid containing **250** mg per 5 mL, what is the dosage in mL?

20 mg/kg · 18 kg = **360** mg

If *x* represents the dosage, then

$$\frac{x}{360} = \frac{5 \text{ mL}}{250}$$

x = **7.2** mL   (5.5 mL = 1 teaspoon)

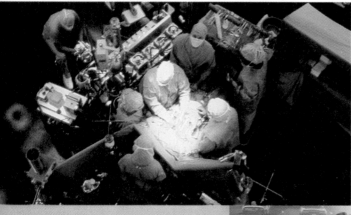

Doctors, nurses, radiologists, researchers, and lab technicians all use the tools of algebra to carry out certain tasks in their work routine. Technology performs most of the repetitive, time-consuming work; but users must understand the math behind the instruments or they will sooner or later misuse the tool. Laboratory technicians

have to standardize and adjust instruments as well as test output for consistency and precision. Many medical personnel have to interpret the results given by these instruments. The manuals that accompany scientific instruments are usually overflowing with formulas and equations that hinder those deficient in algebra.

EXAMPLE 2   Eye doctors tell us that a person's ability to focus his eyes is measured in diopters and is called *accommodation*. Knowing how close someone can hold an object and still see it in focus lets the doctor calculate a person's accommodation, A. If Lana can read a book clearly down to a near point of $n = 9.1$ cm, then her focusing ability is found by

$$A = \frac{100}{n} = \frac{100}{9.1} \approx 11.0 \text{ diopters}$$

At age 45 she will probably have a focusing ability of only 3.2 diopters:

$$\frac{100}{n} = 3.2 \text{ diopters.}$$

Therefore, her near point = 31 cm (a little more than 1 foot).

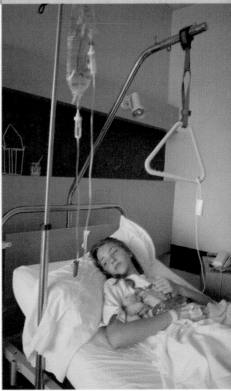

Nurses precisely calculate drip rates and antibiotic dosages for intravenous (IV) fluids to match the doctor's prescriptions.

EXAMPLE 3   A dietetic nurse has a patient who needs 15 mg of iron per day from nonmeat sources. She knows the amount of iron in one cup of kidney beans is 4.5 mg and the amount in one cup of soy beans is 5.5 mg. Write an equation expressing the patient's iron intake and suggest a possible daily routine.

$$4.5k + 5.5s = 15$$

Choosing one cup of kidney beans per day, $4.5(1) + 5.5s = 15$, gives $s = 1.9$ cups of soy beans per day.

Medical lab technicians calculate dilutions to prepare samples for testing. Doctors base treatment plans on these blood chemistry and pathology reports.

Algebra *and* Scripture

In our Christian walk we must prepare by putting on God's armor (Eph. 6:10-18). Likewise we prepare through algebra, developing skill in solving equations and word problems so that we will be ready for future challenges in school and life.

In Luke 14:28-30 Jesus implies that math skills are needed. It's a matter of common sense and good planning to figure costs before a construction project.

1. What other example of common sense does Jesus relate in verses 31-32?

2. Jesus uses these math examples to show us that we should plan ahead too. What should we do to serve Him (verses 26, 27, 33)?

Algebra is a tool that can help you plan. Planning may involve the use of formulas or the solving of equations. Equations are the core of algebra, and each equation expresses a relationship between quantities. Look at some equations in Scripture.

3. Write the equation in Luke 15:4.

4. Genesis 5:3-31 gives nine equations. Write the one with the highest sum. Then write the one with the lowest sum.

THE NTH DEGREE

Write an equation based on the life of Noah using relevant chapters of Genesis.

Monetary transactions also involve the use of math. Of course, each transaction involves arithmetic and numbers. However, business also involves budgets and planning. In ancient times as well as in modern Palestine, transactions involve negotiations to agree on a fair price. Luke gives many examples of people who use math in such business transactions.

For each person using money below, as recorded in Luke, state how he used it. Then decide if the use was proper or improper.

5. Men with debts of 500 pence and 50 pence (7:41; Rom. 13:8)
6. Good Samaritan (10:35)
7. Unjust steward (16:6-7)
8. Zacchaeus (19:8)
9. Two servants (19:13-19)
10. Wicked servant (19:20-23)
11. Widow (21:2)

THE Nth DEGREE

Find a Bible passage in which Jesus used money properly to pay his taxes.

Scriptural Roots

WHAT MAN OF YOU, having an hundred sheep, if he lose one of them, doth not leave the ninety and nine in the wilderness, and go after that which is lost, until he find it?

LUKE 15:4

Solve the following problems.

1. $x - 5 = 126$

2. $4x = 32$

3. $\frac{x}{8} = 19$

4. $x + 8 = 87$

5. $2x - 16 = 74$

6. $\frac{x}{5} - 6 = 84$

7. $6x + 21 = 165$

8. $\frac{x}{9} + 3 = 14$

9. $\frac{y}{-2} = 7 + 3y$

10. $4a = 7 - 4a + 6$

11. $3x + 9 = 10x + 16$

12. $\frac{4k}{9} = 2$

13. $-6(x - 8) = 12$

14. $3(x + 2) = 4(x - 6) + 2(x + 5)$

15. $8x + 4x = 12$

16. $89x + 17 + 6x = 5x - 19$

17. $3y - 10 = 10y$

18. $4(a + 10) - 6(2a + 9) = 146$

19. $5b + (b - 8) = 28$

20. $4c - 2(c + 9) + 10 = -14$

21. $|5x + 9| = 9$

22. $|3x| = 18$

23. $23 = |5x| - 2$

24. $\frac{x}{2} + \frac{4x}{3} = \frac{22}{3}$

25. $\frac{x}{5} + \frac{3x}{10} = \frac{5}{2}$

Solve the following literal equations for *x*.

26. $2x + b = 3c$

27. $x + 5x - 14 = 3y - 12$

28. $\frac{ab}{x} = b$

29. $Rx = H$

30. $x(a + 2b) = 4(ac + b)$

31. Bill has 9 more baseball cards than Jim. If Jim's and Bill's cards total 3 more than three times the number of Jim's cards, how many does each have?

32. Mr. Gonzales is a salesman at the J. N. Car Sales and Service. His salary is $215 per week plus $125 per car that he sells. How many cars must he sell in one week to make $1215?

33. The sum of two numbers is 111, and their difference is 63. What are the two numbers?

34. Find two consecutive integers such that the sum of five times the smaller and three times the larger is 67.

35. Julie drives the 120 miles from Greenup to Newton at 46 mph while Beth drives from Newton to Greenup at 34 mph. How long will it take for Julie and Beth to meet each other if they leave at the same time?

36. A coffee merchant wants to make a mixture of 50 pounds of Colombian and Brazilian coffee that will cost $3.19 per pound. If Colombian coffee sells for $3.35 per pound and Brazilian coffee sells for $2.95 per pound, how much of each type of coffee should be mixed?

37. Craig has a bank that contains only quarters and nickels. How many of each does he have if he has 126 coins worth $24.50?

38. Randy invested twice as much at 10% as he did at 8%. If he earns $30.80 annually, how much did he invest at each rate?

39. Explain the mathematical significance of Luke 15:4.

5 Solving Inequalities

The First National Bank of Newton is holding its annual board meeting. Mr. Lee, the bank president, presents the annual report to the members of the board. Mr. Lee must make wise investments of the bank's funds so that the bank and its stockholders will make a profit. The bank creates income by lending its money to people or companies at a certain interest rate or by investing it in federal or municipal bonds. The profit the bank obtains from these investments pays the interest (calculated at a lower rate than the lending rate) on bank accounts for the use of the money deposited and the rest is then divided among the stockholders as dividends.

The stockholders have a vested interest in the financial plans that Mr. Lee presents at the annual board meeting. Mr. Lee knows that he must gain their confidence in his plans for investing their money. He summarizes investments that will earn $3.4 million in the coming year. He needs to know how much money he must invest in municipal bonds that yield 8% annually so that the total interest income for the bank will be at least an additional $2.1 million.

When Mr. Lee solves these important business problems, he must work with inequalities. Can you find the solution to the bank president's problem? He must solve the inequalities accurately. Where do you think he first learned the basic principles for solving such problems?

After this chapter you should be able to

1. graph inequalities on a number line.
2. solve inequalities.
3. describe the properties of inequalities.
4. solve inequality conjunctions and disjunctions.
5. solve absolute value inequalities.
6. set up and solve inequalities from word problems.

5.1 Inequalities

In an *inequality* two things are not equal. Scripture reminds us of some inequalities. One is the unequal fight between the great God and the lesser created being Satan. Satan seeks equality with God: "I will be like the most High" (Isa. 14:14). The serpent Satan told Eve the lie that she too could be like, or equal to, God (Gen. 3:5), and humanism is the continuation of that lie today. Humanism says that man is his own god, but the Bible teaches that there is only one God (Deut. 4:39). No matter how hard man tries, he cannot make himself equal to God.

The Tall Trees Grove at Redwoods National Park, California, contains the tallest tree in the world (center) at 368 feet high. Thus, $h \leq 368$ where h is any tree height.

The phrases "is greater than," "is not equal to," and "is less than" are phrases that often appear in mathematical inequalities. Symbols, however, are usually used to represent these and other important inequality phrases.

Symbol	Meaning	Example
$<$	is less than	$4 < 6$
$>$	is greater than	$5 > 3$
$\neq$	is not equal to	$2 \neq 4$
$\leq$	is less than or equal to	$3 \leq 3$
$\geq$	is greater than or equal to	$8 \geq 7$

THE SYMBOL $<$ MEANS "LESS THAN." THE SYMBOL $>$ MEANS "GREATER THAN."

Placing a slash mark through any of the symbols results in their negation, just as in the case of the equal sign (example: $\nless$ means not less than).

You already know that $3x + 5 = 10$ is an equation. The equal sign ($=$) is the sign of an equality. The equations studied previously had one or two solutions. A mathematical sentence such as $3x + 5 < 10$ is an inequality and can have many solutions.

Definition

An **inequality** is a mathematical sentence stating that two numbers or expressions are not always equal.

Consider the inequality $x < 5$. How many values can x have? Does $x = -2$ make the inequality true? Yes, but any negative number is a solution as well as numbers such as $\frac{1}{3}$, $1\frac{1}{2}$, and 4. An inequality has an infinite number of solutions, all of which can be indicated on a number line. Since 5 is the smallest whole number that is not a solution, place a circle at 5 on the number line and draw a line with an arrow pointing to the left of 5. You have just indicated that all numbers less than 5 are solutions to the inequality $x < 5$.

EXAMPLE 1   Graph $x \geq -3$.

Answer

1. Draw a number line and label it.
2. Decide if -3 should be included in the solution. Since the symbol means "greater than or equal to," x could equal -3. Therefore, -3 is part of the solution. Put a dot on -3.
3. Draw an arrow to the right to indicate all numbers greater than -3.

Graphing Inequalities

1. Draw a number line and label it.
2. To indicate that the number is part of the solution, place a dot on the number. To indicate that the number is not part of the solution, place a circle on the number.
3. Shade the appropriate portion of the line.

EXAMPLE 2   Graph $x \neq 2$.

Answer

-6 -5 -4 -3 -2 -1 0 1 2 3 4

1. This inequality is not as specific as the others. We know only that x does not equal 2.

2. Therefore, the solutions for this inequality include any number except 2. Draw a circle on 2.

3. Since x could be greater than or less than 2, $x < 2$ or $x > 2$. Draw one arrow pointing to the left and another arrow pointing to the right.

▶ A. Exercises

Look up each reference and write the correct symbols for the equalities and inequalities.

1.	Job 33:12	God	man	
2.	John 13:16	the servant	his lord	
3.	Isaiah 55:8	God's thoughts	man's thoughts	
4.	Matthew 12:42	one (Jesus)	Solomon	
5.	John 5:18	Jesus	God	
6.	Exodus 18:11	the Lord	all gods	
7.	Ephesians 3:8	Paul	least of all saints	
8.	I John 3:20	God	our heart	
9.	Luke 7:28	those born of woman	John the Baptist	
10.	Revelation 21:16	length of city	breadth of city	height of city

Graph each inequality on a separate number line.

11. $x < 4$

12. $x \geq -2$

13. $x \neq 5$

14. $x > -1$

15. $x \leq 22$

16. $x > 3$

17. $x < 6$

18. $x \leq -8$

19. $x < 2$

20. $x \geq 100$

21. $x \neq -4$

22. $x > 7$

23. $x \leq 0$

24. $x \geq 18$

25. $x < -52$

▶ B. Exercises

Graph each pair of inequalities on the same number line.

26. $x > 6$
    $x < 2$
27. $x \leq 1$
    $x > 5$
28. $x \leq 2$
    $x > 4$
29. $x < -3$
    $x \geq 4$
30. $x < -4$
    $x \geq 0$

31. Give a phrase to translate each symbol into words.
    a. $\not>$
    b. $\not<$
    c. $\neq$
    d. $\not\leq$

▶ C. Exercises

32. Which of the original inequalities ($<$, $>$, $\leq$, $\geq$, $\neq$) would mean the same as $\not>$?
33. Which of the original inequalities ($<$, $>$, $\leq$, $\geq$, $\neq$) would mean the same as $\not<$, $\neq$, and $\not\leq$?
34. Which of the original inequalities ($<$, $>$, $\leq$, $\geq$, $\neq$) could be used to translate each phrase below?
    a. "is at most"
    b. "is at least"
35. Group the six verbs ($=$, $<$, $>$, $\leq$, $\geq$, $\neq$) in pairs of opposites. *Hint:* Use exercises 32-33 to identify opposites.

▉ Cumulative Review

Define each term.

36. Prime number
37. Rational number
38. Variable
39. Equation
40. Algebraic expression

Mr. Jenkins, the chemistry teacher, discovered that it took his students only 90 minutes to conduct a certain experiment properly if he wore a blue shirt to class and a whole hour and a half for the same experiment if he wore a white shirt. Can you explain why?

5.2 Properties of Inequality: Addition and Subtraction

Do you suppose that you could add or subtract the same number on both sides of an inequality? Consider a sample case for each of the five inequality symbols.

Finding the number of apples requires the addition of whole, halves, quarters, and eighths.

Case 1	$5 < 7$	Addition
	$5 + 2 < 7 + 2$	If 2 is added to both sides,
	$7 < 9$	the statement is still true.
Case 2	$2 \geq -4$	
	$2 + 5 \geq -4 + 5$	If 5 is added to both sides,
	$7 \geq 1$	the statement is still true.
Case 3	$6 \neq -2$	
	$6 + 3 \neq -2 + 3$	If 3 is added to both sides,
	$9 \neq 1$	the statement is still true.
Case 4	$-9 \leq -3$	Subtraction
	$-9 - 4 \leq -3 - 4$	If 4 is subtracted from both sides,
	$-13 \leq -7$	the statement is still true.
Case 5	$2 > 0$	
	$2 - 9 > 0 - 9$	If 9 is subtracted from both sides,
	$-7 > -9$	the statement is still true.

These samples suggest that inequalities satisfy properties similar to the addition and subtraction properties of equality.

> **Addition Property of Inequality**
>
> If a and b are two real numbers or expressions such that $a < b$ and c is any real number or expression, then
> $$a + c < b + c.$$

> **Subtraction Property of Inequality**
>
> If a and b are two real numbers or expressions such that $a < b$ and c is any real number or expression, then
> $$a - c < b - c.$$

Any inequality symbol can replace the symbol $<$ in these properties without changing the truth of the property.

Use these properties to solve inequalities exactly as you would use them to solve equations. Just think of the inequality as an equation. Solve, keeping the inequality symbol in place.

EXAMPLE 1   Solve and graph $x + 7 < 8$.

Answer

$$
\begin{aligned}
x + 7 &< 8 \\
x + 7 - 7 &< 8 - 7 \qquad \text{Subtract 7 from both sides.} \\
x &< 1
\end{aligned}
$$

EXAMPLE 2   Solve $y - 5 \neq 32$.

Answer

$$
\begin{aligned}
y - 5 &\neq 32 \\
y - 5 + 5 &\neq 32 + 5 \\
y &\neq 37 \qquad \text{Since } y \neq 37,\ y > 37 \text{ or } y < 37.
\end{aligned}
$$

EXAMPLE 3   Solve $x - 6 \geq 12$.

Answer

$$
\begin{aligned}
x - 6 &\geq 12 \\
x &\geq 18 \qquad \text{Add 6 to both sides.}
\end{aligned}
$$

▶ A. Exercises

Solve each inequality. Graph 1 to 5 on number lines.

1. $x + 8 > -4$
2. $x - 2 \leq 3$
3. $y - 10 > 2$
4. $z + 1 \neq -2$
5. $x - 8 < 2$
6. $x + 18 \leq 7$
7. $y - 26 > 82$
8. $z + 5 < -1$
9. $y + 4 \neq 12$
10. $x - 10 \geq 21$

11. $y + 15 \neq 29$

12. $x - 26 \geq 139$

13. $y + 87 < 62$

14. $z - 193 > -149$

▶ **B. Exercises**

Solve each inequality.

15. $3 + x + 4 \leq 5$

16. $4y + 1 - 3y < -3$

17. $-3x + 12 + 4x < 4 \cdot 3$

18. $5x - 4x > 3(2x - 4) - 6x$

19. $2x - (x - 4) \neq 7$

20. $3(x - 1) - 2x \geq 4$

21. $x + 1 > x - 3 - x$

22. $2(y + 5) < y$

23. $8 \leq 5 - (t - 4)$

▶ **C. Exercises**

24. $4x + 5 - (x + 7) > 2(x - 3)$

25. $\frac{4}{3}(x - 6) \leq \frac{1}{3}(x - 9)$

■ **Cumulative Review**

Identify the property used to justify each step. $\frac{1}{3}x + \frac{4}{9} = \frac{1}{6}(3 + x)$

26. $6x + 8 = 3(3 + x)$

27. $6x + 8 = 9 + 3x$

28. $6x + 8 = 3x + 9$

29. $3x = 1$

30. $x = \frac{1}{3}$

5.3 Properties of Inequality: Multiplication and Division

You have probably done experiments in science class. But what is an experiment? It is a test to examine a hypothesis. In mathematics, experiments are frequently examined in cases. Consider these test cases to see if inequalities are always solved like equations.

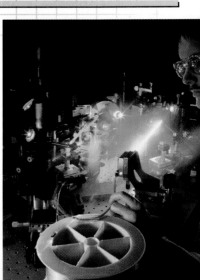

This research scientist performs experiments in fiber optics.

Case 1	Is this statement true?	$3 < 5$
	Now multiply both sides of this inequality by 2.	$3 \cdot 2 < 5 \cdot 2$
	Is this statement true?	$6 < 10$

This experiment illustrates that if you multiply both sides of an inequality by a positive number, the inequality is still true. Is this true for a negative multiplier?

Case 2	Is this statement true?	$4 < 6$
	Multiply both sides by -3.	$4 \cdot -3 < 6 \cdot -3$
	Is the inequality still true? No!	$-12 < -18$
	How could you make this final statement true? If you change the inequality sign to $>$, will the statement then be true?	$-12 > -18$

Case 1 illustrates that if you multiply both sides of an inequality by a positive number, the inequality remains the same. But case 2 illustrates that if you multiply both sides of an inequality by a negative number, the inequality sign must be reversed.

Multiplication Property of Inequality   •

If a, b, and c are real numbers or expressions and
1. $c > 0$ (positive), then $a < b$ implies $ac < bc$.
2. $c < 0$ (negative), then $a < b$ implies $ac > bc$.

Now experiment with division by a positive and then division by a negative.

Case 3	Is this statement true?	$10 > 6$
	Now divide both sides by 2.	$\frac{10}{2} > \frac{6}{2}$
	Is this statement still true?	$5 > 3$
	Yes. Now experiment with the negative case.	

Case 4	Is this statement true?	$18 > 9$
	Divide both sides by -3.	$\frac{18}{-3} > \frac{9}{-3}$
	Is this statement true? No. How can you make the statement true?	$-6 > -3$
	This statement can be made true by reversing the inequality as in multiplication.	$-6 < -3$

Division Property of Inequality

If a, b, and c are real numbers or expressions with $c \neq 0$ and
1. $c > 0$ (positive), then $a < b$ implies $\frac{a}{c} < \frac{b}{c}$
2. $c < 0$ (negative), then $a < b$ implies $\frac{a}{c} > \frac{b}{c}$

By investigating these cases, you have found that multiplying or dividing both sides of an inequality by a negative number changes the direction of the inequality, but multiplying or dividing both sides by a positive number does not change the direction of the inequality. This same idea is true for all inequalities.

EXAMPLE 1 $\frac{x}{-2} > -7$

Answer

$\frac{x}{-2} > -7$

$(-2)\frac{x}{-2} < (-2)(-7)$ Multiply both sides by -2 and reverse the inequality sign.

$x < 14$

EXAMPLE 2 $3x > 9$

Answer

$3x > 9$

$\frac{3x}{3} > \frac{9}{3}$ Divide both sides by 3. Since 3 is positive, the inequality sign remains the same.

$x > 3$

EXAMPLE 3 $-5x \geq 25$

Answer

$-5x \geq 25$

$\frac{-5x}{-5} \leq \frac{25}{-5}$ Divide both sides by -5. Since -5 is negative, you must reverse the inequality sign to keep the statement true.

$x \leq -5$

▶ A. Exercises

Solve for the variable.

1. $\frac{x}{3} < 7$

2. $4x \geq -2$

3. $\frac{y}{-4} \leq -8$

4. $5z > 25$

5. $-7x > -14$

6. $-\frac{y}{4} > 3$

7. $-3x \leq -21$

8. $-z \geq 0$

9. $7x \geq -10$

10. $-2x < 3$

11. $-\frac{y}{8} \geq -12$

12. $\frac{y}{-9} \geq 10$

▶ B. Exercises

Solve after simplifying each side.

13. $\frac{12x}{3} < -4$

14. $6y > -10 - 8$

15. $7x \cdot 2 < -\frac{12}{3}$

16. $2 \cdot 4x < \frac{12}{2}$

17. $10k - 4k \geq 3^2$

18. $-3(x - 4x) \leq -351$

19. $2x - 7x \neq 2^0$

Solve each inequality.

20. $\frac{3x}{-4} > \frac{9}{2}$

21. $\frac{2x}{5} \leq -\frac{4}{15}$

22. $\frac{8}{5} \leq -2x$

23. $-\frac{3x}{4} < -\frac{9}{10}$

▶ C. Exercises

Solve after simplifying each side.

24. $-2(x - 3) \leq 5 - x$

25. $4 - (3x + 2) > 6 - 5x$

◾ Cumulative Review

Simplify.

26. $(5x + 3) - (2x + 7)$

27. $ax + 3a(x + 2) - a$

28. $x^2y - 5xy + xy^2 + xy + x^2y$

29. $2(3x^2 - 7) + 5x(x - 2) - 4(x + 1)$

30. $\frac{3}{56}x - \frac{7}{54}x$

5.4 Solving Inequalities

To solve an inequality, think of it as an equation and solve for the variable, making sure you reverse the inequality sign when multiplying or dividing by a negative number.

$3x < 9$ The graphic solution is shown.
$x < 3$

Van Gogh's Doctor Gachet *sold in 1990 for $82.5 million, the highest price ever paid for a painting sold at auction. Express the price* p *of an auctioned painting as an inequality.*

EXAMPLE 1	$3x + 5 > 20$	
Answer	$3x + 5 > 20$	
	$3x > 15$	1. Subtract 5 from both sides.
	$\frac{3x}{3} > \frac{15}{3}$ $x > 5$	2. Divide both sides by 3. Do not change the inequality sign because you are dividing by a positive number.
EXAMPLE 2	$-4x - 6 \le 18$	
Answer	$-4x - 6 \le 18$	
	$-4x \le 24$	1. Add 6 to both sides.
	$\frac{-4x}{-4} \ge \frac{24}{-4}$	2. When dividing by a negative number, reverse the inequality sign.
	$x \ge -6$	
EXAMPLE 3	$\frac{z}{-3} + 8 \ge 12$	
Answer	$\frac{z}{-3} + 8 \ge 12$	
	$\frac{z}{-3} \ge 4$	1. Subtract 8 from both sides..
	$-3\left(\frac{z}{-3}\right) \le -3(4)$	2. Multiply by the common denominator, -3, to clear the inequality of fractions. Reverse the inequality sign since the multiplier is negative.
	$z \le -12$	

REVERSE THE INEQUALITY SIGN WHEN
MULTIPLYING OR DIVIDING
BY A NEGATIVE!

▶ A. Exercises

Solve for the variable. Graph 1-5 on number lines.

1. $-5x + 3 \geq 13$
2. $8y - 7 > 17$
3. $\frac{z}{-2} - 4 \geq 2$
4. $4x - 6 - 6x > 10$
5. $-3y + 10 < 31$
6. $2z - 9 < 3z + 9$

7. $\frac{x}{6} + 3 \leq -5$
8. $4x + 5 \geq 9x - 2$
9. $4z - 12 < 3z - 142$
10. $-5x - 2x + 6 \geq -6x + 3$
11. $-5x - 10 > -3x - 4$
12. $\frac{2}{3}x \neq 20$

▶ B. Exercises

Solve for the variable.

13. $5(x + 6) - 2x \leq x + 4$
14. $-8x + 4x + 6 < 3x + 6$
15. $6y - 3 + 2y \geq 9y - 7$
16. $\frac{-8z}{3} + 2z - 6 \leq 3z + 2$
17. $x - 5 + 3x \neq 2x - 4$

18. $\frac{11}{8}x + \frac{5}{6} \geq -\frac{1}{4}$
19. $\frac{1}{9} - \frac{3}{30}x < \frac{4}{15}$
20. $-7(x - 1) + x > 9 - 2x$
21. $-\frac{x}{4} - 6 + x \neq 9$
22. $\frac{11}{16}x - \frac{1}{6} \leq \frac{7}{12}x + \frac{5}{8}$

▶ C. Exercises

Solve for the variable.

23. $(2x + 16) - x \neq 5 - (x + 3)$
24. $6(-2x + 4) \leq 3 - 5x + 7$
25. $3x + 3 - 5x \neq 7(2x - 3) - (6x - 4)$

■ Cumulative Review

Identify each type of number.

26. 4.367
27. -5.00
28. $\sqrt{9}$

29. 3.123112233111222333 . . .
30. 37.41414141414141 . . .

5.5 Conjunctions

$x = 4$ and $x < 6$	$x < 3$ or $x \leq -5$
$x > 2$ and $x \leq 4$	$x > -1$ or $x < 8$
$x < -3$ and $x > 7$	$x \neq 5$ or $x < 9$

These mathematical expressions are compound sentences. The three containing the word *and* are called *conjunctions.* The three containing the word *or* are called *disjunctions,* which will be covered in the next section.

Double Arch is one of 2000 arches at Arches National Park, Utah. The park classifies openings with a span of at least 3 feet as an arch. The longest arch in the park is Landscape Arch, 306 feet long. Write a compound inequality for arch spans in the park.

Definition

A **conjunction** is a compound sentence in which the mathematical statements are connected by the word *and,* meaning intersection, and symbolized by $\wedge$.

The solution set to a conjunction is the intersection of the solutions to the separate equations and inequalities in the compound statement. If the intersection is $\varnothing$, then there are no solutions. When you solve conjunctions, graph each separate sentence above the number line and then graph the intersection of the graphs on the number line.

EXAMPLE 1 Solve $x > 2$ and $x \leq 4$.

Answer $x > 2 \wedge x \leq 4$

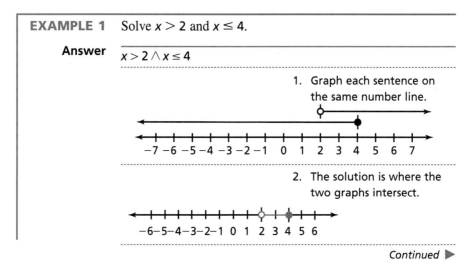

1. Graph each sentence on the same number line.

2. The solution is where the two graphs intersect.

Continued ▶

	Choose any number in the solution and substitute it in both statements.	3. Numbers between 2 and 4 including 4 are solutions. This includes 2.1, 3, and $3\frac{1}{2}$. Write the solution as shown.

$$2 < x \le 4$$

Check.	Using $x = 3$, you get $3 > 2$ and $3 \le 4$.	4. Both original statements are true; therefore, the conjunction is true.

EXAMPLE 2   Solve $x = 4$ and $x < 6$.

Answer $x = 4 \wedge x < 6$

1. Graph $x = 4$ on a number line.

2. Graph $x < 6$ on the same number line.

$x = 4$

3. Write the solution by finding where the two graphs overlap. The two graphs intersect only at 4.

EXAMPLE 3   Solve $x < -3$ and $x > 7$.

Answer

1. Graph both inequalities.

$\varnothing$

2. Since the graphs do not overlap, write the solution as the empty set.

EXAMPLE 4   Solve $x \le 5$ and $x < 0$.

Answer $x \le 5 \wedge x < 0$

$x < 0$

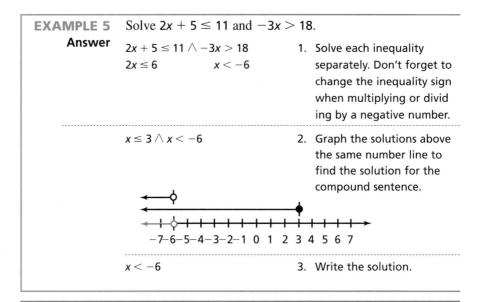

EXAMPLE 5   Solve $2x + 5 \leq 11$ and $-3x > 18$.

Answer

$2x + 5 \leq 11 \wedge -3x > 18$ 1. Solve each inequality
$2x \leq 6$ $x < -6$ separately. Don't forget to
                                          change the inequality sign
                                          when multiplying or divid
                                          ing by a negative number.

$x \leq 3 \wedge x < -6$ 2. Graph the solutions above
                                          the same number line to
                                          find the solution for the
                                          compound sentence.

$x < -6$ 3. Write the solution.

Solving Conjunctions

1. Solve each statement in the compound sentence.
2. Graph both solutions above the same number line.
3. The solution to the conjunction is the intersection of the two graphs.

▶ A. Exercises

Solve.

1. $x > 4$ and $x \geq 2$
2. $x \leq 3$ and $x < 6$
3. $2x > -6$ and $x \leq 1$
4. $x \geq 5$ and $4x < 32$
5. $8x - 12 > 4$ and $2x \geq 14$
6. $x - 3 \leq 4x$ and $2x + 6 < 18$
7. $-5x + 13 > -7$ and $4x - 6 \leq 10$

8. $5x + 3 < 28$ and $6x < 12$
9. $4x - 2 - 5x > 10$ and $3x - 6 \leq 12$
10. $2x - 7 \geq 5$ and $-7x < -49$
11. $x > 3$ and $x \geq 5$
12. $x < 3$ and $x \geq 5$
13. $x < 3$ and $x \leq 5$
14. $x > 3$ and $x \leq 5$

▶ B. Exercises

Solve.

15. $9x + 2 < -7$ and $-2x - 8 \leq 12$
16. $x \neq -3$ and $x = -3$
17. $4x \geq 8$ and $x + 6 \leq 8$
18. $4x + 6 \leq 26$ and $3x \neq 12$
19. $3x + 4 - 2x \leq 12$ and $2x + 6 \neq 8$
20. $8x - 14 + x - 6 \leq 7$ and $x - 16 \geq 0$

► C. Exercises

Solve.

21. $\frac{2x}{3} - 1 < 10$ and $\frac{4x}{5} + 2 > 6$

22. $3(x - 5) + 7 \leq 4 + x - 20$ and $x - 3(x + 1) \leq 5$

■ Cumulative Review

Simplify.

23. $\frac{175}{36} \cdot \frac{45}{140}$

24. $\frac{175}{36} \div \frac{45}{140}$

25. $\frac{175}{36} + \frac{45}{140}$

26. $(2x^3)(3x^2y)$

27. $(5^{-1}x^2)^{-3}$

5.6 Disjunctions

Definition

A **disjunction** is a compound sentence consisting of mathematical statements connected by the word *or,* meaning union, and symbolized by $\vee$.

As stated in Chapter 1, the union of two sets is the set of elements contained in either set, or a combination of the two sets. To solve a disjunction, graph both statements above a number line and find the union of the two sets. Everything shaded will be the solution to the disjunction since a shaded portion will be a solution to one sentence or the other.

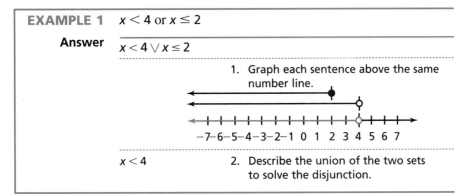

| **EXAMPLE 1** | $x < 4$ or $x \leq 2$ |

Answer $\quad x < 4 \vee x \leq 2$

1. Graph each sentence above the same number line.

$-7\ -6\ -5\ -4\ -3\ -2\ -1\ \ 0\ \ 1\ \ 2\ \ 3\ \ 4\ \ 5\ \ 6\ \ 7$

$x < 4$

2. Describe the union of the two sets to solve the disjunction.

EXAMPLE 2 $x < -4$ or $x > -1$

Answer $x < -4 \lor x > -1$

1. Graph both inequalities.

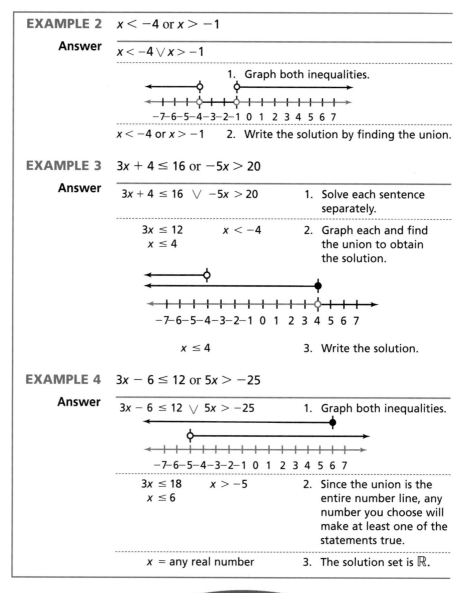

$x < -4$ or $x > -1$ 2. Write the solution by finding the union.

EXAMPLE 3 $3x + 4 \leq 16$ or $-5x > 20$

Answer

$3x + 4 \leq 16 \quad \lor \quad -5x > 20$		1. Solve each sentence separately.
$3x \leq 12 \qquad x < -4$		2. Graph each and find the union to obtain the solution.
$x \leq 4$		

$x \leq 4$ 3. Write the solution.

EXAMPLE 4 $3x - 6 \leq 12$ or $5x > -25$

Answer

$3x - 6 \leq 12 \lor 5x > -25$ 1. Graph both inequalities.

$3x \leq 18 \qquad x > -5$
$x \leq 6$

2. Since the union is the entire number line, any number you choose will make at least one of the statements true.

x = any real number   3. The solution set is $\mathbb{R}$.

REMEMBER THAT X≠5 MEANS
X>5 or X<5

Solving Disjunctions

1. Solve each statement of the disjunction separately.
2. Graph both solutions above the same number line.
3. The solution to the disjunction is the union of the two graphs.

▶ A. Exercises

Solve.

1. $x < 2$ or $x > 5$
2. $x < 2$ or $x < 5$
3. $x > 2$ or $x > 5$
4. $x > 2$ or $x < 5$

5. $x < -4$ or $x > -4$
6. $x < -3$ or $x \leq -2$
7. $x < 5$ or $x \geq 2$
8. $x \leq -1$ or $x > 4$

▶ B. Exercises

Solve.

9. $x \neq 6$ or $x \neq 3$
10. $2x + 5 > 17$ or $x + 2 \leq 8$
11. $x - 6 \leq -6$ or $3x - 5 > 10$
12. $3x + 5 > 2x$ or $6x - 3x + 4 \geq 16$

13. $2x - 6 \geq 14$ or $8x + 2x - 3 > 27$
14. $x - 7 > 0$ or $2x + 16 \leq 2$
15. $3x + 6 \leq -9$ or $x < 6$
16. $2x - 7 > -21$ or $4x + 6 \neq 22$

▶ C. Exercises

Solve.

17. $5x - 1 < 1$ or $3x - 2 \neq 5$
18. $\frac{5}{7}x + \frac{1}{2} < 2$ or $\frac{3}{4}x - \frac{1}{5} \leq \frac{1}{10}$

19. $3x < 4$ or $x > \sqrt{2}$
20. $3x + 1 \geq 6$ or $9(4 - x) \leq 15$

▪ Cumulative Review

21. Graph $x = \frac{5}{3}$ on a number line.
22. Solve and graph $|x| = \frac{7}{3}$.

Solve.

23. $|3x + 1| = 4$
24. $|3x + 1| = 0$

25. $|3x + 1| = -2$

5 Probability and Statistics

Addition Principle of Counting

Disjunction is as important in probability as it is in solving inequalities. You can recognize disjunctions in probability problems by the word *or.*

EXAMPLE 1 Suppose that three roads link Fargo and Rapid City. If two air routes connect them, how many ways can you drive or fly from Fargo to Rapid City?

Answer Since you can drive three ways or fly two ways, there are five routes that you can travel.

> ### Addition Principle of Counting
>
> If *A* can occur in *a* ways and *B* can occur in *b* ways, then either *A* or *B* can occur in $a + b$ ways.

The rule becomes useful when *A* and *B* occur in many ways. It's easy to count the five routes in example 1 on the diagram, but with large numbers the rule enables you to add instead of counting one by one.

EXAMPLE 2 If **788** people saw the school play the first night, and **657** people saw the school play the second night, how many people saw the play (the first night *or* the second night)? Assume that nobody saw the play twice.

Answer Add the attendance of the two nights: $788 + 657 = 1445$ people.

What if the play was performed three nights? You can see that you would add all three attendance figures.

You can use this counting principle to calculate probabilities.

EXAMPLE 3	What is the probability that a randomly selected two-letter abbreviation will begin with either *K* or a vowel?
Answer	Of **676** possible two-letter abbreviations (see Chapter 4), $1 \cdot 26 = 26$ begin with the letter *K* and $5 \cdot 26 = 130$ begin with a vowel. Since $26 + 130 = 156$, we know that **156** of the two-letter abbreviations begin either with *K* or a vowel. The desired probability, then, is $P = \frac{156}{676} = 0.23$.

▶ Exercises

1. Pete needs to go to Seneca, Kansas, from Tampa, Florida. The major airports near Seneca are at Topeka, Kansas, and Lincoln, Nebraska. Pete learns that 7 flights are scheduled from Tampa to Lincoln and 4 to Topeka. How many ways can he fly to either Topeka or Lincoln and then drive to Seneca?

2. Jane has 79 American-made dolls and 34 imported dolls. How many dolls does she have all together?

Ken has 423 football cards, 59 hockey cards, 382 baseball cards, and 167 basketball cards.

3. How many sports cards does he have?

4. If Ken selects one card at random, what is the probability that it will be either a hockey card or a basketball card?

5. During softball season Kathy had 15 hits, walked 12 times, and did not get on base 19 times. How many times did she come to bat?

RENÉ DESCARTES

René Descartes, a frail child, was born on March 31, 1596, in La Haye, France. His mother, Jeanne Brochard, died while René was just a baby. René's father felt a keen sense of responsibility for his children after the death of their mother and provided the best care possible for them. He hired a well-qualified nurse to tend to the children. As René grew older, he spent some time with each of his grandmothers. Throughout his childhood René was inquisitive, constantly asking why things are true.

Because of René's delicate health, his father did not make him study normal school lessons but let him study whatever and whenever he wanted until he was eight. His father then searched out the best school for his young son to begin his formal education. He chose the Jesuit school at La Flèche. The schoolmaster took special interest in René and helped him along through school. He finished his work at the school at age 16.

Descartes's family was well-to-do, and they provided him with a comfortable income for his entire life. Therefore, he never had to worry about making a living. He spent some of his young adulthood studying and then decided to see the world. He partially accomplished this goal by spending several tours on duty as a soldier. In 1621 he had had enough excitement as a soldier and decided to do some traveling and thinking.

One result of his meditations during this time was his resolve never to take anything on authority but to make everything pass through a thorough, methodical examination before accepting it as truth. The concise systematic

$$ax^2 + bx + c = 0$$

proof used in geometry intrigued Descartes, and he attempted to apply mathematical reasoning to all forms of science.

Because of its logical-reasoning quality, mathematics appealed to Descartes. He is probably most famous for his development of the Cartesian plane and a method of locating points in the plane. This discovery led to the development of analytic geometry, which is the study of equations and their visual representations on a Cartesian plane. He also developed an analytic method for the study of loci and formed the "rule of signs," a method for determining the number of positive and negative solutions to a polynomial equation.

Descartes wrote mathematical papers and books but was afraid to publish them because he feared that the Catholic church would declare them heretical. He had seen how the church reacted to Galileo's discoveries, and he thought it not worth the trouble to publish his works. He often compared the laws of nature with the laws of mathematics and was convinced that there was a connection between these laws. In 1637 Descartes's friends convinced him to publish his masterpiece on mathematics and on June 8, 1637, *Discourse on the Method of Reasoning Well and Seeking Truth in the Sciences* was published. This work, often abbreviated to *Method*, exposed analytic geometry to the world.

Descartes spent the rest of his life studying mathematics and tutoring children of royalty in Holland and Sweden. René Descartes died on February 11, 1650, at the age of 54.

He often compared the laws of nature with the laws of mathematics and was convinced that there was a connection between these laws.

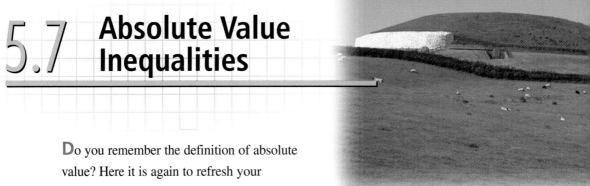

5.7 Absolute Value Inequalities

Newgrange in Ireland dates from 3200 B.C. Its age is $\left|-3200\right| + \left|2000\right| = 5200$ years old.

Do you remember the definition of absolute value? Here it is again to refresh your memory.

$$\left|x\right| = \begin{cases} x, \text{ if } x \geq 0 \\ -x, \text{ if } x < 0 \end{cases}$$

Remember that $\left|4\right| = 4$ and $\left|-4\right| = -(-4) = 4$. You have learned how to solve absolute value equations. Now you will learn how to solve absolute value inequalities. Here is a simple example to get you started.

EXAMPLE 1   Solve $\left|x\right| < 3$.

Answer

What values will make this inequality true?

5?	$\left|5\right| < 3$	no
2?	$\left|2\right| < 3$	yes
0?	$\left|0\right| < 3$	yes
−2?	$\left|-2\right| < 3$	yes
−5?	$\left|-5\right| < 3$	no

Here is the solution on a number line.

$$\leftarrow \!\!\!+\!\!-\!\!\!\diamond\!\!-\!\!+\!\!-\!\!+\!\!-\!\!+\!\!-\!\!+\!\!-\!\!+\!\!-\!\!\diamond\!\!-\!\!+\!\!\rightarrow$$
$$-4\,-3\,-2\,-1\ \ 0\ \ 1\ \ 2\ \ 3\ \ 4$$

It is written as the conjunction $x < 3$ and $x > -3$. Combine these by writing $-3 < x < 3$.

We can solve absolute value inequalities such as example 1 algebraically. In the problem $\left|x\right| < 3$, two possible situations can occur according to the definition of absolute value.

---

1. If $x \geq 0$, then by definition $\left|x\right| = x$. Since $\left|x\right| < 3$, $x < 3$.

2. If $x < 0$, then by definition $\left|x\right| = -x$. Since $\left|x\right| < 3$, $-x < 3$ and $x > -3$.

Remember that absolute value is the distance from zero and that $|x| < 3$ indicates that x is within 3 units of zero ($-3 < x < 3$).

EXAMPLE 2   Solve $|x| < 5$.

Answer

$x < 5$ and $x > -5$	1. Since the inequality sign is $<$, use conjunction.
$-5 < x < 5$	2. Write the compound solution.

So far the solutions have been conjunctions. Whenever the sign in an absolute value inequality is $<$, you can expect the solution to be a conjunction.

If the sign is $>$, what type of compound sentence do you suppose the answer will be?

EXAMPLE 3   Solve $|x| > 1$.

Answer

What values will make this inequality true?

0?	$|0| > 1$	no
4?	$|4| > 1$	yes
-3?	$|-3| > 1$	yes

1. Graph the inequality.

$x < -1$ or $x > 1$ 2. Write the solution.

Remember that absolute value is the distance from zero and that $|x| > 1$ indicates that x is more than one unit from zero and we write $x < -1$ or $x > 1$.

How does the definition of absolute value apply to this example? According to the definition, two possible situations can occur.

1. If $x < 0$, then by definition $|x| = -x$.
   $|x| > 1$
   $-x > 1$
   $x < -1$

2. If $x \geq 0$, then by definition $|x| = x$.
   $|x| > 1$
   $x > 1$

The solution is $x < -1$ or $x > 1$. You cannot combine the inequalities into a single inequality.

EXAMPLE 4   Solve $|x| > 6$.

Answer

$x < -6 \lor x > 6$ 1. Since the symbol is $>$, the solution will be a disjunction. Write the two inequalities.

2. Graph both inequalities.

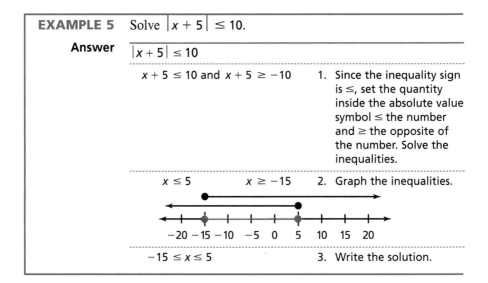

$$-7\,-6\,-5\,-4\,-3\,-2\,-1\;\;0\;\;1\;\;2\;\;3\;\;4\;\;5\;\;6\;\;7$$

$x < -6$ or $x > 6$ 3. Write the solution.

COMPARISON OF THE TWO TYPES OF ABSOLUTE VALUE INEQUALITIES

Name	conjunction	disjunction
Expression x, constant c	$|x| < c$	$|x| > c$
Means	x is less than c units from zero (close to zero)	x is more than c units from zero (far from zero)
Graph		
Solution	$-c < x < c$	$x < -c$ or $x > c$
Description requires	"and" to express between $-c$ and c	"or" to express smaller than the opposite of c or larger than c (not at the same time)
Symbol	$\land$	$\lor$

Sometimes the expression within the absolute value symbols is not just x but can be an algebraic expression such as $x + 5$.

EXAMPLE 5   Solve $|x + 5| \le 10$.

Answer

$|x + 5| \le 10$

$x + 5 \le 10$ and $x + 5 \ge -10$ 1. Since the inequality sign is $\le$, set the quantity inside the absolute value symbol $\le$ the number and $\ge$ the opposite of the number. Solve the inequalities.

$x \le 5$ $x \ge -15$ 2. Graph the inequalities.

$$-20\,-15\,-10\;\;-5\;\;0\;\;5\;\;10\;\;15\;\;20$$

$-15 \le x \le 5$ 3. Write the solution.

EXAMPLE 6 Solve $\left| -3x + 6 \right| > 18$.

Answer Since the symbol is $>$, set the quantity $<$ the opposite of the number and set the quantity $>$ the number. Solve the inequalities and find their union.

$$\left| -3x + 6 \right| > 18$$

$-3x + 6 < -18$	$-3x + 6 > 18$
$-3x < -24$	$-3x > 12$
$x > 8$	$x < -4$
$x < -4$ or	$x > 8$

▶ A. Exercises

Solve each inequality for x.

1. $\left| x \right| < 3$
2. $\left| x \right| \geq 10$
3. $\left| x \right| \leq 5$
4. $\left| x \right| > 7$

5. $\left| 2x \right| > 16$
6. $\left| x - 3 \right| < 10$
7. $\left| x + 6 \right| \geq 5$
8. $\left| x + 4 \right| \leq 2$

▶ B. Exercises

Solve for x.

9. $\left| 2x + 6 \right| \geq 14$
10. $\left| 3x - 10 \right| < 9$
11. $\left| 4x + 17 \right| > 7$
12. $\left| \frac{2x}{3} - 7 \right| \leq 4$
13. $\left| \frac{5x}{9} + 6 \right| > 5$
14. $\left| 2x - 8 \right| < 10$

15. $\left| 4x - 7 \right| \geq 29$
16. $\left| -4x - 8 \right| > 4$
17. $\left| 3x + 2 \right| \leq 6$
18. $\left| 7x + 9 - 6x \right| > 8$
19. $\left| 2x - 6 + 5x \right| < 10$
20. $\left| 4x - 6 \right| < 24$

▶ C. Exercises

Use your knowledge of absolute value to solve these inequalities.

21. $\left| x + 7 \right| \leq 0$
22. $\left| 4x - 5 \right| < 0$
23. $\left| 3x - 1 \right| > 0$

24. $\left| 5x - 3 \right| \geq -2$
25. $\left| 2x - 8 \right| \leq -1$

Translate each phrase.

26. The sum of five and three times a number
27. The distance traveled in *t* hours at 10 mph
28. The value in dollars of *x* nickels and *y* quarters
29. The perimeter of a rectangle that is *x* meters wide and 50 meters long

Translate each sentence; do not solve.

30. The sum of 2 consecutive integers is seventeen.
31. The square of Jim's age is twice the age that he will be four years from now.

Solve the word problem.

32. Eight less than twice a number is twelve. Find the number.

5.8 Word Problems Using Inequalities

When God repeats something, you should take notice, for God does not repeat His promises or warnings without a purpose. For example, salvation through the blood of Jesus Christ, the primary theme of the Bible, is repeated from Genesis to Revelation. Read Ephesians 1:7. God wants everyone to be saved (cf. I Tim. 2:4). He reviews the plan of salvation often so that man will be without excuse.

You will also need to review the steps that you have learned for solving word problems. You can apply the same steps to word problems involving inequalities.

1. **Read** the problem carefully, looking for important words.
   a. Whenever possible make a drawing.
   b. Identify the unknowns and assign variables.
2. **Plan.**
   a. Write down any relevant formulas.
   b. Make a table (if possible).
3. **Solve.**
   a. Write an inequality from two related expressions.
   b. Solve the inequality.

Important words	Meanings
is greater than	$>$
is less than	$<$
is at least	$\geq$
is at most	$\leq$

4. Check.

   a. Answer all questions and interpret each answer in the context of the problem.

   b. Be sure each answer is reasonable.

EXAMPLE 1   How much money must be invested at 7% a year to produce a yearly income of at least $875?

Answer   **1. Read** the problem carefully, noting the phrase "at least."

   2. Plan. Write the formula $Prt = I$. You can make a table or substitute into the formula. Let $x =$ the amount invested.

P	r	t	=	I
x	0.07	1		0.07x

   3. Solve. Since "at least" means $\geq$, the product of the principal P, the rate r, and the time t must be larger than or equal to the interest produced. By substitution you get the inequality $x(0.07)(1) \geq 875$.

$$0.07x \geq 875$$
$$7x \geq 87{,}500$$
$$x \geq 12{,}500$$

   4. Check. Is $\$12{,}500(0.07)(1) \geq \$875$?
   Since $\$12{,}500$ at 7% produces exactly $\$875$, any amount larger than 12,500 will produce a larger amount that will also satisfy the inequality. The answer is reasonable.

EXAMPLE 2   The difference between a number and 25 is less than 82. What could the number be?

Answer

Let $x =$ the number	1. Read. Define the variable.
$x - 25 < 82$	2. Plan. Translate the phrase "difference between a number and 25."
$x < 107$	3. Write and solve the inequality.
Thus, the number can be any number less than 107.	4. Check. Interpret and evaluate the answer.

▶ A. Exercises

1. The sum of two numbers is more than 20, and one number is 4 more than the other number. What are the numbers?

2. A certain number times 23 and added to 15 is greater than 429. What is the number?

3. Find the least positive integer such that 4 more than 7 times the number is greater than 95.

4. Find the largest integer such that 8 more than 6 times the integer is less than −42.

5. Pam wants to buy three times as many cans of green beans, which cost 62¢ per can, as cans of peas, which cost 69¢ per can. If she has no more than $10.00 to spend, what is the maximum number of cans of peas she can buy?

6. The president of the First National Bank is responsible for making wise investments of the bank's funds. He made some investments from which the bank will earn $2.3 million. If he can buy some municipal bonds that yield 8% interest annually, how much money must he invest so that the total interest income for the bank will be at least $2,500,000?

7. For Mr. Rogers to pay his monthly bills he must make at least $1675 each month. He sells cars and makes a guaranteed salary of $850 per month plus $225 commission on each car he sells. What is the least number of cars he must sell each month to meet his monthly obligations?

▶ B. Exercises

8. The sum of two numbers is at most eleven, and their difference is twenty-one. What are the numbers?

9. Paul Bermudez earns twice as much per week as his sister Naomi. If she makes $30 per week more than her brother John and the sum of their salaries is at most $330, what range can their salaries take each week?

10. Each ounce of whole milk contains twice as many calories as an ounce of skim milk. A mixture of 4 ounces of whole milk and 2 ounces of skim milk contains at least 100 calories. What is the minimum number of calories in each ounce of whole and skim milk?

11. Chris is shopping and has $100 cash. She refuses to use a credit card today. She finds a dress costing $66.95 and a pair of earrings costing $15.75. There is also a 5% sales tax to add to the total. How much more can she spend and stay within the limits of her cash?

12. John wants to enclose a garden. He has up to 60 feet of fencing available. If the width must be five more than half the length, what are the possible dimensions?

13. Jeff bikes for three hours and his brother bikes four hours. Although Jeff bikes 15 mph faster, his total distance was at most twice as far as his brother's. How fast does each ride?

C. Exercises

14. Water from the Dead Sea is eight times saltier than the ocean. Fifty gallons of Dead Sea water and 100 gallons of ocean water together contain at least 20 gallons of salt. What is the percentage of salt in each water source?

15. Mr. Stevens invests $2500 between two accounts. One account earns 5% interest, the other 8%. Since he cannot afford the early-withdrawal penalty in the 8% account, he wants to invest as much as possible at 5%. How much should he invest in each account if he wants to earn at least $150 this year in interest?

Write a compound inequality describing land elevation. Hint: *The lowest point on earth is the shore of the Dead Sea.*

■ Cumulative Review

Solve.

16. $x + 8 = 0$

17. $3x + 2 = 17$

18. $\frac{4}{5} + \frac{x}{3} = 2$

19. $8x - 10 = 9x + 4$

20. $2x + 6 - 5x = 3(2x - 7)$

21. $|4x + 7| = 5$

Solve and graph.

22. $3x - 2 > 4$

23. $|x| \leq 5$

24. $x + 3 < -4$ or $\frac{1}{2}x > -1$

25. $-\frac{3}{8}x + 4 \geq \frac{1}{12}$

Algebra *and* Scripture

We already know that math is orderly and builds upon previous principles. This means that each new concept provides opportunity for review of old ones. Inequalities cannot be understood without a clear understanding of equalities. This applies both to solving them and using them to solve word problems.

Why is it important to review things we have learned as we begin a new topic? Answering questions about a new topic will require that we correctly apply what we already know in the new context. In the same way, you must review Scripture before you attempt to defend your faith.

1. How often should we review Scripture and be ready to defend our faith (I Pet. 3:15)?

THE NTH DEGREE

Find 4 verses in II Peter that show that Peter desired to help his readers remember the principles of salvation.

Explain from each passage how God wants us to build upon our Bible knowledge.

2. I Peter 2:2
3. Hebrews 5:12-14
4. Isaiah 28:9-13

In particular, this chapter developed concepts of inequalities. Identify the use of inequalities for general comparisons in the verses below.

5. Mark 4:31
6. I John 4:4

However, you may not have realized that there are also specific numerical inequalities in the Bible. Examine each of these. What is being compared?

7. Exodus 16:16-17
8. Exodus 30:15
9. Judges 16:30

Judges 16:30, then, is perhaps the clearest statement of a numerical inequality in Scripture.

Scriptural Roots

AND SAMSON SAID, Let me die with the Philistines. And he bowed himself with all his might; and the house fell upon the lords, and upon all the people that were therein. So the dead which he slew at his death were more than they which he slew in his life.

JUDGES 16:30

Chapter 5 Review

Graph each inequality on a separate number line.

1. $x \le 10$
2. $y > 4$
3. $a \ne 7$
4. $c < 0$
5. $t \ge 3$

Solve each inequality and graph the solution.

6. $x + 3 \ge 5$
7. $y - 9 < -6$
8. $3x \le 18$
9. $\frac{x}{5} > 2$
10. $-6x < -30$
11. $4x - 7 > 5$
12. $2y + 3 \ne 5$
13. $7 - 3a \ge 21$
14. $\frac{2b}{7} + 1 > 3$
15. $\frac{t}{-3} > 2$

Solve each compound sentence and graph the solution.

16. $x > 2$ and $x \le 5$
17. $y < -3$ or $y > 2$
18. $5x \ge 10$ and $3 + x \le 8$
19. $2x + 7 < 9$ and $-3x \le 6$
20. $12x - 6 \ge 6 \lor x < 5$

Solve each compound inequality.

21. $x > 3$ and $x > 5$
22. $x > -3$ or $x > -2$
23. $x \ge 2$ and $x \le 2$
24. $x \ge -2$ and $x < -4$
25. $-3x + 1 \ne 3 \land 4x + 12 \ge 6$

Solve for the variable.

26. $|x| > 5$
27. $|x - 6| \le 8$
28. $|6x| \ge 45$
29. $|3x - 7| > 11$
30. $\left|\frac{2x}{5} - 4\right| < 9$

Translate each phrase into symbols.

31. Negative two is less than negative 1.
32. A certain number is greater than 5.
33. The square of a number is at least zero.
34. The reciprocal of a natural number is at most 1.
35. The perimeter of a square is no more than 3, using x as the length of a side.

Interpret each absolute value sentence in exercise 36 and 37 as a distance statement.

36. $|x| < 2$
37. $|x| \geq 3$
38. The product of 7 and a number is more than the sum of 7 and the number. What is the number? What is the smallest integer that could be a solution for the number?
39. Bill has scores of 95, 78, and 93 on his English exams. If he wants to get an A on his report card, he must have an average of at least 90. What is the lowest score he can get on his next exam and still have an A?
40. Explain the mathematical significance of Judges 16:30.

6 Relations, Functions, and Graphs

Mr. Johnson took a summer trip to excavate Ciudad Perdida, a lost Tayrona city in the Sierra de Santa Martha of Colombia, South America, as part of an archeological team. Mark was one of five students who accompanied him. The students obtained parental permission and then raised funds for travel and lodging.

Mark learned that preparing the excavation site for digging was very similar to graphing, which he had recently studied in algebra. A reference point, called the datum point, is first selected and marked with a white x in a circle. All other measurements are made from this point. The archeologist then marks off the dig area with a grid of parallel lines, which run both north and south and east and west. The intervals between the lines vary from two to twenty feet. The archeologists then mark the site by driving stakes at the intersection of the lines and stretching tape tautly along each grid line.

The marking enables digging areas to be identified easily. When Mr. Johnson directs Mark to dig in area 3E/2N, Mark knows exactly where to work. The section of grid is identified by the intersection stake at the square's southwest corner. Mark soon unearthed several pieces of pottery and reported his find to Mr. Johnson. Mr. Johnson recorded the location of each find on a piece of graph paper.

After this chapter you should be able to

1. give examples of relations and functions in set form, table form, or circle mapping.

2. define and calculate the slope of a line.

3. graph linear equations and linear inequalities.

4. write equations of lines in standard form or slope-intercept form, given certain information.

5. solve direct variation problems.

6.1 Coordinates in a Plane

Sometimes when you try to find a certain town on a map, you first have to look at the index to find in what general region the town is located. Look at the map shown and find the towns indicated in the index.

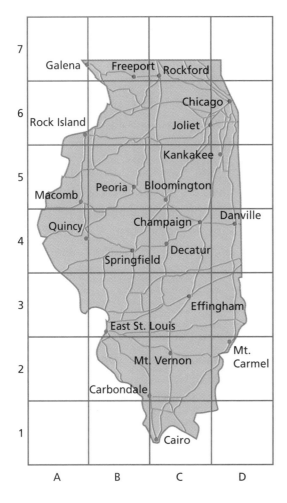

The state capitol in Springfield, Illinois

Index

Bloomington	C-5
Cairo	C-1
Carbondale	B-2
Champaign	C-4
Chicago	D-6
Danville	D-4

On this map a letter and a number indicate a region where you would find these cities. The letter shows the horizontal position and the number the vertical position. In the index, the symbols that represent the location of the towns are actually ordered pairs.

Definition

An **ordered pair** is a pair of symbols for which the order is important.

The two symbols in an ordered pair are called *coordinates.* For each city the first coordinate is a letter from *A* to *D*. The second coordinate is a number from 1 to 7.

All possible locations in Illinois can be represented by ordered pairs. The set of all possible ordered pairs is known as the Cartesian product. The *Cartesian product* is the set of all ordered pairs produced by pairing the elements of set *S*, the set of letters, and set *T*, the set of numbers, such that the first coordinate of the ordered pair is an element of *S* and the second coordinate is an element of *T*.

$$S = \{A, B, C, D\}$$
$$T = \{1, 2, 3, 4, 5, 6, 7\}$$

Thus, the Cartesian product of these two sets, called *S* cross *T*, indicated by $S \times T$, would be this.

$$S \times T = \{(A, 1), (A, 2), (A, 3), (A, 4), (A, 5), (A, 6), (A, 7), (B, 1), (B, 2),$$
$$(B, 3), (B, 4), (B, 5), (B, 6), (B, 7), (C, 1), (C, 2), (C, 3), (C, 4), (C, 5),$$
$$(C, 6), (C, 7), (D, 1), (D, 2), (D, 3), (D, 4), (D, 5), (D, 6), (D, 7)\}$$

The locations in this set represent regions, not points.

In this chapter you will be working with a special Cartesian product described by $\mathbb{R} \times \mathbb{R}$, which simply means the set of all ordered pairs formed when the first coordinate is an element of $\mathbb{R}$ (the set of real numbers) and the second coordinate is also an element of $\mathbb{R}$. In algebra the plane represents $\mathbb{R} \times \mathbb{R}$.

Note that this infinite set of ordered pairs represents every point in the plane, not regions as in the map example. It is called the *Cartesian plane* for its inventor, René Descartes. He was the first to see the connection between lines in a plane and algebraic equations.

Two perpendicular lines (one horizontal, the other vertical) divide the plane into four sections called *quadrants,* which are numbered counterclockwise with roman numerals. See the illustration below.

The **x-axis** is the horizontal reference line in a plane.

The **y-axis** is the vertical reference line in a plane.

The **origin** is the point at which the axes cross.

The *x*-axis is a horizontal number line: positive is right, negative left. The *y*-axis is a vertical number line: positive is up, negative down. The origin is labeled *O*. The process of locating points in a plane is called plotting points or graphing ordered pairs.

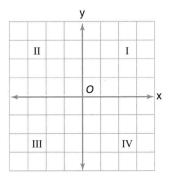

On the map of Illinois (page 218), the horizontal distance was given first and the vertical distance second. In the Cartesian plane the horizontal distance (*x*) always comes first and the vertical distance (*y*) second. The order of the coordinates in an ordered pair is very important.

An ordered pair with unknown coordinates is usually expressed (*x, y*).

Definitions

The **x-coordinate** (abscissa) is the first coordinate of an ordered pair.

The **y-coordinate** (ordinate) is the second coordinate of an ordered pair.

EXAMPLE 1 Graph the ordered pair (2, 1).

Answer 1. Locate the origin.
2. Move right two units (*x*).
3. Move up one unit (*y*).
4. Place a dot at this point.
5. Label the point (2, 1). It is in the first quadrant.

EXAMPLE 2   Graph the ordered pair $(-3, 4)$.

Answer   1. Locate the origin.
2. Move left three units (x).
3. Move up four units (y).
4. Place a dot at this point.
5. Label the point $(-3, 4)$. It
is in the second quadrant.

EXAMPLE 3   Graph the ordered pair $(0, -7)$.

Answer   1. Locate the origin.
2. Since the x-coordinate is 0,
do not move left or right.
3. Move down seven units (y).
4. Place a dot at this point.
5. Label the point $(0, -7)$.
This is on the y-axis.

Plotting Points (x, y)

1. Locate the origin.
2. Move horizontally x units.
3. Move vertically y units from the position found in step 2.
4. Place a dot at the position.
5. Label the point.

EXAMPLE 4   State the coordinates of point A.

Answer   1. Locate the origin.
2. Move right until you are
above point A.
3. Write the x-coordinate (4).
4. Move down to point A.
5. Write the y-coordinate (-3)
6. Write the coordinates as the ordered
pair $(4, -3)$. This point is in the
fourth quadrant.

▶ A. Exercises

Refer to the map of Illinois on the first page of this section.
1. Give the city having the location (index reference) B-4.
2. Give the location of Rock Island.

State the coordinates of each point.
3. A
4. B
5. C
6. D
7. E
8. F
9. G
10. H
11. I
12. J

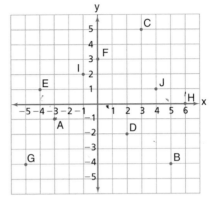

On graph paper draw a set of axes and label them. Then plot the following points and label them.

13. (2, 4)
14. (−2, −5)
15. (5, −4)
16. (−1, 3)
17. (3, 8)
18. (2, −9)
19. (−2, −6)
20. (−4, 1)
21. (0, −4)
22. (−6, 0)

▶ B. Exercises

23. What are the coordinates of the origin?

Give the quadrant or axis of the point described.

24. (−3, 5)
25. (0, 1)
26. (2, −7)
27. (−5, 0)
28. (−1, −11)
29. Both coordinates are positive.
30. Both coordinates are negative.

31. The abscissa is positive and the ordinate is negative.
32. What is true about all the points that have 5 for an ordinate (*y*-coordinate)?

▶ C. Exercises

Let *A* = {*a*, *b*, *c*} and *B* = {0, 1}.
33. Find *A* × *B* and *B* × *A*.
34. Is finding a cross product of two sets a commutative operation? Explain.

Simplify.

35. $-n + n$

36. $(3x^2 + 5x + 4) - 4(2x^2 + x + 1)$

37. $7x + 2y - 3x + 11y + 3(x - y)$

38. $2x + 3x^0 - 5x + 4 - x + (2x)^0$

39. $2ab - 3a^2b + 4ab - 2ab^2 - 11ab$

6.2 Relations and Functions

Do you know what a relation is? Look up the word *relation* in a dictionary and read the definitions. How many relatives do you have? What other relations do you have with people? If you are a Christian, you are related to all

This couple and their boy and girl illustrate several family relationships.

other Christians through salvation in the blood of Jesus Christ. The New Testament commands Christians to love and care for their spiritual brothers. Which of your Christian relations have you prayed for today?

In mathematics, a *relation* is also an association between two or more things. Specifically applied, a relation is any set of ordered pairs.

Definition

A **relation** is any set of ordered pairs.

A common relation that exists is the relation in a grocery store between prices and items. If $A = \{x \mid x$ is all the prices in the store$\}$, and $B = \{y \mid y$ is all the different items in the store$\}$, a relation exists between A and B. The symbolism $\{x \mid x$ is . . . $\}$ means "the set of all x such that x is . . ." The table shows some of the ordered pairs for this relation.

x	y
79¢	gum
89¢	apple
79¢	yogurt

Here is a relation given in three different forms: (1) as a set of ordered pairs, (2) as a table, and (3) as a graph. A graph of a relation is the set of points in the plane that corresponds to the ordered pairs of the relation.

1. $\{(-3, 5), (2, 2), (2, 4), (4, -1)\}$

2.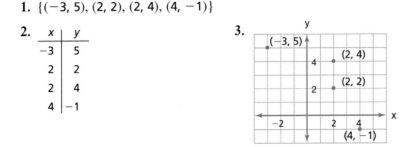

3.

The set of first elements (*x*-coordinates) of the ordered pairs is called the *domain* of the relation. The second set of elements (*y*-coordinates) is called the *range*.

EXAMPLE 1   Find the domain and range of the relation shown above $\{(-3, 5), (2, 2), (2, 4), (4, -1)\}$.

Answer   The domain is $\{-3, 2, 4\}$, and the range is $\{-1, 2, 4, 5\}$.

The domain and range can be illustrated as follows. The lines show the pairing of a number in the domain with a number in the range.

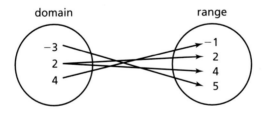

Definitions

The **domain of a relation** is the set of first coordinates of the ordered pairs of a relation.

The **range of a relation** is the set of second coordinates of the ordered pairs of a relation.

There is a special type of relation called a function. A function cannot have two or more ordered pairs with the same first coordinate. Every first element is paired with a unique second element. *Unique* means one and only one, the only one of its kind.

Definition

A **function** is a relation in which each *x*-coordinate is paired with one and only one *y*-coordinate.

A function, because it is a relation, also has a domain and a range. Furthermore, a function is graphed just like a relation. All functions are relations, but not all relations are functions.

EXAMPLE 2   The Cartesian graph and the circle model are two different representations of the same relation. Is the relation a function?

Answer   First, write the set of ordered pairs.
$\{(1, 9), (2, 8), (3, 7)\}$

Notice that each element of the domain is paired with a unique element of the range. Therefore, this relation is a function.

EXAMPLE 3   Is the relation in example 1 a function?
$\{(-3, 5), (2, 2), (2, 4), (4, -1)\}$

Answer   This relation is not a function because two different ordered pairs have the same first element. Not every element of the domain is paired with a unique element of the range. In particular, 2 is an element of the domain that is paired with two different range elements.

You can see the same fact using the circle model, or Cartesian graph, on page 224. In the circle model, the arrows show that 2 is paired with both 2 and 4. On the Cartesian graph, the plotted points (2, 2), and (2, 4) are on the same vertical line. Whenever you see more than one point plotted on a vertical line, the relation is not a function because two ordered pairs have the same *x*-coordinate.

EXAMPLE 4   The local grocery store is having a sale on potato chips. One bag regularly sells for $1, but if you buy two, you get a third one free. Plot the set of ordered pairs on a Cartesian plane. Are these ordered pairs a relation? What is the domain? What is the range? Are these ordered pairs a function?

Answer   Yes, this is a relation since any set of ordered pairs is a relation. The domain is {0, 1, 2, 3, . . . 11, 12} and the range is {0, 1, 2, . . . 7, 8}. No element of the domain relates to more than one element of the range.

x number of bags	cost in $ for *x* bags
0	0
1	1
2	2
3	2
4	3
5	4
6	4
7	5
8	6
9	6
10	7
11	8
12	8

▶ A. Exercises

Tell which of the following are relations; then give the domain and the range of each. Tell whether the relation is also a function, and make a circle model of each relation.

1. {(2, 4), (5, 9), (8, 2)}
2. {3, 4, 7, 9}
3. {(1, 3), (1, 6), (4, 9), (6, 1)}
4. {(−3, 2), (−3, 4), (6, 8), (7, 1)}

5. {(−4, 7), (−2, 5), (3, 7)}
6. {(−5, 1), (−5, 2), (2, 8), (5, 6)}
7. {(1, 3), (2, 3), (4, 7), (8, 1)}

For each set choose the letter of the correct description.
  A. Both a relation and a function.
  B. A relation that is not a function.
  C. Neither a relation nor a function.
  8. {(2, 3), (4, 5)}   11. {(2, 3), (3, 4)}
  9. {2, 3, 4, 5}   12. {(2, 3), (2, 4)}
  10. {(2, 3), (4, 3)}

▶ B. Exercises

Each relation can be expressed in set form, table form, as a graph, and as a circle model. Give the other three forms for each relation and state whether the relation is a function.

13.
x	y
−2	0
−1	4
0	3
1	−1
1	4

15. {(−1, 3), (1, −2)}

14.

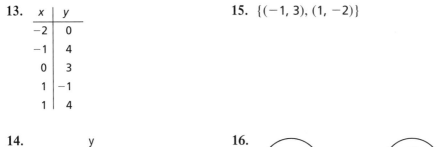

16.

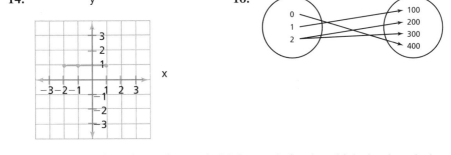

17. Let A = {3, 4} and B = {1, 6, 9}. Make a relation in which the domain is A and the range is B. List it in set form; then make a circle model.

▶ C. Exercises

Let A = {3, 4} and B = {1, 6, 9}.
18. Make two functions in which the domain is A and the range is a proper subset of B. List each function in set form. Then make a circle model.

There is a function called the greatest integer function symbolized by [x].
For any real number x, [x] is the largest integer less than or equal to x.

19. Complete the following table of values for this function.

x	$4\frac{1}{2}$	5	$5\frac{1}{4}$	$6\frac{3}{4}$	$-\frac{1}{2}$	$-2\frac{1}{2}$	$-5\frac{3}{4}$	$\frac{1}{3}$	$-\frac{1}{4}$

■ Cumulative Review

Solve.

20. $h - 5 = 4$

21. $3m + 1 = m$

22. $7a - 13 = 5a + 9$

23. $2(x - 5) + x = 3x - 4(x - 2)$

24. $|y| = 6$

25. $3 - 2x < 8$

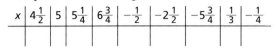

6.3 Graphs of Relations and Functions

What is your relation with Jesus Christ? Is He your personal Savior? If so, you are a child of God and a joint-heir with Christ (Gal. 4:4-7). He should have control over the full range of your life, and He has given you a special function to perform: to show to others that you are like Christ.

State the domain and the range of the relation {(1, 3), (1, 4), (2, 3), (2, 4)}. On a Cartesian plane plot the points indicated by each ordered pair.

Is this relation a function? One way to tell before you graph the relation is to look at the first element of each ordered pair. If any element of the domain is used more than once, the relation is not a function. After you have graphed the relation, you can quickly tell by using the *vertical line test.*

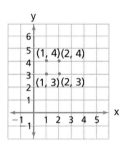

Vertical Line Test for Functions

If any vertical line intersects the graph in more than one point, the relation is not a function. Otherwise, it is a function.

Consider moving an imaginary vertical line across the preceding graph from left to right. The line intersects two points when it gets to the *x*-coordinate 1. Immediately you know that this relation is not a function.

In the following examples, the symbol | is read "such that."

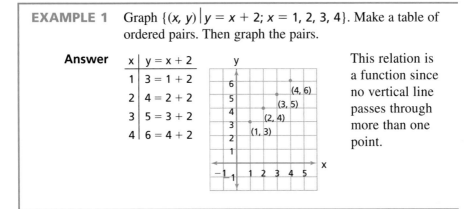

EXAMPLE 1   Graph $\{(x, y) \mid y = x + 2; x = 1, 2, 3, 4\}$. Make a table of ordered pairs. Then graph the pairs.

Answer

x	y = x + 2
1	3 = 1 + 2
2	4 = 2 + 2
3	5 = 3 + 2
4	6 = 4 + 2

This relation is a function since no vertical line passes through more than one point.

TO FIND Y, SUBSTITUTE FOR X AND EVALUATE.

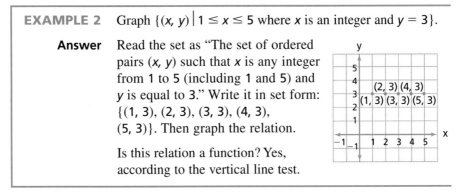

EXAMPLE 2   Graph $\{(x, y) \mid 1 \le x \le 5$ where *x* is an integer and $y = 3\}$.

Answer   Read the set as "The set of ordered pairs (*x*, *y*) such that *x* is any integer from 1 to 5 (including 1 and 5) and *y* is equal to 3." Write it in set form: $\{(1, 3), (2, 3), (3, 3), (4, 3), (5, 3)\}$. Then graph the relation.

Is this relation a function? Yes, according to the vertical line test.

What would happen to the graph in example 2 if the restriction about *x* as an integer were left out?

EXAMPLE 3   Graph $\{(x, y) \mid 1 \leq x \leq 5, y = 3\}$.

Answer   If there is no restriction on *x*, you must consider *x* to be any real number. The graph must contain all possible real values of *x* from 1 to 5 as shown.

This graph indicates that every ordered pair with *x* equal to any real number from 1 to 5 and *y* equal to 3 has been graphed. Included on this segment are ordered pairs such as (2.1, 3), (π, 3) and ($\frac{7}{2}$, 3). The result is a segment from 1 to 5 with an ordinate of 3 for all points.

Relations often can be described in terms of equations or inequalities.

EXAMPLE 4   Graph $\{(x, y) \mid y = \pm\sqrt{x}; x = 1, 4, 9\}$.

Answer   1. Make a table to find ordered pairs. To find the *y* values, substitute the *x* values from the domain in the equation $y = \pm\sqrt{x}$. For each value of *x* you should find two values for *y*.

x	y
1	1
1	−1
4	2
4	−2
9	3
9	−3

2. Graph the set of ordered pairs {(1, 1), (1, −1), (4, 2), (4, −2), (9, 3), (9, −3)}.

3. This relation is not a function because each value of *x* generates two values for *y*.

If the domain had not been restricted, then a smooth curve would have been drawn connecting the points.

EXAMPLE 5 Graph $\{(x, y) \mid y = \pm\sqrt{x}\}$.

Answer

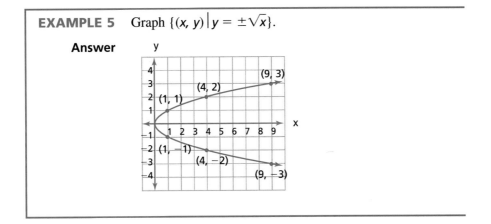

▶ A. Exercises

Is the relation a function?

1.

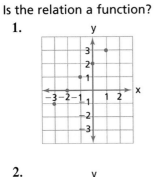

2.

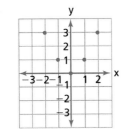

3.

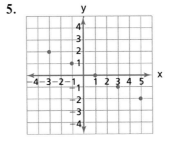

4.

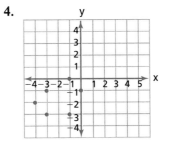

5.

Do the following graphs represent functions?

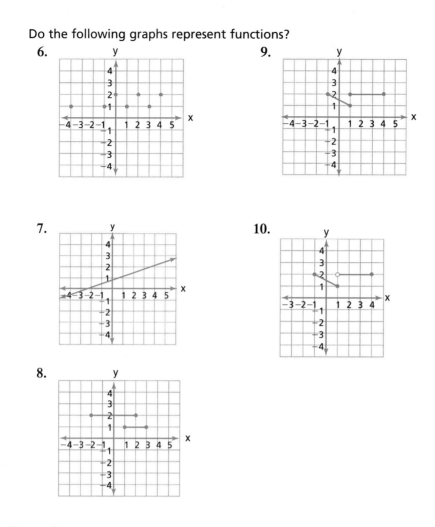

6.

7.

8.

9.

10.

▶ B. Exercises

Make a table and graph each relation. Is it a function?

11. $\{(x, y) \mid y = 3x; x = -1, 0, 1\}$
12. $\{(x, y) \mid y = 3x\}$
13. $\{(x, y) \mid y = x^2; x = -1, 0, 1, 2\}$
14. $\{(x, y) \mid y = x^2\}$
15. $\{(x, y) \mid y = 2x + 3; x = 0, \frac{1}{2}, 1, 2\}$
16. $\{(x, y) \mid y = 2x + 3\}$
17. $\{(x, y) \mid y = -x - 4; x = -2, 0, 2\}$
18. $\{(x, y) \mid y = -x - 4\}$
19. $\{(x, y) \mid x = 2; -1 \leq y \leq 3\}$

▶ C. Exercises

20. Graph $\{(x, y) \mid 0 \leq x \leq 4, -3 \leq y \leq 2,$ and x is an integer$\}$. Is it a function?
21. Graph $\{(x, y) \mid 0 \leq x \leq 4, -3 \leq y \leq 2\}$ Is it a function?

Solve.

22. $\frac{3}{20}x + 4 = \frac{7}{12}$

23. $\left|\frac{1}{9}x + 3\right| = \frac{1}{6}$

24. $\left|5x - \frac{3}{4}\right| \leq \frac{5}{6}$

25. $\frac{1}{2}x > \frac{1}{7}$ or $x + \frac{1}{3} \geq \frac{1}{5}$

26. $\frac{1}{7}x > 5$ and $-\frac{1}{2}x > \frac{1}{16}$

You CAN do it!

Plot the ordered pairs of numbers on a graph and connect them with line segments in the order they are listed. Start a new portion of the picture after the words "end line."

(−4, 5)	(4, 2)	(−6, 10)	(−1, −1)
(−4, 1)	(3, 2)	(−5, 11)	(−1, −2)
(−1, 1)	(3, 1)	(−3, 12)	(1, −2)
(−1, 5)	end line	(3, 12)	(1, −1)
(−4, 5)		(5, 11)	(−1, −1)
end line	(−5, 5)	(6, 10)	end line
	(−3, 7)	(5, 9)	
(−1, 2)	(−2, 7)	(2, 8)	(−4, −3)
(−2, 2)	(−1, 6)	(−2, 8)	(−3, −4)
(−2, 1)	end line	(−5, 9)	(−2, −5)
end line		(−6, 10)	(2, −5)
	(1, 6)	end line	(3, −4)
(1, 5)	(2, 7)		(4, −3)
(4, 5)	(3, 7)	(6, 10)	(2, −4)
(4, 1)	(5, 5)	(6, −7)	(−2, −4)
(1, 1)	end line	(5, −8)	(−4, −3)
(1, 5)		(2, −9)	end line
end line		(−2, −9)	
		(−5, −8)	
		(−6, −7)	
		(−6, 10)	
		end line	

6.4 Graphs and Intercepts of Linear Equations

Many relations and functions can be described in terms of an equation. One such equation is called a *linear equation* because when it is graphed all the points that satisfy it are in a straight line. The *standard form* of a linear equation is $ax + by = c$, where a, b, and c are any real numbers. An example would be $2x + 3y = 8$.

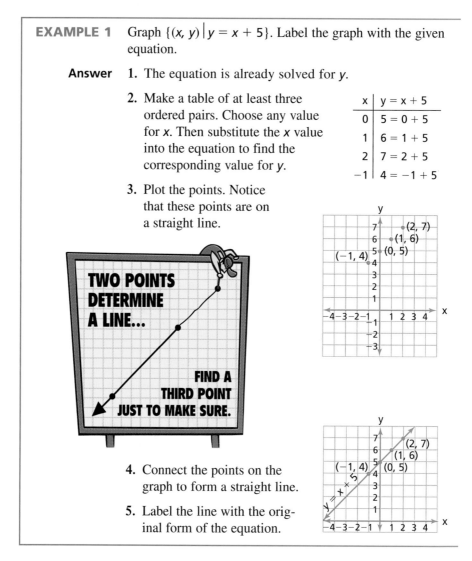

EXAMPLE 1   Graph $\{(x, y) \,|\, y = x + 5\}$. Label the graph with the given equation.

Answer   1. The equation is already solved for y.

2. Make a table of at least three ordered pairs. Choose any value for x. Then substitute the x value into the equation to find the corresponding value for y.

x	y = x + 5
0	5 = 0 + 5
1	6 = 1 + 5
2	7 = 2 + 5
−1	4 = −1 + 5

3. Plot the points. Notice that these points are on a straight line.

TWO POINTS DETERMINE A LINE...

FIND A THIRD POINT JUST TO MAKE SURE.

4. Connect the points on the graph to form a straight line.

5. Label the line with the original form of the equation.

Notice that the equation could also have been expressed in standard form as follows.

$$y = x + 5 \qquad -x + y = 5 \qquad x - y = -5$$

Graphing Linear Equations

1. Solve the linear equation for *y*.
2. Make a table of ordered pairs. Select at least three different values for *x*, substitute them into the equation, and determine the corresponding *y* values.
3. Graph the ordered pairs on a Cartesian plane.
4. Connect the points with a straight line.
5. Label the line with the original equation.

EXAMPLE 2   Graph $x + 3y = 4$.

Answer   1. Solve this equation for *y*. Think of it as a literal equation.

$$x + 3y = 4$$
$$3y = -x + 4$$
$$y = \frac{-x + 4}{3}$$

2. Make a table of ordered pairs.

x	$y = \frac{-x + 4}{3}$
0	$\frac{4}{3} = \frac{0 + 4}{3}$
4	$0 = \frac{-4 + 4}{3}$
1	$1 = \frac{-1 + 4}{3}$

3. Graph these ordered pairs as points.

4. Connect the points with a straight line.

5. Label the line with the original form of the equation. In this example, the equation was originally in standard form.

From the graph of example 2, you can identify where the graph crosses the axes. These points are called intercepts. The *y*-intercept is $(0, \frac{4}{3})$ and the *x*-intercept is $(4, 0)$. The *y*-intercept is important throughout the rest of this chapter.

The **y-intercept** is the point where the line crosses, or intersects, the *y*-axis. The *y*-intercept always has **0** as its first coordinate.

The **x-intercept** is the point where the line crosses, or intersects, the *x*-axis. The *x*-intercept always has **0** as its second coordinate.

You can also find the intercepts from the equation without graphing. Simply locate the point where the other coordinate is zero.

EXAMPLE 3   Find the *x*-intercept and *y*-intercept of the line described by the equation $2x + y = 6$.

Answer   Since the value of *y* must be **0** at the *x*-intercept, substitute **0** for *y* and solve for *x*.

$$2x + y = 6$$
$$2x + 0 = 6$$
$$2x = 6$$
$$x = 3$$

The *x*-intercept is the point **(3, 0)**.

Since the value of *x* must be **0** at the *y*-intercept, substitute **0** for *x* and solve for *y*.

$$2x + y = 6$$
$$2(0) + y = 6$$
$$y = 6$$

The *y*-intercept is the point **(0, 6)**.

Since you can find any three points when graphing a line, it is often convenient to find and graph the intercepts as two of the points.

▶ A. Exercises

For each equation make a table of at least three ordered pairs. Then graph the equation on its own set of axes. Give the *y*-intercept for each graph.

1. $2x + y = 5$
2. $x - y = 6$
3. $3x + 2y = -2$
4. $x = 6y$
5. $x - 3y = 9$

6. $4x + y = 1$
7. $x - 2y = 18$
8. $5x + 2y = 10$
9. $x + y = 8$
10. $2x - 4y = 16$

▶ B. Exercises

Find both intercepts without graphing.

11. $y = 2x + 3$

12. $3x - y = 1$

13. $y = x - 4$

14. $x - 2y = -12$

Solve for y.

15. $x + 5y = 20$

16. $4x + 4y = 3 + 4x + y$

Solve for y and find the intercepts.

17. $x = 3y + 5$

18. $4x - 7y = 2$

19. What is the x-value of every y-intercept?

20. What is the y-value of every x-intercept?

21. On what line is the y-intercept always found?

22. On what line is the x-intercept always found?

▶ C. Exercises

23. Can a function ever have two x-intercepts? two y-intercepts? Explain.

24. Graph the set of equations on the same set of axes. Label each line with the standard form of the linear equation. What do the equations have in common?

$y = x + 1$

$y = 2x + 1$

$y = -2x + 1$

$y = -\frac{1}{2}x + 1$

■ Cumulative Review

Graph on a number line or the Cartesian plane as needed.

25. -5

26. $|x| > 2$

27. $x \leq 1$

28. $(-5, 1)$

29. $|x| = 3$

30. $\{(x, y) \mid x = 3, 1 < y < 2\}$

6.5 Slopes of Lines

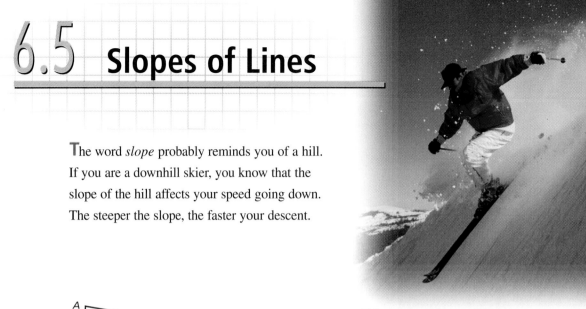

The word *slope* probably reminds you of a hill. If you are a downhill skier, you know that the slope of the hill affects your speed going down. The steeper the slope, the faster your descent.

This skier negotiates a descent of about 45 degrees. Thus, the slope is m = −1.

How is the slope of a ski run measured? Let's try a beginner hill. The top of the hill, *A*, is 2 units high. When you get to *B*, your vertical change will be −2. Your horizontal change will be +12. To find the slope, divide the vertical change (−2) by the horizontal change (+12).

$$\frac{\text{vertical change}}{\text{horizontal change}} = \frac{-2}{12} = -\frac{1}{6}$$

That this slope is a downgrade is shown by the negative sign, and the steepness by the number $\frac{1}{6}$. If $\frac{1}{6}$ were changed to a decimal, the slope would be approximately −0.17 or −17%. This is what is meant by a 17% downgrade.

Actually, slope is any variation from the horizontal. In math any line other than a vertical line will have slope.

Definition

> The **slope of a line** is the change in the *y* values of two points divided by the change in the corresponding *x* values of those two points: the vertical change (rise) divided by the horizontal change (run).

In the following formula for finding the slope of a line going through two points (x_1, y_1) and (x_2, y_2), the slope is indicated by *m*.

$$m = \frac{y_2 - y_1}{x_2 - x_1} \text{ if } x_2 - x_1 \neq 0.$$

EXAMPLE 1   Find the slope of the line that passes through (1, 4) and (2, 2).

Answer   1. Find the vertical change (change in *y*) between the two points. Notice that if you start at (1, 4) and move to (2, 2) you move down two units. So the vertical change is −2.

2. Find the horizontal change (change in *x*). The horizontal change is one unit to the right. So the horizontal change is 1.

3. Therefore, the slope of the line is vertical change (rise) over horizontal change (run).

$$m = \frac{\text{rise}}{\text{run}} = \frac{-2}{+1} = -2$$

If you had started with the point (2, 2) and moved to (1, 4) to find the slope, the vertical change would have been two units up (positive) and the horizontal change would have been one unit left (negative). Since +2 divided by −1 is still equal to −2, the slope is the same. The slope between any two points on a given line will always be the same.

The sign of the slope tells you whether the line slants up or down to the right. In the example above, the slope of −2 is negative, so the line slants down to the right. Lines with positive slopes will have graphs that slope up to the right.

Different notations for slope	
m	$\frac{y_2 - y_1}{x_2 - x_1}$
$\frac{\text{vertical change}}{\text{horizontal change}}$	$\frac{\text{rise}}{\text{run}}$
$\frac{\text{change in } y}{\text{change in } x}$	$\frac{\triangle y}{\triangle x}$

Sometimes you will have to look at the graph of a line to find the slope. You should also be able to determine the slope of a line if you do not have a graph but are given two points on the line.

EXAMPLE 2   Find the slope of the line passing through (4, 1) and (2, −3).

Answer

$(x_1, y_1) = (4, 1)$ $(x_2, y_2) = (2, -3)$	1. Label the points.
$m = \frac{y_2 - y_1}{x_2 - x_1}$ $= \frac{-3 - 1}{2 - 4}$	2. Substitute values into the equation.
$= \frac{-4}{-2}$ $= 2$	3. Evaluate.

The slope of this line is 2, but writing it as $\frac{2}{1}$ helps us to see that the rise is 2 and the run is 1.

EXAMPLE 3   Find the slope of the line passing through (3, 4) and (−1, 5).

Answer $(x_1, y_1) = (3, 4); (x_2, y_2) = (-1, 5)$

$m = \frac{y_2 - y_1}{x_2 - x_1}$

$= \frac{5 - 4}{-1 - 3}$

$= \frac{1}{-4}$

$= -\frac{1}{4}$

USE **X** VALUES IN THE DENOMINATOR IN THE SAME ORDER **THAT** **y** VALUES ARE USED IN THE NUMERATOR

WHEW! HOPE I DON'T GET MANY CALLS FOR THESE SLOPE-SIDE SIGNS!

Finding the Slope of a Line

1. If you are given two points, label them point (x_1, y_1) and point (x_2, y_2). Then find the slope by using $m = \frac{y_2 - y_1}{x_2 - x_1}$ if $x_2 - x_1 \neq 0$.
2. If you are given the graph of a linear equation, count the vertical change and the horizontal change from one point to another point. Then write the vertical change over the horizontal change as a fraction. Reduce if possible.

In the previous examples the lines have been diagonal. What is the slope of a horizontal line?

EXAMPLE 4   Given the two points (2, 4) and (7, 4), determine the slope.

Answer $m = \frac{y_2 - y_1}{x_2 - x_1} = \frac{4 - 4}{7 - 2} = \frac{0}{5} = 0$

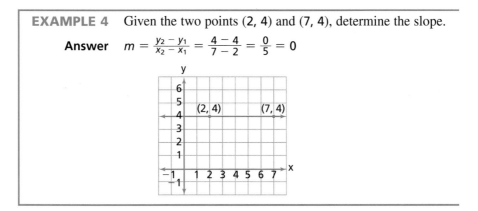

The slope of a horizontal line is always 0 because there is no variation from the horizontal. Now, consider a vertical line.

EXAMPLE 5   Given points (3, 4) and (3, −2), determine the slope.

Answer $m = \frac{y_2 - y_1}{x_2 - x_1} = \frac{4 - (-2)}{3 - 3} = \frac{6}{0}$

Hold it! Division by 0 is undefined. Since the slope of a vertical line is undefined, we say vertical lines have no slope.

► A. Exercises

Find the slope and *y*-intercept of each graph.

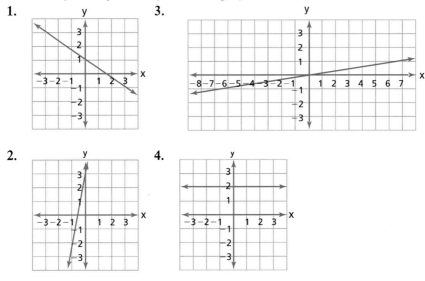

1.

3.

2.

4.

Find the slope of the line going through the given points.

5. $(2, 5), (3, 9)$ 8. $(3, 6), (-4, -1)$
6. $(-1, 8), (3, 4)$ 9. $(2, 7), (3, 7)$
7. $(-2, -5), (1, 0)$ 10. $(-4, -6), (-3, -2)$

► B. Exercises

Find the slope of the line going through the given points.

11. $(2, 5), (2, -3)$ 14. $(3, 6), (1, 9)$
12. $(5, 7), (1, -3)$ 15. $(-4, -1), (-1, 7)$
13. $(-2, 4), (-5, -2)$ 16. $(-1, 7), (-1, 2)$

► C. Exercises

On steep mountain roads the slope ratio is given as a percent to warn
motorists. Find the percent downgrade to the nearest tenth of a percent or
distance to the nearest tenth of a mile for each road (1 mile = 5280 feet).

17. The road descends 800 feet in 2 miles.
18. A sign read "6% downgrade next three miles." How many feet of eleva-
    tion will be lost?
19. A road construction crew must make a road from Barren Pass, elevation
    6030 feet, to Fern Creek, elevation 4502 feet. How long must the road be
    in order to avoid grades over 5%?

Evaluate.

Use $a = -4$, $b = 3$, $c = -2$, $x = 0$, $y = -1$

20. $\frac{bc}{ay}$

21. $\frac{b - c}{a + y}$

22. $\sqrt{ac - y}$

23. $\frac{a^0 + x(b + y)}{yc + b}$

24. $5a - 3y - 4b + 2x^3 + c$

ALGEBRA AND BUSINESS

People in the field of business must do a lot of figuring with numbers, but their most important role is decision making. Good decisions rest upon accurate information, logical analysis of the data collected, and realistic projections based on the analysis. Such projections depend upon algebra.

Those involved with finance regularly use formulas to compute returns on investments. Their computers and calculators are programmed to take investment information entered and display the interest without the user ever knowing or seeing the formulas. In these situations, we could say that algebra works behind the scenes.

Many business decisions cannot be based on the results from existing formulas or functions because the known information exists only as data from real-world applications. The information may be in a table or chart that can be analyzed by a graph that approximates the behavior of the data. Very often a function can be derived from the data that serves as a model for the relationship. The discrete statistical data is input to a graphics calculator and a continuous model derived that fits the data quite well.

Executives meet to brainstorm, plan, and troubleshoot.

EXAMPLE The following table gives the actual sales of a company in millions of dollars. The first year is called zero, or the base year, so that later years can be expressed in terms of a variable *x* that is in years since the base year. Predict the sales after 5 years. 14 years.

Continued ▶

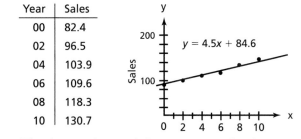

Year	Sales
00	82.4
02	96.5
04	103.9
06	109.6
08	118.3
10	130.7

$y = 4.5x + 84.6$

Answer The dots on the graph form a scatter plot that can be approximated by a line. When the ordered pairs are entered into a scientific calculator, the equation of the line is obtained: $y = 4.47x + 84.57$.

Using this linear equation as a model for trend analysis, sales for the fifth year ($x = 5$) correspond to $y = \$106,900,000$. It also predicts sales in the fourteenth year of $\$147,100,000$.

In the example, the fifth year falls between two given data pairs. Estimating the value for a point between two given data points is called *interpolation*. When the x-value is beyond the last data point, such as the projection for the fourteenth year, the estimation is called *extrapolation*.

In marketing analysis it is often desirable to know the average rate of change (ARC) in sales or costs over a period of years or months.

$\text{ARC} = \dfrac{\text{change during interval}}{\text{length of interval}}$

1. Find the change in sales from year 5 to year 14 using the model.

$\text{ARC} = \dfrac{147,100,000 - 106,900,000}{14 - 5}$

$= \dfrac{40,200,00}{9}$

$= \$4,467,000$

2. Find the per-year increase.

Did you notice that the ARC is the slope of the line? The change during the interval is the rise, and the length of the interval is the run. Slopes have many applications to revenue and cost analysis.

Functions, relations, graphs, and other tools of algebra help the business world make sound financial decisions. Accountants, brokers, financial officers, managers, and sales people all use varying amounts of algebra to analyze complex arrays of data that would otherwise overwhelm them.

Functions, relations, graphs, and other tools of algebra help the business world make sound financial decisions.

A business executive shows graphs at a meeting.

6.6 Slope-Intercept Form of a Linear Equation

Equations of lines can be written in several different forms by applying the properties of equality. You have already learned the standard form of a linear equation: $ax + by = c$. Another form for a line is the *slope-intercept form.*

The slope-intercept form of a linear equation is $y = mx + b$. In this equation, m is the slope of the line, and b is the y-coordinate for the y-intercept (where the line intersects the y-axis).

You can solve for y as you would solve a literal equation. Be sure to arrange the terms on the right side with the x term first and the constant last.

*The square base of the Trans-America Pyramid in San Francisco, California, is **145** feet on each side. Since the height is **786** feet, determine the slope of each side.*

EXAMPLE 1   Write $3x + 2y = 6$ in slope-intercept form. Identify m and b.

Answer

$3x + 2y = 6$	1. Solve for y.
$2y = 6 - 3x$	
$\frac{2y}{2} = \frac{6}{2} - \frac{3x}{2}$	
$y = 3 - \frac{3x}{2}$	

$y = -\frac{3x}{2} + 3$	2. Apply the commutative property of addition to rearrange the right side so that the term with x is first.

$y = -\frac{3}{2}x + 3$	3. Compare this equation with $y = mx + b$ to find m and b.
$m = -\frac{3}{2}$	
$b = 3$	

You can see that the standard form $3x + 2y = 6$ and the slope-intercept form $y = -\frac{3}{2}x + 3$ refer to the same line. They are two different forms of the same equation.

Changing Linear Equations to Slope-Intercept Form

1. Solve the linear equation for *y*.
2. Arrange terms on the right side with the variable term first.

You have already learned how to graph a linear equation by plotting the points from a table of ordered pairs and connecting them to form a line. However, a faster method involves using the slope-intercept form of an equation. Since the equation $y = mx + b$ gives the *y*-coordinate of the *y*-intercept (*b*), you can immediately plot the point (0, *b*). Then you can use the slope *m* to find a second point.

EXAMPLE 2 Graph $y = \frac{1}{2}x + 4$.

Answer

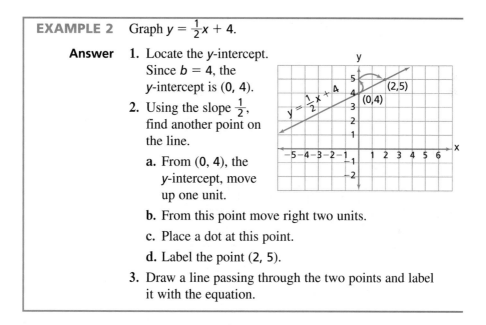

1. Locate the *y*-intercept. Since *b* = 4, the *y*-intercept is (0, 4).

2. Using the slope $\frac{1}{2}$, find another point on the line.

   a. From (0, 4), the *y*-intercept, move up one unit.

   b. From this point move right two units.

   c. Place a dot at this point.

   d. Label the point (2, 5).

3. Draw a line passing through the two points and label it with the equation.

Using Slope-Intercept Form to Graph a Linear Equation

1. Place the equation in slope-intercept form ($y = mx + b$) if it is not already in it.
2. Plot the *y*-intercept (0, *b*) on the graph.
3. Starting at the *y*-intercept, use the slope to locate another point.
4. Draw a line through the two points and label it with the equation.

EXAMPLE 3   Graph $2x + y = -3$.

Answer   1. Write the equation in slope-intercept form.

$$2x + y = -3$$
$$y = -2x - 3$$

2. Locate the y-intercept $(0, -3)$.

3. Since the slope is -2, or $\frac{-2}{1}$, move down two units and right one unit from the y-intercept. (Remember that slope is rise over run.)

4. Draw a line through the points and label the line.

EXAMPLE 4   Graph $2x + 3y = 6$.

Answer $2x + 3y = 6$

$$3y = -2x + 6$$
$$y = -\frac{2}{3}x + 2$$
$$m = -\frac{2}{3}$$
$$b = 2$$

The y-intercept is $(0, 2)$. Beginning at $(0, 2)$, find another point using the slope.

EXAMPLE 5   Write $y = 3$ in slope-intercept form. Identify m and b. Graph the equation.

Answer   1. This equation is already in slope-intercept form because it is solved for y.

2. Compare $y = 3$ with $y = mx + b$. Since there is no x variable in the equation, rewrite $y = 3$ as $y = 0 \cdot x + 3$. Plot the y-intercept $(0, 3)$.

3. Since $m = 0$, the slope is zero and the line is horizontal. Plot another point with a y-coordinate of 3.

4. Draw the horizontal line through the two points.

You can also see that this equation describes a function. Since any vertical line touches the graph of $y = 3$ at only one point, the relation is a function. It is called a *constant function* because the value of y is constantly 3 no matter what x is.

▶ A. Exercises

Graph each linear equation by using its slope-intercept form. Identify m and b.

1. $y = 3x + 4$

2. $y = -\frac{1}{3}x - 2$

3. $y = -x + 1$

4. $y = 4x - 7$

5. $y = -\frac{1}{4}x + 5$

6. $y = -2x + 4$

7. $y = 6$

8. $y = -2$

Write each equation in slope-intercept form. Give the values of m and b.

9. $3x + y = 5$

10. $x - y = -6$

11. $x + 7y = 14$

12. $3x + 7y = 21$

13. $8x - 3y = 9$

14. $28x - 7y = -77$

15. $x = -3$

16. $-5x + y = 2$

▶ B. Exercises

Graph each linear equation by using its slope-intercept form.

17. $2x + y = 5$

18. $x + y = 12$

19. $2x + y = 8$

20. $\frac{1}{2}y = x - 3$

21. $3x + y - 8 = 0$

22. $8x + y + 10 = 0$

23. $x - 3y = -6$

24. $3x + 2y = 8$

25. $3x - y = -9$

26. $3x - 4y = -16$

27. $x + 5y = -20$

28. $6x - y = 12$

29. $7x + 2y = 16$

30. $5x - 2y = 10$

▶ C. Exercises

31. What lines do not represent functions? Explain.

32. Write the equation in slope-intercept form. Give the value of m and b and graph the equation. $4(x - 2) + 7y = 5 - (2x - 3y)$

▪ Cumulative Review

Find the LCM of 15 and 36, and apply it to find answers to the following exercises.

33. Subtract $\frac{13}{36} - \frac{7}{15}$.

34. Solve $\frac{19}{36}x = \frac{8}{15}$.

35. Add $\frac{17}{15} + \frac{5}{36}$.

Find a GCF and use it to calculate the answer.

36. Reduce $\frac{84}{196}$.

37. Multiply $\frac{11}{195} \cdot \frac{156}{85}$.

Rules of Probability

By now you should realize that "and" and "or" are very important words. Look at the contexts in which they are used.

	and	or	see
sets	intersection: $A \cap B$	union: $A \cup B$	Section 2.7
compound inequality	$x < 1$ and $x > 0$	$x < 1$ or $x > 5$	Sections 5.5 and 5.6
counting principle	ab for A and B	$a + b$ for A or B	Chapters 4 and 5 features
probability	$P_A \cdot P_B$	$P_A + P_B$	this feature

You should not be surprised that these words are important clues in probability also. In fact, the rules are similar to the counting rules. Remember that probability is a ratio: $P = \frac{s}{t}$.

EXAMPLE 1   What is the probability of obtaining a head or a tail on one flip of a coin?

Answer   The word *or* tells you to add the probabilities.

$$P_H = \frac{1}{2} \qquad P_T = \frac{1}{2} \qquad P_{H \text{ or } T} = \frac{1}{2} + \frac{1}{2} = 1$$

There is a **100%** likelihood that you will get either heads or tails.

EXAMPLE 2   What is the probability of obtaining heads three times in a row?

Answer   In other words, find the probability of obtaining heads and then heads and then heads again (P_{HHH}). The word *and* warns you to multiply.

$$P_H = \frac{1}{2} \qquad P_{HHH} = \frac{1}{2} \cdot \frac{1}{2} \cdot \frac{1}{2} = \frac{1}{8}$$

These rules should remind you of the addition principle of counting and the multiplication principle of counting.

If P_A is the probability of A and P_B is the probability of B, then

$P_{A \cup B} = P_A + P_B$ (as long as A and B do not intersect)

$P_{A \cap B} = P_A \cdot P_B$ (as long as A and B do not affect each other)

▶ Exercises

Ten students are in a class: Bill Green, Joan Brown, Nancy Wong, Gary Repp, Sandra Peters, Bob Powers, Larry Schultz, Scott King, Steve Sanders, and Ruth Smith. Each student's name is written on a piece of paper and placed in a hat. A slip is drawn and the name is read.

1. What is the probability of selecting a boy? a girl? a last name beginning with S? a last name beginning with K? a last name beginning with P?

Use rules to find each probability. Replace each name in the hat before drawing again.

2. A last name beginning with S or P
3. A last name beginning with S or K
4. A boy and then a girl
5. The same person four times in a row

6.7 Point-Slope Form of Linear Equations

9% GRADE
6 MILES

In previous sections of this chapter, you learned how to graph linear equations. Beginning with this lesson, you will be given certain "facts" from which you must determine the equation of a line. You should be able to find the equation of a line if you know

1. the slope and *y*-intercept of the line,

2. the slope and a point on the line, or

3. two points on the line.

Using the slope and *y*-intercept to find the equation of the line is simple. Just substitute the given values for the appropriate variables in the slope-intercept form of the equation.

A 9% downgrade corresponds to a descent of 9 vertical feet for every 100 horizontal feet, or $-\frac{9}{100}$.

EXAMPLE 1 Find the equation of the line with slope $\frac{2}{3}$ and *y*-intercept (0, 5).

Answer Since $m = \frac{2}{3}$ and $b = 5$, insert these values into the equation $y = mx + b$. The slope-intercept form of the equation is $y = \frac{2}{3}x + 5$.

EXAMPLE 2 Write the equation of the line with slope 3 and *y*-intercept (0, −2).

Answer $y = 3x - 2$

You can also determine the equation of a line from the slope and any given point on the line. Let (x_1, y_1) represent the given point, and substitute (x, y) for (x_2, y_2) in the slope formula. Then (x_1, y_1) represents a specific known point while (x, y) represents any general point on the line.

$$\frac{y - y_1}{x - x_1} = m \qquad \text{1. Apply the slope formula.}$$

$$\frac{y - y_1}{x - x_1}(x - x_1) = m(x - x_1) \qquad \text{2. Multiply both sides of the equation by } (x - x_1) \text{ to clear the fractions.}$$

$$y - y_1 = m(x - x_1) \qquad \text{3. Cancel.}$$

The resulting equation is called *point-slope form*. This form is useful whenever the *y*-intercept is not given.

EXAMPLE 3   Find the equation of the line that passes through the point (1, 5) and has slope 3.

Answer   Substitute the values for *m* and (x_1, y_1) in the point-slope form of the line. Then change to the slope-intercept form.

$$m = 3$$
$$(x_1, y_1) = (1, 5)$$
$$y - y_1 = m(x - x_1)$$

$y - 5 = 3(x - 1)$	1. Substitute into point-slope form.
$y - 5 = 3x - 3$	2. Distribute.
$y = 3x + 2$	3. Solve for *y*.

EXAMPLE 4   Write the equation of the line that has slope $\frac{1}{2}$ and goes through the point (−3, 2).

Answer $y - y_1 = m(x - x_1)$
$y - 2 = \frac{1}{2}[x - (-3)]$
$y - 2 = \frac{1}{2}(x + 3)$
$y - 2 = \frac{1}{2}x + \frac{3}{2}$
$y = \frac{1}{2}x + \frac{7}{2}$

EXAMPLE 5   Write the equation of the line that has slope 0 and goes through the point (−1, 6).

Answer $y - y_1 = m(x - x_1)$
$y - 6 = 0[x - (-1)]$
$y - 6 = 0$
$y = 6$ is a horizontal line

Always simplify your final answer to the slope-intercept form of the equation

---

▶ A. Exercises

Write the equation of the line given the slope and the *y*-intercept.

1. $m = 3, b = \frac{1}{4}$
2. $m = -\frac{1}{3}, b = 3$
3. $m = -5, b = 10$
4. $m = 6, b = -\frac{1}{2}$
5. $m = 0, b = 7$

6. $m = 3, b = 2$
7. $m = 9, b = -\frac{2}{3}$
8. $m = 4, b = -9$
9. $m = \frac{1}{4}, b = 8$
10. $m = -\frac{3}{2}, b = -4$

▶ B. Exercises

Write the equation of the line given the slope and a point through which the line passes.

11. $-\frac{1}{4}, (1, 6)$
12. $8, (-3, 2)$
13. $\frac{3}{5}, (0, 4)$
14. $-3, (2, -5)$
15. $-\frac{1}{8}, (-9, 0)$

16. $\frac{1}{4}, (3, 7)$
17. $-4, (-4, 1)$
18. $\frac{5}{3}, (-3, -1)$
19. $\frac{4}{5}, (-5, 2)$
20. $\frac{9}{4}, (3, 0)$

▶ C. Exercises

Write the equation of the line given the slope and a point through which the line passes.

21. $0.25, (4.1, 3.7)$
22. $-\frac{3}{5}, \left(\frac{15}{7}, -\frac{3}{7}\right)$

■ Cumulative Review

Find the slope of each line.

23. The line passing through $(1, 7)$ and $(-3, 2)$
24. $5x - 4y = 4$
25. Graph both lines above on the same graph. What do you notice?

Refer to $3x - 5y = 10$.

26. Is it a relation? a function?
27. Give the *x*-intercept and *y*-intercept.

6.8 Finding the Equation of a Line Given Two Points

Now that you know how to determine a linear equation by using (1) the slope and the *y*-intercept of a line and (2) the slope and a point on the line, you will learn how to determine an equation given any two points on the line.

On a steep slope, engineers may extend the horizontal distance with a pigtail curve, as on Iron Mountain Road in South Dakota.

EXAMPLE 1 Write the equation of the line that passes through the points (1, 3) and (4, −2).

Answer

$$m = \frac{y_2 - y_1}{x_2 - x_1}$$

$$= \frac{-2 - 3}{4 - 1}$$

$$= -\frac{5}{3}$$

1. First find the slope of the line.

$$y - y_1 = m(x - x_1)$$

$$y - 3 = -\frac{5}{3}(x - 1)$$

$$y - 3 = -\frac{5}{3}x + \frac{5}{3}$$

$$y = -\frac{5}{3}x + \frac{14}{3}$$

2. By using the point-slope form of the equation and the point (1, 3), you can now find the equation of this line. Substitute values for the point and for *m* in the point-slope form of the equation. Simplify.

Now do the same procedure, but use the point (4, −2). Do you get the same equation after changing it to slope-intercept form?

One method of checking your work is to substitute values for the unused ordered pair in your answer and evaluate the expression. In this problem, if you substitute 4 for *x*, and simplify the right side, you get −2, the value of *y* for the given point. Since (4, −2) satisfies it, the linear equation is correct.

EXAMPLE 2   Write the equation of the line passing through $(-5, 2)$ and $(3, -4)$. What is the y-intercept?

Answer

$m = \frac{y_2 - y_1}{x_2 - x_1}$ 1. Find the slope.

$\quad = \frac{-4 - 2}{3 - (-5)}$

$\quad = -\frac{6}{8}$

$\quad = -\frac{3}{4}$

$y - y_1 = m(x - x_1)$ 2. Choose one of the given points

$y + 4 = -\frac{3}{4}(x - 3)$ and use the point-slope form of

$y + 4 = -\frac{3}{4}x + \frac{9}{4}$ the equation to determine the

$\quad\; y = -\frac{3}{4}x - \frac{7}{4}$ slope-intercept form of

the equation.

$2 = -\frac{3}{4}(-5) - \frac{7}{4}$ 3. To check, substitute the other

$2 = \frac{15}{4} - \frac{7}{4}$ point $(-5, 2)$ into the equation.

$2 = \frac{8}{4}$ Since a true statement results,

$2 = 2$ $(-5, 2)$ is also on the line.

The y-intercept is $\left(0, -\frac{7}{4}\right)$. 4. Identify the b value in the

equation.

EXAMPLE 3   Write the equation of the line passing through $(7, 4)$ and $(7, 2)$.

Answer

$m = \frac{y_2 - y_1}{x_2 - x_1}$

$m = \frac{4 - 2}{7 - 7}$

$m = \frac{2}{0}$

The slope is undefined; therefore, the line must be a vertical line. To write the equation of a vertical line, set x equal to the value of the x-coordinates of the ordered pairs. The equation of this line is $x = 7$.

Writing an Equation from Given Information

1. Identify the slope of the line.
2. Substitute the slope and a given point in the point-slope form of the equation.
3. State the resulting equation in slope-intercept form.

Can you see how important the slope of the line is? It is the first thing you must identify whenever you want to find the equation of a line.

Finally, you should be sure that you understand when to use each form of the line. The main application of each is given below.

A. Use slope-intercept form to graph lines.
B. Use point-slope form to find equations of lines.

▶ A. Exercises

Write each equation and give the *y*-intercept for the line that passes through the given points.

1. $(4, 2), (-3, 9)$
2. $(0, 4), (2, 7)$
3. $(2, 7), (1, 8)$
4. $(1, 4), (0, 0)$
5. $(1, 3), (2, 5)$
6. $(1, 3), (-3, 6)$

7. $(-4, 2), (7, 3)$
8. $(-1, -9), (4, 4)$
9. $(-3, 2), (10, -6)$
10. $(2, 8), (-3, 1)$
11. $(3, -1), (-10, -8)$
12. $(-3, 4), (2, 1)$

▶ B. Exercises

Write the equation of the line with the given information.

13. $m = 3, b = 8$
14. $m = \frac{2}{5}$, point $(-1, -3)$
15. points $(1, 3)$ and $(-4, -9)$
16. points $(2, 0)$ and $(6, -5)$

17. points $(2, -8)$ and $(-6, -1)$
18. points $(13, 9)$ and $(-1, 16)$
19. points $(-5, -4)$ and $(3, -4)$

20. Find the equation of the line passing through $(-5, 3)$ and $(-5, 4)$.

▶ C. Exercises

Find the equation of the line through $(-1, 2)$ that is parallel to $3x + 2y = 7$ by following the steps in exercises 21-23.

21. What is the slope of $3x + 2y = 7$?
22. What would the slope of a line parallel to the given line be?
23. Use the point and the slope to find the equation.

Translate each phrase or sentence below. Do not calculate, simplify, or solve.

24. The sum of four more than a number and three more than twice the same number is 20.
25. The sum of four consecutive integers.
26. Thirty coins in dimes and quarters have a total value of at most $4.00. How many of each could there be?
27. The distance between two towns is 40 miles. A motorcycle travels three times the speed of a bicycle and the riders meet after a half-hour. How fast is each traveling?
28. How much pure ammonia should be mixed with 20 gallons of a cleaning solution that is 7% ammonia to increase the cleaning strength to 10% ammonia?

6.9 Direct Variation

Look at the following table. What value for y should come next?

x	y
0	0
1	3
2	6
3	9
4	

This table might represent the amount of commission earned when you make $3 on each item sold. If you sell three items, you earn $9 commission. What equation describes this relation? Since the y value in the table is three times the x value, x and y vary directly. The equation would be $y = 3x$. This equation is a special form of the slope-intercept equation in which b equals 0. Whenever one variable is a multiple of another variable, we say the variables are in direct variation to each other or that they are directly proportional.

Definition

A **direct variation** is a linear function in which one variable is a positive multiple of the other variable.

The general equation of a direct variation is $y = kx$, where k is a positive number called the *constant of variation*. A linear function of the form $y = mx$ is a direct variation. However, $y = 2x + 4$ is not a direct variation.

The perimeter of a square is directly proportional to the length of one side of the square. What is the constant of variation? Since the perimeter equals four times the length of one side, the constant of variation is **4**.

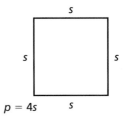

$p = 4s$

EXAMPLE 1

Read the table. Is y a multiple of x? What is the constant of variation? Write an equation expressing the relation.

x	y
0	0
1	7
2	14
3	21

Answer

Yes, y is a multiple of x since each value of y is seven times the x value. The constant of variation is **7**. The equation is $y = 7x$.

EXAMPLE 2

Find k if y varies directly with x and $y = 6$ when $x = 3$. Write the equation that expresses the variation.

Answer

Write the general form of a direct variation. Substitute the values of x and y and solve for k.

$y = kx$

$6 = k(3)$

$\frac{6}{3} = k$

$k = 2$

The direct variation then is $y = 2x$.

EXAMPLE 3

If y varies directly with x and $y = 8$ when $x = \frac{4}{5}$, find y when $x = 3$.

Answer

$y = kx$ 1. Find the constant of variation.

$8 = k\left(\frac{4}{5}\right)$

$\frac{5}{4}(8) = k$

$k = 10$

$y = kx$ 2. To find y when $x = 3$, substitute the

$y = 10x$ values for k and x into the equation.

$y = 10 \cdot 3$

$y = 30$

EXAMPLE 4   If y varies directly with x and $y = \frac{2}{3}$ when $x = 10$, find y when $x = 7\frac{1}{2}$.

Answer

$y = kx$	1. Find k.
$\frac{2}{3} = k(10)$	
$\left(\frac{2}{3}\right)\left(\frac{1}{10}\right) = k$	
$k = \frac{1}{15}$	
$y = \frac{1}{15}x$	2. Find y.
$y = \left(\frac{1}{15}\right)\left(\frac{15}{2}\right)$	
$y = \frac{1}{2}$	

A relation is linear if it can be put in the standard form of a line $ax + by = c$. Direct variation describes certain lines ($y = kx$, $k > 0$), but it also applies to some other relations. Study this example.

EXAMPLE 5   The distance that an object falls varies directly with the square of the time. If an object falls 64 feet in 2 seconds, how far does it fall in 5 seconds?

Answer

$d = kt^2$	1. Write the direct variation between distance d and the square of the time t^2.
$64 = k \cdot 2^2$	2. Substitute $d = 64$ and $t = 2$.
$64 = k \cdot 4$	
$16 = k$	
$d = 16t^2$	3. Substitute 16 in the original equation.
$d = 16 \cdot 5^2$	4. Find d when $t = 5$.
$d = 16 \cdot 25$	
$d = 400$ ft.	

Do you see that $d = kt^2$ is not a linear relationship? This type of direct variation problem arises in gravity problems like example 5 and also in surface area and volume problems as you will see in the exercises.

▶ A. Exercises

Write the equation that describes the variation indicated by each table.
Graph the equation on a Cartesian plane.

1.

x	y
0	0
1	6
2	12
3	18

3.

x	y
0	0
1	2
2	4
3	6

2.

x	y
0	0
1	10
2	20
3	30

4.

x	y
0	0
1	0.5
2	1
3	1.5

5. The formula for the additional pressure resulting from being underwater is $p = 0.433h$, where h is the depth below the surface. Is this a direct variation? If it is, what is the constant of variation? Make a table of at least 3 values.

6. The formula for the circumference of a circle is $C = \pi d$. What is the constant of variation in this formula?

If y varies directly with x, find the value of k when x and y have the values given. Then write the equation that expresses the variation.

7. $x = 9, y = 18$

9. $x = 7, y = 4$

8. $x = 5, y = \frac{1}{2}$

10. $x = 12, y = 2$

11. If y varies directly with x, and $y = 16$ when $x = 4$, find y when $x = 10$.

12. If y varies directly with x, and $y = 3$ when $x = 2$, find y when $x = 7$.

13. If y varies directly with x, and $y = 5$ when $x = 1$, find y when $x = 20$.

14. Write a formula expressing the relationship of the distance (d) a car travels at the rate of 52 mph if the distance varies directly with the time (t) in hours.

▶ B. Exercises

For each item below, answer the following questions. Is it a relation? Is it a function? Is it linear? Is it a direct variation?

15. $y = -3x$

18. $y = \frac{1}{3}x$

16. $x = 2$

19. $y = -2x + 3$

17. $y + 2x$

20. $y = 3x^2$

21. The annual interest of a certain bank account varies directly with the principal. If $200 earns $12 annual interest, how much annual interest will $347 earn?

22. The force exerted to stretch a spring is in direct variation with the distance stretched. If a force of 3 newtons stretches a spring 2 meters, how much force is needed to stretch it 5 meters?

23. For a certain electrical resistance, the force is directly proportional to the current. If the current is 6 amps when the force is 15 volts, find the current when the force is 40 volts.

▶ C. Exercises

24. The speed of a falling object is directly proportional to the square of the elapsed time. If an object is falling at 256 ft. per second after 4 seconds, how fast was it falling after 3 seconds?

25. The volume of a rubber ball varies directly with the cube of the radius. If the volume of a rubber ball is 33.5 cubic inches when the radius is 2 in., find the volume of a ball with a 3 in. radius (nearest cubic inch).

■ Cumulative Review

$A = \{x \mid -5 \le x < 1 \text{ and } x \text{ is an integer}\}$
$B = \{x \mid -3 < x \le 4 \text{ and } x \text{ is an integer}\}$
$C = \{x \mid |x| > 4\}$
$D = \{x \mid x > 4\}$
$E = \{x \mid x < -4\}$

26. List the elements of set A.
27. Find $A \cup B$.
28. Find $B \cap D$.
29. Graph set C on a number line.
30. State the relationship among sets C, D, and E in symbols.

6.10 Graphing Linear Inequalities

Linear inequalities are similar to equations but contain an inequality instead of an equal sign. Remember, an inequality uses the symbols $\ne$, $<$, $>$, $\le$, or $\ge$ and has many solutions.

In the case of $x > 3$, every point to the right of three on the number line is a solution. A linear inequality, such as $2x + y > 3$, will divide the plane into two parts and every point on one side of the line will be a solution. Depending upon the inequality, the points on the line may or may not be solutions.

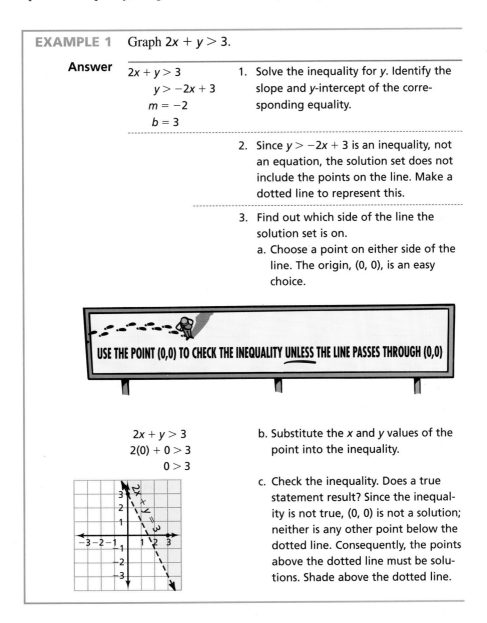

EXAMPLE 1   Graph $2x + y > 3$.

Answer

$2x + y > 3$
$\quad y > -2x + 3$
$\quad\quad m = -2$
$\quad\quad\quad b = 3$

1. Solve the inequality for y. Identify the slope and y-intercept of the corresponding equality.

2. Since $y > -2x + 3$ is an inequality, not an equation, the solution set does not include the points on the line. Make a dotted line to represent this.

3. Find out which side of the line the solution set is on.
   a. Choose a point on either side of the line. The origin, $(0, 0)$, is an easy choice.

USE THE POINT (0,0) TO CHECK THE INEQUALITY UNLESS THE LINE PASSES THROUGH (0,0)

$2x + y > 3$
$2(0) + 0 > 3$
$\quad\quad 0 > 3$

b. Substitute the x and y values of the point into the inequality.

c. Check the inequality. Does a true statement result? Since the inequality is not true, $(0, 0)$ is not a solution; neither is any other point below the dotted line. Consequently, the points above the dotted line must be solutions. Shade above the dotted line.

If the point you chose makes the inequality true, all points on that side of the line will also make the inequality true. In such a case, you would shade the same side as the point you chose. For instance, in the example above, suppose you chose (3, 4), which is above the dotted line.

$$2x + y > 3$$
$$2 \cdot 3 + 4 > 3$$
$$6 + 4 > 3$$
$$10 > 3 \quad \text{So (3, 4) is a solution.}$$

This means that all points above the dotted line are solutions to this inequality. Again, you would shade the area above the dotted line. Notice that there are an infinite number of solutions.

Graphing Inequalities

1. Solve for y and identify the slope and y-intercept of the corresponding equality.
2. If the inequality is $<$ or $>$, use a dotted line to indicate that points on the line are not solutions. If the inequality is $\leq$ or $\geq$, use a solid line since points on the line are solutions.
3. Choose any point not on the line and substitute it in the inequality. If the inequality is true, shade the side where the point is. If the inequality is false, shade the other side.

EXAMPLE 2   Graph $6x - 2y \geq 10$.

Answer

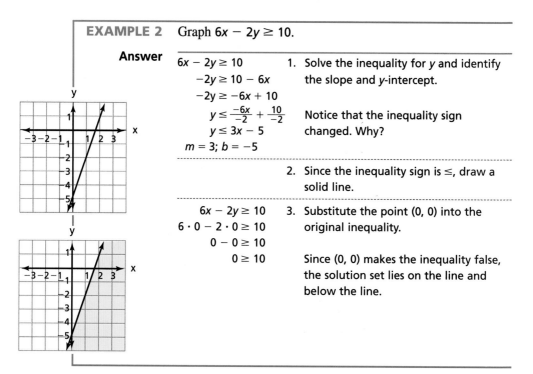

$$6x - 2y \geq 10$$
$$-2y \geq 10 - 6x$$
$$-2y \geq -6x + 10$$
$$y \leq \frac{-6x}{-2} + \frac{10}{-2}$$
$$y \leq 3x - 5$$
$$m = 3; b = -5$$

1. Solve the inequality for y and identify the slope and y-intercept.

   Notice that the inequality sign changed. Why?

2. Since the inequality sign is $\leq$, draw a solid line.

$$6x - 2y \geq 10$$
$$6 \cdot 0 - 2 \cdot 0 \geq 10$$
$$0 - 0 \geq 10$$
$$0 \geq 10$$

3. Substitute the point (0, 0) into the original inequality.

   Since (0, 0) makes the inequality false, the solution set lies on the line and below the line.

As a check, you can try some points in the portion you shaded. Do they make the inequality true?

If the inequality is solved for y, it is easy to determine which side of the line should be shaded. On the y-axis, up means larger values of y and down smaller values of y. Therefore, if $y <$, shade below. If $y >$, shade above. Notice in example 2, $y \leq 3x - 5$, the shading was below the line. *Caution:* For this method to work, the inequality must be in $y = mx + b$ form.

▶ A. Exercises

Graph each of the following inequalities on separate sets of axes.

1. $y > 3x + 2$
2. $y \leq -5x + 7$
3. $y \geq 2x - 6$
4. $3x + y > 12$
5. $2x - y \leq 4$
6. $3x - 2y \geq 6$
7. $x + y > -2$
8. $2x - y > -9$
9. $x + 3y \leq 12$
10. $x - 4y \geq 16$

▶ B. Exercises

11. How many solutions are there to a linear inequality?
12. Are inequalities relations? functions?

Graph each of the inequalities on the Cartesian plane.

13. $y \geq 5$
14. $x < -4$
15. $3y < 7$
16. $-x \leq -2$

Express the following inequalities in symbols and graph the region indicated.

17. The sum of two numbers x and y is at least five.
18. One number, y, is at most five times another number, x.

▶ C. Exercises

Graph the following conjunctions and disjunctions, shading the region that satisfies them.

19. $y \geq 2x + 3$ or $y \leq 2x - 1$
20. $x > 1$ and $x \leq 4$

▪ Cumulative Review

Simplify.

21. $3x^2 - 5x(x + 2) + 10x + 2x^2$
22. $x + y - 3x + y + xy + y + x$
23. $2(5 + 3) - 3 + 5 \cdot 6 + 4^0$

Solve.

24. $5x - 3 = 2(x + 4) - 7$
25. $4 - 3x < 8$

Algebra *and* Scripture

In this chapter we have studied relations. In math, relations are sets of ordered pairs. In general, people are related when they are connected by marriage or ancestry. Spiritually, every Christian is related to Jesus Christ and God the Father (Gal. 4:1-7 and I John 4:14-16) as well as to all other Christians (Eph. 2:19).

We have seen that God is changeless—He doesn't change His mind or Himself (Heb. 13:8). This means that God is faithful in all His relationships. He keeps His promises. Read Numbers 23:19.

1. What phrase implies that God does not change?
2. What phrase shows that God is faithful?
3. What phrase says that God is truth?

Math also reflects these qualities of godliness. Math doesn't change; it is constant and consistent, because it describes with precise notation, principles of God's consistent and orderly creation.

4. Can you think of a lesson in which it was important for us to determine whether a math statement was true or false?

THE NTH DEGREE

What Bible verse says, "it is impossible for God to lie"?

Number relations appear in Scripture too. In Chapters 3 and 4, you found numerical equations and inequalities in the Bible. For a function in Scripture, let's look at the assignment of an order of service to the sons of Aaron (I Chron. 24:1-18). Each son was assigned a number, so the sons form the domain.

5. What is the range of this function?

Another example of a function in the Scripture is the conversion function of Ezekiel 45:11. If x is the number of homers and y is the number of baths . . .

6. Give a function that expresses the relation in the verse.

7. Is it a direct variation?

> ### Scriptural Roots
>
> GOD IS NOT A MAN,
>
> that he should lie;
>
> neither the son of man,
>
> that he should repent:
>
> hath he said, and shall
>
> he not do it? or hath
>
> he spoken, and shall he
>
> not make it good? ❧
>
> NUMBERS 23:19

On a sheet of graph paper, graph the ordered pairs and label each point. Then tell which quadrant the point is in.

1. $(3, -5)$

2. $(-6, 7)$

3. $(2, 9)$

4. $(-3, -1)$

5. $(0, 5)$

6. $(-7, 0)$

State which are relations. Give their domain and range. Then tell if the relation is also a function.

7. $(3, 7), (-2, 4), (1, 8)$

8. $(2, 8), (9, 4), (2, 7)$

9. $(-1, 4), (3, 4), (7, 4)$

Graph these relations. Then state whether they are functions.

10.

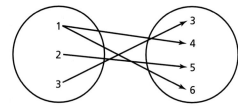

11. $y = x + 4$ with $-4 \leq x \leq 6$

12. $y = x - 5$ with $3 \leq x \leq 8$ and x is an integer

13. $y = \frac{x}{3}$ with $x \in \{-3, 0, 6, 9\}$

14. $A \times B$ if $A = \{1, 3\}$ and $B = \{-1, 1, 2\}$

Find the slope of the line passing through the given points.

15. $(2, 5), (3, -7)$

16. $(5, 7), (-3, -4)$

17. $(-8, -2), (4, -6)$

Place each equation in slope-intercept form. Then give the slope and *y*-intercept of the line.

18. $5x + y = 9$

19. $3x + 2y = 8$

20. $12x + 4y = 16$

Graph each linear equation.
21. $3x + y = 6$
22. $x - 2y = 12$
23. $4x + 3y = 15$
24. $9x - 3y = 12$
25. $5x + y = 9$

Find the equation of the line.
26. with $m = 3$ and $b = -\frac{1}{5}$
27. with $m = \frac{1}{2}$ and passing through (10, 3)
28. passing through (2, 9) and (−1, 4)
29. passing through (11, 2) and (11, 3)
30. passing through (7, 8) and (0, 3)
31. passing through (2, −1) and parallel to $5x + y = 8$

Find the value of the constant of variation when y varies directly with x.
32. $x = 2$
    $y = 10$
33. $x = 6$
    $y = 3$
34. If y varies directly with x and $y = 12$ when $x = 3$, find y when $x = 15$.
35. The sales tax in a certain city varies directly with the cost of the item. $3 tax is assessed on an item costing $42.87. How much tax will there be on a five-dollar item?

Graph.
36. $y \leq x + 7$
37. $6x + 2y < 18$
38. $y > 3x + 4$
39. $y \geq 5x - 1$
40. Explain the mathematical significance of Numbers 23:19.

7 Systems of Equations and Inequalities

Every manufacturing plant depends on a group of accountants and analysts who plan the production process. Each product has a break-even point, which describes the number of items that should be manufactured and sold for the business to break even (make income equal production cost). Since one goal of any company is to make a profit, the company will want to make and sell more items than the break-even number.

Mr. Fitzgerald is starting a company that makes hot-air balloons. He determines that his fixed manufacturing cost will be $30,000 per month (electricity and water bills, rent for office and production space, cleaning, and so forth) plus $7500 per item manufactured. He decides to sell each balloon for $13,500. How many balloons should he make and sell to break even?

He lets x represent the number of items to make and sell. The break-even point is computed by comparing two equations: cost and revenue (income). The cost equation can be expressed by $C = 30,000 + 7500x$. Since each balloon sells for $13,500, the revenue equation is $R = 13,500x$.

Business and other fields require a knowledge of solving systems of equations. In this chapter you will learn methods of solving them. By the end of the chapter you should be able to solve the above problem. More advanced methods build on the basic principles of this chapter.

After this chapter you should be able to

1. solve a system of linear equations by using three different methods: graphing, substitution, and addition.

2. classify a system of equations as consistent or inconsistent, dependent or independent.

3. solve word problems using systems.

4. solve a given system of inequalities.

7.1 Solving Systems of Equations by Graphing

The slope of a side of the pyramid, El Castillo, at Chichén Itzá, Mexico, is greater than the slope of the staircase on that side.

Up to this point all of your work in algebra has consisted of working one equation at a time. First you graphed and solved equations with one variable, or unknown (x). Then you learned to graph equations in two variables (x and y). Now you will learn to find the solution to systems of two equations in two variables. A solution to such a system must satisfy both equations at the same time.

EXAMPLE 1   Is (11, 2) a solution to the system?

$$x - y = 9$$
$$2x + y = 9$$

Answer

$x - y = 9$	$2x + y = 9$
$11 - 2 = 9$	$2(11) + 2 = 9$
$9 = 9$	$24 = 9$

(11, 2) is not a solution since it satisfies only one equation. Is (6, −3) a solution to the system?

$x - y = 9$	$2x + y = 9$
$6 - (-3) = 9$	$2(6) + (-3) = 9$
$9 = 9$	$12 - 3 = 9$
	$9 = 9$

(6, −3) is a solution.

Systems of equations can be solved several ways. To find the solution to a system of equations, you might consider all the ordered pairs that make the first equation true and then identify which one of them would also make the second equation true. Unfortunately infinitely many ordered pairs make the first equation true: for example, (−6, 4) or (−10, 8) or (−1.5, −0.5). But only one of them also makes the second equation true. This method is too time consuming and tedious.

A more appropriate method is to graph both equations on the same set of axes. The solution to the system is the ordered pair for the point where the two lines intersect.

EXAMPLE 2 Solve the system.

$$x + y = -2$$
$$x - y = 4$$

Answer

$$x + y = -2$$
$$y = -x - 2$$

$$x - y = 4$$
$$-y = -x + 4$$
$$y = x - 4$$

1. Change each equation to slope-intercept form.

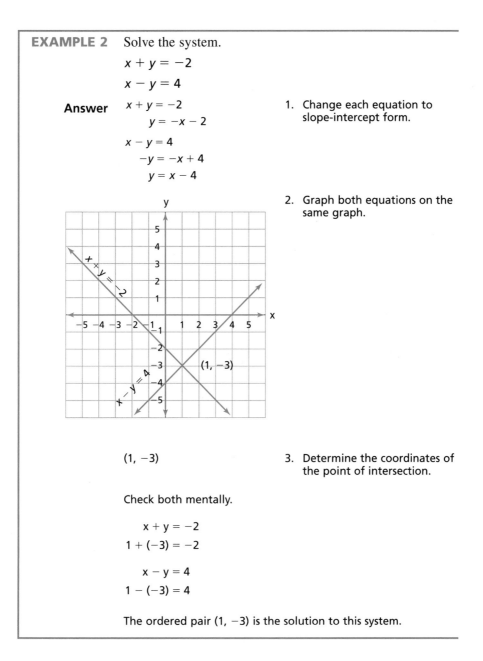

2. Graph both equations on the same graph.

$(1, -3)$

3. Determine the coordinates of the point of intersection.

Check both mentally.

$$x + y = -2$$
$$1 + (-3) = -2$$

$$x - y = 4$$
$$1 - (-3) = 4$$

The ordered pair $(1, -3)$ is the solution to this system.

EXAMPLE 3   Solve.
$$x + y = 5$$
$$3x + y = 7$$

Answer $x + y = 5$

$y = -x + 5$

$3x + y = 7$

$y = -3x + 7$

1. Change both equations to slope-intercept form.

2. Graph both equations.

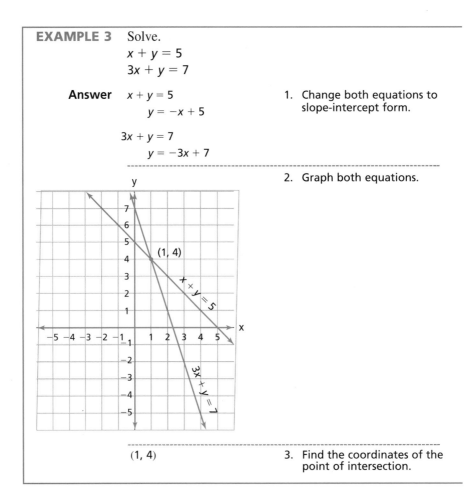

(1, 4)

3. Find the coordinates of the point of intersection.

Solving a System of Linear Equations by Graphing

1. Solve each equation for *y* to obtain slope-intercept form.
2. Graph both equations on the same set of axes and label each line.
3. Find the coordinates of the point of intersection of the two lines.
4. Check the solution in both of the original equations.

Some biblical events happened at the same time. The simultaneous events of Matthew 27:35-54 reveal our access to God through Christ. Before Christ died, only one man, the high priest, entered the presence of God once a year by entering the holy of holies beyond the veil. The veil in the temple symbolized the separation between man and God. But when Jesus died for our sins, "the veil of the temple was rent in twain from the top to the bottom." God ripped the veil simultaneously with the death of Jesus to show that Christ had provided direct access to God (Heb. 4:15-16).

► A. Exercises

Is $(-2, 5)$ a solution to each system?

1. $x + y = 3$
   $2x + y = 1$

2. $x + 2y = 8$
   $3x + y = 1$

3. $x - y = 7$
   $2x + 3y = 4$

4. $3x + 2y = 4$
   $5x + 3y = 5$

For each system determine whether the given point is the solution.

5. $x + 3y = 13; (2, -5)$
   $6x + y = 7$

6. $2x - 5y = 9; (7, 1)$
   $x + y = 8$

7. $x + 2y = 1; (-3, -2)$
   $3x - 2y = 5$

8. $3x - y = -7; (-1, 4)$
   $x - 5y = -19$

9. $5x + 6y = 0; (6, -5)$
   $2x + y = 7$

10. $y = -2; (-2, -8)$
    $y = 4x$

► B. Exercises

Graph each system of linear equations to find its solution.

11. $x + y = 5$
    $x - y = 1$

12. $x - y = -2$
    $4x - y = 4$

13. $6x + y = 7$
    $y = 1$

14. $x + 2y = 10$
    $9x + 2y = -6$

15. $8x - 3y = -12$
    $4x - y = -8$

16. $4x + y = 7$
    $x - 3y = 18$

17. $x + y = 9$
    $11x + y = 19$

18. $9x - y = -5$
    $12x - y = -8$

19. $x - 5y = -30$
    $2x - y = 3$

► C. Exercises

Graph the following equations and estimate the solution of the system.

20. $9x - 2y = 7$
    $3x + 4y = 14$

■ Cumulative Review

Simplify.

21. $\frac{3}{5} + \frac{12}{35} \cdot \frac{49}{9}$

22. $\left| \frac{7}{26} - \frac{14}{39} \right|$

23. $\sqrt[3]{\frac{8}{343}}$

24. $\frac{6^{-2}}{3} \cdot \frac{2^{-1}}{9^{-3}}$

25. $\sqrt{\frac{527}{144} + \frac{1}{72}}$

7.2 Using the Graphing Method

F-16 jets flying parallel courses

If you draw two lines on a piece of paper, one of the following possibilities will result.

The three pairs of lines shown represent the three possible relationships of a system of two linear equations. So far, the two-equation problems you have graphed have produced a pair of intersecting lines. The coordinates of the point of intersection identify the only solution to both equations. Notice in the illustration shown that when the two lines are parallel, no solution to the system exists.

EXAMPLE 1 Solve the system.

$$x + y = 3$$
$$x + y = 7$$

Answer

$x + y = 3$ $\quad y = -x + 3$	1. Obtain slope-intercept form for each equation.
$x + y = 7$ $\quad y = -x + 7$	

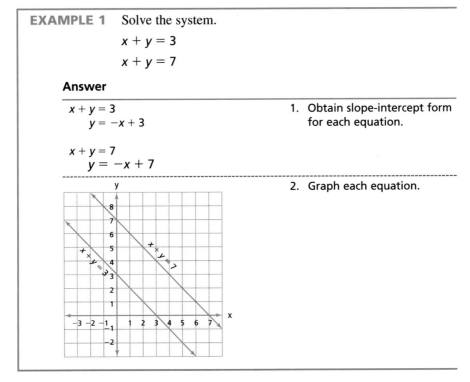

2. Graph each equation.

Since there is no point of intersection for the two parallel lines, the system has no solution.

Every pair of parallel lines represents an inconsistent system of linear equations. All systems without solutions are called inconsistent. In contrast, a system having a solution is called consistent.

EXAMPLE 2   Solve.

$$2x + y = -4$$
$$x - 3y = -9$$

Answer

$$2x + y = -4$$
$$y = -2x - 4$$

$$x - 3y = -9$$
$$-3y = -x - 9$$
$$y = \frac{1}{3}x + 3$$

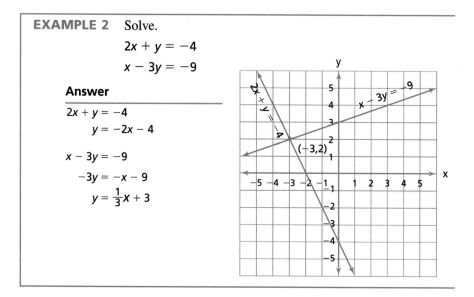

The solution is one point, $(-3, 2)$. The system is consistent and independent. Any system of linear equations that intersect in one point is called consistent. They are also independent: the two equations do not represent the same line.

EXAMPLE 3   Solve simultaneously.

$$x + y = 3$$
$$2x + 2y = 6$$

Answer

$$x + y = 3$$
$$y = -x + 3$$

$$2x + 2y = 6$$
$$2y = -2x + 6$$
$$y = -x + 3$$

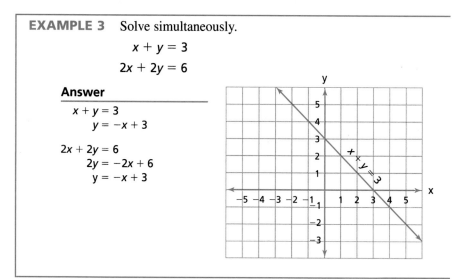

Since the slope-intercept form of these two equations is the same, their graphs are identical. The line described by the equation $y = -x + 3$ is the graph for both equations. Thus, the entire line is the solution to the system. The line contains an infinite number of points all of which are solutions.

Any linear system of equations that produces an infinite number of solutions is called consistent but dependent (not independent).

To summarize, a system of two linear equations may have 0, 1, or an infinite number of solutions. Use the slope-intercept form of the equations to determine the number of solutions.

Definitions

A **consistent system of equations** is a system that has at least one solution.

A **dependent system of equations** is a consistent system that has an infinite number of solutions.

Notice that *inconsistent* means not consistent and *independent* means not dependent.

POSSIBLE SOLUTIONS FOR SYSTEMS OF EQUATIONS

	Consistent		Inconsistent
	Independent	*Dependent*	
Number of solutions	finite	infinite	none
Graphs	graphs intersect	graphs coincide	graphs do not intersect
Applied to lines (number of solutions)	one	all points on the line	none

▶ A. Exercises

Solve each system by graphing and tell whether it is consistent or inconsistent. If the system is consistent, tell whether it is dependent or independent.

1. $x + y = 4$
   $5x + y = 8$

2. $x - y = 3$
   $4x - y = 15$

3. $2x + y = 8$
   $4x + 2y = 16$

4. $3x + y = 5$
   $4x + 3y = 15$

5. $x + 2y - 10 = 0$
   $3x + 2y = 14$

6. $8x - 2y = 6$
   $y = 4x + 3$

7. $x - 2y = 4$
   $3x + 2y = -12$

8. $x + 2y = 8$
   $y = -\frac{x}{2} + 4$

▶ B. Exercises

Solve each system by graphing and tell whether it is consistent or inconsistent. If the system is consistent, tell whether it is dependent or independent.

9. $x = -3$
   $x = 4$

10. $x - y = 6$
    $5x - 5y = 30$

11. $5x - 3y = -12$
    $2x + 3y = -9$

12. $2x - 7y = 21$
    $3x + 7y = 14$

13. $3x + 4y = 20$
    $x + 2y = 8$

14. $x - y = -4$
    $x + 3y = 24$

15. $3x + 4y = 4$
    $x - 2y = 8$

16. $3x + y = 5$
    $y = 3x - 4$

17. $3x - 5y = -15$
    $3x + 5y = 45$

18. $x + y = -4$
    $y = -7$

19. $x - 3y = -15$
    $y = 4$

20. $12x + 4y = 8$
    $3y = 15 - 9x$

▶ C. Exercises

Draw conclusions about the slopes and y-intercepts of the following types of systems of linear equations.

21. inconsistent systems
22. dependent systems
23. independent systems

▮ Cumulative Review

Solve.

24. $x - 5 = 8$

25. $5x - 11 = 2x + 4$

26. $\frac{1}{32}x + \frac{3}{40} = \frac{7}{16}$

27. $4(x - 3) \leq 8x$

28. $\left| 2x + 1 \right| > 19$

7.3 Solving Simple Systems of Equations by Substitution

Substitution refers to replacing one thing with another. As sinful humans, we are condemned to die. But Jesus paid sin's penalty for us through His death and shed blood at Calvary. (Read II Cor. 5:14-15.) If you are saved, thank God continually for providing a substitute for you so that you do not have to face the wrath and judgment of God. If you are not saved, accept the substitutionary death of Jesus as your hope of eternal life in heaven.

The graphing method of solving systems of equations works well if the solutions are small integers, but it becomes awkward when the solutions are large or fractional. A more precise method for solving simultaneous equations is the *substitution method*. With this method you solve one equation for one variable in terms of the other, substitute the solution into the other equation, and then solve for the other variable.

EXAMPLE 1 Solve.

$$x + y = -4$$
$$x - y = 10$$

Answer

$x + y = -4$ $x = -4 - y$	1. Solve the first equation for x in terms of y. The equation says that x equals $-4 - y$.
$x - y = 10$ $(-4 - y) - y = 10$ $-4 - y - y = 10$ $-4 - 2y = 10$ $-2y = 14$ $y = -7$	2. Substitute $-4 - y$ for x in the second equation and solve for y.
$x + y = -4$ $x + (-7) = -4$ $x = -4 + 7$ $x = 3$	3. Substitute your result, $y = -7$, in either equation and solve for x. This is called back-substitution.
$(3, -7)$	4. Write the ordered pair from the values $x = 3$ and $y = -7$.

Continued ▶

Check.

$x + y = -4$	5. Check the solution in the original equations.

$$3 + (-7) = -4 \qquad x - y = 10$$
$$3 - (-7) = 10$$

EXAMPLE 2 Solve.

$$x + y = 5$$
$$3x + y = 7$$

Answer

$3x + y = 7$ $y = -3x + 7$	1. Solve the second equation for y in terms of x.
$x + y = 5$ $x + (-3x + 7) = 5$ $-2x + 7 = 5$ $-2x = -2$ $x = 1$	2. Substitute $-3x + 7$ for y into the first equation and solve for x.
$3x + y = 7$ $3(1) + y = 7$ $y = -3 + 7$ $y = 4$	3. Find y by back-substituting $x = 1$ into the second equation.
The solution is the ordered pair (1, 4).	4. State the solution as an ordered pair.
$1 + 4 = 5$ and $3(1) + 4 = 7$	5. Check your answer mentally.

IT DOESN'T MATTER WHICH EQUATION YOU WORK WITH FIRST OR WHICH VARIABLE YOU SOLVE FIRST...

THE SOLUTION SHOULD ALWAYS BE GIVEN AS AN ORDERED PAIR

EXAMPLE 3 Solve by substitution.

$$x = 4y$$
$$3x + 2y = 8$$

Answer

$x = 4y$	1. The first equation is already solved for x in terms of y.
$3x + 2y = 8$ $3(4y) + 2y = 8$ $12y + 2y = 8$ $14y = 8$ $y = \frac{8}{14}$ $y = \frac{4}{7}$	2. Substitute $4y$ for x in the second equation and solve for y.
$x = 4y$ $x = 4\left(\frac{4}{7}\right)$ $x = \frac{16}{7}$	3. Substitute $\frac{4}{7}$ for y back into the first equation. Solve for x.
The solution is $\left(\frac{16}{7}, \frac{4}{7}\right)$.	4. Give the solution as an ordered pair.
	5. Check mentally.

Solving a System of Equations by the Substitution Method

1. Solve one equation for one variable in terms of the other. Choose the easiest one to solve.
2. Substitute into the other equation by replacing the variable with the equivalent quantity. Solve the equation.
3. Back-substitute the numerical value of the second variable into either original equation. Solve for the other variable.
4. Write the solution as an ordered pair.
5. Check the solution in the original equations.

▶ A. Exercises

Solve each system by substitution. Be sure to give your solution as an ordered pair.

1. $3x + y = 12$
   $x + y = 20$

2. $x + y = 5$
   $x - y = 3$

3. $x + 4y = 30$
   $2x + 5y = 36$

4. $x + 2y = 9$
   $x + y = 28$

5. $x - 5y = 17$
   $2x - 7y = 22$

6. $7x + 3y = 35$
   $x - 2y = 5$

7. $2x + 3y = 25$
   $x - y = -5$
8. $3x + y = 10$
   $x - y = -6$
9. $x - 3y = -5$
   $2x - 5y = -9$

10. $x - y = 1$
    $x - 3y = 9$
11. $x + 8y = 23$
    $x + 3y = 8$
12. $x - y = 2$
    $x + y = 6$

▶ B. Exercises

Solve each system by substitution. Be sure to give your solution as an ordered pair.

13. $3x + 5y = 13$
    $x + 8y = 36$
14. $x + y = 10$
    $y = 2x$
15. $2x - y = -4$
    $x + y = -6$
16. $2x + 4y = 10$
    $3x - y = 18$

17. $x + 3y = 14$
    $x = 2y$
18. $5x - y = 6$
    $6x - y = 9$
19. $13x + 7y = 88$
    $x + 8y = -38$

▶ C. Exercises

Solve each system by substitution. Be sure to give your solution as an ordered pair.

20. $2x - 3y = 16$
    $5x + 9y = -59$

21. $3x + 5y = 8$
    $7x - 2y = 10$

■ Cumulative Review

Multiple choice. Identify the number that

22. is not a real number.
    A. -7 C. $\sqrt{-1}$ E. $\frac{1}{3}$
    B. $\sqrt{5}$ D. 0

23. is not an integer.
    A. -7 C. $4\frac{1}{2}$ E. $\frac{6}{3}$
    B. $\sqrt{4}$ D. 0

24. is not a rational number.
    A. -7 C. $\frac{11}{5}$ E. $2.\overline{34}$
    B. $\sqrt{5}$ D. 0

25. is a natural number.
    A. -7 C. $\frac{3}{2}$ E. $\frac{6}{3}$
    B. $\sqrt{3}$ D. 0

26. is a whole number.
    A. -7 C. $4\frac{1}{2}$ E. 4^{-1}
    B. $\sqrt{3}$ D. 0

7.4 Solving Systems by the Substitution Method

When you graphed a system of equations, how did you determine that it was consistent or inconsistent? When you use the algebraic method, how can you tell if a system is consistent or inconsistent? Watch what happens when you solve this inconsistent system algebraically by substitution.

Sand dunes are classified using systems. If the prevailing wind direction parallels dune length, seif *dunes result. Otherwise,* barchan *dunes form, such as this dune in the Sahara.*

$x + y = 5$
$x + y = 7$

$x + y = 5$ $y = -x + 5$	1. Solve the first equation for y and substitute the derived expression in the second equation.
$x + y = 7$ $x + (-x + 5) = 7$ $5 = 7$	2. Solving the second equation, you find that the variables are gone and the resulting statement is false.

Whenever you solve a system algebraically in which all variable terms vanish and you get a false statement as a solution, the system is inconsistent. It has no solution.

Now look at a consistent, but dependent, system.

$x + y = 2$
$3x + 3y = 6$

$x + y = 2$ $y = 2 - x$	1. Solve this equation for y.
$3x + 3y = 6$ $3x + 3(2 - x) = 6$ $3x + 6 - 3x = 6$	2. Substitute this expression into the second equation.
$6 = 6$	3. The result is a true statement with no variables. The system is consistent and dependent and has an infinite number of ordered pairs as solutions.

EXAMPLE 1 Solve the system.

$2x + 3y = 16$

$4x + 5y = 28$

Answer

$2x + 3y = 16$ $2x = 16 - 3y$ $x = \dfrac{16 - 3y}{2}$	1. Solve one of the equations for one of the variables. Here we solve the first equation for x.
$4x + 5y = 28$ $4\left(\dfrac{16 - 3y}{2}\right) + 5y = 28$ $2(16 - 3y) + 5y = 28$ $32 - 6y + 5y = 28$ $-y = -4$ $y = 4$	2. Now substitute this quantity for x in the second equation.
$2x + 3y = 16$ $2x + 3(4) = 16$ $2x = 4$ $x = 2$ The solution is $(2, 4)$.	3. Substitute 4 for y in the first equation
$2(2) + 3(4) = 16$ $4(2) + 5(4) = 28$	4. Check mentally using $x = 2$ and $y = 4$.

So far, all the systems of equations you have studied in this chapter have been linear systems. Some systems of equations are not linear but can still be solved by the substitution method. The next example shows the solution of a nonlinear system.

EXAMPLE 2   Solve the system.

$$x^2 = y$$
$$x^2 + 3y = 64$$

Answer

$x^2 + 3y = 64$	1. Substitute so that you will get a linear
$y + 3y = 64$	equation with one unknown. Since $x^2 = y$,
$4y = 64$	substitute y for x^2 in the second equation.
$y = 16$	Solve for y.
$x^2 = y$	2. Now find the value of x by substituting
$x^2 = 16$	16 for y in the first equation.
$x = \pm\sqrt{16}$	
$x = \pm 4$	

There are two possible solutions to this problem: (4, 16) and (−4, 16). The system is consistent since it has solutions. It is independent since it has only two solutions rather than infinitely many.

▶ A. Exercises

Solve each system of equations by the substitution method. Tell whether each system is inconsistent or consistent. If the system is consistent, tell whether it is independent or dependent.

1. $x + y = 14$
   $3x + 2(y - 5) = 21$

2. $x + 6y = -9$
   $4x - 7y = -5$

3. $2x - y = 11$
   $6x - 3y = -24$

4. $2x - 3y = -13$
   $x - 11y = 3$

5. $x + 3y = 18$
   $3x - y = -6$

6. $5x + 7y = 38$
   $9x + y = 80$

7. $2(x + y) - 5(x + 1) = 3$
   $-3x + 2y = 8$

8. $x - 3y = -9$
   $x - y = 1$

9. $5x - 4y = 11$
   $3x - y = 1$

10. $4x + 7y = 2$
    $5x - 3y = -21$

▶ B. Exercises

Solve each system of equations by the substitution method.

11. $2x - 8y = 7$
    $3x + y = -2$

12. $4x + 3y = 9$
    $x - 5y = 6$

13. $y^2 = x + 9$
    $4x + y^2 = 209$

14. $3x + 5y = 8$
    $2x - 4y = 7$

15. $10x - 12y = 14$
    $35 + 30y = 25x$

16. $15x - 24y = 7$
    $32y + 9 = 20x$

Write two equations and solve the system by substitution.

17. The sum of two numbers is 63, and their difference is 13. Find the two numbers.
18. The sum of two numbers is 996. The difference of the larger and twice the smaller is 33. Find the two numbers.

▶ C. Exercises

Solve each system by the substitution method.

19. $(x + y)^2 = 36$
    $x + y = 6$

20. $x^2 + y = 5$
    $8x^2 - 2y = 0$

21. $x^2 + y^2 = 25$
    $2x^2 - 3y^2 = 5$

■ Cumulative Review

Graph. Use number lines or Cartesian planes as appropriate.

22. $\{(5, 1), (-1, 2)\}$

23. $x + 5 = 7$

24. $5 - x > 3$

25. $|x| = 2$

26. $y = -5x + 3$

27. $y > 2 - x$

Permutations

The word *permutation* means "arrangement," so the number of permutations is the number of arrangements, which can be applied to such diverse things as books on a shelf to batting order of a baseball team.

Since arrangements are determined by the number of options in each position, the formula derives from the multiplication principle of counting. By considering the number of objects for each position, 7 objects can be arranged in $7 \cdot 6 \cdot 5 \cdot 4 \cdot 3 \cdot 2 \cdot 1$, or **5040**, ways. This calculation is symbolized by 7! (read 7 factorial) and by $_7P_7$. The latter symbol abbreviates 7 objects permuted 7 at a time but is more frequently read "the number of permutations of 7 objects taken seven at a time."

EXAMPLE 1   Each issue of a magazine presents a travel column about a Canadian province. How many ways can three different Canadian provinces be featured?

Lake Louise at Banff National Park in the Canadian Rockies is a world-famous attraction in the province of Alberta.

Answer   First, recall (or look up) the number of provinces in Canada: ten. Next, recognize that the answer to the question is represented by $_{10}P_3$. Finally, calculate the number of permutations of 10 objects taken 3 at a time using the multiplication principle of counting: $10 \cdot 9 \cdot 8 = 720$ possible arrangements.

Notice in the example that the calculation of

$_{10}P_3 = 10 \cdot 9 \cdot 8$ is the same as $\frac{10!}{7!}$ as shown below.

$$10 \cdot 9 \cdot 8 = \frac{10 \cdot 9 \cdot 8 \cdot \cancel{7} \cdot \cancel{6} \cdot \cancel{5} \cdot \cancel{4} \cdot \cancel{3} \cdot \cancel{2} \cdot \cancel{1}}{\cancel{7} \cdot \cancel{6} \cdot \cancel{5} \cdot \cancel{4} \cdot \cancel{3} \cdot \cancel{2} \cdot \cancel{1}}$$

In other words, you can calculate the arrangements of 3 out of 10 objects by calculating the arrangements of 10 objects and dividing out the unused arrangements of the other 7 objects. Do you see that the formula for n objects permuted r at a time is the following ratio?

$$_nP_r = \frac{n!}{(n-r)!}$$

EXAMPLE 2 How many ways can a president, vice president, secretary, and treasurer be chosen from a board of trustees with twelve members.

Answer Calculate $_{12}P_4 = \frac{12!}{(12-4)!}$

$$= \frac{12!}{8!}$$
$$= 12 \cdot 11 \cdot 10 \cdot 9$$
$$= 11{,}880$$

What happens when some of the objects are indistinguishable? In such cases, you can divide out the number of repeats.

EXAMPLE 3 How many different arrangements of the letters of ARKANSAS are there?

Answer Notice that you can switch the two S's without obtaining a different arrangement of letters. This means that you must divide 8! by two in order to avoid counting each spelling twice because of the order of the S's. Similarly, the three A's can be arranged in 3!, or 6, ways, and so we must divide out the 3! repeats of each spelling based on switching the A's. Thus, the number of different arrangements of the letters is given by $\frac{8!}{2!\,3!} = \frac{40{,}320}{2 \cdot 6} = 3360$.

▶ Exercises

1. Find $_{22}P_4$.
2. Find $_8P_8$.
3. How many ways can you arrange 7 out of 11 different books on a shelf?
4. How many arrangements of the letters of MASSACHUSETTS are there?
5. Ten objects are in a box and two will be drawn without looking. What is the probability that you correctly guess the two objects in order?

7.5 Solving Simple Systems of Equations by the Addition Method

So far you have learned to solve systems of linear equations by graphing and by substitution. Another method, called the *addition method,* avoids much of the work with fractions. For this method, add or subtract the two equations (or multiples of them) to eliminate one of the variables. Solve for the remaining variable. The second variable can be found by back-substitution into one of the original equations.

EXAMPLE 1 Solve the system.

$$x + y = 4$$
$$x - y = 10$$

Answer

$x + y = 4$ $x - y = 10$ $2x = 14$	1. Add the two equations to eliminate the y terms (which have opposite signs and the same coefficients). If you add the left sides, you must also add the right sides.
$x = 7$	2. Now solve the resulting equation.
$x + y = 4$ $7 + y = 4$ $y = -3$	3. Back-substitute 7 for x in either of the original equations. Then solve for y.
The solution is $(7, -3)$.	4. The values are $x = 7$ and $y = -3$.

Check.

$x + y = 4$	$x - y = 10$
Does $7 + (-3) = 4$?	Does $7 - (-3) = 10$?

This system is quite easy to solve by the addition method. Other systems may be slightly harder to solve, but any linear system can be solved by the addition method.

EXAMPLE 2   Solve.

$$3x + 2y = 8$$
$$3x + 5y = 14$$

Answer

$3x + 2y = 8$ $\underline{3x + 5y = 14}$ $-3y = -6$	1. Because the signs in front of the x terms are the same and the coefficients are the same, subtract the equations and solve for y. Be sure to subtract each term.
$y = 2$	2. Solve for y.
$3x + 2y = 8$ $3x + 2(2) = 8$ $3x + 4 = 8$ $3x = 4$ $x = \dfrac{4}{3}$	3. Find the value of x by back-substituting 2 for y in either of the original equations and solving for x.
The solution is $\left(\dfrac{4}{3}, 2\right)$.	4. Write the ordered pair.

Check.

$3x + 2y = 8$	$3x + 5y = 14$
$3\left(\dfrac{4}{3}\right) + 2(2) = 8$	$3\left(\dfrac{4}{3}\right) + 5(2) = 14$
$4 + 4 = 8$	$4 + 10 = 14$
$8 = 8$	$14 = 14$

Solving a System of Equations by the Addition Method

1. Add or subtract the equations to eliminate one variable.
   a. If the signs preceding the variable to be eliminated are different, add the equations.
   b. If the signs preceding the variable to be eliminated are the same, subtract the equations.
2. Solve the resulting linear equation for the remaining variable.
3. Substitute the value found into either of the original equations and solve for the other variable.
4. Write the solution as an ordered pair.
5. Check the solution in all original equations.

EXAMPLE 3 Solve the system.

$$4x - 2y = 13$$
$$8x + 2y = 23$$

Answer

$4x - 2y = 13$ $\underline{8x + 2y = 23}$ $12x \quad = 36$	1. Because the *y* variables have the same coefficient and different signs, adding the equations eliminates *y*.
$x = 3$	2. Solve for *x*.
$4x - 2y = 13$ $4(3) - 2y = 13$ $12 - 2y = 13$ $-2y = 1$ $y = -\frac{1}{2}$	3. Back-substitute and solve for *y*.

The solution is $\left(3, -\frac{1}{2}\right)$.   4. Write the solution as an ordered pair.

Check.   Since the ordered pair must satisfy both equations, the ordered pair must be checked in each.

$$8x + 2y = 23 \qquad\qquad 4x - 2y = 13$$
$$8(3) + 2\left(-\tfrac{1}{2}\right) = 23 \qquad 4(3) - 2\left(-\tfrac{1}{2}\right) = 13$$
$$24 - 1 = 23 \qquad\qquad 12 + 1 = 13$$
$$23 = 23 \qquad\qquad\quad 13 = 13$$

▶ A. Exercises

Using the addition method, solve each system of equations.

1. $x + y = 5$
   $x - y = -3$

2. $7x + y = 35$
   $x + y = 5$

3. $2x + y = 9$
   $-2x - 3y = 13$

4. $x + 2y = 13$
   $x + 6y = 45$

5. $2x + 3y = 19$
   $2x + 7y = 47$

6. $2x + 9y = 30$
   $2x + y = -2$

7. $x - y = -2$
   $6x + y = -19$

8. $x + y = -3$
   $x = 1$

9. $9x - 4y = -66$
   $x + 4y = 6$

10. $3x - 5y = 8$
    $5y = 10$

▶ B. Exercises

Use the addition method to solve each system of equations.

11. $5x + y = 17$
    $3x + y = 12$

12. $2x + 6y = 5$
    $2x - 3y = -4$

13. $x + 3y = 8$
    $x - 3y = 10$

14. $2x - 7y = 26$
    $x - 7y = 18$

15. $4x + 3y = 7$
    $4x = 7 - 3y$

16. $x + 2y = 9$
    $3x - 2y = 7$

17. $x + 3y = 11$
    $x + 2y = 11$

18. $x + 3y = 11$
    $x + 3y = 7$

▶ C. Exercises

Using the addition method, solve each system of equations.

19. $3x - y = \frac{23}{5}$
    $15x + 25y = 90$

20. $\frac{1}{2}x + \frac{1}{5}y = 1$
    $\frac{3}{2}x + \frac{1}{5}y = -7$

■ Cumulative Review

Simplify.

21. $3x^3y(2x + 5y^2) - 4xy(x^3 + x^2y^2)$

22. $5x - x^2 + 3x + 4 - 7x + 2 - x^2$

23. $\frac{21}{8} + \left(-\frac{21}{8}\right)$

24. $\frac{3}{y} - 7x^0y + 2y + 3x^0y^{-1} - \frac{4}{y^{-1}}$

25. $5y^2(3x^{-2}y^3z^{-1})^{-3}$

KARL FRIEDRICH GAUSS

Karl Friedrich Gauss (1777-1855) was born in a duchy of what is now western Germany, where his father was a bricklayer. His mother and father were common people who did not see the value of an education for their son but thought he should work as a common laborer to help them financially. Johann Martin Bartels, a professor of math at Dorpat, observed Gauss's unique aptitude for calculation. Professor Bartels told Charles William, duke of Brunswick, about the boy, and the duke decided to educate Karl himself.

In 1792 at age fifteen, Gauss was sent to Caroline College to study. Three years later he knew everything the professors there could teach him. While attending Caroline College, Gauss studied and proved two unsolved problems in advanced mathematics: the method of least squares and the law of quadratic reciprocity. In 1796, he also solved a problem from ancient Greece: constructing a seventeen-sided regular polygon using only a straight-edge and a compass. By the age of nineteen, therefore, Gauss had already solved three problems any one of which would have been the discovery of a lifetime and guaranteed him a spot in mathematical history. But Gauss was just beginning!

By 1798 Gauss was earning a living as a private tutor at Brunswick. In 1799 he published a proof of the fundamental theorem of algebra, which states that every algebraic equation has at least one root (solution). By 1801 these studies led to the publication of his most famous work, *Disquisitiones Arithmeticae,* which dealt with number theory.

One of Gauss's most distinguishing characteristics was that he was one of the last men to have a diversified field of study. He studied not only mathematics but also many math-related fields, such as astronomy, electricity, and optics.

He was the first theoretical astronomer; he calculated the orbits of asteroids between Mars and Jupiter. Because of his study of math and astronomy, Gauss became the director of the Gottingen Observatory and a professor of astronomy there in 1807. From 1830 to 1840 he did research on electricity and magnetism. In 1840 he published his research on optics and systems of lenses.

His broad range of interests extended to all branches of mathematics and he discovered important ideas in each. Because he left many of his discoveries unpublished, others later rediscovered them and received the recognition. Gauss stands, with Archimedes and Sir Isaac Newton, as one of the three greatest mathematicians of all time.

> *He was one of the last men to have a diversified field of study.*

7.6 Solving Systems by the Addition Method

Adding or subtracting two linear equations to eliminate a variable works easily when the coefficients of one of the variables have the same absolute value. However, if the coefficients are different, you can make them the same by applying the multiplication property of equality.

EXAMPLE 1 Solve the system.

$$x + y = 8$$
$$3x + 2y = 22$$

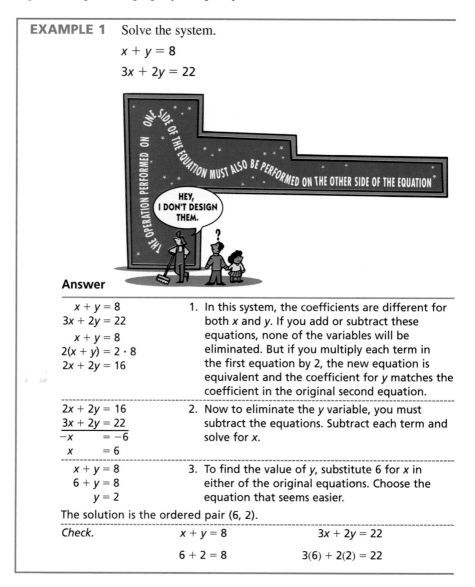

Answer

$x + y = 8$ $3x + 2y = 22$ $x + y = 8$ $2(x + y) = 2 \cdot 8$ $2x + 2y = 16$	1. In this system, the coefficients are different for both x and y. If you add or subtract these equations, none of the variables will be eliminated. But if you multiply each term in the first equation by 2, the new equation is equivalent and the coefficient for y matches the coefficient in the original second equation.
$2x + 2y = 16$ $\underline{3x + 2y = 22}$ $-x \quad\quad = -6$ $x \quad\quad = 6$	2. Now to eliminate the y variable, you must subtract the equations. Subtract each term and solve for x.
$x + y = 8$ $6 + y = 8$ $y = 2$	3. To find the value of y, substitute 6 for x in either of the original equations. Choose the equation that seems easier.

The solution is the ordered pair (6, 2).

Check.	$x + y = 8$	$3x + 2y = 22$
	$6 + 2 = 8$	$3(6) + 2(2) = 22$

Remember, the ordered pair represents the coordinates of the point where the two lines will intersect when you graph them.

Addition Method (Multipliers required)

1. Multiply both sides of one or both equations so that the coefficients of the variable to be eliminated have the same absolute value.
2. Follow the procedure for solving systems of equations by the addition method (compare p. 291).

EXAMPLE 2 Solve the system.

$$2x + 3y = 6$$
$$3x - 2y = 8$$

Answer

$2x + 3y = 6$ $\qquad$ $3x - 2y = 8$		1. To eliminate the y
$2(2x + 3y) = 2(6)$ $\quad$ $3(3x - 2y) = 3(8)$		terms, multiply the first
$4x + 6y = 12$ $\qquad$ $9x - 6y = 24$		equation by 2 and the second
		equation by 3 to obtain
		coefficients of 6 and -6
		respectively for the y terms.

$$\begin{array}{rl} 4x + 6y &= 12 \\ 9x - 6y &= 24 \\ \hline 13x &= 36 \\ x &= \frac{36}{13} \end{array}$$

2. Then add these equations and solve for x.

$$2x + 3y = 6$$
$$2\left(\frac{36}{13}\right) + 3y = 6$$
$$\frac{72}{13} + 3y = 6$$
$$3y = \frac{78}{13} - \frac{72}{13}$$
$$y = \frac{6}{13} \cdot \frac{1}{3}$$
$$y = \frac{2}{13}$$

3. Find y by substituting $\frac{36}{13}$ for x in one of the original equations.

The solution is $\left(\frac{36}{13}, \frac{2}{13}\right)$. This system is consistent and independent.

Check.

$$2x + 3y = 6 \qquad\qquad 3x - 2y = 8$$
$$2\left(\frac{36}{13}\right) + 3\left(\frac{2}{13}\right) = 6 \qquad 3\left(\frac{36}{13}\right) - 2\left(\frac{2}{13}\right) = 8$$
$$\frac{72 + 6}{13} = 6 \qquad\qquad \frac{108 - 4}{13} = 8$$

When you solve systems of equations, all three methods yield the same solution. You can also use any method to determine whether a system is inconsistent, dependent, or independent. The following table summarizes how.

Type of System	Consistent		Inconsistent
	Independent	Dependent	
Number of solutions	finite number (one if linear)	infinite number	none
Graphic solution	lines intersect	lines coincide	lines parallel
Algebraic solution	statement containing a variable and its value (e.g., $x = 6$)	true statement (e.g., $0 = 0$)	false statement (e.g., $0 = 5$)

▶ A. Exercises

Solve each system of equations using the addition method. If the system is not independent, tell whether it is inconsistent or dependent.

1. $3x + 2y = 18$
   $5x - 3y = 11$

2. $x - 3y = 8$
   $x + y = -4$

3. $2x - 7y = 3$
   $-4x + 14y = -6$

4. $x + y = 10$
   $2y = 20 - 2x$

5. $5x - 4y = 7$
   $7x - 3y = 2$

6. $x + y = 18$
   $2x + 2y = 10$

7. $x + y = 14$
   $2x - 3y = -17$

8. $2x + y = 15$
   $x + 2y = 18$

9. $5x - y = -42$
   $-44 + y = 5x$

10. $6x - 11y = -26$
    $x + 3y = -14$

▶ B. Exercises

Solve each system of equations using the addition method. If the system is not independent, tell whether it is inconsistent or dependent.

11. $\frac{x}{2} + y = 9$
    $x + y = 14$

12. $x + 2y = 9$
    $3x + y = 16$

13. $2x + 4y = 5$
    $3x - 2y = 7$

14. $5x - 4y = 3$
    $2x + 3y = 17$

15. $3x - 2y = 5$
    $4x + 3y = 8$

16. $\frac{1}{2}x - 3y = 1$
    $-x + 6y = 2$

17. $3x + y = 6$
    $x + \frac{1}{3}y = 2$

18. The sum of two numbers is 621, and their difference is 109. Find the two numbers.

▶ C. Exercises

Write two equations and solve the system.

19. The difference of two numbers is 62, and the sum of twice the larger and 3 times the smaller is 304. Find the numbers.

20. Four less than five times a number is twelve more than another number. Three times the first number less twice the second number is eight. Find the numbers.

■ Cumulative Review

21. The perimeter of a garden is 90 ft. The width is 7 ft. less than the length. Find the dimensions.

22. Ben is twice as old as Bonnie. Together they are 57 years old. How old are they?

23. The sum of two consecutive integers is at most eight less than five times the smaller. Find the range of the smaller number.

24. Five more than twice a number is forty-one. Find the number.

25. Barry drove to Boise in 3 hours and returned in 4 hours. If he drove 10 mph slower on the way home, how far is it to Boise?

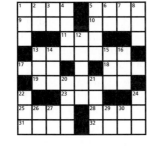

DOWN
1. degrees in a circle
2. normal body temperature on Celsius scale
3. days in a lunar month
4. middle year of the twentieth century
5. 37^2 minus minutes in four hours
6. inches in a yard
7. base of decimal system
8. America's age in 1976
12. 31 in the binary system
13. a multiple of 191
14. CCI
15. the number of the Beast
16. weeks in $18\frac{3}{4}$ years
20. 1020 subtracted from feet in a mile
21. UCDB on the telephone
22. product of two primes < 40 whose difference is 34
24. centimeters in a meter
26. years in two decades
27. eight dozen
29. degrees in a right angle
30. seconds in a minute

ACROSS
1. 36 plus days in nine regular years
5. cups in 82 gallons
9. digits > 5
10. White House street number
11. 2^9
13. date the Eagle landed on the moon
17. chapters in the New Testament
18. $\sqrt{450,000}$ to the nearest integer
19. date Lincoln was shot
23. Fahrenheit temperature at which water boils
25. square inches in a square yard
28. feet in $\frac{3}{4}$ mile
31. sum of all primes < 100
32. pounds in a ton

7.7 Motion Problems

In Chapter 4 you worked motion problems with only one variable. Now that you can solve a system of equations, you can solve motion problems using two variables. Sometimes a problem is easier to solve with two variables than with one. You can solve your system using either the substitution or the addition method. Remember, the basic formula for solving motion problems is $rt = d$.

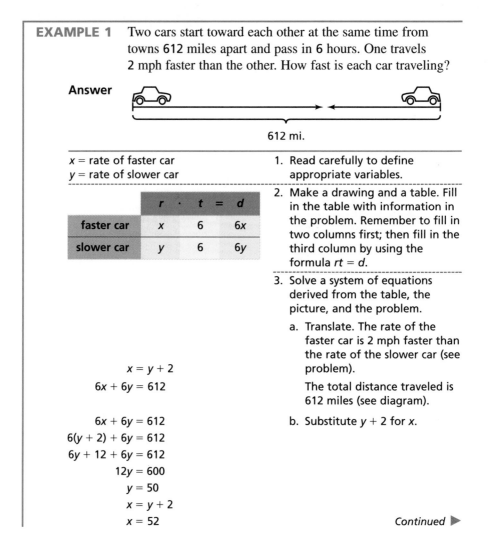

EXAMPLE 1 Two cars start toward each other at the same time from towns **612** miles apart and pass in **6** hours. One travels **2** mph faster than the other. How fast is each car traveling?

Answer

612 mi.

x = rate of faster car
y = rate of slower car

1. Read carefully to define appropriate variables.

	r	$\cdot$	t	$=$	d
faster car	x		6		$6x$
slower car	y		6		$6y$

2. Make a drawing and a table. Fill in the table with information in the problem. Remember to fill in two columns first; then fill in the third column by using the formula $rt = d$.

3. Solve a system of equations derived from the table, the picture, and the problem.

a. Translate. The rate of the faster car is 2 mph faster than the rate of the slower car (see problem).

$$x = y + 2$$
$$6x + 6y = 612$$

The total distance traveled is 612 miles (see diagram).

$$6x + 6y = 612$$
$$6(y + 2) + 6y = 612$$
$$6y + 12 + 6y = 612$$
$$12y = 600$$
$$y = 50$$
$$x = y + 2$$
$$x = 52$$

b. Substitute $y + 2$ for x.

Continued ▶

$$52 = 50 + 2$$
$$6(52) + 6(50) = 312 + 300 = 612$$

The faster car travels 52 mph;
the slower car travels 50 mph.

4. Check that your answers are reasonable.

EXAMPLE 2 When his Sunday school class went canoeing, Bill paddled **12** miles down the river in **3** hours. After paddling back upstream for **2** hours, he had traveled **4** miles. How fast does Bill paddle in still water? What is the rate of the current?

Answer The two unknowns are the rate of the river and the rate Bill is rowing.

Canoe trip on the Colorado River

x = Bill's paddling rate y = rate of the river current	1. Read carefully to define variables.

2. Plan by making a table. Because the current works with Bill as he travels downstream, his overall downstream rate will be the sum of his paddling rate and the current's rate $(x + y)$. His upstream rate, however, will be his paddling rate less the current rate $(x - y)$. Fill in two columns in the table; then complete the third column by using the motion formula.

	r	$\cdot\ t\ =$	d
traveling upstream	$x - y$	2	$2(x - y)$
traveling downstream	$x + y$	3	$3(x + y)$

3. Solve the system of equations.

$$3(x + y) = 12$$
$$2(x - y) = 4$$

a. Translate the information in the third column according to the original problem.

$$(x + y) = 4$$
$$(x - y) = 2$$

b. Instead of multiplying the variables in parentheses by the coefficient, you can divide both sides of the equation by the coefficients.

$$
\begin{aligned}
x + y &= 4 \\
\underline{x - y} &= \underline{2} \\
2x &= 6 \\
x &= 3
\end{aligned}
$$

c. Substituting 3 for x, find y.

$$x + y = 4$$
$$3 + y = 4$$
$$y = 1$$

Bill paddles his canoe 3 mph.
The current flows 1 mph.

4. Check for a reasonable answer.

*Container ships travel at **24** knots and cross the Atlantic in eight to ten days. A ship carrying **600** containers cannot fit through the Panama Canal!*

▶ A. Exercises

Give the correct expression for each rate. Do not solve.

1. A bicyclist riding against a wind of *x* mph if his speed on a calm day is 12 mph

2. A blimp that usually goes *y* mph in still air, when a **10** mph tail wind is blowing

3. A canoe going downstream in a current of *c* mph if the canoe on a lake averages **4** mph

4. A boat traveling upstream on Pine Creek, which has a current of **2** mph. The boat usually goes *z* mph in still water.

5. A plane that goes **500** mph in still air flying into a headwind of *w* mph

Make a table for each problem. Do not solve.

6. A blimp travels **2** hours with the wind and **5** hours against it.

7. Brad rows **6** hours upstream against a current of **3** mph and returns with the current in **4** hours.

8. A pilot flies **150** mph in still air. He flies with the wind **4** hours to Albuquerque and then against the wind **9** hours to Miami.

Use each table to write a system of equations. Do not solve.

9. The ATV traveled a total of **230** miles in **7** hours.

r	t	d
30	x	$30x$
40	y	$40y$

10. The plane flew to Omaha and then returned. The speed of the plane in still air was **100** mph more than the wind speed.

r	t	d
$x + y$	2	$2(x + y)$
$x - y$	3	$3(x - y)$

► B. Exercises

Make a table, and use systems of equations to solve these word problems.

11. The Hiking Club went on a hike one Saturday. In the morning they walked an average speed of 3 mph; in the afternoon they walked an average speed of 2 mph for 1 hour more than the number of hours they had walked in the morning. How many hours did they walk in the morning if they walked a total of 22 miles?

12. Find the rate of two cars traveling in the same direction if they leave the same place at the same time. The rate of one is twice as fast as the other, and after 4 hours the faster car is 80 miles ahead of the slower car.

13. Bob leaves Centerville at 11:00 A.M. and travels west at 45 mph. Lane leaves Centerville at 1:00 P.M. the same day and travels east at 50 mph. At what time will the two be 375 miles apart?

14. Flying with the wind, a plane travels 1200 nautical miles in 4 hours. Flying against the wind, it travels 500 nautical miles in 2 hours. What is the speed of the plane in still air and the speed of the wind?

15. Grandma Vaughn and her son John live 184 miles apart. If they leave their homes at the same time and head toward each other, they will meet in 2 hours. John travels 12 mph faster than Grandma. How fast does each travel?

16. A southbound train travels for 2 hours and meets a northbound train that has been traveling for 4 hours. The trains started from cities 350 miles apart. What is the speed of each train if the northbound train travels 10 mph slower than the southbound?

17. On a calm day Paul can bike to Janesville in 3 hours. Yesterday he made it in two hours with a 12 mph tail wind. How fast does he bike on a completely calm day?

18. A plane leaves the Ligonier Airport and travels west at 230 mph. A second plane leaves 3 hours later and travels east at 215 mph. How long has each plane flown when the two planes are 1135 miles apart?

19. A car leaves Middletown and heads toward Rochester 258 miles away at the same time a car leaves Rochester and heads toward Middletown. If the rate of the first car is 12 mph faster than the rate of the second and if the cars meet in 3 hours, how fast is each traveling?

20. A train leaves City View at 11:00 A.M. and heads east at 38 mph. At 2:00 P.M. another train leaves, traveling east at 53 mph. How long will it take the second train to come within 54 miles of the first train?

21. In 3 hours scouts raft 15 miles downstream from one camp to another, but they take 5 hours to paddle back to their camp upstream. What is the scouts' paddling rate in still water? What is the rate of the current in the stream?

22. Two trains leave the station at the same time, one traveling north and the other traveling south. The express travels 14 mph faster than the local. After 3 hours they are 315 miles apart. What is the rate of each train?

▶ C. Exercises

Use systems of equations to solve these word problems.

23. Mr. Brannon took his Sunday school boys on an camping trip. They bicycled to the trail head and then hiked to their camp. They rode at an average speed of **9** mph and walked at a speed of **2** mph in the **6** hours they traveled. How long did they hike if they traveled a total distance of **40** miles?

24. Young salmon hatch in freshwater streams and then migrate downstream to the ocean at the rate of **70** miles in **8** hours. There they live until they reach spawning age. Then they return upstream to fresh water to spawn and usually die soon after. On the upstream trip, the salmon travel about **58** miles in **8** hours. Find the rate of the salmon swimming in still water and the rate of the current.

■ Cumulative Review

Give the slope of each line.

25. The line connecting (2, 3) and (−5, 4)
26. $y = -3x - 4$
27. $4x - 5y = 7$
28. $y = -2$
29. $x = 4$
30. The line parallel to $y = 5x + 3$

7.8 Interest Problems

Interest problems, like motion problems, can be solved by using systems of equations. The basic formula used to compute simple interest for investment problems is $Prt = I$; P (the principal, or amount invested), r (the annual rate of interest), and t (the length of time in years) are multiplied together to produce I, the interest earned by the investment.

EXAMPLE 1   Dan has $25,000 that he wants to invest, some at **8%** and some at **10%** interest. If his annual interest income is to be $2220, how much should he invest at each interest rate?

Answer

Let x = amount to be invested at 8%   1. **Read.** Let x and y stand for
  y = amount to be invested at 10%   the unknowns, the two
              amounts to be invested.

	P	r	$t =$	I
8% investment	x	0.08	1	0.08x
10% investment	y	0.10	1	0.10y

2. **Plan.** Make a table to organize the information. Fill in the table. Record the rate of interest in decimal form. Since annual interest means interest for one year, the number in the time column will be 1. Fill in the interest column by multiplying across the row.

$$x + y = 25,000$$
$$0.08x + 0.10y = 2,220$$

3. **Solve.** Locate unused information in the problem. The $25,000 is the total invested, so using the principal column, you get $x + y = 25,000$. The $2220 is the interest earned, so using the interest column, you get $0.08x + 0.10y = 2220$. Solve this system.

$$
\begin{aligned}
-10x - 10y &= -250,000 \\
8x + 10y &= 222,000 \\
\hline
-2x &= -28,000 \\
x &= 14,000
\end{aligned}
$$

  Using the addition method, multiply the top equation by -10 and the bottom equation by 100. Then solve for x.

$$14,000 + y = 25,000$$
$$y = 11,000$$

Substitute 14,000 for x and solve for y.

Dan should invest $14,000 at 8% interest and $11,000 at 10% interest to make $2220 interest in one year.

4. **Check.**

As you study the next two problems, think of the reasoning behind the computations.

EXAMPLE 2   The six-month interest check from an 11% investment was $95 more than a six-month interest check from a 9% investment. If $5000 was invested, how much was invested at each rate?

Answer

Let x = amount invested at 11%   1. **Read.**
  y = amount invested at 9%

	P	r	t =	I
first investment	x	0.11	0.5	(0.11)(0.5)x = 0.055x
second investment	y	0.09	0.5	(0.09)(0.5)y = 0.045y

2. **Plan.** Since six months is one-half of a year, complete the table as shown.

$$x + y = 5000$$
$$0.055x = 0.045y + 95$$
$$y = 5000 - x$$
$$1000(0.055x) = 1000(0.045y + 95)$$
$$55x = 45y + 95{,}000$$
By substitution, $55x = 45(5000 - x) + 95{,}000$
$$55x = 225{,}000 - 45x + 95{,}000$$
$$100x = 320{,}000$$
$$x = 3200$$

$$y = 5000 - 3200$$
$$y = 1800$$

3. **Solve.**

$3200 was invested at 11%, and $1800 was invested at 9% interest.

4. **Check.**

EXAMPLE 3 Mike is going to make two investments, and he knows he will receive $770 in interest per year. The interest rate on the $5000 investment is one percent higher than on the $4000 investment. What is the interest rate for each investment?

Answer

Let x = the interest rate on the $4000 investment
y = the interest rate on the $5000 investment

1. **Read** and assign variables.

	P	r	t =	I
first investment	4000	x	1	4000x
second investment	5000	y	1	5000y

2. **Plan** using a table.

$$4000x + 5000y = 770$$
$$y = x + 0.01$$

$$4000x + 5000(0.01 + x) = 770$$
$$4000x + 50 + 5000x = 770$$
$$9000x = 720$$
$$x = 0.08$$

$$y = 0.01 + x$$
$$y = 0.09$$

3. **Solve** the system using substitution.

The interest rate on the $4000 investment is 8%.

The interest rate on the $5000 investment is 9%.

4. **Check** mentally that the answer is reasonable.

► A. Exercises

Complete each row of the table.

	P	r	t	=	I
1.	500	0.12	4		
2.	x	0.045	2		
3.	112	x	0.5		
4.	30	0.04	x		
5.	500		2		50
6.	200	x			200x

Find the interest for each investment.

7. You invest **$400** for four years at **8%** annual interest.

8. Debbie invests **$8437** at $5\frac{1}{2}$% interest for **6 months**.

Use the table to write a system of equations. Do not solve.

9. The income from two accounts is **$30** and the total invested is **$600**.

	P	r	t	=	I
first account	x	0.07	1		
second account	y	0.05	1		

10. The income from the two accounts is the same, but the second account pays a **3%** higher interest rate.

	P	r	t	=	I
first account	341	x	2		
second account	237	y	2		

► B. Exercises

11. Mrs. Hill invests **$15,000** in two accounts. One of the accounts yields an interest rate of **8%** and the other pays **10%**. The total amount of interest paid is **$1330** annually. What is the amount invested at each rate?

12. Mr. Hunt invested a total of **$10,000** in two different accounts. One account yields **10%** interest while the other yields **9.5%** interest. How much did he invest in each account if his total annual interest was **$971**?

13. A total of **$6200** is invested in stock. The preferred stock yields **7%** interest while the common stock yields **5.5%** interest. How much is invested in each type of stock if the total investment brings in **$389** per year?

14. Mark invests **$8000** in an account that pays **12%** interest and **$2000** in one that pays **8%**. If he leaves the money in the accounts for the same length of time, how long must he leave it to gain **$5600** in interest?

15. Mr. Cocrane can invest one sum of money at 7% and a second sum at 10% and get $640 per year. If he invests his first sum at 10% and his second sum at 7%, he will make $550 per year. How much is he going to invest in the separate accounts? Which method of investment is wiser?

16. Dr. Taylor invested $12,500, part at 9% and part at 7.5%. If her annual income from the investments is $1004.70, what was the amount of each?

17. Mary plans to invest a total of $7500 in two types of stocks, one paying 6% interest and the other paying 15% interest. How much does she invest in each type of stock if the total interest gained annually is $585?

18. Scott borrowed $1200 from two different low-interest lending institutions. He pays 7% annual interest on one loan and 8.5% annual interest on the other. The total amount of interest he pays annually is $89.25. How much did he borrow at each interest rate?

19. Miss Parker invested one amount of money at 9.2% interest and another amount $700 more than the first, at 10.4% interest. If the total amount of interest is $425.60 annually, how much money is in each investment?

20. Larry Hall is going to borrow $3000 to buy a computer. He borrowed from two of his brothers, paying 6.5% interest to the older one and 8% interest to the other one. How much does he borrow from each if his annual interest is a total of $213?

21. Gina receives an allowance of $3.00 per week. She has saved her money for three weeks and now wants to make an investment. Her mother promises to pay her 30% interest if she leaves the money for a year. Her father promises to pay 25% interest for a year. If Gina makes an investment in each of her parents offers and receives $2.55 interest at the end of the year, how much did she invest in each parent's offer?

22. The Green Publishing Company invests a total of $27,000 into two new businesses. It expects a return of 14% on one business and 25% on the other business. How much did it invest in each business if it received $5540 in one year?

23. A businessman invests $20,000 in a dry cleaning establishment and $30,000 in a restaurant. What is his expected rate of return, or rate of interest, on each investment if he expects a total of $4600 annually and the average of the two rates is 9%?

▶ **C. Exercises**

24. Bob invests $8000 in one account and $3000 in a different account. The account in which he invested $8000 pays an interest rate 2 percentage points higher than that of the other account. What are the interest rates if the total amount of interest paid after 2 years is $1860?

25. Diane plans to deposit $1200 in one account and $900 in another account. The rate of interest paid on the first account is 2 percentage points more than the second. If the total annual income from the two investments is $223.50, what is the interest rate of each investment?

Give each set below in set notation.

26. The set of all numbers between 5 and 90 inclusive
27. The set of all primes between 20 and 30
28. {2, 3, 4} ∩ {1, 3, 5}
29. {1, 4} ∪ {1, 3, 5}
30. {2, 3, 4} × {1, 4}

7.9 Mixture Problems

You can also solve mixture problems with two variables as you did with motion and interest problems.

Almonds and other nuts for sale at a bazaar at Tunis, Tunisa

EXAMPLE 1 The Nut Shop sells cashews for $8.15 a pound and almonds for $6.95 a pound. The manager wants to make 80 pounds of a cashew and almond mix that sells for $7.25 a pound. How many pounds of each nut should he put in the mix?

Answer

Let x = pounds of cashews
     y = pounds of almonds

1. **Read** and identify the two variables.

2. **Plan** by making a table.

	Number of pounds	Price per pound	Total price
cashews	x	8.15	8.15x
almonds	y	6.95	6.95y
mix	80	7.25	580

$$x + y = 80$$
$$8.15x + 6.95y = 580$$

3. **Solve.**

   a. Write two equations using the columns with variables. The first combines the amount of cashews and almonds to equal the total amount in the mixture. The second combines the total cost of the nuts to equal the total cost of the mixture.

Continued ▶

$$y = 80 - x$$
$$815x + 695y = 58{,}000$$
$$815x + 695(80 - x) = 58{,}000$$
$$815x + 55{,}600 - 695x = 58{,}000$$
$$120x = 2400$$
$$x = 20$$
$$y = 80 - x$$
$$y = 60$$

b. Solve the first equation for y, and eliminate the decimals in the second equation by multiplying both sides by 100.

c. Choose either the substitution method or the addition method for solving the system.

Mix 20 pounds of cashews and 60 pounds of almonds.

4. **Check** your answers in the context of the problem.

Solving Word Problems with Two Variables

1. Read the problem carefully and look for unknown quantities. Use two variables to represent the unknowns.
2. Plan by making a table. Fill in as much information as possible.
3. Solve a system of equations obtained from information in the table and in the problem.
4. Check your answers in the context of the original problem.

As you study the following examples, try to guess the next step before you read it. Reasoning through examples will help you do exercises on your own.

EXAMPLE 2   Emmanuel Christian School sent out 150 pieces of mail. Some of the letters required 40 cents postage while others required 64 cents. If the total postage bill was $71.04, how many pieces of each type were mailed?

Answer

Let x = number of letters with 40¢ postage
y = number of letters with 64¢ postage

1. **Read.**

2. **Plan.**

	Number of pieces	Cost per piece	Total price
40¢	x	0.40	$0.40x$
64¢	y	0.64	$0.64y$

$$x + y = 150$$
$$0.40x + 0.64y = 71.04$$
$$-40x - 40y = -6000$$
$$\underline{40x + 64y = 7104}$$
$$24y = 1104$$
$$y = 46$$
$$x + y = 150$$
$$x + 46 = 150$$
$$x = 104$$

3. **Solve.**

a. Write two equations, one for number of pieces, one for total price.

b. The first equation is multiplied by -40, the second by 100.

104 letters with 40¢ postage and 46 letters with 64¢ postage

4. **Check.**

EXAMPLE 3   If milk that is 3% fat is mixed with fat-free milk to produce 5 gallons of 2%, how much of each should be used?

Answer

Let x = number of gallons of 3%
$\quad\quad y$ = number of gallons of fat-free

1. **Read** and assign variables.

2. **Plan** by making a table.

	gal. of liquid	% of fat	gal. of fat
3% milk	x	0.03	$0.03x$
fat-free	y	0	0
mixture	5	0.02	0.1

3. **Solve.**

$x + y = 5$
$0.03x = 0.1$

a. Make two equations, one for gallons of liquid and one for gallons of fat.

$3x = 10$
$x = \frac{10}{3} = 3\frac{1}{3}$

b. Solve for x in the second equation. Eliminate the decimal by multiplying by 100.

$\frac{10}{3} + y = 5$
$y = \frac{5}{3} = 1\frac{2}{3}$

c. Substitute $\frac{10}{3}$ for x in the first equation and solve for y.

$3\frac{1}{3}$ gallons of 3% milk should be mixed with $1\frac{2}{3}$ gallons of fat-free milk.

4. **Check** the answer in the context.

▶ A. Exercises

Use systems of equations to solve each word problem.

1. Kim wants to make a mix of nuts and raisins for a party. Nuts cost 20¢ per ounce and raisins cost 12¢ per ounce. How many ounces of each should she buy if she wants 48 ounces of a mix that costs 15¢ per ounce?

2. A grocer mixes oranges and bananas to make a 10-pound fruit basket. The oranges cost 75¢ per pound and the bananas cost 60¢ per pound. How many pounds of each should he use if the basket is to cost $6.90?

3. Caramels cost $1.90 per pound, and butterscotch candies cost $1.40 per pound. A 5-lb. bag of mixed candy is to sell for $7.50. How many pounds of each kind of candy should be mixed together?

4. Shawn has a salt water solution that is 30% salt. How many gallons of pure water (0% salt) and salt water solution should he mix to make 40 gallons of a diluted solution that is 9% salt?

5. The florist advertises roses for $2 a bud and carnations for $.75 a flower. If John pays $20.50, excluding tax, for a bouquet of 14 flowers for Teresa, how many of each flower is in the bouquet?

6. A pharmacist is making an antiseptic of iodine and alcohol. The iodine/alcohol mixture he now has is 5% iodine. He wants a mixture that is 6% iodine. How much of a 10% iodine solution and how much of his original antiseptic should he mix to make 50 mL of the new antiseptic?

7. Raisin Rich breakfast cereal is 10% protein. A dietician wants to raise the percentage of protein served in a bowl of cereal to 20%. The high-protein grain that will be mixed with Raisin Rich is 40% protein. How many grams of each should be mixed together to make a 12-gram serving of cereal with the proper percentage of protein?

8. Max Biggs, the gardener, plans to seed the front lawn with a new mix of grass seed. He has a mix that is 80% fescue and 15% winter rye. How much fescue and how much of his previous mix should he blend together to form 50 pounds of an 86% fescue mixture?

9. Concrete is made of cement, water, and aggregate (sand and gravel). Aggregates should make up 75% of the total mass of concrete. If you have a concrete mixture that is 60% aggregate, how many kilograms of this mix and how many kilograms of aggregate should be combined to form 48 kilograms of the concrete mix with the proper percent of aggregate?

10. Chemist John Wetzel has two HNO_3 acid and water solutions. John knows that the percentage of acid in solution I is 20 percentage points less than the percentage of acid in solution II. If he mixes 40 mL of solution I with 60 mL of solution II and obtains a mixture that is 27% acid, what percentage of acid is in each solution?

11. Becky makes an antiseptic of alcohol and water. If she buys a mixture that is 40% alcohol to make a 12.5% alcohol solution, how much water and alcohol should she mix to obtain 128 mL of homemade antiseptic?

12. A factory sells two types of antifreeze. Type A is 40% ethylene glycol, and type B is 52% ethylene glycol. A man wants 200 gallons of antifreeze that would protect his radiator to $-25°$. To protect to $-25°$, the mix must be 45% ethylene glycol. How many gallons (to the nearest tenth) of each should be mixed to get the correct strength of ethylene glycol?

▶ B. Exercises

Use systems of equations to solve each word problem.

13. In District 12, 85% of the voters voted for Mr. Johnson for mayor. In District 13, 43% of the voters voted for him. From the two districts 10,253 voters cast votes for him. How many voted for Mr. Johnson in each district if a total of 16,460 people voted in the districts?

14. A butcher wants to grind round steak and mix it with regular ground beef to make a deluxe ground beef. The round steak sells for $2.59 per pound and the regular ground beef sells for $1.89 per pound. How many pounds of each should he grind together to make 50 pounds of deluxe ground beef that will sell for $2.38 per pound?

15. An ice cream company is going to mix cream that is 40% fat with milk that is $3\frac{1}{2}$% fat to produce 60 gallons of a mixture that is 10% fat. How many gallons of cream and how many gallons of milk should they use?

16. Lea mixes corn syrup and molasses together to make a special syrup that she uses on pancakes. If she can afford to pay 11¢ per ounce for the mix and corn syrup costs 9.5¢ per ounce and molasses cost 12¢ per ounce, how many ounces of each should she mix together to make 12 ounces of the mix?

17. Mr. Lucas, owner of a pet store, wants to mix two different kinds of seed together to form a high-grade birdseed. Seed A sells for 28¢ per pound, seed B sells for 60¢ per pound, and the mixture will sell for 50¢ per pound. If he wants to make 85 pounds of the seed mixture, how much of each seed (to the nearest tenth of a pound) should he mix together?

18. How many pounds of $2.99 per pound coffee and $7.99 per pound coffee must be mixed in order to make 90 pounds of a mixture that will sell for $5 per pound? (Round to the nearest tenth.)

▶ C. Exercises

Use systems of equations to solve each word problem.

19. In ordinary ocean water, sodium chloride (the chemical name for ordinary table salt) represents 2.8% by mass. The Dead Sea, which lies between Israel and Jordan, is about 12% sodium chloride. If a chemist takes a sample of water from the Dead Sea and wants to dilute it with ordinary ocean water, how much ocean water and how much water from the Dead Sea (to the nearest tenth of a liter) should he combine to form 12 liters of a 10% sodium chloride solution?

20. A grain farmer can sell 50 bushels of beans and 100 bushels of corn for $485, or he can sell 20 bushels of beans and 205 bushels of corn for $565.25. What is the selling price of beans and corn per bushel?

Identify the main property used to justify each step in the solution of the inequality shown: $5(3 + x) + 3 \leq 4 \cdot 0$.

21. $5(3 + x) + 3 \leq 0$

22. $(15 + 5x) + 3 \leq 0$

23. $(5x + 15) + 3 \leq 0$

24. $5x + (15 + 3) \leq 0$

25. $-5x + 5x + 18 \leq -5x + 0$

26. $0 + 18 \leq -5x + 0$

27. $18 \leq -5x$

28. $-\frac{1}{5} \cdot 18 \geq -\frac{1}{5}(-5x)$

29. $-\frac{18}{5} \geq 1x$

30. $-\frac{18}{5} \geq x$

7.10 Systems of Inequalities

In Chapter 6 you learned how to graph an inequality with two variables. A system of inequalities generally has an infinite number of solutions. The solution to a system of inequalities can be determined by graphing each inequality on the same pair of axes and identifying the intersection of all the graphs.

Climbers watch an avalanche on the slopes of Mt. Everest.

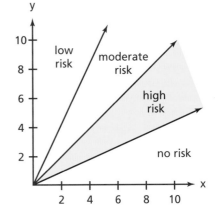

Avalanche Risk for Mountain Slopes

low risk

moderate risk

high risk

no risk

EXAMPLE 1   Solve the system of inequalities.

$$3x + y > 4$$
$$x - y \le 8$$

Answer

$3x + y > 4$
$\quad y > -3x + 4$

$x - y \le 8$ $\quad -y \le -x + 8$ $\quad\quad y \ge x - 8$	1. Place both inequalities in slope-intercept form for easy graphing. Notice the inequality sign change here because the multiplier was negative.
	2. Graph the inequalities on the same set of axes.
	3. The solution set is the darkest shaded area. This solution set is *infinite*. Any point in this shaded area makes both inequalities true.

Check.   To check, choose any point in the shaded area, say (1, 7), and try it in the original inequalities.

$3x + y > 4$	$x - y \le 8$
$3(1) + 7 > 4$	$1 - 7 \le 8$
$10 > 4$	$-6 \le 8$

Solving Systems of Inequalities

1. Graph all inequalities on one set of axes.

2. Find the solution set where the shaded regions intersect.

3. Check your results.

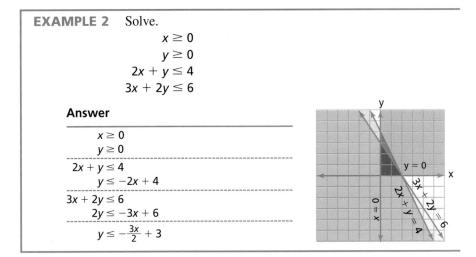

EXAMPLE 2 Solve.

$$x \geq 0$$
$$y \geq 0$$
$$2x + y \leq 4$$
$$3x + 2y \leq 6$$

Answer

$$x \geq 0$$
$$y \geq 0$$

$$2x + y \leq 4$$
$$y \leq -2x + 4$$

$$3x + 2y \leq 6$$
$$2y \leq -3x + 6$$

$$y \leq -\frac{3x}{2} + 3$$

The solution is all points in the darkest shaded region.

▶ A. Exercises

Graph each system of inequalities.

1. $x + y \geq 2$
   $x - y < 4$

2. $5x + y > 2$
   $2x + y \leq 1$

3. $3x - 2y \geq 6$
   $x + y \leq 3$

4. $2x - y < 5$
   $3x + y \geq 4$

5. $x + 5y < 15$
   $3x + 2y \leq 8$

▶ B. Exercises

Graph each system of inequalities.

6. $3x + y > 9$
   $2x + y \geq 6$

7. $x + 2y \geq -4$
   $x + 2y < 6$

8. $x \geq 0$
   $y \geq 0$
   $5x + 6y \leq 30$

9. $x \geq 0$
   $y \geq 0$
   $x + 4y \leq 8$
   $2x + y \leq 4$

10. $x \geq 0$
    $y \geq 0$
    $3x + y \leq 8$
    $x + 2y \leq 6$

11. $x \geq 0$
    $y \leq 2$
    $x + y > 1$

Is each point a solution to the system of inequalities? Do not graph.

12. $5x + 3y \leq 2$; $(1, -2)$
    $x - 2y \geq 4$

13. $3x - y > 4$; $(3, 1)$
    $2x + 6y < 3$

14. $5 - 2x \geq y$; $(-1, -2)$
    $3y + 4 > 2x$

15. $y \geq 2 - x$; $(-3, 5)$
    $3x + 4y < 12$

▶ C. Exercises

Graph the system of inequalities and then name (a) a point that satisfies the system, (b) a point that does not satisfy the system, and (c) a point that lies on the boundary of the region.

16. $x \geq 0$
    $y \geq 0$
    $2x + y \leq 4$
    $x + y \geq 2$

17. $x + y \geq 3$
    $2x < 3y + 1$
    $y \geq 0$
    $y < 2$

■ Cumulative Review

Find the equation of each line if

18. the slope is -3 and the y-intercept is $(0, 2)$.

19. the slope is $\frac{2}{3}$ and it passes through $(2, 5)$.

20. it passes through $(1, 5)$ and $(-2, 2)$.

21. it is vertical and passes through $(-2, -5)$.

22. it is parallel to $y = \frac{1}{2}x - 4$ and passes through $(1, 5)$.

Algebra and Scripture

In this chapter we studied simultaneous conditions (p. 272). We looked for the value that satisfied all the conditions at the same time. Similarly, rocket scientists must identify the time of launch by considering many simultaneous conditions including the moon's position, rocket weight, fuel, and local weather patterns.

Prophetic statements are also conditions that can be fulfilled simultaneously. God told the Israelites that He would send a Messiah and King to rule them in righteousness and then gave them prophecies to identify this Messiah.

1. What does Micah prophesy of Messiah in Micah 5:2?
2. What does Isaiah prophesy of Messiah in Isaiah 7:14?
3. What does David prophesy of Messiah in Psalm 41:9?
4. What does Zechariah prophesy about Messiah's crucified body in Zechariah 12:10?
5. What does David prophesy about Messiah in Psalm 16:10?

Of all the people ever born in Israel, only Jesus fulfills all the prophecies at once. He is the only solution to these simultaneous conditions.

Substitution is another prophecy that Jesus fulfilled. We have already discussed II Corinthians 5:14-15 (p. 280). In each passage below, identify the phrase that shows that Jesus was a substitute— He died in our place.

6. Isaiah 53:6
7. II Corinthians 5:21
8. I Peter 2:24

The idea of substitution recurs in Scripture.

9. Identify the substitute in Genesis 22:13.

THE NTH DEGREE
  Whom did Esther replace?

10. What phrase in each verse of Genesis 36:33-39 shows the substitution of one king for another?

This phrase occurs 57 times in Kings and Chronicles (such as I Chron. 1:44-50) as well as once each in II Samuel and Isaiah to describe royal replacements. The same idea occurs in Exodus 29:30, Leviticus 6:22, and Deuteronomy 10:6 but refers to an office other than king.

11. What office is involved in these three passages?

For a mathematical substitution, the good Samaritan (Luke 10:35) offered to substitute his money for the expenses of the innkeeper. Read another debt substitution below.

12. In Philemon 18, the writer offered to pay any debts that Onesimus might owe to Philemon. Who made the offer?

Let's be sure to apply the principle of substitution in our Christian lives. Replace bad habits with good ones. Put off the old man . . . put on the new (Col. 3:8-14).

> *Scriptural Roots*
>
> **FOR HE HATH MADE** him to be sin for us, who knew no sin; that we might be made the righteousness of God in him.
>
> **II CORINTHIANS 5:21**

Chapter 7 Review

Determine whether $(-2, 3)$ is a solution to each system.

1. $3x + 4y = 6$
$y = 1 - x$

2. $5x - 2y = 7$
$x + y = 1$

3. $x + 2y = 4$
$3x + y = -3$

4. $x + y < 2$
$x + 2y \geq 4$

Use the graphing method to solve each system.

5. $x + y = 11$
$2x - y = -5$

6. $3x - y = 14$
$x + 3y = -12$

7. $x + y = -2$
$3x + y = -10$

8. $x + 3y = 5$
$y = 2$

Use the substitution method to solve each system.

9. $2x + 3y = 8$
$x + 2y = 4$

10. $5x - 3y = 12$
$3x + y = -2$

11. $4x + 3y = -20$
$5x - 2y = -2$

12. $5x + y = 8$
$-10x - 2y = -3$

Use the addition method to solve each system.

13. $x - 2y = -11$
$3x + y = 16$

14. $2x + 3y = 9$
$4x - y = 2$

15. $5x - 3y = -25$
$6x + 2y = -2$

16. $x + y = -2$
$2x + 2y = -4$

Solve each system using any method.

17. $y = 2x - 3$
$y = \frac{1}{3}x + 7$

18. $x - 2y = -42$
$3x - y = -31$

19. $2x + 5y = 8$
$x - 5y = 4$

20. $0.5x - 2.1y = 7.2$
$1.4x + 0.3y = 7.8$

Solve each system using any method. Tell whether each is consistent or inconsistent, dependent or independent.

21. $x + y = 5$
$x = 2 - y$

22. $3x + 5y = 1$
$4x - 3y = 11$

23. $3x + y = 6$
$\frac{2}{3}y = 5 - 2x$

24. $3x + y = 4$
$2y = 8 - 6x$

25. $x + y^2 = 8$
$x = y^2$

Give a symbolic expression for each.

26. The distance traveled by a jet in 12 hours at x mph
27. The upstream speed of a kayaker that goes 3 mph in still water if paddling in a current of c mph
28. The annual interest received from an investment of d dollars at 7%
29. The amount of salt when m gallons of a 20%-salt solution is mixed with n gallons of a 23%-salt solution

Solve algebraically.

30. Sugar Tooth Candy Company needs 300 gallons of a 32% sucrose solution for a certain kind of candy. The company has a solution that is 60% sucrose and a solution that is 25% sucrose. How many gallons of each should the company mix together to obtain the desired solution?
31. Mr. Arnold is going to invest $1550 in two separate accounts. One account pays 7.5%, and the other account pays 8.25%. How much should he invest in each account so that his annual return on his investment will be $121.20?
32. Two fishing boats leave Sandy Cove at the same time traveling in the same direction. One boat is traveling three times as fast as the other boat. After five hours the faster boat is 80 miles ahead of the slower boat. What is the speed of each boat?

Graph each system of inequalities.

33. $2x + y < 6$
    $3x - y \geq 4$
34. $5x + 2y \leq 8$
    $x + y > -5$
35. $3x + 5y \geq 12$
    $2x - 3y < -6$
36. $y \leq \frac{1}{3}x + 4$
    $y > 2$

37. What does the graph of an inconsistent linear system look like?
38. Explain the mathematical significance of II Corinthians 5:21.

8 Polynomials

$$y = mx + b$$

The Sims family, vacationing in Arizona, visits the Grand Canyon. As they view the colorful panorama, Mr. Sims reminds them that the God who created such immense beauty is also interested in and loves each family member. Though the colors of the Grand Canyon change hour by hour, moment by moment, God never changes.

Far below them the Colorado River winds its way 217 miles through the Grand Canyon. The width of the canyon varies from four to eighteen miles, and the height varies also, reaching a maximum of 5700 feet. The Sims select a remote trail for their backpack to the bottom. At the top of a high cliff, Bill, the oldest son, wonders how far it is to the bottom. Bill remembers from physical science that distance can be found by using the formula $d = \frac{1}{2}gt^2$, in which g is the gravitational acceleration of 32 ft./sec.^{2} and t is the amount of time in seconds that an object falls. Bill drops a flare from the top of the cliff and times its drop to the bottom at 6 seconds.

The formula that Bill used has a polynomial in it. By the time the trail reached the lower level for Bill to retrieve the flare, he had calculated the height of the cliff using the formula. You may also be able to find the solution to Bill's problem, but by the end of this chapter you will also be able to perform the four operations on polynomials.

After this chapter you should be able to

1. classify and evaluate any given polynomial.
2. add and subtract polynomials.
3. multiply polynomials of all types.
4. recognize special cases and use shortcuts for multiplying polynomials.
5. divide polynomials.

8.1 Classifying and Evaluating Polynomials

Do you remember what terms are? They were defined in Chapter 3 as a constant, a variable raised to a power (can be first power), or the product of one or more such variables and a constant. Like terms have the same variables with the same exponents. Remember that you can add and subtract like terms only. The algebraic expression $2x^2 + 3x + 5y - 4x$ contains four terms: $2x^2$, $3x$, $5y$, and $-4x$. The like terms in this example are $3x$ and $-4x$. The entire algebraic expression is called a polynomial.

The graph of the polynomial $-0.00037x^3 + 0.049x^2 - 2.19x + 39.49$ models this wave at Waimea Bay, Hawaii.

Definitions

A **polynomial** is an algebraic expression of one or more terms.

A **monomial** is a polynomial with only one term.

A **binomial** is a polynomial with exactly two terms.

A **trinomial** is a polynomial with exactly three terms.

POLYNOMIALS

	Monomial	Binomial	Trinomial	Other Polynomials
one variable	$4y^3$	$2x^2 + 3x$	$5x^2 + 2x - 6$	$x^4 + 2x^3 - x^2 + 9$
two variables	$3x^2y$	$5x^2 + y^3$	$3x^2 + 6xy + 7y^2$	$x^3y + 5xy^2 + 3xy - 7y^5$
three variables	$8ab^2c$	$7a^2b + 5c^5$	$2a^2b^5 + 8c^4 - 2a^5$	$3c^2 + 4c - 8d + 2e - e^2$

Another way to classify polynomials is by the degree of the polynomial.

Definition

The **degree of a term** is the sum of the exponents on the variables.

The degree of the term $5x^3y^2z^4$ is 9, and the degree of the term $4x^2y$ is 3. Remember, a variable without a written exponent has the exponent 1. The degree of the term 8 is 0 because the exponent on the variable is 0. But there is no variable, you may say. Observe the following:

$$8 = 8 \cdot 1$$
$$= 8 \cdot x^0$$

So the exponent on the variable is 0.

Definition

The **degree of a polynomial** is the degree of the term with the highest degree.

EXAMPLE 1   Find the degree of the polynomial $3x^3y + 2x + 4xy^2$.

Answer   First, find the degree of each term.

term	degree
$3x^3y$	$3 + 1 = 4$
$2x$	1
$4xy^2$	$1 + 2 = 3$

Since the highest degree of any term is four, the degree of the trinomial $3x^3y + 2x + 4xy^2$ is four.

Polynomials are easy to evaluate if you follow the substitution principles and the order of operations.

EXAMPLE 2   Evaluate $2x^2 - 5x + 6$ when $x = 3$.

Answer

$2x^2 - 5x + 6$ 1. Substitute 3 for x in the trinomial.
$2(3)^2 - 5(3) + 6$

- -

$2 \cdot 9 - 5 \cdot 3 + 6$ 2. Follow the order of operations to
$\underbrace{18} - \underbrace{15} + 6$ evaluate this expression.
9

EXAMPLE 3   Evaluate $5x^3y + 2x - 3y + 5$ when $x = -2$ and $y = 1$.

Answer $5x^3y + 2x - 3y + 5$

$5(-2)^3(1) + 2(-2) - 3(1) + 5$ Substitute.
$5(-8)(1) + 2(-2) - 3(1) + 5$
$-40 - 4 - 3 + 5$
-42

The vertical method of multiplication is good to start with, but it is quite time consuming and cumbersome. You must learn to multiply binomials quickly and accurately in your head because multiplication of binomials is a very important part of algebra. The process used to multiply binomials mentally is called the *FOIL method. FOIL* stands for **F**irst, **O**uter, **I**nner, **L**ast and relates to the terms of the binomials.

To find the product, multiply the first terms, then the outer terms, then the inner terms, and then the last terms. Combine like terms and remember to arrange them in descending powers of the variable.

First ⌐ Outer

$(x + 7)$ $(x + 2)$

Inner

Last

First $= x^2$

Outer $= 2x$

Inner $= 7x$

Last $= 14$

$x^2 + 2x + 7x + 14$

$x^2 + 9x + 14$

EXAMPLE 4 Multiply $(4x - 5)(x + 3)$.

Answer

1. Multiply by the FOIL method.

$((4x) - 5)((x) + 3)$ product of first terms $= 4x^2$

$((4x) - 5)(x + (3))$ product of outer terms $= 12x$

$(4x (- 5))((x) + 3)$ product of inner terms $= -5x$

$(4x (- 5))(x + (3))$ product of last terms $= -15$

$4x^2 + 12x + (-5x) + (-15)$ 2. Find the sum of the four products.

$4x^2 + 7x - 15$ 3. Combine like terms.

Multiplying Binomials Vertically

1. Multiply each term of one binomial with both terms in the other binomial.
2. Add like terms to obtain the final product.

Multiplying Binomials Mentally

1. Find the product of the first, outer, inner, and last terms.
2. Combine like terms.

> **EXAMPLE 5** Multiply $(2x - 5)(3x - 2)$.
>
> **Answer** $F = 6x^2$
>
> $O = -4x$
>
> $I = -15x$
>
> $L = 10$
>
> $6x^2 - 4x - 15x + 10$
>
> $6x^2 - 19x + 10$

▶ A. Exercises

Use the FOIL method to multiply these binomials.

1. $(x + 5)(x + 2)$
2. $(x - 7)(x + 9)$
3. $(x + 6)(x - 4)$
4. $(x + 2)(x + 1)$
5. $(x - 3)(x - 4)$
6. $(x - 6)(x + 8)$
7. $(x + 1)(x - 5)$
8. $(x - 3)(x - 8)$
9. $(x - 3)(x - 3)$
10. $(x - 4)(x - 4)$
11. $(x - 6)(x + 2)$
12. $(x + 3)(x + 8)$
13. $(x - 6)(x - 7)$
14. $(x - 7)(x - 9)$
15. $(x + 9)(x - 8)$
16. $(x - 5)(x + 5)$
17. $(x + 3)(x - 3)$
18. $(x - 7)(x + 7)$
19. $(x - 10)(x + 10)$
20. $(a - b)(a + b)$
21. $(x - 8)(x - 8)$
22. $(a - b)(a - b)$
23. $(x + 1)(x + 1)$
24. $(x + 9)(x + 9)$
25. $(x + 3)(x + 3)$
26. $(x + 9)(x - 7)$

▶ B. Exercises

Use the FOIL method to multiply these binomials.

27. $(3x + 2)(x + 4)$
28. $(2x - 6)(4x + 1)$
29. $(5x - 6)(3x + 2)$
30. $(2x - 9)(4x - 11)$
31. $(x + 6)^2$
32. $(3x - 2)^2$
33. $(-7x - 10)^2$
34. $(11x + 12)^2$
35. $(8x + 3)^2$
36. $(x + 7)(3x - 4)$
37. $(5x + 6)(2x - 7)$
38. $(3x + 8)(2x - 3)$
39. $(x + 4)(2x - 9)$
40. $(3x + 6)(x - 1)$
41. $(3x + 4)(3x - 4)$
42. $(2x - 13)(2x + 13)$
43. $(2x + 4)(3x - 6)$
44. $(5x + 6)(x - 4)$
45. $(2x + 14)(3x - 7)$
46. $(x + 4)(2x - 11)$

Perform the indicated operations.
47. $(8x + 3)(3x - 2) + (x - 4)(x + 4)$
48. $(-2x - 5)(x - 12) - (3x + 2)(-x + 7)$

■ Cumulative Review

49. Give the multiplicative inverse of $-\frac{3}{7}$.
50. What is the identity for multiplication?

State each property.
51. commutative property of multiplication
52. associative property of multiplication
53. power property of exponents

8.6 Multiplying Polynomials

Multiplying polynomials in which one factor has three or more terms may be done horizontally by the distributive property, but because of the additional products, you may prefer to do it vertically. Example 1 is done vertically, and example 2 horizontally.

EXAMPLE 1	Multiply $(3x^2 - 4x + 9)(x + 2)$.

Answer

$$3x^2 -4x+ 9$$
$$x+ 2$$
1. Check that the polynomials are arranged in descending powers of x. Write the problem vertically.

$$6x^2 -8x+ 18$$
$$3x^3 - 4x^2 +9x$$
2. Multiply each term in the multiplier by each term in the multiplicand. Be sure to use the sign in front of the term. Keep like terms in the same column.

$$3x^3 + 2x^2 + x + 18$$
3. Add.

EXAMPLE 2   Multiply $(7a + 4b - 5c)(2a + b)$.

   Answer $(7a + 4b - 5c)(2a + b)$

   $(7a + 4b - 5c)2a + (7a + 4b - 5c)b$

   $14a^2 + 8ab - 10ac + 7ab + 4b^2 - 5bc$

   $14a^2 + 15ab - 10ac - 5bc + 4b^2$

Multiplying Polynomials

1. Arrange both factors in descending powers of the same variable.
2. Place the factors in vertical form.
3. Multiply each term of the multiplier by each term of the multiplicand and place like terms in the same column.
4. Add like terms to obtain the final product.

EXAMPLE 3   Multiply $(4x^3 - 10x + 5x^2 + 6)(7x - 8 + 3x^2)$.

   Answer

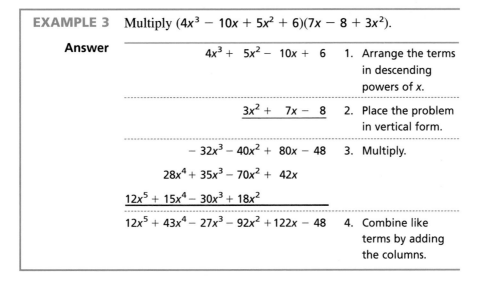

$$4x^3 + 5x^2 - 10x + 6 \qquad \text{1. Arrange the terms in descending powers of } x.$$

$$3x^2 + 7x - 8 \qquad \text{2. Place the problem in vertical form.}$$

$$-32x^3 - 40x^2 + 80x - 48$$
$$28x^4 + 35x^3 - 70x^2 + 42x \qquad \text{3. Multiply.}$$
$$12x^5 + 15x^4 - 30x^3 + 18x^2$$

$$12x^5 + 43x^4 - 27x^3 - 92x^2 + 122x - 48 \qquad \text{4. Combine like terms by adding the columns.}$$

▶ A. Exercises

Multiply the polynomials.

1. $(x^2 + xy + y^2)(x + y)$
2. $(3a^2 - 2a - 4)(a - 7)$
3. $(6x^2 + 3xy - 9y^2)(2x + y)$
4. $(7a + 3b - 9c + d)(a + b)$
5. $(2x^2 - x + 4)(3x - 7)$
6. $(a^2 - 3a - 9)(a + 2)$
7. $(2a + 4b)(3a - 9)$
8. $(4x^2 - 3x - 6)(x + 2)$

9. $(3x - 6)(3x + 5)$
10. $(2x^2 - 5x + 8)(3x + 6)$

▶ B. Exercises

Multiply the polynomials.
11. $(8x^2 + 3x + 4)(x - 6)$
12. $(2x^2 + 5x + 10)(x + 4)$
13. $(5x^2 - 7x + 4)(x - 3)$
14. $(x^2 - 3x - 9)(x^2 + 4x - 6)$
15. $(8x^2 - 2x + 6)(3x + 4)$
16. $(x - 3)(x^2 + 3x + 9)$
17. $(2x^2 + 5)(3x^2 - 9)$
18. $(x - 7)(x - 5)(x - 3)$
19. $(2x + 3)(x - 7) - (3x - 1)(x - 5)$
20. $(2x^2 - 5x + 7)(3x^2 - 7x - 4)$

▶ C. Exercises

The four steps below form a proof of the FOIL method. Give the correct reason for each step.

$\quad (a + b)(c + d)$
21. $(a + b)c + (a + b)d$
22. $ac + bc + (a + b)d$
23. $ac + bc + ad + bd$
24. $ac + ad + bc + bd$

The FOIL method can be thought of as a property itself (since you proved it), or it can be thought of as a special case of the distributive property used repeatedly.

■ Cumulative Review

25. Solve $5(x - 2) = 4 + 3x$.
26. Simplify $(3x^{-2}y)^{-3}$.
27. Solve the system $2x - y = 7$; $3x + 2y = 0$.
28. Simplify $\sqrt{9} + 9^0 - 9$.
29. Solve $|2x + 3| = 4$.

Combinations

Recall that the number of permutations of n objects taken r at a time is given by the following formula.

$$_nP_r = \frac{n!}{(n-r)!}$$

This formula counts arrangements in which order is important. If you arrange 2 out of the 3 objects A, B, and C, you get 6 arrangements: AB, BA, AC, CA, BC, CB. Therefore, $_3P_2 = 6$.

Combinations are the number of collections of r out of n objects. In a collection, order is *not* important. AB and BA are the same set. So there are only 3 combinations of 2 out of 3 objects: {A, B}, {A, C}, and {B, C}.

In this example $_3P_2 = 6$ counts each combination twice, so dividing by 2 gives the number of combinations.

$$_3C_2 = \frac{_3P_2}{2} = \frac{6}{2} = 3$$

You know that $_nP_r$ counts all the arrangements of each set of r objects. Since $r!$ counts the number of ways to arrange r objects, each set has been counted in each possible rearrangement. Divide by $r!$ to get the total number of sets (combinations).

$$_nC_r = \frac{_nP_r}{r!} = \frac{\frac{n!}{(n-r)!}}{r!} = \frac{n!}{(n-r)!} \cdot \frac{1}{r!} = \frac{n!}{(n-r)!r!}$$

EXAMPLE 1 How many study groups containing 8 students are possible in a class of 12?

Answer Since order is not important, calculate $_{12}C_8$.

$$_{12}C_8 = \frac{12!}{4!8!} = \frac{12 \cdot 11 \cdot 10 \cdot 9 \cdot 8!}{4!8!}$$

$$\frac{\overset{3}{\cancel{12}} \cdot 11 \cdot 10 \cdot 9}{\underset{2}{\cancel{24}}} = \frac{990}{2} = 495$$

Remember that order is important in permutations but not in combinations. That is why you must divide out the number of arrangements that repeat in order to find the number of combinations.

You may be surprised to know that combinations also apply to the polynomials that you have discussed in this chapter.

EXAMPLE 2   What is the coefficient of the x^2 term in $(x + 1)^4$?

Answer   One way to answer this question is to expand the polynomial and notice that the desired coefficient is **6**.

$$(x + 1)^4 = (x + 1)(x + 1)(x + 1)(x + 1)$$
$$= (x^2 + 2x + 1)(x^2 + 2x + 1)$$
$$= x^4 + 4x^3 + 6x^2 + 4x + 1$$

Another way to find the answer is to calculate $_4C_2$, which gives the coefficient of the second power term in a fourth power expansion. By this method, we obtain $_4C_2 = \frac{4!}{2!2!} = 6$ as before. Notice that this method is easier. For coefficients in which the exponent is large, such as $(x + 1)^{32}$, the second method is easy, but the first method would take hours.

As you can see, combinations can be used to find coefficients of terms in the expansion of a power of a binomial. For this reason combinations are sometimes called *binomial coefficients*. Some calculators use the symbol $\binom{n}{r}$ instead of $_nC_r$. Also, remember that $0! = 1$.

▶ Exercises

1. Find $_{12}P_7$ and $_{12}C_7$.
2. Find $_9P_9$ and $_9C_9$.
3. Find $_nC_n$. Explain your answer.
4. How many committees of 4 could be made from a club of 10 people?
5. What is the coefficient of x^7 in $(x + 1)^{10}$?

8.7 Special Products

Two special products can serve as shortcuts. Recognizing these binomial products can save you time. The first special product involves squaring a binomial.

As the Suez Canal shortcuts the trip around Africa, recognizing special products will shortcut trial and error factoring

---

EXAMPLE 1 Simplify $(x + 2)^2$.

Answer
$$(x + 2)^2 = (x + 2)(x + 2)$$
$$= x^2 + 2x + 2x + 4$$
$$= x^2 + 4x + 4$$

EXAMPLE 2 Simplify $(3x - 4)^2$.

Answer
$$(3x - 4)^2 = (3x - 4)(3x - 4)$$
$$= 9x^2 - 12x - 12x + 16$$
$$= 9x^2 - 24x + 16$$

EXAMPLE 3 Simplify $(a + b)^2$.

Answer
$$(a + b)^2 = (a + b)(a + b)$$
$$= a^2 + ab + ab + b^2$$
$$= a^2 + 2ab + b^2$$

Squaring a Binomial

1. Square the first term.
2. Multiply the first and last terms together and double the product.
3. Square the last term.
4. Add all three terms.

EXAMPLE 4 Simplify $(2x - 5)^2$.

Answer
$$(2x - 5)^2 = (2x)^2 + 2(2x)(-5) + (-5)^2$$
$$= 4x^2 - 20x + 25$$

Now consider the product of two binomials, one indicating the sum and the other indicating the difference of the same terms.

EXAMPLE 5 Multiply $(x - 4)(x + 4)$.

Answer $(x - 4)(x + 4) = x^2 + 4x - 4x - 16$
$$= x^2 - 16$$

EXAMPLE 6 Multiply $(3x + 5)(3x - 5)$.

Answer $(3x + 5)(3x - 5) = 9x^2 - 15x + 15x - 25$
$$= 9x^2 - 25$$

EXAMPLE 7 Multiply $(x + y)(x - y)$.

Answer $(x + y)(x - y) = x^2 - xy + xy - y^2$
$$= x^2 - y^2$$

Notice that the middle terms are eliminated when finding the product of the sum and difference of the same two quantities.

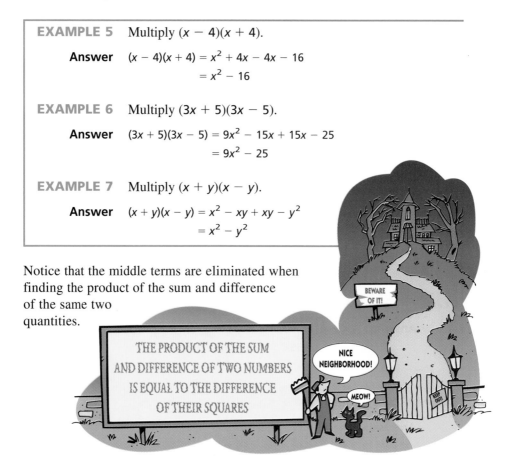

THE PRODUCT OF THE SUM AND DIFFERENCE OF TWO NUMBERS IS EQUAL TO THE DIFFERENCE OF THEIR SQUARES

Obtaining the Difference of Squares

1. Square the first term.
2. Subtract the square of the last term.

EXAMPLE 8 Multiply $(3x + 7)(3x - 7)$.

Answer

$(3x)^2 = 9x^2$	1. Square 3x.
$7(7) = 49$	2. Square 7.
$9x^2 - 49$	3. Write as the difference of the squares.

Finally, you should remember that finding higher powers requires repeated multiplication.

> **EXAMPLE 9** Simplify $(x + 8)^3$.
>
> **Answer** $(x + 8)^3 = (x + 8)(x + 8)(x + 8)$
> $= (x^2 + 16x + 64)(x + 8)$
> $= x^3 + 16x^2 + 64x + 8x^2 + 128x + 512$
> $= x^3 + 24x^2 + 192x + 512$

▶ A. Exercises

Multiply.

1. $(x + 3y)^2$
2. $(5x - 3)(5x + 3)$
3. $(x^2 - 8)(x^2 + 8)$
4. $(3x + 4)(3x - 4)$
5. $(x - 6)^2$
6. $(2x + 3)^2$

7. $(x - 9y)^2$
8. $(x + 2y)(x - 2y)$
9. $(2x + 11)(2x - 11)$
10. $(6x - 12)^2$
11. $(x - 16)^2$
12. $(x + 12)(x - 12)$

▶ B. Exercises

Perform the indicated operation and simplify.

13. $(x + 2)^3$
14. $(5x - 3)(5x + 3)$
15. $(5x - 3)^2$
16. $(x + 3)(x - 3) - (x + 2)^2$
17. $(x + 5)(x + 6) + (x - 2)^2$

18. $(x^2 - 5x)(x + 2) + (3x - 6)(x + 2)$
19. $(x - 6)(x + 2)(x + 6)$
20. $(x - 1)(x + 1)$
21. $(x - 1)^2$
22. $(x - 1)^3$

▶ C. Exercises

Perform the indicated operations and simplify.

23. $(2x^2 + 3x - 5)(x + 3) + (x - 6)(x + 6)$
24. $(3x - 2)^4$

■ Cumulative Review

Simplify.

25. $(3x^2)(5x^3)$
26. $6x(xy + 5z)$

27. $(x + y)(3x + 5)$
28. $(x^2 + x + 1)(x^2 - x + 1)$

29. $(2x^3 - 7x^2 + 8x - 9) + (3x^3 - 2x^2 - 5x + 2)$
30. $(8x^2 - 7x + 4) - (-3x^2 - 7x + 4)$

8.8 Dividing by a Monomial

The Word of God divides (cf. Heb. 4:12-13). It divides right from wrong, good from bad, light from dark, spiritual from unspiritual. The Holy Spirit speaks to the Christian to reveal sin in the Christian's life and to provide guidance and security. If a Christian does not read the Bible regularly and systematically, he cannot maintain fellowship with God as he should. He must read and study the Word of God every day so that he can rightly divide the word of truth to the unsaved world (cf. II Tim. 2:15).

The amount steel expands is $e = \frac{st}{1.1 \cdot 10^5}$, where s is the bridge span and t is the temperature change. In New York City average temperatures vary from 26° to 84°F How much will the 1595-foot span of the Brooklyn Bridge expand?

Dividing monomials is really a review of several concepts that you have already learned. First, you must remember the sign rules for division. In Chapter 1 you learned that dividing two numbers with like signs yields a positive answer and dividing two numbers with unlike signs yields a negative answer. Second, you need to keep in mind the division properties of exponents. When dividing like bases, subtract the exponent of the denominator from the exponent of the numerator. Third, you need to remember that a division problem can be written in the form of a fraction. With these things in mind, you should be able to divide monomials.

EXAMPLE 1 Simplify $32xyz \div 4x$.	**EXAMPLE 2** Simplify $\frac{-18a^2b}{9a}$.
Answer $\dfrac{32xyz}{4x}$	**Answer** $\dfrac{-18a^2b}{9a}$
$\dfrac{2^5xyz}{2^2x}$	$\dfrac{\overset{-2}{\cancel{-18}} \overset{a}{\cancel{a^2}} b}{\underset{1}{\cancel{9}} \underset{1}{\cancel{a}}}$
$\dfrac{2^{\overset{3}{\cancel{5}}} \cancel{x} yz}{2^2 \cancel{x}}$	$-2ab$
$\dfrac{2^3yz}{1}$	
$8yz$	

Dividing Monomials

1. Place in fractional form.
2. Reduce the numerical coefficients.
3. Use the sign rules and the properties of exponents to cancel variable factors.
4. Multiply the remaining coefficient and variable factors.

EXAMPLE 3   Simplify $\dfrac{54x^2yz^3}{3xyz^2}$.

Answer $\dfrac{54x^2yz^3}{3xyz^2}$

$$\dfrac{\overset{18}{\cancel{54}}\ \overset{x}{\cancel{x^2}}\ \overset{1}{\cancel{y}}\ \overset{z}{\cancel{z^3}}}{\underset{1}{\cancel{3}}\ \underset{1}{\cancel{x}}\ \underset{1}{\cancel{y}}\ \underset{1}{\cancel{z^2}}}$$

$18xz$

The principles for dividing polynomials by a monomial are exactly the same as the principles for dividing numbers. Review the basic steps in division before you begin dividing polynomials.

EXAMPLE 4   Simplify $(15 + 27) \div 3$.

Answer

$\dfrac{15 + 27}{3}$	1. Place the problem in fractional form.
$\dfrac{15}{3} + \dfrac{27}{3}$	2. Separate addends.
$5 + 9$	3. Simplify.
14	

Alternate solution: $\dfrac{15 + 27}{3} = \dfrac{42}{3} = 14$

In the alternate solution, the numerators were added first. You get the same answer by either method. If you cannot combine the numerator into one term, you must separate the addends before you divide. Do you know why $\dfrac{a+c}{b} = \dfrac{a}{b} + \dfrac{c}{b}$? Recall from Section 2.2 that $\dfrac{a}{b} = a \cdot \dfrac{1}{b}$. Applying this principle, $\dfrac{a+c}{b} = (a+c) \cdot \dfrac{1}{b}$, which equals $\dfrac{a}{b} + \dfrac{c}{b}$ by the distributive property.

EXAMPLE 5 Simplify $(12x^2 + 20x) \div 4x$.

Answer

$\dfrac{12x^2 + 20x}{4x}$ 1. Place the problem in fractional form.

$\dfrac{12x^2}{4x} + \dfrac{20x}{4x}$ 2. Separate into two addends.

$\dfrac{\overset{3}{\cancel{12}}\overset{x}{\cancel{x^2}}}{\underset{1}{\cancel{4}}\,\underset{1}{\cancel{x}}} + \dfrac{\overset{5}{\cancel{20}}\overset{1}{\cancel{x}}}{\underset{1}{\cancel{4}}\,\underset{1}{\cancel{x}}}$ 3. Simplify the addends.

$3x + 5$

Check your solution by multiplying the quotient that you obtained by the divisor. You should get the dividend.

Check. $4x(3x + 5) = 12x^2 + 20x$

Dividing Polynomials by Monomials

1. Place the problem in fractional form.
2. Separate the expression into monomial terms.
3. Simplify each term as much as possible.
4. Check the solution by multiplying the quotient by the divisor to get the dividend.

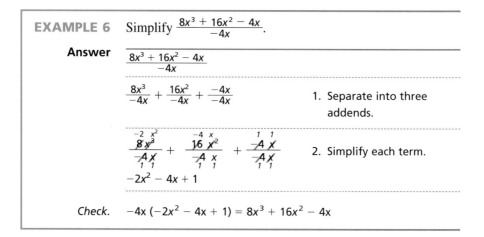

EXAMPLE 6 Simplify $\dfrac{8x^3 + 16x^2 - 4x}{-4x}$.

Answer

$\dfrac{8x^3 + 16x^2 - 4x}{-4x}$

$\dfrac{8x^3}{-4x} + \dfrac{16x^2}{-4x} + \dfrac{-4x}{-4x}$ 1. Separate into three addends.

$\dfrac{\overset{-2}{\cancel{8}}\overset{x^2}{\cancel{x^3}}}{\underset{1}{\cancel{4}}\,\underset{1}{\cancel{x}}} + \dfrac{\overset{-4}{\cancel{16}}\overset{x}{\cancel{x^2}}}{\underset{1}{\cancel{4}}\,x\,\underset{1}{\cancel{x}}} + \dfrac{\overset{1}{\cancel{-4}}\overset{1}{\cancel{x}}}{\underset{1}{\cancel{4}}\,\underset{1}{\cancel{x}}}$ 2. Simplify each term.

$-2x^2 - 4x + 1$

Check. $-4x(-2x^2 - 4x + 1) = 8x^3 + 16x^2 - 4x$

▶ **A. Exercises**

Divide.

1. $\dfrac{3x^2}{3}$

2. $\dfrac{25ab^3}{5a}$

3. $\dfrac{7a^2b}{7ab}$

4. $\dfrac{16x^5y}{8xy}$

5. $\dfrac{-74a^3bc^4}{-2abc^2}$

6. $(5x^2 + 25x) \div 5x$

7. $(x^3 + x^2 - x) \div x$

8. $(24a^2b - 12ab + 9b^2) \div 3b$

9. $(abc + bcd) \div bc$

10. $(8x^3 - 2x) \div 2x$

▶ B. Exercises

Divide.

11. $\dfrac{1}{2}x^3y \div x$

12. $\dfrac{a^4b^3c}{ab^2}$

13. $\dfrac{-42x^5y^4z^{10}}{-6xz^3}$

14. $\dfrac{28a^4bc^5}{-4ac^2}$

15. $\dfrac{x^4y^3z^2}{-xy^2z}$

16. $(81x^3 - 27x^2y + 9xy^3) \div 3x$

17. $(15x^2 - 3x + 27) \div -3$

18. $(-4a^3b^2 + 32ab^3 - 18b^5) \div -2b^2$

19. $(17a^3b^2 - 5a^2b^3 + 2ab^5) \div ab$

20. $(3n^4 - n^2) \div n^2$

21. $(17a^3b - 34ab^2) \div 17a$

22. $(22x^2y + 16xy - 8y) \div 2y$

▶ C. Exercises

Divide.

23. $\dfrac{3}{4}x^3y^4z \div \left(-\dfrac{1}{2}xy^2z\right)$

24. $(6x^4y^3 - 26x^2y^2 - 18xy) \div 2xy$

■ Cumulative Review

Simplify.

25. $\dfrac{0}{5x^2y}$

26. $\dfrac{3x + 2y}{0}$

Evaluate for $x = 2$.

27. $\dfrac{3x^2 + 4}{x}$

28. $3x + 4$

29. $3x + \dfrac{4}{x}$

MIND OVER MATH

Find the missing numbers that will make each division problem correct.

```
        4 _ 2
  _ _ )_ 3 _ _ 4
      = _ 8
      2 2 _
      = _ _ 6
        _ 4
        _ 4
```

```
        7 _ _
  3 _ ) 2 5 _ _ _
      2 _ _
      2 0 _
      = _ _ 0
        _ 0 _
        = = =
```

```
        _ _ _
  _ 1 ) 2 _ 4 _ _
      _ 8 _
      _ 2 _
      = _ _ 4
        6 _ _
        6 _ _
```

8.9 Dividing Polynomials

Dividing with monomials is fairly simple, as you have seen. When the divisor is a binomial, the process becomes more complicated but is still much like dividing by a two-digit number. Divide 1634 by 32.

$$\begin{array}{r} 5\,1\ \text{R.2} \\ 3\,2\,\overline{)1\,6\,3\,4} \\ -1\,6\,0 \\ \hline 3\,4 \\ -3\,2 \\ \hline 2 \end{array}$$

To check, multiply the quotient by the divisor and then add the remainder. If you calculated correctly, you should obtain the original dividend.

$51 \cdot 32 + 2 = 1632 + 2 = 1634$

Now observe a polynomial division. Look for the similarities.

EXAMPLE 1 Divide $(x^2 + 4x - 9) \div (x + 2)$.

Answer

1. First write the problem in long-division form. Be sure that the terms of the dividend and the divisor are in descending powers of one variable.

$$\begin{array}{r} x\phantom{{}+2)x^2+4x-9} \\ x + 2\,\overline{)x^2 + 4x - 9} \\ -(x^2 + 2x) \\ \hline 2x - 9 \end{array}$$

2. Look at the divisor and the first term of the dividend. Divide the first term of the dividend (x^2) by the first term of the divisor x. You get x. Place x in the quotient.

3. Now multiply x by the whole divisor $(x + 2)$ and place the product under the dividend in the proper columns.

4. Subtract to obtain a new dividend.

$$\begin{array}{r} x + 2 \\ x + 2\,\overline{)x^2 + 4x - 9} \\ -(x^2 + 2x) \\ \hline 2x - 9 \\ -(2x + 4) \\ \hline -13 \end{array}$$

5. Divide the divisor into the new dividend.

6. Continue dividing and subtracting until the degree of the new dividend is less than the degree of the divisor.
The quotient is $x + 2$, R. -13.

Check. $(x + 2)(x + 2) - 13 = x^2 + 4x - 9$

Dividing Polynomials

1. Arrange both the dividend and the divisor in descending powers of the same variable.
2. Divide the first term of the dividend by the first term of the divisor to obtain the first term of the quotient.
3. Multiply the quotient by the whole divisor and place the product under the dividend.
4. Subtract this product from the dividend to obtain a new dividend.
5. Go back to step 2 unless the degree of the new dividend is less than the degree of the divisor.
6. Check your results by multiplying the quotient by the divisor and adding the remainder.

EXAMPLE 2   Divide $\dfrac{2x^4 - x^3 + 5x^2 + 9x - 6}{x - 1}$.

Answer   Follow the steps for solving.

$$
\begin{array}{r}
2x^3 + x^2 + 6x + 15 \text{ R.9} \\
x - 1 \overline{) 2x^4 - x^3 + 5x^2 + 9x - 6} \\
\underline{-(2x^4 - 2x^3)} \\
x^3 + 5x^2 \\
\underline{-(x^3 - x^2)} \\
6x^2 + 9x \\
\underline{-(6x^2 - 6x)} \\
15x - 6 \\
\underline{-(15x - 15)} \\
9
\end{array}
$$

The quotient is $2x^3 + x^2 + 6x + 15$, R.9.

Check. $(x - 1)(2x^3 + x^2 + 6x + 15) + 9 = 2x^4 - x^3 + 5x^2 + 9x - 6$

EXAMPLE 3   Divide $(x^3 - 8) \div (x - 2)$.

Answer   Since the x^2 and x terms are missing from the dividend, you will need to show place holders for long division. Insert 0s as coefficients of the missing variables.

$$
\begin{array}{r}
x^2 + 2x + 4 \\
x - 2 \overline{)\, x^3 + 0x^2 + 0x - 8} \\
\underline{-(x^3 - 2x^2)} \\
2x^2 + 0x \\
\underline{-(2x^2 - 4x)} \\
4x - 8 \\
\underline{-(4x - 8)} \\
0
\end{array}
$$

The quotient is $x^2 + 2x + 4$.

WHEN A POLYNOMIAL IS
DIVIDED EVENLY,
AS IN EXAMPLE 3,
BOTH THE DIVISOR
AND THE QUOTIENT
ARE CALLED FACTORS
OF THE POLYNOMIAL

A MASTERPIECE!

EXAMPLE 4   Divide $(3a^3 + 4ab^2 - 5a^2b + 2b^3) \div (a + b)$.

Answer

$$
\begin{array}{r}
3a^2 - 8ab + 12b^2 \text{ R.} -10b^3 \\
a + b \overline{)\, 3a^3 - 5a^2b + 4ab^2 + 2b^3} \\
\underline{-(3a^3 + 3a^2b)} \\
-8a^2b + 4ab^2 \\
\underline{-(-8a^2b - 8ab^2)} \\
12ab^2 + 2b^3 \\
\underline{-(12ab^2 + 12b^3)} \\
-10b^3
\end{array}
$$

1. First arrange the polynomial in descending powers of a.

2. Divide.

The quotient is $3a^2 - 8ab + 12b^2$, R. $-10b^3$.

► A. Exercises

Divide.

1. $(a^2 + 4a + 12) \div (a - 6)$
2. $(x^2 + 8x + 15) \div (x + 2)$
3. $(5x^2 - 2x + 9) \div (x + 1)$
4. $\dfrac{3x^2 + 11x - 15}{3x - 4}$
5. $\dfrac{x^2 + 4x - 3}{x - 1}$
6. $(24x^2 + 13x - 9) \div (x + 3)$

► B. Exercises

Divide. Be careful to use descending order and place holders.

7. $(2 + x^2 - x) \div (3 + x)$
8. $(7x^2 + 8 - 3x) \div (x + 4)$
9. $(x^3 - 2x^2 + 3x) \div (x - 4)$
10. $(4x^2 - 16) \div (x - 2)$
11. $(x^3 + 2x - 8) \div (x + 3)$
12. $(x^3 - 27) \div (x - 3)$
13. $(x^2 - 16) \div (x - 4)$
14. $\dfrac{x^4 - 8x^2 + 16}{x^2 + 4}$
15. $(4t - t^2) \div (t - 1)$
16. $\dfrac{x^2 + 3x + 1}{x^2 + x + 1}$

► C. Exercises

17. $(x^5 - 2x^2 + 6) \div (x^2 + 4)$
18. $(12m^2 - 3m^3 + 4m) \div (3m - 2)$

■ Cumulative Review

19. Graph $x \neq 5$.
20. Find the slope of the line connecting $(5, 1)$ and $(-3, 6)$.
21. Simplify $\dfrac{9}{649} \div \dfrac{33}{118}$.
22. Solve $\dfrac{5}{34}x = \dfrac{3}{4} - \dfrac{2}{51}x$.
23. If r varies directly as s, and $r = 3$ when $s = 12$, find the constant of variation.

Algebra *and* Scripture

$\mathcal{I}$n Chapter 2 we recognized that *whosoever* is like a variable; it enables us to make generalizations about all people without naming them one by one. In the same way, variables can be used to summarize this list of facts:

$$2 \cdot 3 = 3 \cdot 2$$
$$-5 \cdot 4 = 4(-5)$$
$$7(-1) = -1 \cdot 7$$

1. Give the generalization.

In this chapter we have seen how vertical multiplication and long division can be generalized to polynomials. Multiplying polynomials is just like multiplying numbers.

2. Give the multiplication problem in Leviticus 25:8.

Notice that multiplication increases faster than addition:

$$4 + 5 = 9 \text{ but } 4 \cdot 5 = 5 + 5 + 5 + 5 = 20$$

This explains the usage of the word *multiply* in general contexts.

3. What multiplied in Acts 6:1-7?
4. What multiplies for those who follow false gods according to Psalm 16:4?
5. What is supposed to multiply in Genesis 8:17?

THE NTH DEGREE

Find a verse in which God's grace and peace is multiplied.

Read Genesis 1:28. This verse is important in two ways. It stresses both the multiplication of mankind and the dominion of mankind. God commands people both to fill the earth and to subdue it.

6. If the population of the earth were to double in each generation after Creation, counting Adam and Eve as the first generation, how many people would there be in the fourth generation? the eleventh generation?

7. Do populations that double reflect addition or multiplication of the human race?

8. Explain a way in which math helps people to have dominion over the earth in obedience to Genesis 1:28.

Scriptural Roots

And God blessed them, and God said unto them, Be fruitful, and multiply, and replenish the earth, and subdue it: and have dominion over the fish of the sea, and over the fowl of the air, and over every living thing that moveth upon the earth.

Genesis 1:28

Chapter 8 Review

Classify each polynomial below.

1. $x - 5$
2. 7
3. $3x^2y + 4y - 6xy^2$

Evaluate each polynomial if $x = 2$, $y = -1$, and $z = 0$.

4. $4x^3 + 2x - 5z$
5. $8y^4 + 7y^2 + 3y + 9$
6. $3x^2 - 5xz$

Give the degree of each polynomial below.

7. $x^3 + 3x^2 + 5x - 4$
8. $12x$
9. $4x^2y^3 - 3xy^2$
10. 9

Do the indicated operation and simplify.

11. $(2x^2 + 3x - 5) + (7x^2 - 9)$
12. $(5a^2 - ab - 3b^2) - (6a^2 - 7ab + 10b^2)$
13. $(x^2 + y^2) - (x + y^2) + (12x^2 + y)$
14. $(r^2 + 2t) + (r^2 + 6rt - 9t)$
15. $(5x^2y^3)(16xy^4)$
16. $(12ab^5)(-4a^4b)$
17. $(a^5ab^3)^4$
18. $3x(x^2 - 5x + 4)$
19. $7xy^2(3x - 5xy^4)$
20. $-3a^4bc^2(2a^3b + 7abc^5)$
21. $(x + 4)(x - 6)$
22. $(a + 5)(a + 7)$
23. $(3x - 7)(2x + 5)$
24. $(x - 9)(x - 11)$
25. $(a + 3b)(a - 7b)$
26. $(y - 6)(y + 6)$
27. $(x + 3)^2$
28. $(x - 2y)^2$
29. $(x^2 + 3x + 5)(x + 2)$
30. $(x + 3)(x - 3)(x - 3)$
31. $\dfrac{x^5}{x^2}$
32. $8x^2y^3z \div 2xy^2$

33. $\dfrac{7x^2y + 21x^3y^4}{7xy}$

34. $(6x^2 + 21x + 9) \div (x + 3)$

35. $\dfrac{x^2 + 5}{2 + x}$

Use $3x - 5 + x^2$.

36. Give the coefficient of the first term.

37. Give the degree of the second term.

38. Give the coefficient of the last term.

39. Write the polynomial in descending order.

40. Explain the mathematical significance of Genesis 1:28.

9 Factoring Polynomials

$$y = mx + b$$

Glaciers differ from snow fields. While snow fields may become icy or may melt away completely, glaciers consist of solid ice so thick that they persist from year to year and may advance or retreat. The motion derives from the massive weight of the ice, which acts like a mound of dough. Glaciers may advance either by internal deformation (when "dough" folds or faults into a different form) or basal sliding (oozing across the ground).

Glaciologists study basal sliding by staking out a straight line across the glacier. Since the stakes in the center move faster than those near the center, the line of stakes deforms into a curve called a parabola. Comparison of their motions allows the researchers to estimate the velocity of the glacier. The velocity is expressed as a distance from the center line of the glacier.

The Saskatchewan Glacier is part of the Columbia Ice Field in Jasper National Park, Alberta, in the Canadian Rockies. It is 555 meters deep. It moves between 75 and 117 meters per year. Its velocity (m per year) is estimated by the equation given below.

$$y = -0.0001358x^2 + 0.00138x + 80.12$$

The formula factors as follows. This enables you to find the zeros of the function, as you will learn in Chapter 11.

$$y = -\frac{1}{1000}(0.1358x - 105)(x + 763)$$

Glacier temperatures are also modeled using polynomials that can be factored. Temperatures get colder as you go deeper for the first 100 meters, but after that they actually increase.

After this chapter you should be able to

1. factor common monomials from polynomials.

2. factor the difference of two squares.

3. factor perfect square trinomials.

4. factor trinomials as a product of two binomials (when possible).

5. factor completely a given polynomial over the set of integers.

9.1 Factoring Common Monomials

A factor is a quantity (known or unknown) that can be multiplied with another quantity to yield a product. When you learned to find the GCF and the LCM of two numbers, you factored each number into its prime factors. Multiplication begins with the factors and finds the product. *Factoring,* the opposite of multiplication, begins with the product and finds the factors. In this section you will learn to find a common monomial factor in a polynomial and apply the distributive property in reverse.

Definition

A **common monomial factor** is a monomial that is a factor of all the terms in a polynomial.

These skydivers fall according to the monomial $\frac{1}{2}gt^2$.

EXAMPLE 1 Factor $8x^2 - 16$.

Answer

$8x^2 = 2^3x^2$ $16 = 2^4$ GCF of 8 and 16 = 8	1. Factor each term into primes and identify the greatest common factor.
$8x^2 - 16 = 8(x^2 - 2)$	2. Factor 8 out of each term of the polynomial.

Check. $8(x^2 - 2) = 8(x^2) - 8(2) = 8x^2 - 16$

Factoring Common Monomials from a Polynomial

1. Find the GCF of all terms in the polynomial.
2. Divide each term of the polynomial by the GCF (apply the distributive property in reverse) to get the terms of the other factor of the polynomial.
3. Check your solution by multiplying the two factors.

EXAMPLE 2   Factor $3x^2y - 27xy + 9xy^3$.

Answer

$3x^2y - 3^3xy + 3^2xy^3$ GCF $= 3xy$	1. Factor each term, and identify the highest power of each factor that all the terms have in common. The product is the GCF of the terms of the polynomial.
$3xy(x - 9 + 3y^2)$	2. Factor the GCF from each term of the polynomial by dividing the GCF into each term of the polynomial.
$3xy(x - 9 + 3y^2) = 3x^2y - 27xy + 9xy^3$	3. Check mentally using the distributive property.

EXAMPLE 3   Factor $14a^3 + 21a$.

Answer

$14a^3 = 7 \cdot 2 \cdot a^3$ $21a = 7 \cdot 3 \cdot a$	1. By factoring, you can see that the GCF is $7a$.
$7a(2a^2 + 3)$	2. Dividing $14a^3$ by $7a$ gives $2a^2$. Dividing $21a$ by $7a$ gives 3. Check mentally.

EXAMPLE 4   Factor $xa^2 + xy - x$.

Answer $xa^2 + xy - x$
$x(a^2 + y - 1)$

The common monomial here is x.
Factor x out of each term.

▶ A. Exercises

Factor.

1. $7x^2 - 49xy + 28y^2$
2. $a^2 - a$
3. $8x - 32y$
4. $ax + ay$
5. $21x^3 - 6x^2 - 3$
6. $3x + 3y$
7. $15x + 30$
8. $x^2 - 3x$
9. $6a^2 + 48a - 24$
10. $10 - 50x$

▶ B. Exercises

Factor.

11. $6a^2b + 3ab^2$
12. $300x^2 - 100x$
13. $10a^2bc^3 + 5ab^2c$
14. $2\pi x - 4\pi r$
15. $12x^3 - 16xy^2$
16. $20a^3x + 50ax + 10x$
17. $7a^5 - 84a^3 + 21a$
18. $x^5 + x^3 - x^2 + x$

Factor.
19. $6x^4y^5z^3 - 27x^3y^6z^4 + 18x^2y^4z^5$
20. $34a^7b^8c^2 + 51a^3b^5d^4 - 289a^2b^9c^{10}d$

Cumulative Review

Use the circle diagram to answer the following.

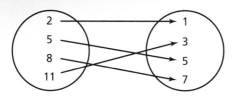

21. Give the domain of the relation.
22. Give the range of the relation.
23. Is the relation a function?
24. Give the relation in set form.
25. Graph the relation.

9.2 Factoring the Difference of Two Squares

In Chapter 8 you learned how to multiply binomials, including the sum and difference of two quantities. The product of the sum $x + y$ and the difference $x - y$ of two numbers is equal to the difference of their squares.

$$(x + y)(x - y) = x^2 - y^2$$

The volume of metal used to make a washer is calculated with a binomial: $V = \pi R^2 t - \pi r^2 t$, *where* R *and* r *are the inner and outer radii and* t *is the thickness.*

Since factoring is the opposite of multiplication, you will get the binomial sum $x + y$ and the binomial difference $x - y$ as factors when you factor any binomial that is the difference of two squares.

EXAMPLE 1 Factor $x^2 - 49$.

Answer Find the square root of each of the two squares. Then express the factors as two binomials, one the sum of the roots and the other the difference of the roots.

$x^2 - 49$
$(x + 7)(x - 7)$

Factoring the Difference of Two Squares

1. Factor any common monomials out of the polynomial.
2. Factor the difference of the two squares into two binomials in which one factor is the sum of the square root terms and the other factor is the difference of the square root terms.
3. Check mentally by multiplying to see if $a^2 - b^2 = (a + b)(a - b)$.

EXAMPLE 2 Factor $5a^2 - 125x^2$.

Answer

$5a^2 - 125x^2$

$5(a^2 - 25x^2)$ 1. Factor the common monomial 5.

$5(a + 5x)(a - 5x)$ 2. Factor the difference of two squares: $a^2 - 25x^2 = (a + 5x)(a - 5x)$.

EXAMPLE 3 Factor $1 - 64y^2$.

Answer $(1 + 8y)(1 - 8y)$

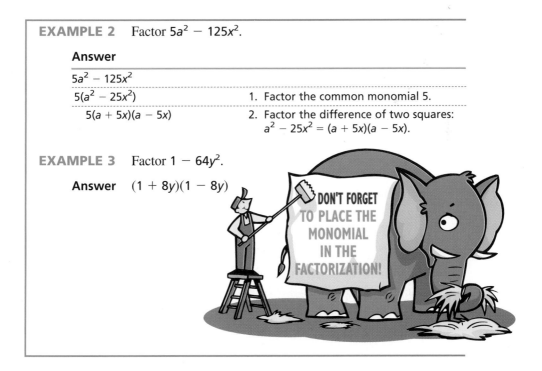

DON'T FORGET TO PLACE THE MONOMIAL IN THE FACTORIZATION!

▶ A. Exercises

Factor.

1. $y^2 - 144$
2. $x^2 - y^2$
3. $49x^2 - 4$
4. $9x^2 - 100$
5. $2a^2 - 242$

6. $25 - 100y^2$
7. $36a^2 - 49$
8. $25x^2 - 49$
9. $a^2 - 225b^2$
10. $a^2x^2 - y^2$

▶ B. Exercises

Factor.

11. $4x^2 - 16$
12. $a^2x^2 - 16x^2$
13. $63x^2 - 175$
14. $147a^2 - 507$

15. $a^4 - a^2b^2$
16. $392a^5 - 200a^3$
17. $16x^2 - 4$
18. $x^7 - x^5$

▶ C. Exercises

Factor.

19. $162a^2b^4c - 18b^4c$
20. $x^6 - x^2$

■ Cumulative Review

21. Evaluate $2x + 4 - 5x + 2$ if $x = 7$.
22. Simplify $2x + 4 - 5x + 2$.
23. Solve $2x + 4 - 5x + 2 = 0$.
24. Graph $y = 2x + 4 - 5x + 2$.
25. Factor $2x + 4$.

MIND OVER MATH

Identify the next five numbers in each sequence and explain the progression.

1. 2, 4, 6, 8, . . .
2. 1, 2, 6, 24, 120, . . .
3. 1, 4, 9, 16, 25, . . .

4. 3, 9, 27, 81, 243, . . .
5. 1, 1, 2, 3, 5, 8, 13, . . .
6. 1, 3, 6, 10, 15, 21, . . .

Identify the next group of letters in each sequence.

1. *ABC, FGH, KLM,* . . .
2. *AZ, BX, CV, DT,* . . .

3. *AAB, ABB, BBC, BCC,* . . .
4. *ABZ, BDZ, DGZ, GKZ,* . . .

Variability

Calculate the mean ($\bar{x}$), the median, and the mode of these ten quiz scores.

7, 6, 9, 5, 8, 8, 4, 10, 8, 7 $\bar{x} = \frac{\Sigma x}{n} = \frac{72}{10} = 7.2$

Notice that the scores are spread out around the mean. Variability measures how much the scores vary or spread out. The *Range* = high score − low score.

EXAMPLE 1   Find the range for the quiz.

Answer   Range = high − low = 10 − 4 = 6, so the scores spread out across a span of six points.

Since the range takes only two scores into account, it is a very rough measurement of variation. Other measures of variability provide a better picture of the spread but require you to calculate the distance of each score from the mean. These distances are called *deviations* and are represented by *d*. For example, the score of 6 has a deviation of $d = |\, x - \bar{x}\,| = |\, 6 - 7.2 \,| = 1.2$ points away from the mean.

The squares of the deviations are more useful. A table can help you organize your calculations of these statistics.

The *average deviation, $\bar{d}$,* is the average of the distances from the mean.

The *variance, s^2,* is an "average" of the squares of the deviations found by dividing the sum of the squared deviations by $n - 1$, where *n* is the number of scores.

The *standard deviation, s,* is the square root of the variance.

EXAMPLE 2   Find the average deviation, the variance, and the standard deviation of the ten quiz scores given previous to example 1.

Answer

n	x	$d = \|\,x - \bar{x}\,\|$	$d^2 = (x - \bar{x})^2$
1	7	0.2	0.04
2	6	1.2	1.44
3	9	1.8	3.24
4	5	2.2	4.84

Continued ▶

5	8	0.8	0.64
6	8	0.8	0.64
7	4	3.2	10.24
8	10	2.8	7.84
9	8	0.8	0.64
10	7	0.2	0.04
total	$\Sigma x = 72$	$\Sigma d = 14$	$\Sigma d^2 = 29.6$
divided total	$\bar{x} = 7.2$	$\bar{d} = 1.4$	$s^2 = 3.29$

From the bottom row of the table, you can read the mean ($\bar{x}$), the average deviation ($\bar{d}$), and the variance (s^2).

$$\bar{d} = \frac{\Sigma d}{n} = \frac{14}{10} = 1.4 \qquad s^2 = \frac{\Sigma d^2}{n-1} = \frac{29.6}{9} = 3.29$$

For the standard deviation, find the square root of the variance.

$$s = \sqrt{s^2} = \sqrt{3.29} = 1.81$$

You will learn more about the variance and standard deviation in future chapters. The standard deviation is often about one-fourth of the range. In such cases, half of the spread will be numerically smaller than the mean and half larger. You can use this estimate of the spread when only the standard deviation is known.

▶ Exercises

Eight students took a 20-point quiz. The scores were 12, 19, 16, 18, 19, 17, 18, 14. Find each statistic below.

1. the mean and range
2. the average deviation
3. variance
4. standard deviation

5. A manufacturer sends a shipment of spokes to a store that assembles and sells bicycles. If the spokes for a 26" wheel are supposed to be 268 mm, those that are too long or too short by more than 1 mm are defective and unusable. Supposing the standard deviation of a sample shipment of these spokes is 0.6 mm, what is the variance? the range? Do you expect some defective spokes?

9.3 Factoring Perfect Square Trinomials

When factoring polynomials, you can save yourself time if you recognize the special cases when you see them. Can you identify a polynomial that is the difference of two squares?

You should also recognize sin in your life. How can you identify sin? You will recognize your sin from reading the Word of God and from the sense of guilt brought by the Holy Spirit. When the Holy Spirit convicts you of sin, you should immediately confess it and forsake it so that God can forgive and cleanse you (I John 1:9). Otherwise, you will grow tolerant and become enslaved by it. Don't allow sin to rule your life (cf. Rom. 6:12-14).

Another special product is the square of a binomial. Review the squaring process (see Chapter 8) and look for characteristic patterns of the product that will identify it.

$$(x + y)^2 = (x + y)(x + y)$$
$$= x^2 + 2xy + y^2$$
$$(y + 4)^2 = (y + 4)(y + 4)$$
$$= y^2 + 8y + 16$$
$$(x + 3)^2 = x^2 + 6x + 9$$
$$(x - 1)^2 = x^2 - 2x + 1$$

What do these four products have in common? First, each is a trinomial. Next, the first and last terms of each trinomial is a perfect square. The middle term is twice the product of the square roots of the first and last terms. Notice that all four follow the same pattern. Anytime you see a trinomial in this pattern, you should recognize it as a perfect square.

Factoring a Perfect Square Trinomial

1. Factor any common monomials from the polynomial before checking for a perfect square.
2. Find the square root of the first and last terms of the trinomial. These are the terms of the binomial factors.
3. The sign between the terms of the binomial factors will be the same as the sign of the middle term in the trinomial.
   $$a^2 + 2ab + b^2 = (a + b)(a + b) = (a + b)^2$$
   $$a^2 - 2ab + b^2 = (a - b)(a - b) = (a - b)^2$$

EXAMPLE 1   Factor $x^2 + 10x + 25$.

Answer

$x^2 + 10x + 25$	1. There are no common factors, but the first and last terms are perfect squares. To be a perfect square trinomial, the middle term must be twice the product of the square roots of the first and last terms. Is it?
$\sqrt{x^2} = x$ $\sqrt{25} = 5$ $2(x)(5) = 10x$	2. Factor by finding the square root of x^2 and of 25. The binomial factor has the terms x and 5.
$(x + 5)^2$	3. Place the sign of the middle term of the trinomial between the terms of the factor.

So the factorization of $x^2 + 10x + 25 = (x + 5)^2$.

EXAMPLE 2   Factor $4x^2 + 12x + 9$.

Answer $\sqrt{4x^2} = 2x$
$\sqrt{9} = 3$
$2(2x)(3) = 12x$
Since the sign of the middle term is positive, the factorization is $(2x + 3)^2$.

BE SURE THE TERMS OF THE TRINOMIAL ARE IN DESCENDING ORDER OF THE VARIABLE BEFORE STARTING TO FACTOR

EXAMPLE 3   Factor $x^2y^2 - 8xyz + 16z^2$.

Answer   Is this a perfect square trinomial?
$\sqrt{x^2y^2} = xy$
$\sqrt{16z^2} = 4z$
$2(xy)(4z) = 8xyz$
Since the sign of the middle term is negative, the factorization is $(xy - 4z)^2$.

EXAMPLE 4   Factor $x^2 - 4x + 9$.

Answer   Is this a perfect square trinomial? No, the middle term is not twice the product of the square roots of the other terms. The trinomial cannot be factored.

▶ A. Exercises

Identify the perfect square trinomials.

1. $x^2 + 6x + 9$
2. $x^2y - 8xy + 16y^2$
3. $x^2 + 14x + 49$
4. $a^2b^2 - 12abc + 36c^2$
5. $4x^2 - 10x + 25$
6. $a^2b^4 + 24ab^2 + 144$
7. $81x^2y^4 + 9xy^2z + z^2$
8. $x^6y^2 - 4x^3yz + 4z^2$
9. $a^2 - 4ab - 4b^2$
10. $16x^2y^8 + 16xy^4 + 4$

Factor.

11. $x^2 - 6x + 9$
12. $16a^2 + 8a + 1$
13. $x^2 - 16x + 64$
14. $m^2 + 24m + 144$
15. $a^2 - 10ab + 25b^2$
16. $a^2 - 14a + 49$

▶ B. Exercises

Factor.

17. $9x^2 + 12x + 4$
18. $36x^2 + 12x + 1$
19. $9x^2 + 30xz + 25z^2$
20. $x^8 + 26x^4 + 169$
21. $x^2t^4 - 20xt^2 + 100$
22. $x^2 + 0.6x + 0.09$
23. $18x^3 + 48x^2 + 32x$
24. $\frac{1}{16}y^2 - 2y + 16$

▶ C. Exercises

Factor.

25. $27x^5y - 72x^3y^2 + 48xy^3$

Factor the polynomial and then express as a division problem.

26. $9x^2 + 48x + 64$

■ Cumulative Review

27. Simplify $23 \cdot 101$.
28. Factor 7373.
29. Write the exercises above as division problems.

Factor each polynomial and then write each as a division problem.

30. $5xy + 20x - 40xy^2$

31. $64x^2 - 9$

9.4 Factoring Trinomials of the Form $x^2 + bx + c$

Most polynomials are neither the difference of two squares nor perfect square trinomials. When you factor a trinomial that is not a perfect square, you must use a trial-and-error method of factoring. You will find factoring becomes much easier with experience. Just remember that factoring is the opposite of multiplying.

EXAMPLE 1   Factor $x^2 + 7x + 12$.

Answer

$x^2 + 7x + 12$

$\qquad x^2 = x \cdot x$
$\qquad$ or
$\qquad x^2 = x^2 \cdot 1$

$(x \quad)(x \quad)$

1. To begin factoring this trinomial, find all possible factors of x^2, the first term. Because this trinomial form requires an x in each factor, you will use $x \cdot x$. Place each x in parentheses, leaving space for the other term.

$12 = 12 \cdot 1$
$12 = -12 \cdot -1$
$12 = 6 \cdot 2$
$12 = -6 \cdot -2$
$12 = 4 \cdot 3$
$12 = -4 \cdot -3$

2. To find the second term in these binomial factors, list all the factors of 12, the last term of the polynomial. The sign on the twelve is positive. This tells you the signs on the constants must be alike.

$(x + 3)(x + 4)$

3. Choose the factors whose sum equals 7, the coefficient of the middle term. Since $3 \cdot 4 = 12$ (the last term) and $3 + 4 = 7$ (the coefficient of the middle term), place 3 in one set of parentheses and 4 in the other.

Check. $(x + 3)(x + 4) = x^2 + 7x + 12$

Factoring $x^2 + bx + c$

1. Factor the first term. Use the factors as the first terms of the binomial factors.
2. Factor c, the last term.
3. Choose the factors of c whose sum is b and place these factors in the factorization as the last terms in the binomial factors.
4. Check the results by multiplying the factors.

EXAMPLE 2   Factor $x^2 + 9x + 8$.

Answer

$x^2 + 9x + 8$

$(x\ \ )(x\ \ )$	1. Factor the first term.
$8 = 1 \cdot 8$ $8 = -1(-8)$ $8 = 2 \cdot 4$ $8 = -2(-4)$	2. Factor the last term.
$8 + 1 = 9$ $(x + 1)(x + 8)$	3. Choose the factors whose sum equals the coefficient of the middle term.

Check. $(x + 1)(x + 8) = x^2 + 9x + 8$

You can do all the steps shown here in your head to save yourself time!

Determining Signs When Factoring

1. If the sign of the last term is positive and the sign of the middle term is positive, the signs between terms in the binomial factors will be positive.
2. If the sign of the last term is positive and the sign of the middle term is negative, the signs between terms will be negative.
3. If the sign of the last term is negative, the sign of one factor will be positive and the other will be negative.

EXAMPLE 3   Factor $x^2 + x - 72$.

Answer

$x^2 + x - 72$	
$(x\ \ )(x\ \ )$	1. Factor the first term.
$-72 = -8 \cdot 9$ $-72 = 8 \cdot -9$	2. Factor the last term. Since the sum must be positive one, you can identify the factors in your head.
$-8 + 9 = 1$ $(x - 8)(x + 9)$	3. Notice that the factors determined the signs. Check mentally.

EXAMPLE 4   Factor $2x^2 + 22x + 48$.

Answer

$2x^2 + 22x + 48$	1. Since this polynomial contains the common monomial factor 2, factor it out first. Factor the trinomial in parentheses as usual.
$2(x^2 + 11x + 24)$	
$2(x\ \ )(x\ \ )$	2. Factor the first term.
$24 = 1 \cdot 24$ $24 = -1 \cdot -24$ $24 = 2 \cdot 12$ $24 = -2 \cdot -12$ $24 = 3 \cdot 8$ $24 = -3 \cdot -8$ $24 = 4 \cdot 6$ $24 = -4 \cdot -6$	3. Factor the last term.
$3 + 8 = 11$ $2(x + 3)(x + 8)$	4. Choose the pair whose sum is 11.
Check. $2(x + 3)(x + 8) = 2x^2 + 22x + 48$	

EXAMPLE 5   Factor $a^2 - 5a - 14$.

Answer $a^2 - 5a - 14$

$(a\ \ )(a\ \ )$

$-7 \cdot 2 = -14$

$-7 + 2 = -5$

$(a - 7)(a + 2)$

▶ A. Exercises

Factor.

1. $x^2 + 4x - 32$
2. $a^2 + 8a + 15$
3. $x^2 - 2x - 3$
4. $a^2 + 2a - 8$
5. $b^2 + b - 20$
6. $x^2 + 15x + 54$
7. $a^2 - 6a + 5$
8. $x^2 - x - 30$
9. $y^2 + 7y + 10$
10. $x^2 + 5x + 4$
11. $a^2 + 3a - 28$
12. $x^2 - 9x + 20$
13. $a^2 - 4a + 3$
14. $x^2 - 8x + 12$
15. $x^2 - 11x + 10$
16. $a^2 - 13a - 30$

▶ B. Exercises

Factor.

17. $4x^2 + 28x + 24$
18. $3x^2 + 24x + 36$
19. $x^2 + 20x + 100$
20. $6b^2 - 42b + 72$
21. $3x^2 - 24x - 27$
22. $x^2 - 16$
23. $ax^2 - 11ax - 12a$
24. $x^2 - 50x + 96$
25. $x^2 - 25$
26. $x^2 + 6x + 9$

▶ C. Exercises

Factor.

27. $-12x^3 + 87x^2 + 72x$
28. $4a^4b - 12a^3b^2 - 40a^2b^3$

■ Cumulative Review

Use the polynomial $6x^3y^3 - 27x^2y^4z + 8x^2y^3$.

29. How many terms are there and what kind of polynomial is it?
30. Give the coefficient of the last term.
31. Give the degree of the first term.
32. Give the degree of the polynomial.
33. Factor the polynomial.

ALBERT EINSTEIN

Albert Einstein was born of Jewish parents on March 14, 1879, in Ulm, a city in southwestern Germany, where Albert's father ran a small electrochemical factory. His mother was an accomplished musician, who encouraged her son to play the violin. He loved classical music and played the violin very well.

While a youngster, Albert did not like formal education. One day his Uncle Jakob introduced him to algebra and the Pythagorean theorem. "Algebra is a merry science," his uncle told him. "We go hunting for a little animal whose name we don't know, so we call it *x*. When we bag our game, we pounce on it and give it its right name." From then on Albert enjoyed pouncing on simple algebraic and geometric problems on his own.

Albert became interested in physics, and at age sixteen he sought admission to the Swiss Polytechnic Institute in Zurich. He had to take the entrance exams twice before he passed them, but he was finally admitted. He graduated from the institute in 1900 after studying math and physics.

Einstein is best known for his theory of relativity and for the formula $E = mc^2$, which he developed in 1905 at the

$$ax^2 + bx + c = 0$$

age of twenty-six. That same year he also developed the study of photoelectric effect, called quantum theory, for which he received the Nobel Prize in physics in 1921. From 1909 to 1933 he was a professor at several European universities and began lecturing abroad. In 1933 Einstein was lecturing in California when Hitler came to power in Germany. Because Einstein was a Jew, the Nazi government confiscated his property and deprived him of his citizenship. He took refuge in the United States and became a professor at the Institute for Advanced Study in Princeton, New Jersey. Einstein became an American citizen in 1940.

Einstein's scientific work laid the foundation for splitting the atom. He is one of the fathers of the atomic age. He arrived at his theories by means of intricate mathematical calculations and equations. But he always insisted that anyone who understood the intricacies of higher math could easily understand his theories. If you continue your study of mathematics, perhaps someday you will study the theories that Einstein developed.

Einstein is best known for his theory of relativity and for the formula $E = mc^2$.

Factoring Trinomials of the Form $ax^2 + bx + c$

To learn how to factor a trinomial of this form, observe the multiplication of two binomials to produce such a trinomial. Multiply the binomials $(3x + 2)(x - 5)$ by the FOIL method and you get $3x^2 - 13x - 10$. The product of the outside terms is called the outer product. The product of the inside terms is called the inner product. When factoring a trinomial of the form $ax^2 + bx + c$, you must factor it into two binomials such that the sum of the outer and inner products equals bx. Find the product of $(3x - 2)(x + 5)$ and compare it to the previous product in which the signs were reversed.

The polynomials in this section differ from those in the last section in that these have a coefficient other than 1 on the x^2 term. The coefficient must be factored with the variable. Study the following examples and notice how to factor a trinomial of this form.

EXAMPLE 1   Factor $3x^2 + 5x + 2$.

Answer

$3x^2 + 5x + 2$	1. Look for a common monomial factor. This polynomial has none.
$3x^2 = x \cdot 3x$	2. Factor $3x^2$. Place these factors in parentheses.
$(3x\ \ )(x\ \ )$ $2 = 1 \cdot 2$ $2 = -1 \cdot -2$	3. Factor the constant 2. Since the sign of the middle term is positive, you must use the positive factors. They can be combined with the other terms in two ways.
$(3x + 1)(x + 2)$ or $(3x + 2)(x + 1)$	

4. Choose the combination of binomials that makes the sum of the outer and inner products (O + I) equal to $5x$.

$(3x + 1)(x + 2)$
x
$+ 6x$
$O + I = 7x \neq 5x$

$(3x + 2)(x + 1)$
$2x$
$+ 3x$
$O + I = 5x$

The solution is $(3x + 2)(x + 1)$.

Check. $(3x + 2)(x + 1) = 3x^2 + 5x + 2$

Factoring $ax^2 + bx + c$ Trinomials

1. Factor any common monomials from the trinomial.
2. Check to see if the trinomial is a perfect square trinomial. If so, factor by the shortcut. If not, factor the first term of the trinomial and place the factors in parentheses.
3. Factor the last term of the polynomial. Choose the binomial factor combination that makes the sum of the outer and inner products equal to the middle term.
4. Check your factorization by multiplying the factors.

EXAMPLE 2   Factor $2x^2 - 9x + 4$.

Answer

$2x^2 - 9x + 4$	1. No common monomials can be factored out.
$2x^2 = x \cdot 2x$ $(x\ )(2x\ )$	2. Factor the first term. Use positive factors.
$4 = 1 \cdot 4$ $4 = -1 \cdot -4$ $4 = 2 \cdot 2$ $4 = -2 \cdot -2$	3. Factor the last term. Since the sign of the middle term is negative, you must use the negative factors and combine them with the first terms of the binomial factors.
$\begin{array}{ll} & \underline{O + I} \\ (x - 1)(2x - 4) & -6x \\ (x - 4)(2x - 1) & -9x \\ (x - 2)(2x - 2) & \end{array}$	4. From the three combinations, choose the one whose sum of the outer and inner products equals $-9x$. Since the second factorization produces the correct middle term, you do not need to check the third combination.

Therefore, $2x^2 - 9x + 4 = (x - 4)(2x - 1)$.

Check. $(x - 4)(2x - 1) = 2x^2 - 9x + 4$

Another reason to rule out the last set of factors above is that the second binomial has a common factor: $2x - 2 = 2(x - 1)$. If you always perform step 1, factoring out any common monomial, then neither binomial factor can have a common factor. This can often substantially reduce the number of possible combinations that you need to check.

As you become more proficient in factoring, you will not need to write down all the factors because you can figure the sums mentally. If you understand the procedures to follow, you can increase your speed with practice.

EXAMPLE 3   Factor $6x^2 - 14x - 40$.

Answer

$6x^2 - 14x - 40$	
$2(3x^2 - 7x - 20)$	1. Remove the monomial factor 2.
$3x^2 = 3x \cdot x$ $2(3x\ \ )(x\ \ )$	2. Factor the first term.
$-20 = -1 \cdot 20 \qquad -20 = -2 \cdot 10$ $-20 = 1 \cdot -20 \qquad -20 = 4 \cdot -5$ $-20 = 2 \cdot -10 \qquad -20 = -4 \cdot 5$	3. Factor the last term. Since the last term (-20) is negative, one factor must be positive and one negative.

	O + I	
$2(3x - 1)(x + 20)$	$59x$	no
$2(3x + 1)(x - 20)$	$-59x$	no
$2(3x - 20)(x + 1)$	$-17x$	no
$2(3x + 20)(x - 1)$	$17x$	no

1, 20 eliminated

4. Find the combination of outer and inner products that produces $-7x$. You may have to try each pair of factors before you find the correct combination. Notice that switching the + and − but keeping the same factors only changes the sign of the middle term. You can use this idea to rule out other possibilities.

$2(3x - 2)(x + 10)$	$28x$	no
$2(3x - 10)(x + 2)$	$-4x$	no

2, 10 eliminated

Reversing signs on these two combinations would give $-28x$ or $4x$, which can be ruled out without writing them down.

$2(3x - 5)(x + 4)$	$7x$	no

opposite of needed factor

$2(3x + 5)(x - 4)$	$-7x$	yes

Therefore, $6x^2 - 14x - 40 = 2(3x + 5)(x - 4)$.

Finally, after several tries, you have found the correct factorization. Sometimes you have to try several combinations before you find the correct one. You can save a lot of time by figuring mentally instead of writing it all down.

▶ A. Exercises

Factor.

1. $2x^2 + 13x - 7$
2. $3x^2 - 14x + 8$
3. $x^2 - 4x - 32$
4. $5x^2 - 14x - 3$
5. $4x^2 + 15x + 9$

6. $9x^2 - 30x + 25$
7. $3x^2 + 5x - 28$
8. $4x^2 - 16$
9. $16a^2 + 40a - 24$
10. $6x^2 + 3x - 30$

▶ B. Exercises

Factor.

11. $9x^2 + 3x - 2$

12. $12x^2 - 8x - 20$

13. $8a^2 - 104a - 112$

14. $2x^2 + 9x + 4$

15. $6a^2 - 5a - 4$

16. $2x^2 + x - 21$

17. $30x^2 - 100x - 250$

18. $5x^2 + 8x - 21$

19. $6x^2 + 5x - 4$

20. $6x^2 - 19x - 20$

▶ C. Exercises

Factor.

21. $144x^2 - 102x + 18$

22. $3a^4b + a^3b^2 - 10a^2b^3$

■ Cumulative Review

23. Simplify $2x(x - 4) + 20x^2 + 3(x^2 - 3) + 8x$.

24. Solve $5x - 7 = 3x + 11$.

25. Divide $\frac{3x^5 - 8x^3 + 2x^2 - 6x + 9}{x - 2}$.

Solve.

26. $x = 8 - y$

    $3x - 8 = 5y$

27. A bus leaves Regina for Raleigh traveling at 50 mph. Two hours later another bus leaves traveling at 55 mph. How long will it take the second bus to catch up with the first bus?

9.6 Factoring Trinomials of the Form $ax^2 + bxy + cy^2$

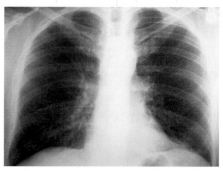

What is different about this form of the trinomial compared to the previous forms you have studied? Did you notice that variables accompany all the terms? To factor a trinomial of this form, follow the same steps you have used, remembering also to factor the variables in the last term.

Just as the x-ray exposes the structure inside this person's chest, so factoring reveals the underlying structure of a polynomial.

EXAMPLE 1   Factor $2x^2 - 3xy - 14y^2$.

Answer

$2x^2 - 3xy - 14y^2$	1. No monomials can be factored out.
$(2x \ )(x \ )$	2. Factor the first term as usual.
$\begin{aligned} -14y^2 &= -14y \cdot y \\ -14y^2 &= 14y \cdot -y \\ -14y^2 &= -7y \cdot 2y \\ -14y^2 &= 7y \cdot -2y \end{aligned}$	3. Factor the last term, including the variables. There are eight possible combinations when switching with $2x$ and x is included.
$\underline{O + I}$	4. Try different ones until you find the one that yields the correct middle term.
$(2x - y)(x + 14y) \quad 27xy \quad$ no	Switching signs will give only $-27xy$ and $12xy$ respectively. Try 2 and 7. $(2x - 2y)(x + 7y)$ will not work. There is no common factor in $2x^2 - 3xy + 14y^2$, so there can be none in either factor. But $2x - 2y$ contains a common factor of 2.
$(2x - 14y)(x + y) \quad -12xy \quad$ no 1, 14 eliminated	
$(2x + 7y)(x - 2y) \quad 3xy \quad$ no opposite of needed term	
$2x^2 - 3xy - 14y^2 = (2x - 7y)(x + 2y)$	Switching the signs will give a positive $3xy$; therefore, $(2x - 7y)(x + 2y)$ is the desired factorization.

Check. $(2x - 7y)(x + 2y) = 2x^2 - 3xy - 14y^2$

EXAMPLE 2 Factor $18a^2 - 57ab + 35b^2$.

Answer

$18a^2 - 57ab + 35b^2$	1. No monomial can be factored out.
$18a^2 = a \cdot 18a$ $18a^2 = 2a \cdot 9a$ $18a^2 = 3a \cdot 6a$	2. Factor the first term of the trinomial. The first terms of the binomial factors will be $(a\ )(18a\ )$, $(2a\ )(9a\ )$, or $(3a\ )(6a\ )$.
$35b^2 = b \cdot 35b$ $35b^2 = -b \cdot -35b$ $35b^2 = 5b \cdot 7b$ $35b^2 = -5b \cdot -7b$	3. Factor the last term. Since the sign before the last term is positive and the sign before the middle term is negative, only the negative factors $-b \cdot -35b$ or $-5b \cdot -7b$ are possible. By now you have some feel for which pairs are more likely to work.

	O + I	
$(2a - b)(9a - 35b)$	$-79ab$	no
$(2a - 5b)(9a - 7b)$	$-59ab$	no
$(3a - 5b)(6a - 7b)$	$-51ab$	no
$(3a - 7b)(6a - 5b)$	$-57ab$	yes

4. $(a - 35b)(18a - b)$ will produce a middle term with a very large absolute value. Since 57 is not relatively large compared to the product of 18 and 35, try 2 and 9 or 3 and 6 first. Try different combinations of factors until you find the one combination that produces $-57ab$.

Check. $(3a - 7b)(6a - 5b) = 18a^2 - 57ab + 35b^2$

▶ A. Exercises

Factor.

1. $x^2 + 4xy - 60y^2$
2. $a^2 + 4ab - 12b^2$
3. $y^2 - 6yz + 9z^2$
4. $a^2 - b^2$
5. $6x^2 + xy - 5y^2$
6. $2y^2 - 3yz + z^2$
7. $m^2 - mn - 20n^2$
8. $a^2 - 4ab - 32b^2$
9. $a^2 + 3ab - 28b^2$
10. $x^2 - xy - 56y^2$

Factor.

11. $3x^2 - 14xy - 5y^2$

12. $3a^2 + 12ab - 36b^2$

13. $18c^2 + 9cd - 6d^2$

14. $6x^2 - 17xy + 12y^2$

15. $21a^2 + 5af - 6f^2$

16. $8a^2 - 26ac - 7c^2$

17. $9x^2 + 6xy - 8y^2$

18. $3a^2 - 11ac + 6c^2$

▶ **C. Exercises**

Factor.

19. $16p^2q - 70pq^2 + 24q^3$

20. $72x^3 - 21x^2 - 18x$

Cumulative Review

21. Graph $y < -\frac{1}{3}x + 5$.

22. Lynn has $5.90 in quarters and dimes. If there are 4 less dimes than quarters, how many of each are there?

23. Write $5 > x$ using a less than sign.

24. One factor of $12x^2 + 5x - 28$ is $4x + 7$. Find the other factor by dividing.

25. One factor of $15x^2 - 4x - 4$ is $3x - 2$. Find the other factor by factoring.

9.7 Factoring Completely

Every polynomial can be factored. All of the factoring you have done has been done over the set of integers. If a polynomial cannot be factored over the set of integers, it can be factored over the set of real numbers or over the complex number system. Sometimes after you factor a polynomial, you can factor the resulting polynomial. In Algebra 1, we will consider a polynomial completely factored

*Cumberland Falls, Kentucky, is **68** feet high. Its flow of **3217** cubic feet per second (cfs) makes it the most powerful waterfall in the South. Determine its energy (horsepower), using **E** = **0.11345rh**, where **r** is the flow in cfs and **h** is the height in feet.*

when it cannot be factored further over the set of integers. From this point on, *factor* means "factor completely over the set of integers."

Factoring Completely over the Set of Integers

1. Factor out any common monomial factors.
2. If the remaining polynomial is a special product, factor by the shortcut learned for that special product. If it isn't a special product, factor by trial and error.
3. Continue factoring until each factor is no longer factorable over the set of integers.
4. Check by multiplying the factors.

EXAMPLE 1   Factor $5ax^5 - 5axy^4$.

Answer

$5ax^5 - 5axy^4$ $5ax(x^4 - y^4)$	1. $5ax$ is a common monomial. Factor it out of the polynomial.
$5ax(x^2 + y^2)(x^2 - y^2)$	2. Now the polynomial in parentheses is the difference of two squares. Factor it.
$5ax(x^2 + y^2)(x - y)(x + y)$	3. Check each new factor. Can any of them be factored over the set of integers? Yes, $x^2 - y^2$ can be factored because it is the difference of two squares. Factor it. None of these factors can be factored over the set of integers.

Check. $5ax(x^2 + y^2)(x - y)(x + y) = 5ax^5 - 5axy^4$

Sometimes a polynomial contains common binomial factors, such as $x + y$ in $3(x + y) - y(x + y)$. Considering $(x + y)$ as one variable and applying the distributive property, you can factor out the whole binomial from the polynomial.

$$3(x + y) - y(x + y) = (x + y)(3 - y)$$

Look at this process another way.

Let $z = x + y$.

Then $3(x + y) - y(x + y) = 3z - yz$.

Now can you factor $3z - yz$? Yes. It has a common monomial, z.

$3z - yz = z(3 - y)$.

Since we let $z = x + y$, we can now substitute $x + y$ back into the factorization in place of z. Therefore, $z(3 - y) = (x + y)(3 - y)$, the very same factorization that we obtained earlier.

EXAMPLE 2   Factor $(am - an) - (pm - pn)$.

Answer

$(am - an) - (pm - pn)$	
$a(m - n) - p(m - n)$	1. Factor the common monomials from each binomial.
$(m - n)(a - p)$	2. Now you can see that the polynomial has the common binomial factor $m - n$. Factor it from the polynomial using the distributive property.

EXAMPLE 3   Factor $x^4 - 9x^2 + 8$.

Answer

$x^4 - 9x^2 + 8$	1. There are no common monomials and no special cases.
$(x^2 - 1)(x^2 - 8)$	2. Factor by trial and error.
$(x - 1)(x + 1)(x^2 - 8)$	3. Factor the first binomial again because it is the difference of two squares. This is the complete factorization over the set of integers.

▶ A. Exercises

Factor completely.

1. $a^2 + 2a + 1$
2. $x^3 - 2x^2 + x$
3. $100 - a^2$
4. $12a^8 - 10a^6$
5. $a^2 + 16a$
6. $x^2 - 6x + 8$
7. $3a^5 - 4a^3$
8. $x^2 - 14x + 49$
9. $5a + 35$
10. $pqx + p$
11. $10x^2 + 50x + 70$
12. $ax^2 - 6ax + 9a$
13. $m^{10} + 2m^5 + 1$
14. $3x^2 - 21x - 180$
15. $25x^2 - 1$
16. $2m^2 - 2m - 112$

▶ B. Exercises

Factor completely.

17. $8a^2 - 48ab^2 + 72b^4$
18. $a^4x^4 - 81$
19. $(2ax^2 + bx^2) - (2ay^2 + by^2)$
20. $3x^3 - 33x^2 + 84x$
21. $a(b + c) - m(b + c)$
22. $a(m + n) + b(m + n) - c(m + n)$
23. $(at - aw) + (bt - bw)$
24. $xy + xz + wy + wz$

► **C. Exercises**

Factor completely.

25. $x^2 + 2xy + y^2 - 9$
26. $x^2 + 2xy + y^2 + 2x + 2y + 1$

■ Cumulative Review

Solve for q.

27. $Aq - 5 = 7n$
28. $q + 12p = 3t$
29. $\frac{q}{6} + \frac{3q}{4} = 2m$
30. $5q + xq = 7$ (*Hint:* Factor the left side first.)
31. $q^2 = R$

Algebra *and* Scripture

Remember that you can convert a multiplication to a division problem by dividing a factor into the product. Likewise, you can use division to help you factor. Factoring polynomials generalizes principles of factoring and dividing integers. Division, the basis of factoring, appears often in Scripture.

1. According to Judges 7:16, how many people were in each group? Write the division problem. Is it consistent with verse 19?

2. In Exodus 21:35, into how many equal portions is the money divided?

3. Write the division problem of I Kings 7:3-5 (the *ranks* in verse 5 tell you the number of pillars per row).

When an army conquered a city, they took all the valuables as reward. These riches are called the booty, the prey, or the spoils of the battle. A dozen Bible passages refer to victors dividing the spoil amongst themselves. Read Joshua 22:8-9 concerning the tribes of Reuben and Gad and the half tribe of Manasseh.

4. What did these tribes of Israel take as the spoils of war?

5. What did they do with the collected booty?

6. What is better than demanding our share of the spoils according to Proverbs 16:19?

THE Nth DEGREE

Find a verse in Isaiah that speaks of dividing the spoils.

In I Samuel 30, the story is told of how the Amalekites conquered David's home, Ziklag. David pursued them and got everything back.

7. What did he promise in verse 24 to the men who guarded their camp?

An understanding of division also helps us to understand the miracle of Jesus' feeding a multitude. Read Mark 6:34-44.

8. The two fishes were divided equally among how many men? How many baskets of scraps were left?

We know that if we divide two fishes among so many people, each one would get only a crumb. Yet Jesus fed them all with much left over! In the normal order, division would not allow you to do this. Therefore, we recognize this as a miracle.

Finally, we sometimes use the word *division* to express "cutting into portions" even if the portions are of unequal sizes. The mathematical meaning is still at the heart of this extended usage. Consider some examples of divisions into unequal parts.

9. Luke 15:12 pictures a father giving his two sons their inheritance. In the Jewish culture of the time, did the sons get equal inheritance?

10. Joshua 18:10 discusses the division of the land for the twelve tribes. Were the portions equal in area according to Numbers 33:54? Which tribe had the biggest portion?

11. Luke 12:52 refers to a separation into two unequal portions. How many were in each?

Scriptural Roots

And He divided the three hundred men into three companies, and he put a trumpet in every man's hand, with empty pitchers, and lamps within the pitchers. ❧

JUDGES 7:16

Chapter 9 Review

Factor completely.

1. $8x^2y^3 + 5xy^2 - 2x$

2. $3r^2 + 5r$

3. $x^4 + 3x^3y + 7x^2$

4. $a^2 - 9b^2$

5. $25x^2 - 144y^2$

6. $24x^2 - 96y^2$

7. $a^2 + 14a + 49$

8. $5b^2 - 50b + 125$

9. $4x^2 - 12xy + 9y^2$

10. $x^2 + 5x - 14$

11. $2x^2 - 30x + 108$

12. $2a^2 + 9a - 18$

13. $6a^2 - 20a + 14$

14. $15x^2 - x - 6$

15. $x^2 - 5x - 84$

16. $15x^2 + xy - 2y^2$

17. $12x^2 + 78xy + 90y^2$

18. $x^2y + xy - 56y$

19. $12x^2 + 22x - 70$

20. $(x + y)^2 - 9$

21. $2x^2 + 9x + 7$

22. $2x^2 + 15x + 7$

23. $9x^2 - 25$

24. $9x^2 - 25x$

25. $9x^2 + 34x + 25$

26. $9x^2 - 50x + 25$

27. $9x^2 + 21x - 8$

28. $9x^2 + 30x + 25$

29. $3x^2 - 17x + 20$

30. $10x^2 - x - 21$

31. $4p^2 - 30pq - 126q^2$

32. $x^2y - xy + x^2 - 1$

33. $x^4 + 3x^2 + 2$

34. $256x^8 - 1$

35. $2x^3 + 2x^2y + 4x^2 + 4xy$

36. $9x^4 - 288x^2 + 2304$

37. $36x^4 - 97x^2 + 36$

38. $x^4 + 6x^2 + 9$

39. Give the mathematical significance of Mark 6:41-43.

10 Radicals

The speed of waves can be calculated according to the formula $V = \sqrt{gh}$, in which V represents the speed, or velocity, of the ocean wave; g is gravitational acceleration of 32 ft./sec.^{2}, and h is the depth of the water in feet. What is the velocity of the tsunami in water that is 60 feet deep? 800 feet deep? 1800 feet deep? By the end of this chapter you will be able to answer these questions.

A tsunami is a large ocean wave. The waves can reach speeds as high as 600 mph out in deep water and produce tidal waves when they hit the shore. The deadliest tidal wave on record claimed over 200,000 lives in November of 1970 in Bangladesh.

Earthquakes on the ocean floor cause tsunamis. Sensors identify such earthquakes and calculate their magnitudes on the Richter scale. Computers use radicals to figure the speed of the wave. From the speed and direction, the computers plot its course and estimate the time when it will reach the shore. People in the area can be warned to go inland to avoid the deadly tidal waves.

After this chapter you should be able to

1. approximate the root of any number using the two nearest integers or using a calculator.
2. convert between radical form and exponential form.
3. simplify any radical.
4. multiply and divide radicals.
5. rationalize the denominator of a fraction when necessary.
6. add and subtract radicals.
7. solve problems using the Pythagorean theorem.
8. develop and use the distance formula.
9. solve a given radical equation.

10.1 Expressing Square Roots

When you studied square roots in Chapter 2, all the radicands were perfect squares. Since you memorized the squares of the first twenty integers, you can identify the positive (principal) root when you see one of those numbers squared. All of the roots of perfect squares are rational numbers.

Reception from a TV tower depends on the height of the tower. The approximate effective radius is $d = \sqrt{1.5h}$.

You will now study radicals that represent irrational numbers. Recall that irrational numbers cannot be expressed as fractions because they are nonrepeating infinite decimals. They can be approximated by rounding at any decimal place or represented exactly by the use of a radical sign (or a fractional exponent). The root sign and π are used to symbolize certain irrational numbers because it is impossible to write them in precise decimal form.

An approximation is an act or process of finding a value near the actual one. Christian education should help Christian young people come nearer to the image of God. Do you know Christ as your Savior? If you do, I Peter 2:21 commands you to become more like Christ. Are you approximating Christ more closely each day?

What does $\sqrt{7}$ equal? God is the only one who knows the exact decimal value of $\sqrt{7}$. In most of your algebraic work you will want to leave the answer in square root form without finding an approximation, but sometimes you will need to know a close approximation to the square root of a number.

To find the whole number approximation of any radicand greater than 0, think of the integers whose squares bound the radicand. For $\sqrt{7}$, $2^2 = 4$ is less than 7 and $3^2 = 9$ is greater than 7. Since $4 < 7 < 9$, it follows that $\sqrt{4} < \sqrt{7} < \sqrt{9}$, which can be simplified to $2 < \sqrt{7} < 3$. Therefore, $\sqrt{7}$ is between 2 and 3. If you are asked to give a more exact approximation of the radical, say for example $\sqrt{7}$ rounded to tenths, use a calculator with a square root button and round the solution to the nearest tenth.

EXAMPLE 1 Find $\sqrt{7}$ to the nearest tenth.

Answer A calculator will give 2.6457513.

Round to the nearest tenth: $\sqrt{7} \approx 2.6$

EXAMPLE 2 Estimate $\sqrt{129}$ to the nearest integer.

Answer $11^2 = 121$ and $12^2 = 144$

Since $121 < \quad 129 < \quad 144$

$\sqrt{121} < \sqrt{129} < \sqrt{144}$

and $\quad 11 < \sqrt{129} < \quad 12$

Exponential form is a method of expressing the exact value of a radical. In the radical $\sqrt[3]{16}$, the index is 3 and the radicand is 16. Since $16 = 4^2 = 2^4$, we could write $\sqrt[3]{16}$ as $\sqrt[3]{4^2}$ or $\sqrt[3]{2^4}$. In general, we could write every radical in the form $\sqrt[b]{x^a}$, where the index is b and the radicand is x^a. In some cases the exponent 1 is understood, as in $\sqrt[3]{7}$. Likewise, when an index is not written, it indicates a square root and an index of 2 is understood, as in $\sqrt{3}$.

Comparing the following computations will show a pattern for changing radicals to their exponential equivalents. Consider these two facts.

$$\sqrt{4}\,\sqrt{4} = 2 \cdot 2 \qquad \text{and} \qquad 4^{\frac{1}{2}} \cdot 4^{\frac{1}{2}} = 4^{\left(\frac{1}{2}+\frac{1}{2}\right)}$$
$$= 4 \qquad\qquad\qquad\qquad\qquad = 4^1$$
$$= 4$$

Since steps 1 and 2 both result in 4, make the substitution in the following proof.

$$\sqrt{4}\,\sqrt{4} = 4^{\frac{1}{2}} \cdot 4^{\frac{1}{2}}$$
$$\left(\sqrt{4}\right)^2 = \left(4^{\frac{1}{2}}\right)^2$$

Taking the square root of each side,

$$\sqrt{4} = 4^{\frac{1}{2}}$$

you can change any radical to exponential form by using the following definition.

Definition

$$x^{\frac{a}{b}} = \sqrt[b]{x^a}$$

From this definition, it follows that

$$\sqrt[b]{x^b} = x^{\frac{b}{b}} = x^1 = x \qquad \text{and} \qquad \left(x^{\frac{1}{b}}\right)^b = x^{\frac{b}{b}} = x^1 = x$$

EXAMPLE 2   Multiply $3\sqrt{2} \cdot 4\sqrt{5}$.

Answer

$3\sqrt{2} \cdot 4\sqrt{5}$

$(3 \cdot 4)(\sqrt{2}\sqrt{5})$ 1. Using the commutative property, arrange the multiplication problem in a different order.

                  2. Multiply the coefficients; then multiply the radicands.

$12\sqrt{10}$ This radical cannot be simplified.

EXAMPLE 3   Multiply $\sqrt{12}\ \sqrt{4}$.

Answer

$\sqrt{12}\ \sqrt{4}$ 1. Simplify each factor.

$\sqrt{2^2 \cdot 3}(2)$

$2\sqrt{3}(2)$

$4\sqrt{3}$ 2. Multiply.

Multiplying Radicals

1. Simplify each radical.
2. Multiply coefficients together. Then multiply radicals together, observing the properties of exponents.
3. Simplify the solution.

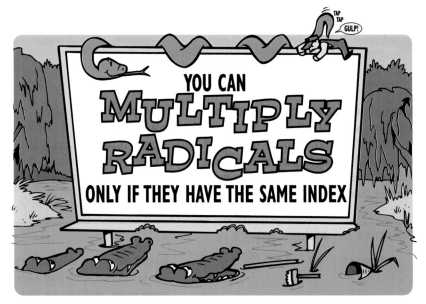

EXAMPLE 4   Multiply $\sqrt[3]{1125}\ \sqrt[3]{63}$.

Answer

$\sqrt[3]{1125}\ \sqrt[3]{63}$

$\sqrt[3]{3^2 \cdot 5^3}\ \sqrt[3]{3^2 \cdot 7}$ 1. Simplify each factor.

$5\sqrt[3]{3^2}\ \sqrt[3]{3^2 \cdot 7}$ 2. Multiply.

$5\sqrt[3]{3^4 \cdot 7}$

$5 \cdot 3\sqrt[3]{3 \cdot 7}$ 3. Simplify again.

$15\sqrt[3]{21}$

EXAMPLE 5   Multiply $\sqrt{6ab}\ \sqrt{2bc}$.

Answer

$\sqrt{6ab}\ \sqrt{2bc}$

$\sqrt{12ab^2c}$

$\sqrt{4b^2 \cdot 3ac}$

$2b\sqrt{3ac}$

EXAMPLE 6   Simplify $\sqrt[3]{4x^2y^5z} \cdot \sqrt[3]{8xy}$.

Answer

$\sqrt[3]{4x^2y^5z}\ \sqrt[3]{8xy}$

$\sqrt[3]{2^2x^2y^5z}\ \sqrt[3]{2^3xy}$ 1. Factor the numbers into primes.

$\sqrt[3]{2^5x^3y^6z}$ 2. Multiply, observing the properties of exponents.

$2^{\frac{5}{3}}xy^2z^{\frac{1}{3}}$ 3. Divide each exponent by the index to determine perfect squares.

$2 \cdot 2^{\frac{2}{3}}xy^2z^{\frac{1}{3}}$

$2xy^2\sqrt[3]{2^2 \cdot z^1}$ 4. Simplify by multiplying all perfect squares and changing fractional exponents to radical form.

$2xy^2\sqrt[3]{4z}$

▶ A. Exercises

Multiply the radicals. State the product in simplest form.

1. $\sqrt{5}\ \sqrt{3}$
2. $\sqrt{8}\ \sqrt{3}$
3. $\sqrt{7}\ \sqrt{5}$
4. $\sqrt{3}\ \sqrt{6}$

5. $\sqrt{18}\ \sqrt{3}$
6. $\sqrt{12}\ \sqrt{5}$
7. $\sqrt{9}\ \sqrt{7}$
8. $\sqrt{126}\ \sqrt{3}$

9. $\sqrt{5}\ \sqrt{118}$
10. $\sqrt{34}\ \sqrt{36}$
11. $\sqrt{28}\ \sqrt{35}$
12. $\sqrt{42}\ \sqrt{16}$

▶ B. Exercises

Multiply the radicals. State the product in simplest form.

13. $\sqrt[5]{32} \ \sqrt[5]{64}$

14. $\sqrt[3]{136} \ \sqrt[3]{42}$

15. $\sqrt[3]{40} \ \sqrt[3]{54}$

16. $\sqrt{539} \ \sqrt{242}$

17. $\sqrt[3]{81} \ \sqrt[3]{64}$

18. $\sqrt{3x^2y^3} \ \sqrt{2xy}$

19. $\sqrt{2a^{15}b^3} \ \sqrt{8ab}$

20. $\sqrt{x^2y} \ \sqrt{xy^2} \ \sqrt{xy}$

21. $\sqrt[3]{4x^5y^7} \ \sqrt[3]{2x^6y}$

22. $\sqrt[3]{25a^4bc^6} \ \sqrt[3]{8abc^3}$

▶ C. Exercises

Multiply the radicals. State the product in simplest form.

23. $\sqrt[3]{55233} \ \sqrt[3]{2907}$

24. $\sqrt[4]{80x^3y^2} \ \sqrt{54x^3y^2}$

■ Cumulative Review

25. Graph $x + y > 3$.

26. Solve $5x - 11 = x + 7$.

27. Approximate to the nearest tenth using a calculator: $\sqrt{17} - 6\sqrt{0.5}$.

28. Simplify $x(3x - 1) + 2(3x - 1)$.

29. Factor $x(3x - 1) + 2(3x - 1)$.

10.4 Dividing Radicals and Rationalizing Denominators

You have learned the product property of radicals, $\sqrt[n]{x} \cdot \sqrt[n]{y} = \sqrt[n]{xy}$, which helps you simplify radicals when you multiply them. A similar rule applies to division, called the *division property*.

$$\sqrt[n]{\frac{x}{y}} = \frac{\sqrt[n]{x}}{\sqrt[n]{y}}$$

Look at this numerical example of the division property.

$$\sqrt{\frac{16}{25}} = \frac{4}{5} \qquad \frac{\sqrt{16}}{\sqrt{25}} = \frac{4}{5}$$

A farmer determines the sprinkler radius for circular irrigation as $r = \sqrt{\dfrac{A}{\pi}}$. *Rationalize the denominator.*

By the substitution principle, $\sqrt{\frac{16}{25}} = \frac{\sqrt{16}}{\sqrt{25}}$.

Do you remember that a division problem can be written in fractional form? So $3 \div 4$ is the same as $\frac{3}{4}$. Therefore, you can express the division of radicals as fractions. Thus $\sqrt{5} \div \sqrt{7}$ is the same as $\frac{\sqrt{5}}{\sqrt{7}}$.

By the division property, $\frac{\sqrt{5}}{\sqrt{7}}$ and $\frac{\sqrt{35}}{7}$ represent the same number. You can see why by following the steps.

$$\frac{\sqrt{5}}{\sqrt{7}} = \frac{\sqrt{5}}{\sqrt{7}} \cdot 1 \qquad \text{identity property of multiplication}$$

$$= \frac{\sqrt{5}}{\sqrt{7}} \cdot \frac{\sqrt{7}}{\sqrt{7}} \qquad \frac{a}{a} = 1 \text{ (using } a = \sqrt{7}\text{)}$$

$$= \frac{\sqrt{35}}{\sqrt{49}} \qquad \text{multiplication property of radicals}$$

$$= \frac{\sqrt{35}}{7} \qquad \text{since } \sqrt{49} = 7$$

According to the division property of radicals $\frac{\sqrt{5}}{\sqrt{7}} = \sqrt{\frac{5}{7}}$ also. If $\frac{\sqrt{5}}{\sqrt{7}}$, $\sqrt{\frac{5}{7}}$, and $\frac{\sqrt{35}}{7}$ all represent the same number, which one is most simplified?

$$\frac{\sqrt{5}}{\sqrt{7}} \approx \frac{2.24}{2.65} \qquad \text{This requires dividing decimals by decimals.}$$

$$\sqrt{\frac{5}{7}} \approx \sqrt{0.71} \qquad \text{This requires finding the square root of a decimal.}$$

$$\frac{\sqrt{35}}{7} \approx \frac{5.92}{7} \qquad \text{This requires dividing a decimal by a natural number.}$$

You can verify that all of the computations result in the same answer, approximately 0.85, and you should also see that it is easier to divide by a natural number than to do the decimal operations. From here on, the third form will be required. "Simplify" means that no radicals should be in the denominator of your answer. The process shown above for eliminating the irrational numbers from the denominator is called *rationalizing the denominator.*

Definition

To **rationalize the denominator** means to eliminate radicals from the denominator by multiplying by 1 in an appropriate form.

The name *rationalizing* comes from making the denominator a *rational* number (instead of irrational). Remember that the fraction is simplified when the denominator is rational because it is easier to divide that way. Study the examples to see how to choose the appropriate form of 1.

EXAMPLE 1 $\sqrt{3} \div \sqrt{6}$

Answer

$\dfrac{\sqrt{3}}{\sqrt{6}}$

$\sqrt{\dfrac{3}{6}}$	1. Use the division property.
$\sqrt{\dfrac{1}{2}}$	2. Reduce the fraction.
$\dfrac{\sqrt{1}}{\sqrt{2}}$ $\dfrac{1}{\sqrt{2}}$	3. Use the division property again.
$\dfrac{1}{\sqrt{2}} \cdot \dfrac{\sqrt{2}}{\sqrt{2}}$ $\dfrac{\sqrt{2}}{\sqrt{2^2}}$	4. Rationalize the denominator by multiplying by 1 in the form $\dfrac{\sqrt{2}}{\sqrt{2}}$ to produce a perfect square in the denominator.
$\dfrac{\sqrt{2}}{2}$	5. Simplify the product.

EXAMPLE 2 Simplify $\dfrac{\sqrt{3}}{\sqrt{12}}$.

Answer

$\dfrac{\sqrt{3}}{\sqrt{12}}$

$\sqrt{\dfrac{3}{12}}$	1. Use the division property.
$\sqrt{\dfrac{1}{4}} = \dfrac{\sqrt{1}}{\sqrt{4}} = \dfrac{1}{2}$	2. Simplify.

EXAMPLE 3 Simplify $\dfrac{\sqrt{2}}{\sqrt{75}}$.

Answer

$\sqrt{2}$ cannot be simplified $\sqrt{75} = \sqrt{3 \cdot 5^2}$ $\qquad = 5\sqrt{3}$ $\dfrac{\sqrt{2}}{\sqrt{75}}$	1. Simplify the numerator and denominator.
$\dfrac{\sqrt{2}}{5\sqrt{3}}$	2. Rationalize the denominator.
$\dfrac{\sqrt{2}}{5\sqrt{3}} \cdot \dfrac{\sqrt{3}}{\sqrt{3}}$	3. Multiply.
$\dfrac{\sqrt{2 \cdot 3}}{5\sqrt{3^2}} = \dfrac{\sqrt{6}}{5 \cdot 3} = \dfrac{\sqrt{6}}{15}$	4. Simplify.

Rationalizing the Denominator (Square Root)

1. Place the radicals in fractional form $\left(\frac{\sqrt{a}}{\sqrt{b}}\right)$ by using the division property.
2. Simplify the numerator and the denominator as much as possible.
3. If a radical is left in the denominator, multiply the numerator and the denominator by a radical that will make the radicand in the denominator a perfect power.
4. Simplify both numerator and denominator to obtain the final answer.

This method of rationalizing the denominator works not only with square roots but also with other roots.

EXAMPLE 4 Simplify $\dfrac{\sqrt[3]{8}}{\sqrt[3]{16}}$.

Answer

$$\frac{\sqrt[3]{8}}{\sqrt[3]{16}}$$

$\sqrt[3]{\dfrac{8}{16}}$	1. Use the division property.
$\sqrt[3]{\dfrac{1}{2}}$	2. Simplify.
$\dfrac{\sqrt[3]{1}}{\sqrt[3]{2}}$	3. Use the division property.
$\dfrac{1}{\sqrt[3]{2}}$	4. Simplify.
$\dfrac{1}{\sqrt[3]{2}} \cdot \dfrac{\sqrt[3]{2^2}}{\sqrt[3]{2^2}}$ $\dfrac{\sqrt[3]{2^2}}{\sqrt[3]{2^3}}$	5. Rationalize. To make the radicand in the denominator a perfect cube, multiply by the power that will produce a perfect cube.
$\dfrac{\sqrt[3]{4}}{2}$	6. Simplify.

EXAMPLE 5 Simplify $\sqrt{18a^2bc^3} \div \sqrt{9\,ab^3c^2}$.

Answer

$$\sqrt{18a^2bc^3} \div \sqrt{9\,ab^3c^2}$$

$\sqrt{\dfrac{18a^2bc^3}{9ab^3c^2}}$	1. Write the division as a fraction.
$\sqrt{\dfrac{\overset{2}{\cancel{18}}\,\overset{a}{\cancel{a^2}}\,\overset{1}{\cancel{b}}\,\overset{c}{\cancel{c^3}}}{\underset{1}{\cancel{9}}\,\underset{1}{\cancel{a}}\,\underset{b^2}{\cancel{b^3}}\,\underset{1}{\cancel{c^2}}}}$	
$\sqrt{\dfrac{2ac}{b^2}} = \dfrac{\sqrt{2ac}}{\sqrt{b^2}} = \dfrac{\sqrt{2ac}}{b}$	2. Simplify.

EXAMPLE 6 Simplify $\dfrac{\sqrt{3x^3}}{4\sqrt{x^5y}}$.

Answer

$$\dfrac{\sqrt{3x^3}}{4\sqrt{x^5y}}$$

$$\dfrac{x\sqrt{3x}}{4x^2\sqrt{xy}}$$

1. Simplify the numerator and the denominator.

$$\dfrac{\cancel{x}\sqrt{3\cancel{x}}}{4\cancel{x}^{2}\sqrt{\cancel{x}y}}$$
$$x$$

$$\dfrac{\sqrt{3}}{4x\sqrt{y}}$$

$$\dfrac{\sqrt{3}}{4x\sqrt{y}} \cdot \dfrac{\sqrt{y}}{\sqrt{y}}$$

2. Rationalize the denominator by multiplying the numerator and the denominator by $\sqrt{y}$.

$$\dfrac{\sqrt{3y}}{4xy}$$

3. Simplify.

▶ A. Exercises

Simplify.

1. $\dfrac{2}{\sqrt{13}}$

2. $\dfrac{2\sqrt{3}}{\sqrt{9}}$

3. $\dfrac{3}{\sqrt{5}}$

4. $\dfrac{3\sqrt{5}}{\sqrt{15}}$

5. $\dfrac{\sqrt{4}}{\sqrt{25}}$

6. $\dfrac{1}{\sqrt{6}}$

7. $\dfrac{\sqrt{15}}{\sqrt{5}}$

8. $\sqrt{3} \div \sqrt{2}$

9. $\sqrt{5} \div \sqrt{4}$

10. $\dfrac{\sqrt{72}}{\sqrt{18}}$

11. $\dfrac{\sqrt{14}}{\sqrt{21}}$

12. $\dfrac{\sqrt{8}}{\sqrt{4}}$

13. $\dfrac{\sqrt{114}}{\sqrt{32}}$

14. $\dfrac{\sqrt{10}}{3\sqrt{5}}$

▶ B. Exercises

Simplify.

15. $\dfrac{\sqrt[3]{9}}{\sqrt[3]{36}}$

16. $\dfrac{\sqrt[3]{16}}{\sqrt[3]{4}}$

17. $\sqrt[3]{\dfrac{1}{8}}$

18. $\dfrac{\sqrt[3]{5}}{\sqrt[3]{25}}$

Perform the indicated operation and give each answer in simplest form.

19. $\sqrt{82x^4y^3} \div \sqrt{14x^3y^5}$

20. $\sqrt{5xy} \div \sqrt{10x^2y^3}$

21. $\sqrt{14x^3t^2z^5} \div \sqrt{7xtz}$

22. $\sqrt{15x^4y^2} \div \sqrt{3xy^3z}$

23. $\sqrt{r^3s^2t} \div \sqrt{rst}$

24. $\sqrt{6mn} \div \sqrt{3mn^2}$

▶ C. Exercises

Simplify.

25. $\dfrac{\sqrt[4]{4096}}{\sqrt[3]{512}}$

26. $\dfrac{\sqrt[4]{567a^4b^3}}{\sqrt{180a^3b^7}}$

■ Cumulative Review

27. Factor $3x^3y^2 - 15xy^3 + 5x^2y$.

28. Graph $y = 3x - 1$.

29. Solve $x - 2 < 5 \lor 2x > 7$.

30. Simplify $(3x^2 + x - 5)(x - 7)$.

31. What property justifies the first step of multiplying these radicals:
$3\sqrt{2} \cdot 5\sqrt{2} = 3 \cdot 5\sqrt{2}\ \sqrt{2} = 15(2) = 30.$

Solve each equation for the variable. Write the solution in the appropriate squares in the grid.

Across

1. $5x + 35 = 3160$
4. $3y - 105 = 342$
7. $6x^2 - 672 = x^2 + 32(979)$
8. $3x - (8 - x) = 2x(5) - 242$
10. $9x - 16 = 227$
12. $\frac{x}{33} + \frac{x}{9} = 42$
13. $x - 100 = -30$
14. $\frac{x}{28} = 157$
16. $\frac{x}{6} + 27x = 263{,}245$
18. $\frac{x}{2} + 10(x - 3) = 568.5$
19. $x^2 = 144$
20. $13x - 15{,}079 = 52{,}755$
22. $2y - 583 = 4293$
24. $\sqrt{4} - 222 = -5x$
25. $\frac{x}{5} + \frac{x}{25} = 54$
26. $z = \sqrt{625} + 2\sqrt{100}$
27. $2^7 = k + 29$
28. $x^2 - 168 = 3313$
30. $16\left(2\sqrt[3]{27}\right) = x - 28$
31. $x = 8(100) + 3$

Down

2. $2x = 7 \cdot 8$
3. $x + 599 = 75^2$
4. $10\sqrt{4900} = x - \left(26^2\right) - 3$
5. $x - 1 = \sqrt{64} \cdot 6$
6. $25^2 - x = 1$
9. $x^2 = 160{,}000$
11. $x \cdot 56^0 = 73{,}524$
13. $40^3 + 25^3 = x + 19^2 + 30$
15. $3x = 2913$
17. $\frac{1}{4}x = \frac{921}{6}$
20. $24^2 = x + 3^3$
21. $t - 669 = 85^2 + 20^2$
22. $50^2 = g - 58$
23. $\frac{6}{z} = \frac{1}{71} \cdot \frac{1}{2}$
27. $10^2 - 2^3 = e$
29. $2 \cdot 3^2 \cdot 5 = z$

Standard Deviations

In Chapter 9 you learned how to find standard deviations. The formula is an application of square roots. Substituting the formula for variance (s^2) into the formula for standard deviation, you obtain the formula for standard deviation.

$$s = \sqrt{s^2} = \sqrt{\frac{\sum(x - \bar{x})^2}{n - 1}}$$

Remember that $\bar{x}$ is the mean, x represents a score, n is the number of scores, and $\sum$ tells you to find the sum. According to the order of operations, you should

1. find each deviation (subtract the mean from the score).
2. square each deviation.
3. find the sum of all these squares.
4. divide by one less than the number of scores.
5. take the square root.

Why is a standard deviation useful? Since it measures the variability of scores around the mean, it is useful for interpreting test scores. You can use it as a unit of comparison. Look again at the ten quiz scores: 7, 6, 9, 5, 8, 8, 4, 10, 8, 7.

Remember that $\bar{x} = 7.2$ and $s = 1.81$.

If Mary scored **9** points on the quiz, her score falls **9** − **7.2**, or **1.8** units above the mean. In other words, she scored $\frac{1.8}{1.81}$, or about **1** standard deviation above the mean. This number, **1**, is called Mary's *z-score*.

$$z = \frac{x - \bar{x}}{s}$$

A *z*-score describes the number of standard deviations above or below the mean for a particular score. You can see that most of the scores are within 1 standard deviation of the mean.

EXAMPLE 1   Ryan forgot to study for the quiz, and he knows he will have to study hard to make up for it. Convert his score of 4 to a *z*-score.

Answer   Ryan's score converts to a *z*-score of $z = \frac{x - \bar{x}}{s} = \frac{4 - 7.2}{1.81} = -1.77$. Thus, his score is more than a standard deviation below the mean.

> **EXAMPLE 2** Scott takes a standardized test for college placement with
> a mean of **500** and a standard deviation of **100**. If his score
> was **572**, compute his *z*-score to interpret his score.
>
> **Answer** Since $\frac{572-500}{100} = 0.72$, Scott scored 0.7 standard
> deviations above the mean. He did well.

▶ Exercises

Test scores for an English class of 12 students are shown.

   87 78 63 82 94 74 75 80 73 68 77 78

1. Find the mean and standard deviation.
2. Which scores are within 1 standard deviation of the mean?
3. Convert Baxter's score of **82** to a *z*-score. How many standard deviations is his score from the mean?
4. Find the *z*-scores for any scores that are over **2** standard deviations from the mean.
5. If Tom has a score of **640** on the standardized test in example 2, interpret his results.

Fossils of Priscacara liops *found near Kemmerer, Wyoming, average 5 inches long with a standard deviation of about $\frac{1}{2}$ inch. What is the typical range of lengths?*

ALGEBRA AND QUALITY CONTROL

What does quality control mean? Of course a manufacturer wishes to minimize costs, but he must do so without sacrificing quality. The company's reputation may be damaged if parts do not meet standardized sizes, fail to function adequately, or are defective. Such poor quality can bankrupt a company when disappointed consumers turn to a competitor.

Quality control standards direct manufacturing and services worldwide. The International Standards Organization pressures industrialized nations to meet its ISO 9000-9004 standards in order to do business internationally. Even companies that do not export may feel pressure from foreign competition. Foreign auto manufacturers with high quality standards forced the American automotive industry to improve the quality of its products just to remain competitive.

Quality control encompasses all aspects of a company—including plant operations, equipment, and products. Those who analyze the plant operations to identify ways to streamline production are called operations research analysts. They look for ways to reduce personnel, time, stages, and handling for a smoother operation. Some of their analysis methods involve algebra.

A scientist examines a computer chip for microscopic defects. Studying defects helps to produce more durable chips.

Maintaining equipment and machines for efficiency and safety is part of making quality products. The machines usually consist of microprocessors; electronic sensors, switches, and control circuits; and, of course, computers. Such maintenance, then, requires knowledge of electronic hardware, which in turn involves algebra.

Of course, the focus of all quality control is the final product. By selecting samples of the items produced, quality control engineers determine whether the product meets the federal or industrial standards. By testing the samples, they can draw statistical conclusions about all items produced. Of course, the statistical formulas are nothing more than algebra.

An engineer tests engines on a production line and records data via computers to generate reports on production quality.

EXAMPLE The thickness of the magnetic coating on audio tapes needs to be **38 ± 4.5** units as measured by an optical instrument. Find the mean and standard deviation of the sample **S** of magnetic coating thicknesses.

$S = \{35.8, 33.2, 39.9, 41.5, 44.1, 39.9, 37.4, 33.6, 36.2, 40.7\}$

$$\bar{x} = \frac{35.8+33.2+39.9+41.5+44.1+39.9+37.4+33.6+36.2+40.7}{10}$$

$\bar{x} = 38.23$ units

$$s^2 = \frac{(35.8-38.23)^2 + (33.2-38.23)^2 + \ldots + (40.7-38.23)^2}{9}$$

$$= 12.70$$

$$s = 3.56$$

An engineer takes notes as he inspects an industrial plant and will later calculate whether the plant meets federal and industry standards.

Recall that the range is roughly four standard deviations, two on each side of the mean. Thus, we may roughly approximate the thicknesses of all the magnetic coatings produced as between the two algebraic expressions $\bar{x} - 2s$ and $\bar{x} + 2s$. In other words, the thickness should be between $38.23 - 2(3.56) = 38.23 - 7.12 = 31.11$ and $38.23 + 2(3.56) = 38.23 + 7.12 = 45.35$. Since the coatings must be within 4.5 units of 38, the quality control engineer has determined that the coatings thicknesses produced (within 7.12) is not according to specifications.

10.5 Adding and Subtracting Radicals

When you add and subtract terms that contain radicals, you must be sure that they are like radicals. Adding and subtracting them is much like adding and subtracting terms containing variables. Just as $2x + 3x = 5x$ because of the distributive property, so $2\sqrt{5} + 3\sqrt{5} = 5\sqrt{5}$. When you add and subtract like radicals, treat them as though they were variables and combine the rational factors.

Definition

Like radicals are radicals that have the same radicand and the same index.

Adding and Subtracting Radicals

1. Simplify each radical.
2. Combine like radicals by adding or subtracting the rational factors.

EXAMPLE 1 Simplify $4\sqrt{3} + 2\sqrt{3}$.

Answer

$4\sqrt{3} + 2\sqrt{3}$	1. Both terms are already simplified.
$\sqrt{3}(4 + 2)$	2. Combine these terms, considering $\sqrt{3}$
$6\sqrt{3}$	as if it were a variable such as x.

EXAMPLE 2 Simplify $\sqrt{5} + 9\sqrt{5} + \sqrt{2}$.

Answer

$\sqrt{5} + 9\sqrt{5} + \sqrt{2}$	1. All terms are in simplest form.
$10\sqrt{5} + \sqrt{2}$	2. Combine like radicals. Only $\sqrt{5}$ terms are similar.

Did you remember that $\sqrt{5}$ means the same as $1\sqrt{5}$? Did you try to combine $\sqrt{5}$ and $\sqrt{2}$? Are they like terms? Observe the following procedure.

Notice that $\sqrt{9} + \sqrt{16} = 3 + 4 = 7$, but $\sqrt{25} = 5$.

Does $\sqrt{9} + \sqrt{16} = \sqrt{25}$?

No, $7 \neq 5$. This proves that $\sqrt{a + b} \neq \sqrt{a} + \sqrt{b}$.

EXAMPLE 3   Simplify $\sqrt{12} - \sqrt{3}$.

Answer

$\sqrt{12} - \sqrt{3} = \sqrt{2^2 \cdot 3} - \sqrt{3}$	1. Simplify each term. $\sqrt{3}$ is already in simplest form.
$2\sqrt{3} - \sqrt{3}$ $\sqrt{3}$	2. Combine like terms.

When the unsaved man looks at a born-again believer, he might consider the Christian to be radical. First Peter 2:9 says, "But ye are a chosen generation, a royal priesthood, an holy nation, a peculiar people; that ye should shew forth the praises of him who hath called you out of darkness into his marvellous light." A Christian should strive to be holy and separate from the world so that nonbelievers can see Christ. Would an unsaved man see you as radically different and be drawn to salvation in Jesus Christ?

EXAMPLE 4   Simplify $2\sqrt{50} - 5\sqrt{8}$.

Answer

$2\sqrt{50} - 5\sqrt{8}$ $2\sqrt{5^2 \cdot 2} - 5\sqrt{2^3}$ $2 \cdot 5\sqrt{2} - 5 \cdot 2\sqrt{2}$	1. Simplify each term.
$10\sqrt{2} - 10\sqrt{2}$ 0	2. Combine like terms.

EXAMPLE 5   Simplify $-8\sqrt{5} + 9\sqrt{20} - 6\sqrt{5}$.

Answer

$-8\sqrt{5} + 9\sqrt{20} - 6\sqrt{5}$ $-8\sqrt{5} + 9\sqrt{2^2 \cdot 5} - 6\sqrt{5}$ $-8\sqrt{5} + 18\sqrt{5} - 6\sqrt{5}$	1. Simplify each term.
$4\sqrt{5}$	2. Combine like terms.

▶ A. Exercises

Simplify.

1. $\sqrt{3} + 5\sqrt{3}$
2. $2\sqrt{6} + 3\sqrt{6}$
3. $\sqrt{3} + 4\sqrt{2} + \sqrt{3}$
4. $2\sqrt{5} - 6\sqrt{5} + 3\sqrt{5}$
5. $\sqrt{8} + 3\sqrt{2} - 4\sqrt{2}$
6. $8\sqrt{7} - 3\sqrt{7}$

7. $\sqrt{20} + 4\sqrt{5}$
8. $5\sqrt{12} - 6\sqrt{3}$
9. $\sqrt{12} - \sqrt{48}$
10. $-3\sqrt{3} + \sqrt{18} + \sqrt{27}$
11. $\sqrt{x^2 y} - x\sqrt{y}$
12. $\sqrt{75} - \sqrt{18}$

► B. Exercises

Simplify.

13. $\sqrt{5} + \sqrt{20} - \sqrt{72}$

14. $\sqrt{x} + 3\sqrt{xy} + 5\sqrt{x}$

15. $4\sqrt{x} + 3\sqrt{y} - 2\sqrt{x}$

16. $a\sqrt{3} - 3a\sqrt{3} + \sqrt{2}$

17. $3\sqrt{ab} + 4\sqrt{a} - 5\sqrt{b} + 5\sqrt{b}$

18. $\sqrt{32a^3} + \sqrt{2a} - 5\sqrt{6}$

► C. Exercises

Simplify.

19. $\sqrt{a^3b} + \sqrt[3]{a^4b} + \sqrt[4]{a^5b} + a\sqrt[6]{a^3b^3}$

20. $\sqrt{x^3 - 8x^2 + 16x} + \sqrt{64x^3} + \sqrt{x^2 + 4x + 4}$

■ Cumulative Review

21. Graph (7, 4).

22. Factor $x^2 - 32x + 256$.

23. Use long division:
$6x^2 + 11x - 31 \div 3x - 5$.

24. Solve $3x - \sqrt{18} = x + \sqrt{50}$.

25. Simplify $3 + 5(2 + 6)$.

10.6 The Pythagorean Theorem

Ancient Egyptian farmers divided their farmland into plots with square corners. Each year when the Nile River flooded, new boundary lines had to be marked and square corners had to be found again. (A square corner is a right angle, which has a measure of **90°**.) The Egyptians found that they could form a right angle by making a triangle whose sides measured **3, 4**, and **5** units. The angle opposite the side **5** units long (the hypotenuse) was always a right angle.

The Nile River

A **right angle** is an angle whose measure is $90°$.

A **right triangle** is a triangle that has a right angle.

The **hypotenuse** is the side of a right triangle opposite the right angle.

A group of Greek philosophers and mathematicians led by Pythagoras began to study the Egyptian's use of triangles. Pythagoras and his followers believed that every right triangle possesses a property that the sum of the squares of the lengths of the legs (two shorter sides) is equal to the square of the length of the hypotenuse. Given any right triangle *ABC* with *c* the hypotenuse, $a^2 + b^2 = c^2$. To check this property, substitute the values into the equation.

$$3^2 + 4^2 = 5^2$$
$$9 + 16 = 25$$
$$25 = 25$$

A mathematical observation can be called a theorem only after it has been proved, or shown to be true for all cases.

Definition

A **theorem** is a statement that has been proved to be always true.

Because Pythagoras may have been the first to prove this property of right triangles, it is called the Pythagorean theorem in his honor.

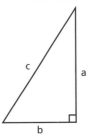

Theorem

Pythagorean theorem. The sum of the squares of the lengths of the legs (*a* and *b*) of a right triangle is equal to the square of the length of the hypotenuse (*c*).

$$a^2 + b^2 = c^2$$

EXAMPLE 1 Find the length of side b in the right triangle ABC.

A

15

b

C 12 B

Answer

Let b = unknown leg length $c = 15$, the hypotenuse $a = 12$	1. After identifying the variable, identify the lengths of the other two sides, making sure that the hypotenuse is c.
$a^2 + b^2 = c^2$ $12^2 + b^2 = 15^2$	2. Substitute the lengths of the sides in the Pythagorean theorem.
$144 + b^2 = 225$ $b^2 = 81$ $\sqrt{b^2} = \sqrt{81}$ $b = \pm 9$	3. Solve for b by isolating b^2 on one side of the equal sign. Then take the square root of both sides.
Therefore, $b = 9$ units.	4. Since you are looking for a length, use only the positive solution.

Solving an Equation of the Form $x^2 = c$

To solve an equation of the form $x^2 = c$, take the square root of both sides of the equation: $x = \pm\sqrt{c}$.

EXAMPLE 2   Find the hypotenuse of right triangle *ABC*.

B, c, 1, A, 2, C

Answer

Let c = length of hypotenuse $a = 1, b = 2$	1. Assign variable and identify known lengths.
$a^2 + b^2 = c^2$ $1^2 + 2^2 = c^2$ $1 + 4 = c^2$	2. Substitute values into the Pythagorean theorem.
$c = \pm\sqrt{5}$	3. To solve for c, take the square root of both sides.
$c = \sqrt{5}$	4. Distance is always positive.

▶ A. Exercises

Find the length of the unknown side of the right triangle.

	a	b	c
1.	4	5	?
2.	3	3	?
3.	2	?	8
4.	1	9	?
5.	3	?	14
6.	2	5	?
7.	?	6	12
8.	?	8	10
9.	7	?	9
10.	?	2	5

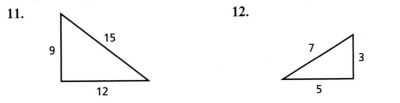

If the sum of the squares of the legs of a triangle equals the square of the hypotenuse, the triangle is a right triangle. Determine whether each triangle is a right triangle by using the Pythagorean theorem.

11.

9, 15, 12

12.

7, 3, 5

13.

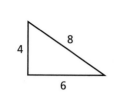

14.

▶ B. Exercises

Find the third side of each right triangle.

15. $a = 3, b = \sqrt{7}$ 17. $b = \sqrt{51}, c = 10$

16. $a = \sqrt{11}, b = \sqrt{13}$

18. A surveyor is measuring between property pins across a pond. He needs to know the distance from A to B. He knows that from A to C is 0.3 miles and from C to B is 0.6 miles. He also knows that $\overline{AC}$ and $\overline{CB}$ form a right angle. What is the distance from A to B?

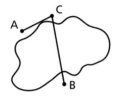

19. A 25-foot-long ladder is placed against the side of a house with its bottom end 6 feet from the house. How high does the ladder reach?

20. The M. T. Container Manufacturing Company is planning to make a new line of boxes 3 inches high and 10 inches long. If the M. T. box measure 14 inches diagonally across the bottom, what is the width of the box?

▶ C. Exercises

21. The dimensions of a rectangular box are length = 15 in., width = 12 in., and height = 9 in. Use the Pythagorean theorem to find (a) the length of a diagonal of the bottom of the box and (b) the length of a diagonal.

22. The dimensions of a rectangular box are *l*, *w*, and *h* for length, width, and height. Use the Pythagorean theorem to derive a formula to find (a) the length of a diagonal of the bottom of the box and (b) the length of a diagonal of the box in terms of *l*, *w*, and *h*.

■ Cumulative Review

Translate using variables.

23. The square root of three less than twice a number
24. The square root of three, less than twice a number
25. Three less than twice the square root of a number
26. Three less than the square root of twice a number
27. Twice the square root of three less than a number

10.7 The Distance Formula

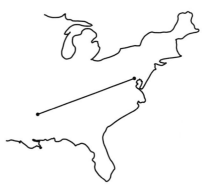

Airlines plan their routes so that the planes can fly in a straight line to the next stop because a straight line is the shortest distance between two points. Can you find the distance from Washington, D.C., to Jackson, Mississippi? Always think of distance as a positive number. Finding the distance between two points on a graph is quite simple if the points are in a horizontal or vertical line.

The USS Nimitz, the largest aircraft carrier in the world, displaces 94,000 metric tons of water when fully loaded with 90 aircraft and a crew of 5,700.

EXAMPLE 1 Find the distance between P_1 (read "P sub 1") and P_2.

Answer To find this horizontal distance, you can either (1) count the number of squares between the points or (2) subtract the values of the x-coordinates and find the absolute value of the difference. If you use absolute value, you will come out with the same value no matter which point you choose first.

$$|5 - 1| = |4| = 4$$
$$|1 - 5| = |-4| = 4$$

EXAMPLE 2   Find the vertical distance between P_1 and P_2.

Answer

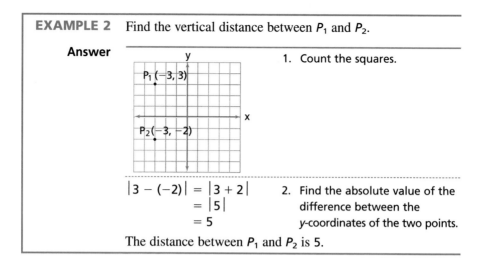

1. Count the squares.

$$|3 - (-2)| = |3 + 2|$$
$$= |5|$$
$$= 5$$

2. Find the absolute value of the difference between the y-coordinates of the two points.

The distance between P_1 and P_2 is 5.

By counting squares, you can easily find horizontal and vertical distances. But can you see any problem with counting squares? Counting squares between $(-5, -127)$ and $(-5, 318)$ would take a lot of time. You can find the distances much faster by subtracting. Horizontal distance is found by $|x_2 - x_1|$ and vertical distance by $|y_2 - y_1|$.

What should you do to find the distance between two points not on a horizontal or vertical line? Since you cannot count the number of squares between the two points, you cannot just subtract x values or y values. You must first locate a third point that is on the same horizontal line as one point and on the same vertical line as the other point. This point will be the vertex of a right angle. By forming a right triangle, you can now use the Pythagorean theorem to find the distance between the two points.

EXAMPLE 3   Find the distance between P_1 $(-3, 1)$ and P_2 $(5, 4)$.

Answer

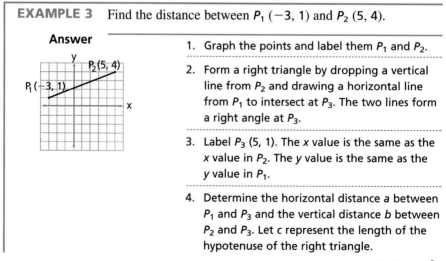

1. Graph the points and label them P_1 and P_2.

2. Form a right triangle by dropping a vertical line from P_2 and drawing a horizontal line from P_1 to intersect at P_3. The two lines form a right angle at P_3.

3. Label P_3 (5, 1). The x value is the same as the x value in P_2. The y value is the same as the y value in P_1.

4. Determine the horizontal distance a between P_1 and P_3 and the vertical distance b between P_2 and P_3. Let c represent the length of the hypotenuse of the right triangle.

Continued ▶

$$a^2 + b^2 = c^2$$
$$8^2 + 3^2 = c^2$$
$$64 + 9 = c^2$$
$$73 = c^2$$
$$\sqrt{73} = c$$

5. Substitute values into the Pythagorean theorem and solve for c.

So the distance between P_1 and P_2 is $\sqrt{73} \approx 8.5$.

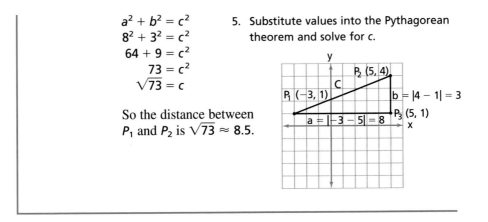

The distance formula was developed from a procedure similar to the one you just followed. Study the following proof.

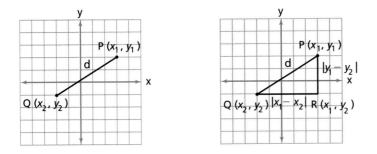

Consider points $P(x_1, y_1)$ and $Q(x_2, y_2)$ in the plane. Find the distance d between these two points.

Form a right triangle and label the vertex of the right angle R. The coordinates of R must be (x_1, y_2). The vertical distance between P and R is $|y_1 - y_2|$ (vertical change); the horizontal distance between Q and R is $|x_1 - x_2|$ (horizontal change). Let d be the distance between P and Q. Using the Pythagorean theorem, you get

$$d^2 = \left(|x_1 - x_2|\right)^2 + \left(|y_1 - y_2|\right)^2.$$

You can drop the absolute value signs since their squares will be positive anyway.

$$d^2 = (x_1 - x_2)^2 + (y_1 - y_2)^2$$

To solve for d, find the square root of both sides.

$$d = \sqrt{(x_1 - x_2)^2 + (y_1 - y_2)^2}$$

Since you can use this formula to find the distance between any two points in a plane, memorize it so that you can use it when you need it.

EXAMPLE 4   Find the distance between (1, 1) and (5, 1).

Answer   Let $(x_1, y_1) = (1, 1)$
$(x_2, y_2) = (5, 1)$

$$d = \sqrt{(x_1 - x_2)^2 + (y_1 - y_2)^2}$$
$$= \sqrt{(1 - 5)^2 + (1 - 1)^2}$$
$$= \sqrt{(-4)^2 + 0^2}$$
$$= \sqrt{16}$$
$$= 4$$

The distance is **4** units.

EXAMPLE 5   Find the distance between $(-2, 9)$ and (7, 5).

Answer   Let $(x_1, y_1) = (-2, 9)$
$(x_2, y_2) = (7, 5)$

$$d = \sqrt{(x_1 - x_2)^2 + (y_1 - y_2)^2}$$
$$= \sqrt{(-2 - 7)^2 + (9 - 5)^2}$$
$$= \sqrt{(-9)^2 + 4^2}$$
$$= \sqrt{81 + 16}$$
$$= \sqrt{97}$$

The distance is $\sqrt{97}$, or approximately **9.8** units.

EXAMPLE 6   Suppose that Washington, D.C., and Jackson, Mississippi, are represented by the ordered pairs shown. Use the distance formula to find the flight distance.

Answer
$$d = \sqrt{(x_1 - x_2)^2 + (y_1 - y_2)^2}$$
$$= \sqrt{(-350 - 400)^2 + (100 - 500)^2}$$
$$= \sqrt{(-750)^2 + (-400)^2}$$
$$= \sqrt{562500 + 160000}$$
$$= \sqrt{722500}$$
$$= 850$$

So the air distance between Washington, D.C., and Jackson, Mississippi, is **850** miles.

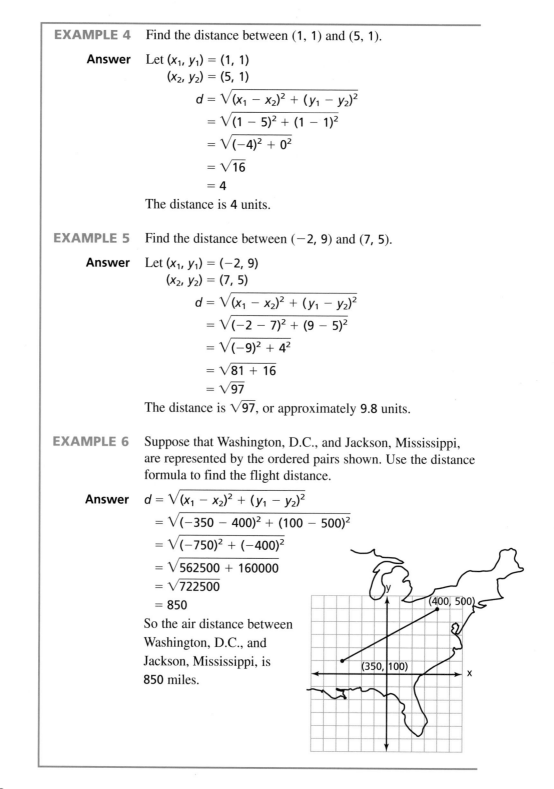

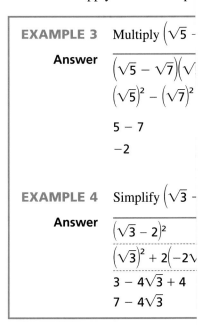

EXAMPLE 1 Multiply $\sqrt{5}(\sqrt{}$

Answer $\sqrt{5}(\sqrt{3} - 2)$

$= \sqrt{15} - 2\sqrt{5}$

EXAMPLE 2 Multiply $(\sqrt{7} -$

Answer $(\sqrt{7} + \sqrt{2})(\sqrt{3}$

$\sqrt{7}\,\sqrt{3} - 6\sqrt{7}$

$\sqrt{21} - 6\sqrt{7} +$

Since no terms
or combined, tl

Just as you must apply two previo
Christian's must also apply various
Spiritual maturity comes only as t
he already knows. God will not re
what He has already revealed. Are
you know that you could obey mo

The special products that you obse
nomials also apply to radical expr

EXAMPLE 3 Multiply $(\sqrt{5} -$

Answer $(\sqrt{5} - \sqrt{7})(\sqrt{}$

$(\sqrt{5})^2 - (\sqrt{7})^2$

$5 - 7$

-2

EXAMPLE 4 Simplify $(\sqrt{3} -$

Answer $(\sqrt{3} - 2)^2$

$(\sqrt{3})^2 + 2(-2\sqrt{}$

$3 - 4\sqrt{3} + 4$

$7 - 4\sqrt{3}$

▶ A. Exercises

Find the distance between the following pairs of points.

1. (2, 7) and (−3, 5)
2. (8, 4) and (−1, −4)
3. (2, 6) and (−4, 5)
4. (−3, −1) and (2, 3)
5. (1, 0) and (4, 2)
6. (3, 4) and (0, 0)

7. (1, 8) and (−2, −5)
8. (−7, 3) and (1, 8)
9. (−2, −6) and (2, 1)
10. (4, 7) and (1, 5)
11. $(2\sqrt{7}, -3)$ and $(\sqrt{7}, 5)$
12. $(5\sqrt{3}, \sqrt{24})$ and $(-\sqrt{12}, \sqrt{54})$

▶ B. Exercises

Find the perimeter of each figure.

13.

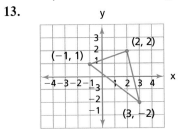

14.

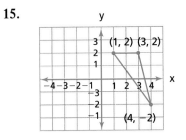

15.

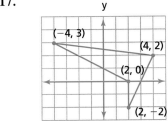

16.

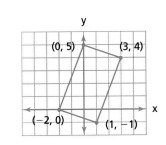

17.

18. If the locations of two cities on a map are indicated by the ordered pairs (73, 132) and (3, −146), what is the distance in air miles between these two cities?

19. A destroyer is located ;
    (15, 3), where the num
    the distance in nautical

▶ C. Exercises

20. A plane flying at 10,00(
    flies over the destroyer
    19. Find its air distance
    deck of the aircraft car
    cal miles (*Note:* 1 nauti
    mile = **6076 ft.**)

21. Determine the perimete
    trapezoid shown to the r

■ Cumulative Review

22. Factor $4xy + 3y + 16x$
23. State the division prope
24. Solve $x\sqrt{7} = \sqrt{11}$.
25. Graph $\sqrt{18}$.
26. Simplify $\frac{4xyz^3}{6xy^3z}$.

10.8 Multip Expre

In Chapter 8 you learned how
you learned to multiply and d
and divide radical expressions

Definition

A **radical expression** is an al;

Some examples of radical ex
$\sqrt[3]{2x^2y}$. Radical expressions :
follow the same rules that yo

▶ B. Exercises

Simplify.

9. $\dfrac{2}{\sqrt{3} - 1}$

10. $\dfrac{\sqrt{5} - 3}{\sqrt{5} + 3}$

11. $\dfrac{5}{\sqrt{2} - \sqrt{6}}$

12. $\dfrac{\sqrt{5} + 1}{\sqrt{7} - 2}$

13. $\dfrac{16}{\sqrt{7} + \sqrt{3}}$

14. $\dfrac{\sqrt{8}}{3\sqrt{2} - \sqrt{3}}$

▶ C. Exercises

Simplify.

15. $\dfrac{\sqrt{2} + \sqrt{5}}{\sqrt{3} - \sqrt{10}}$

16. $\dfrac{3\sqrt{2} - 8\sqrt{7}}{4\sqrt{3} + \sqrt{5}}$

■ Cumulative Review

17. Factor $x^2 + 4xy - 45y^2$.
18. Graph the relation $\{(3, -2), (1, 4), (2, 0), (-3, 5)\}$.
19. Solve $-3x + 2 > 23$.
20. Find x.

21. Simplify $\dfrac{8}{\sqrt[3]{5}}$.

10.10 Radical Equations

Equations such as $\sqrt{x} = 10$, $3 + \sqrt{x} = 24$, and $6\sqrt{x} = 9$ are called radical equations because they contain a variable in the radicand. Equations such as $x + \sqrt{3} = 0$ and $5x - \sqrt{13} = 25$ are not radical equations because the variable is not in the radicand. You can easily solve radical equations, but you must be sure to check all solutions in the original equation. If a solution does not check in the original equation, it is *extraneous* and there is no solution.

Definition

A **radical equation** is an equation that contains a variable in a radicand.

EXAMPLE 1   Solve $\sqrt{x} = 10$.

Answer
$$\sqrt{x} = 10$$
$$\left(\sqrt{x}\right)^2 = \left(10\right)^2$$
$$x = 100$$

Check. $\sqrt{100} = 10$

To eliminate the square root sign, square both sides of the equation. When you square a square root, you get the radicand. That is, $\left(\sqrt{x}\right)^2 = x$.

Solving Radical Equations

1. Isolate the radical (rearrange the equation so that the radical containing the variable is by itself on one side of the equation).
2. Square both sides of the equation.
3. Solve the resulting equation.
4. Check your solutions in the original equation.

EXAMPLE 2   Solve $8 + \sqrt{x - 3} = 4$.

Answer

$8 + \sqrt{x - 3} = 4$	
$\sqrt{x - 3} = -4$	1. Isolate the radical on one side of the equation.
$\left(\sqrt{x - 3}\right)^2 = (-4)^2$	2. Square both sides.
$x - 3 = 16$	3. Solve.
$x = 19$	

Check.

$8 + \sqrt{19 - 3} = 4$	4. Check.
$8 + \sqrt{16} = 4$	
$8 + 4 = 4$	Since $12 \neq 4$, this solution does
$12 \neq 4$	not check. So 19 is extraneous, and there is no solution.

EXAMPLE 3   Solve $\sqrt{2x + 5} = 8$.

Answer

$\sqrt{2x + 5} = 8$	1. The radical is already isolated.
$\left(\sqrt{2x + 5}\right)^2 = 8^2$	2. Square both sides.
$2x + 5 = 64$	3. Solve the resulting equation.
$2x = 59$	
$x = \frac{59}{2}$	

Check.

$\sqrt{2\left(\frac{59}{2}\right) + 5} = 8$	4. Check.
$\sqrt{59 + 5} = 8$	
$\sqrt{64} = 8$	
$8 = 8$	$\frac{59}{2}$ is the solution.

EXAMPLE 4   Solve $10 - 2\sqrt{x} = 0$.

Answer

$10 - 2\sqrt{x} = 0$	1. Get the radical alone on one side.
$-2\sqrt{x} = -10$	
$\sqrt{x} = 5$	
$\left(\sqrt{x}\right)^2 = 5^2$	2. Square both sides.
$x = 25$	3. The equation is solved.

Check.

$10 - 2\sqrt{x} = 0$	4. Check.
$10 - 2\sqrt{25} = 0$	
$10 - 2 \cdot 5 = 0$	
$10 - 10 = 0$	
$0 = 0$	25 is the solution.

► A. Exercises

Solve each radical equation and check your solution.

1. $\sqrt{x} = 4$
2. $\sqrt{y} = 5$
3. $\sqrt{x + 2} = 8$
4. $\sqrt{y - 5} = 2$
5. $3 + \sqrt{x} = 9$

6. $2 - \sqrt{x} = -8$
7. $\sqrt{x} = 3.2$
8. $\sqrt{x + 5} = 0$
9. $\sqrt{x + 5} + 5 = 7$
10. $3 - \sqrt{x - 5} = 4$

► B. Exercises

Solve each radical equation and check your solution.

11. $7 + 3\sqrt{x - 3} = -14$
12. $3 + 4\sqrt{x + 3} = 11$
13. $5 + 2\sqrt{y - 3} = 27$
14. $5 + \sqrt{x + 1} = 7$

15. $14 - \sqrt{x - 3} = 10$
16. $8 + 2\sqrt{x} = 18$
17. $12 - 4\sqrt{x - 3} = 7$
18. $5\sqrt{x} - 13 = 2\sqrt{x} + 26$

► C. Exercises

Solve the following.

19. $5\sqrt{x - 1} + 2\sqrt{x + 1} = 3\sqrt{x + 1} - \sqrt{x - 1}$
20. $\sqrt{5x + 1} - \sqrt{x + 3} = 0$

Cumulative Review

21. Simplify $\dfrac{\sqrt{3}}{2} + \dfrac{\sqrt{3}}{5}$.

22. Solve $\dfrac{x}{3} - \sqrt{14} = \dfrac{5}{2}$.

23. Graph $y = \dfrac{7}{8}$.

24. Factor $x^2 - \dfrac{1}{9}$.

25. Divide $\dfrac{x^3 - x^2 - 18x + 8}{x + 4}$.

$\mathcal{A}$lgebra *and* $\mathcal{S}$cripture

$$3x + x = 4x$$
$$3\sqrt{2} + \sqrt{2} = 4\sqrt{2}$$

In this chapter, you expanded the addition rules to include radicals. Addition is the most important operation since multiplication is just repeated addition, and subtraction and division are the inverses of these. After counting, therefore, addition forms the next building block for arithmetic and math.

The Bible frequently records additions. In Chapter 4 you discovered the addition problems of Genesis 5. Now read Numbers 2.

Fill in the census data for the tribes. Give the subtotals from verses 9, 16, 24, and 31. Also copy the grand total from verse 32.

Tribe	Census	Subtotals	Grand Total
1. Judah			
2. Issachar			
3. Zebulun			
4. Reuben			
5. Simeon			
6. Gad			
7. Ephraim			
8. Manasseh			
9. Benjamin			
10. Dan			
11. Asher			
12. Naphtali			

Add each column to check the grand total.

13. Identify the two addends in Matthew 6:27.

This addition shows us that we must trust in God's sovereign control of our unchangeable circumstances. On the other hand, we must be responsible to change what we can. Just six verses later God tells us to put our efforts into seeking the kingdom of God (6:33).

14. What will be added as a result?

Matthew 6:33 gives us an example of a nonnumerical use of addition. Notice that it is like the general uses of multiplication mentioned in Chapter 8—the idea depends upon the mathematical meaning of addition as uniting the elements of two sets into one. God will add to the set of our possessions whatever elements are lacking to meet our needs. Similarly, God tells us to add to our faith.

15. What qualities must we *add* to our *faith* (give the reference)?

16. A wise man obeys the Scriptures. What will this *add* to him, according to Proverbs 3:1-2 and 16:23?

Read about the growth of the church in Acts 2:37-42 and 6:1-8. Use the mathematical concepts of addition and multiplication to answer the questions about these verses.

THE *N*TH DEGREE

Would the meaning be the same if the words *added* (2:41) and *multiplied* (6:7) were exchanged? Why? What aspects of the mathematical meanings are significant in the contexts?

Scriptural Roots

BUT SEEK YE FIRST the kingdom of God, and his righteousness; and all these things shall be added unto you. ❧

MATTHEW 6:33

Find the approximate value of each of the following square roots by using a calculator and rounding to the nearest tenth.

1. $\sqrt{127}$
2. $\sqrt{0.63}$
3. $\sqrt{243}$
4. $\sqrt{619}$

Change each radical to exponential form.

5. $\sqrt{2x^3}$
6. $\sqrt[4]{3y^2}$
7. $\sqrt[4]{16x^5y}$

Change each expression to radical form.

8. $3^{\frac{2}{3}}a^{\frac{5}{3}}$
9. $(2xy)^{\frac{1}{3}}z^{\frac{4}{3}}$
10. $7^{\frac{1}{2}}x^{\frac{1}{3}}y^{\frac{1}{2}}$

Simplify each radical.

11. $\sqrt{84}$
12. $\sqrt{8}\,\sqrt{2}$
13. $\dfrac{5}{\sqrt{6}}$
14. $\sqrt[3]{216}$
15. $\sqrt{2}+5\sqrt{2}+\sqrt{8}$
16. $\sqrt[3]{21}\,\sqrt[3]{9}$
17. $\dfrac{\sqrt{5}}{\sqrt{15}}$
18. $\sqrt{5x^3y^4}\,\sqrt{15xy^5}$
19. $\sqrt{5}\!\left(\sqrt{7}+3\right)$
20. $\dfrac{\sqrt{7}}{\sqrt{27}}$
21. $\sqrt{6}-\sqrt{24}+5\sqrt{6}$
22. $\dfrac{\sqrt[3]{3}}{\sqrt[3]{27}}$
23. $\sqrt[5]{1632}$

24. $\sqrt{2x^{12}y^3} \div \sqrt{8x^4y^9}$

25. $\sqrt{20} \sqrt{63}$

26. $\sqrt[3]{7} + \sqrt[3]{56} - \sqrt[3]{189}$

27. $\sqrt{11}\left(\sqrt{2} - \sqrt{13}\right)$

28. $\left(\sqrt{2} + \sqrt{3}\right)\left(\sqrt{2} - \sqrt{3}\right)$

29. $\sqrt[3]{9a^5b^2} \sqrt[3]{3ab^4}$

30. $\dfrac{6}{3 + \sqrt{2}}$

Find the distance between each pair of points.

31. (1, 7) and (2, 9)

32. (−3, 2) and (−1, −5)

33. (4, 3) and (−5, 4)

Solve each radical equation.

34. $\sqrt{x} = 16$

35. $\sqrt{x + 5} = 25$

36. $\sqrt{x - 2} + 8 = 57$

37. If the two legs of a right triangle measure 4" and 6", what is the length of the hypotenuse?

38. A straight palm tree fell against another tree, forming a right triangle. The trunks of the two trees were 20 feet apart at the ground. A monkey climbs 53 feet up the leaning tree trunk and then comes down the standing tree trunk. How many feet does the monkey climb in coming down the vertical trunk in order to reach the ground?

39. A grandfather clock has a long pendulum. The time it takes for a pendulum to swing from one side to the other side and back again, a period, is described by the formula $T = 2\pi\sqrt{\dfrac{l}{g}}$ where T is in seconds if l is in cm and $g = 980$ cm/second². How long does it take the pendulum to go through one period if the pendulum is 98 cm long?

40. Explain the mathematical significance of Matthew 6:33.

11 Quadratic Equations

$y = mx + b$

Travis hoped to place first in the javelin toss at a special track and field day in his city. As he practiced, he found that the javelin went farther if he released it at an angle halfway between straight up and straight out. He wondered why and did some internet research.

Travis found that biomechanics laboratories study motions for athletes. Complicated equations describe their body movements. Such analyses identify ideal body positions for optimal distance. One page also gave the two equations for the motion of the center of mass of a projectile such as a shot put or javelin. This type of motion is much simpler to describe.

$$x = 40t$$

$$0 = 40t - 16t^2$$

The first equation tells how far the javelin moves in a given amount of time. The second equation is a quadratic equation in which t is the amount of time that the projectile remains in the air. You will learn methods for solving such problems in this chapter.

After this chapter you should be able to

1. solve quadratic equations by factoring.
2. solve quadratic equations by completing the square.
3. solve quadratic equations by using the quadratic formula.
4. set up and solve word problems requiring quadratic equations.

11.1 Zero Product Property

All of the equations you have solved so far have been linear equations. A linear equation can be put into the general form $ax + b = 0$ (where $a \neq 0$). The polynomial on the left is a binomial with degree 1 (the highest degree of either term). For this reason, linear equations are sometimes called first-degree equations.

Now you will learn to solve quadratic equations. A quadratic equation also has a general form, but the polynomial has degree 2.

Definition

A **quadratic equation** is an equation of the second degree. The general form is $ax^2 + bx + c = 0$, where a, b, and c are real numbers and $a \neq 0$.

To solve quadratic equations, you must first understand the zero product property. It permits you to use your factoring skills to solve them.

Zero Product Property

If the product of two or more factors is 0, at least one of the factors is 0.

What is the value of x in the equation $3x = 0$? If $3x = 0$, then $x = 0$.

In the equation $xy = 0$, either $x = 0$ or $y = 0$, or possibly both equal zero.

In the equation $(x - 1)(x + 3) = 0$, either $x - 1 = 0$ in which case $x = 1$, or $x + 3 = 0$ and $x = -3$. Therefore, the equation $(x - 1)(x + 3) = 0$ has two solutions, 1 and -3.

EXAMPLE 1   Solve $(x - 5)(x + 2) = 0$.

Answer

$(x - 5)(x + 2) = 0$

$x - 5 = 0$ or $x + 2 = 0$ 1. Set each factor equal to 0 using the zero product property.

$x = 5$ or $x = -2$ 2. Solve each linear equation.

Since $x = 5$ or $x = -2$, you can see that this quadratic equation has two solutions: 5 and -2.

The word *or* means union. Most quadratic equations will have two solutions, but the method works regardless of the number of factors.

EXAMPLE 2   Solve $(x - 4)(x + 2)(x - 3) = 0$.

    Answer $(x - 4)(x + 2)(x - 3) = 0$

$$x - 4 = 0 \quad \text{or} \quad x + 2 = 0 \quad \text{or} \quad x - 3 = 0$$
$$x = 4 \quad \text{or} \quad x = -2 \quad \text{or} \quad x = 3$$

The equation has three solutions, -2, 3, and 4.

EXAMPLE 3   Solve $8x^2 - 16x = 0$.

    Answer

$8x^2 - 16x = 0$	
$8x(x - 2) = 0$	1. Factor the polynomial.
$8x = 0 \quad$ or $\quad x - 2 = 0$ $x = 0 \quad$ or $\quad x = 2$	2. Set each factor equal to 0. Solve each equation.
Thus, the solution of the equation is $x = 0$ or $x = 2$.	

    Check.
$$8(0)^2 - 16 \cdot 0 = 0 \qquad 8(2)^2 - 16 \cdot 2 = 0 \qquad 3.\ \text{Check.}$$
$$0 - 0 = 0 \qquad\qquad 8 \cdot 4 - 16 \cdot 2 = 0$$
$$0 = 0 \qquad\qquad\qquad 32 - 32 = 0$$
$$0 = 0$$

EXAMPLE 4   Solve $2(x - 3)(x + 7) = 0$.

    Answer $2(x - 3)(x + 7) = 0$

Since $2 \neq 0$, either
$$x - 3 = 0 \quad \text{or} \quad x + 7 = 0$$
$$x = 3 \quad \text{or} \quad x = -7$$

▶ A. Exercises

Solve.

1. $5x = 0$
2. $(x - 2)(x + 4) = 0$
3. $(y + 5)(y + 2) = 0$
4. $(x - 3)(x - 1) = 0$
5. $2x(x + 7) = 0$
6. $(x + 2)(x + 6) = 0$
7. $(y - 3)(y - 8) = 0$
8. $(x - 2)(x + 1)(x - 6) = 0$
9. $3x(x + 12) = 0$
10. $(x - 7)(x + 4)(x - 6) = 0$
11. $8x(x + 1)(x - 10) = 0$
12. $(x - 2)(x - 2) = 0$

▶ B. Exercises

Solve.

13. $-5x(x - 1)(3x + 2) = 0$

14. $(4x + 1)(3x + 2) = 0$

15. $(2x - 11)(4x - 5) = 0$

16. $x^2 + 5x - 36 = 0$

17. $x^2 - x - 56 = 0$

18. $x^2 - x = 0$

▶ C. Exercises

Solve.

19. $14x^2 - 29x + 12 = 0$

20. $15x^3 - 17x^2 - 42x = 0$

■ Cumulative Review

21. Factor $x^4 - 3x^3 + 2x^2$.

22. Multiply $3x(x - 5)$.

23. Solve $3x - 5 = 0$.

24. Graph $3x - 5 = y$.

25. Evaluate $3x - 5$ if $x = 4$.

11.2 Solving Quadratic Equations by Factoring

You can solve many quadratic equations by factoring. However, always remember to be sure that the equation is in the general form first.

Galileo dropped balls from the Leaning Tower of Pisa and showed that falling objects can be described by a quadratic relationship.

Solving Quadratic Equations by Factoring

1. *Arrange* all terms on one side of the equation in descending powers of the variable and set equal to 0.
2. *Factor* the polynomial side of the equation.
3. *Set* each factor that contains a variable equal to 0 using the zero product property.
4. *Solve* the resulting equations.
5. *Check* your solutions in the original equation.

EXAMPLE 1   Solve $x^2 + 2x - 63 = 0$.

Answer

$x^2 + 2x - 63 = 0$	1. No rearrangement is needed.
$(x + 9)(x - 7) = 0$	2. Factor the left side.
$x + 9 = 0$ or $x - 7 = 0$	3. Set each factor equal to 0.
$x = -9$ or $x = 7$	4. Solve both equations.
Check. $(-9)^2 + 2(-9) - 63 = 0$ $7^2 + 2(7) - 63 = 0$ $81 - 18 - 63 = 0$ $49 + 14 - 63 = 0$ $0 = 0$ $0 = 0$	5. Check.

The solutions are often expressed as a set, called the solution set. The solution set for example 1 is $\{-9, 7\}$.

EXAMPLE 2   Solve $x^2 - 49 = 0$ and give the solution set.

Answer

$x^2 - 49 = 0$	1. It is in general form.
$(x - 7)(x + 7) = 0$	2. Factor the left side.
$x - 7 = 0$ or $x + 7 = 0$	3. Apply the zero product property.
$x = 7$ or $x = -7$	4. Solve both equations.
The solution set is $\{-7, 7\}$.	5. Check mentally and write the solution set.

EXAMPLE 3   Give the solution set to $2x^2 = 7x + 4$.

Answer

$$2x^2 = 7x + 4$$

$2x^2 - 7x - 4 = 0$	1. Move all terms to the left side of the equation to get 0 on the right side.
$(x - 4)(2x + 1) = 0$	2. Factor the left side.
$x - 4 = 0 \qquad$ or $\qquad 2x + 1 = 0$	3. Set each factor equal to 0 using the zero product property.
$\qquad\qquad\quad 2x = -1$ $x = 4 \qquad$ or $\qquad x = -\frac{1}{2}$	4. Solve the linear equations.
$2(4)^2 = 7(4) + 4 \quad$ or $\quad 2\left(-\frac{1}{2}\right)^2 = 7\left(-\frac{1}{2}\right) + 4$	5. Check mentally.

The solution set is $\left\{-\frac{1}{2}, 4\right\}$.

Some word problems require quadratic equations.

EXAMPLE 4   Find the dimensions of a rectangular room 5 feet longer than wide, requiring 204 square feet of carpet.

Answer

Let x = the width $x + 5$ = the length	1. Identify what you are asked to find. In this problem you are asked to find the dimensions of the living room.
  $\boxed{}\,x$ $x + 5$	2. Draw a picture.
$x(x + 5) = 204$	3. Set up an equation. Since 204 square feet of carpet are needed for the room, 204 is the area of the floor. The equation will be $A = lw$, the formula for finding the area of a rectangle.
$x^2 + 5x = 204$ $x^2 + 5x - 204 = 0$ $(x + 17)(x - 12) = 0$ $x + 17 = 0 \qquad$ or $\qquad x - 12 = 0$ $x = -17$ or $\qquad\quad x = 12$	4. Solve. Multiply the left side by using the distributive property. Then move all terms to one side of the equation. Solve the equation by factoring it.
$x = 12$	5. Check in context.

Since you are dealing with dimensions, neither the length nor the width can be negative. Consequently, 12 is the only possible solution. Therefore, the width (x) is 12, and the length ($x + 5$) is 17. Is this a reasonable solution? Does it work in the problem?

▶ A. Exercises

Solve each quadratic equation.

1. $y^2 + 6y + 9 = 0$
2. $a^2 + 2a - 15 = 0$
3. $x^2 - 9 = 0$
4. $p^2 = 2p + 24$
5. $m^2 - 2m = 35$
6. $x^2 + 3x = 0$

Solve each quadratic equation and write the solution set.

7. $x^2 - 7x = 0$
8. $t^2 - 4t + 4 = 0$
9. $x^2 - 10x = -16$
10. $x^2 = 5x$
11. $x^2 - 12 = -4x$
12. $x^2 - 7x = 8$
13. $y^2 = 169$
14. $x^2 + 8 = -6x$
15. $a^2 + 15a = -50$
16. $4x^2 = 9$

▶ B. Exercises

Solve each quadratic equation.

17. $30 = a^2 + 13a$
18. $16y^2 = 9$
19. $8x^2 + 10x = -3$
20. $2r - r^2 = 0$
21. $10t^2 = -7t + 12$
22. $14x^2 - 40 + 19x = 0$

Set up a quadratic equation and solve.

23. The difference of two numbers is 6 and the difference of their squares is 60. Find the two numbers.
24. A farmer planted 168 tomato plants. If he had 2 more plants in a row than the number of rows, how many rows did he have?

▶ C. Exercises

Set up a quadratic equation and solve.

25. Joe said, "If five times my age in 8 years is subtracted from the square of my present age, the result is 86." Find Joe's present age.

26. Brady wants to build a sidewalk around his flower garden that is 52 feet long and 44 feet wide. How wide should the sidewalk be if he retains 1748 square feet for the flower garden?

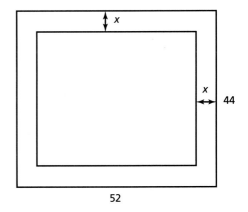

Simplify.

27. $2\sqrt{6} - 5\sqrt{3} + 7\sqrt{12} - \sqrt{3}$

28. $\sqrt{22}(4\sqrt{20} - 3\sqrt{55})$

29. $\sqrt{120472}$

30. $\sqrt[3]{84x^2y^5} \, \sqrt[3]{126x^4y^5}$

31. $\dfrac{\sqrt{3} + 5}{\sqrt{5} - \sqrt{3}}$

11.3 Solving Equations by Taking Roots

In example 2 in the last section, you learned how to solve equations of the form $x^2 - c = 0$. The two solutions to the quadratic equation in example 2 are 7 and -7, usually written ± 7. Review that example; then you will be ready to learn another method of solving these equations.

The second method for solving equations of this form depends upon the following general principle: the *n*th roots of equals are equal.

If $x^2 = 36$, then $\sqrt{x^2} = \pm\sqrt{36} = \pm 6$.

As an example of a higher root,

if $x^3 = 36$, then $\sqrt[3]{x^3} = \sqrt[3]{36} \approx 3.3$.

Solving Equations of the Form $x^2 - c = 0$

1. Isolate the squared term.
2. Find the square roots of both sides (don't forget the $\pm$).
3. Simplify the radicals.

EXAMPLE 1   Solve $x^2 - 49 = 0$.

Answer

$x^2 - 49 = 0$

$x^2 = 49$	1. Isolate the squared term by adding 49 to both sides of the equation.
$\sqrt{x^2} = \pm\sqrt{49}$	2. Find the square roots of both sides.
$x = \pm 7$	3. Simplify the radicals.

Compare this answer with the answer to example 2 of the previous section. You may recall that $\sqrt{x^2} = |x|$. When you take the square root of both sides of the equation, you actually get $|x| = 7$. Therefore, $x = 7$ or $x = -7$. You will not have to show the absolute value step each time as long as you are careful to include the $\pm$ at the square root step each time.

EXAMPLE 2   Solve $2x^2 - 6 = 0$.

Answer

$2x^2 - 6 = 0$ $2x^2 = 6$ $x^2 = 3$	1. Place in the proper form.
$\sqrt{x^2} = \pm\sqrt{3}$ $x = \pm\sqrt{3}$	2. Find the square roots of both sides.
$2(\sqrt{3})^2 - 6 = 0 \qquad 2(-\sqrt{3})^2 - 6 = 0$ $6 - 6 = 0 \qquad\qquad 6 - 6 = 0$ $0 = 0 \qquad\qquad\qquad 0 = 0$	3. Check the solution by substituting $\sqrt{3}$ and $-\sqrt{3}$ in the original equation.

EXAMPLE 3   Solve $(x + 2)^2 = 36$.

Answer

$(x + 2)^2 = 36$	1. The left side already is a perfect square.
$\sqrt{(x + 2)^2} = \pm\sqrt{36}$ $x + 2 = \pm 6$	2. Take the square root of both sides.
$x + 2 = 6 \quad$ or $\quad x + 2 = -6$ $x = 4 \quad$ or $\quad x = -8$	3. Solve these two linear equations.
$(4 + 2)^2 = 36 \qquad (-8 + 2)^2 = 36$	4. Check mentally.

EXAMPLE 4 Solve $7x^2 + 6 = 2x^2 + 8$.

Answer

$7x^2 + 6 = 2x^2 + 8$	1. Solve for the squared term.
$5x^2 = 2$	
$x^2 = \frac{2}{5}$	
$\sqrt{x^2} = \pm\sqrt{\frac{2}{5}}$	2. Find the square root of both sides.
$x = \pm\frac{\sqrt{2}}{\sqrt{5}}$	
$x = \pm\frac{\sqrt{2}\,\sqrt{5}}{\sqrt{5}\,\sqrt{5}}$	3. Rationalize the denominator.
$x = \frac{\pm\sqrt{10}}{5}$	

EXAMPLE 5 Solve $x^2 + 7 = 0$.

Answer

$$x^2 + 7 = 0$$
$$x^2 = -7$$
$$x = \pm\sqrt{-7}$$

Notice that we are now asking what number multiplied times itself gives a negative product? No such number exists in the real number system. Such a number is a complex number and will be covered in Algebra 2. For now write "complex" as your answer to a problem like this one.

▶ A. Exercises

Solve.

1. $x^2 - 100 = 0$

2. $x^2 - 64 = 0$

3. $x^2 = 25$

4. $x^2 - 5 = 31$

5. $x^2 = 6$

6. $x^2 + 5 = 0$

7. $2x^2 - 17 = x^2 + 3$

8. $4x^2 - 16 = 3x^2 + 9$

9. $3x^2 + 10 = x^2 + 24$

10. $(x + 4)^2 = 25$

▶ B. Exercises

Solve.

11. $(x - 6)^2 = 13$

12. $(x + 3)^2 = 121$

13. $(x - 5)^2 + 17 = 0$

14. $(y + 2)^2 = 18$

15. $7q^2 = 11$

16. $5x^2 + x - 2 = x^2 + x + 7$

17. $(4x + 1)^2 = 9$

18. $4(x + 1)^2 = 9$

Solve.

19. $2(5x - 3)^2 = 7$

20. $4x^2 - 20x + 25 = 32$

■ Cumulative Review

21. Factor $2x^3 + x^2 + 4x + 2$.

22. Simplify $3^{\frac{1}{2}} x^2 y^{-3}$.

23. Solve $x + 3 < 5$.

24. Graph the system.
$$x + y \geq 4$$
$$2x - y \leq -7$$

25. Jess invested $30 more at 6% than at 5%. If his total annual interest is $100, how much is invested at each rate?

 MIND OVER MATH

One purpose for studying mathematics is to teach ourselves how to reason correctly. Read the following proofs. Can you detect the faulty reasoning?

Proof that $1 = 2$

Let $a = b$.	$a = b$
Multiply both sides by b.	$ab = b^2$
Subtract a^2 from both sides.	$ab - a^2 = b^2 - a^2$
Factor both sides.	$a(b - a) = (b + a)(b - a)$
Divide both sides by $(b - a)$.	$a = b + a$
Substitute 1 for a.	$1 = b + 1$
Since $a = b$, substitute 1 for b.	$1 = 1 + 1$
Add.	$1 = 2$

Proof that $4 = 8$

The equation is balanced since both sides equal -32. Add 36 to both sides and then factor the perfect square trinomials.

$$16 - 48 = 64 - 96$$
$$16 - 48 + 36 = 64 - 96 + 36$$
$$(4 - 6)^2 = (8 - 6)^2$$

Take the square root of both sides.

$$4 - 6 = 8 - 6$$

Add 6 to both sides.

$$4 = 8$$

JOHN VON NEUMANN

On December 28, 1903, John von Neumann was born in Budapest, Hungary, to Max and Gita von Neumann. John was to become one of the most important mathematicians in the history of the United States and even the world. Although you may have never heard of him, his discoveries brought modern society into both the atomic age and the computer age.

John was born to wealthy parents who appreciated and encouraged their son in his endeavors in mathematics. By the time John was six, he could divide two eight-digit numbers in his head; by ten, he had completed college calculus. His photographic memory enabled him to look briefly at a page of numbers in a telephone book and then recall a whole column of names, addresses, and phone numbers. Despite his unusual mental aptitude, John was considerate and not overly proud. He realized that God had given him a gift for obtaining knowledge. John enjoyed playing with other children but also loved conversations with adults.

When von Neumann finished high school, his father thought he should enter a more lucrative field than mathematics. He submitted to his father's wishes and completed a degree in chemistry at the University of Berlin in 1925. However, his gift and love for mathematics enabled him to earn a Ph.D. in math from the University of Budapest in just one year.

John von Neumann taught at the University of Berlin, from 1926-29 and at the University of Hamburg, 1929-30. In 1930 he came to the United States as a visiting professor at Princeton, and in 1933 he became a professor at the newly established Institute for Advanced Study at Princeton, where Albert Einstein had just become director of the school of mathematics. In 1937 von Neumann became an American citizen.

Von Neumann loved to play with numbers in his spare time. One number game he especially liked was to search for prime numbers on car license plates. He eventually coauthored (with Oscar Morganstern) *Theory of Games and Economic Behavior* in 1944. He later contributed to finite math and mathematical analysis as well.

During World War II, von Neumann was involved with the War Department of the U.S. government. His assignments included submarine warfare projects, economic intelligence projects, and ordnance problems. Each group that he worked with gave him the problems they could not solve. His most famous work came out of secret meetings at Los Alamos, New Mexico, where scientists and mathematicians gathered to develop the atomic bomb. By creating a means of detonating a bomb by an inward burst, von Neumann expedited the development of the atomic bomb by one year.

Von Neumann's wife, Klara, became interested in programming computers and he soon became interested also. When the war was over in 1945, von Neumann became the director of Princeton Institute's Electronic Computer Project, which developed several electronic computers. One of these computers was called MANIAC (mathematical analyzer, numerical integrator and computer). Businesses and government were quick to take advantage of these new high-speed computers. His constant computations to improve his computers led von Neumann to the invention of the H-bomb, which in turn made intercontinental ballistic missiles (ICBMs) possible.

John von Neumann realized that no machine that man could design or build could compare to the intelligence God created in man. Knowing in detail the complex computer circuitry developed by human intelligence, he once said, "There is no comparison between the human nervous system and the most complicated machine that human intelligence has ever devised, or can devise. No man can tell me that behind the complications of the human nervous system there is no such thing as a greater intelligence. For me, that other intelligence is God." Von Neumann continued working with computers until his death February 8, 1957.

His discoveries brought modern society into both the atomic age and the computer age.

11.4 Completing the Square

Some quadratic equations cannot be factored over the set of integers. For instance, $a^2 - 7a - 3 = 0$ cannot be factored so another method is needed to solve it (see example 4). Instead, take square roots on both sides after changing the polynomial into a perfect square trinomial. This method is called *completing the square*. Remember, the middle term of a perfect square trinomial is twice the product of the square roots of the first and last terms.

To complete the square for $x^2 + 10x$, find what to add to the expression to make it a perfect square trinomial. You can find what to add by dividing the absolute value of the numerical coefficient of x by 2 and squaring the result. Dividing 10 by 2, you get 5, and $5^2 = 25$. You must add 25 to $x^2 + 10x$ to get the perfect square trinomial $x^2 + 10x + 25$. Now you can factor the perfect square trinomial into $(x + 5)^2$.

Completing the Square

1. Find half of the absolute value of the numerical coefficient of x (or the variable to the first power).
2. Square the result of step 1 and add the square to the given expression.

EXAMPLE 1 Complete the square and then factor the resulting perfect square trinomial: $a^2 - 16a$.

Answer

$16 \div 2 = 8$	1. Divide the absolute value of -16.
$(8)^2 = 64$	2. Square the result.
$a^2 - 16a + 64$	3. Add the result to the other terms.

The completed square is $a^2 - 16a + 64$ and its factorization is $(a - 8)^2$.

EXAMPLE 2 Complete the square on $x^2 - \frac{3}{5}x$. Then factor the perfect square trinomial.

Answer $\frac{3}{5} \div 2 = \frac{3}{5} \cdot \frac{1}{2} = \frac{3}{10}$

$\left(\frac{3}{10}\right)^2 = \frac{9}{100}$

The completed square is $x^2 - \frac{3}{5}x + \frac{9}{100}$.

The factorization is $\left(x - \frac{3}{10}\right)^2$.

You can use this method to solve any quadratic equation. Remember, however, that if you add a number to one side of the equation you must add the same number to the other side.

EXAMPLE 3 Solve $x^2 + 8x = 9$.

Answer

$x^2 + 8x = 9$	
$x^2 + 8x + 16 = 9 + 16$	1. Complete the square. Think $8 \div 2 = 4$ and $4^2 = 16$. Add 16 to both sides.
$(x + 4)^2 = 25$	2. Write the left side in factored form.
$\sqrt{(x + 4)^2} = \pm\sqrt{25}$ $x + 4 = \pm 5$	3. Solve the equation using the root method.

$x + 4 = 5$ or $x + 4 = -5$
$x = 1$ or $x = -9$

The solution set is $\{1, -9\}$.

Check. $1^2 + 8(1) = 9$ $(-9)^2 + 8(-9) = 9$
$1 + 8 = 9$ $81 - 72 = 9$
$9 = 9$ $9 = 9$

Solving Quadratic Equations by Completing the Square

1. Rearrange terms so that the constant is on one side of the equation and all terms containing variables are on the other side of the equation.
2. Complete the square on the side containing the variable, making sure the same operation is performed on both sides of the equation.
3. Write the side containing the variable in factored form.
4. Take the square root of both sides.
5. Find both solutions by solving the equations.

EXAMPLE 4 Solve $a^2 - 7a - 3 = 0$.

Answer

$a^2 - 7a - 3 = 0$	
$a^2 - 7a = 3$	1. Add 3 to both sides to get the constant on the right.
$a^2 - 7a + \frac{49}{4} = \frac{12}{4} + \frac{49}{4}$	2. Complete the square. $\left(\frac{7}{2}\right)^2 = \frac{49}{4}$
$\left(a - \frac{7}{2}\right)^2 = \frac{61}{4}$	3. Write the left side in factored form.
$\sqrt{\left(a - \frac{7}{2}\right)^2} = \pm\sqrt{\frac{61}{4}}$ $a - \frac{7}{2} = \pm\frac{\sqrt{61}}{2}$	4. Take the square root of both sides.
$a = \frac{7 \pm \sqrt{61}}{2}$	5. Solve the equation.

The solution set is $\left\{\frac{7 + \sqrt{61}}{2}, \frac{7 - \sqrt{61}}{2}\right\}$.

▶ A. Exercises

What number must be added to complete each square?

1. $x^2 + 8x$
2. $x^2 - 12x$
3. $x^2 + 16x$
4. $x^2 - 10x$
5. $x^2 + 52x$
6. $x^2 - 2x$
7. $x^2 + 3x$
8. $x^2 - 5x$
9. $x^2 - 9x$
10. $x^2 - 24x$

Solve each quadratic equation by completing the square.

11. $x^2 + 4x - 5 = 0$
12. $x^2 + 6x + 5 = 0$
13. $a^2 + 2a = 15$
14. $y^2 - 6y = 7$

▶ B. Exercises

Solve by completing the square. Give the solution set.

15. $x^2 - 10x = 24$
16. $a^2 + 6a = 55$
17. $x^2 - 2x - 99 = 0$
18. $m^2 - 14m + 40 = 0$
19. $x^2 + x = 2$
20. $a^2 - 7a = -10$
21. $m^2 - \frac{4}{3}m = 0$
22. $4x = x^2 - 3$

Solve by completing the square.

23. $x^2 + 3x + 1 = 0$ 24. $3m^2 + 15m - 36 = 0$

Cumulative Review

25. Solve $3\sqrt{5 - x} = 12$.
26. Give the solution set for $|x| = 5$.
27. Graph $\{x \mid -2 < x < 3\}$.
28. Simplify $\dfrac{8}{15} - \dfrac{1}{6}$.
29. Find the LCM for 100 and 150.

11.5 Completing the Square with Leading Coefficients

In all of the problems in the preceding section, the numerical coefficient of the squared variable was 1. Completing the square works only if the coefficient of the second-degree variable (x^2) is 1. If it is not 1, you will need to factor the term so that the coefficient becomes 1. You must factor the numerical coefficient of the second-degree variable from both the squared variable and the first-degree variable. You do not, however, factor the constant term but instead transfer it to the other side of the equation beforehand.

EXAMPLE 1   Solve $4x^2 + 8x - 5 = 0$ by completing the square.

Answer

$4x^2 + 8x - 5 = 0$	
$4x^2 + 8x = 5$	1. Add 5 to each side of the equation.
$4(x^2 + 2x) = 5$	2. Factor the 4 from the terms on the left.
$4(x^2 + 2x + 1) = 5 + 4(1)$	3. Complete the square inside the parentheses, being careful to add the same amount to both sides of the equation (in this case 4).

Continued ▶

$4(x + 1)^2 = 9$	4. Write the left side as a perfect square.
$(x + 1)^2 = \frac{9}{4}$	5. Divide both sides by 4.
$\sqrt{(x + 1)^2} = \pm\sqrt{\frac{9}{4}}$	6. Take the square root of each side.
$x + 1 = \pm\frac{3}{2}$ $x = -1 \pm \frac{3}{2}$	7. Solve for x.
$x = \frac{1}{2}, -\frac{5}{2}$	8. Check mentally.

An alternative method is to divide by 4 in step 3 before completing the square.

EXAMPLE 2   Solve $3x^2 - 2x - 1 = 0$ by completing the square.

Answer

$3x^2 - 2x - 1 = 0$	
$3x^2 - 2x = 1$	1. Add 1 to each side of the equation.
$3\left(x^2 - \frac{2}{3}x\right) = 1$	2. Factor the 3 from the terms on the left $\left(2 \div 3 = \frac{2}{3}\right)$.
$3\left(x^2 - \frac{2}{3}x + \frac{1}{9}\right) = 1 + 3\left(\frac{1}{9}\right)$	3. Complete the square inside the parentheses. $\frac{1}{2}\left(\frac{2}{3}\right) = \frac{1}{3}$; $\left(\frac{1}{3}\right)^2 = \frac{1}{9}$. You add the $\frac{1}{9}$ inside the parentheses, which is multiplied by 3. Thus, you really added $3\left(\frac{1}{9}\right)$ to the left side (think of the distributive property). Add the same to the right side.
$3\left(x - \frac{1}{3}\right)^2 = \frac{4}{3}$	4. Write the left side as a perfect square.
$\frac{1}{3} \cdot 3\left(x - \frac{1}{3}\right)^2 = \frac{4}{3} \cdot \frac{1}{3}$ $\left(x - \frac{1}{3}\right)^2 = \frac{4}{9}$	5. Solve this equation. First, multiply both sides by $\frac{1}{3}$ to clear the left side of the constant 3.
$\sqrt{\left(x - \frac{1}{3}\right)^2} = \pm\sqrt{\frac{4}{9}}$ $x - \frac{1}{3} = \pm\frac{2}{3}$	6. Take the square root of both sides.
$x - \frac{1}{3} = \frac{2}{3}$ or $x - \frac{1}{3} = -\frac{2}{3}$	7. Solve the linear equations.
$x = 1$ or $x = -\frac{1}{3}$	8. Check mentally.

Solving Quadratic Equations of the Form $ax^2 + bx + c = 0$ by Completing the Square

1. Add or subtract to put the constant term on the opposite side of the equation from the two variable terms.
2. Factor a from the variable terms.
3. Complete the square inside the parentheses. To the constant term add the product of the number used to complete the square and the factor a.
4. Write the expression inside parentheses as a perfect square of a binomial.
5. Divide both sides of the equation by a.
6. Take the square root of both sides.
7. Solve the resulting linear equations.
8. Check the results.

EXAMPLE 3 Solve $5x^2 - 40x - 25 = 0$ by completing the square.

Answer

$$5x^2 - 40x - 25 = 0$$
$$5x^2 - 40x = 25$$
$$5(x^2 - 8x) = 25$$
$$5(x^2 - 8x + 16) = 25 + 80$$
$$5(x - 4)^2 = 105$$
$$(x - 4)^2 = 21$$
$$\sqrt{(x - 4)^2} = \pm\sqrt{21}$$
$$x - 4 = \pm\sqrt{21}$$
$$x = 4 \pm \sqrt{21}$$

Can you explain the steps in this example?

▶ A. Exercises

What would be added to each side of the equation if you were solving by completing the square? Do not solve.

1. $2x^2 + 4x = 7$
2. $3x^2 + 18x = 2$
3. $-4x^2 - 8x = 18$
4. $4x^2 + 12x = -5$

Solve each quadratic equation by completing the square.

5. $2x^2 + 12x = 4$
6. $x^2 - 4x = 0$
7. $3x^2 - 12x = -3$
8. $4x^2 - 8x - 5 = 0$

▶ B. Exercises

Solve each quadratic equation by completing the square. Give the solution set.

9. $2x^2 + x = 3$

10. $2x^2 - x = 1$

11. $4x^2 - 4x = 11$

12. $2a^2 = -3a - 1$

Solve each equation by completing the square.

13. $6n^2 = 9n + 27$

14. $2x^2 - 6x = -1$

15. $2a^2 - a - 3 = 0$

16. $3z^2 - 2z - 8 = 0$

17. $2x^2 = 3x - 35$

18. $3x^2 = -8x - 5$

19. $2x^2 + 24x + 1 = 0$

20. $3t^2 + 24t + 1 = 0$

▶ C. Exercises

21. Solve $5x^2 + 24x + 1 = 0$.

22. The equation $x^4 + 3x^2 - 2 = 0$ can be solved by completing the square. Let $x^2 = y$ and substitute to get a quadratic equation in y and solve for y. Approximate y to two decimal places. Then try to find x from y.

■ Cumulative Review

23. Evaluate $3[2 \cdot 3 - 4 + (5 - 8) \div (-3)] - 4$.

24. Simplify $\sqrt[3]{378}$.

25. Simplify $(x^{-3})^{-2}$.

26. Evaluate $\left(\frac{1}{2}\right)^{-3} + (2^{-2})^3 + \frac{2}{3^{-4}}$.

27. Simplify $(2x + 5)^2 + \frac{1}{(2x + 5)^{-1}}$.

11.6 The Quadratic Formula

You can solve any quadratic equation by completing the square, but using a formula is much easier. Carefully study the development of the formula, making sure you understand each step.

The sparks from this industrial welding job trace curves called parabolas *that are described by quadratic equations.*

Consider a quadratic equation of the form $ax^2 + bx + c = 0$, in which a, b, and c are numerical coefficients and the constant term and $a \neq 0$. In order to develop the formula, solve for x by completing the square.

1. First subtract the constant term from each side.

   $$ax^2 + bx + c = 0$$
   $$ax^2 + bx = -c$$

2. Factor the a from the variable terms.

   $$a\left(x^2 + \frac{bx}{a}\right) = -c$$

3. Complete the square. Think $\frac{1}{2} \cdot \frac{b}{a} = \frac{b}{2a}$ and $\left(\frac{b}{2a}\right)^2 = \frac{b^2}{4a^2}$. Notice $\frac{b^2}{4a^2}$ is added inside the parentheses but $a\left(\frac{b^2}{4a^2}\right) = \frac{b^2}{4a}$, which is added to the right side.

   $$a\left(x^2 + \frac{bx}{a} + \frac{b^2}{4a^2}\right) = -c + \frac{b^2}{4a}$$

4. Write the perfect square on the left in factored form. Combine terms on the right using the common denominator $4a$.

   $$a\left(x + \frac{b}{2a}\right)^2 = -\frac{4ac}{4a} + \frac{b^2}{4a}$$

5. Rearrange the terms in the numerator so that the positive term appears first.

   $$a\left(x + \frac{b}{2a}\right)^2 = \frac{b^2 - 4ac}{4a}$$

Continued ▶

Multiply both sides by $\frac{1}{a}$ to eliminate the a factor outside the parentheses.	$\frac{1}{a} \cdot a\left(x + \frac{b}{2a}\right)^2 = \frac{1}{a}\left(\frac{b^2 - 4ac}{4a}\right)$
. Simplify.	$\left(x + \frac{b}{2a}\right)^2 = \frac{b^2 - 4ac}{4a^2}$
8. Find the square root of both sides. Since the denominator on the right is a perfect square, it can be removed from the radical sign by taking its root.	$\sqrt{\left(x + \frac{b}{2a}\right)^2} = \pm\sqrt{\frac{b^2 - 4ac}{4a^2}}$ $x + \frac{b}{2a} = \pm\frac{\sqrt{b^2 - 4ac}}{2a}$
9. To solve for x, subtract $\frac{b}{2a}$.	$x = -\frac{b}{2a} \pm \frac{\sqrt{b^2 - 4ac}}{2a}$
10. Since the fractions have like denominators, combine them.	$x = \frac{-b \pm \sqrt{b^2 - 4ac}}{2a}$

In step 1 you assume that you have a quadratic equation in the form $ax^2 + bx + c = 0$. In ten steps you prove that $x = \frac{-b \pm \sqrt{b^2 - 4ac}}{2a}$. Do you remember what a theorem is? You have just proved the theorem resulting in the quadratic formula.

Theorem

Quadratic formula. If $ax^2 + bx + c = 0$ where $a \neq 0$, then

$$x = \frac{-b \pm \sqrt{b^2 - 4ac}}{2a}.$$

Notice that the quadratic formula describes two answers because the root of a radical can be either positive or negative. Be sure to memorize this formula so that you can use it quickly to solve quadratic equations. Notice also that $-b$ should be read "opposite of b."

EXAMPLE 1 Use the quadratic formula to solve $x^2 - 5x - 6 = 0$.

Answer

$a = 1$ $b = -5$ $c = -6$ $x = \frac{-b \pm \sqrt{b^2 - 4ac}}{2a}$	1. Assign the numerical coefficients in this equation to the corresponding letters in the general quadratic equation form, $ax^2 + bx + c = 0$. Notice that each coefficient takes the sign preceding it.

Continued ▶

$$x = \frac{-(-5) \pm \sqrt{(-5)^2 - 4(1)(-6)}}{2(1)}$$

2. Substitute these values into the quadratic formula.

$$x = \frac{5 \pm \sqrt{25 + 24}}{2}$$

3. Simplify the radicand.

$$x = \frac{5 \pm \sqrt{49}}{2}$$

Notice that $-b = -(-5) = 5$.

$$x = \frac{5 \pm 7}{2}$$

$$x = \frac{5 + 7}{2} \quad \text{or} \quad x = \frac{5 - 7}{2}$$

4. Simplify the two answers separately.

$$x = \frac{12}{2} \quad \text{or} \quad x = \frac{-2}{2}$$

$$x = 6 \quad \text{or} \quad x = -1$$

The solution set is $\{-1, 6\}$.

If you solved this equation by factoring or by completing the square, you would get the same solution set. For the remainder of this section, however, use the quadratic formula. Later you can choose the method that you want to use. With practice, you will learn to recognize which equations can be more quickly solved by factoring or using the formula.

EXAMPLE 2 Use the quadratic formula to solve $3x^2 + 4x - 8 = 0$.

Answer

$a = 3$
$b = 4$
$c = -8$

1. Identify coefficients by letter.

$$x = \frac{-b \pm \sqrt{b^2 - 4ac}}{2a}$$

2. Substitute values into the quadratic formula and simplify.

$$x = \frac{-4 \pm \sqrt{(-4)^2 - 4(3)(-8)}}{2(3)}$$

$$x = \frac{-4 \pm \sqrt{16 + 96}}{6}$$

$$x = \frac{-4 \pm \sqrt{112}}{6}$$

3. Simplify the radical.

$$x = \frac{-4 \pm 4\sqrt{7}}{6}$$

$$x = \frac{2(-2 \pm 2\sqrt{7})}{6}$$

4. Since the LCM of -4, 4, and 6 is 2, factor a 2 from the numerator.

$$x = \frac{-2 \pm 2\sqrt{7}}{3}$$

5. Reduce $\frac{2}{6}$ to $\frac{1}{3}$.

The solution set is $\left\{ \frac{-2 + 2\sqrt{7}}{3}, \frac{-2 - 2\sqrt{7}}{3} \right\}$.

Solving Quadratic Equations by the Quadratic Formula

1. Arrange the equation in the form $ax^2 + bx + c = 0$.
2. Identify the values of a, b, and c from the equation.
3. Substitute these values into the quadratic formula and simplify.

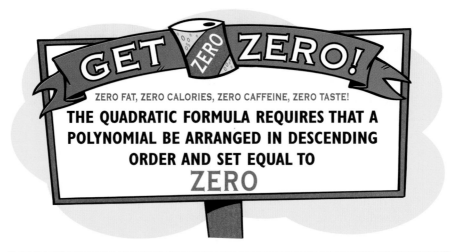

ZERO FAT, ZERO CALORIES, ZERO CAFFEINE, ZERO TASTE!

THE QUADRATIC FORMULA REQUIRES THAT A POLYNOMIAL BE ARRANGED IN DESCENDING ORDER AND SET EQUAL TO

ZERO

EXAMPLE 3 Use the quadratic formula to solve $5x^2 + 3x = 2$.

Answer

$$5x^2 + 3x = 2$$
$$5x^2 + 3x - 2 = 0$$
$$a = 5$$
$$b = 3$$
$$c = -2$$

1. Write the equation in the form $ax^2 + bx + c = 0$. Determine the values of a, b, and c.

$$x = \frac{-b \pm \sqrt{b^2 - 4ac}}{2a}$$

$$x = \frac{-3 \pm \sqrt{3^2 - 4(5)(-2)}}{2(5)}$$

2. Substitute these values into the quadratic formula.

$$x = \frac{-3 \pm \sqrt{9 + 40}}{10}$$

$$x = \frac{-3 \pm \sqrt{49}}{10}$$

$$x = \frac{-3 \pm 7}{10}$$

3. Simplify.

$$x = \frac{-3 + 7}{10} \quad \text{or} \quad x = \frac{-3 - 7}{10}$$

$$x = \frac{4}{10} \quad \text{or} \quad x = \frac{-10}{10}$$

$$x = \frac{2}{5} \quad \text{or} \quad x = -1$$

The solution set to this quadratic equation is $\left\{-1, \frac{2}{5}\right\}$.

A formula expresses a fundamental truth. It is very important that you, as a teenager, use the Bible as the formula book for your life. The Bible is full of fundamental truths. Jesus expressed one to Nicodemus in John 3:3. Read John 3:15-18. What fundamental truth is given in this passage? Find three more passages that give fundamental Bible truths.

▶ A. Exercises

Use the quadratic formula to find the solution set for each equation.

1. $x^2 + 6x + 8 = 0$
2. $x^2 + 4x + 3 = 0$
3. $x^2 + 8x + 15 = 0$
4. $x^2 - 9x + 20 = 0$
5. $x^2 - 9 = 0$
6. $x^2 - 9x = -8$
7. $2x^2 - x - 3 = 0$
8. $x^2 + 3x = 28$
9. $x^2 - 6x = -9$
10. $4x^2 - 5x - 9 = 0$

▶ B. Exercises

Use the quadratic formula to solve each equation.

11. $2x^2 - 9x + 4 = 0$
12. $3x^2 = 2x + 5$
13. $2x^2 - 5x - 10 = 0$
14. $4y^2 - 3y = 8$
15. $7m^2 + 9m = -2$
16. $15x^2 + 22x + 8 = 0$
17. $-3k^2 + 2k + 10 = 0$
18. $4x^2 + 4x + 3 = 0$
19. $8x^2 = 26x + 7$
20. $5r^2 - 7 = 2r$

▶ C. Exercises

Use the quadratic formula to solve each equation. Estimate answers rounded to the nearest hundredth.

21. $-2.5x^2 + 7.4x - 3.8 = 0$
22. $\frac{2}{3}x^2 - \frac{4}{5}x - \frac{1}{2} = 0$

Cumulative Review

Simplify.

23. $x + x$
24. $x \cdot x$
25. $\frac{x}{x}$
26. $x - x$

27. Sara bought a dress for $43 after obtaining a 23% discount. How much was the dress originally?

Empirical Rule

Many sets of numbers that occur in nature, manufacturing, and educational testing can be represented graphically by a mound-shaped curve. This curve shown in the diagram below is often called a *normal curve*.

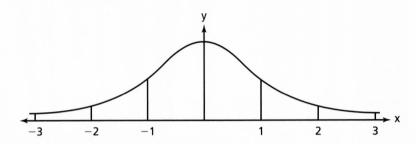

Notice that in this distribution the average or mean ($\bar{x}$) is in the center of the distribution and three standard deviations (1s, 2s, and 3s) are shown on each side of the mean. The graph shows that most students score near the average and few students score either very high or very low. When a set of numbers forms a mound-shaped distribution such as this, the *Empirical Rule* applies to the distribution.

Empirical Rule

Given a mound-shaped distribution of numbers, the approximate percentage of scores will be contained in the following intervals as follows:

$$\bar{x} \pm 1s \qquad 68\%$$

$$\bar{x} \pm 2s \qquad 95\%$$

$$\bar{x} \pm 3s \qquad 100\%$$

The $\bar{x} \pm 1s$ means the lower bound of the interval is $\bar{x} - 1s$ and the upper bound of the interval is $\bar{x} + 1s$.

This rule applies to situations such as the height and weight of people or the size of parts made by a machine in a factory.

EXAMPLE 1 The average weight of a Boston terrier is 19 pounds with a standard deviation of 3 pounds. If the distribution of weights is approximately mound shaped, what percentage of Boston terriers weigh between 13 and 25 pounds?

Answer 1. Convert 13 to a number of standard deviations from the mean (z-score). Since $\bar{x} = 19$ and $s = 3$,

$$z = \frac{13 - 19}{3} = -2.$$

2. Convert 25 to a z-score: $\frac{25 - 19}{3} = 2.$

So, the interval 13 to 25 corresponds to $\bar{x} \pm 2s$. By the Empirical Rule 95% of all Boston terriers weigh between 13 and 25 pounds.

EXAMPLE 2 If there are 254 Boston terriers in the Kennel Club, approximately how many of them will weigh between 13 and 25 pounds?

Answer Find 95% of 254: (.95)(254) = 241.3.

Approximately 241 of the 254 Boston terriers weigh between 13 and 25 pounds.

▶ Exercises

Use the following information to answer the questions. The average cost of operating a car is 34.5 cents per mile and the standard deviation is 3.4 cents per mile. Assume the distribution has a mound-shaped curve.

1. What percentage of cars cost between 31.1 and 37.9 cents per mile to operate?

2. What percentage of cars cost between 24.3 and 44.7 cents per mile to operate?

3. If a large company owns 3249 cars, how many of them cost between 27.7 and 41.3 cents per mile to operate?

4. What percent of cars cost between 34.5 and 41.3 cents per mile to operate?

5. How many of the 3249 cars cost between 27.7 and 37.9 cents per mile to operate?

11.7 Solving Quadratic Equations

When you solve a quadratic equation, choose the method that is easiest and most appropriate for that particular problem.

Joern Utzon designed the "sails" of Australia's Sydney Opera House using a pair of shells, each represented by a quadratic equation.

General Method of Solving Quadratic Equations

1. Place the quadratic equation in the form $ax^2 + bx + c = 0$.
2. If $b = 0$, use the square root method.
3. If the polynomial factors, solve the equation by factoring.
4. Otherwise use the quadratic formula.

Although you never need to complete the square in order to solve quadratic equations, you may still be asked specifically to use it to solve some problems. Its primary importance is in developing the quadratic formula, and it will also be useful for graphing in Chapter 14. Therefore, unless you are instructed to complete the square, you should use one of the other three methods.

▶ A. Exercises

Use any method to find the solution set for each quadratic equation.

1. $a^2 - 2a - 8 = 0$
2. $x^2 - 3x - 5 = 0$
3. $3a^2 + 13a = -4$
4. $x^2 + x = 2$
5. $x^2 - 15x + 54 = 0$
6. $x^2 - 21 = 4x$
7. $6y^2 = 13y - 2$
8. $4x^2 - 5x - 9 = 0$

Use any method to solve each quadratic equation.

9. $2x^2 - 7x + 2 = 0$
10. $x^2 + 2x + 9 = 0$
11. $3a^2 - 5 = -2a$
12. $x^2 + 12x - 45 = 0$
13. $4r^2 - 5 = r$
14. $q^2 + 9q - 4 = 0$
15. $2x^2 + 4x - 6 = 0$
16. $a^2 + 3a = -1$

▶ B. Exercises

Use any method to solve each quadratic equation.

17. $x^2 + 8x - 2 = 0$

18. $x^2 + 3x - 2 = 0$

19. $-t^2 + 4 = 0$

20. $a^2 + 44a + 2 = 0$

21. $x^2 - 4x + 2 = 0$

22. $(3x + 4)(2x - 5) = 4$

23. $(x + 5)(2x - 7) = 9$

24. $(3x - 1)^2 + 6 = 0$

25. $x(5x - 9) + 6 = 0$

26. $(x - 2)^2 + (x - 5) + 1 = 0$

27. $(y + 4)^2 - y(y + 2) = 9$

28. $(x - 6)(x + 2) - (x - 6) = 9$

▶ C. Exercises

Find x rounded to 3 decimal places.

29. $2x^2 - 7x - 8 = 0$

30. $(x - 1)^2 - (3x + 2)(x - 5) = 0$

■ Cumulative Review

31. Solve $\sqrt{5x + 2} = 4$.

32. Name the property: if $ab = 0$, then $a = 0$ or $b = 0$.

33. Graph $y = \frac{-5}{3}x + 7$.

34. Simplify $2\sqrt{3} + 5\sqrt{12} + 7\sqrt{2} + \sqrt{27}$.

35. The perimeter of a rectangle is 98 cm. The length is 2 cm less than 3 times the width. Find the dimensions.

11.8 Word Problems Using Quadratic Equations

A carpenter wants to fit three boards together to form a right triangle to use as a brace. The hypotenuse must be 3 feet longer than one leg and 5 feet longer than the other leg.

EXAMPLE 1 Find the measurements for the sides of the triangle needed by the carpenter. Use the Pythagorean theorem and approximate your answer to the nearest hundredth.

Answer You can solve the above problem using the methods you have learned in this chapter. First, review how to set up word problems (p. 136).

Sketch a right triangle, label the legs *a* and *b* and the hypotenuse *c*.

Now introduce the variables.

> Let x = the hypotenuse
> $x - 3$ = one leg
> $x - 5$ = the other leg

Substitute these variables into the Pythagorean theorem and solve the resulting quadratic equation.

$$a^2 + b^2 = c^2$$
$$(x - 5)^2 + (x - 3)^2 = x^2$$
$$x^2 - 10x + 25 + x^2 - 6x + 9 = x^2$$
$$x^2 - 16x + 34 = 0$$

$$x = \frac{-b \pm \sqrt{b^2 - 4ac}}{2a}$$

Now substitute values into the quadratic formula and evaluate.

$$x = \frac{16 \pm \sqrt{(-16)^2 - 4(1)(34)}}{2(1)}$$

$$x = \frac{16 \pm \sqrt{256 - 136}}{2}$$

$$x = \frac{16 \pm \sqrt{120}}{2}$$

$$x = \frac{16 \pm 2\sqrt{30}}{2}$$

$$x = \frac{2(8 \pm \sqrt{30})}{2}$$

$$x = 8 \pm \sqrt{30}$$

$x \approx 8 \pm 5.48$	Approximate $\sqrt{30}$ so that
$x \approx 8 + 5.48$ $\qquad x \approx 8 - 5.48$	a value for the hypotenuse
$x \approx 13.48$ $\qquad\quad x \approx 2.52$	can be determined.
$x - 3 \approx 10.48$ $\qquad x - 3 \approx -0.48$	
$x - 5 \approx 8.48$ $\qquad x - 5 \approx -2.48$	

The only sensible solution for the hypotenuse is **13.48** feet (13 feet $5\frac{3}{4}$ inches) because **2.52** feet would give negative values for both legs, which is impossible. So **13.48** feet is the length of the hypotenuse, **10.48** feet is the length of one leg, and **8.48** feet is the length of the other leg.

Look again at this problem, this time considering the formulas and processes you had to learn and apply in order to solve it.

1. Represent the dimensions using variables.
2. Apply the Pythagorean theorem.
3. Apply the quadratic formula to solve for *x*.
4. Approximate a square root.

Much of what you learn this year applies to practical problems. Algebra will help you not only in math classes throughout high school and college but also in your future career. You will apply your ability to reason abstractly to problems and issues that you cannot now imagine. Likewise, you should apply your knowledge of Scripture to every decision in life: "be ye doers of the word, and not hearers only" (cf. James 1:22). Do you let the Word of God mold your life, or do you deceive yourself?

EXAMPLE 2   Your dad has asked you to build a rectangular dog pen that contains **600** square feet and is **10** feet longer than it is wide. How much fencing will you need to build the pen?

Answer   Since you want the area to be **600** square feet, you can set up an equation using the formula $A = lw$. Using *w* for width,

$$\text{let } w = \text{the width}$$
$$w + 10 = \text{the length}$$
$$w(w + 10) = 600$$
$$w^2 + 10w - 600 = 0$$
$$(w + 30)(w - 20) = 0$$
$$w + 30 = 0 \quad \text{or} \quad w - 20 = 0$$
$$w = -30 \qquad\qquad w = 20$$

The only positive answer is **20**; therefore, the width is to be **20** feet and the length is $w + 10$ or **30** feet.

Since perimeter is found by $P = 2l + 2w$, we need $2(30) + 2(20) = 100$ feet of fencing.

▶ A. Exercises

The box shown has no top. Use the dimensions of the box to find the following:

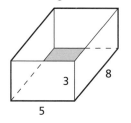

1. the perimeter of the bottom
2. the area of the bottom
3. the volume
4. the surface area
5. the dimensions of the cardboard needed to make the box by cutting out squares from the corners and folding up the sides

The box shown has no top. Use variables to express the following:

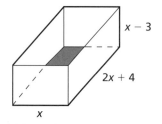

6. the perimeter of the bottom
7. the area of the bottom
8. the volume
9. the surface area

10. Using the variable x, express the three dimensions of a box in two ways if the length of the box is two units longer than three times the width, and the width is seven less than the height. For the first set of answers, let x equal the height. For the second set of answers, let x equal the width.

▶ B. Exercises

Solve, using a quadratic equation.

11. The difference of two numbers is 6, and their product is 216. Find the two numbers.
12. The width of a rectangular patio is 4 feet less than the length. What are the dimensions if the area is 96 square feet?
13. One integer is 2 less than eight times another. The difference of their squares is 884. Find the integers.
14. If one side of a square is increased by 3 inches and the adjacent side is decreased by 1 inch, the rectangle formed has an area of 77 square inches. Find the length of a side of the square.
15. The hypotenuse of a right triangle is 8 inches more than one leg and 3 inches more than the other leg. To the nearest tenth, find the lengths of the sides of the triangle.

16. A box is to be made from a sheet of cardboard 24 inches long and 18 inches wides by cutting squares from each corner and then folding the cardboard up. What is the length of a side of the squares that should be cut out of each corner if the bottom of the box is to have an area of 265 square inches?

17. Mr. Smith is taking the scouts camping, and he has a rope that is to reach from a stake in the ground to the top of a tent pole. If the pole is 8 feet high and the rope is 12 feet long, how far from the pole should he place the stake to make the rope taut?

18. A baseball diamond is a square with an area of 8100 square feet. How far does a catcher have to throw the ball to throw out a runner who is trying to steal second base?

▶ C. Exercises

19. What are the dimensions of a rectangle whose perimeter is 54 inches and whose area is 180 square inches?

20. A rectangular piece of cardboard is made into a box by cutting 3-inch squares from each corner and then folding the cardboard up. The length of the cardboard is 3 inches more than the width. If the volume ($V = lwh$) of the box is 540 cubic inches, what are the dimensions of the original cardboard?

Cumulative Review

21. What property allows you to complete the square on a quadratic equation.

Give the standard form for the following.

22. a linear equation

23. a quadratic equation

24. Simplify $52^{-\frac{1}{2}}$.

25. The sum of three consecutive odd numbers is 333. Find the numbers.

Algebra *and* Scripture

In previous chapters you studied the principles of multiplication, division, and addition in the Bible. Remember that subtraction is the inverse of addition; it is the same as adding the opposite. This is why negative numbers and subtraction are so closely related.

1. Write the subtraction problem from I Kings 6:37-38.
2. Write the subtraction problem from Luke 15:4.
3. Write the subtraction problem from Genesis 18:28.

You recently studied the importance of learning fundamental truths (p. 467) and then applying them (p. 467). You have often applied the concept of subtraction in this book: you subtracted fractions, polynomials, and radicals, and you learned the subtraction properties of equality, inequality, and exponents. Even in this chapter you used subtraction in the quadratic formula to write both solutions ($\pm$). In the Scriptures, the men of Israel applied subtraction to calculate land values for sanctification and redemption.

4. Imagine that Jesse desires to sanctify some land sixteen years after a year of Jubilee; according to Leviticus 25:8-13 and 27:18, what subtraction must he perform in the process of valuation?

Now consider the subtraction of Judas from the apostles.

THE NTH DEGREE

Find a passage listing the twelve apostles and giving their number.

5. What number is used in Mark 14:10 to describe Judas?

6. After Judas betrayed the Lord and hung himself, how do the gospels refer to the apostles (Matt. 28:16; Mark 16:14; Luke 24:9, 33)?

7. What equation represents exercises 5 and 6?

Finally notice that the replacement of Judas by Matthias in Acts 1:15-26 was an addition of one for the purpose of undoing the loss of one. Acts 2:14 shows Peter with the eleven—a total of twelve again.

8. What property does $12 - 1 + 1 = 12 + 0$ illustrate?

Scriptural Roots

PERADVENTURE THERE shall lack five of the fifty righteous: wilt thou destroy all the city for lack of five? And he said, If I find there forty and five, I will not destroy it. 🌿

GENESIS 18:28

Solve by factoring.
1. $(x - 2)(x + 3) = 0$
2. $x^2 + 3x - 10 = 0$
3. $8x^3 - 2x = 0$

Solve by the root method.
4. $x^2 = 6$
5. $3x^2 - 7 = 5$
6. $(x - 4)^2 = 11$

Identify a, b, and c for substitution into the quadratic formula. Do not solve.
7. $x^2 + 4x - 1 = 0$
8. $3x^2 = 2 + x$

Solve using the quadratic formula.
9. $x^2 - 6x + 2 = 0$
10. $3x^2 + 2x - 5 = 0$
11. $4x^2 - 5 = 2x + 1$

Solve by completing the square.
12. $x^2 + 8x + 7 = 0$
13. $x^2 + 5x = 3$
14. $2x^2 - 20x - 5 = 0$

Solve using any method (except completing the square). Give the solution set.
15. $a^2 = 16$
16. $2x^2 + 8x + 9 = 0$
17. $(x - 7)(x + 2) = 0$
18. $x^2 - 9 = 0$
19. $a + 3 = a^2 - 2$
20. $x(5x - 8) = 0$
21. $\sqrt{x + 7} - x = 5$
22. $x^2 + 6x + 9 = 0$

Solve using any method (except completing the square).

23. $y^2 - 17 = 0$
24. $\sqrt{x^2 + 2} = 3$
25. $x^2 - 5x - 24 = 0$
26. $p^2 - 14p - 8 = 0$
27. $5a^2 + 3a = -6$
28. $x + 8 = x^2 - 3$
29. $2x^2 + 9x - 56 = 0$
30. $\sqrt{x} = 2 - x$
31. $a^2 + 7a - 12 = 0$
32. The difference of two numbers is 19; their product is -84. Find the two numbers.
33. The area of a rectangular piece of concrete is 120 square feet, and its perimeter is 46 feet. What are the dimensions of the rectangle?
34. What is the mathematical significance of Genesis 18:28?

12 Rational Expressions

$$y = mx + b$$

Passengers screamed as the roller coaster crested its highest hill and began its descent. At the bottom the riders felt a sinking feeling under a force twice as strong as gravity. Then the coaster sped on through hair-raising bends and dizzying corkscrews.

Roller coaster designers know that a force of 2g is obtained at the bottom of that first hill. In other words, the acceleration at that point is twice the acceleration caused by the pull of gravity and is represented by the formula $a = 2g$. This g force causes the riders to feel the sinking sensation. A 100-pound person is pressed down in his seat with a force of 200 pounds, or 2 g's. The designers doubled the maximum total weight of train and riders to find the force exerted on the track at the end of that first breathtaking drop.

The formula for finding force is $f = \left(\frac{w}{g}\right)a$, where f is the force in pounds, w is the weight in pounds, g is the acceleration caused by gravity (32 ft./sec.^{2}), and a is the acceleration of the moving body. If the coaster can withstand 20,400 pounds of force at the bottom of the big dip accelerating at 64 ft./sec.^{2}, what is the weight per person that designers are allowing for the train and riders?

The force equation contains a rational expression, which you will learn to solve by the end of this ride, uh, chapter. So hang on. Here we go!

After this chapter you should be able to

1. tell when a rational expression will be undefined.

2. simplify rational expressions.

3. multiply and divide rational expressions.

4. add and subtract rational expressions.

5. simplify complex rational expressions.

12.1 Simplifying Rational Expressions

Recall that a rational number is defined as a ratio whose denominator is not zero. Similarly, a rational expression is a ratio of polynomials whose denominator is not zero.

Definition

A **rational expression** is an expression of the form $\frac{P_1}{P_2}$ in which P_1 and P_2 are polynomials and $P_2 \neq 0$.

A few rational expressions are given below. Notice that expressions 1, 3, and 6 have the same degree of polynomial in the numerator as in the denominator. Expressions 2 and 4 have a higher degree in the numerator while expression 5 has a higher degree in the denominator. See page 325 to review degrees of polynomials.

When a larger tube tapers into a smaller one, the taper per inch T is $T = \frac{D - d}{L}$, where L is the length of pipe and D and d are the larger and smaller diameters respectively.

1. $\dfrac{x}{x+2}$

2. $\dfrac{x-4}{5}$

3. $\dfrac{x+6}{x-9}$

4. $\dfrac{3x^2 + 4x - 5}{x}$

5. $\dfrac{x+7}{x^2 + 3x - 9}$

6. $\dfrac{2x^2 + 3x + 6}{x^2 - 8x + 7}$

What would happen in expression 1 if x had a value of -2? Substituting -2 for x, you get $\frac{-2}{-2+2}$, which simplifies to $\frac{-2}{0}$. Since you have already learned that division by 0 is undefined, the rational expression is undefined when $x = -2$. Notice that the variable can equal 0, but the polynomial in the denominator cannot equal 0.

To determine when a rational expression is undefined, you must determine what values of x will make the denominator zero. In expression 2, the denominator has no variables. Since $5 \neq 0$, the rational expression is always defined.

EXAMPLE 1 Determine when the other four expressions (3-6) are undefined.

Answer

3. $\dfrac{x+6}{x-9}$

$x - 9 = 0$

$x = 9$

$\dfrac{x+6}{x-9}$ is undefined

when $x = 9$

4. $\dfrac{3x^2 + 4x - 5}{x}$

$x = 0$

$\dfrac{3x^2 + 4x - 5}{x}$ is undefined

when $x = 0$

5. $\dfrac{x+7}{x^2 + 3x - 9}$

$x^2 + 3x - 9 = 0$

$x = \dfrac{-3 \pm \sqrt{3^2 - 4(1)(-9)}}{2(1)}$

$= \dfrac{-3 \pm \sqrt{45}}{2}$

$= \dfrac{-3 \pm 3\sqrt{5}}{2}$

$\dfrac{x+7}{x^2 + 3x - 9}$ is undefined

when $x = \dfrac{-3 \pm 3\sqrt{5}}{2}$

6. $\dfrac{2x^2 + 3x + 6}{x^2 - 8x + 7}$

$x^2 - 8x + 7 = 0$

$(x - 7)(x - 1) = 0$

$x - 7 = 0$ or $x - 1 = 0$

$x = 7$ or $\quad x = 1$

$\dfrac{2x^2 + 3x + 6}{x^2 - 8x + 7}$ is undefined

when $x = 7$ or $x = 1$

Do you recall how to reduce a fraction such as $\frac{12}{15}$ to lowest terms? First, find common factors of both the numerator and the denominator and then cancel all common factors. When you cancel, you are actually dividing both the numerator and the denominator by the same number. Simplifying is based on the fundamental principle of fractions that you learned in Chapter 2. That principle states that if a is an integer and b and c are nonzero integers, $\frac{a}{b} = \frac{ac}{bc}$.

EXAMPLE 2 Simplify $\frac{4a^3}{8a}$.

Answer Factor and cancel like factors.

$\dfrac{4a^3}{8a}$

$\dfrac{4 \cdot a \cdot a^2}{4 \cdot 2 \cdot a}$

$\dfrac{a^2}{2}$

EXAMPLE 3 Simplify $\frac{180m^3n^2}{27mn}$.

Answer $\dfrac{180m^3n^2}{27mn}$

$\dfrac{9 \cdot 20m^2 \cdot mn \cdot n}{9 \cdot 3 \cdot mn}$

$\dfrac{20m^2n}{3}$

EXAMPLE 4   Simplify $\dfrac{4x^2 + 4x - 48}{x - 3}$, leaving your answer in factored form.

Answer $\dfrac{4x^2 + 4x - 48}{x - 3}$ Factor each polynomial completely.

$\dfrac{4(x^2 + x - 12)}{x - 3}$

$\dfrac{4(x + 4)(x - 3)}{x - 3}$ Cancel common factors.

$4(x + 4)$

EXAMPLE 5   Simplify $\dfrac{x^2 - 4}{x^2 + 4x + 4}$.

Answer $\dfrac{x^2 - 4}{x^2 + 4x + 4}$

$\dfrac{(x + 2)(x - 2)}{(x + 2)(x + 2)}$

$\dfrac{x - 2}{x + 2}$

► A. Exercises

State the value or values for which the rational expression is undefined.

1. $\dfrac{3x + 4}{x}$

2. $\dfrac{x^2 - 3}{x + 4}$

3. $\dfrac{x - 7}{x + 2}$

4. $\dfrac{x + 8}{x - 5}$

5. $\dfrac{x^2 + 3x - 2}{x^2 + 5x - 24}$

6. $\dfrac{x - 5}{x^3 - 3x^2 - 4x}$

7. $\dfrac{x - 7}{x^2 + 7x - 18}$

8. $\dfrac{x + 4}{x^2 - 5x - 24}$

► B. Exercises

Simplify each rational expression, leaving answers in factored form.

9. $\dfrac{3x^2}{15x}$

10. $\dfrac{24x^2y^3}{8xy}$

11. $\dfrac{15a^3bc^2}{27abc^4}$

12. $\dfrac{5xyz + 5z}{10x^2y^2 - 10}$

13. $\dfrac{2x + 3}{2x + 3}$

14. $\dfrac{3x^2 + 3xy}{x^2 - y^2}$

15. $\dfrac{x^3 - 3x^2 - 10x}{x^3 + 2x^2}$

16. $\dfrac{2x - 3}{2x + 3}$

17. $\dfrac{15x^2 - 100x + 60}{3x^2 + x - 2}$

18. $\dfrac{3x^5y - 3x^4y - 60x^3y}{9x^4 + 36x^3}$

19. $\dfrac{2x^2 + x - 45}{9 - 11x + 2x^2}$

20. $\dfrac{x^7y^2 + x^6y^2 - 6x^5y^2}{x^5 - 9x^3}$

Simplify each rational expression, leaving answers in factored form.

21. $\dfrac{x^5 + x^4 - 4x^3 - 4x^2}{x^5 + 4x^4 + 4x^3}$

22. $\dfrac{48x^2 + 34x - 5}{1 - 8x}$ (*Hint:* Factor -1 from denominator.)

■ **Cumulative Review**

23. Graph $\left(-\frac{2}{3}, 2.5\right)$.

24. Solve for m: $mp - r = 0$.

25. Solve for s: $ns^2 + ms + q = 0$.

26. Simplify $\dfrac{3x^2 y \sqrt{20}}{9xy \sqrt{6}}$.

27. Simplify $3^{-1} + 5^{-1}$.

28. Give the slope and the y-intercept of $3x - 5y = 11$.

12.2 Multiplying Rational Expressions

The basic rule for multiplication of rationals is to multiply the numerators and divide by the product of the denominators. You can multiply first and then cancel or cancel first and then multiply. Do you remember which is faster?

A player's batting average is .314, which is calculated using a rational expression $A = \frac{H}{B}$, *where H is the number of hits and B is times at bat.*

EXAMPLE 1 Multiply $\frac{5}{9} \cdot \frac{27}{40}$.

Answer $\dfrac{\cancel{5}}{\cancel{9}} \cdot \dfrac{\overset{3}{\cancel{27}}}{\underset{8}{\cancel{40}}} = \dfrac{3}{8}$

You can multiply rational expressions in the same way. As with rational numbers, it will save time to cancel first.

EXAMPLE 2   Simplify $\dfrac{3a}{2ab} \cdot \dfrac{12a}{18bc}$.

Answer

$$\dfrac{3a}{2ab} \cdot \dfrac{12a}{18bc} \qquad \text{1. Cancel common factors.}$$

$$\dfrac{3\!\!\!/a}{2\!\!\!/ab} \quad \dfrac{\overset{6}{1\!\!\!/2}a}{1\!\!\!/8bc} \qquad \text{2. Multiply.}$$

$$\dfrac{a}{b^2c}$$

EXAMPLE 3   Multiply $\dfrac{5x^2y}{2x^3yz} \cdot \dfrac{24xy^2z^5}{10xy}$.

Answer

$$\dfrac{5x^2y}{2x^3yz} \cdot \dfrac{24xy^2z^5}{10xy}$$

$$\dfrac{\overset{1}{5\!\!\!/}\,\overset{1}{x^2}\,\overset{1}{y\!\!\!/}}{\underset{1}{2\!\!\!/}\,\underset{x}{x^3}\,\underset{1}{y\!\!\!/}\,\underset{1}{z\!\!\!/}} \cdot \dfrac{\overset{6}{\overset{}{2\!\!\!/4}}\,\overset{1}{x\!\!\!/}\,\overset{y}{y^2}\,\overset{z^4}{z^5}}{\underset{\underset{1}{2\!\!\!/}}{10}\,\underset{1}{x\!\!\!/}\,\underset{1}{y\!\!\!/}}$$

$$\dfrac{6yz^4}{x}$$

Multiplying Rational Expressions

1. Factor all algebraic quantities in the numerators and denominators.
   Constants may be reduced without breaking them up into a product of
   primes.
2. Simplify the expressions by dividing (canceling) common factors that
   appear both in a numerator and a denominator.
3. Multiply the numerators and divide by the product of the denominators.

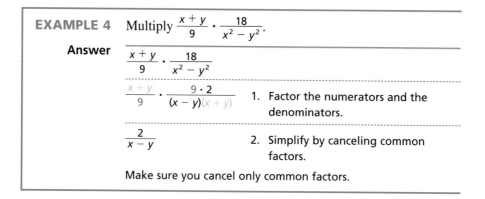

EXAMPLE 4   Multiply $\dfrac{x + y}{9} \cdot \dfrac{18}{x^2 - y^2}$.

Answer

$$\dfrac{x + y}{9} \cdot \dfrac{18}{x^2 - y^2}$$

$$\dfrac{x + y}{9} \cdot \dfrac{9 \cdot 2}{(x - y)(x + y)} \qquad \text{1. Factor the numerators and the}$$
$$\text{denominators.}$$

$$\dfrac{2}{x - y} \qquad \text{2. Simplify by canceling common}$$
$$\text{factors.}$$

Make sure you cancel only common factors.

EXAMPLE 5 Simplify $(x^3 - x^2 - 72x) \cdot \dfrac{3}{x^2 + x - 56}$, leaving the answer in factored form.

Answer $(x^3 - x^2 - 72x) \cdot \dfrac{3}{x^2 + x - 56}$

$x(x^2 - x - 72) \cdot \dfrac{3}{(x + 8)(x - 7)}$ Factor the numerators and denominators; then simplify.

$\dfrac{x(x + 8)(x - 9)}{1} \cdot \dfrac{3}{(x + 8)(x - 7)}$

$\dfrac{3x(x - 9)}{x - 7}$

▶ A. Exercises

Multiply.

1. $\dfrac{2}{5} \cdot \dfrac{19}{28}$

2. $\dfrac{16}{9} \cdot \dfrac{27}{8}$

3. $\dfrac{4}{11} \cdot \dfrac{33}{32}$

4. $\dfrac{2a}{3} \cdot \dfrac{9}{16}$

5. $\dfrac{3a^2}{17b} \cdot \dfrac{34b^2}{6ab}$

6. $\dfrac{5x^2y}{18xy} \cdot \dfrac{3y^3}{9y}$

7. $\dfrac{x^3yz^2}{xy} \cdot \dfrac{x^4y}{x^9y^2z}$

8. $\dfrac{32a^2b}{xy^3} \cdot \dfrac{2xy}{8a^2}$

9. $\dfrac{(x + 2)}{5} \cdot \dfrac{25}{(x + 2)}$

10. $\dfrac{(x - 3)(x + 4)}{x - 1} \cdot \dfrac{x - 1}{(x - 4)(x - 3)}$

▶ B. Exercises

Multiply, leaving your answer in factored form.

11. $\dfrac{x^2 - 5x - 14}{8} \cdot \dfrac{4}{x - 7}$

12. $\dfrac{x^2 + 3x - 18}{x^2 - x} \cdot \dfrac{x^3y}{xy - 3y}$

13. $\dfrac{x^2 + 10x + 16}{x - 4} \cdot \dfrac{x^2 - x - 12}{x + 2}$

14. $\dfrac{x^2 - x - 20}{x^2 - 6x + 5} \cdot \dfrac{x + 3}{x^2 + 7x + 12}$

15. $\dfrac{2x^2 - xy - y^2}{x^2 - y^2} \cdot \dfrac{x^2 + 2xy + y^2}{3x^2 - xy - 4y^2}$

16. $\dfrac{x - 2}{x^3 - 5x^2 + 6x} \cdot \dfrac{xy^2}{xy + 4y}$

17. $\dfrac{a^2 + ab - 2b^2}{a^2 - b^2} \cdot \dfrac{a^2 - 2ab - 3b^2}{a^2 - 3ab}$

18. $\dfrac{2m^2 - mn - 3n^2}{m - n} \cdot \dfrac{m^2 - n^2}{2m^2 - 5mn + 3n^2}$

19. $\dfrac{3x^2 - 19xy + 20y^2}{x + y} \cdot \dfrac{y + x}{2x^2 - 11xy + 5y^2}$

20. $\dfrac{3x^2 - 11xy - 4y^2}{x^3y - 4x^2y^2} \cdot \dfrac{x^2y - 3xy^2}{3x + y}$

21. $\dfrac{3x^2 + xy - 2y^2}{2x^2 - 3xy + y^2} \cdot \dfrac{2x^2 + xy - y^2}{x^2 + 2xy + y^2}$

22. $\dfrac{a^2 + 7ab + 10b^2}{a^2 + ab - 2b^2} \cdot \dfrac{3a^2 - 7ab + 4b^2}{3a^2 + 11ab - 20b^2}$

23. $\dfrac{(x + 3)(x - 2)}{x^2y} \cdot \dfrac{xy}{(x - 2)(x + 5)} \cdot \dfrac{x(x + 5)}{x + 3}$

24. $\dfrac{x^2 - 7x - 18}{x + 4} \cdot \dfrac{x^2 - 5x + 6}{x - 9} \cdot \dfrac{x + 4}{x - 3}$

25. $\dfrac{ax^2}{ax + x} \cdot \dfrac{a^2 - 1}{x}$

26. $\dfrac{x - 1}{x + 3} \cdot \dfrac{x^2 + 9x + 1}{x - 3} \cdot \dfrac{x^2 + x + 1}{x^2 + 9x + 1}$

▶ C. Exercises

Multiply.

27. $\dfrac{x^4 + x^3 - 6x^2}{xy^3 - 2y^3} \cdot \dfrac{x^2 + 2x - 15}{x^2 + 8x + 15} \cdot \dfrac{y^2}{x^3}$

28. $\dfrac{a^2 + 2ab - 3b^2}{a^2b^3} \cdot \dfrac{4ab^4}{a^2 + 8ab + 15b^2} \cdot \dfrac{a^2 + 3ab - 10b^2}{a + 7b}$

■ Cumulative Review

29. Solve $\frac{24}{25}x + 7 = x - \frac{3}{10}$.

30. Simplify $(\sqrt{26} - 4\sqrt{2})(2\sqrt{13} + 5)$.

31. Find the slope of a line parallel to $7x = 4 - 5y$.

32. One less than the square root of one more than a number is 10. Find the number.

33. Graph $2x + 3y = 15$.

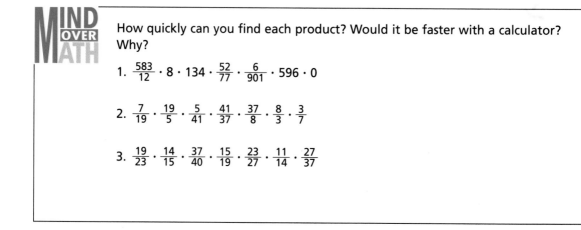

MIND OVER MATH

How quickly can you find each product? Would it be faster with a calculator? Why?

1. $\dfrac{583}{12} \cdot 8 \cdot 134 \cdot \dfrac{52}{77} \cdot \dfrac{6}{901} \cdot 596 \cdot 0$

2. $\dfrac{7}{19} \cdot \dfrac{19}{5} \cdot \dfrac{5}{41} \cdot \dfrac{41}{37} \cdot \dfrac{37}{8} \cdot \dfrac{8}{3} \cdot \dfrac{3}{7}$

3. $\dfrac{19}{23} \cdot \dfrac{14}{15} \cdot \dfrac{37}{40} \cdot \dfrac{15}{19} \cdot \dfrac{23}{27} \cdot \dfrac{11}{14} \cdot \dfrac{27}{37}$

12.3 Dividing Rational Expressions

To divide rational expressions, you must multiply by the reciprocal. The term *reciprocal* refers to a mutual exchange. In math, the reciprocal is an exchange between the numerator and denominator. Christians must also maintain reciprocal relationships, displaying a mutual love for one another (John 13:34). We must receive and admonish one another (Rom. 15:7, 14), forbear and forgive one another (Eph. 4:2, 32), comfort and edify one another (1 Thess. 4:18; 5:11), and serve and submit to one another (1 Peter 4:10; 5:5).

When you divide rational numbers, such as $\frac{1}{2} \div \frac{7}{4}$, find the reciprocal of the second fraction (the divisor) and multiply. So $\frac{1}{2} \div \frac{7}{4} = \frac{1}{2} \cdot \frac{4}{7} = \frac{2}{7}$. Follow this same procedure when you divide rational expressions.

EXAMPLE 1 Divide $\frac{x^2}{3y^2} \div \frac{x}{9y}$.

Answer $\frac{x^2}{3y^2} \div \frac{x}{9y}$

$\frac{x^2}{3y^2} \cdot \frac{9y}{x}$ ⟶ Invert the divisor and multiply.

$\frac{\overset{x}{\cancel{x^2}}}{\underset{y}{\cancel{3y^2}}} \cdot \frac{\overset{3}{\cancel{9y}}}{\cancel{x}}$

$\frac{3x}{y}$

EXAMPLE 2 Simplify $\dfrac{(x + y)^2}{x^2 - 4xy + 4y^2} \div \dfrac{9}{x^2 - xy - 2y^2}$.

Leave the answer in factored form.

Answer $\dfrac{(x + y)^2}{x^2 - 4xy + 4y^2} \div \dfrac{9}{x^2 - xy - 2y^2}$.

$\dfrac{(x + y)^2}{x^2 - 4xy + 4y^2} \cdot \dfrac{x^2 - xy - 2y^2}{9}$ ⟶ Invert the divisor and multiply.

$\dfrac{(x + y)(x + y)}{\cancel{(x - 2y)}(x - 2y)} \cdot \dfrac{\cancel{(x - 2y)}(x + y)}{9}$

$\dfrac{(x + y)^3}{9(x - 2y)}$

Dividing Rational Expressions

1. Invert the divisor and multiply.
2. Factor.
3. Simplify.

EXAMPLE 3 Divide $\dfrac{x^2 + 3xy + 2y^2}{x^2 + xy - 2y^2} \div \dfrac{x^2 + 4xy + 3y^2}{x^2 - y^2}$.

Answer $\dfrac{x^2 + 3xy + 2y^2}{x^2 + xy - 2y^2} \div \dfrac{x^2 + 4xy + 3y^2}{x^2 - y^2}$

$\dfrac{x^2 + 3xy + 2y^2}{x^2 + xy - 2y^2} \cdot \dfrac{x^2 - y^2}{x^2 + 4xy + 3y^2}$ Invert the divisor and multiply.

$\dfrac{(x + 2y)(x + y)}{(x + 2y)(x - y)} \cdot \dfrac{(x + y)(x - y)}{(x + 3y)(x + y)}$

$\dfrac{x + y}{x + 3y}$

▶ A. Exercises

Divide.

1. $\dfrac{4}{5} \div \dfrac{8}{35}$

2. $\dfrac{14}{9} \div \dfrac{28}{27}$

3. $\dfrac{1}{3} \div \dfrac{2}{3}$

4. $\dfrac{3x^3}{5} \div \dfrac{6x^2y}{25}$

5. $\dfrac{8x^4y^2}{x^3y} \div \dfrac{24x}{7y}$

6. $\dfrac{a^2b^3}{x^5y^2} \div \dfrac{a^4b}{xy^3}$

7. $\dfrac{(x + y)^2}{x - y} \div \dfrac{(x + y)(x - y)}{(x - y)^2}$

8. $\dfrac{4(x + 1)}{5(x - 5)} \div \dfrac{3(x + 1)}{x - 5}$

▶ B. Exercises

Divide. Leave answers in factored form.

9. $\dfrac{x^2 - y^2}{(x - y)^2} \div \dfrac{x^2 - 2xy + y^2}{x - y}$

10. $\dfrac{x^2 + 2x}{3x - 9} \div \dfrac{x^3 - 9x}{x - 3}$

11. $(x + 1) \div \dfrac{x^2 + 2x + 1}{x}$

12. $\dfrac{x^2 - 11x + 18}{x - 3} \div \dfrac{x^2 + 6x + 8}{x + 2}$

13. $\dfrac{x^2 - xy - 2y^2}{x^2 - y^2} \div \dfrac{x^2 - 3xy + 2y^2}{3x^2 + 4xy + y^2}$

14. $1 \div \dfrac{x^3 - x^2 + y}{x^5 + xy}$

15. $\dfrac{x^2 + 3x - 54}{x^2 + 5x + 6} \div \dfrac{x^2 - 12x + 36}{x^2 - 3x - 18}$

16. $\dfrac{x^4y - 3x^3y - 10x^2y}{x^2 + 4x + 3} \div \dfrac{x^2y^4 - xy^4 - 2y^4}{x^2 + 7x + 12}$

17. $\dfrac{1}{2x^2 + xy - y^2} \div \dfrac{x^2 + 2xy + y^2}{2x^2 - 3xy + y^2}$

18. $\dfrac{3a^2 - 6a}{7a^3} \div \dfrac{a^2 - 4}{14}$

19. $\dfrac{3m^2 - 2mn - n^2}{m^3 n^2} \div m^2 - 2mn + n^2$

20. $\dfrac{12x^2 - 29xy + 14y^2}{x^2 - xy - 12y^2} \div \dfrac{3x^2 + xy - 2y^2}{x^2 - 2xy - 8y^2}$

▶ C. Exercises

Simplify.

21. $\dfrac{x^2 - 3x - 18}{x^2 - 2x - 48} \div \dfrac{x^2 - x - 12}{x^3 - 12x^2 + 36x} \cdot \dfrac{3x^2 - 6x - 144}{x^2 - 4x}$

22. $\dfrac{(3x + 1)(x - 1) + (5x - 3)(x + 2) - (19x - 12)}{x^2 - 1} \div \dfrac{4x^2 + 7x - 15}{x^2 + 4x + 3}$

▧ Cumulative Review

23. Simplify $\dfrac{11}{25} - \dfrac{6}{25}$.

Use $(6, -3)$ and $(-2, -4)$.

24. Find the slope of the line through the points.

25. Find the distance between points.

26. Graph $2 < x \le 8$.

27. Solve $3(2x - 5) + 2(5x + 1) = 7 - 3x(x - 5)$.

12.4 Adding and Subtracting Rational Expressions

Operations with rational expressions follow the same rules as operations on rational numbers. Now you will add and subtract rational expressions. If two rational numbers must have a common denominator in order to be combined, do rational expressions have to have a common denominator as well? Of course they do. But you will learn how to find a common denominator for two or more rational expressions in the next two sections. This section will be easy because the rational expressions already have a common denominator.

EXAMPLE 1   Simplify $\frac{4}{x} + \frac{9}{x}$.

Answer $\frac{4}{x} + \frac{9}{x} = \frac{13}{x}$

Adding Rational Expressions with a Common Denominator

1. Add the numerators.
2. Simplify the rational expression.

EXAMPLE 2   Add $\frac{3x^2 + 4x - 8}{x + 2} + \frac{x^2 - 3x - 6}{x + 2}$.

Answer

$\frac{3x^2 + 4x - 8}{x + 2} + \frac{x^2 - 3x - 6}{x + 2}$

$\frac{3x^2 + 4x - 8 + x^2 - 3x - 6}{x + 2}$ 1. Add the numerators.

$\frac{4x^2 + x - 14}{x + 2}$ 2. Combine like terms.

$\frac{(4x - 7)(x + 2)}{x + 2}$ 3. Factor and simplify.

$4x - 7$

EXAMPLE 3   Simplify $\frac{2x + 9}{x - 4} + \frac{3x + 2}{x - 4}$.

Answer

$\frac{2x + 9}{x - 4} + \frac{3x + 2}{x - 4}$

$\frac{2x + 9 + 3x + 2}{x - 4}$ 1. Add the numerators.

$\frac{5x + 11}{x - 4}$ 2. Combine like terms. This rational expression cannot be simplified.

To subtract rational expressions, follow the procedure for subtracting rational numbers. When the expressions have a common denominator, combine like terms in the numerator and place them over the common denominator. Then factor and simplify.

EXAMPLE 4   Subtract $\frac{4}{x} - \frac{8}{x}$.

Answer $\frac{4}{x} - \frac{8}{x} = -\frac{4}{x}$

Subtracting Rational Expressions with a Common Denominator

1. Subtract the numerators.
2. Simplify the resulting rational expression.

EXAMPLE 5 Simplify $\dfrac{2+x}{8} - \dfrac{x-9}{8}$.

Answer

$\dfrac{2+x}{8} - \dfrac{x-9}{8}$

$\dfrac{2+x-(x-9)}{8}$ 1. Place the expression being subtracted in parentheses.

$\dfrac{2+x-x+9}{8}$ 2. Remove parentheses by using the distributive property.

$\dfrac{11}{8}$ 3. Combine like terms.

EXAMPLE 6 Simplify $\dfrac{3x^2+3x-20}{2x^2+18x+40} - \dfrac{x^2+x+4}{2x^2+18x+40}$.

Answer

$\dfrac{3x^2+3x-20}{2x^2+18x+40} - \dfrac{x^2+x+4}{2x^2+18x+40}$

$\dfrac{3x^2+3x-20-(x^2+x+4)}{2x^2+18x+40}$ 1. Subtract.

$\dfrac{3x^2+3x-20-x^2-x-4}{2x^2+18x+40}$ 2. Remove parentheses.

$\dfrac{2x^2+2x-24}{2x^2+18x+40}$ 3. Combine like terms.

$\dfrac{2(x+4)(x-3)}{2(x+5)(x+4)}$ 4. Factor.

$\dfrac{x-3}{x+5}$ 5. Cancel common factors.

Finding the GCF of the polynomials $2x^2 + 2x - 24$ and $2x^2 + 18x + 40$ can help you simplify the rational expression in step 4 above. The process is the same as finding the GCF of rational numbers.

Find the GCF of $2x^2 + 2x - 24$ and $2x^2 + 18x + 40$.
1. Factor each polynomial.
   $2x^2 + 2x - 24 = 2(x^2 + x - 12) = 2(x + 4)(x - 3)$
   $2x^2 + 18x + 40 = 2(x^2 + 9x + 20) = 2(x + 5)(x + 4)$
2. Identify all common factors.
   $GCF = 2(x + 4)$

By dividing the numerator and denominator by the GCF, the rational expression can be reduced to lowest terms. We call this canceling all common factors.

▶ A. Exercises

Add or subtract and simplify.

1. $\frac{8}{x} + \frac{6}{x}$

2. $\frac{5}{x+2} + \frac{7}{x+2}$

3. $\frac{4}{x} - \frac{9}{x}$

4. $\frac{3x}{y^2} - \frac{5x}{y^2}$

5. $\frac{7}{2c} - \frac{9}{2c}$

6. $\frac{3x}{8} + \frac{5x}{8}$

7. $\frac{2x}{x-7} - \frac{14}{x-7}$

8. $\frac{6}{a+b} - \frac{3a}{a+b}$

9. $\frac{5x}{x^2+y} + \frac{4x}{x^2+y}$

10. $\frac{x+4}{7} - \frac{x-3}{7}$

11. $\frac{x-5}{x+2} - \frac{x+7}{x+2}$

12. $\frac{4a}{a-b} - \frac{4b}{a-b}$

13. $\frac{9x}{yz} + \frac{3y}{yz}$

14. $\frac{2x}{x+y} - \frac{2y}{x+y}$

15. $\frac{3a}{a^2-b^2} - \frac{3b}{a^2-b^2}$

▶ B. Exercises

Add or subtract and simplify.

16. $\frac{a-2}{a^2-3a+9} + \frac{a+4}{a^2-3a+9}$

17. $\frac{2m^2+4mn+n^2}{m^2+mn-2n^2} + \frac{m^2+3mn+n^2}{m^2+mn-2n^2}$

18. $\frac{5}{a^2+3a-2} - \frac{7}{a^2+3a-2}$

19. $\frac{x+2}{x^2-4x-7} + \frac{x-9}{x^2-4x-7}$

20. $\frac{5x^2+3x-9}{x^2+7x+10} + \frac{2x^2+8x+3}{x^2+7x+10}$

21. $\frac{3x^2+4x-10}{x^2+5x-36} - \frac{2x^2+x+18}{x^2+5x-36}$

Add or subtract and simplify. Leave answers in factored form.

22. $\frac{a^3}{a-b} - \frac{a}{a-b}$

23. $\frac{x+2}{x^2-3x-9} - \frac{x-4}{x^2-3x-9}$

24. $\frac{2x^2-6x+4}{x^2-8x+15} + \frac{x^2-5x-19}{x^2-8x+15}$

25. $\frac{x^2-8x+13}{x^2-4x-12} - \frac{-x^2-4x-1}{x^2-4x-12}$

▶ C. Exercises

Add or subtract and simplify.

26. $\frac{-3x-3}{2x^2-5x-12} - \frac{5x^2-2x+1}{2x^2-5x-12} - \frac{x^2+6x-7}{2x^2-5x-12}$

27. Naming the appropriate properties, explain why $\frac{4x+8}{2x+6}$ can be reduced but $\frac{4x+7}{2x+6}$ cannot.

■ Cumulative Review

Explain why each expression is *not* simplified. Then simplify.

28. $\frac{4\sqrt{7}}{5-\sqrt{2}}$

29. $40^{\frac{1}{3}}$

30. $3x - 5 + 2x + 1$

31. $\frac{9 \pm 3\sqrt{7}}{6}$

32. $\frac{3x^2-15x}{x-5}$

12.5 Adding Rational Expressions with Different Denominators

Before you add or subtract rational numbers that have different denominators, you must change them into equivalent rational expressions that have the same denominator. Here you will learn how to find the LCM of polynomials.

To find the LCM of two or more polynomials, factor them completely. Then find the product of the highest power of each factor.

The total time for a roundtrip hike is the sum of two rational expressions: $t = \frac{d_{uphill}}{r_{uphill}} + \frac{d_{downhill}}{r_{downhill}}$.

EXAMPLE 1   Find the LCM of $x^4 - 3x^3 - 10x^2$ and $3x^2 - 30x + 75$.

Answer

1. Factor each polynomial.

   $x^4 - 3x^3 - 10x^2$ $\qquad\qquad$ $3x^2 - 30x + 75$

   $x^2(x^2 - 3x - 10)$ $\qquad\qquad$ $3(x^2 - 10x + 25)$

   $x^2(x - 5)(x + 2)$ $\qquad\qquad$ $3(x - 5)^2$

   The factors are x, $(x - 5)$, $(x + 2)$, and 3.

2. The LCM is the product of the highest power of each factor.

   $LCM = 3x^2(x - 5)^2(x + 2)$

EXAMPLE 2   Add $\frac{3}{2a} + \frac{5}{8a}$.

Answer

$$2a = 2 \cdot a$$
$$8a = 2^3 \cdot a$$
$$LCM = 2^3 \cdot a = 8a$$

1. To find the common denominator, determine the LCM of $2a$ and $8a$.

$$\frac{3}{2a} + \frac{5}{8a}$$

$$\frac{3}{2a} \cdot \frac{4}{4} + \frac{5}{8a}$$

2. Now you must make equivalent rational expressions with the denominator $8a$. Since $4 \cdot 2a = 8a$, multiply the numerator and the denominator by 4.

$$\frac{12}{8a} + \frac{5}{8a} = \frac{17}{8a}$$

3. Add.

EXAMPLE 3   Simplify $\dfrac{2x-5}{3x} + \dfrac{x-1}{2x} + \dfrac{5x+6}{12x^2}$.

Answer

$$3x = 3 \cdot x$$
$$2x = 2 \cdot x$$
$$12x^2 = 2^2 \cdot 3 \cdot x^2$$
$$\text{LCM} = 2^2 \cdot 3 \cdot x^2 = 12x^2$$

1. Find the common denominator.

$$\dfrac{2x-5}{3x} + \dfrac{x-1}{2x} + \dfrac{5x+6}{12x^2}$$

$$\dfrac{(2x-5)}{3x} \cdot \dfrac{4x}{4x} + \dfrac{(x-1)}{2x} \cdot \dfrac{6x}{6x} + \dfrac{5x+6}{12x^2}$$

$$\dfrac{8x^2-20x}{12x^2} + \dfrac{6x^2-6x}{12x^2} + \dfrac{5x+6}{12x^2}$$

2. Make equivalent rational expressions using $12x^2$ as the denominator.

$$\dfrac{8x^2-20x+6x^2-6x+5x+6}{12x^2}$$

3. Add numerators, and combine like terms.

$$\dfrac{14x^2-21x+6}{12x^2}$$

4. The expression does not reduce.

Adding and Subtracting Rational Expressions with Different Denominators

1. Find the LCM of the denominators.
2. Make equivalent rational expressions having the LCM as common denominator.
3. Combine the numerators and place over the common denominator.
4. Simplify the rational expression.

▶ A. Exercises

Perform the indicated operations and simplify.

1. $\dfrac{3x}{4} + \dfrac{9}{16}$

2. $\dfrac{x}{9} + \dfrac{4x}{7}$

3. $\dfrac{x-3}{18} + \dfrac{x+7}{4}$

4. $\dfrac{x+y}{225} + \dfrac{x}{15}$

5. $\dfrac{a^2+3a}{5} + \dfrac{a^2-9}{2}$

6. $\dfrac{4}{3x} + \dfrac{7}{21x^3}$

7. $\dfrac{9}{3m^3} + \dfrac{14}{8m^2}$

8. $\dfrac{5}{2x^3y^2} + \dfrac{10}{xy}$

9. $\dfrac{3x}{9y} + \dfrac{4x^2}{6y^3}$

10. $\dfrac{x+y}{3x} + \dfrac{x}{27y^2}$

11. $\dfrac{x^2+y^3}{4xy} + \dfrac{x^2+y}{9x^3}$

12. $\dfrac{x^2+xy-y^2}{8x^4} + \dfrac{2x^2+3xy-5y^2}{28x^3y}$

▶ B. Exercises

Perform the indicated operations and simplify.

13. $\dfrac{2x^2 + 3x}{2x + 8} + \dfrac{x^2 + 2x - 28}{3x - 12}$

14. $\dfrac{x^2 - 4}{x^2} + \dfrac{x - y}{x}$

15. $\dfrac{1}{3x - 9} + \dfrac{1}{x} + \dfrac{1}{4x + 16}$

16. $\dfrac{10}{x^2 - 6x - 27} + \dfrac{8}{x^2 - 3x - 18}$

17. $\dfrac{3x^2 - 7x + 3}{x^2 - 8x + 15} + \dfrac{-2x^2 + 2x + 3}{x^2 - 6x + 9}$

18. $\dfrac{3}{x^2 - y^2} + \dfrac{5}{x + y}$

19. $\dfrac{x - 3}{x + 5} + \dfrac{2x - 7}{x + 3} + \dfrac{26}{x^2 + 8x + 15}$

20. $\dfrac{x^2 + 3x - 5}{x^2 + 6x - 16} + \dfrac{x^2 - 4}{x^2 - 6x + 8}$

▶ C. Exercises

Perform the indicated operation and simplify.

21. $\dfrac{4x - 1}{x^2 + 5x + 6} + \dfrac{x + 3}{2x + 6} + \dfrac{3x + 2}{x^2 - 2x - 8}$

22. $\dfrac{4}{x^2 - 3x + 2} + \dfrac{2x}{x^2 - 5x + 6} + \dfrac{1}{x^2 - 7x + 12}$

▮ Cumulative Review

23. Simplify $(5x^{-3}y^2)^2(4x^2y^3)^{-1}$.
24. Graph $y > 2 - x$.
25. Solve $15x^2 + 14x = 16$.
26. One angle of a triangle is 10° more than another. The third angle is 6° less than twice the first. Find the measure of each angle. (*Hint:* The measures of the angles in a triangle always add up to 180°.)
27. A ladder must reach 20 feet up a telephone pole when it is positioned six feet from the base of the pole. How long does the ladder need to be?

ALGEBRA AND ENGINEERING

People's lives depend on the accuracy of an engineer's work.

Civil engineers plan the building that the construction crew erects.

Engineers must face reality—there is no partial credit for some correct calculations if a bridge collapses. People's lives depend on the accuracy of an engineer's work. The type of structure needed requires a particular type of engineer—but all types rely on algebra.

How do civil engineers know how deep to make a foundation? The foundation of a bridge or building must transfer the entire weight of the structure to the ground. Skyscrapers and bridges must be built on bedrock because they have so much weight relative to the size of their foundation. Most houses can be built on undisturbed hard clay soil. Some buildings need pilings that are like posts driven deep into the ground to reach rock or soil that can bear greater weight.

The strength and rigidity of steel beams and columns must be carefully calculated and must include a safety factor to allow for unexpected loads. The manufacturers of steel beams and parts publish the specifications of each. The engineer selects the steel parts with the specifications needed.

The engineer must also compute the load for each beam. The deflection (amount of bend) in an I-beam that has a load

at the midpoint of the beam is given by the following formula.

$$\Delta = \frac{Pl^3}{48EI}$$

A beam in which P is 500 pounds, E is 2×10^6, I is 250, and the length l is 96", has a deflection at the center of the beam of

$$\Delta = \frac{500(96)^3}{48(2 \times 10^6)(250)} = 0.018".$$

Since 0.018" is a very small deflection, we would say this is a very stiff beam.

A civil engineer wants to design a storm drain laid at a slope of 0.35%. His special calculator tells him how much runoff water a concrete pipe with a 24-inch diameter can carry on such a gradual slope. If he needs a greater capacity, he will have to use a steeper slope or select a larger diameter pipe.

If the drain empties into a stream at 215.55 ft. above mean sea level, calculate the inlet elevation for a section of pipe 175 ft. long.

The slope of 0.35% means that the elevation will change 0.0035 ft. for each linear foot of pipe $\frac{0.35}{100} = 0.0035$.

type of engineer	structures designed
civil	buildings, bridges, roads, railroads, tunnels, sewers
chemical	plants for cosmetics, drugs, plastics, soaps, etc.
computer	computers, printers, networks, disks, etc.
electrical	electric motors, circuits, TVs, transformers
industrial	selecting equipment and locations for plants
mechanical	engines, machines, utilities

Road construction crew

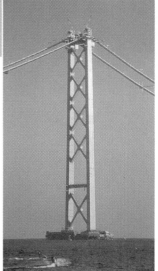

The towers and cables for Japan's Akashi-Kaikyo Bridge now support the longest suspension span in the world.

change in elevation = (0.0035)(175) = 0.61 ft.

inlet elevation = 215.55 + 0.61 = 216.16 ft. above mean sea level

From an elevation of 216.6 ft., the pipe will descend to 215.55 ft. over a distance of 175 ft.

12.6 Subtracting Rational Expressions with Different Denominators

The steps for subtracting rational expressions are the same as for addition, but as in the previous subtraction problems, more care must be taken with signs. As before, the numerator of the polynomial being subtracted should be completely rewritten with all signs changed and like terms collected (added).

Wind resistance reduces normal rates and requires a difference of rational expressions: $r = \frac{d_{normal}}{t_{normal}} - r_{wind}$.

EXAMPLE 1   Simplify $\dfrac{x-3}{x+1} - \dfrac{x-4}{x+2}$, but leave the answer in factored form.

Answer

$\dfrac{x-3}{x+1} - \dfrac{x-4}{x+2}$	1. $x+1$ and $x+2$ have no common factors. The LCM is $(x+1)(x+2)$.
$\dfrac{x-3}{x+1} \cdot \dfrac{(x+2)}{(x+2)} - \dfrac{x-4}{x+2} \cdot \dfrac{(x+1)}{(x+1)}$	
$\dfrac{x^2-x-6}{(x+1)(x+2)} - \dfrac{x^2-3x-4}{(x+1)(x+2)}$	2. Write each expression with a common denominator.
$\dfrac{x^2-x-6-(x^2-3x-4)}{(x+1)(x+2)}$	3. Write a single fraction.
$\dfrac{x^2-x-6-x^2+3x+4}{(x+1)(x+2)}$	4. Rewrite the quantity being subtracted with opposite signs (add the opposite).
$\dfrac{2x-2}{(x+1)(x+2)}$	5. Collect like terms (add).
$\dfrac{2(x-1)}{(x+1)(x+2)}$	6. Factor the numerator and observe that the rational expression does not reduce.

EXAMPLE 2   Simplify $\dfrac{y}{x^2 + xy} - \dfrac{x}{xy + y^2}$.

Answer

$x^2 + xy = x(x + y)$ 1. Find the common

$xy + y^2 = y(x + y)$ denominator.

LCM $= xy(x + y)$

$\dfrac{y}{x^2 + xy} - \dfrac{x}{xy + y^2}$

$\dfrac{y}{x(x + y)} - \dfrac{x}{y(x + y)}$

$\dfrac{y}{x(x + y)} \cdot \dfrac{y}{y} - \dfrac{x}{y(x + y)} \cdot \dfrac{x}{x}$ 2. Make equivalent rational expressions having the common denominator $xy(x + y)$.

$\dfrac{y^2}{xy(x + y)} - \dfrac{x^2}{xy(x + y)}$

$\dfrac{y^2 - x^2}{xy(x + y)}$ 3. Write a single fraction (subtract).

$\dfrac{(y - x)(y + x)}{xy(x + y)}$ 4. Simplify.

$\dfrac{(y - x)\cancel{(x + y)}}{xy\cancel{(x + y)}}$ 5. Since addition is commutative, $y + x = x + y$, rewrite this

$\dfrac{y - x}{xy}$ term and cancel.

What happens to a binomial such as $x - 4$ when you multiply it by -1?

$$-1(x - 4) = -x + 4 = 4 - x$$

Has the value of the expression changed? Yes, it has because $x - 4 \neq 4 - x$. Substitute a few different values for x and you will realize that they are opposites; that is, $-(x - 4)$ is $4 - x$.

Sometimes you may need to change the form of a denominator so that you can find a common denominator. But you must change the form without changing the value of the rational expression.

A rational number can be thought of as having three signs: one in the numerator, one in the denominator, and one preceding the fraction. The rational $-\frac{4}{5}$ can be expressed as follows:

$$\dfrac{-4}{5} \qquad \dfrac{4}{-5} \qquad -\dfrac{4}{5}$$

All of these different forms are equivalent expressions. Sometimes it is easier to simplify a problem like $\frac{3}{5} + \frac{2}{-5}$ if you use another form of the rational. To add $\frac{3}{5}$ and $\frac{2}{-5}$, change $\frac{2}{-5}$ to $\frac{-2}{5}$ and then add. You should be able to change any rational number or rational expression to another form by changing the positions of the signs to yield equivalent expressions. Can you give the three equivalent forms of $\frac{3}{7}$? They are

$$\frac{-3}{-7} \qquad -\frac{3}{-7} \qquad -\frac{-3}{7}$$

This idea may help you see why we are able to change the sign of the operation and the signs of one factor in the denominator without changing the answer.

EXAMPLE 3   Subtract $\dfrac{4x}{x-7} - \dfrac{3x}{7-x}$.

Answer $\dfrac{4x}{x-7} - \dfrac{3x}{7-x}$ Since subtraction is adding the

$\dfrac{4x}{x-7} + \dfrac{3x}{-(7-x)}$ opposite, we can change $\dfrac{3x}{7-x}$

$\dfrac{4x}{x-7} + \dfrac{3x}{x-7}$ into its opposite, $\dfrac{3x}{x-7}$, and add.

$\dfrac{7x}{x-7}$

EXAMPLE 4 $\dfrac{x^2+x-9}{(x+2)(x-5)} - \dfrac{2x^2+x+1}{(x+2)(5-x)}$

Answer $\dfrac{x^2+x-9}{(x+2)(x-5)} + \dfrac{2x^2+x+1}{(x+2)(x-5)}$ 1. Change $5-x$ to $x-5$, which results in the opposite of the denominator. Compensate by changing to the opposite operation (addition).

$\dfrac{x^2+x-9+2x^2+x+1}{(x+2)(x-5)}$ 2. Combine and simplify.

$\dfrac{3x^2+2x-8}{(x+2)(x-5)}$

$\dfrac{(3x-4)(x+2)}{(x+2)(x-5)}$

$\dfrac{3x-4}{x-5}$

▶ A. Exercises

Perform the indicated operations and simplify.

1. $\dfrac{x}{9} - \dfrac{4x}{7}$

2. $\dfrac{x+y}{5} - \dfrac{x}{15}$

3. $\dfrac{4}{3x} - \dfrac{7}{21x^3}$

4. $\dfrac{9}{3m^3} - \dfrac{14}{8m^2}$

5. $\dfrac{3x}{9y} + \dfrac{4x^2}{6y^3}$

6. $\dfrac{3}{x} - \dfrac{4}{x+1}$

7. $\dfrac{x}{(x-2)^2} - \dfrac{3}{x-2}$

8. $\dfrac{2x}{x+5} - \dfrac{3}{x-4}$

9. $\dfrac{2x+10}{(x+5)^2} - \dfrac{3x-5}{x+5}$

10. $\dfrac{1}{2x+8} - \dfrac{x+3}{3x+12}$

▶ B. Exercises

Perform the indicated operations and simplify.

11. $\dfrac{2x}{(x-7)(x+4)} - \dfrac{9}{(x-7)^2}$

12. $\dfrac{4}{x-2} - \dfrac{10}{2-x}$

13. $\dfrac{5x}{x-1} - \dfrac{6x^2}{x^2-1}$

14. $\dfrac{3y}{y^2+7y+10} - \dfrac{2y}{y^2+10y+25}$

15. $\dfrac{7}{(x+2)(x-5)} - \dfrac{9}{(x+2)^2(x+3)}$

16. $\dfrac{x}{x+3} + x - \dfrac{x}{x+5}$

17. $\dfrac{x-3}{(x+2)(4-x)} - \dfrac{x+9}{(x+2)(x-4)}$

18. $\dfrac{a+3}{a+5} - \dfrac{a+2}{a-5} + \dfrac{a}{a^2-25}$

19. $\dfrac{2x}{x+4} - \dfrac{3x}{x^2-5x-36}$

20. $\dfrac{x^4}{x^2+12x+32} - \dfrac{8x^3}{x^4-4x^3-32x^2}$

21. $\dfrac{a+b}{a-b} - \dfrac{4}{a+b} + \dfrac{a^2+3a-10}{a^2-b^2}$

22. $\dfrac{5x^2+3x-7}{x^2+2x-63} - \dfrac{4x^2+8x+7}{x^2-16x+63}$

▶ C. Exercises

23. Explain why you cannot work the following problem by making the change shown. Then work it another way.

$$\dfrac{3x+5}{(x-2)(x-5)} - \dfrac{4x+1}{(2-x)(5-x)} = \dfrac{3x+5}{(x-2)(x-5)} + \dfrac{4x+1}{(x-2)(x-5)}$$

24. Simplify

$$\dfrac{x-1}{(x-3)(x-4)} - \dfrac{x-9}{(x-3)(4-x)} - \dfrac{x-3}{(3-x)(4-x)} - \dfrac{2-x}{(x-3)(x-4)}.$$

■ Cumulative Review

Identify each property or formula.

25. $a^2 + b^2 = c^2$

26. If $ab = 0$, then $a = 0$ or $b = 0$.

27. $\dfrac{a}{b} = \dfrac{ac}{bc}$

28. $a(b+c) = ab + ac$

29. $x = \dfrac{-b \pm \sqrt{b^2-4ac}}{2a}$

Intersecting Sets and Probability

Since probabilities are fractions, word problems involving them can result in rational expressions. In this feature, you will learn a counting rule to help you compute probabilities. Remember that the addition principle of counting says that *A* or *B* can occur in *a* + *b* ways. This rule applies only when *A* and *B* do not overlap—that is, when they are disjoint sets, called *mutually exclusive events*. When *A* and *B* contain some of the same elements, these items get counted twice and you must subtract out the number of elements in the intersection in order to get the correct total.

General Addition Principle

If *A* occurs *a* ways, *B* occurs *b* ways, and $A \cap B$ occurs in *i* ways, then $A \cup B$ occurs in $a + b - i$ ways.

Notice that if $A \cap B = \varnothing$, $i = 0$, so $a + b - 0 = a + b$. In other words, the general addition principle also applies to mutually exclusive events and results in the simple formula that you learned in Chapter 5.

EXAMPLE 1 How many valuable materials are either birthstones or anniversary gifts?

Answer In an almanac, you can find the birthstones that appear below.

Month	Stone	Month	Stone
January	garnet	July	ruby
February	amethyst	August	sardonyx
March	bloodstone	September	sapphire
April	diamond	October	opal
May	emerald	November	topaz
June	pearl	December	turquoise

Wedding anniversary gifts are also listed. For tenth through fourteenth, they are tin, steel, silk, lace, and ivory. From

Continued ▶

fifteenth through sixtieth, they are given in five year increments: crystal, china, silver, pearl, jade, ruby, sapphire, gold, emerald, diamond.

Thus, $a = 15$ anniversary gifts, $b = 12$ birthstones, and $i = 5$ (since pearl, ruby, sapphire, emerald, and diamond each occur in both lists).
$a + b - i = 15 + 12 - 5 = 22$

The same principle applies to probabilities:

$$P_{A \cup B} = P_A + P_B - P_{A \cap B}$$

EXAMPLE 2 Sara collects dolls and has an extensive collection of 218. She has 56 antique dolls, 27 rag dolls, and 81 imported dolls. However, three rag dolls are antique and two are imported, including one that is both antique and imported. Seven other antique dolls are also imported. If she selects a doll at random for display, what is the probability that the doll will be either antique or imported?

Answer Since one rag doll is antique and imported and seven other dolls are also both antique and imported, there are eight dolls in the intersection. The probability $P_{A \cap B} = \frac{8}{218}$. Thus,

$$P_{A \cup B} = P_A + P_B - P_{A \cap B} = \frac{56}{218} + \frac{81}{218} - \frac{8}{218} = \frac{129}{218}.$$

▶ Exercises

1. If there are 12 flights daily from LA to Chicago and 15 from LA to New York but 2 of these make stops in Chicago, how many flights are there from LA to Chicago or New York?
2. How many months have 31 days or precede May?
3. A hat contains 23 slips of paper, 16 of which are green slips, 10 are square slips, and 7 are green squares. What is the probability that a slip drawn will be either green or square?

Consider Sara's doll collection in example 2. Find the probability that she selects a doll as follows.

4. either a rag doll or imported
5. either a rag doll or antique

Give the values of x that make each rational expression undefined.

1. $\dfrac{5}{x - 3}$

2. $\dfrac{2x + 1}{x^2 + 5x}$

3. $\dfrac{x - 8}{x^2 - 4x - 12}$

4. $\dfrac{x - 9}{3x^2 + 16x + 21}$

5. $\dfrac{x - 6}{x^3 - x}$

Find the LCM for each pair of polynomials.

6. $x^2 + 14x + 24 \qquad x^3 + 20x^2 + 96x$

7. $x^2 - 2x - 63 \qquad x^2 - 3x - 54$

8. $4x - 20 \qquad x^2 - 25$

9. $2x^2 + 11x + 5 \qquad 2x^2 - 15x - 8$

10. $x^2 - 16 \qquad x^3 - 4x^2$

Simplify each rational expression. Give answers in factored form.

11. $\dfrac{3x + 4}{6x^2 - 7x - 20}$

12. $\dfrac{12x + 3}{8x + 2}$

13. $\dfrac{x^2 + 7x + 10}{x^2 - x - 6}$

14. $\dfrac{2x - 14}{2x^2 - 22x + 56}$

15. $\dfrac{x^4 - 10x^3}{x^6 + 8x^5 + 15x^4}$

Perform the operations and simplify but leave answers in factored form.

16. $\dfrac{4x^3}{(x - 5)^2} \cdot \dfrac{(x - 5)}{2x}$

17. $\dfrac{2x + 6}{3x + 5} + \dfrac{x + 4}{3x + 5}$

18. $\dfrac{56x^2 - 18}{7x - 5} - \dfrac{7x^2 + 7}{7x - 5}$

19. $\dfrac{(9x + 2)(x - 3)}{(2x - 1)(x + 4)} \div \dfrac{(9x + 2)(x - 6)}{(x - 6)(2x - 1)}$

20. $\dfrac{5x(x - 8)}{(x + 2)(3x + 1)} \cdot \dfrac{3x + 1}{10(x - 8)^2}$

21. $\dfrac{x^2 + 5x + 4}{x^2 + 6x + 8}$

22. $\dfrac{x^2 + 13x + 22}{3} \cdot \dfrac{9}{x + 2}$

23. $\dfrac{x}{x^2 - y^2} + \dfrac{y}{x^2 - y^2}$

24. $\dfrac{5x + 2}{x + 2} - \dfrac{x - 1}{x + 3}$

25. $\dfrac{5x^3}{3x^2 + x - 10} \div \dfrac{15x}{6x^2 + 13x + 2}$

26. $\dfrac{3}{1 - x} + \dfrac{7}{x - 1}$

27. $\dfrac{xy}{5xy^3 - 11x^2} - \dfrac{y^3}{5y^5 - 11xy^2}$

28. $\dfrac{x^2 - 5x - 14}{2x + 3} \cdot \dfrac{2x^2 + x - 3}{x^2 - 7x}$

29. $\dfrac{x - 1}{x^2 + 9x + 18} \div \dfrac{x^2}{x^2 + x - 30}$

30. $\dfrac{4x^2 + 6x}{6x^2 - x - 15} - \dfrac{6x + 9}{15 + x - 6x^2}$

31. $\dfrac{\frac{2x}{y} + 1}{\frac{2x + y}{y^3}}$

32. $\dfrac{x + 1}{x^2 + 2x - 5} - \dfrac{x - 7}{x^2 + 2x - 5}$

33. $\dfrac{x + 2y}{27y} + \dfrac{x}{3}$

34. $\dfrac{\frac{x^2 - 4}{x}}{x + 2}$

35. $\dfrac{x^3 + 4x}{3x^2 + 23x + 14} \div \dfrac{x^4 - 16}{x^2 + 5x - 14}$

Simplify. Leave answers in factored form.

36. $\dfrac{x + 6}{x - 2} \div \dfrac{x^2 + 3x - 10}{x + 1}$

37. $\dfrac{x^2 + 2x + 5}{x^2 - 2x - 24} + \dfrac{-5x - 23}{x^2 - 7x + 6}$

38. $\dfrac{2x^2 + 10x - 28}{x - 6} \cdot \dfrac{2x^2 - 21x + 54}{3x^3 - 5x^2} \cdot \dfrac{x^4}{2x^2 - 5x - 18}$

39. $\dfrac{x + y}{x^2 + 2xy + y^2} + \dfrac{3x}{x - y} - \dfrac{2x + 3y}{x + y}$

40. Give the mathematical significance of Leviticus 6:20.

13 Rational Equations

Looking out across the lake, Glenn Osborne marveled at God's beautiful creation. As a freshwater zoologist for Glacier National Park, he studies the ecology of the park's lakes and ponds. The phantom midge is a larval stage in the life of the Clear Lake gnat. The transparent body of the phantom midge (from which it takes its name) can reach half an inch long. Its two silvery air bladders inflate for the midge to rise to the surface of the lake at night and deflate for descent to the bottom during the day.

Glenn wonders about the water pressures on the midge at various depths. Lowering an apparatus into the lake, he obtains values that he can substitute into the equation $P_2 = \left(\dfrac{P_1 V}{T_1}\right)\left(\dfrac{T_2}{V - W}\right)$.

The letters have the following meanings:

P_1 = atmospheric pressure

P_2 = water pressure at a given depth

V = volume of air in the container before submersion

T_1 = temperature of the air in the container before submersion

T_2 = temperature of the air in the container after submersion

W = volume of water in the container after submersion

Glenn frequently uses rational equations like this one to study the effects of water pressure on aquatic creatures. In this chapter, you will learn to solve such equations.

After this chapter you should be able to

1. identify the difference between a rational equation and an equation containing fractions.

2. solve equations containing fractions.

3. solve rational equations.

4. solve a variety of applied word problems that involve rational equations.

5. solve literal equations.

13.1 Numerical Denominator

In Chapter 4, you solved equations containing fractions. The variables were always in the numerators, and you cleared the fractions by multiplying both sides of each equation by the common denominator (LCM). Then you solved the resulting equations.

EXAMPLE 1 Solve $\dfrac{x+4}{2} + \dfrac{x-6}{3} = \dfrac{1}{6}$.

Answer

$\dfrac{x+4}{2} + \dfrac{x-6}{3} = \dfrac{1}{6}$	1. The least common multiple is 6.
$6\left(\dfrac{x+4}{2} + \dfrac{x-6}{3}\right) = 6\left(\dfrac{1}{6}\right)$	2. Clear the fractions.
$6\left(\dfrac{x+4}{2}\right) + 6\left(\dfrac{x-6}{3}\right) = 6\left(\dfrac{1}{6}\right)$	3. Apply the distributive property.
$\begin{aligned} 3(x+4) + 2(x-6) &= 1 \\ 3x + 12 + 2x - 12 &= 1 \\ 5x &= 1 \\ x &= \tfrac{1}{5} \end{aligned}$	4. Solve.

EXAMPLE 2 Solve $\dfrac{x-7}{7} - \dfrac{x+2}{3} = 1$.

Answer

$\dfrac{x-7}{7} - \dfrac{x+2}{3} = 1$	1. The least common multiple is 21.
$21\left(\dfrac{x-7}{7} - \dfrac{x+2}{3}\right) = 21 \cdot 1$ $21\left(\dfrac{x-7}{7}\right) - 21\left(\dfrac{x+2}{3}\right) = 21$	2. Multiply both sides of the equation by 21 to clear fractions.
$\begin{aligned} 3(x-7) - 7(x+2) &= 21 \\ 3x - 21 - 7x - 14 &= 21 \\ -4x - 35 &= 21 \\ -4x &= 56 \\ x &= -14 \end{aligned}$	3. Solve.

▶ A. Exercises

Solve.

1. $\frac{x}{4} = 10$

2. $\frac{x}{9} = \frac{1}{8}$

3. $\frac{m}{3} = 9$

4. $\frac{a}{6} = \frac{1}{3}$

5. $\frac{x + 1}{3} = 4$

6. $\frac{x - 9}{7} = \frac{1}{14}$

7. $\frac{a + 3}{5} = \frac{a - 2}{10}$

8. $\frac{x - 7}{2} = \frac{x - 3}{4}$

9. $\frac{a - 9}{15} = \frac{a - 6}{5}$

10. $\frac{y + 2}{3} = \frac{y + 9}{2}$

▶ B. Exercises

Solve.

11. $\frac{a + 4}{11} - \frac{a + 2}{3} = 7$

12. $\frac{x - 12}{2} + \frac{x + 7}{5} = \frac{1}{10}$

13. $\frac{m + 5}{7} - \frac{m - 3}{6} = \frac{m + 3}{2}$

14. $\frac{y - 5}{12} + \frac{y + 3}{3} = \frac{2}{24}$

15. $\frac{x + 4}{9} - \frac{x - 7}{3} = 2$

16. The width of a rectangular picture is one-half the length. If the area is 648 square inches, what are the dimensions of the picture?

17. Jack and Erin spent $\frac{1}{4}$ of their money on rides at the fair. They paid $20 for food and transportation and returned with $\frac{4}{7}$ of their money. How much did they take to the fair?

Texas State Fair at Dallas

▶ C. Exercises

Solve.

18. $\frac{x^2}{9} = \frac{x}{3} + 4$

19. $\frac{x^2}{4} - \frac{29x}{8} = 3$

■ Cumulative Review

20. Simplify $\frac{x + 3}{27} - \frac{x + 5}{21}$.

21. Solve $\frac{x + 3}{27} = \frac{x + 5}{21}$.

22. Graph $y < x$.

23. Solve the system.

$$4x + 3y = 9$$
$$3x - 7y = 16$$

24. The hypotenuse of a right triangle is 3 less than twice the length of one side. The other side is 2 less than the hypotenuse. Find the lengths.

Independent and Dependent Probabilities

Finding probabilities with several steps requires the multiplication principle. Determine the factors separately based on whether the probabilities are independent or dependent. *Dependent* means that the first probability affects the second. Such situations occur when you draw objects from a bowl without replacement because the total number of objects in the bowl reduces each time. *Independent* means that the probabilities are not dependent, such as when drawing with replacement.

EXAMPLE 1 Find the probability of drawing (without replacement) **3** red marbles in succession from a bowl containing **9** red, **6** blue, and **2** green marbles.

Answer For the first draw, **9** of the **17** marbles are red, so the probability of drawing a red marble is $\frac{9}{17}$. For the second draw, only **8** red marbles remain of the **16** remaining marbles. Thus, the probability of drawing a red one on the second draw is $\frac{8}{16} = \frac{1}{2}$. By the third draw, only **15** marbles remain of which **7** are red. Applying the multiplication principle, we get

$$P_{\text{RRR}} = \frac{9}{17} \cdot \frac{1}{2} \cdot \frac{7}{15} = \frac{21}{170}.$$

EXAMPLE 2 Find the probability of drawing marbles in the order green, blue, green from the same bowl in example 1.

Answer Notice that the total number of marbles reduces by one each time (without replacement), and the drawing of the first green marble reduces the number of green marbles but not the number of blue marbles.

$$P_{\text{GBG}} = \frac{2}{17} \cdot \frac{6}{16} \cdot \frac{1}{15} = \frac{1}{340}$$

▶ Exercises

Using the bowl of marbles in the examples, find these probabilities if **3** draws are to be made without replacement.

1. P_{BBB}
2. P_{GGR}
3. P_{GGG}
4. P_{BRR}

5. Repeat exercise 3 with replacement.

13.2 Polynomial Denominators

To solve rational equations, apply the same rules that you have already learned for solving an equation containing fractions. The denominator in these rational expressions will be either a first or a second degree polynomial.

Definition

A **rational equation** is an equation containing a rational expression with a variable in the denominator.

EXAMPLE 1 Solve $\frac{9}{x+3} = 9$.

Answer

$\frac{9}{x+3} = 9$	1. The common denominator is $x + 3$.
$(x+3)\frac{9}{x+3} = 9(x+3)$	2. Multiply both sides of the equation by the common denominator.
$9 = 9x + 27$ $-18 = 9x$ $-2 = x$	3. Solve.
$\frac{9}{-2+3} = 9$ $\frac{9}{1} = 9$ $9 = 9$	4. Check.

You must always check your solutions to rational equations in the original equation. Remember that rational expressions may be undefined and when you multiply by an expression to clear the denominators, the new equation may introduce solutions for which the original equation was undefined. Remember that any solution that does not check is extraneous.

EXAMPLE 2   Solve $\dfrac{5}{x+1} = \dfrac{-2}{x-6}$.

Answer

$\dfrac{5}{x+1} = \dfrac{-2}{x-6}$	1. The common denominator (LCM) is $(x+1)(x-6)$.
$(x+1)(x-6)\dfrac{5}{x+1} = (x+1)(x-6)\dfrac{-2}{x-6}$	2. Multiply both sides of the equation by the LCM.
$5(x-6) = -2(x+1)$ $\qquad 5x - 30 = -2x - 2$ $\qquad 7x = 28$ $\qquad x = 4$	3. Solve.
$\dfrac{5}{4+1} = \dfrac{-2}{4-6}$ $\qquad \dfrac{5}{5} = \dfrac{-2}{-2}$ $\qquad 1 = 1$	4. Check. The solution checks.

EXAMPLE 3   Solve $\dfrac{x-12}{x-10} = \dfrac{2}{x} - \dfrac{20}{x^2 - 10x}$.

Answer

$\dfrac{x-12}{x-10} = \dfrac{2}{x} - \dfrac{20}{x^2 - 10x}$	1. The LCM is $x(x-10)$.
$x(x-10)\dfrac{x-12}{x-10} = \left[\dfrac{2}{x} - \dfrac{20}{x(x-10)}\right]x(x-10)$	2. Multiply both sides by the LCM.
$x\cancel{(x-10)}\dfrac{x-12}{\cancel{x-10}} = \dfrac{2}{\cancel{x}}\cancel{x}(x-10) - \dfrac{20}{\cancel{x(x-10)}}\cancel{x(x-10)}$	
$x(x-12) = 2(x-10) - 20$ $x^2 - 12x = 2x - 20 - 20$ $x^2 - 12x = 2x - 40$ $x^2 - 14x + 40 = 0$ $(x-10)(x-4) = 0$ $x - 10 = 0 \quad \text{or} \quad x - 4 = 0$ $\quad\; x = 10 \quad \text{or} \quad\;\; x = 4$	3. Solve the quadratic equation.

Check.

$$\dfrac{10-12}{10-10} = \dfrac{2}{10} - \dfrac{20}{10^2 - 10 \cdot 10} \qquad\qquad \dfrac{4-12}{4-10} = \dfrac{2}{4} - \dfrac{20}{4^2 - 10 \cdot 4}$$

$$\dfrac{-2}{0} = \dfrac{2}{10} - \dfrac{20}{0} \qquad\qquad\qquad \dfrac{-8}{-6} = \dfrac{1}{2} - \dfrac{20}{16 - 40}$$

$$\dfrac{4}{3} = \dfrac{1}{2} - \dfrac{20}{-24}$$

$$\dfrac{4}{3} = \dfrac{1}{2} + \dfrac{20}{24}$$

$$\dfrac{4}{3} = \dfrac{8}{6}$$

$$\dfrac{4}{3} = \dfrac{4}{3}$$

Since division by 0 is undefined,   4 is a solution.
10 is extraneous.

EXAMPLE 4 What number added to both the numerator and the denominator of $\frac{3}{5}$ makes a fraction equal to $\frac{6}{7}$?

Answer

$\frac{3+x}{5+x} = \frac{6}{7}$	1. Let x = the number to be added to the numerator and the denominator. Write the appropriate equation.
$7(5+x)\frac{3+x}{5+x} = \frac{6}{7} \cdot 7(5+x)$ $7(3+x) = 6(5+x)$	2. Multiply both sides of the equation by the LCM $7(5+x)$.
$21 + 7x = 30 + 6x$	3. Solve.
$x = 9$	4. Check your solution.

▶ A. Exercises

Solve each rational equation.

1. $\frac{2}{x} = 8$

2. $\frac{9}{x} = 3$

3. $\frac{8}{y} = 16$

4. $\frac{20}{m} = 4$

5. $\frac{8}{x+2} = 3$

6. $\frac{10}{a-5} = 7$

7. $\frac{36}{a+5} = 6$

8. $\frac{x+3}{x-2} = 1$

9. $\frac{x-5}{x-4} = 2$

10. $\frac{m+4}{m-9} = 2$

▶ B. Exercises

Solve.

11. $\frac{2}{a-7} = \frac{9}{a+3}$

12. $\frac{4}{3x} + 7 = \frac{1}{6x}$

13. $\frac{6x+5}{2x} - \frac{8x+3}{9x} = \frac{5}{18}$

14. $\frac{5}{x+9} = \frac{7}{x-8}$

15. $\frac{a-3}{4} - \frac{5}{a+2} = 1$

16. $\frac{x+3}{x-4} = \frac{4}{x} + \frac{28}{x^2-4x}$

17. $\frac{m+4}{m-9} = \frac{m-3}{m-6}$

18. $\frac{x+12}{x-2} - \frac{4}{x} = \frac{-4}{x^2-2x}$

19. What number must be added to the numerator and the denominator of $\frac{5}{11}$ to make a rational number equivalent to $\frac{3}{4}$?

20. What number must be added to the numerator and subtracted from the denominator of $\frac{1}{2}$ to make a rational number equivalent to $-\frac{8}{7}$?

21. One number is six less than another number. The quotient of the larger divided by the smaller is $\frac{5}{2}$. What are the two numbers?

22. Divide 84 into two parts so that the smaller part divided by the larger part is equal to $\frac{3}{4}$.

Solve.

23. $\dfrac{4}{x^2 - 8x + 15} = \dfrac{1}{x^2 - 3x - 10}$

24. $\dfrac{1}{x^2 - 2x - 8} - \dfrac{4}{x^2 - x - 12} = \dfrac{2}{x^2 - 2x - 8}$

■ Cumulative Review

25. Solve $\dfrac{6yp - t}{q} = n$ for y.

26. What values make $\dfrac{x}{3x + 5}$ undefined?

27. Simplify $\dfrac{8}{x} - \dfrac{5}{x + 2}$.

28. Solve $\dfrac{8}{x} - \dfrac{5}{x + 2} = 0$.

29. Graph the system.
$$y \le 2x + 3$$
$$y \ge x - 2$$

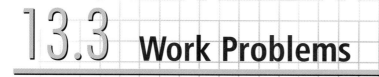

13.3 Work Problems

Work is a God-given responsibility (Gen. 3:19). Paul and his associates worked "night and day" for their room and board so as not to be a burden to others. He reprimanded some sluggards: "if any would not work, neither should he eat" (II Thess. 3:8-10). Every Christian has a responsibility to work hard because he serves not just a teacher, employer, or parent, but the Lord Jesus Himself (cf. Rom. 12:11).

Management supervisors realize that some jobs can be done faster if more than one machine or person works on the project. The work problems in this section can help you analyze some of the everyday jobs in which you might be involved.

EXAMPLE 1   The yearbook advisor knows that Suzette can proof fifteen pages in 60 minutes. Shawn can proof the same amount in 75 minutes. If a fifteen-page section needs to be checked, how long will it take them to finish the project if they work together?

Answer   First READ the problem carefully. In this problem, you are looking for the number of minutes it will take Suzette and Shawn to do the job together. Let x = the number of minutes required to do the job together.

Next, PLAN—make a table that indicates the amount of work each does in one minute as well as the time it takes each one to do all the work. If Suzette can do the job in 60 minutes, she does $\frac{1}{60}$ of the job in 1 minute. If Shawn can do the job in 75 minutes, she does $\frac{1}{75}$ of the job in 1 minute. Since they can do the job together in x minutes, they can do $\frac{1}{x}$ of the job in 1 minute.

	minutes to do all the work	part of work done in one minute
Suzette	60	$\frac{1}{60}$
Shawn	75	$\frac{1}{75}$
together	x	$\frac{1}{x}$

Once the table is complete, you must SOLVE an equation. $\frac{1}{60} + \frac{1}{75}$ equals the part of work the girls do together in one minute, or $\frac{1}{x}$ of the total work. The equation is

$$\frac{1}{60} + \frac{1}{75} = \frac{1}{x}$$

Continued ▶

Since the common denominator is **300x**,

$$300x\left(\frac{1}{60}\right) + 300x\left(\frac{1}{75}\right) = \frac{300x}{x}$$

$$5x + 4x = 300$$

$$9x = 300$$

$$x = 33\tfrac{1}{3}$$

Finally, you must CHECK your answer. Working together, the girls can complete the project in $33\tfrac{1}{3}$ minutes.

Can you see how knowing the time it will take for workers to finish a project is helpful to a company or business trying to get a particular job done? When the labor cost can be estimated, the marketing manager can determine how to price and promote products. As you study the next example, remember to READ, PLAN, SOLVE, and CHECK.

EXAMPLE 2   Bill and Jim, who mow lawns in the summer, have a big job coming up. Bill figures that doing the job by himself will take **10** hours but doing the job with Jim will take only **4** hours. How long would it take Jim to mow the whole lawn by himself?

Answer

Let x = the amount of time it takes Jim alone

1. ***Read.*** What are you looking for?

2. ***Plan.*** Make a table.

	hours for whole job	part of work done in one hour
Bill	10	$\frac{1}{10}$
Jim	x	$\frac{1}{x}$
together	4	$\frac{1}{4}$

$$\frac{1}{10} + \frac{1}{x} = \frac{1}{4}$$

$$20x\left(\frac{1}{10} + \frac{1}{x}\right) = \frac{1}{4}(20x)$$

$$20x\left(\frac{1}{10}\right) + 20x\left(\frac{1}{x}\right) = \frac{1}{4}(20x)$$

$$2x + 20 = 5x$$

$$-3x = -20$$

$$x = 6\tfrac{2}{3}$$

3. ***Solve.*** Form the equation from the information in the right-hand column. Solve this equation.

It takes Jim $6\tfrac{2}{3}$ hours to mow the whole lawn.

4. ***Check.*** Does the answer fit the context?

▶ A. Exercises

1. Peter takes **3** hours to mow the lawn and Jon takes **6** hours. How long will it take them working together?

2. Sheila and Susan can each wash their parents car in one hour. How long will it take them working together?

3. Brian can plant his acreage in **74** hours. His neighbor can do the same amount of acreage with his larger equipment in **50** hours. How long will it take to plant Brian's field if they work together on it?

4. Darla figured that making puppets for vacation Bible school would take her **4** hours. If she worked with her sister, who would take **6** hours for the job, she could get finished faster. If the girls work together, how long will it take them to finish the puppets?

5. The junior class is getting ready for the spring play, and Larry is in charge of painting the sets, which will take **52** hours if he paints them by himself. Larry knows that John is a good artist and could paint the sets in **36** hours. If he decides to ask John to help him, how long will it take the two guys to paint the sets?

6. It takes **9** hours for one water pipe to fill a swimming pool. If another pipe is added and both pipes work together, the pool fills in only **3** hours. How long would it take the second pipe to fill the pool if it were the only one used?

▶ B. Exercises

Solve to the nearest tenth.

7. Phil can load a truck in **2** hours. With Bob's help they finished loading one in **45** minutes. How long would it take Bob working alone?

8. A certain computer can grade **2000** objective-answer exams in **10** minutes. A new computer can grade the **2000** exams in less time. If the two computers together can grade **2000** in **3** minutes, how long does it take the new computer to grade the **2000** exams?

9. If Sam, who takes twice as long as Brent to remove the tassels from an acre of corn, works with Brent, he and Brent can do an acre in **50** minutes. How long does it take each one to do the job alone?

10. Ron, Mike, and Tim are going to paint a house together. Ron can paint one side of the house in **4** hours. To paint an equal area, Mike takes only **3** hours and Tim **2** hours. If the men work together, how long will it take them to paint one side of the house?

11. Joy takes **3** hours longer than Fran to clean the house. If the girls work together, they can get the work done in **4** hours. How long does it take each girl working alone to clean the house?

12. Dan can reshingle a roof in **10** hours, Rob in **8**. Dave has never done the job alone, but last time he helped with a similar job it took the three men $3\frac{1}{3}$ hours working together. How long would it take Dave alone?

13. How long will it take the Swansons to weed their vegetable garden if all four of them work together? They estimate that working alone it would take Mr. Swanson **4** hours, Mrs. Swanson **4** hours, Brenda **6** hours, and Glen **7** hours.

14. At 1 P.M. Mrs. Fanelli tells Joey and Marcy that they can play mini-golf if they get the chores done (properly!). Joey usually takes **5** hours doing the chores, and Marcy does them in **4** hours. If they work together, how long will it take them to do the job? If the course closes at 5 P.M. and it takes **14** minutes to drive to it, how long will they have to play?

▶ C. Exercises

Solve to the nearest tenth.

15. A machine at a light-bulb factory produces metal bases for light bulbs. The company has a rush order that needs to be filled in **24** hours. After **7** hours the machine breaks down, and another machine is used to complete the job in **5** hours. It would have taken **15** hours to do the job using the first machine alone. How long would it have taken to do the job using only the second machine?

16. Pam takes **2** hours longer than Carla to make a dress. Together they can finish the dress in **4** hours. How long does each take working alone?

▪ Cumulative Review

Factor.

17. $7x^4 + 11x^2 + 4$
18. $3x^4 - 31x^2 + 36$
19. $x^8 - y^8$
20. $xy^2 + 2x^2 - 2xy - y^3$
21. $3x^6 - 3x^4 + 6x^2 - 6$

13.4 Investment Problems

In Luke 19:11-27 Jesus told a parable about a nobleman who gave each of his ten servants a certain amount of money to manage. Two of the ten servants increased the amount given them. A third servant, afraid he would lose what he had, hid the money. When the nobleman returned, he was very angry with the third servant, who could at least have invested the money and returned it with interest. Have you developed the talents that God has given you and invested them in His service?

The main formula that you must remember when solving investment problems is the simple interest formula $I = Prt$: I stands for the interest gained on an investment, P is the principal (amount invested), r is the interest rate per year in decimal form, and t is the time of the investment in years.

EXAMPLE 1 Mr. Williams invested $5000 in a bank account paying 8% simple interest and left it there for $2\frac{1}{2}$ years. How much interest did he gain?

Answer

$I = Prt$	Using the formula $I = Prt$, substitute values for P, r, and t.
$I = (5000)(0.08)(2.5)$	$P = 5000$ is the amount invested. $r = 0.08$ is the decimal form for 8%. $t = 2.5$ is the decimal form for $2\frac{1}{2}$.
$I = 400(2.5)$	
$I = 1000$	

EXAMPLE 2 The freshmen saved money for their senior trip. At the end of their freshman year, they invested one-third of their money in a savings account yielding $5\frac{1}{2}$% interest and one-half of their money in an account yielding 8% interest. The rest was put in a checking account, yielding 5% interest. If the total interest per year from all three accounts is $40, how much money did the freshman class invest?

Continued ▶

Answer

	P	r	t	=	I
first	$\frac{x}{3}$	0.055	1		$\frac{x}{3}(0.055)$
second	$\frac{x}{2}$	0.08	1		$\frac{x}{2}(0.08)$
third	$\frac{x}{6}$	0.05	1		$\frac{x}{6}(0.05)$

1. **Read.** Let x represent the total amount of money the freshman class invested.

2. **Plan.** Use a table to organize the information.

$$\left(\frac{x}{3}\right)(0.055) + \left(\frac{x}{2}\right)(0.08) + \left(\frac{x}{6}\right)(0.05) = 40$$

3. **Solve.** Since the total interest is $40, you can set up an equation.

$$6\left[\left(\frac{x}{3}\right)(0.055) + \left(\frac{x}{2}\right)(0.08) + \left(\frac{x}{6}\right)(0.05)\right] = 6(40)$$
$$2x(0.055) + 3x(0.08) + x(0.05) = 240$$
$$0.11x + 0.24x + 0.05x = 240$$

This equation has fractions and decimals. We will eliminate the fractions first. The common denominator is 6.

$$100[0.11x + 0.24x + 0.05x] = 100(240)$$
$$11x + 24x + 5x = 24,000$$
$$40x = 24,000$$
$$x = 600$$

To eliminate the decimals, multiply both sides by 100.

The freshman class invested $600 that year.

4. **Check** the answer in the context.

▶ A. Exercises

How much interest is earned from
1. $200 invested for 6 years at 6%?
2. $200 invested for $6\frac{1}{2}$ years at $5\frac{1}{2}$%?
3. $600 invested for 21 months at 6%?
4. At 5% how long will it take Joe to earn $100 in interest from his $200 investment?
5. Jenny has $350 to invest and wants to earn $90 interest in the next 5 years. What interest rate must she find?
6. Steve's bank pays 7% interest. How much must he invest to earn $151 interest in the next 4 years?

Use the table as the basis to write a system of equations. Do not solve.

P	r	t	=	I
x	0.06	1		0.06x
y	0.05	1		0.05y

7. Sarah invests the same amount in each account and earns a total of $250 annually.

8. Sarah invests **$100** more at **5%** than at **6%**, but the two accounts earn the same annual interest.

Use two variables to make a table for each problem. Do not work them out.

9. Ted invests **$600**, part at **8%** and part at **5%** for 2 years.

10. Tracy invests **$500** in a CD account and **$200** in a savings account, each for a year.

▶ B. Exercises

11. Mr. Willis has one-fifth of his savings invested at **6%**, three-fifths at **8%**, and the rest at **10%**. His total interest from savings is **$1078** annually. How much does he have invested at each rate?

12. Mary invested **$2000**, part at $5\frac{1}{2}$**%** and part at **7%**. If the total yearly income from the two investments is **$115.22**, how much is invested in each account?

13. Mrs. Lopez has a sum of money invested at **9%** and another sum equaling one-third of the first sum invested at $5\frac{3}{4}$**%**. The yearly income from the **9%** investment exceeds the interest of the $5\frac{3}{4}$**%** investment by **$425**. How much is invested at each rate?

14. Grace plans to invest her **$10,000** in three kinds of bonds. She will invest half as much in bond *A* as in *B* and the rest in bond *C*. Their yields are **4%**, **7%**, and **11%** respectively. If her total interest for a year is **$830**, how much will she invest in bonds *A*, *B*, and *C*?

New York Stock Exchange

15. The yearly interest income from two investments is **$1050**. If **$3000** is invested at a rate two percentage points higher than that of an **$8000** investment, what are the interest rates for the two investments?

16. The Stees plan to invest a total of **$8500** in two accounts, the first paying **8%** interest and the second paying $6\frac{1}{2}$**%** interest. How much should they invest in each account in order to gain **$3302.50** in 5 years?

17. Paul plans to buy some stocks in a new computer company. He can buy preferred stock, which yields an average of **11%** interest, and he can buy common stock, which yields an average of **9%** interest. If he invests three-fourths of his money in preferred stock and one-fourth in common stock, he will gain **$1312.50** in $2\frac{1}{2}$ years. How much must Paul invest?

18. Doug will make two **$8000** investments. If one account yields **11%**, what should the interest rate be on the other account to make a yearly total of **$1720** in interest?

19. Mr. and Mrs. Beach opened a retirement account that will yield $9\frac{1}{2}\%$ interest annually. They also invested a certain amount in a passbook savings account that pays $5\frac{3}{4}\%$ interest. If their total investment is $2200 and they gain a total of $171.50 annually in interest, how much did they invest in each account?

20. An investment of at least $2500 pays $6\frac{1}{2}\%$ interest, while an investment of less than $2500 pays $5\frac{1}{2}\%$. Two people invest in this opportunity, one investing $1080 more than the other, and the annual interest of one is $88.90 more than that of the other. Find how much was invested at each rate.

■ Cumulative Review

Solve and graph.

21. $3x = 15$

22. $7 - 5x \leq 22$

23. $7 + 5x \leq 9 \vee 5x + 3 > 7$

24. $2x - 3 > 5 \wedge 5x - 1 < 9$

25. $\frac{5x - 9}{x - 2} - 1 = \frac{13}{3} + \frac{1}{x + 2}$

Three computer programmers stopped at a hotel on their way to a computer exhibition. The night clerk charged them $30 for the room, so each man paid $10. In the morning the men did some minor repairs on the manager's computer, which had broken down during the night, so the manager decided to knock $5 off their room rate. While the men were at breakfast, the waiter came to them and gave each man $1, keeping the other $2 for himself. The men actually paid only $9 apiece, or a total of $27, for the room; the waiter kept $2, making a total of $29. What happened to the other $1?

13.5 Motion Problems

Do you remember the basic equation that you used to solve the motion problems in Chapters 4 and 7? Remember always to make a table and fill in two columns, using variables and information from the problem. Fill in the third column from the other two columns; then make an equation using the last column you filled in and any unused information from the problem.

EXAMPLE 1 If Lisa flies home for vacation, she will arrive $12\frac{1}{2}$ hours earlier than if she drives the 780 miles. Find the average speed of the plane if the speed the car could travel is one-sixth the speed of the plane.

Answer

Let x = the speed of the plane

$\frac{x}{6}$ = the speed of the car

1. **Read.** What are you looking for?

2. **Plan.** Make a table to aid in the solution of this problem.

   a. Fill in two columns of the table.

   b. When two columns are full, fill in the third column without looking at the problem.

	r	t =	d
by car	$\frac{x}{6}$		780
by plane	x		780

	r	t =	d
by car	$\frac{x}{6}$	$\frac{780}{\frac{x}{6}}$	780
by plane	x	$\frac{780}{x}$	780

3. **Solve.** Reread the problem to find information about the time column since it was the last one filled in. Since flying is $12\frac{1}{2}$ hours shorter than driving, write an equation.

$$\frac{780}{\frac{x}{6}} = \frac{780}{x} + 12\frac{1}{2}$$

$$\frac{4680}{x} = \frac{780}{x} + \frac{25}{2}$$

Simplify all terms in the equation.

$$2x\left(\frac{4680}{x}\right) = 2x\left(\frac{780}{x} + \frac{25}{2}\right)$$

$$2x\left(\frac{4680}{x}\right) = 2x\left(\frac{780}{x}\right) + 2x\left(\frac{25}{2}\right)$$

$$9360 = 1560 + 25x$$

$$7800 = 25x$$

$$312 = x$$

Multiply both sides of the equation by the common denominator and solve.

The plane travels 312 mph.

4. **Check.** Does the answer fit the context of the problem?

Did you follow all of the steps in example 1? If not, go back and read it again. These problems differ from those you worked earlier only in that they often contain rational expressions. If you set up the table correctly, you will have little difficulty in solving them.

EXAMPLE 2   A canoe race at summer camp requires each team of canoeists to paddle down the river, which flows at the rate of **3** mph, to a certain marker and back. The winning team, which paddles **5** mph in still water, made the trip from the starting line to the marker and back in **5** hours. How far down the river is the marker?

Answer

	r	t	=	d
downstream	8			x
upstream	2			x

1. **Read.** What are you looking for? You are looking for distance, *x*.

---

2. **Plan.** Is the distance going to the marker the same as the distance from the marker?

   a. Make a table.

   b. Fill in the third column from the table.

	r	t	=	d
downstream	8	$\frac{x}{8}$		x
upstream	2	$\frac{x}{2}$		x

$$\frac{x}{8} + \frac{x}{2} = 5$$

$$8\left(\frac{x}{8} + \frac{x}{2}\right) = 5 \cdot 8$$

$$8\left(\frac{x}{8}\right) + 8\left(\frac{x}{2}\right) = 40$$

$$x + 4x = 40$$

$$5x = 40$$

$$x = 8$$

3. **Solve.** Does the problem contain any information about time that has not been used yet? Yes, the total time is 5 hours.

The distance from the starting line to the marker is 8 miles.

4. **Check.**

▶ A. Exercises

Make a table for exercises 1 and 2 but do not solve.

1. Becky drove the 200 miles to her aunt's house at a speed 3 mph faster than she returned.

2. Brian biked against a 5 mph wind for 50 miles and then returned with the wind.

Make a table and solve.

3. At 7:00 A.M. Joe started walking to school at a rate of 5 mph. At 7:30 his brother Tom started riding a bicycle to school. If Tom rode at a rate of 10 mph, how far did Joe walk before Tom caught up with him?

4. The girls' bus for the senior trip left the school $\frac{1}{2}$ hour later than the boys' bus, which traveled at an average speed of 45 mph. When it finally got going, the girls' bus averaged 50 mph. How long did it take the girls' bus to catch up with the boys' bus?

▶ B. Exercises

5. Two flights left Karr Airport at the same time. One plane flew 250 mph. The other plane flew 375 mph. The faster plane went 750 miles farther than the slower plane and traveled one hour longer. How far did each plane travel?

6. Mr. Truman drove to his cottage in the mountains at a rate of 45 mph. On the way back from the cottage he drove at a speed of 50 mph but took a route 15 miles shorter than the route he traveled to the cottage. How many total miles did he travel on this trip if it took him $\frac{1}{2}$ hour longer to go than to return?

The Seward Special in Alaska

7. Jim and Mike walked 45 minutes to the bicycle repair shop. Their ride home took an hour, but it was 3 miles longer than their walk. If their riding rate was 2 mph faster than their walking rate, how fast did they walk and ride?

8. Lee walks $\frac{1}{10}$ as fast as a train travels. It takes 1.5 hours longer for Lee to walk 12 miles than for the train to travel 60 miles. Find the speed of each.

9. An airplane flew **700** miles with the wind in the same amount of time that it flew **625** miles against the wind. The average speed of the plane with no wind is **265** mph. What was the wind speed?

10. Donna and Evan canoed a total of **14** miles upstream and back. The round trip took **8** hours. If they row at a rate of **4** mph in still water, how fast is the current?

11. The Smiths biked **15** miles from Brattleboro to Keene with a tail wind of **2** mph. If the return trip against the wind took **2** hours longer, how fast would they bike on a calm day?

12. A bicycle club took a weekend trip to a national forest and rode **60** miles at a certain average rate. On their return trip over the same route, they traveled **4** mph faster and took **4** hours less. What were their average rates going and returning?

▶ C. Exercises

13. A touring bus traveling to and from a historical site covers **200** miles in $4\frac{1}{2}$ hours. If the rate returning was **10** mph faster than the rate going, find the rate each way. Also find the amount of time it took to reach the site.

14. Mr. Johnson drives a semitrailer truck. On one trip to a city **275** miles from his home, he traveled $\frac{1}{2}$ hour longer going than he did returning along the same route. How long did it take him to make the trip each way if his rate going was **5** mph slower than his rate returning? How fast did he travel each way?

■ Cumulative Review

Use (1, 3) and (−2, 5) to find

15. the slope of the line through these points.

16. the length of the segment connecting the points.

17. Divide $x^4 - 4x^3 + 3x^2 - 2x + 9$ by $x^2 - 3x + 5$.

18. A chemist wanted to prepare a solution of potassium iodide for an experiment in order to use up some previously prepared solutions of different concentrations. How many grams of a **28%** solution and how many grams of a **60%** solution must she mix in order to prepare **800** grams of a **40%** solution?

19. A gardener has **80** pounds of a lime/fertilizer mixture that is **25%** fertilizer. How much lime should he add to produce a mixture that is **20%** fertilizer?

13.6 Literal Equations

What does *literal* mean? Look up the word in a dictionary. Does *literal* mean what you thought it meant?

In Matthew 5:18, Jesus claimed that the words and letters of the inspired Bible will all be fulfilled exactly as it says. This is what we mean when we say that the Bible is literally true. If you believe something literally, you believe it word for word and letter by letter in context. Since the Bible uses the words "heaven" and "hell" to refer to real places (Matt. 25:40-46), we must believe that they are real places, and we say that there is a *literal* heaven and a *literal* hell.

Electricians use the rational equation called Ohm's law to determine the current I in amps when the resistence R in Ohms and the electromotive force E in volts are known: $I = \frac{E}{R}$.

In a similar way, mathematical sentences contain letters or symbols that have meaning in the context of an equation. The solved equation is equivalent to the original equation. Do you remember solving some literal equations in Chapter 4?

EXAMPLE 1   Solve $F = \frac{WH}{L}$ for H.

Answer

$$F = \frac{WH}{L}$$

$$L \cdot F = \frac{WH}{L} \cdot L \qquad \text{1. The common denominator is } L.$$
$$\text{Multiply both sides by } L.$$

$$LF = WH \qquad \text{2. Now divide both sides by } W.$$

$$\frac{LF}{W} = H$$

EXAMPLE 2 Solve $d = 0.07v^2$ for v.

Answer

$d = 0.07v^2$	
$100d = 7v^2$	1. Clear equations of decimals (multiply by 100).
$\dfrac{100d}{7} = v^2$	2. Divide both sides by 7.
$\pm\sqrt{\dfrac{100d}{7}} = v$ $\dfrac{\pm 10\sqrt{d}}{\sqrt{7}} = v$	3. To find v, you must take the square root of each side and simplify.
$\dfrac{\pm 10\sqrt{7d}}{7} = v$	4. Rationalize the denominator.

EXAMPLE 3 Solve $3a + bx = \dfrac{4x}{5}$ for x.

Answer

$3a + bx = \dfrac{4x}{5}$	
$5(3a + bx) = \dfrac{4x}{5} \cdot 5$	1. Multiply by the denominator.
$15a + 5bx = 4x$ $5bx - 4x = -15a$	2. Get all terms that contain x on one side of the equation.
$x(5b - 4) = -15a$	3. Factor the variable from the left side.
$x = \dfrac{-15a}{5b - 4}$	4. Divide both sides by the coefficient of x.

You have solved a literal equation only when the variable for which you are solving is on one side and all other terms are on the other side. The variable cannot appear on both sides in the final solution.

Solving a Literal Equation

1. Clear the equation of fractions.
2. Perform any indicated operations and combine like terms.
3. Place all terms containing the variable on one side of the equation and all other terms on the other side.
4. If the variable is raised to a power, find the proper root or power to solve for it. Otherwise, factor the variable from all the terms.
5. Divide both sides by the coefficient of the variable.

EXAMPLE 4   Solve $v = e^3$ for e.

Answer $v = e^3$

$\sqrt[3]{v} = \sqrt[3]{e^3}$ Find the cube root of both sides.

$\sqrt[3]{v} = e$

▶ A. Exercises

Solve for the stated variable.

1. $e = mc^2$ for c
2. $s = 16t^2$ for t
3. $p = 0.433h$ for h
4. $I = Prt$ for r
5. $d = rt$ for t
6. $w = \frac{11(h - 40)}{2}$ for h

7. $C = 2\pi r$ for r
8. $w = s + cp$ for p
9. $P = 3s$ for s
10. $V = \pi r^2 h$ for h
11. $A = \pi r^2$ for r
12. $P = 2b + 2h$ for b

▶ B. Exercises

Solve for the stated variable.

13. $V = \frac{4}{3}\pi r^3$ for r
14. $v + 10 = \frac{t}{v} - \frac{25}{v}$ for t
15. $P = \frac{d^2 n}{2.5}$ for d
16. $\frac{nx}{b} - n = x$ for x

17. $\frac{3a}{x - a} = y$ for x
18. $\frac{a}{3 + z} = \frac{b}{3 - z}$ for z
19. $2y - 3x = ay - 2x$ for y
20. $\frac{x}{b} - \frac{x}{c} = x$ for b

▶ C. Exercises

Solve for the stated variable.

21. $Lx^2 - 5nx + 4q = 0$ for x
22. $\frac{3}{v} + R = tv$ for v

■ Cumulative Review

23. Twice a number is eleven. Find the number.
24. The absolute value of four less a number, is less than six. Find the number.
25. The square of a number reduced by twice the number is 15. Find the number.
26. The difference of two numbers is 808, and the sum is 950. Find the numbers.
27. If A varies directly with B and A is 48 when B is 56. Find A when B is 49.

Algebra *and* Scripture

You have seen that there are many fractions in the Bible. If you paid attention to the units, you also noticed that fractions in the Bible describe distance, area, volume, time, and money. In Leviticus the priests had to use fractions for preparing sacrifices, and they even had to work with complex fractions.

Read Numbers 31:25-31. In this passage Moses and Eleazar had to calculate with fractions. The description of their work continues through verse 47.

1. What fraction of the spoil did the soldiers receive?
2. What fraction of the soldiers' portion did the Lord receive?
3. What complex fraction of all the spoil is this? Simplify it.
4. What fraction of the spoil did the rest of the people receive?
5. What fraction did the Levites get from the people's portion?
6. What complex fraction of the spoil is this? Simplify it.

THE *N*TH DEGREE

Find a passage in which the people of Israel listened to the reading of the Old Testament for a fourth of the day and then confessed their sins and worshiped the Lord for another fourth of the day.

Read Ezekiel 5. Notice that Ezekiel's hair forms the whole in verses 1-4.

7. What fractional addition equation can you write from these verses?

8. Write the equation above in multiplication form.

9. What property is illustrated in exercise 8?

Starting in verse twelve of Ezekiel 5, God explains the symbolic meaning of the three portions of Ezekiel's hair. Complete the table.

	fraction	hair (v. 2)	symbolizes (v. 12)
10.	whole	hair	
11.	first part		death by famine and pestilence
12.	second part	hair clipped with knife	
13.	third part		scattering of refugees

14. Use the portions in verse 12 to write another fractional equation. Is it the same?

Chapter 13 Review

Solve the following problems.

1. $\dfrac{x+8}{6} + \dfrac{x-6}{2} = 1$

2. $\dfrac{x^2}{4} = \dfrac{13x}{8} + 3$

3. $\dfrac{5}{x} = 25$

4. $\dfrac{6}{x-3} = 3$

5. $\dfrac{x+8}{2x-6} = \dfrac{17}{23}$

6. $\dfrac{12x-3}{x^2+4x-5} - \dfrac{5}{x+5} = \dfrac{6}{x-1}$

7. $\dfrac{3}{8x} + \dfrac{1}{4} = \dfrac{5}{6x}$

8. $\dfrac{-5x+8}{x^2-9} + \dfrac{5}{x+3} = \dfrac{7x}{2x-6}$

9. $\dfrac{2x-2}{x^4-x^2} = \dfrac{x-5}{x^3+x^2}$

10. $\dfrac{6}{x^2-x-2} = \dfrac{-1}{x^2+x-6} - \dfrac{4}{x^2+4x+3}$

Solve each literal equation.

11. $\dfrac{R}{n} = n$ for n

12. $3x + 4z = n$ for z

13. $\dfrac{3A}{R-A} = S$ for R

14. $\dfrac{3A}{R-A} = S$ for A

15. $\dfrac{1}{M} + \dfrac{1}{N} = \dfrac{1}{Q}$ for M

16. $r^2 - 3r = K$ for r

Complete each table and write an equation.

17.

	r	t	=	d
going	x − 5	7		
returning	x + 5	4		

18.

	hours alone	portion of job/hour
first	5	
second	x	
together	2	

19. total time = 7 hours

	r	t	=	d
going	x + 3			40
returning	x			50

20.

	hours alone	part done in one hour
Ben	x	
Sarah	2x	
Joe	x + 5	
together	8	

Solve.

21. What number must be added to both the numerator and the denominator of $\frac{7}{8}$ to produce a fraction equivalent to $\frac{12}{13}$?

22. Dana has decorated the church for Christmas in 5 hours and Carla has done it in 3 hours. If they work together, how long will it take them?

23. Joan can wallpaper a living room in 9 hours. Kelly is inexperienced at wallpapering, but she wants to learn. If they work together on wallpapering the living room, it takes 6 hours. How long would it take Kelly to wallpaper the living room by herself?

24. Paul bikes 40 miles in the same time that Mary drives 100 miles. If Mary travels 12 mph more than twice Paul's rate, how fast does each travel?

25. Sandy invested $1000, part at 11% and part at 7%. If she earned $100 annually, how much is invested at each rate?

26. Ken and Dave can each paint the house in 12 hours, but Stan can do it in 10 hours. If the 3 work together, how long will it take?

27. What is the mathematical significance of Ezekiel 5:12?

14 Quadratic Functions

$y = mx + b$

Shasta Dam is among the ten highest dams in the United States. This dam on the Sacramento River in northern California is 602 feet high and 3460 feet across. Its 6.3 million cubic yards of concrete weighs 15 million tons. Shasta Lake, the reservoir behind the dam, contains 6.25 billion tons of water and offers water sports and habitat for fish and game. The base of the dam is 883 feet wide to withstand the thousands of pounds of water pressure per square foot.

Shasta Dam has seven hydroelectric generators that produce two billion kilowatt-hours of electricity annually, which supplies energy to residents of northern California. The water that pours through the dam creates a waterfall 487 feet high or 2.5 times the height of Niagara Falls.

Before construction began on Shasta Dam, engineers had to make detailed topographical maps and perform extensive geological studies. One of these civil engineers has said, "Algebra seems like the *ABC*'s to us. Algebra seems so easy that we don't even think about what we're doing." You are not yet able to understand the complex equations used to design Shasta Dam, but you can learn these *ABC*'s now. Quadratic functions, such as $f(x) = 3x^2 + 2x - 5$, are used often in the engineering field. By the end of this chapter, you should be able to find the zeros of this function and graph it. These concepts are also important in the mathematical field of calculus, which engineers also use.

After this chapter you should be able to

1. use function notation.

2. graph quadratic functions.

3. place quadratic functions in the proper form for graphing.

4. find the zeros of a quadratic function.

5. apply quadratic functions to word problems.

14.1 Quadratic Functions of the Form $f(x) = ax^2$

When you studied linear equations, you learned that a relation is a set of ordered pairs, and a function is a special kind of relation. Therefore, any function, linear or quadratic, is a special set of ordered pairs. In a linear equation such as $y = x + 5$, the value of y depends upon the value of x. Thus, y is called a function of x, abbreviated $f(x)$, and when described as a set is written $\{(x, y) | y = x + 5\}$, which is read "the set of ordered pairs (x, y) such that y equals x plus 5." To graph such a function, you first make a table of values.

x	y
0	5
1	6
2	7

Another way to express a function is to use function notation. Thus, $f = \{(x, y) | y = x + 5\}$ would be written $f(x) = x + 5$ and read "f of x is equal to x plus 5." Since y and $f(x)$ are the same, the table looks almost the same using function notation.

x	f(x)
0	5
1	6
2	7

To evaluate a function, simply substitute the value of x into the expression for $f(x)$.

EXAMPLE 1   For $f(x) = x - 8$, find $f(x)$ when $x = 4$, $x = -2$, and $x = 6$.

Answer
$$f(x) = \ \ x - 8$$
$$f(4) = \ \ 4 - 8 = -4$$
$$f(-2) = -2 - 8 = -10$$
$$f(6) = \ \ 6 - 8 = -2$$

Substitute values of x into the function to find the values of $f(x)$.

Thus, $f(4) = -4$, $f(-2) = -10$, and $f(6) = -2$.

Function notation can also be written as a set of ordered pairs.

EXAMPLE 2   If $f(x) = x^2 + 8$, evaluate $f(2)$, $f(-4)$, and $f(0)$. Then express the answers as ordered pairs.

Answer

$f(x) = x^2 + 8$
$f(2) = 2^2 + 8 = 4 + 8 = 12$
$f(-4) = (-4)^2 + 8 = 16 + 8 = 24$
$f(0) = 0^2 + 8 = 0 + 8 = 8$

x	$f(x)$
2	12
-4	24
0	8

$\{(-4, 24), (0, 8), (2, 12)\}$

You can easily graph a quadratic function on a Cartesian plane using the y-axis as the $f(x)$ axis. Notice that a quadratic function, like a quadratic equation, involves a second-degree polynomial.

Definition

A **quadratic function** is a function of the form $f(x) = ax^2 + bx + c$, where a, b, and c are real numbers and $a \neq 0$.

Consider now some quadratic functions of the form $f(x) = ax^2$.

EXAMPLE 3   Graph $f(x) = 3x^2$.

Answer

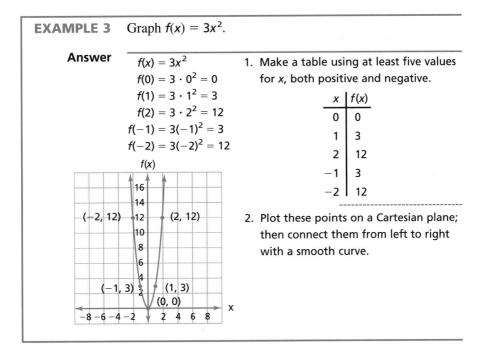

$f(x) = 3x^2$
$f(0) = 3 \cdot 0^2 = 0$
$f(1) = 3 \cdot 1^2 = 3$
$f(2) = 3 \cdot 2^2 = 12$
$f(-1) = 3(-1)^2 = 3$
$f(-2) = 3(-2)^2 = 12$

1. Make a table using at least five values for x, both positive and negative.

x	$f(x)$
0	0
1	3
2	12
-1	3
-2	12

2. Plot these points on a Cartesian plane; then connect them from left to right with a smooth curve.

Notice the shape of the graph. It is not a straight line because the equation is not a linear equation. This figure is called a *parabola*. The graph of any quadratic function is a parabola.

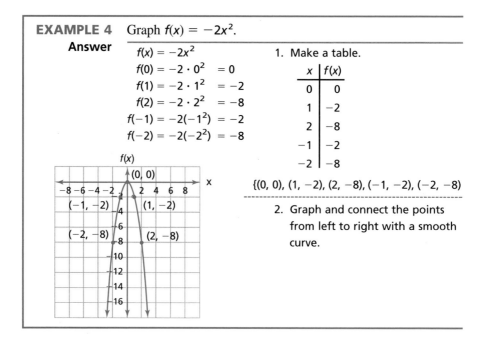

EXAMPLE 4 Graph $f(x) = -2x^2$.

Answer

$f(x) = -2x^2$

$f(0) = -2 \cdot 0^2 \quad = 0$

$f(1) = -2 \cdot 1^2 \quad = -2$

$f(2) = -2 \cdot 2^2 \quad = -8$

$f(-1) = -2(-1^2) \quad = -2$

$f(-2) = -2(-2^2) \quad = -8$

1. Make a table.

x	$f(x)$
0	0
1	-2
2	-8
-1	-2
-2	-8

$\{(0, 0), (1, -2), (2, -8), (-1, -2), (-2, -8)\}$

2. Graph and connect the points from left to right with a smooth curve.

The arrows at the ends of the parabola indicate that the parabola will extend without limit. The highest or lowest point of the parabola is called the *vertex*. The vertex of the parabolas in examples 3 and 4 is (0, 0).

Graphing Quadratic Equations of the Form $f(x) = ax^2$

1. Find at least five ordered pairs that satisfy the function.
2. Plot the ordered pairs on a Cartesian plane.
3. Connect the ordered pairs from left to right with a smooth curve.

▶ A. Exercises

Find $f(0)$, $f(2)$, $f(-1)$, and $f(4)$ for each function.

1. $f(x) = x + 3$
2. $f(x) = -x - 6$
3. $f(x) = 2x$
4. $f(x) = -2x + 6$
5. $f(x) = x^2$

6. $f(x) = x^2 - 4$
7. $f(x) = x^2 + 5$
8. $f(x) = 2x^2$
9. $f(x) = 3x^2 - 7$
10. $f(x) = 2x^2 - 8$

Graph each quadratic function.

11. $f(x) = x^2$

12. $f(x) = 2x^2$

▶ B. Exercises

Graph each quadratic function.

13. $f(x) = \frac{1}{2}x^2$

14. $f(x) = -\frac{1}{3}x^2$

15. $f(x) = -10x^2$

16. $f(x) = \frac{2}{3}x^2$

17. Where is the vertex in each graph? Where is the vertex of any quadratic function of the form $f(x) = ax^2$?

18. The *axis of symmetry* of a parabola is the vertical line across which the parabola may be reflected. What is the axis of symmetry in the equations you graphed?

19. Does the graph open upward or downward if $a > 0$?

20. Give the *y*-intercept of the graphs above.

Let $f(x) = 3x^2 - 7x - 18$.

21. Find $f(-1)$.

22. Find $f(0)$.

23. Find $f\left(\sqrt{11}\right)$.

24. For what value of x does $f(x) = 2$?

▶ C. Exercises

25. Given $f(x) = 0.2x^2 + 0.3$,
    a. find $f(x)$ for $x = \pm1, \pm2$, and ±3.
    b. graph the function.
    c. give the coordinates of the vertex.
    d. give the equation of the axis of symmetry.

Cumulative Review

26. Simplify $-4 - \{-[-3 + (-7)] + [-5(-9 - 1)]\} \div (-5)$.

27. Solve $3 - (-x + 2) = 10 \div 2$.

28. Jay has $3.41 in pennies and dimes. How many of each are there if there are five more than six time as many pennies as dimes?

29. If 97 is at least 3 more than twice a number, what could the number be?

30. Sales tax varies directly with the cost of an item. If a $527 item is taxed $36.89, how much tax will you pay on an item costing $297?

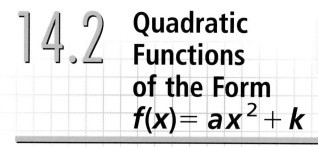 

14.2 Quadratic Functions of the Form $f(x) = ax^2 + k$

Model rockets follow a parabolic trajectory.
The vertex is at the maximum height of the rocket.

In the last section you learned about function notation and that the graph of a quadratic function forms a parabola. How does the quadratic function $f(x) = ax^2 + k$ differ from the ones in the last section? How will the extra term affect the graph of the function? As you study the examples, notice what happens to the vertex and axis of symmetry for these graphs.

EXAMPLE 1 Graph $f(x) = 2x^2 + 4$.

Answer

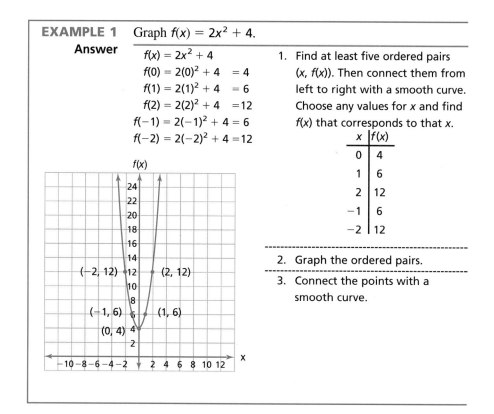

$f(x) = 2x^2 + 4$
$f(0) = 2(0)^2 + 4 = 4$
$f(1) = 2(1)^2 + 4 = 6$
$f(2) = 2(2)^2 + 4 = 12$
$f(-1) = 2(-1)^2 + 4 = 6$
$f(-2) = 2(-2)^2 + 4 = 12$

1. Find at least five ordered pairs $(x, f(x))$. Then connect them from left to right with a smooth curve. Choose any values for x and find $f(x)$ that corresponds to that x.

x	$f(x)$
0	4
1	6
2	12
−1	6
−2	12

2. Graph the ordered pairs.

3. Connect the points with a smooth curve.

EXAMPLE 2 Graph $f(x) = -3x^2 - 2$.

Answer

$f(x) = -3x^2 - 2$

$f(0) = -3(0)^2 - 2 = -2$

$f(1) = -3(1)^2 - 2 = -5$

$f(2) = -3(2)^2 - 2 = -14$

$f(-1) = -3(-1)^2 - 2 = -5$

$f(-2) = -3(-2)^2 - 2 = -14$

x	f(x)
0	-2
1	-5
2	-14
-1	-5
-2	-14

Recall the form of the equations here, $f(x) = ax^2 + k$, and notice that if $a > 0$ the curve opens up as in example 1, and if $a < 0$ it opens down as in example 2. Did you recognize that the extra term $+k$ moves the vertex of the parabola up or down k units?

▶ A. Exercises

Graph each quadratic function.

1. $f(x) = x^2 + 2$
2. $f(x) = x^2 - 7$
3. $f(x) = x^2 - 1$
4. $f(x) = x^2 + 3$

5. $f(x) = -x^2 + 2$
6. $f(x) = -x^2 - 5$
7. $f(x) = 2x^2 - 3$
8. $f(x) = -5x^2 + 1$

9. $f(x) = 2x^2 + 3$
10. $f(x) = \frac{1}{2}x^2 + 5$

Study exercises 1-10. Can you tell from the equation where the vertex will be and which direction it will open? Check your theory by identifying the vertex and direction of each parabola below without graphing.

11. $f(x) = x^2 + 1$
12. $f(x) = -x^2 + 4$

13. $f(x) = -3x^2 - 5$
14. $f(x) = 3x^2 - 9$

▶ B. Exercises

Graph each quadratic function without making a table of values.

15. $f(x) = \frac{1}{4}x^2 + 2$
16. $f(x) = -3x^2 + 4$

17. $f(x) = \frac{2}{3}x^2 - 6$
18. $f(x) = -\frac{1}{5}x^2 + 4$

19. $f(x) = 7x^2 - 1$

20. What was the axis of symmetry in all of these graphs?

▶ C. Exercises

21. Make a table of values for $x = y^2$, and graph it.
    a. Which way does it open?
    b. Where is the vertex?
    c. What is the equation of the axis of symmetry?
    d. In what way is it fundamentally different from the previous parabolas graphed?

Cumulative Review

22. Solve $5 - x > 8$.
23. Multiply $(x - 4)(x^4 + 4x^3 + 16x^2 + 64x + 256)$.
24. Factor $18x^3 + 33x^2 - 105x$.
25. Solve the system.
    $$4x + 3y = 8$$
    $$2x - y = -1$$
26. One number is 32 more than twice another. The difference between them is 103. Find the numbers.

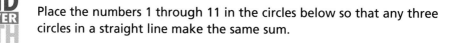

Place the numbers 1 through 11 in the circles below so that any three circles in a straight line make the same sum.

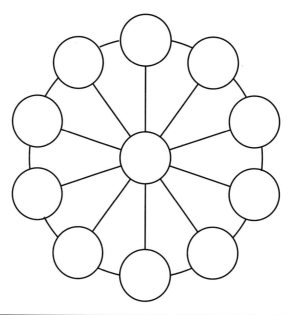

14.3 Quadratic Functions of the Form $f(x) = a(x-h)^2 + k$

The final type of quadratic function is of the form $f(x) = a(x - h)^2 + k$. You learned in the last section that the k term in the function $f(x) = ax^2 + k$ moved the graph vertically from the origin. If $k > 0$, the parabola moved up k units; if $k < 0$, the parabola moved down k units. Another term has been added to the same basic function. What do you think the value h might do to the graph? Watch the examples to see what happens to the graph now.

EXAMPLE 1 Graph $f(x) = (x - 2)^2 + 4$.

Answer

$a = 1$
$h = 2$
$k = 4$

1. Determine the value of a, h, and k to find the maximum or minimum value of the parabola.

$f(-1) = (-1 - 2)^2 + 4 = 13$
$f(0) = (0 - 2)^2 + 4\ \ = 8$
$f(1) = (1 - 2)^2 + 4\ \ = 5$
$f(2) = (2 - 2)^2 + 4\ \ = 4$
$f(3) = (3 - 2)^2 + 4\ \ = 5$
$f(4) = (4 - 2)^2 + 4\ \ = 8$
$f(5) = (5 - 2)^2 + 4\ \ = 13$

2. Choose some values for x and make a table of ordered pairs for this function.

x	$f(x)$
−1	13
0	8
1	5
2	4
3	5
4	8
5	13

3. Graph these ordered pairs, and connect them with a smooth curve from left to right.

What happened to the parabola? How does this graph vary from the graph in the previous section? The k value moved the vertex vertically as before. In example 1 k was four and the graph moved up 4 units. In this example, the graph moved 2 units to the right of the y-axis. Notice that $h = 2$ in the equation, and the axis of symmetry is the line $x = 2$.

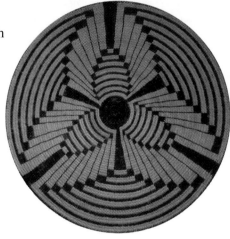

EXAMPLE 2   Graph $f(x) = -2(x - 3)^2 + 1$.

Answer $f(1) = -2(1 - 3)^2 + 1 = -7$
$f(2) = -2(2 - 3)^2 + 1 = -1$
$f(3) = -2(3 - 3)^2 + 1 = 1$
$f(4) = -2(4 - 3)^2 + 1 = -1$
$f(5) = -2(5 - 3)^2 + 1 = -7$

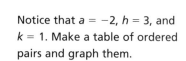

Notice that $a = -2$, $h = 3$, and $k = 1$. Make a table of ordered pairs and graph them.

x	$f(x)$
1	-7
2	-1
3	1
4	-1
5	-7

In this example, $h = 3$ and $k = 1$. Notice that the vertex is $(h, k) = (3, 1)$.

Graphing Quadratic Equations of the Form $f(x) = a(x - h)^2 + k$

1. Make a table of ordered pairs and graph them. The vertex will be (h, k).
2. Connect the ordered pairs from left to right with a smooth curve.

Where would the vertex be if the equation was $f(x) = (x + 3)^2 - 1$? Since $x + 3 = x - (-3)$, $h = -3$, and $(h, k) = (-3, -1)$.

If a quadratic function is not in the form $f(x) = a(x - h)^2 + k$, you can change it to the proper form by following a procedure very similar to the completing-the-square procedure that you learned in Chapter 11.

EXAMPLE 3   Graph $f(x) = x^2 - 6x + 10$.

Answer

1. Since this quadratic function is not in the correct form, you must place it in the correct form by completing the square on the right. Leave the constant term on the outside of the parentheses.
$$f(x) = (x^2 - 6x) + 10$$

2. Complete the square of the terms inside the parentheses by taking $\frac{1}{2}$ of the coefficient of x and squaring it. Since you are adding 9 in the parentheses, you must subtract 9 outside of the parentheses.
$$\frac{1}{2} \cdot 6 = 3$$
$$3^2 = 9$$
$$f(x) = (x^2 - 6x + 9) + 10 - 9$$

3. Factor inside the parentheses and add the constants outside.
$$f(x) = (x - 3)^2 + 1$$

4. Now the function is in the proper form and can be graphed easily. Identify a, h, and k. The vertex is (h, k), or (3, 1), and the graph opens upward because $a > 0$. Find four more ordered pairs and graph them.

$a = 1$
$h = 3$
$k = 1$

x	$f(x)$
1	5
2	2
3	1
4	2
5	5

EXAMPLE 4   Graph $f(x) = -2x^2 - 12x - 19$.

Answer

$f(x) = -2x^2 - 12x - 19$

1. This function must be placed in the form $f(x) = a(x - h)^2 + k$ by completing the square.

$f(x) = -2(x^2 + 6x) - 19$

2. Group the first two terms together. Then factor -2 from these two terms.

Continued ▶

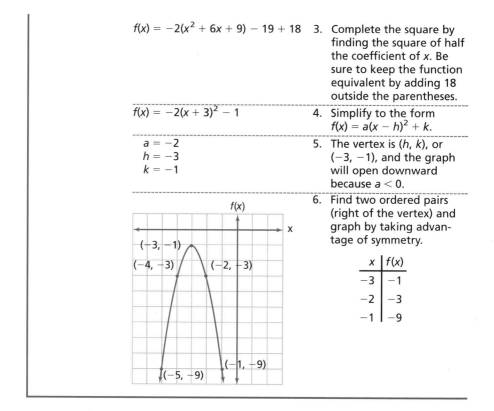

$f(x) = -2(x^2 + 6x + 9) - 19 + 18$ 3. Complete the square by finding the square of half the coefficient of x. Be sure to keep the function equivalent by adding 18 outside the parentheses.

$f(x) = -2(x + 3)^2 - 1$ 4. Simplify to the form $f(x) = a(x - h)^2 + k$.

$a = -2$
$h = -3$
$k = -1$

5. The vertex is (h, k), or $(-3, -1)$, and the graph will open downward because $a < 0$.

6. Find two ordered pairs (right of the vertex) and graph by taking advantage of symmetry.

x	$f(x)$
-3	-1
-2	-3
-1	-9

▶ A. Exercises

Graph each quadratic function.

1. $f(x) = (x - 4)^2 + 2$
2. $f(x) = (x - 2)^2$
3. $f(x) = (x - 1)^2 - 3$
4. $f(x) = -2(x - 2)^2 + 5$
5. $f(x) = (x + 3)^2$

6. $f(x) = (x + 1)^2 - 2$
7. $f(x) = -(x + 4)^2 + 1$
8. $f(x) = (x - 3)^2 - 8$
9. $f(x) = 3(x + 1)^2 + 4$
10. $f(x) = \frac{-1}{2}(x - 2)^2 + 3$

▶ B. Exercises

Place each quadratic function in the form $f(x) = a(x - h)^2 + k$.

11. $f(x) = x^2 + 4x - 12$
12. $f(x) = x^2 - 6x + 8$
13. $f(x) = x^2 - 3x$
14. $f(x) = x^2 + 14x + 40$
15. $f(x) = x^2 - 8x + 15$

16. $f(x) = x^2 + 10x + 24$
17. $f(x) = x^2 + x - 6$
18. $f(x) = x^2 - x + 2$
19. $f(x) = x^2 - x - 12$
20. $f(x) = x^2 + 4x - 5$

Give the vertex, tell whether the graph opens upward or downward, and give the axis of symmetry.

21. $f(x) = 3(x - 2)^2 + 4$ 23. $f(x) = x^2 - x - 30$
22. $f(x) = -4(x + 3)^2 - 2$ 24. $f(x) = 3x^2 - 2x - 8$

▶ C. Exercises

25. Given $f(x) = \frac{1}{3}x^2 + 2x + \frac{3}{2}$,
    a. find the vertex.
    b. tell which way it opens.
    c. write the equation of the axis of symmetry.
    d. graph the function.

■ Cumulative Review

Simplify.

26. $\dfrac{x}{x + \sqrt{5}}$

27. $\dfrac{8}{x + 1} - \dfrac{3}{x}$

Solve.

28. $3x + 8 = 5x + 9$

29. $2x^2 - 3x + 1 = 0$

30. $\dfrac{8}{x + 1} - \dfrac{3}{x} = 1$

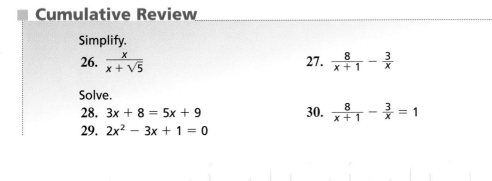

14.4   Zeros of a Function

$\mathbf{D}$o you remember what the y-intercept is? It is the point at which the graph crosses the y-axis. The value of x at this point is always 0. Likewise, the point at which the graph crosses the x-axis is called the x-intercept. The value of y at this point is always 0. Since $f(x)$ in function notation corresponds to y, the value of x at the point at which the graph crosses the x-axis is called the zero of the function.

Definition

A **zero of a function (x-intercept)** is the value of x at the point at which the graph of the function crosses the x-axis.

A linear function has one real zero unless it is a horizontal line, but a quadratic function can have up to two real zeros. To find the zeros of a function algebraically, set the function equal to **0** and solve for *x*.

EXAMPLE 1 Find the zeros of this quadratic function.

f(x)

Answer Since the graph crosses the *x*-axis at (**1, 0**) and (**4, 0**), the zeros of the function are *x* = **1** and *x* = **4**.

EXAMPLE 2 Find the zeros of $f(x) = x^2 - 5x - 6$ algebraically.

Answer

$$f(x) = x^2 - 5x - 6$$
$$x^2 - 5x - 6 = 0$$

1. Set the function equal to zero and solve for *x*.

$$(x - 6)(x + 1) = 0$$

2. Factor and set each factor equal to 0.

$$x - 6 = 0 \qquad x + 1 = 0$$
$$x = 6 \qquad\quad x = -1$$

The zeros of this function are *x* = 6 and *x* = −1.

EXAMPLE 3 Find the zeros of $f(x) = x^2 - 2x - 5$.

Answer $x^2 - 2x - 5 = 0$

$$x = \frac{2 \pm \sqrt{(-2)^2 - 4(1)(-5)}}{2(1)}$$

$$x = \frac{2 \pm \sqrt{24}}{2}$$

$$x = \frac{2 \pm 2\sqrt{6}}{2}$$

$$x = \frac{2(1 \pm \sqrt{6})}{2}$$

$$x = 1 \pm \sqrt{6} \approx 3.45 \text{ and } -1.45$$

Since the quadratic will not factor, the quadratic formula must be used.

You should recognize that a quadratic function has one zero when the vertex is on the *x*-axis (see Section 14.1). There are no zeros when the graph does not cross the *x*-axis (see the graphs in Section 14.2).

► A. Exercises

Graph each function and find its zeros.

1. $f(x) = x^2 + 3$
2. $f(x) = (x - 3)^2$
3. $f(x) = 2(x + 1)^2 - 8$
4. $f(x) = -2(x + 3)^2 - 2$
5. $f(x) = x^2 - 2x - 8$
6. $f(x) = -x^2 - 6x - 9$

Identify the y-intercept of each function.

7. $f(x) = 3x - 5$
8. $f(x) = x^2 + 8$
9. $f(x) = 4x^2 - 5x$
10. $f(x) = 3x^2 - 2x + 1$

► B. Exercises

Find the zeros of each function algebraically.

11. $f(x) = x^2 - 16$
12. $f(x) = x^2 - 7x + 12$
13. $f(x) = (x + 2)^2 - 3$
14. $f(x) = x^2 - 5x + 6$
15. $f(x) = x^2 + 3x$
16. $f(x) = x^2 - 4x - 4$
17. $f(x) = x^2 - 8x + 16$
18. $f(x) = x^2 + 6x - 9$

► C. Exercises

19. Given $f(x) = -1.5x^2 - 7x + 12$,
    a. find the vertex algebraically.
    b. tell which way it opens.
    c. find all zeros by using the quadratic formula.

■ Cumulative Review

20. Graph $f(x) = -3x$.
21. Find the distance between $(2, 5)$ and $(-3, 7)$.
22. A passenger train, going 30 mph faster than a freight train, travels 560 miles in 6 hours less time. Find their speeds.

Canadian Pacific Railway

23. Simplify $(x^2 + 3x) + (2x^2 - 5x + 4)$.
24. Solve $x^2 + 3x = 2x^2 - 5x + 4$.

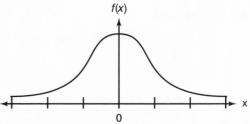

Standard Normal Distribution

The bell-shaped curve is a special function called the *standard normal distribution*. This equation, graphed below, uses the number e. The value of e is approximately 2.7.

$$f(x) = \frac{1}{\sqrt{2\pi}} e^{-\frac{1}{2}x^2}$$

The function above is called an exponential function since the variable is in the exponent.

The formula above does not tell us how to find the percentage of scores at various distances from the mean. Using calculus, mathematicians have calculated the table of z-scores on page 593. Notice that the first decimal point of the z-score is on the left margin and the second decimal point is across the top. The graph reminds you that you are finding an area that represents the percentage of the whole.

EXAMPLE 1   Gas consumption for compact cars averages **30.3** miles per gallon with a standard deviation of **4.4** mpg. What percentage of compact cars get between **25** and **30.3** miles per gallon?

Answer   Sketch a normal curve with a mean at **30.3**. Label **25** and shade from **25** to **30.3** as shown.

Next, find the z-scores. Since **30.3** is the mean, it has a z-score of zero. For the value of **25**,

$$z = \frac{x - \bar{x}}{s} = \frac{25 - 30.3}{4.4} = -\frac{5.3}{4.4} \approx -1.20.$$

Consult the table on page 593 under **1.20** to obtain **0.3849**, or about **38.5%**. This represents the percentage of scores between z = 0 and z = 1.2. By symmetry this percentage is the same as the desired percentage. So **38.5%** of compact cars get between **25** and **30.3** mpg.

EXAMPLE 2   An elevator designer knows that the total weight of eight passengers averages 1200 pounds with a standard deviation of 99 pounds. What is the probability that the total weight exceeds 1350 pounds?

Answer   Compute the *z*-score for 1350:

$$z = \frac{x - \bar{x}}{s} = \frac{1350 - 1200}{99} = 1.52.$$

Look up 1.52 on the table on page 593 to obtain the percentage 0.4357, or about 44%. Remember that this number represents weights between 1200 and 1350. To find weights exceeding 1350, we must subtract from 50%, as you can see from the sketch: 50% − 43.6% = 6.4%.

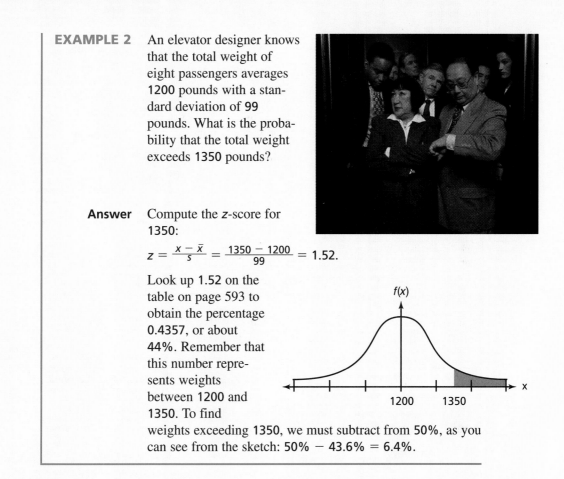

▶ Exercises

1. Find *f*(−1) for the standard normal distribution.

What percentage of scores have *z*-scores between

2. 0 and 2.38?   3. −0.56 and 1.23?

4. While the 6.4% in example 2 is quite low, it is still too high a probability when human lives are in jeopardy. What is the probability that the weight exceeds 1500 pounds?

5. The daily revenue of a small restaurant averages $530 with a standard deviation of $120. If the restaurant has daily costs of $310, on what percentage of the days do they lose money?

14.5 Applications of Quadratic Functions

Quadratic functions are often used to solve maximum or minimum problems. The maximum or minimum of a quadratic function is the value of the function at its vertex. If the parabola opens upward, the quadratic has a minimum point; that is, *y* has a smallest value. If the parabola opens downward, the quadratic has a maximum point (largest value for *y*). Do you remember how to tell if a parabola opens upward or downward? When the quadratic function is of the form $f(x) = a(x - h)^2 + k$, the *a* will tell whether the vertex is the maximum or minimum point of the function.

If $a > 0$, $f(x)$ opens upward and has a minimum point.

If $a < 0$, $f(x)$ opens downward and has a maximum point.

Remember, to graph a quadratic function, make sure that it is in the form $f(x) = a(x - h)^2 + k$.

Now you are ready to solve word problems involving quadratic functions. You should have these steps memorized. For review, turn to page 132.

EXAMPLE 1   A farmer wants to fence in a rectangular pen along the bank of a stream but does not want to use any fencing on the bank. If he has **60** yards of fencing altogether, what should be the dimensions of the pen to allow for maximum area?

Answer

Let *x* = the width of the pen

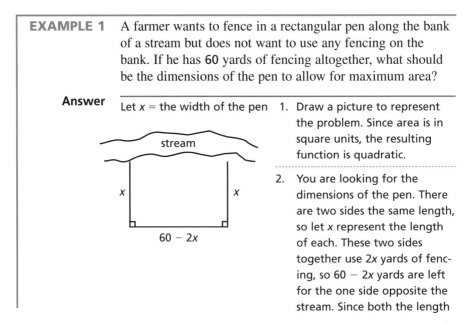

1. Draw a picture to represent the problem. Since area is in square units, the resulting function is quadratic.

2. You are looking for the dimensions of the pen. There are two sides the same length, so let *x* represent the length of each. These two sides together use 2*x* yards of fencing, so 60 − 2*x* yards are left for the one side opposite the stream. Since both the length

Continued ▶

and the width are in terms of x, the area is a function of x. Next find the area of the rectangle using the formula $A = lw$.

$60 - 2x =$ the length of the pen
$$f(x) = x(60 - 2x)$$
$$f(x) = 60x - 2x^2$$
$$f(x) = -2x^2 + 60x$$

3. The quadratic function needs to be placed in the form $f(x) = a(x - h)^2 + k$ so that you can find the vertex quickly. Factor -2 from the variable terms. Then complete the square.

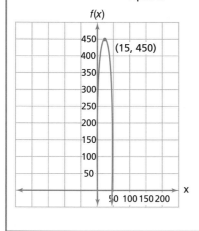

$$f(x) = -2(x^2 - 30x)$$
$$f(x) = -2(x^2 - 30x + 225) + 450$$
$$f(x) = -2(x - 15)^2 + 450$$

The value of $a = -2$, $h = 15$, and $k = 450$. Now graph the parabola. The vertex is (h, k), or $(15, 450)$. It is a maximum point because a is less than 0. What do the values at this point represent? The first number in the ordered pair, 15, is x, the width of the pen. The second number, 450, is $f(x)$, which represents the area. To find the length of the pen, substitute 15 for x in $60 - 2x$.

$$60 - 2(15) = 60 - 30 = 30$$

The function has a maximum of 450 when $x = 15$. In other words, for a maximum area of 450 square yards, the pen should be 15 yards wide and 30 yards long.

EXAMPLE 2   The distance that a ball thrown into the air travels depends upon time, gravity, and velocity. The equation $f(t) = -16t^2 + 96t$ includes the factors of gravity and velocity and is written in terms of time in seconds, where $f(t)$ is the height in feet the ball reaches at a particular time. Find the maximum height the ball reaches and the number of seconds it will take the ball to reach this height.

Answer   Factor -16 out of the quadratic function and complete the square.

$$f(t) = -16t^2 + 96t$$
$$= -16(t^2 - 6t)$$
$$= -16(t^2 - 6t + 9) + 144$$
$$= -16(t - 3)^2 + 144$$

Continued ▶

The vertex is (**3, 144**), and it is a maximum point because *a* is less than **0**. Since the function is a function of *t*, the ordered pair (**3, 144**) is of the form (*t*, *f(t)*). So *t* = **3** and *f(t)* = **144**. The ball will reach a maximum height of **144** feet in **3** seconds. Notice that if the quadratic function is in the form $f(x) = a(x - h)^2 + k$, you do not need to graph the parabola. Simply identify *k* from the vertex (*h, k*) as the maximum or minimum value. This maximum (or minimum) occurs when *x = h*.

▶ A. Exercises

1. Find the dimensions of a rectangular rug that has a perimeter of **80** feet and the maximum possible area.

2. Pastor Kliewer wants to fence in an area beside the pond on the church property to make a rectangular recreation area for the church. If he has **50** yards of fencing to enclose an area bordering the pond and he wants to make sure he has the maximum area, what should be the dimensions of the area?

3. Of all the pairs of numbers whose difference is **8**, only one pair has a product smaller than any other pair. Find this pair of numbers.

4. The difference of two numbers is **12**, and their product is a minimum. What are the two numbers?

5. Julie wants to place **44** feet of picket fencing around a garden to create the largest area possible. What dimensions should her garden be to have the maximum area?

The revenue resulting from manufacturing and selling a product is represented by $R(x) = -\frac{1}{4}(x - 200)^2 + 750$, where *x* is the number manufactured and *R(x)* is the income generated.

6. How much income is gained (or lost) by manufacturing **100** items? **250** items?

7. How many should be produced for maximum profit?

8. What would the maximum profit be?

▶ B. Exercises

9. If the height a ball reaches when thrown into the air can be given by the equation $f(t) = -16t^2 + 64t$, where *t* is time in seconds and *f(t)* the height in feet, how long will it take the ball to reach its maximum height? What is the maximum height?

10. The cost equation used by the R & E Manufacturing Co. is $C(x) = 2x^2 - 8x + 12$, where x represents the number of hours it takes to produce a particular product and $C(x)$ represents the cost of production in hundreds of dollars. What would be the minimum cost possible?

11. The accountants at the new microwave oven company have found that the equation $P(x) = -x^2 + 600x + 500$ relates the amount of profit that the company makes to the number of items made. How many ovens should the company produce to make the maximum profit? What will that profit be?

12. The B & J Co. wants to produce items at a minimum cost to the company. If the cost of the items follows the equation $C(x) = x^2 - 140x + 5700$, where x is the number of items produced, how many items should they make to keep the cost to a minimum? What is the minimum cost?

13. Ross wants to create a rectangular pasture that has a maximum area and borders a river so that no fencing is required on that side of the pasture. What should the dimensions of the pasture and the maximum area of the pasture be if he has only 120 yards of fencing material available?

▶ C. Exercises

14. Given x feet of fencing, which shape would give maximum area, a square or a circle?
    a. Express the length s of a side of a square, and the radius r of a circle, in terms of x.
    b. Express the area of the square and of the circle in terms of x.
    c. Answer the original question and justify your answer.

Cumulative Review

15. Divide $x^2 + 5x - 7$ by $x + 1$.
16. Graph $y \le \frac{1}{2} x - 2$.
17. Graph $3x + 2y > 4$.
18. Solve $3x^2 + 7x - 5 = 0$.
19. Find the slope of $5x + 7y = 8$.
20. Find the zeros of $f(x) = x^2 + 4x + 4$.

Algebra and Scripture

When graphing quadratic equations, draw arrows at the ends of the curve to show that the curve continues. If the parabola has a minimum, *y* increases very quickly as *x* increases. In this case, the arrows represent larger and larger numbers. Are large numbers found in the Bible?

Identify the large numbers in each verse below.

1. I Samuel 4:10
2. II Samuel 24:15
3. I Kings 20:29
4. II Kings 5:5
5. I Chronicles 21:5
6. II Chronicles 13:17

The Bible rounds off some large numbers but not others. This is exactly what we do in daily speech, depending on how precise the information needs to be.

7. How do you know that the large number in Judges 16:27 is rounded off?
8. Explain why we know the large number in Jeremiah 52:28 is not rounded.
9. What is the largest number you found in exercises 1-8?

THE Nth DEGREE

Probably the largest number in Scripture is in the first half of Revelation. Can you find it?

In Matthew 14:15-21, Jesus miraculously fed a large crowd when there was only a little food available. Notice that the number of men is rounded off and that women and children were also present. Since the men comprised only a part of the people present, a round figure was especially appropriate.

Scriptural Roots

AND THEY THAT HAD EATEN were about five thousand men, beside women and children. 🙠

MATTHEW 14:21

Chapter 14 Review

If $f(x) = x^2 + 5x - 7$, find the following.

1. $f(2)$
2. $f(-1)$

Find $f(3)$ if

3. $f(x) = 2x^2 - 7x + 1$.
4. $f(x) = \sqrt{x + 1}$.

Find the value of each function when $x = -5$, $x = 3$, and $x = 10$.

5. $f(x) = 12x - 7$
6. $f(x) = x^2 + 2x - 3$

Use $f(x) = 3x^2 - x - 14$. Do not graph.

7. Find $f(3)$.
8. Find the y-intercept.
9. Does it open up or down?
10. Find the zeros.
11. Find the vertex.
12. Find the axis of symmetry.
13. What is the minimum or maximum?
14. Can the graph cross the line $y = -20$? Why?

Graph, giving the vertex and the zeros of each quadratic function.

15. $f(x) = 5x^2$
16. $f(x) = \frac{1}{3}x^2 + 6$
17. $f(x) = \frac{1}{4}x^2$
18. $f(x) = 3x^2 - 7$
19. $f(x) = -2x^2 + 12$
20. $f(x) = (x + 6)^2$
21. $f(x) = -3(x - 2)^2$
22. $f(x) = \frac{1}{2}(x + 4)^2$
23. $f(x) = -5(x - 7)^2 - 3$
24. $f(x) = \frac{2}{3}(x + 6)^2 + 2$
25. $f(x) = x^2 + 6x + 1$
26. $f(x) = x^2 - 14x + 37$

Use the graph to answer each.

27. Find $f(2)$.

28. Find $f(5)$.

29. Give the vertex.

30. Give the axis of symmetry.

31. Give the zeros.

32. What is the maximum or minimum value?

33. Frank runs a hot dog distribution warehouse that distributes hot dogs to the local grocery stores. The amount of profit that he makes depends on the number of boxes of hot dogs he sells. The profit follows the equation $P(x) = -x^2 + 140x - 3940$. What is his maximum profit, and how many boxes must he sell to make the maximum profit?

34. What is the mathematical significance of Matthew 14:21?

Glossary

absolute value   The number of units that a number is from 0 on the number line. More formally, the absolute value of a number is equal to that number if it is greater than or equal to 0 and is equal to the opposite of that number if it is less than 0.

addition method   A method of solving simultaneous equations by adding the equations to cause one of the variables to be eliminated.

addition property of inequality   The principle that if a, b, and c are real numbers such that $a < b$, then $a + c < b + c$.

additive identity   The number 0; the value such that when added to another number yields the same number.

additive identity property   The principle that adding zero to a number gives the original number. For any real number a, $a + 0 = a = 0 + a$

additive inverse property   The principle that for any real number a, $a + (-a) = 0$.

additive inverses   Numbers that when located on a number line are the same distance from 0 but on opposite sides of it. Their sum is 0, the additive identity element.

algebraic expression   The result of performing mathematical operations on any collection of variables and constants.

associative property of addition   The principle that addends can be grouped in any order without affecting the sum. For any real numbers a, b, and c, $a + (b + c) = (a + b) + c$.

associative property of multiplication   The principle that factors can be grouped in any order without affecting the product. For any real numbers a, b, and c, $a(bc) = (ab)c$.

axis   A reference line in a plane.

base   A term that is raised to a power indicated by an exponent. In the expression a^3, the base a is raised to the third power.

binomial   A polynomial with exactly two terms.

Cartesian plane   The plane formed by a Cartesian product described by $\mathbb{R} \times \mathbb{R}$ on which algebraic equations are graphed.

Cartesian product   The set $A \times B$ of all possible ordered pairs where the first coordinate comes from A and the second comes from B.

coefficient   The constant factor accompanying the variables in a term.

combinations   The number of possible ways to select items in which order is not important.

common denominator   The least common multiple of the denominators.

common monomial factor   A factor of a polynomial common to all of its terms.

commutative property of addition   The principle that addends can be arranged in any order without affecting the sum. For any numbers a and b, $a + b = b + a$.

commutative property of multiplication   The principle that factors can be arranged in any order without affecting the product. For numbers a and b, $ab = ba$.

completing the square   A method for obtaining a perfect square trinomial.

complex rational expression   An algebraic expression of the form $E = \frac{c}{d}$ where either c or d or c and d are rational expressions.

composite number   A positive integer greater than 1 that is not prime.

compound sentence   A mathematical relationship defined in terms of two or more equations or inequalities connected by the word *and* or the word *or*.

conjugate of a radical expression   The radical expression with the opposite sign between the terms. For example, the conjugate of $\sqrt{2} - 1$ is $\sqrt{2} + 1$.

conjunction   A compound sentence consisting of sentences connected by the word *and*, meaning intersection, and symbolized by $\wedge$.

consistent system of equations   A system of equations that has a solution.

constant   A symbol that represents a fixed number.

constant of variation   The constant relating two variables in a direct variation. In the expression $y = kx$, k is the constant of variation.

coordinate   The number that corresponds to a point on a number line.

cube root   One of a number's three equal factors.

degree of a polynomial   The degree of the highest-degree term in a polynomial.

degree of a term   The sum of the exponents on the variables.

dependent system of equations   A consistent system of equations that has an infinite number of solutions.

direct variation   A linear function in which one variable is a multiple of the other variable.

disjunction   A compound sentence consisting of sentences connected by the word *or*, meaning union, and symbolized by $\vee$.

distance formula   The formula $d = \sqrt{(x_1 - x_2)^2 + (y_1 - y_2)^2}$, which is used to find the distance d between the two points (x_1, y_1) and (x_2, y_2).

distributive property   The principle that the sum of two numbers multiplied by a factor is equal to the two numbers individually multiplied by the factor and then added. For any numbers a, b, and c, $a(b + c) = ab + ac$.

division property (for exponents)   Subtract exponents to divide with like bases: $x^a \div x^b = x^{a-b}$.

division property of inequality   The principle that if a, b, and c are real numbers such that $a < b$ and $c \neq 0$, then $\frac{a}{c} < \frac{b}{c}$ if $c > 0$ and $\frac{a}{c} > \frac{b}{c}$ if $c < 0$.

division property of radicals   The principle that roots of numerators and denominators under a radical can be found separately; for real numbers x and y with $y \neq 0$, $\sqrt[n]{\frac{x}{y}} = \frac{\sqrt[n]{x}}{\sqrt[n]{y}}$.

domain   The set of first coordinates of the ordered pairs of a relation.

elements   The components of a set.

empty set   A set that has no elements.

equation   A mathematical sentence stating that two expressions are equal.

evaluate   To calculate the value of a numerical expression.

exponent   A superscript written to the right of a term (the base), indicating the number of times the base is to be used as a factor. In the expression a^3, 3 is the exponent.

exponential form   A simplified form of writing repeated multiplication.

extraneous   An apparent solution to an equation, but one that does not check.

factor   n. A number that when multiplied with another number gives a product.
v. To find the numbers that have been multiplied to give a product.

finite set   A set in which the elements can be numbered.

FOIL method   A quick method of mentally multiplying binomials by finding the products of the first, outer, inner, and last terms and then combining like terms.

formula   An equation that describes a relationship among physical quantities.

function   A relation in which each x-coordinate is paired with one and only one y-coordinate.

function notation   A means of expressing the dependence of one variable upon another. For example, $y = x + 5$ can be expressed as $f(x) = x + 5$, indicating that y depends upon x.

graph   A visual representation on a number line or on the coordinate plane.

greatest common factor (GCF)   The largest positive integer that divides evenly into two given integers.

hypotenuse   The side of a right triangle that is opposite the right angle.

inconsistent system of equations   A system of equations that has no solution.

independent system of equations   A consistent system of equations that has a finite number of solutions.

index   The small number above the radical sign that indicates the root to be taken.

inequality   A mathematical sentence that states that two numbers or expressions are not always equal.

infinite set   A set that is not finite.

integers   The set of whole numbers and their opposites. $\mathbb{Z} = \{\ldots, -4, -3, -2, -1, 0, 1, 2, 3, 4, \ldots\}$

intersection of sets   The set of all elements that appear in all of the sets.

irrational numbers   Numbers that cannot be expressed as a ratio of two integers.

least common multiple (LCM)   The smallest positive integer that is a multiple of two given integers.

like terms   Terms that have the same variables with the same exponents.

linear equation   An equation having a line as its graph.

linear function   A function described by the equation $f(x) = mx + b$.

literal equation   An equation with two or more variables.

mathematical property   An equation or statement that is true for any value of the variable.

monomial   A polynomial with only one term.

multiplication property (for exponents)   Add exponents to multiply with like bases: $x^a \cdot x^b = x^{a+b}$.

multiplication property of inequality   The principle that if a, b, and c are real numbers such that $a < b$, then $ac < bc$ if $c > 0$ and $ac > bc$ if $c < 0$.

multiplicative identity   The number 1; a value such that when multiplied by a number gives the number.

multiplicative identity property   The principle that multiplying by 1 gives the original number. For any real number a, $a \cdot 1 = a = 1 \cdot a$.

multiplicative inverse property   The principle that for any number $b \neq 0$, $b \cdot \frac{1}{b} = 1$.

multiplicative inverses   Two numbers that when multiplied have a product of 1.

natural numbers   The set of counting numbers. $\mathbb{N} = \{1, 2, 3, 4, \ldots\}$

null set   See empty set.

number line   A graphical representation of numbers using equal intervals along a line.

opposite numbers   Numbers that when located on a number line are the same distance from 0 but on opposite sides of 0.

order of operations   The order for evaluating expressions: parentheses are first, exponentials are evaluated second, multiplication and division operations are performed left to right next, and addition and subtraction operations are done last from left to right.

ordered pair   A pair of coordinates in which the order is important.

origin   The point at which the axes of a coordinate plane cross.

parabola   The graph of a quadratic function.

perfect square trinomial   A trinomial that is the square of a binomial.

perimeter   The sum of the lengths of the sides of a polygon.

permutations   The number of possible arrangements of a set of items (order is important).

plane   A flat surface that extends infinitely and has an infinite number of points.

point-slope form   A linear equation in the form $y - y_1 = m(x - x_1)$, where m is the slope of the line and (x_1, y_1) is a given point.

polynomial   An algebraic expression with one or more terms.

power property (for exponents)   Multiply exponents to raise exponentials to powers: $(x^a)^b = x^{ab}$.

prime factorization   A number expressed as the product of prime numbers.

prime number   An integer greater than 1 whose only positive factors are 1 and itself.

probability   The likelihood of something occuring, expressed as a decimal or ratio between zero and one.

product property of radicals   The principle that the root of a product under a radical can be found by taking the root of the factors separately. For real numbers x and y, $\sqrt[n]{xy} = \sqrt[n]{x}\ \sqrt[n]{y}$.

Pythagorean theorem   The sum of the squares of the lengths of the legs of a right triangle is equal to the square of the length of the hypotenuse.

quadrant   One of four sections into which two perpendicular lines divide a plane.

quadratic equation   An equation of the second degree in one variable.

quadratic formula   The formula $x = \frac{-b \pm \sqrt{b^2 - 4ac}}{2a}$ used to solve quadratic equations in the form $ax^2 + bx + c = 0$, with $a \neq 0$.

quadratic function   A function described by the equation $f(x) = ax^2 + bx + c$, with $a \neq 0$.

radical   An expression in the form $\sqrt[n]{x}$.

radical equation   An equation that contains a variable in the radicand.

radical expression   An algebraic expression containing at least one radical.

radical sign   The symbol $\sqrt{}$ for the principal (positive) square root.

radicand   The number under a radical sign whose root is to be found.

range   The set of second coordinates of the ordered pairs of a relation.

ratio   The comparison of two numbers by division.

rational equation   An equation containing a rational expression with a variable in the denominator.

rational expression   An algebraic expression that is a ratio of two polynomials, with the polynomial in the denominator not equal to zero.

rational number   A number that can be expressed as a ratio of two integers, with the denominator not equal to zero.

rationalizing the denominator   A procedure for removing a radical from the denominator of a fraction.

real numbers   The union of the sets of rational and irrational numbers.

reciprocals   Two numbers whose product is 1.

relation   Any set of ordered pairs.

relatively prime numbers   Two numbers whose greatest common factor is 1.

right angle   An angle whose measure is 90°.

right triangle   A triangle that contains a right angle.

set   A group or collection of objects or numbers.

simplify   To perform all indicated operations and express the result in standard mathematical form.

solve   To find the values that make a mathematical statement true.

square root   One of a number's two equal factors.

standard deviation   A measure of the variability in a set of data.

statistics   A measurement describing a set of data.

substitution   The process of replacing one quantity with another quantity equal to it.

substitution method   A method for solving simultaneous equations by solving one equation for one variable, substituting the solution into the other equation, and then solving for the other variable.

subtraction property of inequality   The principle that if a, b, and c are real numbers such that $a < b$, then $a - c < b - c$.

system of equations   Two or more equations in two or more variables to be solved simultaneously.

term   A variable, constant, variable raised to a power, or product of a constant and one or more variables.

theorem   A proven statement that is always true.

trinomial   A polynomial with exactly three terms.

union of sets   The set of all the elements that appear in any of the sets.

variable   A symbol used to represent any number of a given set of numbers.

variance   The square of the standard deviation.

vertex   The point at which a parabola reaches its highest or lowest point.

vertical line test   The method of moving a vertical line across a graph of a relation to determine if the relation is also a function.

whole numbers   The set of natural numbers together with 0. $\mathbb{W} = \{0, 1, 2, 3. \ldots\}$

***x*-axis**   The horizontal reference line in a Cartesian plane.

***x*-coordinate**   The first coordinate of an ordered pair.

***x*-intercept**   The point at which a graph of an equation crosses, or intersects, the *x*-axis.

***y*-axis**   The vertical reference line in a plane.

***y*-coordinate**   The second coordinate of an ordered pair.

***y*-intercept**   The point at which a line crosses, or intersects, the *y*-axis.

zero product property   The principle that if the product of two or more factors is 0, at least one of the factors is 0.

zero property of multiplication   The principle that when 0 is a factor, the product will always be 0. For any number a, $a \cdot 0 = 0$.

zeros of a function   The *x*-coordinates of any points at which a graph of a function crosses the *x*-axis.

Selected Answers

Chapter 1—Integers

1.1

1.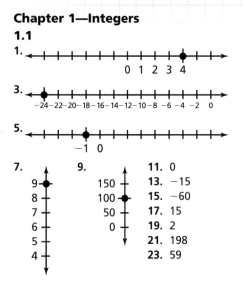

3.

5.

7.

9.

11. 0
13. −15
15. −60
17. 15
19. 2
21. 198
23. 59

1.2

1. −38 3. −42 5. −134 7. 412 9. 5 11. 8
13. 382 15. 0 17. 84 19. 4 21. 315 23. 857 25. 15
27. 12 29. 76 31. same 35. 4 [1.1] 37. 0 [1.1]
39. −5 [1.1]

1.3

1. 24 3. −2 5. −91 7. 4 9. 55 11. 360 13. 0
15. −14 17. 1032 19. −4510 21. 20 23. −6 25. 0
27. 4 + 9 29. 8 + 3 31. identity property of addition
33. −6°F 39. 4 [1.2] 41. 10 [1.2] 43. no [1.2]

1.4

1. 5 3. −17 5. −24 7. −2 9. −130 11. 14 13. −329
15. 275 17. −753 19. 17° 21. 7 − 4 23. 5 − 16
25. −19 27. −14 33. 5 [1.2] 35. no, 5 − 3 ≠ 3 − 5;
2 ≠ −2 [1.3]

1.5

1. −6 3. 24 5. 3 7. 36 9. 287 11. 125 13. −38,920
15. −17,112 17. 351,934 19. −16,014 21. 5 · 4
23. 2 · 9 25. 6 · 8 27. increased by $83 33. 4 [1.2]
35. 15 [1.5]

1.6

1. 9 3. undefined 5. −9 7. −9 9. −6 11. $\frac{8}{3}$ 13. $\frac{9}{2}$
15. $\frac{11}{4}$ 17. undefined 19. 83 21. −43 27. −25 [1.4]
29. identity property of addition [1.3] 31. associative
property of addition [1.3]

1.7

1. $4 \cdot 4 \cdot 4 = 64$ 3. $(-3)(-3)(-3)(-3)(-3) = -243$
5. 1 7. 7^4 9. 4^2 11. 3^5 13. 8^{15} 15. 12^9 17. 7^{11}
19. 8^4 21. 3^8 23. 28^8 25. 2^2 27. $10^6(-2)^9$
29. negative 31. 2^7 33. 6^{10} 35. 4^3 39. 521 [1.3]
41. −27 [1.6] 43. −59 [1.3] 45. −140 [1.3]

1.8

1. $2^4 \cdot 3$ 3. $3^2 \cdot 97$ 5. $2^2 \cdot 5 \cdot 41$ 7. $2^3 \cdot 173$
9. $2 \cdot 47$ 11. $3^4 \cdot 7^3$ 13. $2^6 \cdot 3^2 \cdot 5 \cdot 7$ 15. $2^7 \cdot 3 \cdot 7$
17. $23 \cdot 47$ 19. 13^4 27. −193 [1.4] 29. −764 [1.4]
31. −864 [1.5] 33. −125 [1.6] 35. −305 [1.4]

1.9

1. 2 3. 8 5. 420 7. 2380 9. 190 11. 22,176
13. GCF = $2^3 \cdot 3^4$; LCM = $2^5 \cdot 3^4 \cdot 5^2 \cdot 7$ 15. 8 + 5
17. 5 · 8 19. 5 − 8 27. −9 [1.6] 29. 89 [1.4]
31. −42 [1.4] 33. −2555 [1.6] 35. 76 [1.4]

Chapter 1 Review

1.

3.

5. −29
7. 13
9. −4
11. −20
13. 4
15. 1
17. 444
19. 4^{11}
21. $3 \cdot 5^2$

23. 72
25. 4
27. H
29. A
31. D
33. E
35. B
37. 5 − 8
39. $4 + 9^2$

Chapter 2—Real Numbers

2.1

1. 5.5 3. 0.23 5. $0.\overline{714285}$ 7. $\frac{43}{10}$ 9. $\frac{3}{1}$
11-19.

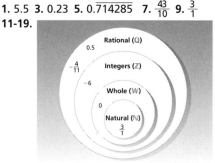

21.
number line: points 0 1 2 3 4 5, filled dot at 3

23. no; no **25.** yes, 1; no **27.** rational
29. $\frac{1}{2}(12)$ [1.6] **31.** $\frac{26}{30}$ [1.6] **33.** $7 + 8$ [1.3]

2.2
1. $\frac{5}{7}$ **3.** $\frac{1}{3}$ **5.** $\frac{36}{81}$ **7.** $\frac{40}{56}$ **9.** $\frac{42}{105}$ **11.** $\frac{24}{48}$ **13.** $\frac{18}{48}$ **15.** $\frac{7}{9}$
17. $\frac{50}{9}$ **19.** $-\frac{17}{88}$ **21.** $\frac{82}{21}$ **23.** $\frac{103}{35}$ **25.** 15.316 **27.** 849.83
29. $\frac{5}{8}$ **33.** associative property of addition [1.3]
35. rational number [2.1]

2.3
1. $\frac{5}{21}$ **3.** $\frac{49}{8}$ **5.** $\frac{12}{5}$ **7.** $\frac{4}{9}$ **9.** $\frac{1}{68}$ **11.** 78.96 **13.** 282
15. 0.87 **17.** $-\frac{7}{33}$ **19.** $\frac{3}{8}$ **21.** $1\frac{2}{3}$ gallons
23. $1\frac{1}{2}$ inches **25.** $5 \cdot \frac{1}{2}$
31. [1.1]
number line: −1 0 1 2 3 4, filled dot at 3

33. 4.3 [1.2] **35.** $\frac{0}{a} = 0$ [1.6]

2.4
1. 17 **3.** 11 **5.** 7 **7.** 8 **9.** −1 **11.** 9 **13.** 22 **15.** 0
17. −13 **19.** 14 **21.** $2 \cdot 4^2 + 5$ **23.** $9 + 11$
25. $9 - |2 + (-15)|$ **29.** $-\frac{1}{2}$ [2.3] **31.** −24 [1.4]

2.5
1. 45 **3.** 75 **5.** $\frac{253}{2}$ or $126\frac{1}{2}$ **7.** 20 **9.** 1389 **11.** 30
13. −6 **15.** 9 **17.** 2 **19.** $(2 + 4) \cdot 7 \div 2$ **21.** $5(6 + 7)$
23. $20^2 - 13^2$ **25.** $2 + 5 \cdot 6$ **29.** −32 [1.7]
31. $2^{13} \cdot 3^{11}$ [1.7]

2.6
1. 7 **3.** 9 **5.** 1 **7.** $\frac{9}{5}$ **9.** $\frac{3}{4}$ **11.** −15 **13.** 19 **15.** 6
17. −3 **19.** 7 **21.** $4^2 = 16$ **23.** $\sqrt{121} = 11$ **25.** −3
27. 30 **29.** −68 **33.** 7, natural [2.1]
35. −8, integer [2.1] **37.** $\sqrt{2}$, real (irrational) [2.1]

2.7
1. {1, 3} **3.** {−1} **5.** {1, 3, 5} **7.** False, but $\varnothing \subseteq B$
9. False **11.** {MN, WI, IA, IL, MO, KY, TN, AR, MS, LA,
ME, MA, MD, MI, MT} **13.** {ME, MA, MD, MI, MN,
MO, MS, MT, TX, LA, AL, FL} **15.** {MN, MO, MS}
17. $\varnothing$ **19.** {TX, LA, MS, AL, FL, WA, ID, MT, ND, MN,
NY, VT, NH, ME} **21.** {0, 1, 2, 3, . . .}
23.
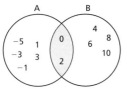

29. $2 \cdot 3^2 \cdot 31$ [1.8] **31.** $2^3 \cdot 3^2 \cdot 11 \cdot 31 = 24{,}552$ [1.9]
33. −11 [2.7]

Chapter 2 Review
1. D **3.** A **5.** B **7.** $(ab)c = a(bc)$ **9.** $a \cdot 1 = a$ and $1 \cdot a = a$
11. $a \cdot \frac{1}{a} = 1$ and $\frac{1}{a} \cdot a = 1$ **13.** 14 **15.** 6 **17.** $\frac{32}{21}$
19. 15 **21.** $-\frac{11}{72}$ **23.** −2 **25.** 2 **27.** −29 **29.** $\frac{1}{2}$
31. {2, 4, 6, 8, 10, 14, 20, 26, 32, . . .} **33.** {2, 4}
35. {0, 1, 2, 3, 4, 5, 6, 8, 10} **37.** 31 and 36 are
infinite; the others are finite **39.** A

Chapter 3—The Language of Algebra
3.1
1. $8x$ **3.** $325n$ **5.** $2y$; if $y =$ Lynn's speed
7. $24 + 24 + w + w$ or $2(24) + 2(w)$ or $2w + 48$
9. {−8, −3, −1, 4} **11.** {−12, 3, 9, 24}
13. $\left\{-2, \frac{1}{2}, \frac{3}{2}, 4\right\}$ **15.** V: x; C: 3, 6 **17.** V: c, d; C: −5
19. commutative property of addition
21. associative property of multiplication
23. commutative property of multiplication
27. −12 [1.4] **29.** 3 [1.6]

3.2
1. $n - 17$ **3.** $x + y$ **5.** $2x + 6$ **7.** $n + 24$ **9.** $\sqrt{n}$
11. $\frac{m + n}{2}$ **13.** s^3 **15.** $h^3 + h^2$ **17.** $126 - n(n - 1)$
19. $a^2 + b^2$ **21.** $6d + 12h$ **23.** $3x + 2y + z$
29. $A \subseteq \mathbb{N}$, $C \subseteq \mathbb{N}$ [2.8] **31.** {3, 5, 7, 11, 13, 17, 19, 23,
29, . . .} [2.8] **33.** {1, 2, 3, 4, 5, 7, 9, 11, 13, 16, 17, 19,
23, 25, 29, 31, 37, . . .} [2.8]

3.3
1. a^3 **3.** k^2 **5.** d^2p^4 **7.** v^7 **9.** rua^2 **11.** $xxxxx$ **13.** ccc
15. $tttttt$ **17.** $\frac{1}{x^5}$ **19.** $\frac{1}{y^2}$ **21.** $\frac{1}{4^3}$ **23.** 8^{-2} **25.** $x^{-2}y^{-9}$
27. $x^{-2}y^{-1}z^{-3}$ **29.** 4^7 **31.** 9^2 **33.** $\frac{1}{4^3}$ **35.** 1 **37.** $\frac{1}{y^2}$
39. x^{10} **43.** $2^3 \cdot 3 = 24$ [1.9] **45.** 0 [1.7]
47. undefined [1.6]

3.4
1. −32 **3.** −2 **5.** −5 **7.** 37 **9.** −59 **11.** −36 **13.** a^4
15. −1 **17.** $\frac{3}{16}$ **19.** $\frac{-31}{80}$ **21.** $\frac{17}{12}$ **25.** J [1.3] **27.** I [1.4]
29. B [2.6] **31.** G [2.6]

3.5
1. 3, 4, −5; $3x$, $4x$ **3.** 1, −2, −9; xy, $-2xy$, $-9xy$
5. 2, −17, 5; $2x^3$, $5x^3$ **7.** $6k$ **9.** $19b$ **11.** $-3d + 10f$
13. $14ab$ **15.** $14x^2 + 3x^2y - 4x$ **17.** $3y^2 - 8y$
19. $3x + y$; 3 **21.** cannot be simplified; −3
23. $1 + xy^2 + x$; 21 **27.** identity property of
multiplication [1.5] **29.** distributive property [1.5]

3.6
1. $6a + 9$ **3.** $4x + 8y$ **5.** $-2x + 23$ **7.** $-6a - 8b$
9. $5a - 4b$ **11.** $b - 18$ **13.** $5x^2 + 5xy$ **15.** $2x$
17. $5a^2 - 10a - 3z + 56$ **19.** $5m^2 - 15m + 24$
21. $-4r^2 + 6r$ **23.** $-u^2 - 20u - 18x^2 + 2xy + y^2$
25. $x^2 + 2xy + y^2$ **29.** x^5 [1.7] **31.** $\frac{1}{x^3}$ [3.3]

3.7
1. 13.856 psi **3.** 160 feet **5.** 12.56 ft. **7.** 60 cu. in.
9. 94 miles **11.** $37.92 **13.** $4257 **15.** $161 **17.** $135
19. $403.75 **21.** $7.50 **23.** $P = a + b + c$
25. Five is less than seven. **27.** The empty set is a subset of the natural numbers. **29.** Pi is not equal to 3.14 ($\pi \approx 3.14$) **33.** −4 [2.5] **35.** 6 [3.4]

3.8
1. add 5 **3.** add 2 **5.** multiply (2 + 3) by 2
7. divide by 2 **9.** divide by 5 **11.** False **13.** True
15. No **17.** Yes **19.** division property of equality
21. multiplication property of equality
23. $x - 10 = a - 6$ **25.** $2(19 + 20) = 78$
27. $\sqrt{400} + 5 = 5^2$ **31.** 5 [3.7] **33.** 390 [3.7]
35. $\frac{9}{2}$ [3.7]

3.9
1. $12x = 780$ **3.** $\frac{3x}{16} = 12$ **5.** $0.15x = 41$
7. $x + (x + 12) = 100$ **9.** $2x + x = 96$
11. $x + (x + 2) = 178$ **13.** $3x + x + (x + 120) = 180$
15. $(2x + 4) + x = 22$ **17.** $x + (x + 7) = 31$ or
$x + (x - 7) = 31$ **19.** $x + (x + 2) + (x + 4) = 57$
23. $4s = 108$ [3.7] **25.** $2(x + 7) + 2x = 74$ [3.7]

Chapter 3 Review
1. {−12, −6, −5, 0} **3.** {−22, 8, 13, 38} **5.** V: x; C: 3, −4
7. V: a; C: 4, 3, −7 **9.** $\frac{1}{x^8}$ **11.** 3^{-2} **13.** x^{-4} **15.** $\frac{1}{7^6}$
17. −432 **19.** 1 **21.** 58 **23.** $-2a + 3b$ **25.** $6a - 9b$
27. $-8a - 3b$ **29.** $3x^2 - 3x + 1$ **31.** $5x - 8y$
33. $4m + 4p + 2n$ **35.** $3x + x^2$ **37.** 64 cubic inches
39. $6x + 2 = 20$

Chapter 4—Solving Equations
4.1.
1. $x = 9$ **3.** $a = -10$ **5.** $x = 8$ **7.** $y = -56$ **9.** $x = 41$
11. $m = 34$ **15.** $y = -10$ **17.** $y = -9$ **19.** $m = -292$
21. $x = 6$ **23.** $b = 28$ **25.** $x = 4$ **27.** $a = 125$
29. $x = \frac{d}{r}$ **31.** $x = 0.49$ **33.** $x = \frac{1}{4}$ **35.** $x = 8$
37. $x = 34$ **39.** $x = 0.3$ **41.** $x = 3.2$ **47.** associative property of addition [1.3] **49.** additive inverse property [1.3]

4.2
1. −41 **3.** 84 **5.** 14 **7.** 6 quarts **9.** 8 mph **11.** 5¢
13. 31 and 124 **15.** −83 **17.** $8.00
23. [1.1]

25. 9 [3.4]

4.3
1. $x = 8$ **3.** $x = 5$ **5.** $x = -8$ **7.** $x = -355$ **9.** $b = 41$
11. $x = 14$ **13.** $m = \frac{31}{3}$ **15.** $n = 35$ **17.** 20 pieces

19. 110 newspapers **21.** $3 \frac{3}{4}$ **25.** 51 [1.4] **27.** 0 [1.6]
29. 1 [1.6]

4.4
1. $x = 1$ **3.** $x = 2$ **5.** $x = 7$ **7.** $x = -3$ **9.** $x = -2$
11. $x = -7$ **13.** $x = -14$ **15.** $x = -6$ **17.** $x = 2$
19. $x = -\frac{b}{2}$ **21.** 26 boys; 37 girls **23.** $49.50 camera; $37.50 calculator **25.** 6' wide and 11' long **27.** $3.\overline{74}$
29. $\frac{907}{10}$ **33.** ∅ [2.7] **35.** {−13, −5, 1, 4, 9, 17} [2.7]
37. {5, 10, 15, 20} [2.7]

4.5
1. $x = 2$ **3.** $x = 3$ **5.** $x = 1$ **7.** $x = 4$ **9.** $b = \frac{3}{2}$ **11.** $n = \frac{4}{3}$
13. $x = 7$ **15.** $a = 2$ **17.** $t = -3$ **19.** $z = -22.18$
21. $x = \frac{2n}{m}$ **23.** $x = \frac{Pn + r}{q}$ **25.** $x = r^2$ **27.** −3, −2
31. 2^{12} [1.8] **33.** 1024 [1.9] **35.** $\frac{67}{258,048}$ [2.2]

4.6
1.

3. $x = -12, 2$

5. $x = -7, 5$

7. $x = \pm 129$ **9.** $x = 22$, or $x = -6$
11. $x = 19$, or $x = -14$ **13.** $x = \frac{12}{5}$, or $x = \frac{-36}{5}$
15. $x = 2$, or $x = \frac{-7}{6}$ **17.** $x = 4$, or $x = \frac{-8}{7}$
21. 12 [1.2] **23.** 30 [1.2] **25.** $|ab| = |a| \, |b|$ [1.2]

4.7
1. $x = 2$ **3.** $x = 21$ **5.** $y = \frac{50}{3}$ **7.** $b = -4$ **9.** $x = 12$
11. $x = -44$ **13.** $y = 1$ **15.** $b = 5$ **17.** $a = 22$
19. $m = 7$ **21.** $P = \frac{14r}{3x}$ **23.** $P = \frac{q + mr}{s}$ or $\frac{mr + q}{s}$
25. An equation has an equal sign. **29.** $x = -1$ [4.4]
31. $7x + 20$ [3.6]

4.8
1. 14 nickels, 26 pennies, 9 dollar bills
3. 26 quarters, 208 pennies **5.** 7 dimes, 27 nickels
7. 11 quarters, 16 dimes, 7 nickels. **9.** 8 dollar bills, 24 dimes, 12 quarters **11.** $3750, $7500, $11,250
13. $4500 at 7%, $4000 at 5% **15.** $6200 at 4%, $7500 at 6% **17.** $1800 for 9 months, $2500 for $1\frac{1}{2}$ years **21.** 19 [2.6] **23.** ±4 [2.6] **25.** $\frac{7}{8}$ [2.6] **27.** 6 [2.6]

4.9
1. $d = 54$ **3.** $t = \frac{x}{19}$ **5.** $r = 20$ **7.** $r = x$ **9.** $d = 7ab$
11. 125 mi. **13.** 400 mph **15.** $\frac{3}{4}$ hour **17.** 1 hour
19. 6 hours **21.** uphill: 10 ft./sec.; downhill: 80 ft./sec. **23.** 2 hours **25.** Jay: $7\frac{1}{3}$ yards/sec.; John: 7 yards/sec. for 31.4 sec. **29.** $x = 112$ [4.7]

31. $x = \frac{-1}{9}$ [4.7] **33.** $x = 17$ [4.4] **35.** $x = \frac{4}{3}$ [4.5]

4.10
1. Amount of salt = 14 gal. **3.** Amount of salt = 7.2 oz.
5. Amount of mixture = 80 liters **7.** Total value = $5.21x$ **9.** Amount of ingredient = $0.50x$ liters
11. 18 gallons; 7.6 gallons; about 42% **13.** 42 gallons of 33% acid **15.** 4 lb. butterscotch, 16 lb. cinnamon balls **17.** 21 lb. Chinese tea, 14 lb. Indian tea
19. 2 gal. **21.** $\frac{2}{15}$ liter **23.** 11% **25.** 3 cans of grapefruit, 4 cans of pineapple **29.** $x = -12$ [4.3]
31. $x = 2$ [4.5] **33.** $x = 16$ [4.7]

Chapter 4 Review
1. $x = 131$ **3.** $x = 152$ **5.** $x = 45$ **7.** $x = 24$
9. $y = -2$ **11.** $x = -1$ **13.** $x = 6$ **15.** $x = 1$
17. $y = \frac{-10}{7}$ **19.** $b = 6$ **21.** $x = \frac{-18}{5}, 0$ **23.** $x = \pm 5$
25. $x = 5$ **27.** $x = \frac{3y+2}{6}$ **29.** $x = \frac{H}{R}$ **31.** Bill, 15; Jim, 6
33. 24, 87 **35.** $1\frac{1}{2}$ hours **37.** 91 quarters, 35 nickels

Chapter 5—Solving Inequalities
5.1
1. $>$ **3.** $\neq$ **5.** $=$ **7.** $<$ **9.** $\not>$
11.
13.
15.
17.
19.
21.
23.
25.
27.
29.
31. a. not greater than b. not less than
c. not greater than or equal to
d. not less than or equal to

37. A number that can be expressed as a ratio of two integers when the denominator is not equal to zero [2.1]
39. A mathematical sentence stating that two expressions are equal [3.8]

5.2
1. $x > -12$
3. $y > 12$
5. $x < 10$

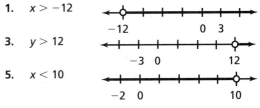

7. $y > 108$ **9.** $y \neq 8$ **11.** $y \neq 14$ **13.** $y < -25$
15. $x \leq -2$ **17.** $x < 0$ **19.** $x \neq 3$ **21.** $x > -4$
23. $t \leq 1$ **27.** distributive property [1.5]
29. subtraction property of equality [3.8]

5.3
1. $x < 21$ **3.** $y \geq 32$ **5.** $x < 2$ **7.** $x \geq 7$ **9.** $\geq \frac{-10}{7}$
11. $y \leq 96$ **13.** $x < -1$ **15.** $x < \frac{-2}{7}$ **17.** $k \geq \frac{3}{2}$
19. $x \neq \frac{-1}{5}$ **21.** $x \leq \frac{-2}{3}$ **23.** $x > \frac{6}{5}$ **27.** $4ax + 5a$ [3.6]
29. $11x^2 - 14x - 18$ [3.6]

5.4
1. $x \leq -2$ **3.** $z \leq -12$ **5.** $y > -7$ **7.** ≤ -48
9. $z < -130$ **11.** $x < -3$ **13.** $x \leq -13$ **15.** $y \leq 4$
17. $x \neq \frac{1}{2}$ **19.** $x > \frac{-14}{9}$ **21.** $x \neq 20$ **27.** integer [2.1]
29. real (irrational) [2.1]

5.5
1. $x > 4$ **3.** $-3 < x \leq 1$ **5.** $x \geq 7$ **7.** $x < 4$ **9.** $x < -12$
11. $x \geq 5$ **13.** $x < 3$ **15.** $-10 \leq x < -1$ **17.** $x = 2$
19. $x \leq 8, x \neq 1$ **23.** $\frac{25}{16}$ [2.3] **25.** $\frac{653}{126}$ [2.2]
27. $\frac{125}{x^6}$ [3.3]

5.6
1. $x < 2$ or $x > 5$ **3.** $x > 2$ **5.** $x \neq -4$ **7.** $\mathbb{R}$ **9.** $\mathbb{R}$
11. $x \leq 0$ or $x > 5$ **13.** $x > 3$ **15.** $x < 6$
21. [1.1]
23. $x = \frac{-5}{3}$, or $x = 1$ [4.6] **25.** $\emptyset$ [4.6]

5.7
1. $-3 < x < 3$ **3.** $-5 \leq x \leq 5$ **5.** $x < -8$ or $x > 8$
7. $x \leq -11$ or $x \geq -1$ **9.** $x \leq -10$ or $x \geq 4$
11. $x < -6$ or $x > \frac{-5}{2}$ **13.** $x < \frac{-99}{5}$ or $x > \frac{-9}{5}$
15. $x \leq \frac{-11}{2}$ or $x \geq 9$ **17.** $\frac{-8}{3} \leq x \leq \frac{4}{3}$
19. $\frac{-4}{7} < x < \frac{16}{7}$ **27.** $10t$ [4.9] **29.** $2x + 100$ [3.7]
31. $x^2 = 2(x + 4)$ [4.2]

5.8

1. $x > 8$; $x + 4 > 12$ **3.** 14 **5.** 3 cans **7.** 4 cars
9. Naomi earns $\leq \$90$; Paul earns $\leq \$180$; John earns $\leq \$60$. **11.** $13.16 **13.** His brother bikes at least 9 mph; Jeff bikes at least 24 mph. **17.** $x = 5$ [4.3]
19. $x = -14$ [4.5] **21.** $x = \frac{-1}{2}$, or $x = -3$ [4.6]
23. $-5 \leq x \leq 5$ [5.7]

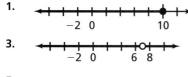

25. $x \leq \frac{94}{9}$ [5.4]

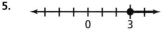

Chapter 5 Review

1.

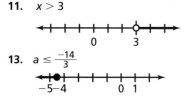

3.

5.

7. $y < 3$

9. $x > 10$

11. $x > 3$

13. $a \leq \frac{-14}{3}$

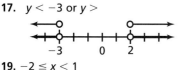

15. $t < -6$

17. $y < -3$ or $y >$

19. $-2 \leq x < 1$

21. $x > 5$ **23.** $x = 2$ **25.** $x \geq \frac{-3}{2}$ but $x \neq \frac{-2}{3}$
27. $-2 \leq x \leq 14$ **29.** $x > 6$ or $x < \frac{-4}{3}$
31. $-2 < -1$ **33.** $x^2 \geq 0$ **35.** $4x \leq 3$ **37.** A number is at least 3 units from zero. **39.** 94

Chapter 6—Relations, Functions, and Graphs

6.1
1. Springfield **3.** $(-3, -1)$ **5.** $(3, 5)$ **7.** $(-4, 1)$
9. $(-5, -4)$ **11.** $(-1, 2)$
13.

15.

17.

19.

21.

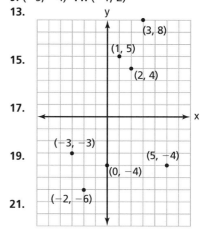

23. $(0, 0)$ **25.** y-axis **27.** x-axis **29.** I **31.** IV **35.** 0 [3.5]
37. $7x + 10y$ [3.6] **39.** $-3a^2b - 5ab - 2ab^2$ [3.5]

6.2
1. relation, $D = \{2, 5, 8\}$, $R = \{2, 4, 9\}$, function

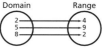

3. relation, $D = \{1, 4, 6\}$, $R = \{1, 3, 6, 9\}$, not a function

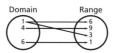

5. relation, $D = \{-4, -2, 3\}$, $R = \{5, 7\}$, function

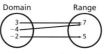

7. relation, $D = \{1, 2, 4, 8\}$, $R = \{1, 3, 7\}$, function

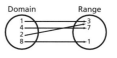

9. C **11.** A **13.** {(−2, 0), (−1, 4), (0, 3), (1, −1), (1, 4)}; not a function

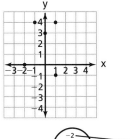

15. function

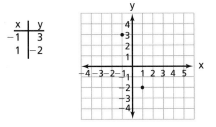

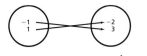

17. Answers will vary. **21.** $m = \frac{-1}{2}$ [4.3]
23. $x = \frac{9}{2}$ [4.5] **25.** $x > \frac{-5}{2}$ [5.4]

6.3

1. yes **3.** no **5.** yes **7.** yes **9.** no
11. yes

x	y = 3x
−1	−3
0	0
1	3

13. yes

x	y = x²
−1	1
0	0
1	1
2	4

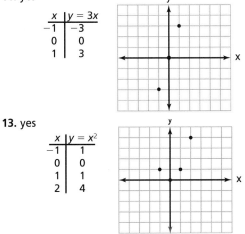

15. yes

x	y = 2x + 3
0	3
$\frac{1}{2}$	4
1	5
2	7

17. yes

x	y = −x − 4
−2	−2
0	−4
2	−6

19. no

x	y
2	−1
2	0
2	1
2	2
2	3

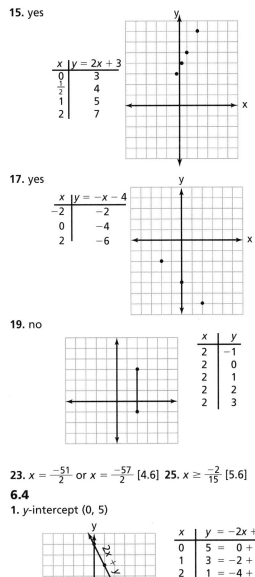

23. $x = \frac{-51}{2}$ or $x = \frac{-57}{2}$ [4.6] **25.** $x \geq \frac{-2}{15}$ [5.6]

6.4

1. y-intercept (0, 5)

x	y = −2x + 5
0	5 = 0 + 5
1	3 = −2 + 5
2	1 = −4 + 5

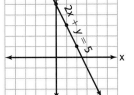

3. *y*-intercept (0, −1)

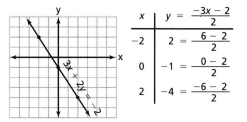

x	$y = \dfrac{-3x - 2}{2}$
−2	$2 = \dfrac{6 - 2}{2}$
0	$-1 = \dfrac{0 - 2}{2}$
2	$-4 = \dfrac{-6 - 2}{2}$

5. *y*-intercept (0, −3)

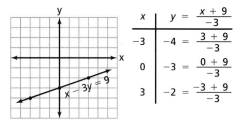

x	$y = \dfrac{x + 9}{-3}$
−3	$-4 = \dfrac{3 + 9}{-3}$
0	$-3 = \dfrac{0 + 9}{-3}$
3	$-2 = \dfrac{-3 + 9}{-3}$

7. *y*-intercept (0, −9)

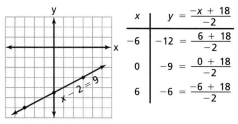

graph: marked off by 2's

x	$y = \dfrac{-x + 18}{-2}$
−6	$-12 = \dfrac{6 + 18}{-2}$
0	$-9 = \dfrac{0 + 18}{-2}$
6	$-6 = \dfrac{-6 + 18}{-2}$

9. *y*-intercept (0, 8)

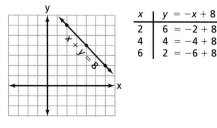

x	$y = -x + 8$
2	$6 = -2 + 8$
4	$4 = -4 + 8$
6	$2 = -6 + 8$

11. *x*: $\left(\dfrac{-3}{2}, 0\right)$, *y*: (0, 3) **13.** *x*: (4, 0), *y*: (0, −4)
15. $y = -\dfrac{1}{5}x + 4$ **17.** $y = \dfrac{x - 5}{3}$, *x*: (5, 0), *y*: $\left(0, \dfrac{-5}{3}\right)$
19. 0 **21.** y-axis or x = 0
25. [1.1]

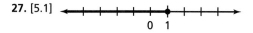

27. [5.1]

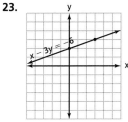

29. [1.2]

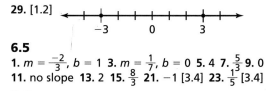

6.5
1. $m = \dfrac{-2}{3}$, $b = 1$ **3.** $m = \dfrac{1}{7}$, $b = 0$ **5.** 4 **7.** $\dfrac{5}{3}$ **9.** 0
11. no slope **13.** 2 **15.** $\dfrac{8}{3}$ **21.** −1 [3.4] **23.** $\dfrac{1}{5}$ [3.4]

6.6
1. $m = 3$, $b = 4$

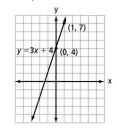

3. $m = -1$, $b = 1$

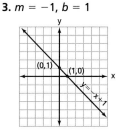

5. $m = \dfrac{-1}{4}$, $b = 5$

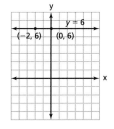

7. $m = 0$, $b = 6$

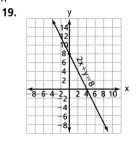

9. $y = -3x + 5$; $m = -3$, $b = 5$ **11.** $y = -\dfrac{1}{7}x + 2$; $m = \dfrac{-1}{7}$, $b = 2$ **13.** $y = \dfrac{8}{3}x - 3$; $m = \dfrac{8}{3}$, $b = -3$
15. no slope intercept form
17.

19.

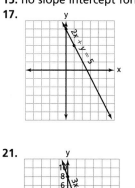

21.

23.

25.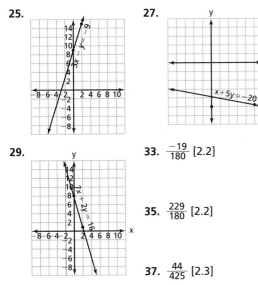

27.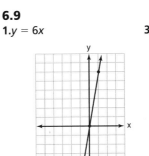

29.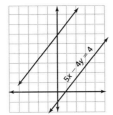

33. $\frac{-19}{180}$ [2.2]

35. $\frac{229}{180}$ [2.2]

37. $\frac{44}{425}$ [2.3]

6.7

1. $y = 3x + \frac{1}{4}$ **3.** $y = -5x + 10$ **5.** $y = 7$
7. $y = 9x - \frac{2}{3}$ **9.** $y = \frac{1}{4}x + 8$ **11.** $y = \frac{-1}{4}x + \frac{25}{4}$
13. $y = \frac{3}{5}x + 4$ **15.** $y = -\frac{1}{8}x - \frac{9}{8}$ **17.** $y = -4x - 15$
19. $y = \frac{4}{5}x + 6$ **23.** $\frac{5}{4}$ [6.5]
25. The lines are parallel. [6.4]

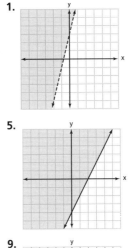

27. x-intercept $\left(\frac{10}{3}, 0\right)$; y-intercept $(0, -2)$ [6.4]

6.8

1. $y = -x + 6$; $b = 6$ **3.** $y = -x + 9$; $b = 9$
5. $y = 2x + 1$; $b = 1$ **7.** $y = \frac{1}{11}x + \frac{26}{11}$; $b = \frac{26}{11}$
9. $y = \frac{-8}{13}x + \frac{2}{13}$; $b = \frac{2}{13}$
11. $y = \frac{7}{13}x - \frac{34}{13}$; $b = -\frac{34}{13}$ **13.** $y = 3x + 8$
15. $y = \frac{12}{5}x + \frac{3}{5}$ **17.** $y = -\frac{7}{8}x - \frac{25}{4}$
19. $y = -4$ **25.** $x + (x + 1) + (x + 2) + (x + 3)$ [4.2]
27. $\frac{1}{2}x + \frac{3}{2}x = 40$ [4.9]

6.9

1. $y = 6x$

3. $y = 2x$

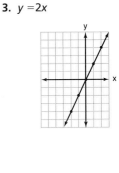

5. yes; $k = 0.433$ **7.** $k = 2$; $y = 2x$ **9.** $k = \frac{4}{7}$; $y = \frac{4}{7}x$
11. 40 **13.** 100 **15.** yes, yes, yes, no **17.** no, no, no, no
19. yes, yes, yes, no **21.** \$20.82 **23.** 16 amps
27. $\{-5, -4, -3, -2, -1, 0, 1, 2, 3, 4\}$ [2.7]
29. [5.7]

6.10

1.

3.

5.

7.

9.

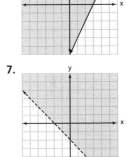

11. an infinite number

13.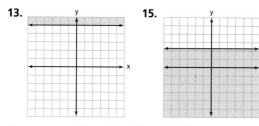

15.

17. $x + y \geq 5$ **21.** 0 [3.6] **23.** 44 [3.2]
25. $x > \frac{-4}{3}$ [5.4]

Chapter 6 Review

1. IV

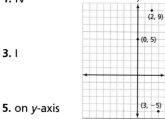

3. I

5. on y-axis

7. relation; function $D = \{-2, 1, 3\}$, $R = \{4, 7, 8\}$
9. relation; function $D = \{-1, 3, 7\}$, $R = \{4\}$
11. yes

13. yes

15. $m = -12$ **17.** $m = \frac{-1}{3}$ **19.** $y = \frac{-3}{2}x + 4$;
$m = \frac{-3}{2}$; $b = 4$

21.

23.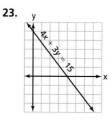

25.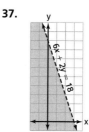

27. $y = \frac{1}{2}x - 2$

29. $x = 11$

31. $y = -5x + 9$

33. $\frac{1}{2}$

35. $0.35

37.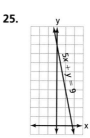

39.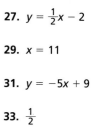

Chapter 7—Systems of Equations and Inequalities

7.1

1. yes **3.** no **5.** no **7.** no **9.** yes
11. 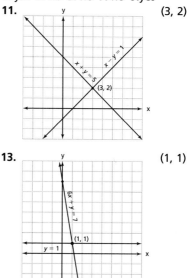 (3, 2)

13. (1, 1)

15.

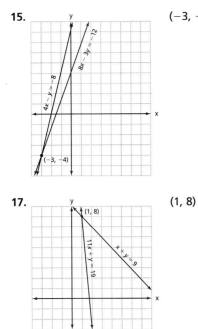

$(-3, -4)$

17. $(1, 8)$

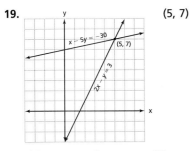

19. $(5, 7)$

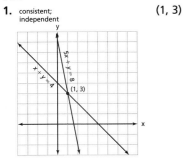

21. $\frac{37}{15}$ [2.3] **23.** $\frac{2}{7}$ [2.6] **25.** $\frac{23}{12}$ [2.6]

7.2

1. consistent; independent $(1, 3)$

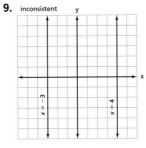

3. consistent; dependent entire line

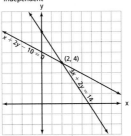

5. consistent; independent $(2, 4)$

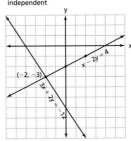

7. consistent; independent $(-2, -3)$

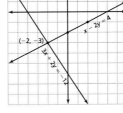

9. inconsistent no solution

11. consistent; independent $(-3, -1)$

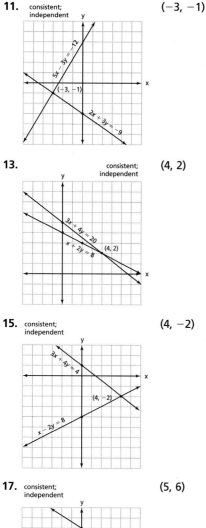

13. consistent; independent $(4, 2)$

15. consistent; independent $(4, -2)$

17. consistent; independent $(5, 6)$

19. consistent; independent $(-3, 4)$

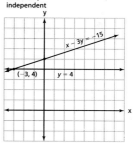

25. $x = 5$ [4.5] **27.** $x \geq -3$ [5.4]

7.3

1. $(-4, 24)$ **3.** $(-2, 8)$ **5.** $(-3, -4)$ **7.** $(2, 7)$ **9.** $(-2, 1)$
11. $(-1, 3)$ **13.** $(-4, 5)$ **15.** $\left(\frac{-10}{3}, \frac{-8}{3}\right)$ **17.** $\left(\frac{28}{5}, \frac{14}{5}\right)$
19. $(10, -6)$ **23.** C [2.1] **25.** E [2.1]

7.4

1. $(3, 11)$; consistent, independent **3.** no solution; inconsistent **5.** $(0, 6)$; consistent, independent **7.** entire line; consistent, dependent **9.** $(-1, -4)$; consistent, independent **11.** $\left(\frac{-9}{26}, \frac{-25}{26}\right)$
13. $(40, 7)$, $(40, -7)$ **15.** entire line **17.** 38, 25

23. [4.1]

25. [4.6]

27. [6.10]

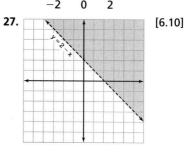

7.5

1. $(1, 4)$ **3.** $(10, -11)$ **5.** $(-1, 7)$ **7.** $(-3, -1)$ **9.** $(-6, 3)$
11. $\left(\frac{5}{2}, \frac{9}{2}\right)$ **13.** $\left(9, \frac{-1}{3}\right)$ **15.** entire line **17.** $(11, 0)$
21. $2x^4y + 11x^3y^3$ [3.6] **23.** 0 [2.2] **25.** $\frac{5x^6z^3}{27y^7}$ [3.3]

7.6

1. $(4, 3)$ **3.** entire line; dependent
5. $(-1, -3)$ **7.** $(5, 9)$ **9.** no solution; inconsistent
11. $(10, 4)$ **13.** $\left(\frac{19}{8}, \frac{1}{16}\right)$ **15.** $\left(\frac{31}{17}, \frac{4}{17}\right)$
17. entire line; dependent
21. 19 ft. $\times$ 26 ft. [4.2] **23.** $x \geq 3$ [5.8]
25. 120 mi. [4.9]

7.7

1. $12 - x$ **3.** $4 + c$ **5.** $500 - w$

7.

	r	t	$=$	d
upstream	$x - 3$	6		$6(x - 3)$
downstream	$x + 3$	4		$4(x + 3)$

9. $x + y = 7$; $30x + 40y = 230$ **11.** 4 hours **13.** 4 P.M.
15. Grandma, 40 mph; John, 52 mph **17.** 24 mph
19. first car, 49 mph; second car, 37 mph **21.** scouts,
4 mph; stream, 1 mph **25.** $\frac{-1}{7}$ [6.5] **27.** $\frac{4}{5}$ [6.6]
29. no slope [6.8]

7.8

1. $I = 240$ **3.** $I = 56x$ **5.** $r = 0.05$ **7.** $128
9. $x + y = 600$; $0.07x + 0.05y = 30$ **11.** $8500 at 8%;
$6500 at 10% **13.** $3200 at 7%; $3000 at $5\frac{1}{2}$%
15. $2000 (first sum) at 7%; $5000 (second sum) at
10%; the first method **17.** $6000 at 6%; $1500 at 15%
19. $1800 at 9.2%; $2500 at 10.4% **21.** $6 in
Mother's 30% offer; $3 in Father's 25% offer
23. 8% for dry cleaning investment; 10% for
restaurant investment **27.** {23, 29} [2.7]
29. {1, 3, 4, 5} [2.7]

7.9

1. 18 oz. nuts; 30 oz. raisins **3.** 1 lb. caramels; 4 lb.
butterscotch **5.** 8 roses; 6 carnations **7.** 8 g Raisin
Rich cereal; 4 g high-protein grain **9.** 30 kg of
original concrete mixture; 18 kg of aggregate
11. 40 mL of 40% alcohol; 88 mL of water
13. 6426 in District 12; 3827 in District 13 **15.** 10.7
gal. of cream, 49.3 gal. of milk **17.** approx. 26.6 lb.
of A; 58.4 lb. of B **21.** zero property of multiplication
[1.5] **23.** commutative property of addition [1.3]
25. addition property of inequality [5.2] **27.** identity
property of addition [1.3] **29.** multiplicative inverse
property [2.3]

7.10

1.
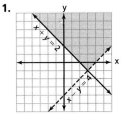

3.
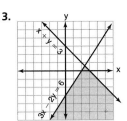

5.
7.

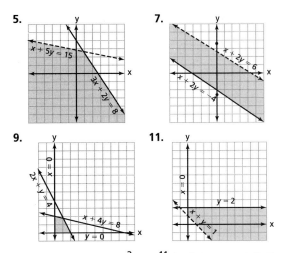

9.
11.

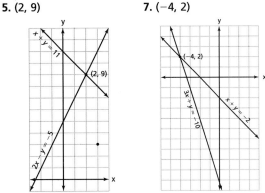

13. no **15.** yes **19.** $y = \frac{2}{3}x + \frac{11}{3}$ [6.7] **21.** $x = -2$ [6.8]

Chapter 7 Review

1. yes **3.** yes
5. (2, 9)   **7.** (−4, 2)

9. (4, 0) **11.** (−2, −4) **13.** (3, 7) **15.** (−2, 5)
17. (6, 9) **19.** (4, 0) **21.** no solution; inconsistent
23. no solution; inconsistent **25.** (4, −2), (4, 2);
consistent, independent **27.** $3 - c$ **29.** $0.2m + 0.23n$
31. $890 at 7.5%; $660 at 8.25%

33.

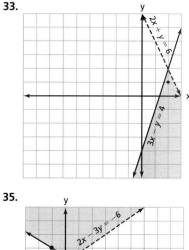

35.

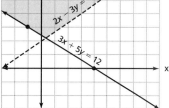

37. 2 parallel lines

Chapter 8—Polynomials

8.1

1. trinomial; 2 **3.** monomial; 2 **5.** trinomial; 4
7. monomial; 6 **9.** trinomial; 7 **11.** 27 **13.** -132
15. 207,360 **17.** 84 **21.** A [3.5] **23.** E [5.6] **25.** B [2.6]

8.2

1. $19m - 6$ **3.** $7m^2 + 10m - 5$ **5.** $2m + n + p$
7. $5x^3 + 9x^2 + 2x - y + 15$ **9.** $-4x^2 - 2xy + 18\,y^2$
11. $-4x^3 + 2x^2 - 2x + 9$ **13.** $-11x^3 + 2x^2 + 7x + 6$
15. $\frac{7}{3}x - \frac{3}{5}y + \frac{8}{7}$ **17.** $14n - 6$ **19.** $3x^2 + 3x - 27$
23. 36 [1.3] **25.** $\frac{19}{66}$ [2.2] **27.** if $a < b$ then
$a + c < b + c$ [5.2]

8.3

1. $3a + 8$ **3.** $-3x + 10y - 6$ **5.** $-7a^3 + 12a^2 - 14a - 7$
7. $x - 16$ **9.** $-4x + 7y + 9$ **11.** 0 **13.** $x^5 - 2x^4 + 6x - 5$
15. $-2x + 5y + 16$ **17.** $-6x^3 - x^2y + xy^2 + y^3 - 2y^4$
19. $-x^5y - 12xy^2 - 3xy^4$ **21.** $5x + 8y$ **25.** -1 [1.7]
27. $a - c = b - c$ if $a = b$ [4.1]
29. $8 - 3 = 5$ but $3 - 8 = -5$ [1.4]

8.4

1. $32x^3y^3z$ **3.** $-12a^3b^3$ **5.** $-108m^3n^{12}$ **7.** $-20ab - 40b^2$
9. $-56k^3 - 63k^2 - 42k$ **11.** $-90a^2b^3$ **13.** $27a^9$
15. $-12a^4b^2c^2$ **17.** $12a^6 + 15a^3 - 54a^2$
19. $-8b^4 + 24b^3 + 32ab^2$ **21.** $5a^5 + 3a^4 - 10a^2$
23. $4x^3 + 2x^2y + 8x$ **27.** 0 apples [1.3] **29.** undefined
slope [6.5] **31.** 1 is the exponent [1.7]

8.5

1. $x^2 + 7x + 10$ **3.** $x^2 + 2x - 24$ **5.** $x^2 - 7x + 12$
7. $x^2 - 4x - 5$ **9.** $x^2 - 6x + 9$ **11.** $x^2 - 4x - 12$
13. $x^2 - 13x + 42$ **15.** $x^2 + x - 72$ **17.** $x^2 - 9$
19. $x^2 - 100$ **21.** $x^2 - 16x + 64$ **23.** $x^2 + 2x + 1$
25. $x^2 + 6x + 9$ **27.** $3x^2 + 14x + 8$ **29.** $15x^2 - 8x - 12$
31. $x^2 + 12x + 36$ **33.** $49x^2 + 140x + 100$
35. $64x^2 + 48x +$ **37.** $10x^2 - 23x - 42$
39. $2x^2 - x - 36$ **41.** $9x^2 - 16$ **43.** $6x^2 - 24$
45. $6x^2 + 28x - 98$ **49.** $\frac{-7}{3}$ [2.3] **51.** $ab = ba$ [1.5]
53. $(a^m)^n = a^{mn}$ [1.7]

8.6

1. $x^3 + 2x^2y + 2xy^2 + y^3$ **3.** $12x^3 + 12x^2y - 15xy^2 - 9y^3$
5. $6x^3 - 17x^2 + 19x - 28$ **7.** $6a^2 - 18a + 12ab - 36b$
9. $9x^2 - 3x - 30$ **11.** $8x^3 - 45x^2 - 14x - 24$
13. $5x^3 - 22x^2 + 25x - 12$
15. $24x^3 + 26x^2 + 10x + 24$ **17.** $6x^4 - 3x^2 - 45$
19. $-x^2 + 5x - 26$ **25.** $x = 7$ [4.5] **27.** $(2, -3)$ [7.6]
29. $x = \frac{1}{2}$ or $x = \frac{-7}{2}$ [4.6]

8.7

1. $x^2 + 6xy + 9y^2$ **3.** $x^4 - 64$ **5.** $x^2 - 12x + 36$
7. $x^2 - 18xy + 81y^2$ **9.** $4x^2 - 121$ **11.** $x^2 - 32x + 256$
13. $x^3 + 6x^2 + 12x + 8$ **15.** $25x^2 - 30x + 9$
17. $2x^2 + 7x + 34$ **19.** $x^3 + 2x^2 - 36x - 72$
21. $x^2 - 2x + 1$ **25.** $15x^5$ [8.4]
27. $3x^2 + 5x + 3xy + 5y$ [8.5]
29. $5x^3 - 9x^2 + 3x - 7$ [8.2]

8.8

1. x^2 **3.** a **5.** $37a^2c^2$ **7.** $x^2 + x - 1$ **9.** $a + d$ **11.** $\frac{1}{2}x^2\,y$
13. $7x^4y^4z^7$ **15.** $-x^3yz$ **17.** $-5x^2 + x - 9$
19. $17a^2b - 5ab^2 + 2b^4$ **21.** $a^2b - 2b^2$ **25.** 0 [1.6]
27. 8 [3.4] **29.** 8 [3.4]

8.9

1. $a + 10$ $R.72$ **3.** $5x - 7$ $R.16$
5. $x + 5$ $R.2$ **7.** $x - 4$ $R.14$ **9.** $x^2 + 2x + 11$ $R.44$
11. $x^2 - 3x + 11$ $R.-4$ **13.** $x + 4$ **15.** $-t + 3$ $R.3$

19.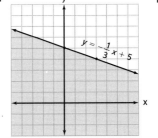

A number line with points from -1 to 7, open circle at 5, arrow extending left. [5.4]

21. $\frac{6}{121}$ [2.3] **23.** $k = \frac{1}{4}$ [6.9]

Chapter 8 Review

1. binomial **3.** trinomial **5.** 21 **7.** 3 **9.** 5
11. $9x^2 + 3x - 14$ **13.** $13x^2 - x + y$ **15.** $80x^3y^7$
17. $a^{24}b^{12}$ **19.** $21x^2y^2 - 35x^2y^6$ **21.** $x^2 - 2x - 24$
23. $6x^2 + x - 35$ **25.** $a^2 - 4ab - 21b^2$
27. $x^2 + 6x + 9$ **29.** $x^3 + 5x^2 + 11x + 10$
31. x^3 **33.** $x + 3x^2y^3$ **35.** $x - 2, R.9$
37. 0 **39.** $x^2 + 3x - 5$

Chapter 9—Factoring Polynomials

9.1
1. $7(x^2 - 7xy + 4y^2)$ **3.** $8(x - 4y)$ **5.** $3(7x^3 - 2x^2 - 1)$
7. $15(x + 2)$ **9.** $6(a^2 + 8a - 4)$ **11.** $3ab(2a + b)$
13. $5abc(2ac^2 + b)$ **15.** $4x(3x^2 - 4y^2)$
17. $7a(a^4 - 12a^2 + 3)$ **21.** $D = \{2, 5, 8, 11\}$ [6.2]
23. yes [6.2]
25. [6.3]

A graph with points (5, 5), (8, 7), (11, 3), (2, 1) plotted.

9.2
1. $(y - 12)(y + 12)$ **3.** $(7x - 2)(7x + 2)$
5. $2(a - 11)(a + 11)$ **7.** $(6a - 7)(6a + 7)$
9. $(a - 15b)(a + 15b)$ **11.** $4(x - 2)(x + 2)$
13. $7(3x - 5)(3x + 5)$ **15.** $a^2(a - b)(a + b)$
17. $4(2x - 1)(2x + 1)$ **21.** -15 [3.4]
23. $x = 2$ [4.4] **25.** $2(x + 2)$ [9.1]

9.3
1. yes **3.** yes **5.** no **7.** no **9.** no **11.** $(x - 3)^2$
13. $(x - 8)^2$ **15.** $(a - 5b)^2$ **17.** $(3x + 2)^2$
19. $(3x + 5z)^2$ **21.** $(xt^2 - 10)^2$ **23.** $2x(3x + 4)^2$
27. 2323 [1.5] **29.** $\frac{2323}{23} = 101$, $\frac{7373}{73} = 101$ [1.6]
31. $(8x - 3)(8x + 3)$, $\frac{64x^2 - 9}{8x - 3} = 8x + 3$ [9.2]

9.4
1. $(x + 8)(x - 4)$ **3.** $(x + 1)(x - 3)$ **5.** $(b + 5)(b - 4)$
7. $(a - 5)(a - 1)$ **9.** $(y + 5)(y + 2)$ **11.** $(a + 7)(a - 4)$
13. $(a - 3)(a - 1)$ **15.** $(x - 10)(x - 1)$
17. $4(x + 6)(x + 1)$ **19.** $(x + 10)^2$ **21.** $3(x - 9)(x + 1)$
23. $a(x - 12)(x + 1)$ **25.** $(x + 5)(x - 5)$

29. 3, trinomial [8.1] **31.** 6 [8.1]
33. $x^2y^3(6x - 27yz + 8)$ [9.1]

9.5
1. $(2x - 1)(x + 7)$ **3.** $(x + 4)(x - 8)$
5. $(4x + 3)(x + 3)$ **7.** $(3x - 7)(x + 4)$
9. $8(2a - 1)(a + 3)$ **11.** $(3x - 1)(3x + 2)$
13. $8(a + 1)(a - 14)$ **15.** $(2a + 1)(3a - 4)$
17. $10(3x + 5)(x - 5)$ **19.** $(3x + 4)(2x - 1)$
23. $25x^2 - 9$ [8.4]
25. $3x^4 + 6x^3 + 4x^2 + 10x + 14$ R. 37 [8.9]
27. 20 hrs. [7.7]

9.6
1. $(x + 10y)(x - 6y)$ **3.** $(y - 3z)^2$ **5.** $(x + y)(6x - 5y)$
7. $(m - 5n)(m + 4n)$ **9.** $(a - 4b)(a + 7b)$
11. $(3x + y)(x - 5y)$ **13.** $3(6c^2 + 3cd - 2d^2)$
15. $(3a + 2f)(7a - 3f)$ **17.** $(3x - 2y)(3x + 4y)$
21. [6.10]

A graph showing the line $y = -\frac{1}{3}x + 5$ with the region below shaded.

23. $x < 5$ [5.1] **25.** $5x + 2$ [9.5]

9.7
1. $(a + 1)^2$ **3.** $(10 - a)(10 + a)$ **5.** $a(a + 16)$
7. $a^3(3a^2 - 4)$ **9.** $5(a + 7)$ **11.** $10(x^2 + 5x + 7)$
13. $(m^5 + 1)^2$ **15.** $(5x - 1)(5x + 1)$ **17.** $8(a - 3b^2)^2$
19. $(2a + b)(x - y)(x + y)$ **21.** $(b + c)(a - m)$
23. $(a + b)(t - w)$ **27.** $q = \frac{7n + 5}{A}$ [4.4]
29. $q = \frac{24m}{11}$ [4.7] **31.** $q = \pm\sqrt{R}$ [7.4]

Chapter 9 Review
1. $x(8xy^3 + 5y^2 - 2)$ **3.** $x^2(x^2 + 3xy + 7)$
5. $(5x - 12y)(5x + 12y)$ **7.** $(a + 7)^2$ **9.** $(2x - 3y)^2$
11. $2(x - 9)(x - 6)$ **13.** $2(3a - 7)(a - 1)$
15. $(x - 12)(x + 7)$ **17.** $6(2x + 3y)(x + 5y)$
19. $2(3x - 5)(2x + 7)$ **21.** $(2x + 7)(x + 1)$
23. $(3x - 5)(3x + 5)$ **25.** $(9x + 25)(x + 1)$
27. $(3x - 1)(3x + 8$ **29.** $(3x - 5)(x - 4)$
31. $2(2p - 21q)(p + 3q)$ **33.** $(x^2 + 2)(x^2 + 1)$
35. $2x(x + 2)(x + y)$ **37.** $(2x - 3)(2x + 3)(3x - 2)(3x + 2)$

Chapter 10—Radicals

10.1
1. $5^{\frac{1}{2}}$ **3.** $2^{\frac{1}{3}}x^{\frac{2}{3}}$ **5.** $7^{\frac{3}{10}}x^{\frac{1}{10}}y^{\frac{2}{5}}$ **7.** $\sqrt[3]{7^2bc^4}$ or $c\sqrt[3]{7^2bc}$
9. $\sqrt[9]{5a^2b^5}$ **11.** between 4 and 5 **13.** between 3 and 4
15. 3.5 **17.** 6.6 **19.** 12.2 **21.** 2.71 **23.** 2.11 **25.** 4.59
27. 2.78
31. 3.9 [1.1]

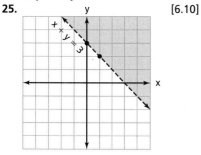

33. $7(x + 4)(x - 4)$ [9.2] **35.** $x = \pm\,14$ [7.4]

10.2
1. $4\sqrt{2}$ **3.** $3\sqrt[3]{2}$ **5.** cannot be simplified **7.** $2\sqrt{3}$
9. $7\sqrt{2}$ **11.** $2\sqrt[3]{20}$ **13.** $3x\sqrt{2y}$ **15.** $5x^2y^4\sqrt{3}$
17. $xy^2z\sqrt[3]{10z^2}$ **21.** $x > -\frac{2}{3}$ [5.4]
23. $(x + 11)(x - 17)$ [9.4] **25.** $170 + \sqrt{11} \approx 173.3$ [3.4]

10.3
1. $\sqrt{15}$ **3.** $\sqrt{35}$ **5.** $3\sqrt{6}$ **7.** $3\sqrt{7}$ **9.** $\sqrt{590}$ **11.** $14\sqrt{5}$
13. $4\sqrt[5]{2}$ **15.** $6\sqrt[3]{10}$ **17.** $12\sqrt[3]{3}$ **19.** $4a^8b^2$
21. $2x^3y^2\sqrt[3]{x^2y^2}$
25.

[6.10]

27. -0.1 [10.1] **29.** $(x + 2)(3x - 1)$ [9.7]

10.4
1. $\frac{2\sqrt{13}}{13}$ **3.** $\frac{3\sqrt{5}}{5}$ **5.** $\frac{2}{5}$ **7.** $\sqrt{3}$ **9.** $\frac{\sqrt{5}}{2}$ **11.** $\frac{\sqrt{6}}{3}$
13. $\frac{\sqrt{57}}{4}$ **15.** $\frac{\sqrt[3]{2}}{2}$ **17.** $\frac{1}{2}$ **19.** $\frac{\sqrt{287x}}{7y}$ **21.** $xz^2\sqrt{2t}$
23. $r\sqrt{s}$ **27.** $xy(3x^2y - 15y^2 + 5x)$ [9.1] **29.** $\mathbb{R}$ [5.6]
31. commutative property of multiplication [1.5]

10.5
1. $6\sqrt{3}$ **3.** $2\sqrt{3} + 4\sqrt{2}$ **5.** $\sqrt{2}$ **7.** $6\sqrt{5}$ **9.** $-2\sqrt{3}$
11. 0 **13.** $3\sqrt{5} - 6\sqrt{2}$ **15.** $2\sqrt{x} + 3\sqrt{y}$
17. $3\sqrt{ab} + 4\sqrt{a}$

21.

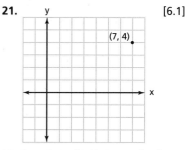

[6.1]

23. $2x + 7$ R.4 [8.9] **25.** 43 [2.5]

10.6
1. $\sqrt{41}$ **3.** $2\sqrt{15}$ **5.** $\sqrt{187}$ **7.** $6\sqrt{3}$ **9.** $4\sqrt{2}$ **11.** yes
13. no **15.** $c = 4$ **17.** $a = 7$ **19.** $\sqrt{589}$ ft. ≈ 24.27 feet
23. $\sqrt{2x - 3}$ [3.2] **25.** $2\sqrt{x} - 3$ [3.2]
27. $2\sqrt{x} - 3$ [3.2]

10.7
1. $\sqrt{29}$ **3.** $\sqrt{37}$ **5.** $\sqrt{13}$ **7.** $\sqrt{178}$ **9.** $\sqrt{65}$ **11.** $\sqrt{71}$
13. $\sqrt{10} + \sqrt{17} + 5$ **15.** $7 + \sqrt{17}$
17. $5\sqrt{5} + \sqrt{65} + 2$ **19.** 12.5 nautical miles
23. If $a = b$, then $\frac{a}{c} = \frac{b}{c}$ (if $c \neq 0$). [3.8]
25. [1.1 and 10.1]

10.8
1. $\sqrt{6} - \sqrt{3}$ **3.** $7\sqrt{3} + \sqrt{14}$ **5.** -8 **7.** $\sqrt{15} + \sqrt{6}$
9. $17 - 2\sqrt{70}$ **11.** $28 - 7\sqrt{11} + 4\sqrt{3} - \sqrt{33}$
13. $12 + 6\sqrt{5} - 4\sqrt{10} - 10\sqrt{2}$ **15.** $-4\sqrt{2} - 4$
17. $5\sqrt{105} + 10\sqrt{7} + 25\sqrt{3} + 10\sqrt{5}$
19. $x^2\sqrt{3} + 2\sqrt{3x} - 5x^2 - 10\sqrt{x}$
21. $5\sqrt{3} - 6\sqrt{15} - 5\sqrt{2} + 6\sqrt{10}$ **23.** $12\sqrt{5}$
27. $x = \frac{\sqrt{17} - \sqrt{5}}{2} < 0.94$ [4.3]
29. 1R. $-2x + 1$ [8.9]
31.

(1, 3) [7.1]

10.9
1. $-3 - \sqrt{5}$ **3.** $\frac{15 - 3\sqrt{7}}{18}$ **5.** $\sqrt{33} - \sqrt{22}$ **7.** $\frac{27 - 9\sqrt{2}}{7}$
9. $\sqrt{3} + 1$ **11.** $\frac{-5\sqrt{2} - 5\sqrt{6}}{4}$ **13.** $4\sqrt{7} - 4\sqrt{3}$
17. $(x + 9y)(x - 5y)$ [9.4]
19. $x < -7$ [5.4] **21.** $\frac{8\sqrt[3]{25}}{5}$ [10.4]

10.10

1. $x = 16$ **3.** $x = 62$ **5.** $x = 36$ **7.** $x = 10.24$ **9.** $x = -1$
11. none (52 is extraneous) **13.** $y = 124$ **15.** $x = 19$
17. $x = \frac{73}{16}$ **21.** $\frac{7\sqrt{3}}{10}$ [2.2]

23.

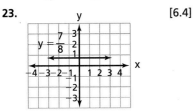

[6.4]

25. $x^2 - 5x + 2$ [8.9]

Chapter 10 Review

1. 11.3 **3.** 15.6 **5.** $2^{\frac{1}{2}}x^{\frac{3}{2}}$ **7.** $2x^{\frac{5}{4}}y^{\frac{1}{4}}$
9. $\sqrt[3]{2xyz^4}$ (or $z\sqrt[3]{2xyz}$) **11.** $2\sqrt{21}$ **13.** $\frac{5\sqrt{6}}{6}$
15. $8\sqrt{2}$ **17.** $\frac{\sqrt{3}}{3}$ **19.** $\sqrt{35} + 3\sqrt{5}$
21. $4\sqrt{6}$ **23.** $2\sqrt[5]{51}$ **25.** $6\sqrt{35}$ **27.** $\sqrt{22} - \sqrt{143}$
29. $3a^2b^2$ **31.** $\sqrt{5}$ **33.** $\sqrt{82}$ **35.** $x = 620$ **37.** $\sqrt{52}$
39. 1.99 seconds

Chapter 11—Quadratic Equations

11.1

1. $x = 0$ **3.** $y = -5$, or $y = -2$ **5.** $x = 0$, or $x = -7$
7. $y = 3$, or $y = 8$ **9.** $x = 0$, or $x = -12$
11. $x = 0$, $x = -1$, or $x = 10$
13. $x = 0$, $x = 1$, or $x = \frac{-2}{3}$ **15.** $x = \frac{11}{2}$, or $x = \frac{5}{4}$
17. $x = -7$, or $x = 8$ **21.** $x^2(x - 1)(x - 2)$ [9.4]
23. $x = \frac{5}{3}$ [4.3] **25.** 7 [3.4]

11.2

1. $y = -3$ **3.** $x = \pm 3$ **5.** $m = -5$, or $m = 7$ **7.** $\{0, 7\}$
9. $\{2, 8\}$ **11.** $\{-6, 2\}$ **13.** $\{-13, 13\}$ **15.** $\{-10, -5\}$
17. $a = 2$, or $a = -15$ **19.** $x = \frac{-3}{4}$, or $x = \frac{-1}{2}$
21. $t = \frac{-3}{2}$, or $t = \frac{4}{5}$ **23.** 2, 8
27. $8\sqrt{3} + 2\sqrt{6}$ [10.5] **29.** $74\sqrt{22}$ [10.2]
31. $\frac{\sqrt{15} + 3 + 5\sqrt{5} + 5\sqrt{3}}{2}$ [10.9]

11.3

1. $x = \pm 10$ **3.** $x = \pm 5$ **5.** $x = \pm\sqrt{6}$ **7.** $x = \pm 2\sqrt{5}$
9. $x = \pm\sqrt{7}$ **11.** $x = 6 \pm \sqrt{13}$ **13.** complex
15. $q = \frac{\pm\sqrt{77}}{7}$ **17.** $x = -1$, or $x = \frac{1}{2}$
21. $(x^2 + 2)(2x + 1)$ [9.7] **23.** $x < 2$ [5.2]
25. 892.73 at 5%; 922.73 at 6% [4.8 and 7.8]

11.4

1. 16 **3.** 64 **5.** 676 **7.** $\frac{9}{4}$ **9.** $\frac{81}{4}$ **11.** $x = 1$, or $x = -5$
13. $x = 3$, or $x = -5$ **15.** $\{-2, 12\}$ **17.** $\{-9, 11\}$

19. $\{-2, 1\}$ **21.** $\left[0, \frac{4}{3}\right]$ **25.** $x = -11$ [10.10]

27.

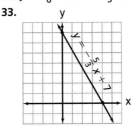

[5.4]

29. 300 [1.9]

11.5

1. 2 **3.** -4 **5.** $x = -3 \pm \sqrt{11}$ **7.** $x = 2 \pm \sqrt{3}$ **9.** $\left\{\frac{-3}{2}, 1\right\}$
11. $\left\{\frac{1 - 2\sqrt{3}}{2}, \frac{1 + 2\sqrt{3}}{2}\right\}$ **13.** $n = 3$, or $n = \frac{-3}{2}$
15. $a = \frac{3}{2}$, or $a = -1$ **17.** complex **19.** $x = \frac{-6 \pm \sqrt{142}}{2}$
23. 5 [2.5] **25.** x^6 [3.3] **27.** $4x^2 + 22x + 30$ [8.7]

11.6

1. $\{-2, -4\}$ **3.** $\{-3, -5\}$ **5.** $\{-3, 3\}$ **7.** $\left\{\frac{3}{2}, -1\right\}$ **9.** $\{3\}$
11. $x = 4$, or $x = \frac{1}{2}$ **13.** $x = \frac{5 \pm \sqrt{105}}{4}$
15. $m = -1$, or $m = \frac{-2}{7}$ **17.** $k = \frac{1 \pm \sqrt{31}}{3}$
19. $x = \frac{-1}{4}$, or $x = \frac{7}{2}$ **23.** $2x$ [3.5] **25.** 1 [2.3]
27. \$55.84 [4.2]

11.7

1. $\{4, -2\}$ **3.** $\left\{\frac{-1}{3}, -4\right\}$ **5.** $\{6, 9\}$ **7.** $\left\{2, \frac{1}{6}\right\}$
9. $x = \frac{7 \pm \sqrt{33}}{4}$ **11.** $a = 1$, or $a = \frac{-5}{3}$
13. $r = \frac{5}{4}$, or $r = -1$ **15.** $x = -3$, or $x = 1$
17. $x = -4 \pm 3\sqrt{2}$ **19.** $t = \pm 2$ **21.** $x = 2 \pm \sqrt{2}$
23. $x = \frac{-11}{2}$, or $x = 4$ **25.** complex
27. $y = \frac{-7}{6}$ **31.** $x = \frac{14}{5}$ [10.10]

33.

y

$y = \frac{-5}{3}x + 1$

x

[6.6]

35. width is $\frac{51}{4} = 12.75$ cm; length is $\frac{145}{4} = 36.25$ cm [4.2]

11.8

1. 26 in. **3.** 120 in³ **5.** 14 in. by 11 in. **7.** $2x^2 + 4x$
9. $8x^2 - 6x - 24$ **11.** 12, 18 or -12, -18
13. 4, 30 **15.** 17.9, 14.9, 9.9 in. **17.** $4\sqrt{5} \approx 8.9$ ft.
21. addition property of equality [3.1]
23. $ax^2 + bx + c = 0$ [11.6] **25.** 109, 111, 113 [3.9]

Chapter 11 Review

1. $x = 2$, or $x = -3$ **3.** $x = 0$, $x = \frac{1}{2}$, or $x = \frac{-1}{2}$
5. $x = \pm 2$ **7.** $a = 1$, $b = 4$, $c = -1$
9. $x = 3 \pm \sqrt{7}$ **11.** $x = \frac{3}{2}$, or $x = -1$

13. $x = \frac{-5 \pm \sqrt{37}}{2}$ 15. $\{-4, 4\}$ 17. $\{-2, 7\}$

19. $\frac{1 + \sqrt{21}}{2}, \frac{1 - \sqrt{21}}{2}$ 21. $\{-3\}$ (-6 is extraneous)

23. $y = \pm \sqrt{17}$ 25. $x = -3$, or $x = 8$ 27. complex

29. $x = -8$, or $x = \frac{7}{2}$ 31. $a = \frac{-7 \pm \sqrt{97}}{2}$

33. 8 ft. by 15 ft.

Chapter 12—Rational Expressions

12.1
1. 0 3. -2 5. 3, -8 7. $-9, 2$ 9. $\frac{x}{5}$
11. $\frac{5a^2}{9c^2}$ 13. 1 15. $\frac{x-5}{x}$ 17. $\frac{5(x-6)}{x+1}$
19. $\frac{x+5}{x-1}$
23. [6.1]

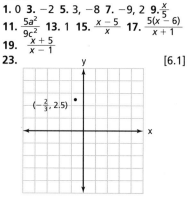

$\left(-\frac{2}{3}, 2.5\right)$

25. $s = \frac{-m \pm \sqrt{m^2 - 4nq}}{2n}$ [11.6] 27. $\frac{8}{15}$ [3.3]

12.2
1. $\frac{19}{70}$ 3. $\frac{3}{8}$ 5. a 7. $\frac{z}{x^3y}$ 9. 5 11. $\frac{x+2}{2}$ 13. $(x+8)(x+3)$
15. $\frac{2x+y}{3x-4y}$ 17. $\frac{a+2b}{a}$ 19. $\frac{3x-4y}{2x-y}$ 21. $\frac{3x-2y}{x-y}$ 23. 1
25. $a(a-1)$ 29. $x = \frac{365}{2}$ (or 182.5) [4.7] 31. $\frac{-7}{5}$ [6.7]
33. [6.6]

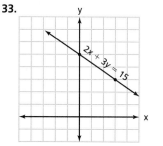

$2x + 3y = 15$

12.3
1. $\frac{7}{2}$ 3. $\frac{1}{2}$ 5. $\frac{7y^2}{3}$ 7. $x + y$ 9. $\frac{x+y}{(x-y)^2}$ 11. $\frac{x}{x+1}$
13. $\frac{(3x+y)(x+y)}{(x-y)^2}$ 15. $\frac{x+9}{x+2}$ 17. $\frac{(x-y)}{(x+y)^3}$
19. $\frac{3m+n}{m^3n^2(m-n)}$ 23. $\frac{1}{5}$ [2.2] 25. $\sqrt{65}$ [10.7]
27. $x = \frac{-1 \pm \sqrt{241}}{6}$ [11.6]

12.4
1. $\frac{14}{x}$ 3. $\frac{-5}{x}$ 5. $\frac{-1}{c}$ 7. 2 9. $\frac{9x}{x^2+y}$ 11. $\frac{-12}{x+2}$
13. $\frac{3(3x+y)}{yz}$ 15. $\frac{3}{a+b}$ 17. $\frac{3m+n}{m-n}$ 19. $\frac{-2x-7}{x^2-4x-7}$
21. $\frac{x+7}{x+9}$ 23. $\frac{6}{x^2-3x-9}$ 25. $\frac{2(x^2-2x+7)}{(x-6)(x+2)}$
29. contains fractional exponent $2\sqrt[3]{5}$ [10.1]
31. fraction not reduced $\frac{3 \pm \sqrt{7}}{2}$ [11.6]

12.5
1. $\frac{12x+9}{16}$ 3. $\frac{11x+57}{36}$ 5. $\frac{7a^2+6a-45}{10}$
7. $\frac{7m+12}{4m^3}$ 9. $\frac{xy^2+2x^2}{3y^3}$ 11. $\frac{9x^4+4x^2y+9x^2y^3+4y^2}{36x^3y}$
13. $\frac{8x^3-3x^2-76x-224}{6(x+4)(x-4)}$ 15. $\frac{19x^2+19x-144}{12x(x-3)(x+4)}$
17. $\frac{x^3-4x^2+17x-24}{(x-3)^2(x-5)}$ 19. $\frac{3(x-2)}{x+5}$ 23. $\frac{25y}{4x^8}$ [3.3]
25. $x = \frac{2}{3}$ or $x = \frac{-8}{5}$ [11.2] 27. $2\sqrt{109} \approx 20.9$ ft. [10.6]

12.6
1. $\frac{-29x}{63}$ 3. $\frac{4x^2-1}{3x^3}$ 5. $\frac{xy^2+2x^2}{3y^3}$ 7. $\frac{-2x+6}{(x-2)^2}$
9. $\frac{-3x+7}{x+5}$ 11. $\frac{2x^2-23x-36}{(x-7)^2(x+4)}$ 13. $\frac{-x^2+5x}{(x-1)(x+1)}$
15. $\frac{7x^2+26x+87}{(x+2)^2(x+3)(x-5)}$ 17. $\frac{-2x-6}{(x+2)(x-4)}$
19. $\frac{2x^2-21x}{(x+4)(x-9)}$ 21. $\frac{2a^2-a+2ab+4b+b^2-10}{(a-b)(a+b)}$
25. Pythagorean theorem [10.6]
27. fundamental property of fractions [2.2]
29. quadratic formula [11.6]

12.7
1. $\frac{2}{5}$ 3. $\frac{a-b}{a+b}$ 5. $\frac{5(x-y)}{x+y}$ 7. $\frac{x}{x-y}$ 9. $\frac{x^2}{x+1}$
11. $(m+n)^2$ 13. $2(x+3)^2$
17. Find common denominator, $\frac{10x+1}{x}$. [12.5]
19. Eliminate negative exponent, $\frac{3}{x^2}$. [3.3]
21. Reduce radical, $5\sqrt{2}$. [10.2]

Chapter 12 Review
1. 3 3. $-2, 6$ 5. 0, 1, -1 7. $(x+6)(x+7)(x-9)$
9. $(2x+1)(x+5)(x-8)$ 11. $\frac{1}{2x-5}$ 13. $\frac{x+5}{x-3}$
15. $\frac{x-10}{x(x+3)(x+5)}$ 17. $\frac{3x+10}{3x+5}$ 19. $\frac{x-3}{x+4}$
21. $\frac{x+1}{x+2}$ 23. $\frac{1}{x-y}$ 25. $\frac{x^2(6x+1)}{3(3x-5)}$ 27. 0
29. $\frac{(x-1)(x-5)}{x^2(x+3)}$ 31. y^2 33. $\frac{x+9xy+2y}{27y}$
35. $\frac{x}{(3x+2)(x+2)}$ 37. $\frac{x^3-4x^2-40x-97}{(x-6)(x+4)(x-1)}$
39. $\frac{x^3+x^2+3x^2y+5xy^2-y^2+3y^3}{(x+y)^2(x-y)}$

Chapter 13—Rational Equations

13.1

1. $x = 40$ **3.** $m = 27$ **5.** $x = 11$ **7.** $a = -8$ **9.** $a = \frac{9}{2}$
11. $a = \frac{-241}{8}$ **13.** $m = \frac{-6}{11}$ **15.** $x = \frac{7}{2}$ **17.** \$112
21. $x = -12$ [13.1]
23.

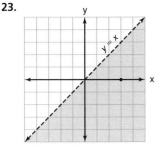

[6.10]

13.2

1. $x = \frac{1}{4}$ **3.** $y = \frac{1}{2}$ **5.** $x = \frac{2}{3}$ **7.** $a = 1$ **9.** $x = 3$
11. $a = \frac{69}{7}$ **13.** $x = \frac{-13}{11}$ **15.** $a = \frac{5 \pm \sqrt{161}}{2}$
17. $m = \frac{51}{10}$ **19.** 13 **21.** 4, 10 **25.** $y = \frac{nq + t}{6p}$ [4.3]
27. $\frac{3x + 16}{x(x + 2)}$ [12.6]
29.

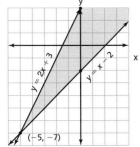

[7.10]

13.3

1. 2 hours **3.** 29.8 hours **5.** 21.3 hours **7.** 1.2 hours
9. Brent, 75 minutes; Jim, 150 minutes **11.** Fran, 6.8
hours; Joy, 9.8 hours **13.** 1.2 hours **17.** $(7x^2 + 4)$
$(x^2 + 1)$ [9.7] **19.** $(x^4 + y^4)(x^2 + y^2)(x + y)(x - y)$ [9.7]
21. $3(x^4 + 2)(x - 1)(x + 1)$ [9.7]

13.4

1. \$72 **3.** \$63 **5.** 5.1% **7.** $0.06x + 0.05y = 250$; $y = x$
9.

	P	r	t	=	d
1st account	x	0.08	2		0.16x
2nd account	y	0.05	2		0.1y

11. \$2695 at 6%, \$8085 at 8%, \$2695 at 10%

13. \$6000 at 9%, \$2000 at $5\frac{3}{4}$% **15.** 11% for \$3000
investment, 9% for \$8000 investment **17.** \$5000;
\$3750 in preferred stock, \$1250 in common stock
21. $x = 5$ [4.1]

23. $x \le \frac{2}{5}$ or $x > \frac{4}{5}$ [5.6]

25. $x = \pm 4$ [13.2]

13.5

1.

	r	t	=	d
going	x + 3	$\frac{200}{x + 3}$		200
return	x	$\frac{200}{x}$		200

3. 5 miles **5.** slower plane, 750 miles; faster plane,
1500 miles **7.** 4 mph walking, 6 mph riding **9.** 15
mph **11.** $\sqrt{34} \approx 5.8$ mph **15.** $\frac{-2}{3}$ [6.5]
17. $x^2 - x - 5$ R: $- 12x + 34$ [8.9] **19.** 20 lb. of lime
[4.10]

13.6

1. $c = \frac{\pm \sqrt{em}}{m}$ **3.** $h = \frac{p}{0.433}$ **5.** $t = \frac{d}{r}$ **7.** $r = \frac{c}{2p}$
9. $s = \frac{P}{3}$ **11.** $r = \frac{\pm \sqrt{A\pi}}{\pi}$ **13.** $r = \frac{\sqrt[3]{6\pi^2 V}}{2\pi}$
15. $d = \frac{\pm \sqrt{2.5nP}}{n}$ **17.** $x = \frac{a(3 + y)}{y}$ **19.** $y = \frac{x}{2 - a}$
23. $\frac{11}{2}$ [4.2] **25.** $-3, 5$ [11.8] **27.** 42 [6.9]

Chapter 13 Review

1. $x = 4$ **3.** $x = \frac{1}{5}$ **5.** $x = 26$ **7.** $x = \frac{11}{6}$ **9.** $x = 7$
11. $n = \pm \sqrt{R}$ **13.** $R = \frac{3A + SA}{S}$ **15.** $M = \frac{NQ}{N - Q}$
17. $7(x - 5) = 4(x + 5)$ **19.** $\frac{40}{x + 3} + \frac{50}{x} = 7$ **21.** 5
23. 18 hours **25.** \$750 at 11%; \$250 at 7%

Chapter 14—Quadratic Functions

14.1

1. 3, 5, 2, 7 **3.** 0, 4, -2, 8 **5.** 0, 4, 1, 16 **7.** 5, 9, 6, 21
9. -7, 5, -4, 41

11.

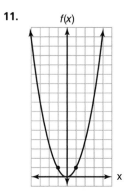

f(x)

13.

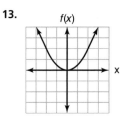

f(x)

x

5.

f(x)

x

7.

f(x)

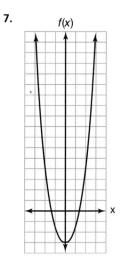

x

15.

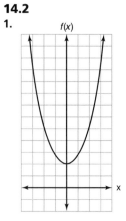

f(x)

x

17. origin (0, 0);
origin (0, 0)
19. upward **21.** −8
23. $15 - 7\sqrt{11}$
27. $x = 4$ [4.4]
29. $x \le 47$ [5.8]

9.

f(x)

x

11. (0, 1) up

13. (0, −5) down

14.2

1.

f(x)

x

3.

f(x)

x

15.

f(x)

x

17.

f(x)

x

19.

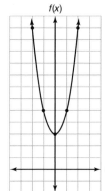

f(x)

x

23. $x^5 - 1024$ [8.6]

25. $\left(\frac{1}{2}, 2\right)$ [7.6]

14.3

1.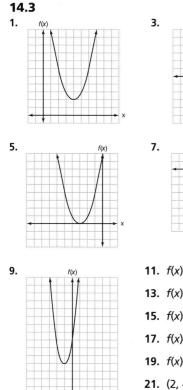

3.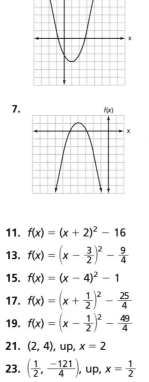

5.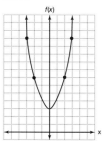

7.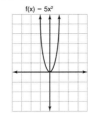

9.

11. $f(x) = (x + 2)^2 - 16$

13. $f(x) = \left(x - \frac{3}{2}\right)^2 - \frac{9}{4}$

15. $f(x) = (x - 4)^2 - 1$

17. $f(x) = \left(x + \frac{1}{2}\right)^2 - \frac{25}{4}$

19. $f(x) = \left(x - \frac{1}{2}\right)^2 - \frac{49}{4}$

21. $(2, 4)$, up, $x = 2$

23. $\left(\frac{1}{2}, \frac{-121}{4}\right)$, up, $x = \frac{1}{2}$

27. $\frac{5x - 3}{x^2 + x}$ [12.6]

29. $x = \frac{1}{2}$, or $x = 1$ [11.2]

14.4

1. no zeros

3. $1, -3$

5. $-2, 4$

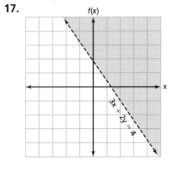

7. $(0, -5)$

9. $(0, 0)$

11. ± 4

13. $-2 \pm \sqrt{3}$

15. $-3, 0$

17. 4

21. $\sqrt{29}$ [10.7]

23. $3x^2 - 2x + 4$ [8.2]

14.5

1. 20 ft. $\times$ 20 ft. **3.** $-4, 4$ **5.** 11 feet by 11 feet
7. 200 items **9.** time, 2 sec.; height 64 ft.
11. 300 ovens; $90,500 profit **13.** 30 yards wide, 60 yards long **15.** $x + 4$ R.-11 [8.9]

17. [6.10]

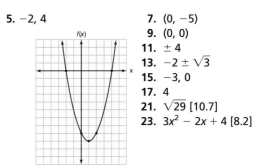

19. $\frac{-5}{7}$ [6.6]

Chapter 14 Review

1. 7 **3.** -2 **7.** 10 **5.** $-67, 29, 113$ **7.** 10 **9.** up **11.** $\left(\frac{1}{6}, \frac{-169}{12}\right)$ **13.** minimum of $\frac{-169}{12} = -14\frac{1}{12}$ when $x = \frac{1}{6}$
15. $(0, 0)$; 0 **17.** $(0, 0)$; 0

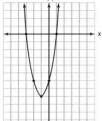

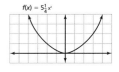

19. $(0, 12)$; $\pm\sqrt{6}$

$f(x) = -2x^2 + 12$

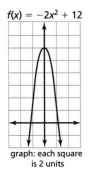

graph: each square is 2 units

21. $(2, 0)$; 2

$f(x) = -3(x - 2)^2$

23. $(7, -3)$; no zeros

25. $(-3, -8)$; $-3 \pm 2\sqrt{2}$

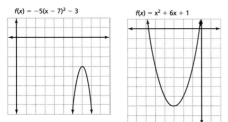

$f(x) = -5(x - 7)^2 - 3$

$f(x) = x^2 + 6x + 1$

27. 0 **29.** $(3, 1)$ **31.** 2 and 4 **33.** $960; 70 boxes

Normal Curve Table

AREAS UNDER THE STANDARD NORMAL CURVE

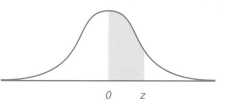

Percent of area under the curve between 0 and z.

	.00	.01	.02	.03	.04	.05	.06	.07	.08	.09
.0	.0000	.0040	.0080	.0120	.0160	.0199	.0239	.0279	.0319	.0359
.1	.0398	.0438	.0478	.0517	.0557	.0596	.0636	.0675	.0714	.0753
.2	.0793	.0832	.0871	.0910	.0948	.0987	.1026	.1064	.1103	.1141
.3	.1179	.1217	.1255	.1293	.1331	.1368	.1406	.1443	.1480	.1517
.4	.1554	.1591	.1628	.1664	.1700	.1736	.1772	.1808	.1844	.1879
.5	.1915	.1950	.1985	.2019	.2054	.2088	.2123	.2157	.2190	.2224
.6	.2257	.2291	.2324	.2357	.2389	.2422	.2454	.2486	.2517	.2549
.7	.2580	.2611	.2642	.2673	.2704	.2734	.2764	.2794	.2823	.2852
.8	.2881	.2910	.2939	.2967	.2995	.3023	.3051	.3078	.3106	.3133
.9	.3159	.3186	.32f2	.3238	.3264	.3289	.3315	.3340	.3365	.3389
1.0	.3413	.3438	.3461	.3485	.3508	.3531	.3554	.3577	.3599	.3621
1.1	.3643	.3665	.3686	.3708	.3729	.3749	.3770	.3790	.3810	.3830
1.2	.3849	.3869	.3888	.3907	.3925	.3944	.3962	.3980	.3997	.4015
1.3	.4032	.4049	.4066	.4082	.4099	.4115	.4131	.4147	.4162	.4177
1.4	.4192	.4207	.4222	.4236	.4251	.4265	.4279	.4292	.4306	.4319
1.5	.4332	.4345	.4357	.4370	.4382	.4394	.4406	.4418	.4429	.4441
1.6	.4452	.4463	.4474	.4484	.4495	.4505	.4515	.4525	.4535	.4545
1.7	.4554	.4564	.4573	.4582	.4591	.4599	.4608	.4616	.4625	.4633
1.8	.4641	.4649	.4656	.4664	.4671	.4678	.4686	.4693	.4699	.4706
1.9	.4713	.4719	.4726	.4732	.4738	.4744	.4750	.4756	.4761	.4767
2.0	.4772	.4778	.4783	.4788	.4793	.4798	.4803	.4808	.4812	.4817
2.1	.4821	.4826	.4830	.4834	.4838	.4842	.4846	.4850	.4854	.4857
2.2	.4861	.4864	.4868	.4871	.4875	.4878	.4881	.4884	.4887	.4890
2.3	.4893	.4896	.4898	.4901	.4904	.4906	.4909	.4911	.4913	.4916
2.4	.4918	.4920	.4922	.4925	.4927	.4929	.4931	.4932	.4934	.4936
2.5	.4938	.4940	.4941	.4943	.4945	.4946	.4948	.4949	.4951	.4952
2.6	.4953	.4955	.4956	.4957	.4959	.4960	.4961	.4962	.4963	.4964
2.7	.4965	.4966	.4967	.4968	.4969	.4970	.4971	.4972	.4973	.4974
2.8	.4974	.4975	.4976	.4977	.4977	.4978	.4979	.4979	.4980	.4981
2.9	.4981	.4982	.4982	.4983	.4984	.4984	.4985	.4985	.4986	.4986
3.0	.4987	.4987	.4987	.4988	.4988	.4989	.4989	.4989	.4990	.4990
3.1	.4990	.4991	.4991	.4991	.4992	.4992	.4992	.4992	.4993	.4993
3.2	.4993	.4993	.4994	.4994	.4994	.4994	.4994	.4995	.4995	.4995
3.3	.4995	.4995	.4995	.4996	.4996	.4996	.4996	.4996	.4996	.4997
3.4	.4997	.4997	.4997	.4997	.4997	.4997	.4997	.4997	.4997	.4998
3.5	.4998									
4.0	.49997									
4.5	.499997									
5.0	.4999997									

TABLE 3 **593**

Symbols

$+$	addition, positive	$\lvert x \rvert$	absolute value of x	$\subset$	is a proper subset of
$-$	subtraction, negative	$=$	is equal to	$\varnothing$	empty set
$\times$	multiplication (times)	$\neq$	is not equal to	$\cup$	union
$\cdot$	multiplication	$\approx$	is approximately equal to	$\cap$	intersection
$\div$	division	$>$	is greater than	$\times$	cross product
$\frac{p}{q}$	division, fraction	$<$	is less than	$\vee$	or
$0.\overline{3}$	repeating decimal	$\geq$	is greater than or equal to	$\wedge$	and
$\mathbb{N}$	natural number	$\leq$	is less than or equal to	$/$	cancellation
$\mathbb{W}$	whole number	$\bar{x}$	average (mean) of x values	$\sqrt{}$	square root
$\mathbb{Z}$	integers	Σ	sum (summation notation)	$\sqrt[3]{}$	cuberoot
$\mathbb{Q}$	rational number	s	standard deviation	$\sqrt[n]{}$	nth root
$\mathbb{R}$	real numbers	$\{\ \}$	set braces	$!$	factorial
$^\circ$	degrees	$\{x \mid \ldots\}$	the set of x such that . . .	$_nP_r$	permutations
$\pm$	plus or minus	$\in$	is an element of	$_nC_r$	combinations
$\%$	percent	$\notin$	is not an element of	$f(x)$	function of x
π	pi	$\subseteq$	is a subset of		

Index

Abscissa 220
Absolute value
  defined 7, 151
  equations 150–52
  inequalities 204–6
Addition
  associative property of 12, 24
  commutative property of 12, 24
  of integers 9, 12
  of like terms 101
  of polynomials 327–28
  of radicals 416
  of rational expressions 492, 495–96
  of rational numbers 51, 54
  on a number line 9–11
  properties of 12
Addition property
  of equality 116
  property of inequality 186

Additive identity 12, 24
Additive inverse 12, 24
Algebraic expressions
  defined 87
  evaluation of 96-97
  polynomial 324
  radical 428
  rational 482
Al-Khwarizmi viii
Associative property
  of addition 12, 24
  of multiplication 20, 24
Average 61
Axis
  of coordinate plane 220
  of symmetry 547, 548
Bernoulli family 118–19
Binomials
  defined 324
  difference of squares 348, 367
  multiplication of 338–39

  by the FOIL method 340
    squaring 347
Braces 66, 76
Brackets 66
Cartesian plane 219
Cartesian product 219
Coefficient 100, 456
Coin problems 157–58
Combinations 345
Combining like terms 101
Commutative property
  of addition 12, 24
  of multiplication 20, 24
Common denominators 54
Completing the square 456–67
Complex rational expressions 506–8
Composite number 31
Compound sentence.
  See Conjunction; Disjunction

Conjugate 432
Conjunctions 194, 206
Consistent system 278, 298
Constant 87
Constant of variation 258
Coordinates
  on a number line 3
  on a Cartesian plane 219
Cube root 71, 398
Degree
  of polynomials 325, 444
  of terms 324
Dependent system 278, 298
Descartes, René 202–3
Difference of squares 348, 367
Direct variation 258
Disjunctions 197, 206
Distance formula 425
Distributive property 20, 24, 100
Division
  by monomials 351–52
  by zero 24

of integers 23–24
of polynomials 354–56
of radicals 406–8
of radical expressions
    431–33
of rational expressions
    489–90, 509
of rational numbers 58
Division property
of equality 116
of exponents 29
of inequality 190
Domain 86, 224
Einstein, Albert 378–79
Element 76
Ellipsis 76
Empty set 76
Equality, properties of 116
Equations
    absolute value 150–52
    defined 115
    forms of 234, 246, 253,
        444
    linear 234, 246, 252
    literal 132, 535–36
    numerical 115
    quadratic 444
    radical 435
    rational 519–20
    solving 115, 132, 140,
        148, 155
    systems of 273
    with two variables 132,
        273
Evaluating
    algebraic expressions 96–97
    exponential forms 28
    numerical expressions 64
Exponential form 27, 93–94,
    397
Exponents
    base of 27
    defined 27
    negative 93–94
    properties of 29
    rational 397
    zero 29
Extraneous 435–36, 519
Factoring
    common monomials 364–
        65
    completely 386–88
    difference of two
        squares 366–67
    into primes 32
    perfect square trinomials
        371–72
    using the ladder method 33

using the tree method 32
to solve quadratic
    equations 446–48
trinomials 374–76,
    380–82, 384–85
Factors
    common monomial
        364–65
    defined 31
    prime 31
Finite set 76
FOIL method 340
Formulas
    defined 107
    distance 425
    quadratic 464
    slope 238
    solving 132, 335–36
    using 108
Fractions
    clearing equations of
        154–55, 516
    complex 506
    fundamental principle of
        52, 483
    operations with 57–58
Function
    defined 225
    domain of 224–25
    graphing 546, 548, 552
    greatest integer 228
    linear 234
    maximum 560
    minimum 560
    notation 544
    quadratic 545
    range of 224–25
    vertical line test for 228
    zeros of a 555
Fundamental principle of
    fractions 52, 483
Gauss, Karl Friedrich 294–95
Graphing
    equations 235, 247
    inequalities 183, 204–6,
        262–64
    on a Cartesian plane 219
    on a number line 3
    ordered pairs 221
    quadratic functions 546,
        548, 552
    relations 224
    systems of equations
        273–78
    systems of inequalities
        314–16
Greatest common factor
    (GCF) 35

Greatest integer function 228
Grouping symbols 66
Hypotenuse 419
Identity
    additive 12, 24
    multiplicative 20, 24
Inconsistent system 278, 298
Independent system 278, 298
Inequalities
    absolute value 204–6
    conjunctions 194–96
    defined 183
    disjunctions 197
    graphing 183, 204–6,
        262–64
    linear 262–64
    properties 186–90
    solving 192
    symbols 182, 594
    systems of 314–15
Infinite set 76
Integers
    addition of 9–12
    defined 46
    division of 23–24
    multiplication of 20–21
    subtraction of 14–16
Intercepts
    x-intercept 236, 555
    y-intercept 236
Interest problems 159–60,
    304–6, 527
Intersection 77, 194
Inverse
    additive 12, 24
    multiplicative 58
    operations 130
Irrational numbers 48, 396
Least common denominator.
    See Least common
    multiple
Least common multiple
    (LCM) 37
Like radicals 416
Like terms 99
Line
    direct variation 258
    equation of 234
    graph of 235, 247
    of symmetry 547–58
    slope of 238
Linear equations
    defined 234
    graphing 235, 247
    point-slope form 254
    slope-intercept form 246
    standard form 234
    systems of 272, 278

Linear inequalities 262–64
Literal equations 132, 535–36
Mathematical property 12
Maximum 560
Minimum 560
Mixture problems 169–71,
    309–11
Monomials
    defined 324
    division by 351–52
    factoring common 364–65
    multiplication by 332–34
Motion problems 163–66,
    300–1, 531–32
Multiplication
    associative property of 20,
        24
    by monomials 332–34
    commutative property of
        20, 24
    of binomials 338–39
        by the FOIL method
            340
    of integers 20–21
    of polynomials 342–43
    of radicals 403–4
    of radical expressions
        428–30
    of rational expressions
        485–86
    of rational numbers 56–57
    properties of 20
    special products 347–49
Multiplication property
    of equality 116
    of exponents 29
    of inequality 189
    of zero 20, 24
Multiplicative identity 20, 24
Multiplicative inverse 57–58
Natural numbers 46
Negative exponents 93–94
Negative numbers 46
Neumann, John von 454–55
Newton, Isaac 18–19
Null set 76
Number line
    addition on 9–11
    coordinates 3
    graphing 3
    subtraction on 15
Number systems 49
Numbers
    complex 46, 49, 452
    composite 31
    integers 46
    irrational 48, 396
    natural 46

negative 46
opposite 6
prime 31
rational 47
real 49
types of 46, 49
whole 46
Opposite numbers 6
Ordered pairs
defined 219
graphing 221
Order of operations 63–64
Ordinate 220
Origin 220
Parabola
defined 546
line (axis) of symmetry 547
Parentheses
equations containing 144
grouping 66
removing 103–4
Perfect power 347, 371–72
Perfect square trinomials 400
Permutations 288–89
Plane. *See* Cartesian plane
Point-slope form 253
Polynomials
addition of 327–28
defined 324
degree of 325
division of 351–56
multiplication of 332–43
subtraction of 330
terms of 324
types of 324
Powers. *See* Exponents
Prime factorization
defined 32
using the ladder method 33
using the tree method 32
Prime numbers
defined 31
relatively prime 36
Principal square root 70
Probability 26, 113
Property
associative 12, 20, 24
commutative 12, 20, 24
defined 12
distributive 20, 24
identity 12, 20, 24
inverse 12, 24, 58
of equality 116
of exponents 29, 94
of inequality 186–90
zero product 444
Pythagorean theorem 419

Quadrants 219–20
Quadratic equations
defined 444
general form 444
solving
by completing the square 456–61
by factoring 446–48, 470
by taking square roots 450–52, 470
by the quadratic formula 463–66, 470
word problems using 471–74
Quadratic formula 464
Quadratic functions
graphing 546, 548, 552
value of 544–45
vertex 546
Radical expressions
addition of 417–18
conjugate 432
defined 428
division of 431–33
multiplication of 428–30
subtraction of 417–18
Radicals
addition of 416
division of 406–8
division property of 406–10
equations 435
exponential equivalents of 397
index of 71
like 416
multiplication of 403–4
product property 400
rationalizing the denominator 407
simplification 400, 407
subtraction of 416–17
Radical sign 71
Radicand 69
Range 224
Rational equations
solving 519–20
word problems using 522–32
Rational expressions
addition of 492, 495–96
complex 506
defined 482
division of 489–90, 507
multiplication of 485–86
simplification of 483–84, 507

subtraction of 493, 496, 500
undefined 482
Rational numbers
addition of 51, 54
defined 47
division of 58
multiplication of 56–57
subtraction of 54
Rationalizing the denominator 407
Real numbers 49
Reciprocals 57
Relations
defined 223
domain 224
graphing 224
range 224
Relatively prime numbers 36
Right angle 419
Right triangle 419
Rise 238
Run 238
Sets
elements of 76
intersection of 77
operations 77
symbols for 76
union of 77
Simplification
of complex fractions 506–7
of radicals 400
of rational expressions 483–84
of rational numbers 51–52
Slope 238
Slope formula 238
Slope-intercept form 246
Square roots
defined 69
principal 70
simplifying 400, 409
Standard deviation 369
Statistics 26
Substitution 97
Subtraction
defined 14
of integers 14–16
of polynomials 330
of radicals 417–18
of rational expressions 493, 496, 500
of rational numbers 54
property of equality 116
property of inequality 187

Systems
consistent 278, 298
dependent 278, 298
graphing 273–78
inconsistent 278, 298
independent 278, 298
of equations 273
of inequalities 314–16
solutions to 273
solving
by addition 290–91, 296–97
by graphing 273–78
by substitution 280–85
word problems using 300–11
Terms
combining like 101
degree of 324
Theorem
defined 419
Pythagorean 419
Trinomials
defined 324
factoring 381
perfect square 347, 371–72
Union 77, 197
Variables 86–87, 130, 482
Variance 369
Variation, direct 258
Vertex 546
Vertical line test 228
Whole numbers 46
Word problems 90, 120, 136–38, 208, 258–60, 300–11, 471–74, 522–32, 560–62
Work problems 522–24
x-axis 220
x-coordinate 220
x-intercept 236
y-axis 220
y-coordinate 220
y-intercept 236
Zero as an exponent 29
Zero product property 444
Zero property of multiplication 20, 24
Zeros of a function 555

Photo Credits

The following agencies and individuals have furnished materials to meet the photographic needs of this textbook. We wish to express our gratitude to them for their important contribution.

Suzanne Altizer
Aramco World
Bob Jones University
(BJU) Press Files
Bridge and Offshore
Engineering Association
Bureau of Reclamation,
Washington, D.C.
Lewis Carl
Cedar Point
CERN
George R. Collins
Corbis
Corel Corporation
Dartmouth College
Victor Englebert
Stan Evans
Dan Feicht
Frazier Photography
Kenneth Frederick
Greyhound Lines, Inc.
Brian D. Johnson
Kromer Company
Tim McCabe
Joe Mehling
National Aeronautics and
Space Administration
(NASA)
National Institutes of
Health (NIH)
National Park Service (NPS)
New York Stock Exchange
(NYSE)
Photo Disc, Inc.
Planet Art
Dr. Margene Ranieri
Rinker Materials
Corporation
South Dakota Tourism
Springfield Illinois
Convention & Visitors
Bureau
State Fair of Texas
Stem Labs, Inc.
Ron Tagliapietra
Graeme Teague
United States Air Force
(USAF)
United States Department
of Agriculture (USDA)
United States Navy
Unusual Films
Kay Washer

Dawn L. Watkins
Nik Wheeler
http://www.arttoday.com

Cover
Corel Corporation:
Blackback butterfly fish,
fireworks, apples; Stan
Evans: snowboarder; BJU
Press Files: aerial view of a
city; Photo Disc, Inc.:
gears, leaf; Corbis: Sydney
Opera House

Title Page
Corel Corporation:
Blackback butterfly fish,
fireworks, apples; Stan
Evans: snowboarder in
mountains

Introduction
Nik Wheeler viii; Unusual
Films ix(top); Corbis ix
(bottom)

Chapter 1
Graeme Teague x-1; Photo
Disc, Inc. 2, 14, 26; Corel
Corporation 7(top), 9, 23;
Corbis 7 (bottom); USDA
20

Chapter 2
Stem Labs, Inc. 44-45;
Photo Disc, Inc. 46, 56,
62, 69, 75(bottom);
Corbis 47; BJU Press Files
51; Planet Art 63; NASA
74; CERN 75(top); Corel
Corporation 77

Chapter 3
Corel Corporation 84-85,
86, 107, 111; Corbis 92;
Photo Disc, Inc. 96, 99,
114; NPS 123

Chapter 4
Corel Corporation 128-29,
138, 159; Photo Disc, Inc.
130, 134, 136, 142, 163,
175 (top); Corbis 143;

Kromer Co. 154; Unusual
Films 158; NIH 174, 175
(bottom)

Chapter 5
Suzanne Altizer 180-81;
NPS 182; Corel
Corporation 186, 204;
Photo Disc, Inc. 188, 194;
Planet Art 192; Unusual
Films 201, 211

Chapter 6
Victor Englebert 216-17;
Springfield Illinois
Convention & Visitors
Bureau 218; Photo Disc,
Inc. 223, 244, 245, 246;
Corel Corporation 252;
South Dakota Tourism 255

Chapter 7
Corel Corporation 270-71,
284, 301, 302, 309;
Corbis 272, 314; USAF
276; Photo Disc, Inc. 288,
304; Kenneth Frederick
299

Chapter 8
Photo Disc, Inc. 322-23,
330, 336, 338, 347, 350;
Corel Corporation 324;
Kay Washer 332; Dr.
Margene Ranieri 334;
Frazier Photography 337

Chapter 9
Corel Corporation 362-63;
Photo Disc, Inc. 364, 366,
370, 384; Greyhound
Lines, Inc. 383; Ron
Tagliapietra 386

Chapter 10
Corel Corporation 394-95;
Photo Disc, Inc. 396, 414,
415(all); George R. Collins
400; USDA, photo by Tim
McCabe 406; Brian D.
Johnson 413; Aramco
World 418; U.S. Navy 423;
Dartmouth College, Joe
Mehling 431

Chapter 11
Photo Disc, Inc. 442-43,
463, 470, 471; Lewis Carl
446

Chapter 12
Dan Feicht, courtesy of
Cedar Point 480-81;
Photo Disc, Inc. 482, 495,
498, 504; Corel
Corporation 485, 506(bot-
tom); Bridge and Offshore
Engineering Assoc.
499(bottom); Rinker
Materials Corp. 499(top);
Corbis 500, 506(top)

Chapter 13
Photo Disc, Inc. 514-15;
State Fair of Texas 517;
Dawn L. Watkins 518;
Unusual Films 525, 535;
NYSE 529; Corel
Corporation 533

Chapter 14
Bureau of Reclamation,
Washington, D.C. 542-43;
Brian D. Johnson 548;
Planet Art 552; Corel
Corporation 557; Photo
Disc, Inc. 559; Suzanne
Altizer 563

Algebra Around Us border
(74-75, 174-75, 244-45,
336-37, 414-15, 498-
99); www.arttoday.com:
computer monitor; Corel
Corporation: moon, jet;
Photo Disc, Inc.: cars,
computer circuit, electro-
cardiogram; Unusual
Films: stopwatch, key-
board, caliper